STEP-BY-STEP RESUMES

For All

CONSTRUCTION TRADES POSITIONS

STEP-BY-STEP RESUMES

For All

CONSTRUCTION TRADES POSITIONS

Evelyn U. Salvador

EMAIL: CareerCatapult@aol.com | **PHONE:** 631-698-7777 | **WEBSITE:** ResumeProducts.com | StepByStepResumes.com

First Edition 2016 – Originally Published by PAGE PUBLISHING, INC.

Printed in the United States of America.

Library of Congress Control Number: 2019913950

ISBN   Paperback   978-1-64361-851-7
              eBook   978-1-64361-852-4

Westwood Books Publishing LLC
11416 SW Aventino Drive
Port Saint Lucie, FL 34987

www.westwoodbookspublishing.com

Dedicated to my husband, John C. Salvador, who is there to encourage me and cheer me on as I continue to author each profession-specific book in the Step-by-Step Resumes book series in which this multiyear endeavor required forgoing much of my income stream.

ABOUT THE AUTHOR
EVELYN U. SALVADOR, NCRW, JCTC
Certified Resume Writer & Career Coach | Personal Branding Pioneer
Multiaward-winning Resume Product Innovator | Author

EVELYN U. SALVADOR, Certified Resume Writer and Career Coach, is a Personal Branding pioneer (since 1990) and the world's leading, multiaward-winning resume product innovator who has helped revolutionize the resume writing industry. She is the author of **Step-by-Step Resumes: Build an Outstanding Resume in 10 Easy Steps!** and **Step-by-Step Cover Letters: Build a Cover Letter in 10 Easy Steps Using Personal Branding** *(both published by JIST Publishing).* Evelyn is in the throes of authoring 23 **Step-by-Step Resumes** books in every profession. She is also a contributing author to **Interview Magic** *(Susan Britton-Whitcomb, JIST Publishing)* and **The Complete Job Search Guide for Latinos** (Murray Mann, Barons Publishing) and has been interviewed for and/or quoted in various other books, numerous publications, talk shows, and Websites.

As a credentialed career management expert and thought leader, Evelyn is one of the top Professional Resume Writers in the world. She is a former **National Resume Writers' Association** *Advertising and Public Relations Chair* as well as its *Eastern Regional Representative.* Her award-winning resume and career products used worldwide by professional resume writers, career coaches, colleges and universities, the military, Departments of Labor, jobseekers, and others can be found at ResumeProducts.com.

Evelyn has been positioning careerists in the top 2 percent in their industry for 25 years. As such, her clients succeed a lot quicker and earn more than their average counterparts. She achieves this by identifying and defining their Personal Brands and leveraging it across all marketing platforms through marketing-savvy wordsmithing and design that compels hiring managers to seek them out over other candidates. This Book shows you step by step how to do this for yourself.

Evelyn is the founder of CreativeImageBuilders.com a personal and business-branding firm, where she spearheads the development of visionary strategies and innovative solutions to meet her clients' target audiences' needs that help position businesses and individuals at the top. She develops self-promotional marketing materials that sell the product...*you.* Whether "you" are a business or an individual and whether your marketing communications are your resume or brochure, web portfolio or website, or LinkedIn or company profile.

When Evelyn first started her practice in 1990, she created branding materials for businesses. When she was asked by family and friends to craft their resumes, they immediately received calls for interviews. She first chalked it up to being "lucky." When that occurred time and again and became the norm, she realized it wasn't luck at all. Their success was due to her applying the same methodology to writing and designing resumes as she was for businesses in creating their marketing materials—that is, selling their features, benefits, competitive edge, value proposition, and return on investment along with their matching achievements—in a designer resume format.

She imparts upon you in this **Step-by-Step Resumes** Book how to define and leverage your own unique brand and has put her resume-writing verbiage and methods into each of the scientific tools it contains so you can do the same to position yourself head and shoulders above your peers. Her own brand characteristics of being visionary, scientific, creative / artistic, strategic, marketing savvy, comprehensive, detail-oriented, and organized is what helps her showcase her clients and readers so desirably to their target audience. *(You will identify your own top 10-15 brand attributes in Step 3: Check Off Your Personal Attributes and Capabilities.)*

Evelyn's work in the career management field has been referred to as *"revolutionary," "groundbreaking," "a labor of love,"* and *"I don't know how I did without it"* by her resume writer peers. Jobseekers refer to her books as *"amazing," "right-on,"* and *"very easy."* And clients state their resumes have helped them *"realize their own worth,"* made them feel *"confident and empowered"* in their job search and that human resource professionals have told them they had *"the best resume"* they had ever seen.

Evelyn attended New York Institute of Technology and started her career in banking where she progressed to Assistant Vice President in charge of bank policies and procedures, after which she worked for a top advertising agency as a Graphic Designer prior to starting her business. She is a member of The National Resume Writers' Association and Career Directors International. Her creative talents encompass writing and editing, design, fine art, and photography. *(Evelyn's Web Portfolio and resume are viewable at EvelynSalvador.com.)*

POSITION TITLES
THIS BOOK COVERS

ADMINISTRATIVE

- Administrator & Coordinator
- Construction & Service Coordinator
- Construction Administrative Coordinator
- Construction Administrator
- Construction Coordinator
- Construction Customer Service Manager
- Construction Expeditor
- Construction Materials Technician
- Construction Office Manager
- Construction Project Administrator
- Construction Project Coordinator
- Construction Project Specialist
- Construction Project Supervisor
- Construction Representative
- Construction Services Assistant
- Construction Services Manager
- Contract Administrator
- Customer Service Representative Construction
- Customer Service Superintendent
- Inventory Control Assistant – Construction
- Inventory Control Manager – Construction
- Lead Project Coordinator
- Material Coordinator
- Office Administrator – Construction
- Office Manager – Construction
- Planning & Coordination Specialist
- Project Control Coordinator
- Project Coordination Specialist
- Project Coordinator
- Project Management Administrator
- Project Material Coordinator
- Project Principal Work Planner
- Project Scheduler
- Project Specialist
- Resident Project Representative
- Services Manager
- Support Specialist
- Other related positions

BUILDING OPERATIONS

- General Manager – Construction
- Operations Manager – Construction
- Building Engineer
- Building Operations Supervisor
- Building Operations Manager
- Building Program Specialist
- Commercial Construction Office Manager
- Construction Operations Manager
- Operations Manager – Construction
- Operations Supervisor
- Other related positions

BUILDING MAINTENANCE

- Area Maintenance Supervisor
- Assistant Building Superintendent
- Building & Grounds Laborer
- Building & Grounds Mechanic
- Building Handyman
- Building Maintenance Attendant
- Building Maintenance Engineer
- Building Maintenance Manager
- Building Maintenance Mechanic
- Building Maintenance Supervisor
- Building Maintenance Technician
- Building Maintenance Worker
- Building Manager
- Building Service Engineer
- Building Technician
- Custodian
- Custodian Engineer
- Facilities Maintenance Mechanic
- General Maintenance Mechanic
- General Maintenance Technician
- General Maintenance Worker
- Janitor
- Maintenance & Operations Supervisor
- Maintenance Engineer
- Maintenance Helper
- Maintenance Journeyman
- Maintenance Mechanic
- Maintenance Project Superintendent
- Maintenance Project Supervisor
- Maintenance Repair Worker
- Maintenance Repair Worker Assistant
- Maintenance Specialist
- Plant Maintenance Mechanic

BUILDING MAINTENANCE
(Cont'd)

- Senior Building Facilities Technician
- Senior Building Maintenance Mechanic
- Senior Building Maintenance Technician
- Senior Building Maintenance Worker
- Senior Building Technician
- Senior Facilities Maintenance Mechanic
- Senior Maintenance Mechanic
- Senior Plant Maintenance Mechanic
- Superintendent of Facilities Maintenance
- Other related positions

CARPENTRY

- Acoustical Carpenter
- Acoustical Ceiling Installer
- Acoustical Ceiling Technician
- Acoustical Ceiling Mechanic
- Cabinetmaker
- Carpenter
- Carpenter / Crew Leader
- Carpenter / Form Setter
- Carpenter / Repairman
- Carpenter Apprentice
- Carpenter Assistant
- Carpenter Lead Hand
- Carpenter, General Foreman
- Carpenter-Contractor
- Carpentry Contractor
- Carpentry Foreman
- Carpentry Supervisor
- Carpet Fitter
- Carpet Installer
- Carpet Layer
- Ceiling Installer
- Ceiling Tile Installer
- Commercial / Industrial Painter
- Commercial Construction Carpenter
- Commercial Glazing Estimator
- Commercial Project Manager
- Craftsman
- Deck Builder
- Deck Installer
- Deck Worker
- Demolition Foreman
- Demolition Worker

POSITION TITLES COVERED (Continued)

CARPENTRY (Cont'd)

- Door & Window Installer
- Driller Drywall & Ceiling Tile Installer
- Drywall & Make-ready Technician
- Drywall Applicator
- Drywall Boardhanger
- Drywall Carpenter
- Drywall Finisher
- Drywall Hanger
- Drywall Installer
- Drywall Mechanic
- Drywall Metal Stud Worker
- Drywall Sander
- Drywall Stripper
- Drywall Taper
- Drywall Worker
- Drywaller
- Elevator Installer
- Fence Builder
- Finish Carpenter
- Finish Superintendent
- Fire Sprinkler Designer
- Fire Sprinkler Fitter
- Fire Sprinkler Helper
- Fire Sprinkler Installer
- Flat Glass Glazier Technician
- Floor Installer
- Floor Layer
- Floor Systems Carpenter
- Foreman
- Framer
- Framing Carpenter
- Furniture Maker
- General Construction Laborer
- General Foreman
- Glass Combo Technician
- Glass Fitter
- Glass Installer
- Glass Setter
- Glass Technician
- Glazier
- Glazier Contractor
- Glazier Supervisor
- Glazing Project Manager
- Handyman
- Handyman / Service Technician
- Installation / Service Technician
- Installation Supervisor
- Installer
- Installer Technician
- Insulation Installer
- Insulation Worker
- Interior Finish Carpenter
- Journeyman Carpenter
- Journeyman Construction Carpenter

CARPENTRY (Cont'd)

- Journeyman Fire Sprinkler Fitter
- Labor Foreman
- Labor Supervisor
- Laborer
- Lath & Plaster
- Lath Hand
- Lather
- Lather Apprentice
- Lead Carpenter
- Lead Glazer
- Maintenance Carpenter
- Master Carpenter
- Metal Framer
- Metal Furrer
- Metal Lather
- Metal Roofing Technician
- Metal Stud Framer
- Multiskilled Craftsman / Remodeler
- Painter
- Painter – Commercial
- Painter – Industrial
- Painter – Residential
- Painter / Crew Leader
- Painter Helper / Prepper
- Painter Leader
- Painting Contractor
- Painting Foreman
- Plaster Lather
- Plasterer
- Prefabricated Structures Carpenter
- Remodeling Tradesman
- Restoration Carpenter
- Rock Lather
- Rockboard Lather
- Roofer
- Roofing Apprentice
- Roofing Carpenter
- Roofing Foreman
- Scaffold Builder
- Scaffold Construction Manager
- Scaffold Erector
- Scenic Carpenter
- Sheetrock Applicator
- Sheetrock Applier
- Sheetrock Finisher
- Sheetrock Hanger
- Sheetrock Installer
- Sheetrock Layer
- Sheetrock Nailer
- Sheetrock Sander
- Sheetrock Worker
- Sheetrocker
- Siding Foreman
- Skilled Carpenter

CARPENTRY (Cont'd)

- Solar Heating Cooling System Installer
- Solar Installation / Production Manager
- Solar Photovoltaic Installer
- Tile Installer
- Window Washer
- Wire Lather
- Wood Lather
- Working Foreman
- Other related positions

CONCRETE WORK

- Cement Gun Operator
- Cement Mason
- Cement Mason Apprentice
- Cement Patcher
- Cementer
- Concrete & Terrazzo Finisher
- Concrete Finisher
- Concrete Finisher Apprentice
- Concrete Floater
- Concrete Floor Installer
- Concrete Form Setter
- Concrete Form Laborer
- Concrete Grinder Operator
- Concrete Installer
- Concrete Laborer
- Concrete Layer
- Concrete Materials Tester
- Concrete Placement Equipment Operator
- Concrete Pointer
- Concrete Polisher
- Concrete Smoother
- Concrete Safety Manager
- Concrete Stone Finisher
- Concrete Swimming Pool Installer
- Concreting Supervisor
- Construction Form Setter
- Curb Builder
- Finish-Pour Assistant
- Joint Finisher
- Joint Setter
- Structural Concrete Superintendent
- Swimming Pool Installer
- Other related positions

CONSTRUCTION

- Apprentice Lineman
- Apprenticeship Manager
- Assistant Builder
- Assistant Commercial Construction Superintendent
- Assistant Construction Manager
- Assistant Multifamily Superintendent

POSITION TITLES COVERED (Continued)

CONSTRUCTION (Cont'd)

- Assistant Superintendent
- Building Construction Laborer
- Cement Finisher
- Cement Laborer
- Civil Foreman
- Civil Superintendent
- Commercial Construction Laborer
- Commercial Construction Manager
- Commercial Construction Superintendent
- Concrete Foreman
- Construction Area Manager
- Construction Assistant Superintendent
- Construction Carpenter
- Construction Field Engineer
- Construction Field Estimator
- Construction Field Supervisor
- Construction Foreman
- Construction Journeyman
- Construction Journeyman Electrician
- Construction Laborer
- Construction Manager
- Construction Operations Supervisor
- Construction Site Manager
- Construction Site Superintendent
- Construction Supervisor
- Construction Tradesman
- Construction Trainee
- Construction Worker
- Contract (Site) Manager
- Contractor
- Crew Chief
- Demolition Superintendent
- Dirt Foreman / Superintendent
- Drilling Foreman
- Field Foreman
- Foreman / Foreperson
- General Contractor
- General Foreman – Civil
- General Laborer
- General Superintendent
- Hazardous Materials Removal Worker
- Heavy Civil Project Engineer
- Home Building Superintendent
- Independent Contractor
- Job Superintendent
- Journey Lineworker
- Junior Site Surveyor
- Junior Superintendent
- Land Construction Manager
- Land Development Manager
- Lead Superintendent
- Leadman / Lead Person
- Leadman Construction Laborer

CONSTRUCTION (Cont'd)

- Multifamily Construction Project Supervisor
- Multifamily Superintendent
- New Homes Superintendent
- Preconstruction Manager
- Preconstruction Manager – Renovation
- Project Superintendent
- Property Manager – Construction
- Public Works Manager
- Regional Property Manager
- Residential Construction Project Manager
- Retail Construction Manager
- Sheet Metal Helper
- Sheet Metal Worker
- Site Manager
- Site Superintendent
- Site Supervisor
- Site Surveyor
- Sitework Manager
- Skilled Trades Apprentice
- Skilled Trades Specialist
- Skilled Trades Worker
- Structural Trades Superintendent
- Structural Tradesworker
- Superintendent – Concrete
- Superintendent – Installation
- Superintendent – Specialty Construction
- Superintendent – Steel
- Superintendent – White Paving
- Supervisor of Building Trades
- Tile Setter
- Trade Professional Manager
- Union Carpenter
- Utility Line Locator
- Utility Maintenance Worker
- Vocational Assistant / General Laborer
- Waterproofer
- Working Superintendent
- Working Superintendent – Retail / Commercial
- Other related positions

ELECTRICAL WORK

- Apprentice Electrician
- Commercial Electrician
- Construction Electrician Journeyman
- Electric Service Worker
- Electrical Apprentice
- Electrical Construction Foreman
- Electrical Design Engineer
- Electrical Engineering Technician
- Electrical Foreman

ELECTRICAL WORK (Cont'd)

- Electrical Project Manager
- Electrical Systems Design Engineer
- Electrical Systems Supervisor
- Electrician
- Electrician Apprentice
- Electrician Contractor
- Electrician Foreman
- Electrician Helper
- Electrician Supervisor
- Engineer – Electrical Systems Design
- Industrial Electrician
- Journeyman Electrician
- Lead Electrician
- Licensed Journeyman Electrician
- Maintenance Electrician
- Master Electrician
- Residential Electrical Foreman
- Wiring Technician
- Other related positions

EQUIPMENT OPERATIONS

- Asphalt Paving Equipment Operator
- Asphalt Paving-Patching Equipment Operator
- Backhoe / Loader Operator
- Backhoe Operator / Excavator
- Bulldozer Operator
- CDL Driver / Equipment Operator
- Certified Crane Operator
- Compact Track Loader Operator
- Concrete & Asphalt Equipment Operator
- Construction Equipment Operator
- Construction Labor / Equipment Operator
- Crane Manager
- Crane Operator
- Crane Rigger
- Directional Bore Operator
- Directional Drill Operator
- Dragline Operator
- Dredge Operator
- Dredger
- Dump Truck Backhoe Operator
- Dump Truck Driver
- Engineering Equipment Operator
- Equipment Operator
- Excavating Machine Operator
- Excavator Operator
- Forklift Operator
- Front-End Loader Operator
- General Construction Equipment Operator
- Gradall Operator
- Grader Operator

POSITION TITLES COVERED (Continued)

EQUIPMENT OPERATIONS
(Cont'd)

- Heavy Equipment Operator
- Heavy Equipment Operator Apprentice
- Horizontal Directional Drill Operator
- Landfill Heavy Equipment Operator
- Loader Operator
- Loading Machine Operator
- Low Boy Driver
- Motor Grader Operator
- Multiterrain Loader
- Paving Equipment Operator
- Pay Loader Operator
- Pile-Driver Operator
- Side Boom Tractor Operator
- Skid Steer Loader Operator
- Surfacing Equipment Operator
- Tamping Equipment Operator
- Track Hoe Operator
- Trencher Operator
- Truck Driver / Equipment Operator
- Utility Worker – Heavy Equipment
- Other related positions

ESTIMATING

- Assistant Estimator – High-end General Construction
- Chief Commercial Roofing Estimator
- Commercial Flooring Estimator
- Construction & Estimator Assistant
- Construction Cost Estimator
- Construction Estimator
- Commercial Estimator
- Cost Analyst
- Cost Estimator
- Estimator
- Estimator – High-end General Construction
- Estimator Project Manager
- Estimating / Bidding Assistant
- Estimating / Change Manager
- Estimating Assistant
- Estimating Supervisor
- Estimator – Specialty Construction
- Estimator – Structural & Miscellaneous Steel Fabrication
- Estimator / Assistant Project Manager
- Estimator / Purchaser
- Junior Construction Estimator
- Junior Estimator
- Mid-level Estimator
- Residential Construction Estimator
- Senior Estimator
- Senior Estimator, Home Building Commercial Construction

ESTIMATING (Cont'd)

- Senior Project Manager / Estimator
- Other related positions

FACILITIES

- Facilities Construction Trades Worker
- Facilities Construction Coordinator
- Facilities Foreperson
- Facilities Generalist
- Facilities Construction Project Specialist
- Facilities Superintendent
- Facility Maintenance Specialist
- Facility Operations Project Manager
- Manager Construction Projects, Facility Engineering
- Territory Facilities Manager
- Other related positions

FIELD WORK

- Field Construction Coordinator
- Field Helper
- Field Install Site Supervisor
- Field Manager
- Field Manager – Homebuilding
- Field Manager – Residential Construction
- Field Operations Supervisor
- Field Representative
- Field Superintendent
- Field Supervisor
- Field Survey Specialist
- Field-based Construction Manager
- Field-based Facilities Manager
- Senior Field Manager
- Other related positions

GENERAL CONTRACTING

- Commercial Contractor
- Concrete Contractor
- Demolition Contractor
- Electrical Contractor
- Excavating Contractor
- Excavator Foreman
- Floor Laying Contractor
- General Building Contractor
- General Contractor
- General Engineering Contractor
- Glass & Glazing Contractor
- Home Improvement Contractor
- Home Remodeling Contractor
- HVAC Contractor
- Maintenance Contractor
- Masonry & Stone Setting Contractor
- Owner / Operator (Contractor)

GENERAL CONTRACTING
(Cont'd)

- Painting Contractor
- Plastering, Drywall, Acoustical & Insulation Contractor
- Plumbing Contractor
- Plumbing, Heating & Air Conditioning Contractor
- Remodel Contractor
- Residential General Contractor
- Roofing & Siding Contractor
- Roofing Contractor
- Sheet Metal Contractor
- Special Trade Contractor
- Specialty Contractor
- Structural Contractor
- Subcontractor
- Other related positions

GROUNDSKEEPING & GREENSKEEPING

- Athletic Field Custodian
- Cemetery Warden
- Greens Foreman
- Greens Superintendent
- Greenskeeper Foreman
- Groundskeeper Foreman
- Park Foreman
- Property Manager – Groundskeeping
- Brush Cutter
- Building & Grounds Attendant
- Building & Grounds Technician
- Cemetery Keeper
- Cemetery Laborer
- Cemetery Worker
- Golf Course Keeper
- Golf Course Laborer
- Grass Cutter
- Grass Mower
- Greens Cutter
- Greens Laborer
- Greenskeeper
- Ground Crewman
- Ground Worker
- Grounds Caretaker
- Grounds Cleaner
- Groundskeeper
- Groundskeeping Maintenance Worker
- Hedge Trimmer
- Maintenance Groundsman
- Park Caretaker
- Park Caretaker Keeper
- Park Caretaker Worker
- Park Crew Chief
- Park Keeper
- Park Worker

POSITION TITLES COVERED (Continued)

GROUNDSKEEPING & GREENSKEEPING (Cont'd)

- Pesticide Handler
- Pesticide Sprayer
- Pruner
- Shrub Trimmer
- Tree Maintenance Worker
- Tree Pruner
- Tree Specialist
- Tree Surgeon
- Tree Trimmer
- Weed Controller
- Weed Inspector
- Weed Sprayer
- Weeder
- Yard Work Laborer
- Yard Worker
- Other related positions

See also "Landscaping."

HIGHWAY & BRIDGE WORK

- Bridge Construction Laborer
- Bridge Foreman
- Bridge Maintenance Mechanic
- Bridge Superintendent
- Crew Leader – Maintenance
- General Highway Worker
- Highway Construction Inspector
- Highway Foreman
- Highway Maintenance Foreman
- Highway Maintenance Laborer
- Highway Maintenance Lead Worker
- Highway Maintenance Technician
- Highway Maintenance Worker
- Highway Safety Specialist
- Highway Technician
- Maintenance of Traffic
- Roadway Construction Laborer
- Tradesworker – Bridges
- Other related positions

INSPECTIONS & COMPLIANCE

- Boiler Inspector
- Bridge Inspector
- Build-It-Back Plumbing Inspector
- Building & Housing Inspector
- Building & Safety Inspector
- Building & Trade Inspector
- Building Engineering Inspector
- Building Equipment Inspector
- Code Inspector
- Combination Inspector
- Commercial Building Inspector

INSPECTIONS & COMPLIANCE (Cont'd)

- Commercial Inspector
- Commissioning Engineer
- Construction & Building Inspector
- Construction Inspector
- Construction Quality Assurance / Quality Control Engineer
- Construction Quality Assurance Inspector
- Construction Quality Control Manager
- Construction Quality Specialist
- Dredging Inspector
- Electrical Inspector
- Field Inspector
- Gas Inspector
- Grade Checker
- Highway Inspector
- Home Inspector
- Housing Inspector
- HVAC-R Inspector
- Inspecting Engineer
- Inspector
- Paving Inspector
- Plumbing Inspector
- Plumbing / Mechanical Inspector
- Plumbing Inspector / Plans Reviewer
- Property Compliance Inspector
- Public Works Inspector
- Other related positions

JANITORIAL / CUSTODIAL

- Cleaner / Janitor
- Custodial Manager
- Custodial Supervisor
- Custodial Worker
- Custodian
- Custodian / Cleaner
- Custodian Engineer
- Custodian / Janitor
- Janitorial Manager
- Janitorial Supervisor
- Janitor
- Janitor / Custodian
- Janitor Cleaner Custodian
- Other related positions

LABOR RELATIONS

- Chief Steward
- Director, Labor Relations
- Labor Business Representative
- Labor Organization Representative
- Labor Organizer
- Labor Relations Director
- Labor Union Business Representative

LABOR RELATIONS (Cont'd)

- Shop Steward
- Steward
- Trade Union Representative
- Union Business Representative
- Union Negotiator
- Union Organizer
- Union Representative
- Union Staff Representative
- Union Steward
- Other related positions

LANDSCAPING

- Crew Leader
- Greenhouse Foreman
- Landscape Foreman
- Landscape Management Technician
- Nursery Manager
- Planting Foreman
- Property Manager – Landscaping
- Principal Landscape Architect
- Garden Center Worker
- Gardener
- Greenhouse Worker
- Horticulturist
- Indoor Gardener
- Irrigation Project Superintendent
- Landscape Gardener
- Landscape Laborer
- Landscape Irrigation Project Superintendent
- Landscape Maintenance Worker
- Landscape Technician
- Landscaper
- Landscaper Helper
- Landscape Design & Build Project Manager
- Lawn Caretaker
- Lawn Maintenance Laborer
- Lawn Mower Operator
- Lawn Service Worker
- Lawn Sprinkler Installer
- Lawn Sprinkler Servicer
- Maintenance Aide
- Maintenance Worker
- Nursery Helper
- Plant-Care Worker
- Property Maintenance Worker
- Shrub Planter
- Sprinkler Fitter
- Other related positions

See also "Groundskeeping & Greenskeeping."

POSITION TITLES COVERED (Continued)

HVAC / HVAC-R

- Air Conditioning Foreman
- Air Conditioning Installer
- Air Conditioning Mechanic
- Air Conditioning Specialist
- Air Conditioning Technician
- Commercial HVAC Foreman
- Commercial HVAC Technician
- Heating Foreman
- Heating Installer
- Heating Mechanic
- Heating Specialist
- Heating Technician
- HVAC / Skilled Tradesman
- HVAC Foreman
- HVAC Helper
- HVAC Installer & Service Technician
- HVAC Mechanic
- HVAC Project Manager
- HVAC Service Technician
- HVAC Specialist
- HVAC Systems Foreman
- HVAC Technician
- HVAC/R Service Technician
- HVAC/R Mechanic
- HVAC/R Specialist
- HVAC/R Technician
- Refrigeration Apprentice
- Refrigeration Foreman
- Refrigeration Installer
- Refrigeration Mechanic
- Refrigeration Specialist
- Refrigeration Technician
- Trades Specialist – HVAC
- Zone Chief (HVAC)
- Other related positions

MASONRY

- Block Mason
- Blocklayer
- Blocklayer Apprentice
- Brick Laborer
- Brick Mason
- Brick Mason Foreman
- Brick Mason Laborer
- Bricklayer
- Bricklayer Apprentice
- Carpentry & Masonry Specialist
- Cement Contractor
- Cement Mason
- Commercial Journeyman Mason
- Commercial Masonry Foreman
- Concrete Finisher
- Construction Mason
- Industrial Brick Mason Foreman
- Marble Setter
- Mason
- Mason Carpenter
- Mason Laborer

MASONRY (Cont'd)

- Mason Tender
- Mason-Plasterer
- Masonry Contractor
- Masonry Foreman
- Masonry Outfitter
- Masonry Specialist
- Masonry Superintendent
- Masonry Tuck-pointer Laborer
- Masonry Worker
- Stonemason
- Stonesetter
- Swimming Pool Installer
- Terrazzo Contractor
- Terrazzo Finisher
- Terrazzo Grinder
- Terrazzo Setter
- Terrazzo Worker
- Other related positions

PLUMBING

- Apprentice Plumber
- Lead Plumber
- Licensed Plumber
- Master Plumber
- Plumber
- Plumber Apprentice / Helper
- Plumbing Contractor
- Plumbing Designer
- Plumbing Foreman
- Plumbing Foreman (Multifamily)
- Plumbing Installer
- Service Plumber
- Other related positions

PURCHASING

- Assistant Purchasing Estimator – Construction
- Assistant Purchasing Manager – Construction
- Purchasing / Estimating Assistant
- Purchasing Administrator
- Purchasing Agent – Construction
- Purchasing Manager – Construction
- Purchasing Trade Agent
- Regional Purchasing Administrator
- Regional Purchasing Manager
- Other related positions

PROJECT MANAGEMENT

- Assistant Project Superintendent / Engineer
- Commercial Project Manager
- Commercial Solar Project Manager
- Construction Manager
- Construction Project Engineer
- Construction Project Manager
- Construction Project Manager / Designer

PROJECT MANAGEMENT (Cont'd)

- Construction Project Manager / Site Superintendent
- Construction Superintendent
- Construction Supervisor
- Land Assistant Project Manager
- Project Assistant – Jobsite
- Project Associate – Construction
- Project Engineer – Electrical
- Project Engineer / Finish Carpenter
- Project Environmental Engineer
- Project Foreman
- Project Lead
- Project Leader
- Project Manager
- Project Manager – Electrical
- Project Manager – HVAC
- Project Manager – Metal Construction
- Project Manager – Plumbing
- Project Manager – Residential Remodeling
- Project Manager – Sheet Metal
- Project Manager / General Contractor
- Project Manager / Installation Manager
- Project Manager / Site Superintendent
- Project Manager Assistant
- Project Superintendent
- Project Superintendent / Engineer
- Project Supervisor
- Solar Project Manager
- Structural Superintendent
- Other related positions

WELDING / STEAMFITTING

- Arc Welder
- Blowtorch Operator
- Blowtorch Welder
- Boiler Welder
- Combination Welder
- Gas Welder
- Hand Arc Welder
- Helliarc Welder
- Iron Worker
- Lead Welder
- Metal Welder
- Pipe Welder
- Pipefitter
- Pipefitter Helper
- Pipefitter Trade Foreman
- Spot Welder
- Steamfitter
- Tack Welder
- Torch Welder
- Tradesworker – Welding
- Welder
- Welding Contractor
- Other related positions

TABLE OF CONTENTS

19

Step 6: PULL YOUR RESUME TOGETHER — 281

Index of all Position Titles — 301

Career Management Resources — 307

Next: See how easy it is to use this book!

HOW TO USE THIS BOOK

Congratulations. You have taken the first, most important step towards advancing your career and becoming more successful!

INTRODUCTION

You are about to embark on a self-discovery process that will help you to not only craft an exemplary resume step by step but better understand what you have to offer prospective employers in order to land the job you seek quickly and garner your highest salary. This book also includes the steps to take to develop your personal brand with lots of foundations already prepared for you where you can just check off boxes and fill in your information.

The *Step-by-Step Resumes* Book series is an extension of Evelyn Salvador's more generalized *Step-by-Step Resumes: Build an Outstanding Resume in 10 Easy Steps!* book *(JIST Publishing)* in that it is profession specific to not only your field and position, but contains numerous functions for each position, resume bullets for each function, as well as achievement samples. This Book includes everything you need to easily craft an exemplary resume to help position you in the top percentage in your field—as if you hired a Certified Resume Writer to craft it for you. You can use it time and again to update your resume throughout your career.

Everything in this book is written in what I call its "lowest common denominator," that is, extremely content rich but in the most concise way possible so you don't have to do a lot of reading, writing, or research.

WHAT YOU NEED TO SUCCEED

Years ago, an excellent resume got a jobseeker's foot in the door. In today's world of work, careerists need three things to succeed: (1) an outstanding resume that highlights your skills and achievements, (2) a well-defined, unique personal brand that showcases your value proposition, and (3) a positive online identity for when employers check your Web presence prior to calling you in for an interview or making a job offer.

THE DIFFERENCE BETWEEN A TEMPLATE AND A FOUNDATION

Templates are generally very basic. They provide a starting point where you have to fill in all relative information in your own words. They do not help you write an interview-generating resume. Unlike resume templates where you have to ponder what you did, Evelyn Salvador's books contain *foundations*. These foundations provide not only the framework that shapes and structures your resume, but all possible options that may be relative to a particular function. Each bullet foundation in this Book includes all of the necessary information required to complete it, whereas very little writing is necessary. All you need to do is just check off what is relative to your own background and fill in the blanks.

HOW TO USE THIS BOOK

This resource is best used as a workbook by identifying everything that is applicable to you. The tools in each chapter will take you step by step to complete your resume in order to highlight your strengths and showcase your value proposition in the best of light to hiring managers. The more thoroughly you complete the sections, the better your end result, the more interviews you will receive, the faster your job turnaround can be, and the higher your salary potential.

Thousands of hours of research and writing went into creating the *Step-by-Step Resumes* Book series so that most everything prospective employers seek in a job candidate would be covered—from your scope of work to each job function and achievement you performed—and includes the largest resource of all relative and current keywords in your industry to help your resume be "screened in" by human resources professionals.

YOUR ACHIEVEMENTS

Since achievement statements are the most powerful in every resume, Evelyn Salvador has included numerous achievement samples throughout this Book. Each individual, however, will have his or her own unique set of accomplishments, so be sure to include any you may not see. The most important rule in resume development—*and this is where 98% of the general public falls short*—is to include **CAR *(Challenge–Action–Result)* Statements**. To the extent possible, this is already done for you.

Don't just say what you did, state how well you accomplished it, the actions you took to make it happen, the end results it derived, and the benefits to your employer and/or its clients (in dollars and percentages wherever possible).

Following are the Steps (chapters) this book contains:

THE EASY STEP-BY-STEP PROCESS

INTRODUCTION

This **Step-by-Step Resumes** Book is divided into six sections, or primary steps:

Step 1: START YOUR RESUME   Pg. 25

The **Resume Worksheet** in this step is where you will start to compile your resume. This section covers your employment, responsibilities, achievements, education and training, professional affiliations, and other related information. During the course of the Book, you will be selecting and transferring over applicable information (such as your professional summary, keywords, and resume bullets) to complete your resume.

Step 2: CHECK OFF YOUR RESUME KEYWORDS (CORE COMPETENCIES)   Pg. 37

Resume Keywords are critical to include in your resume so it can get in the hands of hiring managers. Scroll through the category lists and check off those core competencies you are proficient and knowledgeable in as they relate to your targeted position. You will be including your Primary Keywords within your *"Professional Summary,"* your Secondary Keywords listed in a *"Core Competencies"* or *"Areas of Expertise"* section, and all remaining keywords infused within the body of your resume. Applicable keywords are already included for you in all of the **Resume ClipBullets** found in **Step 5**, and additional keyword instructions are contained in **Step 6: Pull Your Resume Together**.

Step 3: CHECK OFF YOUR PERSONAL ATTRIBUTES   Pg. 73

In this step you will be identifying your personal attributes (your assets / features) and honing in on your top ten attributes that match your prospective employer's needs. Those would be your unique qualities, characteristics, attributes, capabilities, and skills that can be valuable to an employer. You will use these attributes in **Step 4: Develop Your Personal Brand and Professional Summary**.

Step 4: DEVELOP YOUR PERSONAL BRAND & PROFESSIONAL SUMMARY   Pg. 79

Personal Branding is what puts you head and shoulders above your peers and helps position you in the top percentage in your field of expertise. You will first complete the **Personal Branding Worksheet** that will allow you to identify your **Personal Brand** components *(your assets, benefits, competitive edge, value proposition, and return on investment)*, then develop your brand message that includes those elements in five formats: your personally branded **Biography, LinkedIn Profile, Elevator Pitch, Slogan,** and **Professional Summary**. This step is thought provoking because it allows you to delve into yourself as to what you have to offer prospective employers. *Don't skip it*…take the time you need to really get to understand your own unique value you bring to the table. The end result will empower you to obtain the job you seek!

Step 5: SELECT YOUR RESUME CLIPBULLETS™   Pg. 111

Resume ClipBullets™ are prewritten, customizable bullet foundations for the *"Professional Experience"* section of your resume. This step covers most all of the functions, responsibilities, and achievements you will be using to compile your employment information. Select applicable bullets and options as they relate to your specific position(s). You will include those bullets under your applicable employers / job titles in **Step 6: Pull Your Resume Together.**

Step 6: PULL YOUR RESUME TOGETHER   Pg. 281

This step provides step-by-step instructions to compile and edit the information you completed throughout this Book to construct and finalize your resume. It contains a list of **Action Verbs** and **Descriptive Adjectives** and **Adverbs** to infuse within your resume, how to write your **Company and Position Descriptors**, **Resume Design Layout Samples,** and a **Resume Foundation**. And to be sure you've left no stone unturned, read the article *"100 Components of an Exemplary Resume: How Does Your Resume Fare?"* at the end. Just follow the instructions and you're done!

Ready? Grab yourself a cup of coffee, and let's get started!

STEP 1
START YOUR RESUME

CONTENTS OF STEP 1

☐ Fill in the Resume Worksheet

- Personal Information
- Licenses & Certifications
- Professional Summary
- Core Competencies / Skills
- Professional Experience (Your Employment History)
- Education & Training
- Professional Affiliations
- Other Categories (such as Publications, Community Activities, Military, Foreign Languages, or Related Hobbies)

FILL IN THE RESUME WORKSHEET

INSTRUCTIONS

The **Resume Worksheet** you are about to complete will start your resume compilation process. It includes areas for your skills, education, employment, responsibilities, achievements, licenses and certifications, professional affiliations, and other related information. During the course of this Book, you will be adding your "Core Competencies" from **Step 2: Check Off Your Resume Keywords**, the "Professional Summary" from **Step 4: Develop Your Personal Brand and Professional Summary**, and your "Professional Experience" bullets from **Step 5: Select Your Resume ClipBullets**. It is recommended that you complete the Worksheet to the best of your ability so you can be sure that all of your pertinent information has been included when you get to **Step 6: Pull Your Resume Together** where you will be finalizing and editing your resume.

Personal Information

NAME: ADDRESS:

HOME PHONE: CELL PHONE: EMAIL:

WEB PORTFOLIO: LINKEDIN:

OTHER SOCIAL MEDIA:

Licenses & Certifications (if any)

TITLE	YEAR OBTAINED

Professional Summary

This information will be garnered from **Step 4: Develop Your Personal Brand and Professional Summary**.

Core Competencies / Areas of Expertise

List below all of your core competencies / areas of expertise as they relate to your targeted position.
*In **Step 2: Check Off Your Resume Keywords,** you will be developing a comprehensive list of these keywords.*

CORE COMPETENCIES / AREAS OF EXPERTISE

_____   _____   _____   _____
_____   _____   _____   _____
_____   _____   _____   _____
_____   _____   _____   _____
_____   _____   _____   _____

TECHNICAL SKILLS

_____   _____   _____   _____
_____   _____   _____   _____

Personal Attributes / Soft Skills

List below all of your personal attributes / soft skills you have that are helpful to you in your targeted position.
*In **Step 3: Check Off Your Personal Attributes & Capabilities,** you will be developing a comprehensive list of these keywords.*

PERSONAL ATTRIBUTES / SOFT SKILLS

_____   _____   _____   _____
_____   _____   _____   _____
_____   _____   _____   _____

Professional Experience (Your Employment History)

List your current and former positions starting with your most recent. It is not necessary to go back further than 10 to 15 years unless your relevant experience is not shown within that timeframe or position progression is important to note.

JOB #1 – POSITION TITLE: _____

COMPANY: _____ **CITY, STATE:** _____ **START & END YEARS:** _____

Type of Firm: _____   Revenues: $ _____   No. Locations: _____   No. Employees: _____

No. Direct Reports & Titles: _____   No. Indirect Reports & Titles: _____

Your scope of responsibility / main job functions: _____

Describe all of your job functions and how well you accomplished each against company or industry standards.

1. _____
2. _____
3. _____

4. _____

5. _____

6. _____

7. _____

8. _____

9. _____

10. _____

11. _____

12. _____

13. _____

14. _____

15. _____

Fully explain each of your achievements in terms of the challenges you were faced with, the actions you took, and end results.

ACHIEVEMENT #1

YOUR CHALLENGE: _____

_____

YOUR ACTIONS: _____

_____

YOUR RESULTS _____

_____

ACHIEVEMENT #2

YOUR CHALLENGE: _____

_____

YOUR ACTIONS: _____

_____

YOUR RESULTS _____

_____

ACHIEVEMENT #3

YOUR CHALLENGE: _____

_____

YOUR ACTIONS: _____

_____

YOUR RESULTS _____

_____

ACHIEVEMENT #4

YOUR CHALLENGE:

YOUR ACTIONS:

YOUR RESULTS

ACHIEVEMENT #5

YOUR CHALLENGE:

YOUR ACTIONS:

YOUR RESULTS

OTHER ACHIEVEMENTS

JOB #2 – POSITION TITLE: _____

COMPANY: **CITY, STATE:**   **START & END YEARS:**

Type of Firm: Revenues: $ No. Locations: No. Employees:

No. Direct Reports & Titles: No. Indirect Reports & Titles:

Your scope of responsibility / main job functions:

Describe all of your job functions and how well you accomplished each against company or industry standards.

1.

2.

3.

4.

5. _____

6. _____

7. _____

8. _____

9. _____

10. _____

11. _____

12. _____

Fully explain each of your achievements in terms of the challenges you were faced with, the actions you took, and end results.

ACHIEVEMENT #1

YOUR CHALLENGE: _____

_____

YOUR ACTIONS: _____

_____

YOUR RESULTS _____

_____

ACHIEVEMENT #2

YOUR CHALLENGE: _____

_____

YOUR ACTIONS: _____

_____

YOUR RESULTS _____

_____

ACHIEVEMENT #3

YOUR CHALLENGE: _____

_____

YOUR ACTIONS: _____

_____

YOUR RESULTS _____

_____

ACHIEVEMENT #4

YOUR CHALLENGE: _____

_____

YOUR ACTIONS:

_____

_____

YOUR RESULTS

_____

OTHER ACHIEVEMENTS

_____

_____

_____

_____

_____

_____

_____

JOB #3 – POSITION TITLE: _____

COMPANY: CITY, STATE: START & END YEARS:

Type of Firm: Revenues: $ No. Locations: No. Employees:

No. Direct Reports & Titles: No. Indirect Reports & Titles:

Your scope of responsibility / main job functions:

_____

Describe all of your job functions and how well you accomplished each against company or industry standards.

1. _____

2. _____

3. _____

4. _____

5. _____

6. _____

7. _____

8. _____

9. _____

10. _____

Fully explain each of your achievements in terms of the challenges you were faced with, the actions you took, and end results.

ACHIEVEMENT #1

YOUR CHALLENGE:

_____

YOUR ACTIONS:

YOUR RESULTS

ACHIEVEMENT #2

YOUR CHALLENGE:

YOUR ACTIONS:

YOUR RESULTS

ACHIEVEMENT #3

YOUR CHALLENGE:

YOUR ACTIONS:

YOUR RESULTS

OTHER ACHIEVEMENTS

JOB #4 – POSITION TITLE: _____

COMPANY: | **CITY, STATE:** | **START & END YEARS:**

Type of Firm: | Revenues: $ | No. Locations: | No. Employees:

No. Direct Reports & Titles: | No. Indirect Reports & Titles:

Your scope of responsibility / main job functions:

Describe all of your job functions and how well you accomplished each against company or industry standards.

1.

2.

3. _____

4. _____

5. _____

6. _____

7. _____

8. _____

9. _____

10. _____

Fully explain each of your achievements in terms of the challenges you were faced with, the actions you took, and end results.

ACHIEVEMENT #1

YOUR CHALLENGE: _____

_____

YOUR ACTIONS: _____

_____

YOUR RESULTS _____

_____

ACHIEVEMENT #2

YOUR CHALLENGE: _____

_____

YOUR ACTIONS: _____

_____

YOUR RESULTS _____

_____

ACHIEVEMENT #3

YOUR CHALLENGE: _____

_____

YOUR ACTIONS: _____

_____

YOUR RESULTS _____

_____

OTHER ACHIEVEMENTS

_____

_____

JOB #5 – POSITION TITLE: _____

COMPANY: **CITY, STATE:**   **START & END YEARS:**

Type of Firm: Revenues: $ No. Locations: No. Employees:

No. Direct Reports & Titles: No. Indirect Reports & Titles:

Your scope of responsibility / main job functions:

_____

Describe all of your job functions and how well you accomplished each against company or industry standards.

1. _____

2. _____

3. _____

4. _____

5. _____

Fully explain each of your achievements in terms of the challenges you were faced with, the actions you took, and end results.

ACHIEVEMENT #1

YOUR CHALLENGE: _____

YOUR ACTIONS: _____

YOUR RESULTS _____

ACHIEVEMENT #2

YOUR CHALLENGE: _____

YOUR ACTIONS: _____

YOUR RESULTS _____

OTHER ACHIEVEMENTS

_____

_____

_____

_____

Education & Training

COLLEGE / UNIVERSITY	CITY & STATE	DEGREE / COURSEWORK	GPA	YEAR(S)

TRAINING / SEMINAR TITLES	SPONSORED BY	CITY & STATE	YEAR(S)

Professional Affiliations

Use this section to include all memberships and affiliations related to your targeted position.

ORGANIZATIONS	MEMBERSHIP / OFFICES HELD	YEAR(S)

Other

Use this section for other categories such as Publications, Community Activities, Military, Foreign Languages, Related Hobbies, etc.

Next: Check off your Resume Keywords.

STEP 2
CHECK OFF YOUR RESUME KEYWORDS
(CORE COMPETENCIES)

CONTENTS OF STEP 2

- ☐ Resume Keyword Instructions
- ☐ List Your Resume Keywords
  - Primary Keywords
  - Secondary Keywords
  - Remaining Keywords
- ☐ Resume Keywords for Your Profession
  - Account Base Establishment & Maintenance
  - Bidding Process
  - Building Inspection & Compliance
  - Building Maintenance
  - Building Services
  - Business & Administrative Functions
  - CAD (Computer-aided Design) Drafting
  - Carpentry
  - Ceiling, Lathing, Insulation & Drywall Installation
  - Construction
  - Contracts & Negotiations
  - Cost Management
  - Custodial / Janitorial Services
  - Customer & Client Servicing
  - Electrical
  - Electrical Engineering
  - Environmental Compliance
  - Equipment, Machinery, Tools & Testing Devices
  - General Contracting / Trades Management
  - Glazier Projects & Functions
  - Heavy Equipment Operations
  - HVAC / HVAC-R
  - Inspections & Compliance
  - Labor Relations
  - Landscaping & Groundskeeping
  - Masonry
  - Plumbing
  - Project Management
  - Trades Coordination & Oversight
  - Welding / Steamfitting
- ☐ Technical Skills

RESUME KEYWORD INSTRUCTIONS

INTRODUCTION

Resume Keywords are industry buzz words and phrases that prospective employers use to search resumes for the right candidates to fill their open positions. Keywords include core competencies *(your areas of expertise)*, position titles you've held, job-specific skills, soft skills *(personal attributes and capabilities)*, industry credentials *(licenses, certifications, degrees, training)*, and knowledge areas.

Resume Keywords are essential to include in your resume as most hiring managers use Applicant Tracking Software (ATS) to determine whether to "screen in" or "screen out" job candidates by scanning for keywords that match the position they wish to fill. They also search Internet job sites and LinkedIn profiles to find suitable candidates using these job-related keywords. If your resume does not contain important keywords relative to the position you seek, it may never be seen by human eyes. This Book contains the largest keywords resource available for your profession. The more applicable keywords you include in your resume, the higher your probability of being called in for interviews.

INSTRUCTIONS

Scroll through the category lists in this chapter and check off all core competencies you are proficient and/or knowledgeable in as they relate to your targeted position. Then to be sure you've left no stone unturned, search job boards for positions that interest you to ensure you have captured all keywords contained in those postings. In Step 3: Check Off Your Personal Attributes, you will determine your soft skills.

You will be including your primary keywords in your *"Professional Summary,"* your secondary keywords under *"Core Competencies,"* and remaining keywords within your employment bullets under *"Professional Experience."* You can also include a personally branded slogan containing some of your primary keywords under your resume header.

SAMPLE USE OF KEYWORDS IN YOUR RESUME

Following is an example of how resume keywords *(underlined)* can be infused within the various sections of your resume:

YOUR NAME
123 FIRST AVENUE, TOWN, ST 00000 | (000) 000-0000
Email: xxxx@xxxxxx.com | LinkedIn: linkedin.com/xxxxxx | Web Portfolio: YourName.com

Completing Quality Projects on Time and Within Budget...Every Time

PROFESSIONAL SUMMARY

A results-oriented, profitability-conscious Project Manager with more than 12 years of experience spanning all aspects of project management, trades coordination, labor relations management, and structural problem solving via action-driven leadership, direction, and support. Extensive background in managing major commercial construction projects including high-rise buildings, corporate offices, colleges and universities, public buildings, hospitals, and shopping malls. Adept at coordinating multiple subcontractors simultaneously and in developing tactical action plans that direct high-producing teams to overcome boundaries and successfully meet all challenges.

CORE COMPETENCIES

- Full Project Lifecycle Management
- Functional Specifications Development
- Project Time Tracking
- Quality Management

- Cost Estimate Preparation
- Proposals Review & Approval
- Client Presentations
- Scope Change Requests

- Budget Monitoring & Control
- Resource Allocation
- Customer Satisfaction
- Change Management

PROFESSIONAL EXPERIENCE

2012-Present: CONSTRUCTION PROJECT MANAGER | ABC Company | Town, ST

- Provide <u>construction management leadership and direction</u> in the design and build of <u>commercial building projects</u> ranging $1.5 to $5 million for this multimillion-dollar leading <u>construction management firm</u> with three locations.

- Effectively plan, manage, and lead <u>commercial projects</u> from <u>inception through close-out</u>, directing the activities of all <u>trades</u> to ensure projects are completed with <u>high quality</u> <u>on time</u> and <u>within budget</u>.

- Facilitate various <u>project management functions</u> including the review and/or modification of <u>construction drawings</u>, development of <u>job estimates</u>, securing <u>competitive bids</u>, handling <u>contract negotiations</u>, scheduling and coordinating <u>trades</u>, and processing <u>change orders</u>—to the customers' complete satisfaction.

…and so on

Let's get started selecting your Resume Keywords…

LIST YOUR RESUME KEYWORDS

INSTRUCTIONS

After you check off your applicable keywords in this section, come back to this page to list them, as follows:

- Your **Primary Keywords** are those functions you are most proficient in as they relate to your targeted field. They will be included within your *"Professional Summary"* section at the top of your resume (as described in **Step 6: Pull Your Resume Together**) as well as in your Personally Branded Bio and LinkedIn Profile.

- Your **Secondary Keywords** are more "explanatory" as to what your primary keywords involve. These will be listed in your *"Core Competencies"* section of your resume.

- All **Remaining Keywords** should be infused within the bullets in your *"Professional Experience"* section where they are applicable to the functions you handled. These are already included in the bullets contained in **Step 5: Select Your Resume ClipBullets**. *(See sample on preceding page.)*

Note: Less important keywords—such as those performed in lower-level positions—can be omitted unless, for example, hands-on performance of those skills are mentioned as "required" in the job descriptions you researched.

PRIMARY KEYWORDS

SECONDARY KEYWORDS

REMAINING KEYWORDS

SELECT RESUME KEYWORDS FOR YOUR PROFESSION

INSTRUCTIONS: *Place one "X" before all areas of expertise in which you are knowledgeable.*
Place "XX" before all areas in which you are highly proficient and they directly target your profession.

Account Base Establishment & Maintenance

ACCOUNT BASE ESTABLISHMENT & MAINTENANCE – GENERAL

- ☐☐ Account Base Establishment
- ☐☐ Account Services Management
- ☐☐ Accounts Receivable
- ☐☐ Budget Monitoring
- ☐☐ Clients Goals Identification
- ☐☐ Client Meetings
- ☐☐ Client Trust Building
- ☐☐ Cost Expenditure Monitoring
- ☐☐ Customer Service Support
- ☐☐ Existing Accounts Maintenance
- ☐☐ High Return on Investment
- ☐☐ Long-Term Business Planning
- ☐☐ New Client Relationships
- ☐☐ Payment Acceptance
- ☐☐ Presentations
- ☐☐ Repeat Business
- ☐☐ Sales Promotions
- ☐☐ Solutions Selling
- ☐☐ Strong Follow-Up
- ☐☐ Work-In-Progress Records

- ☐☐ Account Profitability
- ☐☐ Account Servicing
- ☐☐ Administrative Support
- ☐☐ Client Account Support
- ☐☐ Client Leads Generation
- ☐☐ Client Needs Assessment
- ☐☐ Closing Sales
- ☐☐ Customer Billing
- ☐☐ Daily Administration
- ☐☐ Expenditure Monitoring
- ☐☐ High-end Project Sales
- ☐☐ New Account Base Establishment
- ☐☐ New Prospects Solicitation
- ☐☐ Payment Schedules Establishment
- ☐☐ Quality Control Systems Development
- ☐☐ Reputation Management
- ☐☐ Sales Strategy
- ☐☐ Strategic Leadership & Direction
- ☐☐ Strong Phone Sales
- ☐☐ Other: _____

- ☐☐ Account Service-Related Documents
- ☐☐ Accountability Systems Development
- ☐☐ Budget Development
- ☐☐ Client Follow-up & Advisement
- ☐☐ Client Needs Assessment
- ☐☐ Client Support
- ☐☐ Contract Negotiations
- ☐☐ Customer Relationship Building
- ☐☐ Data Management
- ☐☐ High Referral Base
- ☐☐ Key Account Sales
- ☐☐ New Account Development
- ☐☐ Overdue Accounts Receivable Reduction
- ☐☐ Per-Project Sales Increase
- ☐☐ Relationship Building
- ☐☐ Sales Forecasting
- ☐☐ Sales Tracking
- ☐☐ Strategy Execution
- ☐☐ Territory Expansion

58

Bidding Process

BIDDING PROCESS

- ☐☐ Acquisition Methods
- ☐☐ Construction Methods Compliance
- ☐☐ Cost Estimating
- ☐☐ Price Change Evaluations
- ☐☐ Product Delivery Resolution
- ☐☐ Vendor Performance Monitoring
- ☐☐ Vendor Reliability Cost Analyses

- ☐☐ Bid Specification Preparation
- ☐☐ Construction Proposals
- ☐☐ Customer Satisfaction
- ☐☐ Pricing & Payment Terms
- ☐☐ Production Bids
- ☐☐ Solutions Development
- ☐☐ Weighted Value Procedures

- ☐☐ Awards Issuance
- ☐☐ Contract Negotiation
- ☐☐ Lifecycle Costing
- ☐☐ Materials Costing
- ☐☐ Proposal Evaluations
- ☐☐ Value Analysis
- ☐☐ Vendor Evaluations

- ☐☐ Construction Bids
- ☐☐ Contractor Selection
- ☐☐ Manufacturing Bids
- ☐☐ Product Requirements
- ☐☐ Purchasing Alternatives
- ☐☐ Vendor Bids
- ☐☐ Other: _____

27

Building Inspection & Compliance

BUILDING INSPECTION / COMPLIANCE

- ☐☐ Air Quality
- ☐☐ Asphalt Paving & Grading Operations
- ☐☐ Construction Contract Administration
- ☐☐ Corporate Buildings
- ☐☐ Drain, Waste & Vent Lines
- ☐☐ Energy Conservation Requirements
- ☐☐ Environmental, Health & Safety Standards
- ☐☐ Fire Regulations

- ☐☐ Alarms & Smoke Control Systems
- ☐☐ Building Code Regulations Compliance
- ☐☐ Construction Site Development
- ☐☐ Ditches & Dredging
- ☐☐ Electrical Wiring
- ☐☐ Energy Efficiency Measures
- ☐☐ Excavation & Fill Operations
- ☐☐ Fire Sprinklers

- ☐☐ Asbestos Abatement Procedures
- ☐☐ Commercial Roofing Systems
- ☐☐ Contract Specifications
- ☐☐ Demolition & Remodel Procedures
- ☐☐ Elevator & Escalator Inspections
- ☐☐ Enforcement Activities
- ☐☐ Fire Protection Equipment
- ☐☐ Food Product Safety

- ☐☐ Gas & Oil Piping
- ☐☐ Hazardous Materials Pollution Control
- ☐☐ Home Systems
- ☐☐ Plumbing Systems
- ☐☐ Reinforced Concrete Structures
- ☐☐ Sewer & Water System Inspections
- ☐☐ Structural Quality & Safety
- ☐☐ Water Supply & Distribution Systems
- ☐☐ Chlorofluorocarbon & Hydrochlorofluorocarbon Refrigerant Control
- ☐☐ Commercial Construction Repair Practices, Materials & Equipment

- ☐☐ Gas-fired & Oil-fired Appliances
- ☐☐ Health Care Quality
- ☐☐ Ordinance Violations
- ☐☐ Quality Assurance
- ☐☐ Safety Practices
- ☐☐ Stop Work Orders
- ☐☐ Structural Steel
- ☐☐ Zoning Laws & Regulations

- ☐☐ Gasoline & Butane Tanks
- ☐☐ HVAC Systems
- ☐☐ OSHA Standards
- ☐☐ Quality Control
- ☐☐ Security Systems
- ☐☐ Street & Highway Inspections
- ☐☐ Water Rights Adjudication
- ☐☐ Other: _____

53

Building Maintenance

BUILDING MAINTENANCE

- ☐☐ Boiler & Chiller Inspections & Repair
- ☐☐ Carpentry/Construction Work
- ☐☐ Construction Oversight
- ☐☐ Cost Reductions & Savings
- ☐☐ Emergency Lighting System
- ☐☐ Executive Office Facilities
- ☐☐ Facility Surveys
- ☐☐ Generator Operations
- ☐☐ Inspections & Compliance
- ☐☐ Machinery Maintenance & Repair
- ☐☐ Office Relocations
- ☐☐ Painting
- ☐☐ Renovations
- ☐☐ Safety & Responsibility for Others
- ☐☐ Sprinkler System Installation / Repair
- ☐☐ Work Collaboration

- ☐☐ Building Maintenance & Repair
- ☐☐ Client Relations
- ☐☐ Continuous Office Space Planning
- ☐☐ Custodial Services
- ☐☐ Environmental, Health & Safety
- ☐☐ Facility Functioning
- ☐☐ Furniture & Equipment Purchasing
- ☐☐ Groundskeeping
- ☐☐ Inventory Control
- ☐☐ Messenger & Courier Services
- ☐☐ Office Renovation & Furnishing
- ☐☐ Plumbing
- ☐☐ Repairs
- ☐☐ Security Systems
- ☐☐ Telecommunications Systems
- ☐☐ Work Inspections

- ☐☐ Building Management
- ☐☐ Company Relocations
- ☐☐ Corporate Office Relocations
- ☐☐ Electrical Wiring
- ☐☐ Equipment Installation & Moves
- ☐☐ Facility Record Maintenance
- ☐☐ Floor Plans
- ☐☐ HVAC Operations
- ☐☐ Maintenance & Repair Reports
- ☐☐ Mailroom Operations
- ☐☐ OSHA Compliance
- ☐☐ Productivity Improvement
- ☐☐ Roofing Repairs
- ☐☐ Special Event Set-ups
- ☐☐ Warehousing
- ☐☐ Other: _____

47

BUILDING MAINTENANCE SYSTEM TYPES

- ☐☐ Boilers (Gas / Electric / Open Flame)
- ☐☐ Commercial Plumbing Systems
- ☐☐ Energy Management Control System (EMCS)
- ☐☐ Energy Related Equipment & Control Systems
- ☐☐ Gas & Electric Heating Systems
- ☐☐ Heating, Cooling & Ventilation Systems
- ☐☐ Industrial Plumbing Systems
- ☐☐ Residential Plumbing Systems
- ☐☐ Water Systems

- ☐☐ Building Management Systems
- ☐☐ Distribution Systems & Controls
- ☐☐ Domestic Plumbing Systems
- ☐☐ Fire Sprinkler Systems
- ☐☐ HVAC Electric Systems
- ☐☐ In-Door Plumbing Systems
- ☐☐ Refrigeration Systems
- ☐☐ Split Systems
- ☐☐ Winterizing Systems

- ☐☐ Cooling Systems
- ☐☐ Drainage Systems
- ☐☐ Gas Systems
- ☐☐ Heating Systems
- ☐☐ HVAC Systems
- ☐☐ Piping Systems
- ☐☐ Plumbing Systems
- ☐☐ Sprinkler Systems
- ☐☐ Other: _____

26

Building Services

BUILDING SERVICES ENGINEERING

- ☐☐ BREEAM (BRE Environmental Assessment Method)
- ☐☐ CIBSE Low Carbon Consultants (LCC) Status
- ☐☐ Construction Suitability Assessments
- ☐☐ Energy Management
- ☐☐ Environmental Impact Minimization
- ☐☐ Fire Detection & Protection
- ☐☐ Information Technology Networking
- ☐☐ Whole Lifecycle Costing Techniques

- ☐☐ Building Sustainability
- ☐☐ Conservation Methods
- ☐☐ Energy Assessors (LCEA) Status
- ☐☐ Engineering Integration
- ☐☐ Environmentally Friendly Operation
- ☐☐ Health & Safety Compliance
- ☐☐ Low Carbon Technologies
- ☐☐ Other: _____

- ☐☐ Carbon Emissions Reduction
- ☐☐ Cost Efficiency
- ☐☐ Energy Distribution
- ☐☐ Engineering Systems
- ☐☐ Environmentally Sustainable
- ☐☐ Lightning Protection
- ☐☐ Sustainable & Green Design

BUILDING SERVICES SPECIALIZATIONS

- ☐☐ Construction
- ☐☐ Design
- ☐☐ Development
- ☐☐ Implementation
- ☐☐ Maintenance
- ☐☐ Monitoring
- ☐☐ Operation
- ☐☐ Other: _____

7

BUILDING ENGINEERING SYSTEMS

- ☐☐ Air Filtration
- ☐☐ Alarm Systems
- ☐☐ Building Facades
- ☐☐ Communication Lines
- ☐☐ Distribution Boards
- ☐☐ Electrical
- ☐☐ Environmental
- ☐☐ HVAC
- ☐☐ Low Voltage (LV) Systems
- ☐☐ Mechanical
- ☐☐ Natural & Artificial Lighting
- ☐☐ Plumbing
- ☐☐ Refrigeration
- ☐☐ Renewable Energy
- ☐☐ Security
- ☐☐ Sustainable Energy
- ☐☐ Water, Draining & Plumbing
- ☐☐ Ventilation
- ☐☐ Others: _____

18

BUILDING MAINTENANCE SYSTEM TYPES

- ☐☐ Boilers (Gas / Electric / Open Flame)
- ☐☐ Building Management Systems
- ☐☐ Cooling Systems
- ☐☐ Commercial Plumbing Systems
- ☐☐ Distribution Systems & Controls
- ☐☐ Drainage Systems
- ☐☐ Energy Management Control System (EMCS)
- ☐☐ Domestic Plumbing Systems
- ☐☐ Gas Systems
- ☐☐ Energy Related Equipment & Control Systems
- ☐☐ Fire Sprinkler Systems
- ☐☐ Heating Systems
- ☐☐ Gas & Electric Heating Systems
- ☐☐ HVAC Electric Systems
- ☐☐ HVAC Systems
- ☐☐ Heating, Cooling & Ventilation Systems
- ☐☐ In-Door Plumbing Systems
- ☐☐ Piping Systems
- ☐☐ Industrial Plumbing Systems
- ☐☐ Refrigeration Systems
- ☐☐ Plumbing Systems
- ☐☐ Residential Plumbing Systems
- ☐☐ Split Systems
- ☐☐ Sprinkler Systems
- ☐☐ Water Systems
- ☐☐ Winterizing Systems
- ☐☐ Other: _____

26

Business & Administrative Functions

ADMINISTRATION & GENERAL BUSINESS

- ☐☐ Account Servicing
- ☐☐ Administration
- ☐☐ Administration Management
- ☐☐ Administrative Support
- ☐☐ Appointment Scheduling
- ☐☐ Back-office Operations
- ☐☐ Benefits Administration
- ☐☐ Bids Preparation
- ☐☐ Billing
- ☐☐ Bookkeeping
- ☐☐ Budget Administration
- ☐☐ Budget Database Updating
- ☐☐ Budget Development
- ☐☐ Building / Lease Contracts
- ☐☐ Business Analysis
- ☐☐ Business Plans
- ☐☐ Certificates of Insurance Monitoring
- ☐☐ Cash Receipts Recording
- ☐☐ Claims Avoidance Handling
- ☐☐ Claims & Litigations Research
- ☐☐ Client Correspondence
- ☐☐ Client Interface
- ☐☐ Client Needs Assessment
- ☐☐ Client Relations
- ☐☐ Communications
- ☐☐ Compliance Oversight
- ☐☐ Computer Troubleshooting
- ☐☐ Contract Development & Review
- ☐☐ Contract Issue Resolution
- ☐☐ Contract Negotiations
- ☐☐ Contract Records & Reports
- ☐☐ Correspondence Composition
- ☐☐ Cost Reductions & Savings
- ☐☐ Customer Handling
- ☐☐ Customer Service
- ☐☐ Data Entry
- ☐☐ Database Maintenance
- ☐☐ Deliveries
- ☐☐ Departmental Support
- ☐☐ Deposits Preparation
- ☐☐ Dispute Resolution
- ☐☐ Document Filing
- ☐☐ Document Preparation
- ☐☐ Document Processing
- ☐☐ Document Scanning
- ☐☐ Emailing
- ☐☐ Executive Assistance
- ☐☐ Expense Report Processing
- ☐☐ Expense Reporting
- ☐☐ Facility Management
- ☐☐ Faxing
- ☐☐ Financial Data Research
- ☐☐ Fulfillment
- ☐☐ General Office Administration
- ☐☐ Goods Transfers
- ☐☐ Grant Applications Development
- ☐☐ Interdisciplinary Team Meetings
- ☐☐ Internet Research
- ☐☐ Inventory Management & Control
- ☐☐ Invoicing
- ☐☐ Job Assignments
- ☐☐ Job Cost Reporting
- ☐☐ Labor Relations
- ☐☐ Legal Records Maintenance
- ☐☐ Logistics Management
- ☐☐ Mail Processing
- ☐☐ Maintenance Activities
- ☐☐ Management Support
- ☐☐ Material Requisitioning
- ☐☐ Materials Distribution
- ☐☐ Materials Scheduling
- ☐☐ Meeting Agenda
- ☐☐ Negotiations
- ☐☐ Networking
- ☐☐ Office Management
- ☐☐ Office Services
- ☐☐ Office Space Planning
- ☐☐ Office Supplies Purchasing
- ☐☐ Operations Management
- ☐☐ Order Processing
- ☐☐ Payment Requisition Processing

☐☐ Payroll Issues Resolution
☐☐ Procedures Development
☐☐ Progress Update Reports
☐☐ Project Management Support
☐☐ Quality Assurance
☐☐ Records Management
☐☐ Risk Management
☐☐ Shipping & Receiving
☐☐ Subcontracts Monitoring
☐☐ Switchboard Operations
☐☐ Transportation
☐☐ Vendor Relations
☐☐ Work Flow Coordination

☐☐ Pricing Strategies Development
☐☐ Procurement
☐☐ Project Planning & Coordination
☐☐ Project Scheduling / Timelines
☐☐ Quality Control
☐☐ Report Generation
☐☐ Sales Progress Tracking
☐☐ Spreadsheets Preparation
☐☐ Supplies Reordering
☐☐ Time Cards Approval
☐☐ Travel Arrangements
☐☐ Word Processing
☐☐ Workflow Management

☐☐ Printing
☐☐ Productivity Improvement
☐☐ Project Life Cycle
☐☐ Purchasing
☐☐ Recordkeeping
☐☐ Research & Analysis
☐☐ Security
☐☐ Stock Distribution
☐☐ Support Staff Training
☐☐ Trades Work Direction
☐☐ Vendor Communications
☐☐ Work Collaboration
☐☐ Other: _____

119

ADMINISTRATIVE MANAGEMENT

☐☐ Accounting & Financial Recordkeeping
☐☐ Budget Development & Expenditure Control
☐☐ Contracts Administration
☐☐ Customer Service Management
☐☐ Employee Benefit Programs Administration
☐☐ Health & Safety Program Development
☐☐ Inventory Management & Control
☐☐ Productivity Improvement
☐☐ Presentation Preparation
☐☐ Staff Training

☐☐ Administrative Management
☐☐ Compensation Management
☐☐ Contract Negotiations
☐☐ Database Set-up & Management
☐☐ Facility Management
☐☐ Office Management
☐☐ Personnel Management
☐☐ Purchasing Management
☐☐ Risk Management
☐☐ Workflow Management

☐☐ Change Management
☐☐ Contractor Bids Issuance
☐☐ Cost Reductions & Savings
☐☐ Dispute Resolution
☐☐ Human Resource Management
☐☐ Operations Management
☐☐ Policies & Procedures Development
☐☐ Records Management
☐☐ Staff Management
☐☐ Other: _____

29

INVENTORY MANAGEMENT & CONTROL

☐☐ Access Control Installation
☐☐ Access Control Support
☐☐ Bookkeeping Assistance
☐☐ Collaborative Vendor Forecasting
☐☐ Control Inventory Management System
☐☐ Customer Access Control
☐☐ Digital Video
☐☐ Electronic Security Systems
☐☐ File Organizing & Maintenance
☐☐ Integrated Systems
☐☐ Inventory Accounting Tools Software
☐☐ Inventory Control Management
☐☐ Inventory Control Software
☐☐ Inventory Control Spreadsheet
☐☐ Inventory Management Software
☐☐ Office Practices & Procedures
☐☐ Personnel Accountability
☐☐ Policies, Procedures, Processes & Forms
☐☐ Production Planning Inventory Control
☐☐ Software License Transactions
☐☐ Spreadsheet & Database Tools

☐☐ Access Control Inventory
☐☐ Asset Protection
☐☐ Business Letter Writing
☐☐ Computer Networking
☐☐ Control Inventory Module Software
☐☐ Detailed Clerical Work Accurately
☐☐ Direct Importing
☐☐ Employee Safety
☐☐ Grammar & Punctuation
☐☐ Inventory Access Control
☐☐ Inventory Accuracy Software
☐☐ Inventory Control Processing
☐☐ Inventory Control System
☐☐ Inventory Shrinkage Reduction
☐☐ Inventory Tracking Software
☐☐ Online Stock Control
☐☐ Quality Control Access Inventory
☐☐ Recordkeeping
☐☐ Security & Asset Protection
☐☐ Spare Parts Inventory Control
☐☐ Statistical Process Control

☐☐ Access Control Maintenance
☐☐ Bill Paying
☐☐ Card Control Inventory
☐☐ Control Form Inventory
☐☐ Correct English Usage
☐☐ Customer Service
☐☐ Distribution Process
☐☐ Facilities
☐☐ Human Resources
☐☐ Inventory Accounting
☐☐ Inventory Control Point
☐☐ Invoice Process
☐☐ Loss Reduction
☐☐ Order Entry
☐☐ Operating Equipment
☐☐ Order Processing
☐☐ Quality Control
☐☐ Secure Asset Storage
☐☐ Stock Control
☐☐ Tool Control & Inventory
☐☐ Other: _____

62

OFFICE SUPPORT

☐☐ Activity Coordination
☐☐ Assignment Oversight
☐☐ Budget Monitoring
☐☐ Conference Coordination
☐☐ Customer Complaint Handling
☐☐ Document Processing

☐☐ Administrative Functions
☐☐ Billing
☐☐ Complex Tasks
☐☐ Confidential Matters
☐☐ Customer Service & Support
☐☐ Discretion Exercising

☐☐ Appointment Scheduling
☐☐ Bookkeeping
☐☐ Complex Info. Interpretation
☐☐ Correspondence Writing
☐☐ Dictation & Transcription
☐☐ Email Generation

☐☐ Event Coordination
☐☐ Financial Transactions
☐☐ Keyboarding
☐☐ Management Liaison
☐☐ Memoranda
☐☐ Multiple Projects Handling
☐☐ Office Support
☐☐ Public Relations Contacts
☐☐ Report Preparation
☐☐ Screening Callers & Visitors
☐☐ Support Staff Supervision

☐☐ Filing
☐☐ Greeting Visitors
☐☐ Legal Secretarial Support
☐☐ Medical Secretarial Support
☐☐ Meeting Scheduling
☐☐ Nonroutine Secretarial Functions
☐☐ Problem Resolution
☐☐ Record Keeping
☐☐ Research & Analysis
☐☐ Shorthand
☐☐ Telephone Answering

☐☐ Financial Record Keeping
☐☐ Independent Judgment
☐☐ Letter Composition
☐☐ Medical Terminology
☐☐ Minutes of Meetings
☐☐ Office Management
☐☐ Procedure Development
☐☐ Report Generation
☐☐ Sales Contracts
☐☐ Spreadsheets
☐☐ Other: _____

50

PURCHASING

☐☐ Acquisition Management
☐☐ Bidding
☐☐ Client Interface
☐☐ Competitive Bidding
☐☐ Delivery Scheduling
☐☐ Expediting
☐☐ Leasing
☐☐ Office Supplies
☐☐ Order Processing
☐☐ Production Materials
☐☐ Request for Proposal (RFP)
☐☐ Supplier Management
☐☐ Vendor Relations
☐☐ Warehouse Management

☐☐ Adjustments
☐☐ Blanket Orders
☐☐ Client & Vendor Records Maintenance
☐☐ Computer Equipment
☐☐ Contract Terms & Negotiations
☐☐ High Volume Processing
☐☐ Logistics Management
☐☐ Materials Replenishment Ordering
☐☐ Pricing Negotiations
☐☐ Promotional Items
☐☐ Request for Quotation (RFQ)
☐☐ Trade Shows
☐☐ Vendor Partnerships
☐☐ Other: _____

☐☐ Barter Arrangements
☐☐ Capital Equipment Acquisition
☐☐ Comparative Cost Analyses
☐☐ Contract Change Orders
☐☐ Distribution Management
☐☐ Inventory Control / Management
☐☐ Materials Management
☐☐ Office Machinery
☐☐ Procurement
☐☐ Purchase Orders
☐☐ Strong Follow-up
☐☐ Vendor Bids
☐☐ Warehousing

43

CAD (Computer-aided Design) Drafting

CAD DRAFTING – GENERAL

☐☐ Administrative Functions
☐☐ Architectural Drawings & Renderings
☐☐ Client Meeting & Strategizing
☐☐ Cost Reductions & Savings
☐☐ Customer Service & Problem Resolution
☐☐ Interdisciplinary/Project Team Member
☐☐ Project Prioritization & Demand Balancing
☐☐ Recordkeeping
☐☐ Other: _____

☐☐ Architectural Drafting
☐☐ Architectural Engineering
☐☐ Client Billing
☐☐ Client Relations
☐☐ Design-and-Build Projects
☐☐ Project Time Tracking
☐☐ Quality Assurance
☐☐ Work Collaboration

☐☐ Architectural Drafting Management
☐☐ Assessments & Evaluations
☐☐ Client Presentations & Proposals
☐☐ Project Development & Initiation
☐☐ Project Management Support
☐☐ Project Planning & Coordination
☐☐ Structural Engineering
☐☐ Zoning & Building Codes

24

CAD DRAFTING TYPES

☐☐ 3D & Sectional Views
☐☐ Construction Documents
☐☐ Drafting Principles & Standards
☐☐ Horizontal & Vertical Grounds Design
☐☐ Interior Designer Coordination
☐☐ Land Development
☐☐ Parts Specifications
☐☐ Preliminary Drawings
☐☐ Profile Sheet Plotting & Drafting
☐☐ Quantity & Cost Estimates
☐☐ Technical Details
☐☐ Topographical Overlays

☐☐ Architectural Renderings
☐☐ Cross-sections
☐☐ Exterior Elevations
☐☐ Flow Sheets
☐☐ Interior Elevations
☐☐ Layout Diagrams
☐☐ Overlays
☐☐ Plans
☐☐ Profile Drawings
☐☐ Schematic Designs
☐☐ Technical Reports
☐☐ Working Plans

☐☐ Base Drawings
☐☐ Drawings
☐☐ Field Surveys
☐☐ Illustrations
☐☐ Isometrics
☐☐ Maps
☐☐ Perspective Drawings
☐☐ Presentations
☐☐ Rough Sketches
☐☐ Specifications
☐☐ Thumbnails
☐☐ Other: _____

35

CAD DRAFTING PROJECT TYPES

Commercial Drafting

☐☐ Building Complexes	☐☐ Building Lobbies	☐☐ Churches & Temples	☐☐ College Campuses
☐☐ Clean Rooms	☐☐ Commercial Buildings	☐☐ Communities	☐☐ Corporate Buildings
☐☐ Corporate Offices	☐☐ Drive-Up Units	☐☐ Elevators	☐☐ Escalators
☐☐ Financial Institutions / Banks	☐☐ Government Agencies	☐☐ Healthcare Facilities	☐☐ Hotels	Resorts
☐☐ Industrial Parks	☐☐ Interior Design	☐☐ Interior Renovation	☐☐ Laboratories
☐☐ Landmark Restorations	☐☐ Landscape Design	☐☐ Manufacturing Plants	☐☐ New Construction
☐☐ Office Space Planning	☐☐ Private Buildings	☐☐ Public Buildings	☐☐ Public	Private Schools
☐☐ Renovations	☐☐ Restaurants	☐☐ Restorations	☐☐ Retail Stores
☐☐ Shopping Malls	☐☐ Stores	☐☐ Universities	☐☐ Other: _____

35

Public / Civil Drafting

☐☐ Aerospace	☐☐ Agricultural Systems	☐☐ Airport Terminals	☐☐ Bridges
☐☐ Dams	☐☐ Flood Control Projects	☐☐ Government Buildings	☐☐ Ground Water Systems
☐☐ Highways & Roadways	☐☐ Irrigation Systems	☐☐ Marinas & Docks	☐☐ Municipal Projects
☐☐ Museums	☐☐ Nuclear	☐☐ Petroleum	☐☐ Pipelines
☐☐ Power Plants	☐☐ Public Utilities	☐☐ River Basin Systems	☐☐ Sewage Systems
☐☐ Surface Water Systems	☐☐ Transit Systems	☐☐ Transportation Systems	☐☐ Urban Centers
☐☐ Water Resource Management	☐☐ Water Distribution Systems	☐☐ Water Quality Systems	☐☐ Other: _____

27

Residential Drafting

☐☐ Apartment Buildings	☐☐ Condominiums	☐☐ Custom-built Baths	☐☐ Custom-built Kitchens
☐☐ Extensions	☐☐ Interior Design	☐☐ High-Rise Buildings	☐☐ Finished Attics
☐☐ Finished Basements	☐☐ Home Construction	☐☐ Home Improvements	☐☐ Landscape Design
☐☐ Room Additions	☐☐ Patios & Decks	☐☐ Room Remodeling	☐☐ Playgrounds
☐☐ Other: _____			

16

Electrical Drafting

☐☐ Electrical Systems	☐☐ Electromagnetic Systems	☐☐ Electronic Systems	☐☐ Electronic Equipment
☐☐ Electronic Facilities	☐☐ Electronic Products	☐☐ Exterior Lighting	☐☐ Interior Lighting
☐☐ Cable Systems	☐☐ Voltage Transformers	☐☐ Proximity Systems	☐☐ Fuel Systems
☐☐ Cargo Systems	☐☐ Power Systems	☐☐ Other: _____	

14

Electronics Drafting

☐☐ Electronic Parts	☐☐ Telecommunications Equipment	☐☐ Station Equipment	☐☐ Computer Hardware
☐☐ Advanced Electronic Equipment	☐☐ Terminal Equipment	☐☐ PC Support Equipment	☐☐ Electric Power Generators
☐☐ Electric Motors	☐☐ Industrial Control Systems	☐☐ Communications Systems	☐☐ Aircraft
☐☐ Machinery Controls	☐☐ Broadcast Systems	☐☐ Navigations Systems	☐☐ Other: _____

14

Manufacturing & Industrial Drafting

☐☐ Industrial Projects	☐☐ Products – Type: _____	☐☐ Environmental Projects
☐☐ Materials Projects	☐☐ Equipment – Type: _____	☐☐ Electrical Projects
☐☐ Electronics Projects	☐☐ Systems – Type: _____	☐☐ Mechanical Projects
☐☐ Structural Projects	☐☐ Services – Type: _____	☐☐ Other: _____

11

Mechanical Drafting

☐☐ Machinery	☐☐ Sheet Metal Steel Fabrication	☐☐ Structures	☐☐ Tooling
☐☐ Module Assemblies	☐☐ Engines	☐☐ Products	☐☐ Factories

☐☐ Mechanical Electrical Systems	☐☐ Mechanical Products	☐☐ Production Equipment	☐☐ Robotics
☐☐ Machine Processes	☐☐ Commercial Assembly	☐☐ Test Processes	☐☐ Fabrication Processes
☐☐ Plastic Processing	☐☐ Injection Molding	☐☐ Thermoforming	☐☐ Castings
☐☐ Other: _____			

20

Other Drafting

☐☐ Biomedical	☐☐ Chemical	☐☐ Environmental	☐☐ Geotechnical
☐☐ Industrial	☐☐ Information Technology	☐☐ Machine Tools	☐☐ Machinery
☐☐ Material Handling	☐☐ Mechanical	☐☐ Other: _____	

10

Carpentry

CARPENTRY / CONSTRUCTION SPECIALIZATIONS

☐☐ Acoustical Ceilings	☐☐ Alarms Systems	☐☐ Asbestos Abatement	☐☐ Blueprint Reading
☐☐ Color Concrete Surfaces	☐☐ Brattices	☐☐ Cabinet Making	☐☐ Carpeting
☐☐ Ceilings / Lathing	☐☐ Concrete Foundations	☐☐ Copper Flashings	☐☐ Columns
☐☐ Concrete & Steel Reinforcement	☐☐ Concrete Castings	☐☐ Demolition	☐☐ Decking
☐☐ Concrete Beams & Forms	☐☐ Ditches & Dredging	☐☐ Drywall Installation	☐☐ Elevators
☐☐ Excavation & Fill Operations	☐☐ Doors & Door Jambs	☐☐ Escalators	☐☐ Fences
☐☐ Exposed Aggregate Walls	☐☐ Fire Sprinklers	☐☐ Firebrick Linings	☐☐ Flooring
☐☐ Floor-to-Floor Build-outs	☐☐ Foundations	☐☐ Framing	☐☐ Gratings
☐☐ Irrigation Systems	☐☐ Hardware	☐☐ Insulation	☐☐ Landscaping
☐☐ Maintenance & Repair Projects	☐☐ Materials Transport	☐☐ Metal Stud Framing	☐☐ Millwork
☐☐ Masonry (Brick/Stone/Cement)	☐☐ Painting	☐☐ Paneling	☐☐ Partitions
☐☐ Paving & Grading	☐☐ Platforms	☐☐ Podiums	☐☐ Ramps
☐☐ Reinforced Concrete Structures	☐☐ Refractory Tile	☐☐ Roofing	☐☐ Scaffolding
☐☐ Roof-top Installations	☐☐ Security Systems	☐☐ Sheetrocking	☐☐ Siding Installation
☐☐ Sidewalks & Walkways	☐☐ Skylights	☐☐ Soaking Pits	☐☐ Solar Panels
☐☐ Smoke Control Systems	☐☐ Steel Reinforcement	☐☐ Steps / Stairs	☐☐ Stone Walls
☐☐ Steel & Concrete Construction	☐☐ Taping & Spackling	☐☐ Tiling	☐☐ Trim work
☐☐ Structural Insulated Wall Panels	☐☐ Weather Stripping	☐☐ Walls & Partitions	☐☐ Wall Coverings
☐☐ Waterproofing	☐☐ Windows / Glazing	☐☐ Other: _____	

74

CARPENTRY & MASONRY MATERIALS

☐☐ Black Iron	☐☐ Brick	☐☐ Brick Veneer	☐☐ Cal Shake	☐☐ Cedar Shake
☐☐ Cement Products	☐☐ Concrete	☐☐ Concrete Pavers	☐☐ Copings	☐☐ Drainage Supplies
☐☐ Face Brick	☐☐ Flashing	☐☐ Glass	☐☐ Granite	☐☐ Grout
☐☐ Hardy Shake	☐☐ Limestone	☐☐ Marble	☐☐ Metal Studs	☐☐ Masonry Ties
☐☐ Mortar	☐☐ Plywood	☐☐ Sheetrock	☐☐ Stone	☐☐ Structural Steel
☐☐ Stucco	☐☐ Terrazzo	☐☐ Tiles	☐☐ Vinyl Siding	☐☐ Wood Studs
☐☐ Other: _____				

30

CARPENTRY & CONSTRUCTION TOOLS

☐☐ Atlas Machines	☐☐ Axes	☐☐ Brush Hooks	☐☐ Bush Axes
☐☐ Carpet Knives & Shears	☐☐ Chainsaws	☐☐ Drill Presses	☐☐ Drills
☐☐ Grinders	☐☐ Hammers	☐☐ Hand Shovels	☐☐ Heat Irons
☐☐ Loop Pile Cutters	☐☐ Heliarc	☐☐ Knee Kickers	☐☐ Lathes
☐☐ Mechanical Soil Compactors	☐☐ Machine Saws	☐☐ Mallets	☐☐ Manifolds
☐☐ Mattocks	☐☐ Picks	☐☐ Post Hole Diggers	☐☐ Power Ladders
☐☐ Power Stretchers	☐☐ Power Tools	☐☐ Power Wet Saws	☐☐ Rakes
☐☐ Sanding Machines	☐☐ Saws	☐☐ Screw Guns	☐☐ Sheathing Guns
☐☐ Sledge Hammers	☐☐ Stages	☐☐ Staple Guns	☐☐ Testing Devices
☐☐ Torches	☐☐ Trowels	☐☐ Wall Trimmers	☐☐ Other: _____

CONSTRUCTION EQUIPMENT, MACHINERY & TOOLS

Refer to "Equipment, Machinery, Tools & Testing Devices."

Ceiling, Lathing, Insulation & Drywall Installation

CEILING, LATHING, INSULATION & DRYWALL INSTALLATION

☐☐ Acoustical Tiles Mounting	☐☐ Ceiling Framing	☐☐ Ceiling Installation
☐☐ Decorative Trim Installation	☐☐ Dry Lines Hanging	☐☐ Drywall & Plaster Applications
☐☐ Drywall Installation	☐☐ Drywall Mounting	☐☐ Drywall Mounting
☐☐ Energy Consumption Reductions	☐☐ Furring Inspections	☐☐ Furring Strips Installation
☐☐ Installation Methods	☐☐ Installation Preparation	☐☐ Insulation Installation
☐☐ Joint Sealing	☐☐ Lathing Installation	☐☐ Man Hour Time Reductions
☐☐ Masonry Inspections	☐☐ Materials Determination	☐☐ Metal Casings Installation
☐☐ Metal Frame Support Welding	☐☐ One-Person Drywall Ceiling Installations	☐☐ Partition Framing
☐☐ Plaster, Drywall, Paneling Removal	☐☐ Productivity Improvement	☐☐ Safety Guidelines
☐☐ Sealing Compound	☐☐ Shock-Absorbing Materials	☐☐ Surface Measurement & Marking
☐☐ Tile Installation	☐☐ Wall Framing	☐☐ Wallboard Fitting & Fastening
☐☐ Wire-Tie Lathing	☐☐ Work Coordination	☐☐ Other: _____

35

INSULATION TYPES

☐☐ Cellulose	☐☐ Fiberglass	☐☐ Foam	☐☐ Rock Wool Batt	☐☐ Other: _____

4

PROJECTS

☐☐ Attics	☐☐ Boilers	☐☐ Buildings	☐☐ Ceiling Concrete Surfaces
☐☐ Ceiling Joists	☐☐ Ceiling Partitions	☐☐ Ceilings	☐☐ Exterior Walls
☐☐ Paneling	☐☐ Plaster Walls	☐☐ Steam & Hot Water Pipes	☐☐ Storage Rooms
☐☐ Tanks	☐☐ Vats	☐☐ Other: _____	

14

Construction

CONSTRUCTION LEADERSHIP

☐☐ Account Management	☐☐ Approval Management	☐☐ Budget Development
☐☐ Building Codes Enforcement	☐☐ Building Inspectors Interface	☐☐ Building Site Inspections
☐☐ Business Operations Management	☐☐ Capital Improvement Projects	☐☐ Change Orders Negotiation
☐☐ Client Proposals Approval	☐☐ Client Relationship Management	☐☐ Codes Compliance
☐☐ Construction Documents Archival	☐☐ Competitive Bids	☐☐ Construction Cost Estimating
☐☐ Construction Documents Oversight	☐☐ Construction Drawings Review	☐☐ Construction Inspections
☐☐ Construction Management Leadership	☐☐ Construction Management Operations	☐☐ Construction Planning
☐☐ Construction Management Oversight	☐☐ Construction Methods Compliance	☐☐ Construction Timetables
☐☐ Construction Project Designs Execution	☐☐ Construction Progress Evaluation	☐☐ Construction Risk Mitigation
☐☐ Contract Administrative Management	☐☐ Construction Submittals Approval	☐☐ Contract Negotiations
☐☐ Cost-effective, Functional Completed Projects	☐☐ Construction Projects Oversight	☐☐ Design Guidelines Development
☐☐ Department of Transportation Inspections	☐☐ Department Procedures Development	☐☐ Design-and-build Oversight
☐☐ Department Standards Development	☐☐ Engineering Research & Analysis	☐☐ Dispute Resolution
☐☐ Environmental Quality Act	☐☐ Field Supervision Activities Oversight	☐☐ Financial Management
☐☐ Fire Regulations Compliance	☐☐ Fiscal Planning	☐☐ General Contracting Oversight
☐☐ Goals Establishment	☐☐ Health & Safety Regulations Compliance	☐☐ Job Estimates Development
☐☐ Key Customers Management	☐☐ Land Development Proposals	☐☐ Local Ordinances Compliance
☐☐ Municipal Regulatory Entities Oversight	☐☐ Management Practices Direction	☐☐ Municipal Permit Attainment
☐☐ Occupational Safety & Health Act compliance	☐☐ New Business Development	☐☐ Operating Plans Execution

- ☐☐ On-site Construction Supervision
- ☐☐ Project Management Practices Establishment
- ☐☐ Project Scheduling Oversight
- ☐☐ Quality Management
- ☐☐ Senior-level Construction Planning
- ☐☐ Specifications Compliance
- ☐☐ Strategic Goals & Priorities Establishment
- ☐☐ Teaming Alliances
- ☐☐ Zoning Laws Compliance

- ☐☐ Price/Cost Management
- ☐☐ Project Coordination Oversight
- ☐☐ Quality Assurance
- ☐☐ Regulatory Inspections Oversight
- ☐☐ Risk Management
- ☐☐ Specifications Standards Development
- ☐☐ Strategy Execution
- ☐☐ Trades Scheduling & Coordination
- ☐☐ Other: _____

- ☐☐ Procurement Processes Oversight
- ☐☐ Project Delivery Management
- ☐☐ Quality Control Ensurance
- ☐☐ Resource Acquisition
- ☐☐ Safety Codes Enforcement
- ☐☐ Strategic Business Planning
- ☐☐ Structural Stability Oversight
- ☐☐ Trades Supervision

82

CONSTRUCTION – GENERAL

- ☐☐ Administrative Management
- ☐☐ Budget Development & Expense Control
- ☐☐ Building & Safety Codes Enforcement
- ☐☐ Business Conduct Policies & Practices
- ☐☐ Construction Management Staff Supervision
- ☐☐ Construction Leadership & Oversight
- ☐☐ Construction Submittals Approval
- ☐☐ Contracts Development & Review
- ☐☐ Corporate Governance Systems Management
- ☐☐ Design Guidelines Development
- ☐☐ Employment Policies & Procedures Oversight
- ☐☐ Environmental Services Management
- ☐☐ Financial Recordkeeping Oversight
- ☐☐ Geospatial Information Services Oversight
- ☐☐ Long-range Goals Establishment
- ☐☐ Municipal Permit Attainment
- ☐☐ New Business Development Initiatives
- ☐☐ New Division / Department Start-up
- ☐☐ Performance Recognition Leadership
- ☐☐ Materials Procurement Oversight
- ☐☐ Policies & Procedures Development
- ☐☐ Project Lifecycle Oversight
- ☐☐ Project Planning & Coordination
- ☐☐ Project Resource Requirements
- ☐☐ Project Management Practices
- ☐☐ Resource Acquisition Direction
- ☐☐ Senior-level Construction Planning
- ☐☐ Specifications Standards Development
- ☐☐ Team Leadership & Direction
- ☐☐ Strategy Execution

- ☐☐ Asset Utilization Management
- ☐☐ Bidding Process Oversight
- ☐☐ Capital Improvement Projects
- ☐☐ Business Goals & Priorities Setting
- ☐☐ Claims Negotiation & Settlement
- ☐☐ Client Meeting & Strategizing
- ☐☐ Client Presentations & Proposals
- ☐☐ Client Relationship Building
- ☐☐ Construction Risk Mitigation
- ☐☐ Cost Reductions & Savings
- ☐☐ Distribution Support
- ☐☐ Engineer Management
- ☐☐ Field Supervision Oversight
- ☐☐ Increased Sales & Profitability
- ☐☐ Inspections & Compliance
- ☐☐ Job Bidding Oversight
- ☐☐ Key Customer Management
- ☐☐ Operating Plans Execution
- ☐☐ Profit & Loss Accountability
- ☐☐ Project Prioritization
- ☐☐ Project Development & Initiation
- ☐☐ Procurement Management
- ☐☐ Project Lifecycle Management
- ☐☐ Proposed Land Developments
- ☐☐ Regulatory Inspections
- ☐☐ Regulatory & Legal Standards
- ☐☐ Safety & Health Promotion
- ☐☐ Safety Program Execution
- ☐☐ Site Analysis
- ☐☐ Other: _____

- ☐☐ Approval Management
- ☐☐ Closeout Processing
- ☐☐ Construction Inspections
- ☐☐ Construction Timetables
- ☐☐ Corporate Affairs
- ☐☐ Contract Negotiations
- ☐☐ Cost Control
- ☐☐ Cost Estimating
- ☐☐ Cost Management
- ☐☐ Employee Retention
- ☐☐ Estimating Oversight
- ☐☐ Ethics & Compliance
- ☐☐ Field Quality Assurance
- ☐☐ Financial Management
- ☐☐ Increased Account Base
- ☐☐ Management Recruitment
- ☐☐ New Business Start-up
- ☐☐ Productivity Improvement
- ☐☐ Operations Management
- ☐☐ Organization Strategy
- ☐☐ Project Team Leadership
- ☐☐ Report Monitoring
- ☐☐ Research Management
- ☐☐ Property Management
- ☐☐ Property Purchases
- ☐☐ Proposal Presentations
- ☐☐ Quality Assurance
- ☐☐ Risk Assessment
- ☐☐ Strategic Planning

88

RESIDENTIAL PROJECTS

- ☐☐ Apartment Buildings
- ☐☐ Extensions
- ☐☐ Finished Basements
- ☐☐ Room Additions
- ☐☐ Other: _____

- ☐☐ Condominiums
- ☐☐ Interior Design
- ☐☐ Home Construction
- ☐☐ Patios & Decks

- ☐☐ Custom-built Baths
- ☐☐ High-Rise Buildings
- ☐☐ Home Improvements
- ☐☐ Room Remodeling

- ☐☐ Custom-built Kitchens
- ☐☐ Finished Attics
- ☐☐ Landscape Design
- ☐☐ Playgrounds

COMMERCIAL PROJECTS

- ☐☐ Building Complexes
- ☐☐ Clean Rooms
- ☐☐ Corporate Offices
- ☐☐ Financial Institutions
- ☐☐ Industrial Parks
- ☐☐ Landmark Restorations
- ☐☐ Office Space Planning

- ☐☐ Building Lobbies
- ☐☐ Commercial Buildings
- ☐☐ Drive-Up Units
- ☐☐ Government Agencies
- ☐☐ Interior Design
- ☐☐ Landscape Design
- ☐☐ Private Buildings

- ☐☐ Churches & Temples
- ☐☐ Communities
- ☐☐ Elevators
- ☐☐ Healthcare Facilities
- ☐☐ Interior Renovation
- ☐☐ Manufacturing Plants
- ☐☐ Public Buildings

- ☐☐ College Campuses
- ☐☐ Corporate Buildings
- ☐☐ Escalators
- ☐☐ Hotels / Resorts
- ☐☐ Laboratories
- ☐☐ New Construction
- ☐☐ Public / Private Schools

☐☐ Renovations   ☐☐ Restaurants   ☐☐ Restorations   ☐☐ Retail Stores

☐☐ Shopping Malls   ☐☐ Stores   ☐☐ Universities   ☐☐ Other: _____

PUBLIC WORKS PROJECTS

☐☐ Aerospace / Aeronautical	☐☐ Agricultural Systems	☐☐ Airport Runways	☐☐ Airport Terminals
☐☐ Atmospheric Sciences	☐☐ Bicycle Paths	☐☐ Biomechanics	☐☐ Bridges
☐☐ Buildings	☐☐ Canals	☐☐ Coastal & Ocean	☐☐ Complexes
☐☐ Construction	☐☐ Dams	☐☐ Disposal Systems	☐☐ Earth Science
☐☐ Earthquake	☐☐ Embankments	☐☐ Environmental	☐☐ Forensic
☐☐ Energy Management Systems	☐☐ Flood Control projects	☐☐ Geodesy	☐☐ Geophysics
☐☐ Environmentally-friendly Systems	☐☐ Government Buildings	☐☐ Geotechnical	☐☐ Harbors
☐☐ Ground Water Systems	☐☐ Highway Maintenance	☐☐ High-Speed Trains	☐☐ Light Rails
☐☐ High-Voltage Underground Cables	☐☐ Highways & Roadways	☐☐ Irrigation Systems	☐☐ Marinas & Docks
☐☐ Manufacturing Plants	☐☐ Materials Management	☐☐ Maritime Facilities	☐☐ Materials Science
☐☐ Metering Systems	☐☐ Metros	☐☐ Military	☐☐ Mining
☐☐ Monorails	☐☐ Municipal Projects	☐☐ Municipal Pumps	☐☐ Museums
☐☐ Pedestrial Safety Management System	☐☐ Parking Facilities	☐☐ Pipelines	☐☐ Ports
☐☐ Power Generation Systems	☐☐ Power Plants	☐☐ Public Buildings	☐☐ Public Utilities
☐☐ Railroads	☐☐ Retaining Walls	☐☐ Rights-of-Way	☐☐ Structural
☐☐ Pressure Reducing Chambers	☐☐ River Basin Systems	☐☐ Sewage Systems	☐☐ Traffic Control
☐☐ Sewage Treatment Facilities	☐☐ Surveying	☐☐ Tolling	☐☐ Water Systems
☐☐ Stand-by Power Generation	☐☐ Transit Systems	☐☐ Tunnels	☐☐ Wells
☐☐ Storage & Delivery Systems	☐☐ Transportation Systems	☐☐ Urban Centers	
☐☐ Storm Water Treatment Facilities	☐☐ Water Distribution Systems		☐☐ Water Main Crossings
☐☐ Sub-Soil Investigation & Earthing Systems	☐☐ Surface & Ground Water Systems		☐☐ Water Pumping Stations
☐☐ Water Resource Management Systems	☐☐ Water Quality Systems		☐☐ Water Supply Systems
☐☐ Water Storage Tanks & Delivery Systems	☐☐ Water Transmission & Distribution Mains		☐☐ Other: _____

86

Contracts & Negotiations

CONTRACT AREAS OF EXPERTISE

☐☐ Acquisition Documentation	☐☐ Award Fee Plans Development	☐☐ Accounting Principles
☐☐ Acquisition Process Automated Tools	☐☐ Business Writing	☐☐ Claims Avoidance
☐☐ Approved Acquisition Strategies Development	☐☐ Clinical Development	☐☐ Clinical Trials
☐☐ Approved Acquisition Strategies Execution	☐☐ Commercial Contracting	☐☐ Cost/Price Analysis
☐☐ Cost Accounting Principles	☐☐ Cost Components & Factors	☐☐ Customer Interface
☐☐ Cost Accounting Standards (CAS)	☐☐ Cost Proposal Oversight	☐☐ Data Entry
☐☐ Cost Proposal Preparation & Coordination	☐☐ CSA Contracts Structure	☐☐ Fixed Price Contracts
☐☐ Evaluation Criteria Development	☐☐ Facility Contract Management	☐☐ Government Contracting
☐☐ Federal Acquisition Regulations (FAR)	☐☐ Legal Correspondence Drafting	☐☐ Negotiations & Mediation
☐☐ Network Real Estate Principles & Practices	☐☐ Paralegal Certification	☐☐ Partner Management
☐☐ Post-Award Contract Management	☐☐ Pre-Solicitation Documentation	☐☐ Proposal Preparation
☐☐ Pre-Award Contract Management	☐☐ Quality Criteria Adherence	☐☐ Risk Mitigation
☐☐ Service Contract Administration	☐☐ Security Clearance	☐☐ Software Licensing
☐☐ Source Selection Plans Development	☐☐ Service Contract Management	☐☐ Task Order Closeouts
☐☐ Subcontract Administration	☐☐ Terms & Conditions Negotiation	☐☐ Other: _____
☐☐ Subcontractor Proposal Evaluation		

45

CONTRACTUAL PROCESS

☐☐ Contract Administration	☐☐ Contract Analysis	☐☐ Contract Approval
☐☐ Contract Closeout Processing	☐☐ Contract Practices & Procedures	☐☐ Contract Consistency
☐☐ Contract Development	☐☐ Contract Documentation	☐☐ Contract Drafting
☐☐ Contract Editing	☐☐ Contract Execution	☐☐ Contract Guidelines
☐☐ Contract Interpretation	☐☐ Contract Issues Response	☐☐ Contract Key Element Extraction
☐☐ Contract Language	☐☐ Contract Law	☐☐ Contract Management

© 2015–PRESENT EVELYN U. SALVADOR   **50**

☐☐ Contract Modifications   ☐☐ Contract Negotiations   ☐☐ Contract Performance Monitoring
☐☐ Contract Regulations   ☐☐ Contract Review Process   ☐☐ Contract Revisions
☐☐ Contract Set-Up   ☐☐ Contract Templates   ☐☐ Contract Terms & Conditions
☐☐ Contract Writing   ☐☐ Document Review & Redlining   ☐☐ Financial Aspects of Contracts
☐☐ Other: _____

30

CONTRACT & LEGAL DOCUMENT TYPES

☐☐ Agreements   ☐☐ Amendments   ☐☐ Best Practices
☐☐ Bids   ☐☐ Bidding Process, Formal   ☐☐ Bidding Review Procedures
☐☐ Briefings   ☐☐ Business Initiatives Support   ☐☐ Client Estimates
☐☐ Client Agreements   ☐☐ Clinical Trial Agreements   ☐☐ Consulting Services
☐☐ Contractual Documents   ☐☐ Estimates   ☐☐ Government Contracts
☐☐ Grant Requests   ☐☐ Integrated Requirements Documents   ☐☐ Guarantees
☐☐ Legal Correspondence   ☐☐ Legal Documents   ☐☐ Legal Standards
☐☐ License Agreements   ☐☐ Maintenance Services   ☐☐ Memoranda of Understanding
☐☐ Plans   ☐☐ Nondisclosure Agreements (NDAs)   ☐☐ Price Negotiation Memoranda
☐☐ Proposals   ☐☐ Requests for Comment (RFC)   ☐☐ Requests for Information (RFI)
☐☐ Software Agreements   ☐☐ Risk Mitigation & Management   ☐☐ Service Agreements
☐☐ Side Letters Preparation   ☐☐ Requests for Proposal (RFP)   ☐☐ Source Selection Reports
☐☐ Specifications   ☐☐ Subcontract Agreements   ☐☐ Subcontracting Procedures
☐☐ Subcontractor Agreements   ☐☐ Teaming Agreements   ☐☐ Technical Documents
☐☐ Technology Services   ☐☐ Warrantees   ☐☐ Other: _____

44

CONTRACTS ADMINISTRATION – CONSTRUCTION

☐☐ Architectural Principles   ☐☐ Pricing Strategy Development   ☐☐ Contractor Claims & Litigations
☐☐ Client Interface   ☐☐ Construction Requirements   ☐☐ Contractor Claims & Litigation Research
☐☐ Data Entry   ☐☐ Claims Avoidance   ☐☐ Design & Construction Law
☐☐ Bids Preparation   ☐☐ Dispute Resolution Methods   ☐☐ Electrical & Plumbing Codes
☐☐ Facility Service Contracts   ☐☐ Fire & Life Safety Codes   ☐☐ Identifying Risks
☐☐ Leasing Options   ☐☐ Legal Obligations Records   ☐☐ License Agreements & Amendments
☐☐ Monitoring Contract Status   ☐☐ Negotiating Contracts   ☐☐ Payment Vouchers Processing
☐☐ Proposal Terms Preparation   ☐☐ State & Local Building Codes   ☐☐ Rental Payment Amounts
☐☐ Real Estate Leases   ☐☐ Uniform Building Code   ☐☐ Terms & Conditions Interpretation
☐☐ Updating Budget Databases   ☐☐ Risk Mitigation Strategies   ☐☐ Other: _____

29

CONTRACT COMPLIANCE / QUALITY CONTROL

☐☐ Accounting Principles   ☐☐ Best Practices Compliance   ☐☐ Change Control
☐☐ Claims Litigation   ☐☐ Contract Management   ☐☐ Contractual Appropriations
☐☐ Contractual Issues   ☐☐ Corporate Policies   ☐☐ Cost Evaluations
☐☐ Data Security   ☐☐ Departmental Practices   ☐☐ Federal Contracting Law
☐☐ Issue Identification   ☐☐ Past Performance Factors   ☐☐ Preproposal Conferences
☐☐ Pricing Strategies   ☐☐ Proactive Quality Monitoring   ☐☐ Project Scope & Requirements
☐☐ Proposal Evaluations   ☐☐ Proposals Development   ☐☐ Regulations Compliance
☐☐ Federal Acquisition Regulations (FAR)   ☐☐ Risk Mitigation   ☐☐ Service Contract Act (SCA)
☐☐ FAR & DFAR, Agency FAR Supplements   ☐☐ Government Contracts Administration   ☐☐ Other: _____

26

GRANTS

☐☐ Cost Data Benchmarking   ☐☐ Electronic Grant Submissions   ☐☐ Government Procedures
☐☐ Grant Application Processing   ☐☐ Grant Application Writing   ☐☐ Grant Contracts
☐☐ Grant Programs   ☐☐ Grant Research   ☐☐ Grant Submission Coordination
☐☐ Grant Submission Processing   ☐☐ Legal Document Interpretation   ☐☐ Private Grants
☐☐ Procedures Administration   ☐☐ Procedures Development   ☐☐ Other: _____

14

CONSTRUCTION CONTRACTS ADMINISTRATION

- ☐☐ Architectural Principles
- ☐☐ Client Interface
- ☐☐ Contractor Claims & Litigations
- ☐☐ Developing Pricing Strategies
- ☐☐ Facility Service Contracts
- ☐☐ Leasing Options
- ☐☐ Monitoring Contract Status
- ☐☐ Proposal Terms Preparation
- ☐☐ State & Local Building Codes
- ☐☐ Updating Budget Databases

28

- ☐☐ Bids Preparation
- ☐☐ Construction Requirements
- ☐☐ Data Entry
- ☐☐ Dispute Resolution Methods
- ☐☐ Fire & Life Safety Codes
- ☐☐ Legal Obligations Records
- ☐☐ Negotiating Contracts
- ☐☐ Real Estate Leases
- ☐☐ Terms & Conditions Interpretation
- ☐☐ Other: _____

- ☐☐ Claims Avoidance
- ☐☐ Contractor Claims & Litigation Research
- ☐☐ Design & Construction Law
- ☐☐ Electrical & Plumbing Codes
- ☐☐ Identifying Risks & Risk Mitigation Strategies
- ☐☐ License Agreements & Amendments
- ☐☐ Payment Vouchers Processing
- ☐☐ Rental Payment Amounts
- ☐☐ Uniform Building Code

CONTRACT DATABASE SET-UP & MAINTENANCE

- ☐☐ Contracts Database
- ☐☐ Customer Files
- ☐☐ Database Set-up
- ☐☐ Locate Executed Contracts
- ☐☐ Pricing Tools
- ☐☐ Other: _____

15

- ☐☐ Correspondence
- ☐☐ Database Maintenance
- ☐☐ Electronic Files Management
- ☐☐ Management Information System Development
- ☐☐ Terms Determination

- ☐☐ Corresponding Logs
- ☐☐ Database Management
- ☐☐ Keep Current With Amendments
- ☐☐ Payment Schedules
- ☐☐ Track Contract Status

TYPE OF CONTRACTS & LEGAL DOCUMENTS

- ☐☐ Agreements
- ☐☐ Bids
- ☐☐ Briefings
- ☐☐ Client Agreements
- ☐☐ Contractual Documents
- ☐☐ Grant Requests
- ☐☐ Legal Correspondence
- ☐☐ License Agreements
- ☐☐ Plans
- ☐☐ Proposals
- ☐☐ Software Agreements
- ☐☐ Side Letters Preparation
- ☐☐ Specifications
- ☐☐ Subcontractor Agreements
- ☐☐ Technology Services

44

- ☐☐ Amendments
- ☐☐ Bidding Process, Formal
- ☐☐ Business Initiatives Support
- ☐☐ Clinical Trial Agreements
- ☐☐ Estimates
- ☐☐ Integrated Requirements Documents
- ☐☐ Legal Documents
- ☐☐ Maintenance Services
- ☐☐ Nondisclosure Agreements (NDAs)
- ☐☐ Requests for Comment (RFC)
- ☐☐ Risk Mitigation & Management
- ☐☐ Requests for Proposal (RFP)
- ☐☐ Subcontract Agreements
- ☐☐ Teaming Agreements
- ☐☐ Warrantees

- ☐☐ Best Practices
- ☐☐ Bidding Review Procedures
- ☐☐ Client Estimates
- ☐☐ Consulting Services
- ☐☐ Government Contracts
- ☐☐ Guarantees
- ☐☐ Legal Standards
- ☐☐ Memoranda of Understanding
- ☐☐ Price Negotiation Memoranda
- ☐☐ Requests for Information (RFI)
- ☐☐ Service Agreements
- ☐☐ Source Selection Reports
- ☐☐ Subcontracting Procedures
- ☐☐ Technical Documents
- ☐☐ Other: _____

Cost Management

COST MANAGEMENT

- ☐☐ Alternative Design Solutions
- ☐☐ Bills of Quantities & Materials
- ☐☐ Change Management
- ☐☐ Commercial Returns Analysis
- ☐☐ Cost Estimate System Development
- ☐☐ Cost Forecasting & Reporting
- ☐☐ Cost-to-Complete Reports
- ☐☐ Financing Arrangements
- ☐☐ Invoice Validation
- ☐☐ Mediation & Arbitration Costs
- ☐☐ Profit Improvement Activities

- ☐☐ Analytical Costing Studies
- ☐☐ Budget Development
- ☐☐ Change Management Processes
- ☐☐ Corrective Actions
- ☐☐ Cost Estimates
- ☐☐ Cost Management Processes
- ☐☐ Expenditure Control
- ☐☐ Functional Cost Analysis
- ☐☐ Market Analysis
- ☐☐ Procurement Management
- ☐☐ Profitability Analysis

- ☐☐ Bid Analysis Preparation
- ☐☐ Change Impact Estimations
- ☐☐ Closeout Administration
- ☐☐ Cost Control Estimates
- ☐☐ Cost Estimates
- ☐☐ Cost Reporting
- ☐☐ Feasibility Studies
- ☐☐ Insurance Replacement Cost Assessments
- ☐☐ Material Costs
- ☐☐ Procurement Services
- ☐☐ Project Budget Establishment

- [ ][ ] Project Budget Requirements
- [ ][ ] Project Cost Estimations
- [ ][ ] Project Execution Cost Management
- [ ][ ] Project Viability Determination
- [ ][ ] Requests for Proposals (RFPs)
- [ ][ ] Risk Analysis
- [ ][ ] Other: _____

- [ ][ ] Project Change Management System
- [ ][ ] Project Earned Value Analyses
- [ ][ ] Project Management Costs
- [ ][ ] Property Condition Reports
- [ ][ ] Reserve Fund Studies
- [ ][ ] Tentative Budget Establishment

- [ ][ ] Project Controls System Establishment
- [ ][ ] Project Economic Viability
- [ ][ ] Project Outcome Predictions
- [ ][ ] Reimbursable Cost Determination
- [ ][ ] Revenue Forecasts
- [ ][ ] Value Engineering

51

Custodial / Janitorial Services

CUSTODIAL / JANITORIAL SERVICES

- [ ][ ] Cleaning Agents and Possible Reactions
- [ ][ ] Custodial Methods and Materials
- [ ][ ] Departmental Policies and Procedures Adherence
- [ ][ ] Electrical Systems and Equipment
- [ ][ ] Federal and State Health and Safety Codes
- [ ][ ] Health and Safety Codes Compliance
- [ ][ ] Infection-Control Standards Compliance
- [ ][ ] Plumbing Systems and Equipment
- [ ][ ] Remodel Work
- [ ][ ] Safety Practices Adherence
- [ ][ ] Securing of Premises

- [ ][ ] Cleaning Supplies Requisitions
- [ ][ ] Custodial Records Updating
- [ ][ ] Damage or Repair Needs Reporting
- [ ][ ] Equipment Purchasing
- [ ][ ] Equipment Replacement
- [ ][ ] Health or Safety Danger Reporting
- [ ][ ] HVAC Systems and Equipment
- [ ][ ] Quality Assurance
- [ ][ ] Repair Work
- [ ][ ] Sanitation and Infection Control
- [ ][ ] Supplies Ordering

- [ ][ ] Custodial Equipment Care
- [ ][ ] Custodial Safety Practices
- [ ][ ] Equipment Maintenance
- [ ][ ] Equipment Repair
- [ ][ ] Fire Hazards Reporting
- [ ][ ] Maintenance Work
- [ ][ ] Preventive Maintenance
- [ ][ ] Records Maintenance
- [ ][ ] Reports Generation
- [ ][ ] Safety Regulations
- [ ][ ] Other: _____

32

CUSTODIAL / JANITORIAL SERVICES MANAGEMENT

- [ ][ ] Administrative Management
- [ ][ ] Building Cleaning Scheduling and Coordination
- [ ][ ] Cleaning Management and Oversight
- [ ][ ] Custodial Assignments
- [ ][ ] Custodial Policies and Procedures Development
- [ ][ ] Custodial Services Expenditures Monitoring
- [ ][ ] Custodial Services Planning
- [ ][ ] Custodial Staff Training and Development
- [ ][ ] Equipment and Supplies Specifications Development
- [ ][ ] Facility Cleaning Plans Development
- [ ][ ] Facility Operations Ensurance
- [ ][ ] Inventory File Maintenance
- [ ][ ] Licensing and Inspection Agency Standards
- [ ][ ] New Product Evaluations
- [ ][ ] Performance Evaluations
- [ ][ ] Product and Equipment Catalogs Maintenance
- [ ][ ] Purchases File Maintenance
- [ ][ ] Quality Assurance Verification
- [ ][ ] Records Maintenance Oversight
- [ ][ ] Repair Work Management and Oversight
- [ ][ ] Safety Standards Setting
- [ ][ ] Work Assignment Scheduling
- [ ][ ] Work Priorities Establishment
- [ ][ ] Other: _____

- [ ][ ] Budget Planning and Development
- [ ][ ] Cleaning and Maintenance Supervision
- [ ][ ] Cost-Cutting Procedures
- [ ][ ] Custodial Care Plans Preparation
- [ ][ ] Custodial Requisitions File Maintenance
- [ ][ ] Custodial Services Management
- [ ][ ] Custodial Staff Hiring
- [ ][ ] Custodial Work Oversight
- [ ][ ] Facilities Inspections
- [ ][ ] Facility Cleaning Schedules Development
- [ ][ ] Inventory Control Management
- [ ][ ] Job Cost Estimating
- [ ][ ] Maintenance Management and Oversight
- [ ][ ] Optimum Work Quality
- [ ][ ] Problem Resolution
- [ ][ ] Productivity Levels Adherance
- [ ][ ] Quality Assurance Programs Development
- [ ][ ] Quality of Work Consistency
- [ ][ ] Remodel Work Planning and Scheduling
- [ ][ ] Repair Work Planning and Scheduling
- [ ][ ] Sanitation and Safety Levels Inspection
- [ ][ ] Work Order Reviews
- [ ][ ] Work Schedules Coordination

46

TYPES OF CLEANING

- [ ][ ] Buffing
- [ ][ ] Floor Finishing
- [ ][ ] Polishing
- [ ][ ] Shampooing

- [ ][ ] Cleaning
- [ ][ ] Garbage Disposal
- [ ][ ] Sanding
- [ ][ ] Snow Removal

- [ ][ ] Disinfecting
- [ ][ ] Graffiti Removal
- [ ][ ] Sanitizing
- [ ][ ] Stripping

- [ ][ ] Dispenser Refilling
- [ ][ ] Landscaping
- [ ][ ] Scrubbing
- [ ][ ] Sweeping

- [ ][ ] Dusting
- [ ][ ] Mopping
- [ ][ ] Sealing
- [ ][ ] Vacuuming

☐☐ Washing   ☐☐ Waste Removal   ☐☐ Waxing   ☐☐ Other: _____

23

ITEMS CLEANED

☐☐ Draperies	☐☐ Exterior Cleaning	☐☐ Facilities	☐☐ Fire Extinguishers	☐☐ Fixtures
☐☐ Floors	☐☐ Furniture	☐☐ Glass Items	☐☐ Grounds	☐☐ Interiors
☐☐ Light Fixtures	☐☐ Premises	☐☐ Property	☐☐ Shades	☐☐ Walls
☐☐ Windows	☐☐ Woodwork	☐☐ Others: _____		

17

Customer & Client Servicing

CUSTOMER SERVICE

☐☐ Appeasing Difficult Customers	☐☐ Asset Protection	☐☐ Building Rapports
☐☐ Calls Screening	☐☐ Cash Management & Control	☐☐ Client Billing
☐☐ Client Needs and Priorities Identification	☐☐ Client Consultation	☐☐ Client Options
☐☐ Client Risks vs. Benefits	☐☐ Consumer Trends	☐☐ Contract Negotiations
☐☐ Converting Customer Desires into Needs	☐☐ Cross-selling	☐☐ Customer Complaints Resolution
☐☐ Cross-sell and Upsell Opportunities Identification	☐☐ Customer Loyalty Increase	☐☐ Customer Orders Facilitation
☐☐ Customer Service Delivery Quality	☐☐ Customer Satisfaction	☐☐ Customer-focused Sales
☐☐ Daily Operations	☐☐ Data Entry	☐☐ Inventory Control
☐☐ Merchandising	☐☐ Monthly Statements Preparation	☐☐ Point-of-Sale Control
☐☐ Post-sales Support	☐☐ Product Encoding	☐☐ Product Research
☐☐ Productivity Improvement	☐☐ Project Scheduling	☐☐ Project-Related Questions
☐☐ Referrals	☐☐ Relationship Development	☐☐ Repeat Business
☐☐ Requests Processing and Expediting	☐☐ Sales Orders Processing	☐☐ Sales Orders Tracing
☐☐ Solutions Development to Meet Needs	☐☐ Shipping and Receiving	☐☐ Solutions Selling
☐☐ Staff Progress Monitoring and Evaluating	☐☐ Training and Development	☐☐ Value-added Sales
☐☐ Supplier and Vendor Telephone Contact	☐☐ Upselling Higher-end Services	☐☐ Other: _____

47

CUSTOMER SERVICE MANAGEMENT

☐☐ Auditing	☐☐ Cash Control and Management	☐☐ Client Solutions Development
☐☐ Compliance with all Policies and Procedures	☐☐ Credit Problems Resolution	☐☐ Customer Service Management
☐☐ Customer Satisfaction Levels Increase	☐☐ Data Entry Oversight	☐☐ Field Research
☐☐ Customer Service Associates Recruitment	☐☐ Intercompany Supply Oversight	☐☐ Inventory Management
☐☐ Customer Service Program Development	☐☐ Loss Prevention	☐☐ Merchandising Management
☐☐ Monthly Statements Review	☐☐ Operations Management	☐☐ Order Processing Oversight
☐☐ Payroll Processing	☐☐ Product Development	☐☐ Product Promotions
☐☐ Receivables Monitoring and Reporting	☐☐ Project Plans Development	☐☐ Sales Associates Recruitment
☐☐ Service Implementation	☐☐ Shipment Delays Resolution	☐☐ Staff Scheduling
☐☐ Stock Level Control	☐☐ Supply Flow Streamlining	☐☐ Tactical Marketing
☐☐ Theft Protection Program Development	☐☐ Other: _____	

31

CUSTOMER RELATIONSHIP MANAGEMENT (CRM)

☐☐ At-risk Clients Retention	☐☐ Attrition Reduction
☐☐ Brand Management	☐☐ Client Expectations Meeting / Exceeding
☐☐ Client Issues and Concerns Resolution	☐☐ Client Issues Coordination
☐☐ Client Program Data Monitoring and Measuring	☐☐ Client Programs Design and Deployment
☐☐ Client Relations Management	☐☐ Client Relationship Strategy Setting
☐☐ Client Relationships Development	☐☐ Client Requests Coordination and Management
☐☐ Client Solutions Development	☐☐ Cost Reduction Opportunities Strategizing
☐☐ Cost Reduction Solutions Deployment	☐☐ Credit Checks
☐☐ Cross-functional Work Collaboration	☐☐ Customer Advocacy
☐☐ Customer Analytical Measurement	☐☐ Customer Experience Post-sales
☐☐ Customer Feedback Procedures Development	☐☐ Customer Relations Satisfaction Ensurance
☐☐ Customer Relationship Building	☐☐ Customer Relationship Enhancement

- ☐☐ Customer Retention
- ☐☐ Customer Service Improvement Enhancements
- ☐☐ Customer Service Statistics Analysis
- ☐☐ High Net Worth Clientele
- ☐☐ Leads Generating and Disposition
- ☐☐ Membership Adoption
- ☐☐ Order Processing Management
- ☐☐ Primary Point of Contact
- ☐☐ Problems Investigation Escalation
- ☐☐ Sales and Revenue Goals Meeting
- ☐☐ Territory Management
- ☐☐ Tier-two Client Support
- ☐☐ Other: _____

- ☐☐ Customer Satisfaction Measurement Methods Development
- ☐☐ Customer Service Policies and Standards Improvement
- ☐☐ Customer Service Support
- ☐☐ Issues Escalation and Prioritization
- ☐☐ Management Leadership Skills Development
- ☐☐ New Accounts Acquisition and Sign-ups
- ☐☐ Portfolio Reviews
- ☐☐ Problem Identification and Resolution
- ☐☐ Products / Services Promotion
- ☐☐ Solutions Adoption Optimization
- ☐☐ Tier-one Client Support
- ☐☐ Trust-based Client-business Relationships

48

CLIENT RELATIONS

- ☐☐ Alternative Budget-friendly Solutions Strategizing
- ☐☐ Client Presentations Development
- ☐☐ Client Proposals Development
- ☐☐ Contract Negotiations and Development
- ☐☐ Customer and Project Staff Liaison
- ☐☐ Fortune 100 to 1000 Client Relations
- ☐☐ Needs Identification
- ☐☐ Problem-solving Challenges to Clients' Satisfaction
- ☐☐ Project Plans Development
- ☐☐ Project Scope Identification
- ☐☐ Resources Coordination
- ☐☐ Service Quality Ensurance
- ☐☐ Tradeoffs Communication

- ☐☐ Automated solutions Development
- ☐☐ Client Priorities Identification
- ☐☐ Client Support, Service, and Follow-up
- ☐☐ Cost Estimates Preparation
- ☐☐ Excellent Client Relations Cultivation
- ☐☐ Long-term Client Relationships
- ☐☐ Primary Client Contact
- ☐☐ Project Milestones Communication
- ☐☐ Project Plans Execution
- ☐☐ Project Strategies Development
- ☐☐ Scope Changes Identification and Processing
- ☐☐ Technical Support and Advice
- ☐☐ Other: _____

25

Electrical

See also "Electrical Engineering."

ELECTRICIAN, GENERAL

- ☐☐ Atmospheric Dynamics
- ☐☐ Electrical Contract Specifications
- ☐☐ Electrical Controls Diagnoses & Repair
- ☐☐ Electrical Maintenance & Repair
- ☐☐ Electrical Testing & Inspections
- ☐☐ Emergency Customer Callbacks
- ☐☐ Engineering Proposals
- ☐☐ Estimating Job Costs
- ☐☐ Industrial Motor Control Centers
- ☐☐ Installation Process Oversight
- ☐☐ Inventory Management & Control
- ☐☐ Material Lists Compilation
- ☐☐ Parts Specifications
- ☐☐ Preventive & Seasonal Maintenance
- ☐☐ Programmable Logic Controllers
- ☐☐ Safety & Responsibility for Others
- ☐☐ Seasonal Maintenance & Repair Work
- ☐☐ Telemetry Theory & Application
- ☐☐ Trades Coordination & Oversight
- ☐☐ Work Orders Preparation

- ☐☐ Contractor Bid Selections
- ☐☐ Electrical Construction Practices
- ☐☐ Electrical Formula Computations
- ☐☐ Electrical Parts Ordering
- ☐☐ Electrical Tools & Equipment Usage
- ☐☐ Electrician Job Preparation
- ☐☐ Equipment Adaptation
- ☐☐ First Aid & CPR
- ☐☐ Inspections & Compliance
- ☐☐ Inventory Control Programs
- ☐☐ Maintenance Staff Assistance
- ☐☐ Operating Efficiency
- ☐☐ Physical Principles & Laws
- ☐☐ Process Control Application
- ☐☐ Scheduling Electrical Work
- ☐☐ Seasonal Overhauls
- ☐☐ Sewer Rooters
- ☐☐ Technical Devices
- ☐☐ Tools & Testing Devices
- ☐☐ Other: _____

- ☐☐ Cost Estimates Preparation
- ☐☐ Defect Isolation
- ☐☐ Electrical Installations
- ☐☐ Electrical Principles
- ☐☐ Electrician Training
- ☐☐ Engineering Data
- ☐☐ Equipment Improvements
- ☐☐ Flaw Detection & Repair
- ☐☐ Instrumentation Theory
- ☐☐ Measuring Instruments
- ☐☐ Operating Cost Reduction
- ☐☐ Parts & Materials Ordering
- ☐☐ Project Time Tracking
- ☐☐ Purchasing Requests
- ☐☐ Record Keeping
- ☐☐ Seasonal Transitions
- ☐☐ Shop Drawings
- ☐☐ Technology Design
- ☐☐ Work Collaboration

58

ELECTRICAL PROJECTS

- ☐☐ Electrical Systems
- ☐☐ Electromagnetic Systems
- ☐☐ Electronic Systems
- ☐☐ Electronic Equipment

- Electronic Facilities
- Cable Systems
- Cargo Systems

14

- Electronic Products
- Voltage Transformers
- Power Systems

- Exterior Lighting
- Proximity Systems
- Other: _____

- Interior Lighting
- Fuel Systems

ELECTRICAL FUNCTIONS

- Adjusting
- Calibrating
- Disconnects
- Fabrication
- Lubricating
- Preventive Maintenance
- Replacement
- Testing
- Specialized Electrical Work

33

- Air Balancing
- Climate Control
- Electrical Wiring
- Fine-Tuning
- Machinery Testing
- Regulating
- Rewiring
- Time Scheduling
- Other: _____

- Alteration
- Cost Estimating
- Equipment Testing
- Inspections
- Maintenance
- Remodeling
- Temperature Balancing
- Troubleshooting

- Cable Splicing
- Diagnosis
- Estimating
- Installation
- Overhauling
- Repair
- Servicing
- Winterizing

ELECTRICAL SYSTEMS

- Bus Bar Systems
- Computer Systems
- Electrical Communications Systems
- Energy Management Systems
- High-Tension Distribution Systems
- Industrial Systems
- Low-Voltage Electrical Systems
- Public Address Systems
- Signaling Systems
- Other: _____

35

- Climate Control Systems
- Conduit Systems
- Electrical Systems
- Fiber Optic Electrical Systems
- High-Voltage Electrical Systems
- Intercom Systems
- Motor Control Systems
- Refrigeration Systems
- Telephone Systems

- Communications Systems
- Digital Systems
- Electronic Systems
- Fire Alarm Systems
- Heating Systems
- Lighting Systems
- Pneumatic Tube Systems
- Security Systems
- Video Systems

ELECTRICAL WORK / EQUIPMENT & COMPONENT TYPES

- AC & DC Motors
- Above-ground Conductors
- Conductors
- Data Communications Devices
- Double-phase Electric Cables
- Electrical Accessories
- Electrical Equipment
- Electrical Instruments
- Electrical Switches
- Generator Equipment
- High-voltage Electrical Work
- Inside Electrical Services
- Lighting Fixtures
- Low-voltage Electrical Work
- Motor Controllers
- Overhead Lines
- Power Lines & Poles
- Programmable Controllers
- Secondary Service Laterals
- Transmission Equipment
- Underground Cable Locators
- Single-phase Electric Cables
- Triple-phase Electric Cables
- Underground Electrical Services

72

- Air Compressors
- Above-ground Conduit
- Cables
- Conduits
- DC Speed Control
- Electronic Controllers
- Electrical Components
- Electrical Motors
- Electronic Controls
- Generators
- Heating Units
- Outside Conductors
- Junction Boxes
- Plumbing Components
- Motor Controls
- Phase Electric Cables
- Primary Power Lines
- Receptacles
- Switchboards
- Underground Conduit
- Water Pumps
- Secondary Service Laterals
- Telecommunications Wiring/Cable
- Other: _____

- Air Conditioning Units
- Circuit Breakers
- Circuit Breakers
- Connectors
- Electric Lines
- Electrical Fuses
- Electrical Controls
- Electrical Panels
- Electronic Controllers
- Fiber-optic
- Inside Conductors
- Outside Conduit
- Mechanical Equipment
- Primary Power Lines
- Motors
- Plumbing Equipment
- Pull Boxes
- Street Lights
- Terminations
- Transformers
- Outside Electrical Services
- Specialized Electrical Work
- Underground Conductors

- Bus Bar
- Control Wiring
- Coax Cables
- Conveyors
- Electrical Apparatus
- Fire Alarms
- Electrical Fixtures
- Electrical Starters
- Elevators
- Fuses
- Inside Conduit
- Overhead Lines
- Microprocessors
- Power Circuits
- Outlet Boxes
- Power Circuits
- Pumps
- Switches
- Traffic Signals
- Water Heaters

ELECTRICAL COMPLIANCE TESTING & QUALITY CONTROL

☐☐ Assembly & Installation Inspections	☐☐ Building Codes Compliance	☐☐ Company Policies
☐☐ Compliance Monitoring	☐☐ Component Safety	☐☐ Contract Compliance
☐☐ Customer Specifications	☐☐ Defect Detection	☐☐ Emergency Procedures
☐☐ Electrical Codes Compliance	☐☐ Electrical Compatibility	☐☐ Faulty Wires Detection
☐☐ Electrical Installation Tracking	☐☐ Environmental Regulations	☐☐ Facilities Inspection
☐☐ Electrical Standards & Practices	☐☐ Handicap Accessibility	☐☐ Maintenance Logs Upkeep
☐☐ Life-Safety Codes Compliance	☐☐ Occupational Hazards Avoidance	☐☐ Loose Connections Repair
☐☐ National Electric Code Compliance	☐☐ On-Site Field Inspections	☐☐ OSHA Compliance
☐☐ Proper Operation Testing	☐☐ Quality Compliance	☐☐ Quality Control Standards
☐☐ Specifications Conformance	☐☐ Safety Precautions	☐☐ Safety Regulations
☐☐ Underground Faults Location	☐☐ Worksite Inspections	☐☐ Other: _____

32

ELECTRICIAN TOOLS & EQUIPMENT USAGE

Refer to "Equipment, Machinery, Tools & Testing Devices."

Electrical Engineering

See also "Engineering – General."

ELECTRICAL ENGINEERING – GENERAL

☐☐ Blueprint / Wiring Schematic Analysis	☐☐ Client Relations	☐☐ Digital Messaging Systems
☐☐ Electrical & Mechanical Defect Resolution	☐☐ Electrical Control Systems	☐☐ Electrical Equipment
☐☐ Electrical Estimating	☐☐ Electrical Installations	☐☐ Electrical Repairs
☐☐ Electrical Systems	☐☐ Electrical Wires	☐☐ Electronic Controls
☐☐ Installation / Inspection	☐☐ Machinery Controls	☐☐ Maintenance Schedules
☐☐ National Electrical Code (NEC)	☐☐ Pipe Bending	☐☐ Service & Repairs
☐☐ System Upgrades	☐☐ Testing	☐☐ Wiring Diagrams
☐☐ Electrical Engineering Design & Development	☐☐ Electrical Plans Development	☐☐ Electrical Systems
☐☐ Electrical Equipment Development & Testing	☐☐ Electrical Testing	☐☐ Electromagnetic Systems
☐☐ Electrical System Design Modifications	☐☐ Installation & Testing	☐☐ Project Development Services
☐☐ Electrical Systems Development & Testing	☐☐ Specifications Development	☐☐ Other: _____

32

ELECTRICAL SYSTEMS

☐☐ Access Control Systems	☐☐ Bus Bar Systems	☐☐ Cable Systems
☐☐ Cargo Systems	☐☐ Climate Control Systems	☐☐ Communications Systems
☐☐ Computer Systems	☐☐ Conduit Systems	☐☐ Digital Messaging Systems
☐☐ Electrical Communications Systems	☐☐ Electrical Systems	☐☐ Electromagnetic Systems
☐☐ Energy Management Systems	☐☐ Exterior Lighting	☐☐ Fiber Optic Electrical Systems
☐☐ Fire Alarm Systems	☐☐ Fuel Systems	☐☐ Heating Systems
☐☐ High-Tension Distribution Systems	☐☐ High-Voltage Electrical Systems	☐☐ Industrial Systems
☐☐ Intercom Systems	☐☐ Interior Lighting	☐☐ Lighting Systems
☐☐ Low-Voltage Switching Systems	☐☐ Motor Control Systems	☐☐ Pneumatic Tube Systems
☐☐ Power Systems	☐☐ Proximity Systems	☐☐ Public Address Systems
☐☐ Refrigeration Systems	☐☐ Security & Personal Protection Systems	☐☐ Signaling Systems
☐☐ Telecommunication Systems	☐☐ Transformers & Generators	☐☐ Video Systems
☐☐ Voltage Transformers	☐☐ Other: _____	

37

COMPLIANCE TESTING & QUALITY CONTROL

☐☐ Assembly & Installation Inspections	☐☐ Building Codes Compliance	☐☐ Company Policies
☐☐ Compliance Monitoring	☐☐ Component Safety	☐☐ Contract Compliance
☐☐ Customer Specifications	☐☐ Defect Detection	☐☐ Emergency Procedures
☐☐ Electrical Codes Compliance	☐☐ Electrical Compatibility	☐☐ Faulty Wires Detection

- [ ] [ ] Electrical Installation Tracking
- [ ] [ ] Electrical Standards & Practices
- [ ] [ ] Life-Safety Codes Compliance
- [ ] [ ] National Electric Code Compliance
- [ ] [ ] Proper Operation Testing
- [ ] [ ] Specifications Conformance
- [ ] [ ] Underground Faults Location

- [ ] [ ] Environmental Regulations
- [ ] [ ] Handicap Accessibility
- [ ] [ ] Occupational Hazards Avoidance
- [ ] [ ] On-Site Field Inspections
- [ ] [ ] Quality Compliance
- [ ] [ ] Safety Precautions
- [ ] [ ] Worksite Inspections

- [ ] [ ] Facilities Inspection
- [ ] [ ] Maintenance Logs Upkeep
- [ ] [ ] Loose Connections Repair
- [ ] [ ] OSHA Compliance
- [ ] [ ] Quality Control Standards
- [ ] [ ] Safety Regulations
- [ ] [ ] Other: _____

32

EQUIPMENT & COMPONENT TYPES

- [ ] [ ] AC & DC Motors
- [ ] [ ] Above-ground Conductors
- [ ] [ ] Conductors
- [ ] [ ] Data Communications Devices
- [ ] [ ] Double-phase Electric Cables
- [ ] [ ] Electrical Accessories
- [ ] [ ] Electrical Equipment
- [ ] [ ] Electrical Instruments
- [ ] [ ] Electrical Switches
- [ ] [ ] Generator Equipment
- [ ] [ ] High-voltage Electrical Work
- [ ] [ ] Inside Electrical Services
- [ ] [ ] Lighting (Exterior / Interior)
- [ ] [ ] Low-voltage Electrical Work
- [ ] [ ] Motor Controllers
- [ ] [ ] Overhead Lines
- [ ] [ ] Power Lines & Poles
- [ ] [ ] Programmable Controllers
- [ ] [ ] Secondary Service Laterals
- [ ] [ ] Transmission Equipment
- [ ] [ ] Underground Cable Locators
- [ ] [ ] Single-phase Electric Cables
- [ ] [ ] Triple-phase Electric Cables
- [ ] [ ] Underground Electrical Services

- [ ] [ ] Air Compressors
- [ ] [ ] Above-ground Conduit
- [ ] [ ] Conduits
- [ ] [ ] Conduits
- [ ] [ ] DC Speed Control
- [ ] [ ] Electronic Controllers
- [ ] [ ] Electrical Components
- [ ] [ ] Electrical Motors
- [ ] [ ] Electronic Controls
- [ ] [ ] Generators
- [ ] [ ] Heating Units
- [ ] [ ] Outside Conductors
- [ ] [ ] Junction Boxes
- [ ] [ ] Plumbing Components
- [ ] [ ] Motor Controls
- [ ] [ ] Phase Electric Cables
- [ ] [ ] Primary Power Lines
- [ ] [ ] Receptacles
- [ ] [ ] Switchboards
- [ ] [ ] Underground Conduit
- [ ] [ ] Water Pumps
- [ ] [ ] Secondary Service Laterals
- [ ] [ ] Telecommunications Wiring / Cable
- [ ] [ ] Wiring Pulling & Termination

- [ ] [ ] Air Conditioning Units
- [ ] [ ] Circuit Breakers
- [ ] [ ] Control Wiring
- [ ] [ ] Connectors
- [ ] [ ] Electric Lines
- [ ] [ ] Electrical Fuses
- [ ] [ ] Electrical Controls
- [ ] [ ] Electrical Panels
- [ ] [ ] Electronic Controllers
- [ ] [ ] Fiber-optic
- [ ] [ ] Inside Conductors
- [ ] [ ] Outside Conduit
- [ ] [ ] Mechanical Equipment
- [ ] [ ] Primary Power Lines
- [ ] [ ] Motors
- [ ] [ ] Plumbing Equipment
- [ ] [ ] Pull Boxes
- [ ] [ ] Street Lights
- [ ] [ ] Terminations
- [ ] [ ] Transformers
- [ ] [ ] Outside Electrical Services
- [ ] [ ] Specialized Electrical Work
- [ ] [ ] Underground Conductors
- [ ] [ ] Other: _____

- [ ] [ ] Bus Bar
- [ ] [ ] Cables
- [ ] [ ] Coax Cables
- [ ] [ ] Conveyors
- [ ] [ ] Electrical Apparatus
- [ ] [ ] Fire Alarms
- [ ] [ ] Electrical Fixtures
- [ ] [ ] Electrical Starters
- [ ] [ ] Elevators
- [ ] [ ] Fuses
- [ ] [ ] Inside Conduit
- [ ] [ ] Overhead Lines
- [ ] [ ] Microprocessors
- [ ] [ ] Power Circuits
- [ ] [ ] Outlet Boxes
- [ ] [ ] Power Circuits
- [ ] [ ] Pumps
- [ ] [ ] Switch Gears
- [ ] [ ] Traffic Signals
- [ ] [ ] Water Heaters

91

Environmental Compliance

ENVIRONMENTAL COMPLIANCE REGULATIONS

- [ ] [ ] Abandoned Mine Lands (AML)
- [ ] [ ] Continuous Emission Monitoring System (CEMS)
- [ ] [ ] CERCLA Hazardous Substances Sec. 101(14)
- [ ] [ ] Chemical Compliance
- [ ] [ ] Clean Water Act (CWA)
- [ ] [ ] Contract Laboratory Program (CLP)
- [ ] [ ] Contract Required Quantitation Limit (CRQL)
- [ ] [ ] Designated for Drinking Water Use [Sec. 305(a)
- [ ] [ ] Emergency Planning and Community Right-to-Know Act
- [ ] [ ] Environmental Protection Agency (EPA)
- [ ] [ ] Federal Insecticide, Fungicide & Rodenticide Act
- [ ] [ ] Hazard Ranking System Guidance Manual (HRSGM)
- [ ] [ ] Maximum Contaminant Level (MCL)
- [ ] [ ] Method Detection Limit (MDL)
- [ ] [ ] National Ambient Air Quality Standard (NAAQS)
- [ ] [ ] National Environmental Policy Act (NEPA)
- [ ] [ ] National Institute for Occupational Safety & Health (NIOSH)
- [ ] [ ] National Pollution Discharge Elimination System (NPDES)

- [ ] [ ] Ambient Aquatic Life Advisory Concentration (AALAC)
- [ ] [ ] CERCLA Environmental Data Management
- [ ] [ ] CERCLA Pollutant or Contaminant Sec. 101(33)
- [ ] [ ] Clean Air Act (CAA)
- [ ] [ ] Code of Federal Regulations (CFR)
- [ ] [ ] Contract Required Detection Limit (CRDL)
- [ ] [ ] EDM Operations & Process of the Clean Water Act
- [ ] [ ] Environmental Management System (EMS)
- [ ] [ ] Environmental Protection Act (EPA)
- [ ] [ ] Environmental Site Assessments (ESAs)
- [ ] [ ] Hazardous Air Pollutants (HAP)
- [ ] [ ] Maximum Achievable Control Technology (MACT)
- [ ] [ ] Maximum Contaminant Level Goal (MCLG)
- [ ] [ ] National Contingency Plan (NCP)
- [ ] [ ] National Emission Standards for Hazardous Air Pollutants (NESHAP)
- [ ] [ ] National Security Personnel System (NSPS)
- [ ] [ ] National Pollutant Discharge Elimination System (NPDES)
- [ ] [ ] Occupational Safety & Health Act (OSHA)

☐☐ Oil Pollution Act (OPA)
☐☐ OSHA Hazard Communication Standard
☐☐ RC14001 Implementation
☐☐ Reciprocating Internal Combustion Engine (RICE)
☐☐ Resource Conservation & Recovery Act (RCRA)
☐☐ Safe Drinking Water Act (SDWA)
☐☐ Superfund Accelerated Cleanup Model (SACM)
☐☐ Superfund Chemical Data Matrix (SCDM)
☐☐ Title V
☐☐ Wastewater Compliance
☐☐ Comprehensive Environmental Response, Compensation & Liability Act (CERCLA)

☐☐ OSHA Air Quality Regulations
☐☐ Pollution Prevention Act (PPA)
☐☐ RCRA Permitting
☐☐ Remedial Investigation Work Plan (RIWP)
☐☐ Resource Conservation & Recovery Act (RCRA)
☐☐ SARA Title III - Community Right to Know
☐☐ Superfund Amendments & Reauthorization Act
☐☐ Title 27 Permitting
☐☐ Toxic Substances Control Act (TSCA)
☐☐ Other: _____

56

ENVIRONMENTAL COMPLIANCE

☐☐ Air Emissions
☐☐ Chemical, Biological, & Radiological Hazards
☐☐ Cost Effective Remediation Methods
☐☐ Environmental Assessments
☐☐ Environmental Cost Estimating
☐☐ Environmental Field Investigations
☐☐ Environmental Modeling
☐☐ Environmental Regulations
☐☐ Federal & State Environmental Laws
☐☐ Federal Facilities Environmental Compliance
☐☐ Indoor And Outdoor Air & Water Systems
☐☐ Phase II Investigations
☐☐ Process Safety Management
☐☐ Remediation Services
☐☐ Scenario Development & Evaluation
☐☐ Soil & Groundwater Sampling
☐☐ Tank Removal & Installation
☐☐ Watershed Analysis

☐☐ Air Pollution
☐☐ Compliance Permitting
☐☐ Emission Inventory
☐☐ Environmental Engineering
☐☐ Environmental Field Work
☐☐ Environmental Investigations
☐☐ Environmental Principles
☐☐ Environmental Report Writing
☐☐ OSHA Monitoring
☐☐ Legal Due Process System
☐☐ OSHA HAZWOPER Training
☐☐ Plant Site Compliance
☐☐ Project Installations
☐☐ Remediation Systems
☐☐ Risk Management Plans
☐☐ Soil & Water Cleanup
☐☐ Toxic Industrial Chemicals
☐☐ Wetland Restoration

☐☐ Compliance Issues
☐☐ Compliance Systems
☐☐ Engineering Analysis
☐☐ Environmental Audits
☐☐ EPA Performance
☐☐ Equipment Changes
☐☐ Environmental Sciences
☐☐ New Regulations
☐☐ Permit Obtainment
☐☐ Permit Applications
☐☐ Phase I Assessments
☐☐ Pollution Monitoring
☐☐ Regulatory Reports
☐☐ Risk Assessments
☐☐ Site Assessments
☐☐ Waste Disposal
☐☐ Waste Management
☐☐ Other: _____

53

ENVIRONMENTAL PROTECTION OFFICES

☐☐ Nuclear Regulatory Commission (NRC)
☐☐ Office of Air Quality (OARM)
☐☐ Office of Environmental Justice (OEJ)
☐☐ Office of Regulatory Enforcement (ORE)
☐☐ Other: _____

☐☐ Office of Administration & Resource Management (OARM)
☐☐ Office of Compliance (OC)
☐☐ Office of General Counsel (OGC)
☐☐ Office of Solid Waste & Emergency Response (OSWER)

8

Equipment, Machinery, Tools & Testing Devices

See also "Heavy Equipment Operations."

CARPENTRY & CONSTRUCTION TOOLS

☐☐ Atlas Machines
☐☐ Carpet Knives & Shears
☐☐ Grinders
☐☐ Loop Pile Cutters
☐☐ Mechanical Soil Compactors
☐☐ Mattocks
☐☐ Power Stretchers
☐☐ Sanding Machines
☐☐ Sledge Hammers
☐☐ Torches

☐☐ Axes
☐☐ Chainsaws
☐☐ Hammers
☐☐ Heliarc
☐☐ Machine Saws
☐☐ Picks
☐☐ Power Tools
☐☐ Saws
☐☐ Stages
☐☐ Trowels

☐☐ Brush Hooks
☐☐ Drill Presses
☐☐ Hand Shovels
☐☐ Knee Kickers
☐☐ Mallets
☐☐ Post Hole Diggers
☐☐ Power Wet Saws
☐☐ Screw Guns
☐☐ Staple Guns
☐☐ Wall Trimmers

☐☐ Bush Axes
☐☐ Drills
☐☐ Heat Irons
☐☐ Lathes
☐☐ Manifolds
☐☐ Power Ladders
☐☐ Rakes
☐☐ Sheathing Guns
☐☐ Testing Devices
☐☐ Other: _____

39

CEILING, LATHING, INSULATION & DRYWALL TOOLS & EQUIPMENT

☐☐ Brushes ☐☐ Compressor Hoses ☐☐ Insulation Compressors ☐☐ Knives

☐☐ Pliers   ☐☐ Power Saws   ☐☐ Saws   ☐☐ Stapling Guns
☐☐ T-Braces   ☐☐ Trowels   ☐☐ Welding Machines   ☐☐ Other: _____

11

ELECTRICIAN EQUIPMENT, TOOLS & TESTING DEVICES

☐☐ Ampmeters	☐☐ Bead Blasters	☐☐ Boom Trucks	☐☐ Bucket Trucks
☐☐ Cable Locating Meters	☐☐ Cement Cutters	☐☐ Conduit Bending	☐☐ Cutting Torches
☐☐ Digger Derricks	☐☐ Drill Presses	☐☐ Drills	☐☐ Electric Drills
☐☐ Equipment Threading	☐☐ Fault Locators	☐☐ Forklifts	☐☐ Grinders
☐☐ Hacksaws	☐☐ Hand & Power Tools	☐☐ Hoists	☐☐ Hydraulic Boom Lifts
☐☐ Hydraulic Pipe Benders	☐☐ Jackhammers	☐☐ Knockout Punches	☐☐ Lift Trucks
☐☐ Measuring Devices	☐☐ Megger Meters	☐☐ Ohmmeters	☐☐ Oscilloscopes
☐☐ Pickup Trucks	☐☐ Pipe Cutters	☐☐ Pipe Threaders	☐☐ Portable Compressors
☐☐ Portable Generators	☐☐ Propane Torches	☐☐ PVC Benders	☐☐ Sand Blasters
☐☐ Skill Saws	☐☐ Test Lamps	☐☐ Testing Instruments	☐☐ Voltmeters
☐☐ Volt-Ohm Meters	☐☐ Welding Equipment	☐☐ Wire & Cable Winches	☐☐ Other: _____

43

GLAZIER EQUIPMENT

☐☐ Beveling Machines	☐☐ Drills	☐☐ Glass Cutters	☐☐ Glazing Knives
☐☐ Grinders	☐☐ Polishing Machines	☐☐ Power Saws	☐☐ Sanding Machines
☐☐ Suction Cups	☐☐ Other: _____		

9

HVAC EQUIPMENT, TOOLS & TESTING DEVICES

☐☐ Acetylene Torches	☐☐ Backhoes	☐☐ Electric Drills	☐☐ Forklifts
☐☐ Hand Tools	☐☐ Manometers	☐☐ Measurement Gauges	☐☐ Metal Snips
☐☐ Pipe Benders	☐☐ Pipe Cutters	☐☐ Power Tools	☐☐ Pressure Gauges
☐☐ Propane Torches	☐☐ Sewer Rooters	☐☐ Thermometers	☐☐ Trenchers
☐☐ Voltmeters	☐☐ Welding Equipment	☐☐ Other: _____	

16

LANDSCAPING & MASONRY EQUIPMENT & MACHINERY

☐☐ Backhoes	☐☐ Boom Trucks	☐☐ Bulldozers	☐☐ Cement Mixers
☐☐ Cement Trucks	☐☐ Compressors	☐☐ Cranes	☐☐ Crawlers
☐☐ Dozers	☐☐ Dump Bodies	☐☐ Force-feed Loaders	☐☐ Forklifts
☐☐ Front Loaders	☐☐ Gear-cutting Machines	☐☐ Graders	☐☐ Heavy Dump Trucks
☐☐ Hoists	☐☐ Hook Lift Hoists	☐☐ Hook Lifts	☐☐ Hydraulic Excavators
☐☐ Mowers	☐☐ Municipal Dump Bodies	☐☐ Orange Peelers	☐☐ Paving Equipment
☐☐ Payloaders	☐☐ Pick-up Trucks	☐☐ Piggy-back Forklifts	☐☐ Platforms
☐☐ Plow Trucks	☐☐ Rand paving Equipment	☐☐ Rear Loaders	☐☐ Road Milling Machines
☐☐ Roadrangers	☐☐ Roll-offs	☐☐ Roof Mowers	☐☐ Sewer Jets
☐☐ Side Loaders	☐☐ Snow Plows	☐☐ Spreaders	☐☐ Steam Rollers
☐☐ Street Sweepers	☐☐ Sweepers	☐☐ Tiger Mowers	☐☐ Tractors
☐☐ Trenchers	☐☐ Truck Loaders	☐☐ Truck-mounted Lifts	☐☐ Other: _____

47

LANDSCAPING & MASONRY TOOLS

☐☐ Axes	☐☐ Chain Saws	☐☐ Clippers	☐☐ Electric Clippers
☐☐ Handsaws	☐☐ Hedge Trimmers	☐☐ Power Pruners	☐☐ Power Tools
☐☐ Pruning Hooks	☐☐ Pruning Saws	☐☐ Rakes	☐☐ Saws
☐☐ Shears	☐☐ Shovels	☐☐ Snow Blowers	☐☐ Sod Cutters
☐☐ Other: _____			

16

PLUMBING TOOLS & EQUIPMENT

☐☐ Acetylene Torches	☐☐ Backhoes	☐☐ Carbon Dioxide Testers	☐☐ Electric Drills
☐☐ Equipment Maintenance	☐☐ Equipment Safety	☐☐ Equipment Use	☐☐ Forklifts
☐☐ Hand & Power Tools	☐☐ Hand & Power Tools	☐☐ Measurement Gauges	☐☐ Metal Snips
☐☐ Oxygen Testers	☐☐ Pipe Benders	☐☐ Plumbing Machinery	☐☐ Pipe Cutters

☐☐ Propane Torches   ☐☐ Sewer Rooters   ☐☐ Trenchers   ☐☐ Welding Equipment
☐☐ Other: _____

20

WELDING / STEAMFITTING MACHINERY, TOOLS & TESTING DEVICES

☐☐ Acetylene Torches	☐☐ Atlas Machines	☐☐ CNC Machines	☐☐ Drill Presses
☐☐ Carbon Dioxide Testers	☐☐ Gear Cutting Machines	☐☐ Electric Drills	☐☐ Hand & Power Tools
☐☐ Centrifugal Chiller Machines	☐☐ Measurement Gauges	☐☐ Metal Snips	☐☐ Micrometers
☐☐ Metal Forming Equipment	☐☐ Milling Machines	☐☐ Oxygen Testers	☐☐ Pipe Benders
☐☐ Metal-removing Machines	☐☐ Pipe Cutters	☐☐ Propane Torches	☐☐ Protractors
☐☐ Steam Absorption Machines	☐☐ Vernier Calipers	☐☐ Welding Devices	☐☐ Other: _____

23

General Contracting / Trades Management

GENERAL CONTRACTING MANAGEMENT

☐☐ Accident Reports Preparation	☐☐ Accounts Payable & Receivable	☐☐ Advertising Campaigns
☐☐ Accounting & Financial Recordkeeping	☐☐ Administrative Management	☐☐ Bid Development
☐☐ Architectural Planning & Design	☐☐ Asbestos Removal / Abatement	☐☐ Bid Specifications
☐☐ Blueprint Reading & Interpreting	☐☐ Bidding Process	☐☐ Business Analysis
☐☐ Blueprint Review &/or Modification	☐☐ Business Development	☐☐ Business Start-up
☐☐ Budget Development & Expense Control	☐☐ Building Maintenance & Repair	☐☐ Cash Control
☐☐ Capital Improvements & Expansions	☐☐ Building Operations Management	☐☐ Client Invoicing
☐☐ Carpentry / Construction Projects Oversight	☐☐ Client Meeting & Strategizing	☐☐ Client Relations
☐☐ Change Order Negotiation & Processing	☐☐ Client Needs Assessment	☐☐ Closeout Processing
☐☐ Computer Hardware & Software	☐☐ Client Presentations & Proposals	☐☐ Competitive Analysis
☐☐ Construction Leadership & Direction	☐☐ Compensation Management	☐☐ Competitive Bids
☐☐ Construction Oversight & Supervision	☐☐ Computer Layout & Design	☐☐ Construction Drawings
☐☐ Construction Project Management	☐☐ Contract Negotiations	☐☐ Contracting Costs
☐☐ Contracts Development & Review	☐☐ Contracts & Leases	☐☐ Cost Analyses
☐☐ Cost Estimate Preparation	☐☐ Cost Management	☐☐ Cost Factoring
☐☐ Cost Reductions & Savings	☐☐ Crew Assignments	☐☐ Crew Supervision
☐☐ Customer Service & Problem Resolution	☐☐ Customer Service Management	☐☐ Customer Satisfaction
☐☐ Database Set-up & Management	☐☐ Design-and-Build Projects	☐☐ Design Conceptualization
☐☐ Employee Benefit Programs Administration	☐☐ Dispute Mediation & Resolution	☐☐ Employee Retention
☐☐ Environment & Safety Health Management Compliance	☐☐ Estimating Timeframes	☐☐ Expense Control
	☐☐ Facilities Management	☐☐ Final Cost Estimates
☐☐ Estimating Material & Labor Costs	☐☐ Floor-to-Floor Build-outs	☐☐ Forecasting Costs
☐☐ Field Labor & Subcontractor Supervision	☐☐ Hiring & Coordinating Trades	☐☐ Increased Account Base
☐☐ General Contractor Office Management	☐☐ Human Resource Management	☐☐ Inspecting Work Areas
☐☐ Increased Sales & Profitability	☐☐ Inspections & Compliance	☐☐ Insurance Costs
☐☐ Interdisciplinary/Project Team Member	☐☐ Inventory Management & Control	☐☐ Invoicing / Client Billing
☐☐ Machinery & Equipment Maintenance	☐☐ Job Bidding	☐☐ Job Estimating
☐☐ Maintenance & Repair Projects	☐☐ Job Site Preparation	☐☐ Job Preparation
☐☐ New Business Development	☐☐ New Business Start-up	☐☐ Job Scheduling
☐☐ On-site Construction Supervision	☐☐ Labor Supervision	☐☐ Land & Building Surveys
☐☐ Operations Management	☐☐ Long-range Planning	☐☐ Low Staff Turnover
☐☐ Performance Recognition Leadership	☐☐ Materials Purchasing	☐☐ Media Analysis
☐☐ Preventive & Seasonal Maintenance	☐☐ Office Management	☐☐ Overhead Costs
☐☐ Project Coordination with Contractors	☐☐ Payroll Processing	☐☐ Permits Obtainment
☐☐ Project Lifecycle Management	☐☐ Post Construction Services	☐☐ Procedure Development
☐☐ Project Resources & Staffing Requirements	☐☐ Productivity Improvement	☐☐ Project Initiation
☐☐ Profit & Loss Responsibility	☐☐ Project Development	☐☐ Project Estimating
☐☐ Project Planning & Coordination	☐☐ Project Management	☐☐ Project Prioritization
☐☐ Punch List Preparation & Completion	☐☐ Project Time Tracking	☐☐ Project Time Tracking
☐☐ Quality Control Programs Development	☐☐ Purchasing	☐☐ Quality Assurance
☐☐ Safety & Responsibility for Others	☐☐ Quality Control	☐☐ Recordkeeping
☐☐ Safety Practices Compliance	☐☐ Research & Analysis	☐☐ Sales Forecasting
☐☐ Staff Collaboration & Team Influence	☐☐ Scheduling & Coordinating Trades	☐☐ Site Locating
☐☐ Strategic Planning & Direction	☐☐ Space Planning	☐☐ Staff Recruitment

- ☐☐ Subcontractor Influence & Collaboration
- ☐☐ Subcontractor Negotiations
- ☐☐ Team Building & Development
- ☐☐ Team Leadership & Direction
- ☐☐ Trades Coordination & Oversight
- ☐☐ Work Area Inspections
- ☐☐ Workers' Compensation Program Administration
- ☐☐ Workflow Planning & Coordination

- ☐☐ Staff Training & Development
- ☐☐ Subcontractor Project Coordination
- ☐☐ Supply Requests Monitoring
- ☐☐ Technical Construction Assistance
- ☐☐ Training & Development
- ☐☐ Trend Forecasting
- ☐☐ Work Collaboration
- ☐☐ Work Scheduling

- ☐☐ Staff Supervision
- ☐☐ Strategizing Client Needs
- ☐☐ Tools & Equipment Usage
- ☐☐ Trades Scheduling
- ☐☐ Trades Supervision
- ☐☐ Welding/Steamfitting
- ☐☐ Work Order Completion
- ☐☐ Other: _____

96

Glazier Projects & Functions

GLAZIER PROJECTS

- ☐☐ Aluminum Curtain Walls
- ☐☐ Blast Resistant Windows
- ☐☐ Display Cases
- ☐☐ Glass Panels
- ☐☐ Mounting Sashes
- ☐☐ Skylights
- ☐☐ Tempered Glass
- ☐☐ Other: _____

- ☐☐ Aluminum Storefronts
- ☐☐ Commercial Projects
- ☐☐ Entrance Enclosures
- ☐☐ Glass Railing Systems
- ☐☐ Residential Projects
- ☐☐ Storefronts
- ☐☐ Unique Designs

- ☐☐ Automotive Projects
- ☐☐ Decorative Finishes
- ☐☐ Glass Doors
- ☐☐ Metal Framework Extrusions
- ☐☐ Security Windows
- ☐☐ Sun Rooms
- ☐☐ Windows

- ☐☐ Backsplashes
- ☐☐ Decorative Room Dividers
- ☐☐ Glass Insulations
- ☐☐ Mirrors
- ☐☐ Shower Enclosures
- ☐☐ Table Tops
- ☐☐ Windshields

28

GLAZIER – GENERAL

- ☐☐ Benchmark Setting
- ☐☐ Calculation Measurement
- ☐☐ Contract Review & Approval
- ☐☐ Equipment Costing
- ☐☐ Industry Standards
- ☐☐ Manufacturer's Installation Instructions
- ☐☐ Materials Lead Time Planning
- ☐☐ Photographing Progress & Results
- ☐☐ Project Cost Estimating
- ☐☐ Project Scheduling
- ☐☐ Project Status Reports
- ☐☐ Quality Work Standards
- ☐☐ Safety Program Compliance
- ☐☐ Work Monitoring & Inspections

- ☐☐ Bid Proposal Preparation
- ☐☐ Change Order Processing
- ☐☐ Contractual Obligations
- ☐☐ Equipment Requirements Estimating
- ☐☐ Invoice Approval
- ☐☐ Material Deliveries Scheduling
- ☐☐ Materials Ordering & Scheduling
- ☐☐ Precision-Cutting Methods
- ☐☐ Project Drawings Review & Verification
- ☐☐ Project Scope & Requirements
- ☐☐ Purchase Orders Issuance
- ☐☐ Records Management
- ☐☐ Scope Changes
- ☐☐ Work Scheduling

- ☐☐ Blueprints Reading & Interpreting
- ☐☐ Closeout Processing
- ☐☐ Customer Satisfaction
- ☐☐ Frames Installation
- ☐☐ Labor Coordination
- ☐☐ Material Quotes
- ☐☐ Negotiating Vendor Pricing
- ☐☐ Progress Records
- ☐☐ Project Management
- ☐☐ Project Specifications
- ☐☐ Quality Installations
- ☐☐ Risks & Liabilities Determination
- ☐☐ Specifications Interpretation
- ☐☐ Other: _____

37

Heavy Equipment Operations

See also "Equipment, Machinery, Tools & Testing Devices."

HEAVY EQUIPMENT

- ☐☐ Airport Runways Lighting
- ☐☐ Athletic Field Lighting
- ☐☐ Brush & Tree Stumps Clearing
- ☐☐ Concrete Pouring & Paving
- ☐☐ Data Verification
- ☐☐ Distribution Powerlines
- ☐☐ Energy Conducting
- ☐☐ Equipment Maintenance & Repair
- ☐☐ Equipment Safety
- ☐☐ Excavating, Backfilling & Grading
- ☐☐ High-voltage Transmission Systems
- ☐☐ Land Reclamation
- ☐☐ Materials Handling
- ☐☐ Mobile Equipment
- ☐☐ Personnel Resource Management

- ☐☐ Asphalt Batching & Paving
- ☐☐ Blueprint Reading & Understanding
- ☐☐ Building Construction
- ☐☐ Concrete Spreading & Leveling
- ☐☐ Demolishing & Rebuilding
- ☐☐ Driveway Construction
- ☐☐ Equipment Cleaning & Lubricating
- ☐☐ Equipment Operation & Control
- ☐☐ Equipment Selection
- ☐☐ Foundation Pouring & Leveling
- ☐☐ Highway & Roadway Construction
- ☐☐ Low-Voltage Lighting Systems
- ☐☐ Materials Loading & Moving
- ☐☐ Outdoor Areas
- ☐☐ Piers Construction

- ☐☐ Asphalt Spreading & Leveling
- ☐☐ Bridge Construction
- ☐☐ Concrete Batch Plant Operations
- ☐☐ Data Compilation
- ☐☐ Demolition
- ☐☐ Earth Moving
- ☐☐ Equipment Inspections
- ☐☐ Equipment Operation Monitoring
- ☐☐ Equipment Troubleshooting
- ☐☐ Curves & Shoulders Grading
- ☐☐ Information Compiling
- ☐☐ Map Reading
- ☐☐ Mechanized Equipment & Devices
- ☐☐ Parking Lots
- ☐☐ Preoperational Equipment Checks

- ☐☐ Quarrying
- ☐☐ Road-building
- ☐☐ Soil Compacting
- ☐☐ Systems Operation & Control
- ☐☐ Underground Services Locating
- ☐☐ Weight Handling

- ☐☐ Records Maintenance
- ☐☐ Safety Protocols
- ☐☐ Stationary Equipment
- ☐☐ Taxiways Lighting
- ☐☐ Water Wells
- ☐☐ Other: _____

- ☐☐ Retaining Walls
- ☐☐ Sand, Rock & Gravel Removal
- ☐☐ Structures Erecting
- ☐☐ Traffic Signal Systems
- ☐☐ Waterways Excavation

61

HEAVY EQUIPMENT OPERATIONS

- ☐☐ 10-wheelers
- ☐☐ A-frame Mowers
- ☐☐ Backup Trucks
- ☐☐ Bush Hogs
- ☐☐ Compressors
- ☐☐ Crawlers
- ☐☐ Distributors
- ☐☐ Excavators
- ☐☐ Gradalls
- ☐☐ Hook Lifts
- ☐☐ Hydraulic Cranes
- ☐☐ Landfill Heavy Equipment
- ☐☐ Loading Machines
- ☐☐ Multiterrain Loaders
- ☐☐ Paving Equipment
- ☐☐ Pile Drivers
- ☐☐ Pneumatic Asphalt Tampers
- ☐☐ Roadmilling Machines
- ☐☐ Scrubbing Machines
- ☐☐ Sewer Jets
- ☐☐ Single-blade Plows
- ☐☐ Snow Plows
- ☐☐ Street Sweepers
- ☐☐ Tamping Equipment
- ☐☐ Tractor Mowers
- ☐☐ Vertical Drills
- ☐☐ Wing Plows

- ☐☐ 18-Ton Hydraulic Crane
- ☐☐ Airport Sweepers
- ☐☐ Belly Dumpers
- ☐☐ Catch Basin Cleaners
- ☐☐ Concrete Equipment
- ☐☐ Crysteel Dump Bodies
- ☐☐ Draglines
- ☐☐ Forcefeed Loaders
- ☐☐ Graders
- ☐☐ Hooklift Hoists
- ☐☐ Hydraulic Excavators
- ☐☐ Lane Closure Trucks
- ☐☐ Low Boys
- ☐☐ Municipal Dump Bodies
- ☐☐ Payloaders
- ☐☐ Pilot Cars
- ☐☐ Post Pounders
- ☐☐ Roadrangers
- ☐☐ Seeders
- ☐☐ Side Boom Tractors
- ☐☐ Skid Steer Loaders
- ☐☐ Sprayers
- ☐☐ Stump Grinders
- ☐☐ Tandem Axle Dump Trucks
- ☐☐ Tractors
- ☐☐ Viking Plows
- ☐☐ Others: _____

- ☐☐ 18-wheel Semi-trucks
- ☐☐ Asphalt Paving Equipment
- ☐☐ Boom Trucks
- ☐☐ Cement Mixers
- ☐☐ Crane Riggers
- ☐☐ Directional Bores
- ☐☐ Dredgers
- ☐☐ Forklifts
- ☐☐ Heavy Dump Trucks
- ☐☐ Horizontal Directional Drills
- ☐☐ Hydraulic Truck Cranes
- ☐☐ Large Rollers
- ☐☐ Mechanical Sweepers
- ☐☐ Orange Peelers
- ☐☐ Pick-up Trucks
- ☐☐ Platforms
- ☐☐ Rear Loaders
- ☐☐ Roll-offs
- ☐☐ Semi-truck Trailers
- ☐☐ Side Loaders
- ☐☐ Skid Steer Machines
- ☐☐ Spreaders
- ☐☐ Surfacing Equipment
- ☐☐ Tankers
- ☐☐ Trenchers
- ☐☐ Water Trucks

- ☐☐ 6-wheelers
- ☐☐ Backhoes
- ☐☐ Bulldozers
- ☐☐ Churn Drills
- ☐☐ Cranes
- ☐☐ Directional Drills
- ☐☐ Dump Truck Backhoes
- ☐☐ Front-end Loaders
- ☐☐ Hoists
- ☐☐ Hydraulic Boom Trucks
- ☐☐ Land Drilling Rigs
- ☐☐ Loaders
- ☐☐ Motorgraders
- ☐☐ Patch Rollers
- ☐☐ Piggyback Forklifts
- ☐☐ Plow Trucks
- ☐☐ Road Watering Equipment
- ☐☐ Roof and Tiger Mowers
- ☐☐ Sewer Cleaners
- ☐☐ Single Axle Dump Trucks
- ☐☐ Skip Loaders
- ☐☐ Steam Rollers
- ☐☐ Sweepers
- ☐☐ Track Hoes
- ☐☐ Truck Loaders
- ☐☐ Wideners

105

HVAC / HVAC-R

HVAC LICENSES & CERTIFICATIONS

- ☐☐ HVAC-related Journeyman's License
- ☐☐ HVAC Certificate

- ☐☐ ICBO HVAC Inspector Certification
- ☐☐ Other: _____

3

HVAC (Heating, Ventilation & Air Conditioning)

- ☐☐ Air Balancing
- ☐☐ Air Quality Testing
- ☐☐ Air Quality Control
- ☐☐ Boiler, Pump & Valve Maintenance
- ☐☐ Central Air Conditioning Systems
- ☐☐ Compressors / Compressor Overhauls
- ☐☐ Digital HVAC Systems
- ☐☐ Energy Management Equipment
- ☐☐ Filter & Duct Replacements
- ☐☐ Freon / Refrigerant Charging
- ☐☐ Generator Testing & Maintenance
- ☐☐ Heating Seasonal Performance Factor (HSPF)
- ☐☐ High Pressure Steam Boilers

- ☐☐ Air Conditioning Systems
- ☐☐ Air Distribution Systems
- ☐☐ Air Quality Testing
- ☐☐ Attic Duct Work
- ☐☐ Compliance with Regulations
- ☐☐ Customer Service & Support
- ☐☐ Duct Work & Cleaning
- ☐☐ Electric Burners
- ☐☐ Firing & Fuel Ratio Controls
- ☐☐ Fuel System Components
- ☐☐ Gas Burners
- ☐☐ Heat Exchangers
- ☐☐ HVAC System Balancing

- ☐☐ Air Conditioning Servicing
- ☐☐ Air Handlers
- ☐☐ Airborne Contaminants
- ☐☐ Climate Control
- ☐☐ Coil & Condenser Cleaning
- ☐☐ Condensing Units
- ☐☐ Duct Flow Readings
- ☐☐ Evaporators
- ☐☐ Fuel & Water Supply Lines
- ☐☐ Furnaces
- ☐☐ Geothermal Pumps
- ☐☐ Heating Systems
- ☐☐ Hot Water Heaters

- ☐☐ HVAC Installation
- ☐☐ HVAC Fans, Piping, Gauges & Indicator Lights
- ☐☐ HVAC Maintenance & Repair Work
- ☐☐ Microprocessor Fan Control
- ☐☐ Pneumatic Piping Systems
- ☐☐ Preventive & Seasonal Maintenance
- ☐☐ Preventive Maintenance Program Development
- ☐☐ Production & Injection Systems
- ☐☐ Seasonal Energy Efficiency Ratio (SEER)
- ☐☐ Solid Fuel Heating Systems
- ☐☐ Supplies & Equipment Ordering
- ☐☐ Temperature & Humidity Control
- ☐☐ Water Softener Adjustments
- ☐☐ Chlorofluorocarbon & Hydrochlorofluorocarbon Refrigerant Control
- ☐☐ Electrical Wiring of Furnaces, Unit Heaters & Cooling Units
- ☐☐ HVAC/HVAC-R & Plumbing Tools & Equipment Usage

83

- ☐☐ Improved Energy Efficiency
- ☐☐ Installation, Service & Repair
- ☐☐ HVAC Monitoring & Testing
- ☐☐ New HVAC System Designing
- ☐☐ Oil Burners
- ☐☐ Pipe Calibration
- ☐☐ Refrigerant Lines & Air Ducts
- ☐☐ Sand Traps
- ☐☐ Service & Maintenance Contracts
- ☐☐ Sump & Chemical Pumps
- ☐☐ Switches & Light Fixtures
- ☐☐ Water Treatment Testing
- ☐☐ Water Tower Treatment
- ☐☐ Inspections & Compliance
- ☐☐ Project Time Tracking
- ☐☐ Other: _____

- ☐☐ HVAC Testing
- ☐☐ HVAC Installations
- ☐☐ Metal & Fiberglass Ducts
- ☐☐ Natural Gas Piping
- ☐☐ Outlet Box Installations
- ☐☐ Refrigerant Systems
- ☐☐ Roof-top Installations
- ☐☐ Solar Panels
- ☐☐ Split Systems
- ☐☐ Testing Devices
- ☐☐ Thermostat Inspections
- ☐☐ Water Loops
- ☐☐ Ventilation

HVAC / HVAC-R SYSTEMS

- ☐☐ Air Conditioning Systems
- ☐☐ Commercial Plumbing Systems
- ☐☐ Energy Management Control System (EMCS)
- ☐☐ Energy Related Equipment & Control Systems
- ☐☐ Heating, Cooling & Ventilation Systems
- ☐☐ Industrial Plumbing Systems
- ☐☐ Refrigeration Systems
- ☐☐ Residential Plumbing Systems
- ☐☐ Ventilation Systems
- ☐☐ Other: _____

27

- ☐☐ Building Management Systems
- ☐☐ Distribution Systems & Controls
- ☐☐ Domestic Plumbing Systems
- ☐☐ Gas & Electric Heating Systems
- ☐☐ HVAC Electric Systems
- ☐☐ In-Door Plumbing Systems
- ☐☐ Piping Systems
- ☐☐ Split Systems
- ☐☐ Water Systems

- ☐☐ Cooling Systems
- ☐☐ Drainage Systems
- ☐☐ Fire Sprinkler Systems
- ☐☐ Gas Systems
- ☐☐ Heating Systems
- ☐☐ HVAC Systems
- ☐☐ Plumbing Systems
- ☐☐ Sprinkler Systems
- ☐☐ Winterizing Systems

HVAC EQUIPMENT

Refer to "Equipment, Machinery, Tools & Testing Devices."

Inspections & Compliance

INSPECTIONS & COMPLIANCE – GENERAL

- ☐☐ Alarms & Smoke Control Systems
- ☐☐ Asbestos Abatement Requirements
- ☐☐ Asphalt Paving & Grading Operations
- ☐☐ Building Code Regulations Compliance
- ☐☐ Code Requirements Verification
- ☐☐ Compliance Awareness Training
- ☐☐ Construction Contract Administration
- ☐☐ Contract Specifications Compliance
- ☐☐ Design Specifications Compliance
- ☐☐ Energy Efficiency Measures
- ☐☐ Energy Conservation Requirements
- ☐☐ Environmental Regulations Compliance
- ☐☐ Government Regulations
- ☐☐ Energy Conservation Requirements
- ☐☐ Environmental, Health & Safety Standards
- ☐☐ Hazardous Materials Pollution Control
- ☐☐ Health & Safety Program Administration
- ☐☐ Health & Safety Program Development
- ☐☐ International Code Council (ICC) Compliance
- ☐☐ Internal & External Review Processes
- ☐☐ Policies & Procedures Compliance
- ☐☐ Quality Testing of Construction Materials

- ☐☐ Air Quality Testing
- ☐☐ Audit Plan Development
- ☐☐ Audit Studies & Analyses
- ☐☐ Building Inspections
- ☐☐ Comprehensive Final Inspections
- ☐☐ Construction Site Development
- ☐☐ Corporate Operations
- ☐☐ Documentation Review
- ☐☐ Electrical Codes Compliance
- ☐☐ Enforcement Activities
- ☐☐ HVAC Systems Compliance
- ☐☐ Fire Protection Equipment
- ☐☐ Life-safety Codes Compliance
- ☐☐ Health Care Quality
- ☐☐ Inventory Audits
- ☐☐ Manual Procedures
- ☐☐ Operations Audits
- ☐☐ OSHA Standards Compliance
- ☐☐ P&L Statements Analysis
- ☐☐ Plumbing Codes Compliance
- ☐☐ Project Progress Meetings
- ☐☐ QA / QC Conceptualization

- ☐☐ Audit Management
- ☐☐ Audit Reports
- ☐☐ Automated Procedures
- ☐☐ Control Programs
- ☐☐ Corrective Actions
- ☐☐ Cost Reductions
- ☐☐ Data Integrity
- ☐☐ Efficiency Evaluations
- ☐☐ Energy Audits
- ☐☐ Financial System Audits
- ☐☐ Investigations
- ☐☐ Operational Compliance
- ☐☐ Fire Regulations
- ☐☐ In-process Testing
- ☐☐ Management Protocols
- ☐☐ Methods Development
- ☐☐ Ordinance Violations
- ☐☐ Policy Effectiveness
- ☐☐ Preventive Maintenance
- ☐☐ QA / QC Documentation
- ☐☐ Quality Control
- ☐☐ Site Inspections

- ☐☐ QA / QC Implementation
- ☐☐ Quality Control Process Development
- ☐☐ Record Accuracy Verification
- ☐☐ Safety Practices
- ☐☐ Safety Regulations Compliance
- ☐☐ State & Local Building Codes
- ☐☐ Structural Quality & Safety
- ☐☐ Uniform Building Code (UBC) Compliance
- ☐☐ Other: _____

- ☐☐ QA / QC Programs & Systems
- ☐☐ QA Performance Reports
- ☐☐ Quality Assurance Audits
- ☐☐ Security Systems
- ☐☐ Specifications Compliance
- ☐☐ Survey Instruments, Use of
- ☐☐ Stop Work Orders
- ☐☐ Work Logs & Reports Maintenance

- ☐☐ Specifications Compliance
- ☐☐ Records Examinations
- ☐☐ Regulatory Compliance
- ☐☐ Stability Studies
- ☐☐ Standards Compliance
- ☐☐ Workmanship Quality
- ☐☐ Testing Systems
- ☐☐ Zoning Laws

90

BUILDINGS & STRUCTURES COMPLIANCE

- ☐☐ Air Quality
- ☐☐ Commercial Construction & Repair Practices
- ☐☐ Commercial Construction Materials & Equipment
- ☐☐ Corrective Actions Recommendations
- ☐☐ Drain, Waste & Vent Lines
- ☐☐ Elevator & Escalator Inspections
- ☐☐ Environmental, Health & Safety Standards
- ☐☐ Fire Protection Equipment
- ☐☐ Footings Positioning & Depth
- ☐☐ Gas-fired & Oil-fired Appliances
- ☐☐ Handicap Accessibility Compliance
- ☐☐ Hazardous Materials Pollution Control Methods
- ☐☐ Irrigation Systems
- ☐☐ Plan Change Architectural Negotiations
- ☐☐ Quality Testing of Construction Materials
- ☐☐ Reinforced Concrete Structures
- ☐☐ Sewer & Water System Inspections
- ☐☐ Structural Quality, Stability & Safety
- ☐☐ Waste & Vent Lines
- ☐☐ Water Supply & Distribution Systems

- ☐☐ Alarm Systems
- ☐☐ Commercial Roofing Systems
- ☐☐ Construction Problems Identification
- ☐☐ Disposal Systems
- ☐☐ Drainage Systems
- ☐☐ Energy Conservation Requirements
- ☐☐ Excavation & Fill Operations
- ☐☐ Fire Exits
- ☐☐ Fire Sprinklers
- ☐☐ Gas & Oil Piping
- ☐☐ Grading Operations
- ☐☐ HVAC Systems & Equipment
- ☐☐ Ordinance Violations
- ☐☐ Plumbing Fixtures, Traps & Systems
- ☐☐ Quality Assurance
- ☐☐ Roofing Systems
- ☐☐ Security Systems
- ☐☐ Soil Conditions
- ☐☐ Water Distribution Systems
- ☐☐ Zoning Laws & Regulations

- ☐☐ Concrete Forms & Foundations
- ☐☐ Corporate Buildings
- ☐☐ Demolition & Remodel Procedures
- ☐☐ Ditches & Dredging
- ☐☐ Electrical Wiring
- ☐☐ Energy Efficiency Measures
- ☐☐ Enforcement Activities
- ☐☐ Fire Regulations
- ☐☐ Food Product Safety
- ☐☐ Gasoline & Butane Tanks
- ☐☐ Home Systems
- ☐☐ Insulation
- ☐☐ OSHA Standards
- ☐☐ Preventive Maintenance
- ☐☐ Quality Control
- ☐☐ Safety Practices
- ☐☐ Smoke Control Systems
- ☐☐ Stop Work Orders
- ☐☐ Water Rights Adjudication
- ☐☐ Other: _____

52

Labor Relations

LABOR RELATIONS

- ☐☐ Adherence to Labor Codes
- ☐☐ Bargaining Table Meetings
- ☐☐ Capacity-building Objectives Development
- ☐☐ Collective Bargaining Agreement Enforcement
- ☐☐ Complex Contract Language Interpretation
- ☐☐ Contract Settlement Administration
- ☐☐ Contractual Terms Compliance
- ☐☐ Employee Engagement Increase
- ☐☐ Employee Engagement Advice
- ☐☐ Employee Engagement Programs
- ☐☐ Employee Rights & Responsibilities
- ☐☐ Employer | Employee-related Concerns
- ☐☐ External Communications Strategy
- ☐☐ Grievance Procedures Execution
- ☐☐ Grievance Research & Evaluation
- ☐☐ Health & Safety Issues Resolution
- ☐☐ Health & Safety Procedures Development
- ☐☐ Labor Agreement Interpretation
- ☐☐ Labor Agreements Administration
- ☐☐ Legally Compliant Job Descriptions
- ☐☐ Member Development Goals Establishment
- ☐☐ Membership Rallies Organization
- ☐☐ National Labor Relations Board Liaison

- ☐☐ Arbitration Hearings
- ☐☐ Budget & Expense Proposals
- ☐☐ Circumstance Mitigation
- ☐☐ Communication Networks
- ☐☐ Contract Campaigns
- ☐☐ Contract Negotiations
- ☐☐ Demonstrations Organizing
- ☐☐ Departmental Operations
- ☐☐ Employee Advocate
- ☐☐ Employer Relations
- ☐☐ Fair Wages & Benefits
- ☐☐ Health & Safety Regulations
- ☐☐ Human Resources Oversight
- ☐☐ Innovative Problem-solving
- ☐☐ International Labor Relations
- ☐☐ Labor Laws
- ☐☐ Labor Organization Direction
- ☐☐ Labor Relations Support
- ☐☐ Liability Reports Review
- ☐☐ Membership Coordination
- ☐☐ Local Membership Promotion
- ☐☐ New Union Activists Training
- ☐☐ Memorandum Agreements

- ☐☐ Benefits Orientations
- ☐☐ Coalition Building
- ☐☐ Collective Agreements
- ☐☐ Collective Bargaining
- ☐☐ Contract Enforcement
- ☐☐ Contract Ratification
- ☐☐ Cost Determinations
- ☐☐ Dispute Resolution
- ☐☐ Employee Relations
- ☐☐ Employment Laws
- ☐☐ Grievance Handling
- ☐☐ Investigations
- ☐☐ Job Placement
- ☐☐ Job Safety Workshops
- ☐☐ Job Security Provisions
- ☐☐ Labor Movement
- ☐☐ Labor Relations
- ☐☐ Local Labor Relations
- ☐☐ Mediation
- ☐☐ Meeting Arrangements
- ☐☐ National Labor Relations
- ☐☐ Negotiations
- ☐☐ Organization Counseling

- ☐☐ National Occupational Standards
- ☐☐ New Union Activists Identification
- ☐☐ Operations Management Oversight
- ☐☐ Organizing Campaigns Implementation
- ☐☐ Policy Change Recommendations
- ☐☐ Press Representatives Relationships
- ☐☐ Program Goals Establishment
- ☐☐ Regulatory Compliance Oversight
- ☐☐ Safety & Health Measures Development
- ☐☐ Union Contract Specifications Adherence
- ☐☐ Union Member Job Performance Enhancement
- ☐☐ Union Membership Benefits Meetings
- ☐☐ Work Lives Quality Improvement
- ☐☐ Workers Compensation Board Regulations
- ☐☐ Workplace Issues Resolution
- ☐☐ Workplace Organization

- ☐☐ Negotiations with Stakeholders
- ☐☐ New Employees Orientation
- ☐☐ New Union Membership Growth
- ☐☐ Organizing Campaigns Planning
- ☐☐ OSHA Compliance Ensurance
- ☐☐ OSHA Standards & Compliance
- ☐☐ Past Practices Establishment
- ☐☐ Plant Production Measures
- ☐☐ Protection of Employee Rights
- ☐☐ Program Goals Formulation
- ☐☐ Side Letter Agreements (SLA)
- ☐☐ Sponsored Events & Rallies
- ☐☐ Union | Management Meetings
- ☐☐ Union Policies & Activities
- ☐☐ Work Site Visits
- ☐☐ Other: _____

- ☐☐ Organizing Plans
- ☐☐ Personnel Policies
- ☐☐ Productivity Improvement
- ☐☐ Political Activity
- ☐☐ Program Cost Monitoring
- ☐☐ Research Compilation
- ☐☐ Pro-employer Campaigns
- ☐☐ Release Agreements
- ☐☐ Risk Mitigation Solutions
- ☐☐ Shop Steward Meetings
- ☐☐ Solutions Development
- ☐☐ Subject Matter Expert
- ☐☐ Union Leadership
- ☐☐ Union Meetings
- ☐☐ Union Relationships

104

Landscaping & Groundskeeping

LANDSCAPING MANAGEMENT

Refer to "General Contracting / Trades Management."

LANDSCAPE ARCHITECTURE

- ☐☐ 3D & Sectional Views
- ☐☐ Architectural Design / Drawings
- ☐☐ Budget Development & Administration
- ☐☐ Client Presentations & Proposals
- ☐☐ Civil Landscape Drafting
- ☐☐ Competitive Bid Solicitation & Analysis
- ☐☐ Contract / Agreement Enforcement
- ☐☐ Contracts Development & Review
- ☐☐ Contract Change Order Preparation
- ☐☐ Contractor Selection
- ☐☐ Customer Service & Problem Resolution
- ☐☐ Design / Build Project Management
- ☐☐ Dimension Preparation
- ☐☐ Environmental Impact Studies
- ☐☐ Hazardous Conditions Evaluations
- ☐☐ Horizontal & Vertical Grounds Design
- ☐☐ Interior Landscaping Design
- ☐☐ Landscaping Construction Direction
- ☐☐ Landscaping Site Inspections
- ☐☐ Long-range Planning
- ☐☐ Print, Mylar & Sepia Preparation
- ☐☐ Priority Establishment & Scheduling
- ☐☐ Project Resources & Staffing Requirements
- ☐☐ Quality Work Standards
- ☐☐ Topographical & Relief Map Overlays
- ☐☐ Structural Features
- ☐☐ Trades Scheduling
- ☐☐ Use of Sun, Earth & Water Power
- ☐☐ Working Plan Development

- ☐☐ Aesthetic & Functional Design
- ☐☐ Architectural Rendering Drafting
- ☐☐ Client Consultation & Interface
- ☐☐ Client Invoicing
- ☐☐ Client Relations
- ☐☐ Client Meeting & Strategizing
- ☐☐ Client Needs Assessments
- ☐☐ Contract Negotiations
- ☐☐ Contract Award Procedures
- ☐☐ Cross-section Plotting
- ☐☐ Cost Reductions & Savings
- ☐☐ Design Conceptualization
- ☐☐ Documents Preparation
- ☐☐ Feasibility Studies
- ☐☐ Field Work Coordination
- ☐☐ Hiring and Coordinating Trades
- ☐☐ Land Development
- ☐☐ Landscaping Management
- ☐☐ Landscaping Plans
- ☐☐ On-site Inspections
- ☐☐ Post Construction Services
- ☐☐ Project Coordination
- ☐☐ Project Life Cycle
- ☐☐ Project Time Tracking
- ☐☐ Scheduling
- ☐☐ Structural Inspections
- ☐☐ Surveying
- ☐☐ Sketches & Thumbnails
- ☐☐ Other: _____

- ☐☐ Bidding Process
- ☐☐ Blueprints Preparation
- ☐☐ CAD Drawings
- ☐☐ Client Presentations
- ☐☐ Closeout Processing
- ☐☐ Client Satisfaction
- ☐☐ Contract Administration
- ☐☐ Cost Management
- ☐☐ Contract Negotiations
- ☐☐ Cost Analyses
- ☐☐ Design Development
- ☐☐ Electrical Drafting
- ☐☐ Estimating
- ☐☐ Fee Negotiations
- ☐☐ Issue Defining
- ☐☐ Land Use Studies
- ☐☐ Landscape Bidding
- ☐☐ Landscape Design
- ☐☐ Layout Diagrams
- ☐☐ Permit Obtaining
- ☐☐ Plumbing Systems
- ☐☐ Project Estimating
- ☐☐ Project Planning
- ☐☐ Project Prioritization
- ☐☐ Schematics
- ☐☐ Recordkeeping
- ☐☐ Wiring Diagrams
- ☐☐ Zoning Laws

85

LANDSCAPING EQUIPMENT & MACHINERY

Refer to "Equipment, Machinery, Tools & Testing Devices."

LANDSCAPING & GROUNDSKEEPING

- Account Servicing & Administration
- Blueprint Interpreting & Updating
- Cost / Expenditure Estimates
- Dethatching & Aerating Lawns
- Full-service Landscape Maintenance
- Commercial Landscape Maintenance Services
- Landscaping Equipment Operation & Maintenance
- Painting Outdoor Furniture & Structures
- Plant Damage Resolution
- Property Potential Maximizing
- Snow Removal / Plowing
- Swimming Pool Maintenance
- Trades Coordination & Oversight
- Transplanting Trees & Shrubs
- Weed, Disease & Insect Control
- Work Functions Coordination
- Other: _____

- Cash Management
- Grounds Maintenance
- Customer Service Inquiries
- Inspections & Compliance
- Landscape Installations
- Lawn Mowing & Edging
- Mulching Planting Areas
- New Garden Plantings
- Pest Management Techniques
- Raking / Mulching Leaves
- Soil Composition Testing
- Sprinkler Systems
- Trades/Crew Supervision
- Troubleshooting
- Weekly Grounds Maintenance
- Pesticide, Herbicide, Fungicide, Insecticide Applications

- Client Database
- Fertilizing
- Irrigation Systems
- Landscape Design
- Lighting Systems
- Masonry Projects
- Property Grading
- Purchasing
- Safety Practices
- Raw Material Use
- Shrub Pruning
- Sod Harvesting
- Work Collaboration
- Sod Planting
- Tree Trimming

47

Masonry

MASONRY PROJECT TYPES

- Landscape Designs
- Sidewalks, Walkways & Paths
- Concrete Casting & Forms
- Ponds & Waterfalls
- Stone Walls
- Walls & Partitions

- Retainer Walls
- Concrete Foundations
- Flooring
- Retaining Walls
- Solar Panels
- Other: _____

- Decorative Patios
- Fireplaces
- Refractory Tile
- Roof-top Installations
- Tiling

- Driveways
- Chimneys
- Steps
- Roadways
- Trim Work

21

MASONRY WORK

- Blueprint Reading
- Color Concrete Surfaces
- Concrete & Steel Reinforcement
- Excavation & Fill Operations
- Steel & Concrete Construction
- Masonry (Brick/Stone/Cement)
- Reinforced Concrete Structures
- Other: _____

- Brattices
- Concrete Foundations
- Concrete Beams & Forms
- Exposed Aggregate Walls
- Job Estimating
- Paving & Grading
- Soaking Pits

- Concrete Castings
- Ditches & Dredging
- Firebrick Linings
- Irrigation Systems
- Job Scheduling
- Refractory Tile
- Structural Insulated Wall Panels

- Columns
- Demolition
- Foundations
- Job Bidding
- Millwork
- Painting

28

MASONRY EQUIPMENT & MACHINERY

Refer to "Equipment, Machinery, Tools & Testing Devices."

Plumbing

PLUMBING LICENSES & CERTIFICATIONS

- EPA - CFC Certification
- Master plumber's License
- Plumbing Contractor License

- HVAC-Related Journeyman's License
- Plumber Apprenticeship Certificate
- Universal CFC Certification

- Licensed Journeyman Plumber
- Plumber's License
- Other: _____

8

PLUMBING AREAS OF EXPERTISE

- Air Conditioning
- Apprentice Monitoring

- Air Handlers
- Architectural Drawings

- Air Quality
- Asbestos Removal

- ☐☐ Bid Coordination & Selection
- ☐☐ Building & Safety Codes
- ☐☐ Building Code Specifications
- ☐☐ Building Plans Interpretation
- ☐☐ Client Meeting & Strategizing
- ☐☐ Contracting / Subcontracting
- ☐☐ Control System Efficiency
- ☐☐ Direct Digital Controls
- ☐☐ Engineering Drawings
- ☐☐ Estimating Job Times, Materials & Costs
- ☐☐ Federal & State Laws & Regulations
- ☐☐ Grounds, Top-Out & Finish
- ☐☐ Hazardous Waste Handling & Disposal
- ☐☐ Hazardous Waste Transportation
- ☐☐ HVAC Heat Return & Main Water Lines
- ☐☐ HVAC Maintenance & Repair
- ☐☐ HVAC Systems, Digitally Controlled
- ☐☐ Inspecting Piping Systems
- ☐☐ Material Shipment Monitoring
- ☐☐ Material Handling
- ☐☐ OSHA, EPA, MSDS & ADA
- ☐☐ Performance Monitoring
- ☐☐ Piping System Inspections
- ☐☐ Plumbing Equipment
- ☐☐ Plumbing Kitchen Facilities
- ☐☐ Plumbing Plans Interpretation
- ☐☐ Plumbing Tools, Materials & Supplies
- ☐☐ Preventive Maintenance Scheduling
- ☐☐ Quality Standards
- ☐☐ Refrigerant Recovery
- ☐☐ Safety Procedure Enforcement
- ☐☐ Specifications
- ☐☐ Temperature Adjustment
- ☐☐ Temperature Controls Verification
- ☐☐ Water System Inspections
- ☐☐ Winterizing Piping Systems
- ☐☐ HVAC Computer-Based Monitoring & Control Devises

- ☐☐ Blueprint Interpretation
- ☐☐ Building Automation
- ☐☐ Building Systems Repair
- ☐☐ Client Emergency Response
- ☐☐ Code Violations Assessment
- ☐☐ Contract Negotiations
- ☐☐ Cooling Water
- ☐☐ Dampers
- ☐☐ Equipment Inspections
- ☐☐ Fabrication
- ☐☐ Faucet & Valve Repair
- ☐☐ Gas Line Installation
- ☐☐ HVAC / HVAC-R
- ☐☐ HVAC Equipment
- ☐☐ HVAC Troubleshooting
- ☐☐ In-Ground Pools Installation
- ☐☐ Inventory Ordering & Issuing
- ☐☐ Job Cost Accountability
- ☐☐ Materials & Hardware Selection
- ☐☐ Materials Shipping
- ☐☐ Microelectronics
- ☐☐ National Plumbing Code
- ☐☐ Plumbing Codes
- ☐☐ Plumbing Installation
- ☐☐ Plumbing Practices & Techniques
- ☐☐ Plumbing Tools & Equipment
- ☐☐ Plumbing Safety Practices
- ☐☐ Punch List Handling
- ☐☐ PVC / EPDM
- ☐☐ Radiant Heating
- ☐☐ Regulatory Requirements
- ☐☐ Safety Requirements
- ☐☐ Sewer Inspections
- ☐☐ Uniform Plumbing Code
- ☐☐ Water Consumption
- ☐☐ Winterizing Sprinkler Systems
- ☐☐ Plumbing Systems Compatibility Determination

- ☐☐ Blueprint Modification
- ☐☐ Client Billing
- ☐☐ Client Relations
- ☐☐ Combustion Analyses
- ☐☐ Compressed Air
- ☐☐ Contract Specifications
- ☐☐ Cost Estimating
- ☐☐ Diffusers
- ☐☐ Equipment Monitoring
- ☐☐ Fans
- ☐☐ Gas Consumption
- ☐☐ Humidification
- ☐☐ HVAC Codes
- ☐☐ HVAC Installation
- ☐☐ HVAC Parts
- ☐☐ Isometric Drawings
- ☐☐ Job Preparation
- ☐☐ Job Scheduling
- ☐☐ Material Bids Review
- ☐☐ Mechanical Operations
- ☐☐ Multi-Family Dwellings
- ☐☐ Plumbing Agreements
- ☐☐ Plumbing Construction
- ☐☐ Plumbing Permits
- ☐☐ Plumbing Specifications
- ☐☐ Potable Water
- ☐☐ Procurement Policies
- ☐☐ Purchasing
- ☐☐ Materials Estimates
- ☐☐ Registers
- ☐☐ Safety Practices
- ☐☐ Schematics
- ☐☐ Technical Drawings
- ☐☐ Ventilation
- ☐☐ Water Heaters
- ☐☐ Other: _____

116

PLUMBING SYSTEMS

- ☐☐ Boilers (Gas / Electric / Open Flame)
- ☐☐ Commercial Plumbing Systems
- ☐☐ Distribution Systems & Controls
- ☐☐ Energy Management Control System (EMCS)
- ☐☐ Energy Related Equipment & Control Systems
- ☐☐ Heating, Cooling & Ventilation Systems
- ☐☐ In-Door Plumbing Systems
- ☐☐ Residential Plumbing Systems
- ☐☐ Water Systems

- ☐☐ Building Management Systems
- ☐☐ Domestic Plumbing Systems
- ☐☐ Fire Sprinkler Systems
- ☐☐ Gas & Electric Heating Systems
- ☐☐ Industrial Plumbing Systems
- ☐☐ HVAC Electric Systems
- ☐☐ Piping Systems
- ☐☐ Split Systems
- ☐☐ Winterizing Systems

- ☐☐ Cooling Systems
- ☐☐ Drainage Systems
- ☐☐ Gas Systems
- ☐☐ Heating Systems
- ☐☐ HVAC Systems
- ☐☐ Plumbing Systems
- ☐☐ Refrigeration Systems
- ☐☐ Sprinkler Systems
- ☐☐ Other: _____

26

PLUMBING COMPONENTS & DEVICES

- ☐☐ Air Compressors
- ☐☐ Building Mechanical Systems
- ☐☐ Chlorine Gas Feeders
- ☐☐ Cooling System Maintenance
- ☐☐ Electronic Controls
- ☐☐ Emergency Lighting System
- ☐☐ Gas & Electric Stoves & Ovens

- ☐☐ Backflow Devices
- ☐☐ Boiler & Steam Controls
- ☐☐ Commodes
- ☐☐ Dishwashers
- ☐☐ Emergency Generator
- ☐☐ Fixtures
- ☐☐ Freezers

- ☐☐ Bearing Assemblies
- ☐☐ Circulation Pumps
- ☐☐ Compressors
- ☐☐ Electric Boilers
- ☐☐ Filtration Pumps
- ☐☐ Flush Valves
- ☐☐ Garbage Disposals

- ☐☐ Cesspool Lines
- ☐☐ Coils
- ☐☐ Condensers
- ☐☐ Electric Motors
- ☐☐ Fittings
- ☐☐ Fountains
- ☐☐ Gas Boilers

68

- ☐☐ Heating System Boilers
- ☐☐ Monitoring & Control Devices
- ☐☐ Pipes, Fittings, Valves & Fixtures
- ☐☐ Plumbing System Equipment
- ☐☐ Plumbing Malfunction Source Identification
- ☐☐ Programmable Logic Controls
- ☐☐ Pump Seals, Bearings & Couplings
- ☐☐ Sewage Collection Systems
- ☐☐ Soda Ash & Chlorine Gas Feeders
- ☐☐ Standard Inspection Procedures
- ☐☐ Swimming Pool Filtration Pumps
- ☐☐ Water Supply & Drain Lines

- ☐☐ Gas & Oil Piping
- ☐☐ Heat Return Lines
- ☐☐ Main Water Lines
- ☐☐ Open Flame Boilers
- ☐☐ Pneumatic Valves
- ☐☐ Roof Drains
- ☐☐ PVC Pipe Installation
- ☐☐ Sheet Metal Handling
- ☐☐ Specialty Plumbing Items
- ☐☐ Steam Lines & Controls
- ☐☐ Toilets / Urinals
- ☐☐ Water Heaters
- ☐☐ Other: _____

- ☐☐ Heat Exchangers
- ☐☐ Heating Pipes
- ☐☐ Mixing Valves
- ☐☐ Package Units
- ☐☐ Pressure Testing
- ☐☐ Rooftop Units
- ☐☐ Sewer Lines
- ☐☐ Steam Boilers
- ☐☐ Steam Lines
- ☐☐ Storm Drains
- ☐☐ Univents
- ☐☐ Water Softeners

- ☐☐ Grills
- ☐☐ Microwaves
- ☐☐ Pumps
- ☐☐ Refrigerators
- ☐☐ Retro-Fittings
- ☐☐ Septic Tanks
- ☐☐ Sinks & Faucets
- ☐☐ Steam Cookers
- ☐☐ Steam Traps
- ☐☐ Thermostats
- ☐☐ Valves

80

PLUMBING ASSOCIATED SERVICES

- ☐☐ Computer Programming
- ☐☐ Consulting
- ☐☐ Facilities Maintenance
- ☐☐ Home Heating Conversions
- ☐☐ Pipe Cutting & Threading
- ☐☐ Preventive Maintenance
- ☐☐ Time & Materials Estimating
- ☐☐ Work Assignment Delegating

- ☐☐ Carpentry
- ☐☐ Copper Soldering
- ☐☐ Engineering
- ☐☐ Maintenance & Repair
- ☐☐ Plumbing Inspections
- ☐☐ Servicing
- ☐☐ Trades Coordination
- ☐☐ Work Prioritization

- ☐☐ Connecting
- ☐☐ Dismantling
- ☐☐ Installations
- ☐☐ Pipe Soldering
- ☐☐ Plumbing Repairs
- ☐☐ Supplies Ordering
- ☐☐ Troubleshooting
- ☐☐ Work Scheduling

- ☐☐ Construction
- ☐☐ Duct Work
- ☐☐ Outdoor Plumbing
- ☐☐ Pipefitting
- ☐☐ Project Planning
- ☐☐ Take-offs
- ☐☐ Welding
- ☐☐ Other: _____

31

PLUMBING EQUIPMENT

Refer to *"Equipment, Machinery, Tools & Testing Devices."*

Project Management

PROJECT LIFECYCLE MANAGEMENT

- ☐☐ Project Budgeting
- ☐☐ Project Definition
- ☐☐ Project Planning
- ☐☐ Project Scope
- ☐☐ Project Timelines
- ☐☐ Full Lifecycle Project Integration

- ☐☐ Project Close-out
- ☐☐ Project Deliverables
- ☐☐ Project Prioritization
- ☐☐ Project Specifications
- ☐☐ Project Time Tracking
- ☐☐ Project Resources & Staffing Requirements

- ☐☐ Project Coordination
- ☐☐ Project Development
- ☐☐ Project Resource Allocation
- ☐☐ Project Strategizing
- ☐☐ Project Strategizing & Initiation

- ☐☐ Project Costing
- ☐☐ Project Objectives
- ☐☐ Project Scheduling
- ☐☐ Project Time Frames
- ☐☐ Other: _____

21

PROJECT MANAGEMENT FUNCTIONS

- ☐☐ Change Management Plan Development
- ☐☐ Cross-Disciplinary Project Management
- ☐☐ Cross-Functional Solutions Development
- ☐☐ Cross-Functional Team Coordination
- ☐☐ Cross-Organizational Project Deployment
- ☐☐ Functional Specifications Development
- ☐☐ Full-Scope Solutions Plan Development
- ☐☐ Management Consulting Support
- ☐☐ Operational Specifications Development
- ☐☐ Plan Development Facilitation
- ☐☐ Project Deliverables Coordination & Control
- ☐☐ Project Financial Administration
- ☐☐ Project Financial Development & Planning
- ☐☐ Project Logistical Support & Planning
- ☐☐ Project Management Coordination
- ☐☐ Project Management Plan Development
- ☐☐ Project Management Repository Establishment
- ☐☐ Project Performance Management

- ☐☐ Budget Control
- ☐☐ Business Case Reviews
- ☐☐ Client Relationship Building
- ☐☐ Global Project Management
- ☐☐ Issue Escalation & Resolution
- ☐☐ Issues Escalation Management
- ☐☐ Materials Submittal Management
- ☐☐ New Work Process Development
- ☐☐ Payment Applications Coordination
- ☐☐ Project Activity Management
- ☐☐ Project Closure & Acceptance
- ☐☐ Project Design & Development
- ☐☐ Project Issues & Risks Tracking
- ☐☐ Project Logistics Determination
- ☐☐ Project Objectives Setting
- ☐☐ Project Operational Development
- ☐☐ Project Plan Development
- ☐☐ Project Resource Interdependence

- ☐☐ Change Control
- ☐☐ Cost Assessments
- ☐☐ Cost Control
- ☐☐ Efficiency Reviews
- ☐☐ Logistics Planning
- ☐☐ Materials Procurement
- ☐☐ Process Improvement
- ☐☐ Partnership Leveraging
- ☐☐ Process Modeling
- ☐☐ Project Communication
- ☐☐ Project Documentation
- ☐☐ Project Execution
- ☐☐ Project Initiation
- ☐☐ Project Implementations
- ☐☐ Project Needs Analysis
- ☐☐ Project Plan Execution
- ☐☐ Project Prioritization
- ☐☐ Project Scheduling

☐☐ Project Proposals Review & Approval
☐☐ Project Resource Deployment & Management
☐☐ Project Scoping & Estimating
☐☐ Quality Standards Compliance
☐☐ Reengineering Management
☐☐ Risk Management Strategizing
☐☐ Schedule Creation & Management
☐☐ Subcontract Agreements Preparation
☐☐ System Integration
☐☐ Team Selection
☐☐ Tracking & Reporting
☐☐ Work Plan Management

☐☐ Project Risk Deliverables
☐☐ Project Tracking & Reporting
☐☐ Project Variance Management
☐☐ Quality Deliverables Control
☐☐ Risk Identification & Mitigation
☐☐ Risks & Controls Management
☐☐ Scope Change Management
☐☐ Solutions Development
☐☐ Task Management
☐☐ Time Management
☐☐ Use Cases Development
☐☐ Other: _____

☐☐ Project Testing
☐☐ Quality Management
☐☐ Requirements Elicitation
☐☐ Resource Allocation
☐☐ Resource Management
☐☐ Scope Change Requests
☐☐ Scope Management
☐☐ Status Reporting
☐☐ Task Planning & Scheduling
☐☐ Time Management
☐☐ Value Proposition

88

PROJECT MANAGEMENT FUNCTIONS – ARCHITECTURE & ENGINEERING

☐☐ Budget Control
☐☐ Client Relationship Building
☐☐ Functional Specifications Development
☐☐ Materials Submittal Management
☐☐ Project Activity Management
☐☐ Project Deliverables Coordination & Control
☐☐ Project Issues & Risks Tracking
☐☐ Project Objectives Setting
☐☐ Project Plan Development
☐☐ Project Scheduling
☐☐ Project Tracking & Reporting
☐☐ Quality Standards Compliance
☐☐ Risk Identification & Mitigation
☐☐ Risks & Controls Management
☐☐ Scope Management
☐☐ Status Reporting
☐☐ Tracking & Reporting

☐☐ Change Orders
☐☐ Cost Control
☐☐ Issues Escalation Management
☐☐ Payment Applications Coordination
☐☐ Project Communication
☐☐ Project Documentation
☐☐ Project Implementations
☐☐ Project Needs Analysis
☐☐ Project Prioritization
☐☐ Project Proposals Review & Approval
☐☐ Quality Management
☐☐ Quality Deliverables Control
☐☐ Resource Management
☐☐ Schedule Creation & Management
☐☐ Subcontract Agreements Preparation
☐☐ Team Selection
☐☐ Other: _____

☐☐ Cost Assessments
☐☐ Issue Escalation & Resolution
☐☐ Materials Procurement
☐☐ Plan Development Facilitation
☐☐ Project Close-outs
☐☐ Project Design & Development
☐☐ Project Management Coordination
☐☐ Project Plan Execution
☐☐ Project Performance Management
☐☐ Project Risk Deliverables
☐☐ Project Scoping & Estimating
☐☐ Resource Allocation
☐☐ Risk Management Strategizing
☐☐ Scope Change Management
☐☐ Solutions Development
☐☐ Time Management

49

PROJECT MANAGEMENT ANALYSIS

☐☐ Alternatives Analysis
☐☐ Customer-Centric Analytics
☐☐ Portfolio Theory Analysis
☐☐ Risk Analysis and Management

☐☐ Conjoint Measurement Analysis
☐☐ Portfolio Analyzer
☐☐ Return on Investment Analysis
☐☐ Value and Risk Analysis

☐☐ Cost/Benefit Analysis
☐☐ Portfolio Level Analysis
☐☐ Value and Cost Analysis
☐☐ Other: _____

11

PROJECT MANAGEMENT METHODOLOGIES

☐☐ Analytical Problem-Solving Methodology
☐☐ Project Management Framework
☐☐ Project Methodology
☐☐ Structure-Disciplined Project Management

☐☐ Change Management Methodologies
☐☐ Deliverables-based PM Methodology
☐☐ Mitigation Strategies

☐☐ Best Practice Leveraging
☐☐ Facilities Methodology
☐☐ Other: _____

9

PROJECT MANAGEMENT, OTHER

☐☐ ANSI Standards
☐☐ Complexity Management
☐☐ Complex Business Problems Resolution
☐☐ Contingency Planning Orchestration
☐☐ Dual Reporting Relationships
☐☐ Earned Value Management Systems
☐☐ Functional Requirements Documentation
☐☐ Information Technology Outsourcing
☐☐ Large Multichannel Retailer Interface
☐☐ Management & Scheduling Techniques
☐☐ Multiple & Large Project Execution
☐☐ Operating Level Agreements (OLAs)

☐☐ Change Orders Estimating
☐☐ Communications Channels & Tools
☐☐ Conjoint Measurement Systems
☐☐ Contract Negotiations
☐☐ Cost Performance Indexing
☐☐ Functional Improvement Changes
☐☐ Functional Managers' Priorities
☐☐ Management by Objectives
☐☐ Management by Exception
☐☐ Manual Processing Procedures
☐☐ On-Time Delivery Ensurance
☐☐ Organizational Change Management

☐☐ Client Relations Management
☐☐ Computer Science
☐☐ Conflict Resolution
☐☐ Contract Writing
☐☐ Efficient Frontiers
☐☐ Methodology Adoption
☐☐ Multi-Month Timelines
☐☐ Multi-Year Timelines
☐☐ Order Management
☐☐ Portfolio Management
☐☐ Proactive Management
☐☐ Program Management

☐☐ Planning & Scheduling Techniques
☐☐ Project Team Management
☐☐ Risk Management Framework
☐☐ Schedule Performance Indexing
☐☐ Skills Categorization Hierarchies
☐☐ Strategic Initiatives Implementation
☐☐ Tactical Elements Organization
☐☐ Vendor Negotiations
☐☐ Other: _____

☐☐ Planned Versus Actual Variance
☐☐ Process & Data Flow Modeling
☐☐ Relationship Management
☐☐ Service Level Agreements
☐☐ Strategic Business Planning
☐☐ Supply Chain Management
☐☐ Underpinning Contracts (UCs)
☐☐ Work Prioritization

☐☐ Project Charter
☐☐ Service Delivery
☐☐ Service Management
☐☐ Storyboards Creation
☐☐ Vendor Management
☐☐ Vendor Relations
☐☐ Vendor Bids
☐☐ Workflow Processes

60

Trades Coordination & Oversight

TRADES COORDINATION & OVERSIGHT

☐☐ Carpentry
☐☐ Facilities Maintenance
☐☐ Welding / Steamfitting

☐☐ Construction
☐☐ HVAC / HVAC-R
☐☐ Other: _____

☐☐ Concrete Pouring
☐☐ Landscaping

☐☐ Dismantling
☐☐ Masonry

☐☐ Electrical
☐☐ Plumbing

9

ELECTRICAL SYSTEMS

☐☐ Bus Bar Systems
☐☐ Climate Control Systems
☐☐ Conduit Systems
☐☐ Electrical Systems
☐☐ Exterior Lighting
☐☐ Fuel Systems
☐☐ High-Voltage Electrical Systems
☐☐ Interior Lighting
☐☐ Motor Control Systems
☐☐ Proximity Systems
☐☐ Security Systems
☐☐ Video Systems

☐☐ Cable Systems
☐☐ Communications Systems
☐☐ Digital Systems
☐☐ Electromagnetic Systems
☐☐ Fiber Optic Electrical Systems
☐☐ Heating Systems
☐☐ Industrial Systems
☐☐ Lighting Systems
☐☐ Pneumatic Tube Systems
☐☐ Public Address Systems
☐☐ Signaling Systems
☐☐ Voltage Transformers

☐☐ Cargo Systems
☐☐ Computer Systems
☐☐ Electrical Communications Systems
☐☐ Energy Management Systems
☐☐ Fire Alarm Systems
☐☐ High-Tension Distribution Systems
☐☐ Intercom Systems
☐☐ Low-Voltage Electrical Systems
☐☐ Power Systems
☐☐ Refrigeration Systems
☐☐ Telephone Systems
☐☐ Other: _____

35

HVAC / HVAC-R SYSTEMS

☐☐ Air Conditioning Systems
☐☐ Commercial Plumbing Systems
☐☐ Energy Management Control System (EMCS)
☐☐ Energy Related Equipment & Control Systems
☐☐ Heating, Cooling & Ventilation Systems
☐☐ Industrial Plumbing Systems
☐☐ Refrigeration Systems
☐☐ Residential Plumbing Systems
☐☐ Ventilation Systems
☐☐ Other: _____

☐☐ Building Management Systems
☐☐ Distribution Systems & Controls
☐☐ Domestic Plumbing Systems
☐☐ Gas & Electric Heating Systems
☐☐ HVAC Electric Systems
☐☐ In-Door Plumbing Systems
☐☐ Piping Systems
☐☐ Split Systems
☐☐ Water Systems

☐☐ Cooling Systems
☐☐ Drainage Systems
☐☐ Fire Sprinkler Systems
☐☐ Gas Systems
☐☐ Heating Systems
☐☐ HVAC Systems
☐☐ Plumbing Systems
☐☐ Sprinkler Systems
☐☐ Winterizing Systems

27

MASONRY & LANDSCAPE PROJECTS

☐☐ Landscape Designs
☐☐ Sidewalks, Walkways & Paths
☐☐ Concrete Casting & Forms
☐☐ Ponds & Waterfalls
☐☐ Stone Walls
☐☐ Walls & Partitions

☐☐ Retainer Walls
☐☐ Concrete Foundations
☐☐ Flooring
☐☐ Retaining Walls
☐☐ Solar Panels
☐☐ Other: _____

☐☐ Decorative Patios
☐☐ Fireplaces
☐☐ Refractory Tile
☐☐ Roof-top Installations
☐☐ Tiling

☐☐ Driveways
☐☐ Chimneys
☐☐ Steps
☐☐ Roadways
☐☐ Trim Work

21

PLUMBING SYSTEMS

☐☐ Boilers (Gas / Electric / Open Flame)
☐☐ Commercial Plumbing Systems

☐☐ Building Management Systems
☐☐ Domestic Plumbing Systems

☐☐ Cooling Systems
☐☐ Drainage Systems

- ☐☐ Distribution Systems & Controls
- ☐☐ Energy Management Control System (EMCS)
- ☐☐ Energy Related Equipment & Control Systems
- ☐☐ Heating, Cooling & Ventilation Systems
- ☐☐ In-Door Plumbing Systems
- ☐☐ Residential Plumbing Systems
- ☐☐ Water Systems

- ☐☐ Fire Sprinkler Systems
- ☐☐ Gas & Electric Heating Systems
- ☐☐ Industrial Plumbing Systems
- ☐☐ HVAC Electric Systems
- ☐☐ Piping Systems
- ☐☐ Split Systems
- ☐☐ Winterizing Systems

- ☐☐ Gas Systems
- ☐☐ Heating Systems
- ☐☐ HVAC Systems
- ☐☐ Plumbing Systems
- ☐☐ Refrigeration Systems
- ☐☐ Sprinkler Systems
- ☐☐ Other: _____

26

WELDING / STEAMFITTING SYSTEM TYPES

- ☐☐ Boilers (Gas / Electric / Open Flame)
- ☐☐ Cooling Systems
- ☐☐ Drainage Systems
- ☐☐ Energy Related Equipment & Control Systems
- ☐☐ Heating Systems
- ☐☐ HVAC Electric Systems
- ☐☐ Piping Systems
- ☐☐ Residential Plumbing Systems
- ☐☐ Water Systems

- ☐☐ Building Management Systems
- ☐☐ Distribution Systems & Controls
- ☐☐ Energy Management Control System
- ☐☐ Gas & Electric Heating Systems
- ☐☐ Heating, Cooling & Ventilation Systems
- ☐☐ In-Door Plumbing Systems
- ☐☐ Plumbing Systems
- ☐☐ Split Systems
- ☐☐ Winterizing Systems

- ☐☐ Commercial Plumbing Systems
- ☐☐ Domestic Plumbing Systems
- ☐☐ Fire Sprinkler Systems
- ☐☐ Gas Systems
- ☐☐ HVAC Systems
- ☐☐ Industrial Plumbing Systems
- ☐☐ Refrigeration Systems
- ☐☐ Sprinkler Systems
- ☐☐ Other: _____

26

Welding / Steamfitting

WELDING / STEAMFITTING

- ☐☐ Atlas Machines
- ☐☐ All Phases of Building Trades
- ☐☐ Blueprint Reading
- ☐☐ CNC Machines
- ☐☐ Compressed Air Systems
- ☐☐ Core Drilling
- ☐☐ Cutting & Threading Pipe
- ☐☐ Drill Presses
- ☐☐ Domestic Water Systems
- ☐☐ Gear Cutting Machines
- ☐☐ Hydraulic Pistons & Seals
- ☐☐ Hydraulic Oil Pressure
- ☐☐ Hydraulic Systems
- ☐☐ Industrial Welding
- ☐☐ Lathes
- ☐☐ Milling Machines
- ☐☐ Industrial Plumbing
- ☐☐ Modified Torch Down Systems
- ☐☐ Rigging
- ☐☐ Pipefitting
- ☐☐ Soldering
- ☐☐ Torch Cutting
- ☐☐ Welding & Arc Welding

- ☐☐ Air Handling Units (Motors, Pneumatic Controls & Coil Units)
- ☐☐ Air Compressor & Sanitary Piping
- ☐☐ Centrifugal Chiller & Steam Absorption Machines
- ☐☐ Cooling Tower Maintenance
- ☐☐ Connecting Water, Steam, Gas, Oxygen, Vacuum & Air Lines
- ☐☐ Computerized Energy Management Building System Program
- ☐☐ HVAC & Sterilization Equipment
- ☐☐ Exotic Metals: Carbon, Stainless, Aluminum, Tungsten & Cast Iron
- ☐☐ Gas Dangers & Safety Requirements
- ☐☐ Gases: Argon, Helium, Oxygen & Acetylene
- ☐☐ Fire Suppression Sprinkler Systems
- ☐☐ HVAC Piping, Equipment & Duct Work
- ☐☐ MIG, TIG, Plasma, Heliarc, Brazing
- ☐☐ Installation, Service & Repair
- ☐☐ Joint Welding: Groove, Bead, Edge, Plug, Slot, Fillet & Arc-Seam
- ☐☐ Medical Gas Piping: Oxygen, Nitrogen, Medical Air & Vacuum Piping
- ☐☐ Low Pressure & High Pressure Boilers / Steam Lines
- ☐☐ Service, Repair & Maintenance
- ☐☐ Precision-measuring Instruments
- ☐☐ Roto Rooter, Jetter & Lift Operator
- ☐☐ Sterilization & Sanitation Equipment
- ☐☐ Wet, Dry & Deluge Sprinkler Systems
- ☐☐ Other: _____

45

SYSTEM TYPES

- ☐☐ Boilers (Gas/Electric/Open Flame)
- ☐☐ Cooling Systems
- ☐☐ Drainage Systems
- ☐☐ Energy Related Equipment & Control Systems
- ☐☐ Heating, Cooling & Ventilation Systems
- ☐☐ HVAC Electric Systems
- ☐☐ Piping Systems
- ☐☐ Residential Plumbing Systems
- ☐☐ Water Systems

- ☐☐ Building Management Systems
- ☐☐ Distribution Systems & Controls
- ☐☐ Energy Management Control System
- ☐☐ Gas & Electric Heating Systems
- ☐☐ Heating Systems
- ☐☐ In-Door Plumbing Systems
- ☐☐ Plumbing Systems
- ☐☐ Split Systems
- ☐☐ Winterizing Systems

- ☐☐ Commercial Plumbing Systems
- ☐☐ Domestic Plumbing Systems
- ☐☐ Fire Sprinkler Systems
- ☐☐ Gas Systems
- ☐☐ HVAC Systems
- ☐☐ Industrial Plumbing Systems
- ☐☐ Refrigeration Systems
- ☐☐ Sprinkler Systems
- ☐☐ Other: _____

20

STEP 3
CHECK OFF YOUR PERSONAL ATTRIBUTES & CAPABILITIES

CONTENTS OF STEP 3

- [ ] Personal Attributes for Trade Positions
- [ ] Personal Attributes for Managers
- [ ] Personal Attributes for Professionals
- [ ] Social and General Attributes
- [ ] List Your Top 10-15 Attributes

Hone in on 10 of your best Personal Attributes or Assets that benefit your audience

Identify your Assets/Features
THAT MATCH YOUR AUDIENCE'S NEEDS

- Able to help others • **Able to overcome obstacles** • Accessible • Accommodating • Accountable • Action-driven leader
- Approachable • Assertive • Attentive • Autonomous • Calm • Candid • **Challenge Seeker** • Client focused • Collaborative
- Committed • Communicative • **Competitive** • Comprehensive • Confident • **Connected** • Consistent • Convincing
- Cooperative • Credible • Dedicated • Dependable • Diligent • Down-to-earth • Driven • Dynamic • Efficient • Empathetic
- **Empowering** • Engaging • Entertaining • Ethical • Expeditor • Fair • Flexible • Friendly • Genuine
- Goal driven • Good Listener • Hardworking • Helpful • Honest • Impartial • Influencer • Insightful
- Inspiring • Intuitive • Investigative • Leader • Logical thinker • Mediator • Mentor • Morale builder
- Motivated • Motivator • **Negotiator** • Nonjudgmental • Objective • Opportunistic • Optimistic
- Organized • Outcome focused • Outgoing • Outside-the-box thinker • People oriented • Perceptive
- Persevering • Planner • Positive • Proactive • **Problem solver** • Process oriented • Productive
- Professional • Project oriented • Promoter • Punctual • Quality conscious • Rapport builder • Realistic
- Reasonable • **Relationship builder** • Reliable • Resilient • Resourceful • Respected • Responsive
- Results oriented • Role model • Savvy • Self-confident • Self-directed • Self-motivated • Self-starter
- Sense of humor • Sensible • Sensitive to others • Service oriented • Sincere • Skilled interpersonally
- Sociable • Sound decision maker • Straightforward • **Strategic thinker** • Success driven • Successful
- Supportive • Tactful • Team builder • Team player • Thorough • **Time manager** • Trendsetter
- Troubleshooter • Trustworthy • Understanding • Versatile • Warm • Well rounded

PERSONAL ATTRIBUTES & CAPABILITIES

INTRODUCTION

In this step you will be identifying your personal attributes (your assets / features) and honing in on your top 10 to 15 attributes that match your prospective employers' needs. Those would be your unique qualities, characteristics, attributes, capabilities, and/or skills that can be valuable to an employer. You will use these attributes in *Step 4: Develop Your Personal Brand and Professional Summary*.

Below are the primary attributes, capabilities, and skills employers seek in candidates in this profession as obtained from actual job postings. You will want to be sure to include in your resume the primary ones that are applicable to you. Place one **"X"** before the attributes you feel you own. Then, review the ones you checked off, and double check (**"XX"**) those that are most important to your specific targeted position.

Personal Attributes for Trade Positions

☐☐ Ability to adjust the eye to bring an object into sharp focus		☐☐ Ability to apply knowledge of codes and regulations
☐☐ Ability to balance to structures		☐☐ Ability to climb scaffolds and ladders
☐☐ Ability to communicate effectively		☐☐ Ability to drive a vehicle safely
☐☐ Ability to interpret a variety of complex instructions		☐☐ Ability to lift and/or move up to 50 to 100 pounds
☐☐ Ability to manage change efficiently and responsibly		☐☐ Ability to manage multiple projects simultaneously
☐☐ Ability to observe critically and obtain accurate data		☐☐ Ability to organize and coordinate work of a unit or laborers
☐☐ Ability to perform strenuous daily activities		☐☐ Ability to read and interpret plans and specifications
☐☐ Ability to read blueprints and drawings		☐☐ Ability to solve practical problems
☐☐ Ability to stay calm in stressful situations		☐☐ Ability to stoop, twist, turn, crouch, and reach
☐☐ Ability to train and instruct others in related work		☐☐ Ability to walk, crawl, and bend for extended periods
☐☐ Ability to sit, kneel, and stand for extended periods		☐☐ Ability to work in inclement weather conditions
☐☐ Ability to work without supervision		☐☐ Basic Computer Skills
☐☐ Current driver's license and acceptable driving record		☐☐ Good balance and physical strength

☐☐ Active Listening	☐☐ Adaptable / Flexible	☐☐ Analytical	☐☐ Arm-Hand Steadiness
☐☐ Attention to Detail	☐☐ Attention to Detail	☐☐ Auditory Attention	☐☐ Communication skills
☐☐ Control Precision	☐☐ Cooperation	☐☐ Coordination	☐☐ Deductive Reasoning
☐☐ Critical Thinking	☐☐ Customer Focused	☐☐ Decision Making	☐☐ Dependable
☐☐ Depth Perception	☐☐ Detail-oriented	☐☐ Dynamic Strength	☐☐ Independent
☐☐ Hard Working	☐☐ High Degree of Concentration	☐☐ Information Processing	☐☐ Initiative
☐☐ Initiative	☐☐ Innovation	☐☐ Judgment	☐☐ Manual Dexterity
☐☐ Math Skills	☐☐ Mathematical Reasoning	☐☐ Mechanical Aptitude	☐☐ Multilimb Coordination
☐☐ Multitasker	☐☐ Near & Far Vision	☐☐ Oral Expression	☐☐ Organized
☐☐ Persistence	☐☐ Problem Sensitivity	☐☐ Problem Solver	☐☐ Quality Control Analysis
☐☐ Rate Control	☐☐ Reaction Time	☐☐ Reasoning Ability	☐☐ Resourceful
☐☐ Responsible	☐☐ Self Control	☐☐ Self-Management	☐☐ Service Orientation
☐☐ Teamworker			

INSTRUCTIONS FOR ADDITIONAL PERSONAL ATTRIBUTES

Below are comprehensive lists of attributes people in general may have. Not all attributes are applicable to all jobseekers or positions. Even though attributes are categorized by executives and managers, professionals, and social and general attributes, review each list as a number of attributes cross over into other categories and may be applicable to your targeted position. Again, place one **"X"** before those attributes you feel come closest to who you are and two **"Xs"** for those assets that are most important in your position.

Personal Attributes for Managers

☐☐ Action-Driven Leadership	☐☐ Approachable / Nonthreatening	☐☐ Authoritative
☐☐ Brainstormer	☐☐ Budget Conscious	☐☐ Career Developer
☐☐ Change Agent / Manager	☐☐ Collaborative	☐☐ Command Presence
☐☐ Commitment to Quality & Safety	☐☐ Commitment to Team Success	☐☐ Concept Formulator
☐☐ Conceptualizer	☐☐ Conflict Manager	☐☐ Continuous Improvement Skills
☐☐ Critical Thinker	☐☐ Cultivator	☐☐ Cultivator
☐☐ Customer Intimacy	☐☐ Decisive	☐☐ Deductive Reasoning

- ☐☐ Delegator
- ☐☐ Direction Provider
- ☐☐ Drive for Value-Added Results
- ☐☐ Exercise Good Judgment
- ☐☐ Handling People with Diplomacy
- ☐☐ Influential
- ☐☐ Inspirational
- ☐☐ Long-Term Success Minded
- ☐☐ Morale Builder
- ☐☐ Organizational Developer
- ☐☐ Overcoming Adversity
- ☐☐ People Manager
- ☐☐ Proactive Problem-Solver
- ☐☐ Project Leadership
- ☐☐ Regrouping Skills
- ☐☐ Responsive
- ☐☐ Solutions Developer
- ☐☐ Strategic Agility & Thinking
- ☐☐ Talent Leader
- ☐☐ Thirst for Innovation
- ☐☐ Visionary Mindset

- ☐☐ Developing Loyalty in Staff
- ☐☐ Director of High Producing Teams
- ☐☐ Effective Communicator
- ☐☐ Exercise Insightful Judgment
- ☐☐ Idea Incubator
- ☐☐ Initiator
- ☐☐ Leadership Developer
- ☐☐ Mediator
- ☐☐ Motivator / Motivational
- ☐☐ Outcome Focused
- ☐☐ Overcoming Boundaries
- ☐☐ Planner & Conceptualizer
- ☐☐ Profitability-Conscious
- ☐☐ Rapport Builder
- ☐☐ Relationship Builder
- ☐☐ Risk Taker
- ☐☐ Sound Decision-Maker
- ☐☐ Tackling Challenges & Obstacles
- ☐☐ Team Approach to Solving Problems
- ☐☐ Top Performer
- ☐☐ Other: _____

- ☐☐ Directing High Producing Teams
- ☐☐ Diversity Management
- ☐☐ Effective Presenter
- ☐☐ Forward-Thinker
- ☐☐ Improvement-oriented
- ☐☐ Innovative
- ☐☐ Leadership Skills
- ☐☐ Mentor
- ☐☐ Negotiator / Mediator
- ☐☐ Outside-the-Box Thinker
- ☐☐ People Development Skills
- ☐☐ Presenter
- ☐☐ Profitability-Conscious
- ☐☐ Recruiting
- ☐☐ Resourceful
- ☐☐ Role Model
- ☐☐ Straight Forward
- ☐☐ Tactical Action Planner
- ☐☐ Team Builder & Leader
- ☐☐ Transformational

Personal Attributes for Professionals

- ☐☐ Ability to Handle Pressure
- ☐☐ Accepting of Responsibility
- ☐☐ Aesthetic Sensibility
- ☐☐ Attentive to Detail
- ☐☐ Big Picture Thinker
- ☐☐ Changeable
- ☐☐ Commitment to Excellence
- ☐☐ Communicator
- ☐☐ Conflict Handler
- ☐☐ Conviction, person of
- ☐☐ Cost Conscious
- ☐☐ Deal well with Ambiguity
- ☐☐ Diplomatic / Tactful
- ☐☐ Employee Retainer
- ☐☐ Exhibits Conviction
- ☐☐ Expert
- ☐☐ Follow-up Oriented
- ☐☐ Hypothesizer
- ☐☐ Integrity
- ☐☐ Learning-oriented
- ☐☐ Mathematical Reasoning
- ☐☐ Open Thinker
- ☐☐ People-oriented
- ☐☐ Political
- ☐☐ Priority Setter
- ☐☐ Progressive
- ☐☐ Quality-oriented
- ☐☐ Sales-oriented
- ☐☐ Service Oriented
- ☐☐ Strong Work Ethic
- ☐☐ Team Player
- ☐☐ Time Manager
- ☐☐ Troubleshooter
- ☐☐ Visualizer

- ☐☐ Academic-oriented
- ☐☐ Accurate
- ☐☐ Affiliated
- ☐☐ Autocratic as needed
- ☐☐ Broad Thinker
- ☐☐ Child-focused
- ☐☐ Commitment to Quality
- ☐☐ Community-oriented
- ☐☐ Conjecturing
- ☐☐ Coordinator
- ☐☐ Criteria Evaluator
- ☐☐ Deductive
- ☐☐ Educated / Degreed
- ☐☐ Entrepreneurial
- ☐☐ Expansive
- ☐☐ Facilitator
- ☐☐ Fundraiser
- ☐☐ Inclusive
- ☐☐ Interpersonal Skills
- ☐☐ Left- & Right-brained Thinker
- ☐☐ Multicultural
- ☐☐ Open to Change
- ☐☐ Perceptive / Perceptual
- ☐☐ Powerful
- ☐☐ Proactive
- ☐☐ Project-Oriented
- ☐☐ Quantitative
- ☐☐ Scientific-minded
- ☐☐ Simplistic in Complex Ideas
- ☐☐ Synergetic
- ☐☐ Technically Competent
- ☐☐ Time-conscious
- ☐☐ Urgency-oriented
- ☐☐ Willing to Try New Things

- ☐☐ Accepting of Criticism
- ☐☐ Active Listener
- ☐☐ Altruistic
- ☐☐ Awareness
- ☐☐ Bureaucratic
- ☐☐ Client Focused
- ☐☐ Commitment to Safety
- ☐☐ Computer Literate
- ☐☐ Connected
- ☐☐ Coping Ability
- ☐☐ Customer-focused
- ☐☐ Detail-oriented
- ☐☐ Educational Leader
- ☐☐ Error Conscious
- ☐☐ Expeditor
- ☐☐ Fact Finder
- ☐☐ Goal-oriented
- ☐☐ Independent Judgment
- ☐☐ Interpreter
- ☐☐ Logical Thinker
- ☐☐ Negotiator
- ☐☐ Originator
- ☐☐ Persistent / Sustaining
- ☐☐ Predictor
- ☐☐ Problem Recognizer
- ☐☐ Psychological Well-being
- ☐☐ Researcher
- ☐☐ Sense of Proportion
- ☐☐ Social Networker
- ☐☐ Tackle Obstacles
- ☐☐ Technologically Literate
- ☐☐ Tolerance for Uncertainty
- ☐☐ Value Analyzer
- ☐☐ Work-oriented

- ☐☐ Accepting of Others
- ☐☐ Adaptable to Change
- ☐☐ Analytical
- ☐☐ Bias Detector
- ☐☐ Challenger
- ☐☐ Client Service-Oriented
- ☐☐ Common Sense Thinker
- ☐☐ Conciliator
- ☐☐ Connector
- ☐☐ Correlation Reasoning
- ☐☐ Deadline-conscious
- ☐☐ Differentiator
- ☐☐ Efficiency-oriented
- ☐☐ Evaluator
- ☐☐ Experimentally-Inclined
- ☐☐ Flexible / Adaptable
- ☐☐ Goodwill Oriented
- ☐☐ Inductive Reasoning
- ☐☐ Knowledgeable
- ☐☐ Mastermind
- ☐☐ Networker
- ☐☐ Outcome Focused
- ☐☐ Personal Presentation
- ☐☐ Presenter
- ☐☐ Problem-solver
- ☐☐ Qualitative
- ☐☐ Results Driven
- ☐☐ Sense of Urgency
- ☐☐ Statistical Thinker
- ☐☐ Task-oriented
- ☐☐ Tech-savvy
- ☐☐ Tolerance of Ambiguity
- ☐☐ Value-oriented
- ☐☐ Other: _____

Social & General Attributes

The following attributes generally answer the question, *"What kind of a person are you?"* Think about how you view yourself as well as how others view you. Different attributes are applicable to different positions. For example, being aggressive, diligent, determined, and methodical would be applicable for an Internal Revenue Services Manager, but definitely not for a Social Worker who would need to be caring, compassionate, empathetic, inspiring, and concerned for others.

Accommodating	Accomplished	Accountable	Adventurous
Advocate	Aggressive	Alert	Ambitious
Animated	Approachable	Articulate	Artistic
Aspiring	Assertive	Attentive	Authoritative
Autonomous	Balanced	Bold	Bright
Calm / Level-headed	Candid	Careful / Cautious	Caring
Challenge Seeker	Charismatic	Cheerful	Clear Thinker
Coachable	Collaborative	Colorful	Committed
Compassionate	Competent	Competitive	Composed
Comprehensive	Conceptual	Concerned for Others	Concise
Confident	Congenial	Conscientious	Conservative
Considerate / Thoughtful	Consistent	Constructive	Contemporary
Convincing	Cooperative	Courageous	Courteous
Creative	Credible	Critical Thinker	Curious
Decisive	Dedicated	Delegator	Democratic
Dependable	Determined	Devoted	Diligent
Discerning	Disciplined	Discoverer	Discreet
Dramatic	Driven	Dynamic	Earnest
Easygoing	Eclectic	Efficient	Elaborative
Eloquent	Emotionally Stable	Empathetic	Empowered
Empowering	Encouraging	Engaging	Enterprising
Enthusiastic	Ethical	Exciting	Expressive
Extroverted	Exuberant	Fair / Impartial	Faithful
Fast Learner	Focused	Foresighted	Forgiving
Friendly	Frugal	Generous	Gentle
Genuine	Giving	Good Judgment	Good Listener
Grateful	Gregarious	Harmonious	Healthy Perspective
Helpful	Honest / Trustworthy	Humble	Humorous
Imaginative	Independent	Industrious	Influential
Initiator	Inquisitive	Insightful	Intellectual
Interactive	Interested	Interesting	Introspective
Intuitive	Inventive	Judgment, Good	Judicious
Kind	Life-long Student	Likable	Literate
Loyal	Mature	Methodical	Meticulous
Mindful	Modest	Moral Minded	Motivated
Multitasker	Nondiscriminatory	Nonjudgmental	Objective
Observant	Open	Open-minded	Optimistic
Organized	Original	Outgoing	Participative
Particular	Passionate	Patient	Perfectionist
Perseverant	Personable	Persuasive	Philosophical
Pioneer	Planner	Poised	Positive
Practical	Pragmatic	Precise	Prestigious
Productive	Professional	Prolific	Promise Keeper
Promotable	Punctual / Prompt	Quick Learner	Quick-Witted
Rational	Realistic	Reasonable	Refined
Reflective Thinker	Relate well with others	Reliable	Resilient
Resourceful	Respected by Others	Respectful	Responsible
Responsive	Sassy	Savvy	Self-assessor
Self-assured	Self-confident	Self-controlled	Self-correcting
Self-directed	Self-disciplined	Self-esteem	Selfless
Self-manager	Self-motivated	Self-reliant	Self-sacrificing

☐☐ Self-starter
☐☐ Sincere
☐☐ Spiritual Values
☐☐ Strong Willed
☐☐ Sympathetic
☐☐ Tenacious
☐☐ Traditional
☐☐ Truthful / Truth Teller
☐☐ Unique
☐☐ Well-rounded
☐☐ Worldly

☐☐ Sense of Humor
☐☐ Sociable
☐☐ Stamina
☐☐ Success-Driven
☐☐ Systematic
☐☐ Thorough
☐☐ Traveler
☐☐ Unconventional
☐☐ Unpretentious
☐☐ Willing to Learn
☐☐ Zen-like

☐☐ Sensible
☐☐ Sophisticated
☐☐ Story Teller
☐☐ Successful
☐☐ Tactful
☐☐ Thoughtful
☐☐ Trusted by others
☐☐ Understanding
☐☐ Values, Person of
☐☐ Willpower
☐☐ Other: _____

☐☐ Sensitive
☐☐ Spirited
☐☐ Striving
☐☐ Supportive
☐☐ Talented
☐☐ Tolerant
☐☐ Trusting
☐☐ Unintimidating
☐☐ Versatile
☐☐ Wise

LIST YOUR TOP 10-15 PERSONAL ATTRIBUTES

INSTRUCTIONS

Select from above and list *in order of importance* your **top 10 to 15 assets / features** you possess that help you in your profession. Those would be your unique qualities, characteristics, attributes, capabilities, or skills that can be valuable to an employer and/or its clients. (Check these against the positions you Googled in **Step 1: Start Your Resume** to see which attributes your targeted employers seek.)

These attributes will be used in **Step 4: Develop Your Personal Brand & Professional Summary.**

YOUR TOP 10-15 ASSETS / FEATURES

ASSET #1: _____

ASSET #2: _____

ASSET #3: _____

ASSET #4: _____

ASSET #5: _____

ASSET #6: _____

ASSET #7: _____

ASSET #8: _____

ASSET #9: _____

ASSET #10: _____

ASSET #11: _____

ASSET #12: _____

ASSET #13: _____

ASSET #14: _____

ASSET #15: _____

STEP 4
DEVELOP YOUR PERSONAL BRAND
& PROFESSIONAL SUMMARY

CONTENTS OF STEP 4

- [ ] Branding Forever Changes You!
  - Once You Identify and Define Your Brand, It Becomes a Catharsis!
  - 10 Reasons Why Personal Branding is Essential
  - Something Magical Happens when You Identify Your Brand!

- [ ] The 5 Critical Components of Successful Branding
  - Introduction
  - Definitions and Examples

- [ ] Complete the Personal Brand Worksheet

- [ ] Develop Your Personal Brand Biography: *To Use as Your Sell Sheet for Networking & Interviews*
  - Introduction
  - Biography Foundation #1 (with Sample)
  - Biography Foundation #2 (with Sample)
  - Biography Foundation #3 (with Samples)
  - Biography Foundation #4 (with Sample)
  - Additional Biography Paragraphs

- [ ] Create Your LinkedIn Profile: *For Use in Your Social Media*
  - Introduction
  - LinkedIn Profile Foundation #1 (with Sample)
  - LinkedIn Profile Foundation #2 (with Sample)
  - LinkedIn Profile Foundation #4 (with Sample)
  - LinkedIn Profile Foundation #3 (with Sample)

- [ ] Develop Your Elevator Pitch: *For Use in all of Your Networking & Interviews*
  - Introduction
  - Personal Brand "Before and After" Example
  - Start Developing Your Elevator Pitch
  - Elevator Pitch Foundation #1 (with Samples)
  - Elevator Pitch Foundation #2 (with Samples)
  - Elevator Pitch Foundation #3 (with Sample)
  - Elevator Pitch Foundation #4 (with Sample)
  - Create Your Unique Elevator Pitch

- [ ] Write Your Slogan / Tag Line: *For Use in Your Resume & Other Career Marketing Materials*
  - Introduction
  - Sample Slogans
  - Write Your Slogan

- [ ] Create Your Professional Summary: *For Your Resume*
  - Introduction
  - Professional Summary Foundation #1 (with Samples)
  - Professional Summary Foundation #2 (with Samples)
  - Professional Summary Foundation #3 (with Samples)
  - Professional Summary Foundation #4 (with Samples)
  - Professional Summary Foundation #5 (with Samples)
  - Additional Professional Summary Sentences

- [ ] Continue to Evolve, Build, and Enhance Your Brand
  - Manage Your Brand
  - Pick Your Brand Colors

BRANDING FOREVER CHANGES YOU

ONCE YOU IDENTIFY AND DEFINE YOUR BRAND, IT BECOMES A CATHARSIS!

Your **Personal Brand** plays a strategic role in managing your career much the same way as a brand does for a business. Knowing what your unique brand is and how it helps you in your profession is critical to your career success. The good news is that everyone already has a Personal Brand whether they are aware of it or not. The secret is to discover what it is and use it to your advantage. This chapter will show you how to identify and define your own unique brand.

Personal Branding is an essential career marketing tool that creates a credible identity so hiring managers who view your brand know your value proposition and are compelled to seek you out over your competition. A well-defined brand will capture the interest of hiring managers, set you apart from other candidates, and help position you in the top percentage in your area of expertise. The five critical components of successful branding include your **Assets / Features, Benefits, Competitive Edge, Value Proposition,** and **Return on Investment** and are explained in this section.

INSTRUCTIONS

The information you compile in the **Personal Branding Worksheet** that follows will help you develop your **Personal Brand Message** in four formats: **(1) Personal Brand Biography, (2) LinkedIn Profile, (3) Elevator Pitch,** and **(4) Slogan** so you can incorporate it into all of your career marketing materials and use it in your networking and interviews. Use the supplied foundations and samples as a guide to spur the development of your brand.

You will then **Create Your Professional Summary** for the top portion of your resume. That section also contains foundations where you can input your unique information along with sample completed summaries for various professions. Finally, at the end of this chapter, you will find a guide to help you **Establish and Evolve Your Brand** going forward.

10 REASONS WHY PERSONAL BRANDING IS ESSENTIAL

Personal branding is essential to your personal growth and career success. Here are ten reasons why effective Personal Branding is important and why you should be sure to develop your unique brand:

1. *Personal Branding* helps position you in the Top 2 Percent of candidates in your field of expertise!
2. *Personal Branding* empowers you with confidence and selling power to sell yourself because you will feel the full value of your worth.
3. *Personal Branding* invites readers in to want to read your career marketing materials and learn more about you.
4. *Personal Branding* allows you to significantly stand out from the competition and receive many more interview calls.
5. *Personal Branding* compels prospective employers to seek you out and call you ahead of other applicants.
6. *Personal Branding* helps you network successfully.
7. *Personal Branding* establishes you as an expert in your niche and helps you build a solid reputation.
8. *Personal Branding* takes less time to fulfill your goals.
9. *Personal Branding* provides for higher earnings potential.
10. *Personal Branding* allows you to become successful more quickly and earn much more!

SOMETHING MAGICAL HAPPENS WHEN YOU DISCOVER AND DEFINE YOUR BRAND!

Something magical truly does happen when you discover and define your brand. For those who have, they call it a *"catharsis,"* an *"epiphany,"* and a *"revelation."* It provides you with self-empowerment, confidence, and selling power to go after and achieve your goals because you know the value of your full worth and what you bring to the table. Hiring managers will seek you out, and it provides high earnings potential.

Identifying and defining your unique brand puts you on the road to unlimited success!

*Stand out from your competition. Discover and define **your** unique brand.*

THE 5 CRITICAL COMPONENTS OF SUCCESSFUL BRANDING

INTRODUCTION

The five critical components of successful business and personal branding that are essential for any brand to be effective include your: **(1) Assets / Features, (2) Benefits, (3) Competitive Edge, (4) Value Proposition,** and **(5) Return on Investment** along with your matching achievements. Keep in mind that you are the product / brand you are selling. All successful brands use this strategy.

Following are definitions and examples of each:

DEFINITIONS AND EXAMPLES

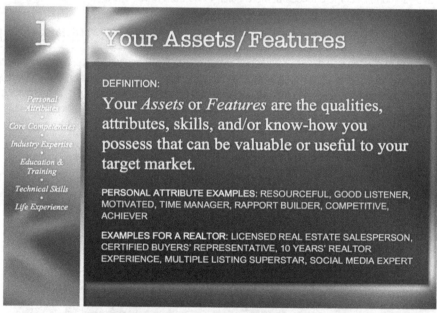

1 Your Assets/Features

Personal Attributes
•
Core Competencies
•
Industry Expertise
•
Education & Training
•
Technical Skills
•
Life Experience

DEFINITION:

Your *Assets* or *Features* are the qualities, attributes, skills, and/or know-how you possess that can be valuable or useful to your target market.

PERSONAL ATTRIBUTE EXAMPLES: RESOURCEFUL, GOOD LISTENER, MOTIVATED, TIME MANAGER, RAPPORT BUILDER, COMPETITIVE, ACHIEVER

EXAMPLES FOR A REALTOR: LICENSED REAL ESTATE SALESPERSON, CERTIFIED BUYERS' REPRESENTATIVE, 10 YEARS' REALTOR EXPERIENCE, MULTIPLE LISTING SUPERSTAR, SOCIAL MEDIA EXPERT

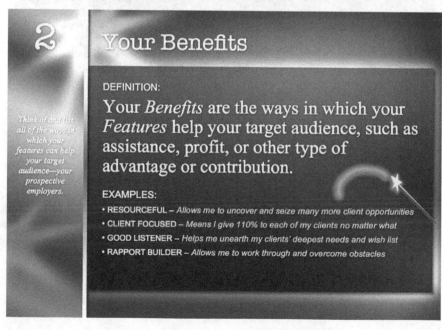

2 Your Benefits

Think of and list all of the ways in which your features can help your target audience—your prospective employers.

DEFINITION:

Your *Benefits* are the ways in which your *Features* help your target audience, such as assistance, profit, or other type of advantage or contribution.

EXAMPLES:

• RESOURCEFUL – *Allows me to uncover and seize many more client opportunities*
• CLIENT FOCUSED – *Means I give 110% to each of my clients no matter what*
• GOOD LISTENER – *Helps me unearth my clients' deepest needs and wish list*
• RAPPORT BUILDER – *Allows me to work through and overcome obstacles*

3 Your Competitive Edge

Everyone has a Personal Brand whether they are aware of it or not. It is who you are, your own unique, authentic self.

It is a matter of discovering those unique qualities you have that set you apart from others.

DEFINITION:

Your *Competitive Edge* is a clear advantage you have over others by way of certain unique strengths or aspects of *you* that make you stand out in your industry. It is your individual *marketing mix* of *Assets and Benefits* that others may not possess.

EXAMPLES:

RESOURCEFUL – *Able to unearth hidden buying or selling opportunities. As a highly connected social media expert, networking helps me find houses for sale and buyers ready to purchase before they are available to others.*

CLIENT FOCUSED – *I don't wait for opportunities to pop up for my clients; I work hard at connecting buyers with sellers 60+ hours a week.*

4 Your Value Proposition

Maintain a complete and up-to-date list of all of your accomplishments in the field.

Select the ones that match your Value Proposition.

DEFINITION:

Your *Value Proposition* is the total worth of all of the *Benefits* you can offer your audience by way of *promised deliverables* backed by *matching achievements*.

EXAMPLE BENEFIT & VALUE PROPOSITION:

RESOURCEFUL – *Other agents are not as able to unearth hidden buying or selling opportunities. As a highly connected social media expert, networking helps me find houses for sale and buyers ready to purchase sometimes before they are even on the open market.*

MATCHING ACHIEVEMENT – *While searching for a home for a couple who enjoyed entertaining, their wish list included buying a house with a resort-like backyard. Through my connections, I seized an opportunity for my buyer that included a large deck, cabana, built-in pool, hot tub, pond, and bridge at an unheard-of price. They were thrilled!*

5 Your Return on Investment

The higher your ROI, the more apt you are to obtain more clients and earn more and your clients to receive more interviews and job offers at their highest salary potential.

DEFINITION:

Your ROI is the measurement of your *contributions (expected future value)* to your target audience. You can get this number by dividing the amount of money or time you have saved or earned *(or similar measurement)* for past clients/employers by the cost of hiring you.

EXAMPLE ROI:

Houses on the market for $375,000 I've negotiated down to $325,000, saving my clients $50,000 and providing them with a 1,667% ROI. (Based on a $3,000 commission rate.)

$50,000 ÷ $3,000 = 1666.6%

COMPLETE THE PERSONAL BRAND WORKSHEET

1. DESCRIBE YOUR CAREER GOALS AND DREAM JOB.

What are your long-term career goals?

What position title(s) are you seeking now?

In what industry do you prefer to work?

Are there any specific (types of) firms where you would like to work?

What type of work do you prefer to handle?

What activities would you prefer not to do?

2. RESEARCH JOB DESCRIPTIONS IN YOUR PROFESSION.

Conduct an Internet search of job descriptions for your most sought-after position(s). *[Google "Job Descriptions for (Position Title)."]* List the job functions and requirements from the top three job postings that interest you in order of your preference. **"X"** each listed function in which you have the experience and qualifications. In compiling your resume later, be sure you include those functions under the position(s) where you actually performed them and include how well you did.

JOB DESCRIPTION #1 – Position Title: _____

JOB FUNCTIONS:

☐
☐
☐
☐
☐
☐
☐
☐
☐
☐

JOB DESCRIPTION #2 – Position Title: _____

JOB FUNCTIONS:

☐
☐
☐
☐
☐
☐
☐
☐
☐
☐

JOB DESCRIPTION #3 – Position Title: _____

JOB FUNCTIONS:

	☐
	☐
	☐
	☐
	☐
	☐
	☐
	☐
	☐
	☐

3. LIST YOUR PRIMARY ASSETS / FEATURES.

From the attributes you selected in **Step 3: Check Off Your Personal Attributes**, list below your top 10 assets that are of most importance to your targeted profession.

EXAMPLES: *a good listener, resourceful, strategic, innovative, organized, customer service oriented, and so on.*

ASSET #1:	ASSET #6:
ASSET #2:	ASSET #7:
ASSET #3:	ASSET #8:
ASSET #4:	ASSET #9:
ASSET #5:	ASSET #10:

4. DETERMINE YOUR BENEFITS.

Describe the benefits of your top 10 assets. In what ways do each of them help you to conduct your work, solve problems on the job, or otherwise benefit a company or its clients?

EXAMPLES: *Being a **good listener** helps me to unearth my clients' deepest needs and sell to match those needs.*
*Being **resourceful** allows me to uncover and seize many more client opportunities that my peers may not be aware of.*

BENEFIT OF ASSET #1:

BENEFIT OF ASSET #2:

BENEFIT OF ASSET #3:

BENEFIT OF ASSET #4:

BENEFIT OF ASSET #5:

BENEFIT OF ASSET #6:

BENEFIT OF ASSET #7:

BENEFIT OF ASSET #8:

BENEFIT OF ASSET #9:

BENEFIT OF ASSET #10:

5. FIGURE OUT YOUR VALUE PROPOSITION.

Explain the deliverables a prospective employer can expect to obtain from hiring you by indicating below the results your top benefits obtain. For each benefit listed in No. 4 above, ask yourself, *"How does that help?"* Keep asking that question and documenting your answers until there are no more answers left for each. This becomes your value proposition.

EXAMPLE *for a **good listener**: After unearthing my clients' deepest needs, I apply in-depth product knowledge coupled with my industry experience to provide matching solutions to their challenges.* ***How does that help?*** *They see value in the product as it solves their problems and meets their needs.* ***How does that help?*** *Prospects are more apt to purchase.* ***How does that help?*** *It increases sales and referrals for my employer.*

VALUE OF BENEFIT #1:

VALUE OF BENEFIT #2:

VALUE OF BENEFIT #3:

VALUE OF BENEFIT #4:

VALUE OF BENEFIT #5:

VALUE OF BENEFIT #6:

VALUE OF BENEFIT #7:

VALUE OF BENEFIT #8:

VALUE OF BENEFIT #9:

VALUE OF BENEFIT #10:

6. INCLUDE YOUR MATCHING ACHIEVEMENTS.

What have you accomplished in your career that proves your value? Check the Achievements you included under your employers in ***Step 1: Start Your Resume***. If these match your value, skip to the next section. Otherwise...

For each achievement, document what your original CHALLENGE was, the problem-solving ACTIONS you took to meet the challenge, and the end RESULTS and BENEFITS your efforts derived. Use numbers (amounts, dollars, percentages, and so on) wherever possible. Then put that information into a sentence that starts with your achievement to create your resume bullets.

EXAMPLE *for a **Good Listener**:*
Your Challenge: *To sell customized IT solutions to Fortune 500 firms.*

Your Actions: *Met with, assessed, and determined a Fortune 100 prospect's greatest needs by listening carefully to their goals and challenges, brainstorming all possible scenarios, providing options, and customizing solutions that solved their problems.*

Your Results / Benefits: *Saved the client $250,000 annually while bringing in $.5 million in sales for my employer. Also increased my employer's competitive edge in the marketplace by adding a high-profile firm to their client market list.*

Your Resume Bullet: *Saved a Fortune 100 client $250,000 while bringing in $.5 million in sales for employer and increasing the firm's competitive edge in the marketplace by assessing the client's greatest needs, listening carefully to their goals and challenges, providing options, and selling customized IT solutions that met their goals.*

ACHIEVEMENT THAT PROVES VALUE #1:

Your Challenge:

Your Actions:

Your Results / Benefits:

Your Resume Bullet:

ACHIEVEMENT THAT PROVES VALUE #2:

Your Challenge:

Your Actions:

Your Results / Benefits:

Your Resume Bullet:

ACHIEVEMENT THAT PROVES VALUE #3:

Your Challenge:

Your Actions:

Your Results / Benefits:

Your Resume Bullet:

ACHIEVEMENT THAT PROVES VALUE #4:

Your Challenge:

Your Actions:

Your Results / Benefits:

Your Resume Bullet:

ACHIEVEMENT THAT PROVES VALUE #5:

Your Challenge:

Your Actions:

Your Results / Benefits:

Your Resume Bullet:

OTHER ACHIEVEMENTS THAT PROVIDED VALUE:

7. IDENTIFY YOUR COMPETITIVE EDGE.

What unique qualities do you possess that differentiates you from others in your field and what advantage does this provide a prospective employer? Consider and list all areas you excel over your counterparts.

FOR EXAMPLE: What do you do better, faster, bigger, or more strategically, creatively, productively, or other in your profession than others in your profession? Think about what your superiors have praised you for, what is documented in your performance evaluations, and/or what others have stated that sets you apart from your peers.

DIFFERENTIATOR #1:

DIFFERENTIATOR #2:

DIFFERENTIATOR #3:

DIFFERENTIATOR #4:

DIFFERENTIATOR #5:

8. DETERMINE YOUR RETURN ON INVESTMENT (ROI).

Employers have a "what's in it for me" approach. Explain why a hiring manager should hire you. What measurement of your contributions *(expected future value)* do you bring to the table? What promise can you make based on what you have accomplished in the past? Think about how your contributions equate to being able to help an employer, such as by increasing sales, cutting costs, streamlining operations, elevating productivity, increasing customer service levels, and the like. Use dollars, numbers, and percentages.

EXAMPLE for a Real Estate Salesperson: Say that due to your excellent negotiation and interpersonal skills, you show more houses to more buyers and/or bring in more leads to more sellers, on average you (1) save buyers $35,000-$50,000 on houses they purchase, (2) are able to obtain a sellers' asking price 85% of the time, (3) sell houses 6 to 9 months sooner in a market where the norm is 1.5 years, (4) have a 65% faster turnaround time. These numbers become your ROI (expected future value) and will attract your target audience.

9. INCLUDE YOUR TESTIMONIALS.

Testimonials are optional but extremely helpful in catching the attention of hiring managers as they add credence to your resume content and showcase qualities others have found in you and your work. Include below any positive comments you have received from others which speaks to how well you perform(ed) your job. Try to include a variety of endorsements that address the brand components you included above. *(If you do not have these now, don't hesitate to ask others to provide them.)*

EXAMPLE: Include comments obtained from letters of recommendation, LinkedIn endorsements, customer thank you letters, performance evaluations, and other means received from superiors, customers, vendors, peers, and others.

TESTIMONIAL #1:

TESTIMONIAL #2:

_____

_____

_____

_____

_____

_____

TESTIMONIAL #3:

_____

_____

_____

_____

_____

_____

10. NEXT, YOU WILL DEVELOP YOUR PERSONAL BRAND MESSAGE IN 5 FORMATS.

In the next section, you will be applying the information you compiled above to create your *Personal Brand Message* in five formats for use in your resume, career marketing materials, networking, social media, and interviews. Each serves its own purpose, as follows:

- **Personal Brand Biography** for use as your Sell Sheet in your Networking and as a leave-behind for your Interviews
- **LinkedIn Profile** for your LinkedIn account and other Social Media
- **Elevator Pitch** for use in all of your Networking and Interviews (can also be included in your Cover Letter)
- **Slogan / Tag Line** for your Resume, Cover Letter, Business Cards, and other Career Marketing Materials
- **Professional Summary** for the top portion of your Resume

Foundations are included for each Brand Message format for you to fill in with your brand components and related information, along with sample completed messages in various professions.

When I develop Personal Brands for clients, I start off with their full Biography, then condense it for the LinkedIn Profile, further condense it for an Elevator Pitch, and lastly create the Slogan and Professional Summary. Using this method in the sequence in this chapter will help with that process.

DEVELOP YOUR PERSONAL BRAND BIOGRAPHY
To Use as Your Sell Sheet for Networking & Interviews

INTRODUCTION

Here is where you will create your *Personal Brand Biography (Sell Sheet)* to use in all of your networking and as an interview leave-behind. Your Sell Sheet will become an important part of your career marketing repertoire. Circulating it to all those with whom you network can help put your brand in the hands of influential professionals and ultimately hiring managers.

You can use the following foundations as a guide to develop your own unique Biography. Mix and match the paragraphs in the various foundations as they pertain to you. Then expand upon the content as it is applicable to your profession, expertise, knowledge, achievements, education, professional affiliations, publications, and/or other pertinent career information. Be sure to incorporate all of your brand elements you developed in this chapter: your features, benefits, competitive edge, value proposition, and return on investment. Tell your story in your biography.

BRING OVER YOUR PERSONAL BRAND COMPONENTS

Start out by opening a blank document and keying in all of your primary Features *(from #3 above)*, Benefits *(from #4)*, Value Proposition *(from #5)*, Competitive Edge *(from #7)*, and Return on Investment *(from #8)*. Having all of your relevant branding information in front of you will help you start the process of creating your *Personal Brand* in its various formats. You can use the Foundations that follow or you can create sentences on your own. Just be sure your brand message includes all five of your personal branding components.

BIOGRAPHY FOUNDATION #1

Biography of: _____ [Name]

_____ [your full name] **is a** _____ [title] **and the/a** [□ world's | □ nation's | □ region's | □ other: _____] [□ leading | □ multiaward-winning | □ highly knowledgeable | □ creative | □ strategic | □ responsive | □ other attributes: _____] _____ [your profession] [□ executive | □ professional | □ other: _____] **who has** _____, _____, **and** _____ [include your value proposition and matching achievements].

As a credentialed _____ [what title or field?] [□ expert | □ thought leader | □ other: _____], _____ [your first name] **is one of the top** _____ [your field of expertise]. **He/She is a** _____, _____, **and** _____ [noteworthy professional affiliation positions you hold] **and author of** _____, _____, **and** _____ [publication titles].

_____ [first name] **is the founder of** _____ [business name], **a** _____ [type of] **firm in** _____ [town], _____ [state] **where he/she** _____ [does what?] **for** _____ [what purpose?]. **He/She** [□ spearheads | □ develops | □ facilitates | □ performs | □ creates | □ conducts | □ other: _____] _____ [what?] **for** _____ [whom?]. _____ [first name] **has been** _____, _____, **and** _____ [doing what?] **by** _____ [how you do it well]. **His/Her services include** _____, _____, **and** _____ [services], **and he/she also provides** _____, _____, **and** _____ [other services].

His/Her _____ [type of] **work in the** _____ [which?] **field has been referred to as** "_____," "_____," **and** "_____" **by her** [□ superiors | □ peers | □ clients | □ others: _____] **and** _____ [who?] **refers to her** _____ [what work?] **as** "_____," **and** "_____" [testimonial excerpts].

_____ [name] [□ attended | □ obtained his/her (□ master's / □ bachelor's / □ associate's) degree(s) at] _____ [college] **and started his/her career in** _____ [which?] **field where he/she progressed to** _____ [title], **after which** _____ [name] _____ [did what type of work?] **prior to** [□ starting his/her business | □ other: _____].

Write a paragraph or two concerning your own unique value proposition and competitive edge: _____.

He/She is a member of _____, _____, **and** _____ [professional affiliations]. **His/Her talents encompass** _____, _____, **and** _____ [what areas?].

_____ [name] **Web Portfolio and resume are viewable at** _____.com).

SAMPLE FOR A CAREER MANAGEMENT LEADER

(The Author's biography at the beginning of the book is a sample of how this foundation can be applied.)

BIOGRAPHY FOUNDATION #2

_____ *[Name]* Biography
Your Slogan / Tagline

_____ *[your full name]* **balances** _____ *[type of]* **experience with** _____, _____, **and** _____ *[type of]* [□ knowledge | □ expertise | □ abilities | □ skills | □ other:_____] **to** [□ develop | □ execute | □ perform | □ other: _____] **successful** _____ *[type of]* [□ strategies | □ programs | □ solutions | □ projects | □ processes | □ other: _____] **that** _____, _____, **and** _____ *[do what?]*.

Coupled with _____' *[first name]* [□ Master's | □ Bachelor's | □ Associate's | □ other: _____] **Degree(s) in** _____ *[what?]*, **his/her** _____ *[type of]* **experience and** _____ *[which?]* **abilities allow him/her to** _____ *[do what?]* **that helps** _____ *[accomplish what?]* **for** _____ *[type of]* [□ firms | □ clients | □ customers | □ patrons | □ others: _____].

_____' *[first name]* _____ *[type of]* **areas of expertise include** _____, _____, **and** _____ *[what areas?]* **with additional proficiencies in** _____, _____, **and** _____ *[what areas?]*.

With a proven track record of [□ exceeding goals and expectations | □ increasing sales _____% *(percentage)* | □ catapulting profits $_____ *(amount)* | □ maximizing revenues $_____ *(amount)* | □ elevating productivity _____% *(percentage)* | □ expanding market share | □ increasing customer service levels | □ other: _____] **for his/her** [□ employers | □ clients], **notable achievements include** _____, _____, **and** _____ *[your top matching achievements]*.

As a [□ results-oriented | □ client-focused | □ solutions-oriented | □ revenue-focused | □ detail-oriented | □ other:_____] *[your primary attributes]* _____ *[type of]* **professional, he/she believes that** _____, _____, **and** _____ *[your profession-related beliefs or mission statement]*.

Write a paragraph or two concerning your own unique value proposition and competitive edge: _____.

_____ *[name]* **is proficient in** _____, _____, **and** _____ *[computer programs]*, **which allows him/her to** _____ *[do what?]*. **He/She has participated in** _____, _____, **and** _____ *[what other functions?]* **and brings** [□ experience | □ enthusiasm | □ drive | □ other: _____] **to all of his/her** [□ projects | □ functions | □ other: _____].

SAMPLE FOR A MARKETING SPECIALIST

The following up-and-coming Marketing Specialist with dual Bachelor's Degrees in Marketing and Business Administration had experience in sales, publishing, and graphic design, but not so much in marketing—yet. There was no question he was going to succeed in his career endeavors because he is smart, marketing savvy, technically inclined, a quick learner, and has in-depth Internet marketing knowledge.

The following sample also depicts how you can turn a "negative" situation into a "positive" asset. I developed his slogan into a "true statement" by coupling it with a silhouette of a business person on a balancing beam: ***"Balancing Marketing Experience with Sales, Graphic Design, and Publishing Expertise to Develop Successful Marketing Campaigns."*** The client received a number of job opportunities, landed his first noninternship position as a Marketing Specialist, and further progressed to a more challenging position at a larger firm where he handles more of the Internet Marketing analytics functions he enjoys.

His bio was designed into a Sell Sheet that was also used as his Web Portfolio home page.

Kenshin Friedman
BIOGRAPHY

KENSHIN FRIEDMAN balances marketing experience with sales, graphic design, and publishing expertise to develop successful online and print marketing campaign strategies and programs that generate leads, procure new target markets, and maximize return on investment for companies and clients alike.

Coupled with Kenshin's dual Bachelor's Degrees in Marketing and Business Administration, his nine years' successful marketing and sales experience and creative abilities allow him to develop innovative marketing programs that help establish brand recognition, product visibility, and consumer awareness for small to large businesses within highly competitive business markets.

Kenshin's Internet Marketing and online advertising areas of expertise include SEO, SEM, PPC management, and digital content management with additional proficiencies in brand management, social media management, multiplatform advertising, and the publishing market.

With a proven track record of exceeding goals and expectations for his employers and clients, notable achievements include developing effective marketing collateral, creating strategic PowerPoint virtualization presentations, and coordinating lead-generating events.

As a client-focused and solutions-oriented marketing professional, Kenshin believes that unearthing target audience needs, presenting product options that meet those needs, and delivering to exceed expectation is the key to success. And that networking, building strong client relationships and key account leadership solidifies long-term connections that maximize that success!

He is proficient in Adobe Photoshop, Illustrator, and InDesign; Microsoft PowerPoint and Excel; as well as SharePoint, which allows him to creatively conceptualize and design unique marketing collateral that meet client needs. He has participated in trend research, analysis, tracking, and forecasting in the launch of new services.

Kenshin brings experience, enthusiasm, and drive to all of his projects.

> *"I had the pleasure of collaborating with Kenshin through our company's interest in his internet knowledge. Through our growth, Kenshin gave us excellent feedback on markets to target, helping to grow each company's Internet presence, which helped us to focus on areas with the highest ROI for our market. His marketing knowledge was able to find us new avenues to target larger companies, which were monumental in growing our business, and track our marketing campaigns for success."*
>
> **JOHN GELBERG, Account Manager**
> **EFGH Internet Marketing**

> *Kenshin was one of our brightest young account managers at ABCD Print Solutions. He is a great self starter and is driven to succeed. I was impressed with Kenshin's intellect and his inquisitive nature as he learned about our business and sought to develop his territory. I believe Kenshin is mature beyond his years and handles himself very well in business and professional settings.*
>
> **MARGE JONES, Executive Vice President, CFO Treasurer, ABCD Print Solutions**

CONTACT KENSHIN AT:

Phone: (000) 000-0000
Email: KFriedman@xxxxx.com
Mail: 1234 Any Road
Any Town, State 00000

CONNECT WITH KENSHIN ON:

Balancing Marketing Experience with Sales, Graphic Design, and Publishing Expertise to Develop Successful Marketing Campaigns

Personal Brand Marketing by CareerCatapult.com

BIOGRAPHY FOUNDATION #3

_____ *[Name]*
Your Slogan / Tagline

As a(n) _____ **and** _____ *[your primary attributes]* _____ *[your title or profession],* _____ *[your full name]* _____ *[does what?].* **He/She works hard to** _____ *[achieve what?].*

With his/her expert knowledge of [☐ the market place | ☐ _____ *(type of)* products | ☐ competitive pricing | ☐ technology | ☐ other expertise: _____] **coupled with exceptional** [☐ relationship-building | ☐ negotiation | ☐ diversity management | ☐ people development | ☐ other: _____] *[your primary skills]* **skills,** _____ *[your first name]* **is able to** [☐ negotiate better prices | ☐ develop cost-effective solutions | ☐ successfully manage _____ *(type of)* projects | ☐ other: _____] **and as a result** _____ *[what you accomplish / the end result].*

_____ *[Name]* **is** _____ *[your competitive edge].* **Unlike most** _____ **s** *[your title],* **he/she** _____ *[does what?].*

As a _____, _____, **and** _____ *[your secondary attributes]* _____ *[title],* **he/she always** _____, _____, **and** _____ *[does what?].* _____ *[explanation of how you do this well].* _____ **and** _____ *[additional attributes],* _____ *[name]* **is** [☐ trusted | ☐ well-respected | ☐ well-liked | ☐ other: _____] **in the industry and** _____ *[does what?].*

Being [☐ positive | ☐ unbiased | ☐ optimistic | ☐ other: _____] **and** [☐ having a sense of humor | ☐ other: _____], **helps** _____, _____, **and** _____ *[with what?].*

_____ *[Name]* **constantly keeps abreast of current** [☐ market conditions | ☐ updated technology | ☐ other: _____] **that can affect** _____ *[what?]* **which helps him/her** _____ *[do what?].*

Write a paragraph or two concerning your own unique value proposition and competitive edge: _____.

_____ *[Name]* **is** [☐ accessible | ☐ approachable | ☐ reliable | ☐ accountable | ☐ other *(your secondary)* attributes: _____] **to/for** _____ *[what?].* **As a** [☐ friendly | ☐ genuine | ☐ impartial | ☐ other: _____] **person, he/she is** _____ *[attributes]* **and helps his/her** [☐ firm | ☐ clients | ☐ other: _____] **achieve their goals by way of** _____ *[doing what?].*

Take Your First Step: Contact _____ *[name]* **at 000-000-0000 or email him/her at** _____ **@** _____.

SAMPLE FOR A REALTOR

Following is an example of a branded bio that includes all five elements of personal branding. See if you don't agree that you would select *this* realtor over any others.

Jane Murphy

LICENSED REAL ESTATE SALESPERSON & CERTIFIED BUYERS' REPRESENTATIVE

House turnaround expert who accelerates results, gets the best prices for her clients in competitive real estate markets, ensures the process goes smoothly, and makes the overall experience enjoyable.

Most people think they should find a house they like and then go with whichever agent advertised that home. Truth is, most agents have access to the same homes for sale. The better method is to first interview and select the realtor who you feel will work hard for you at buying or selling your home, and then go forward with your search for a home or a buyer.

*Since 10% of all agents sell 80% of the houses on the market and 90% sell the remainder, as a **Top Real Estate Producer** who is often in the **Top 10** of the **No. 1** producing real estate firm on Long Island, Jane Murphy is more able to help you buy or sell your home than 90% of other agents.*

With 7 years in the field, she has built a solid reputation of honesty, fairness, and professionalism. With hundreds of homes for sale, her geographic area covers all of Suffolk County.

As both a Licensed Real Estate Salesperson and a Certified Buyers' Rep, Jane Murphy lists, markets, and sells more houses and finds more homes for buyers that match their needs than her average counterpart. She works hard to turn around your sale or purchase more quickly and smoothly in the shortest timeframe using all resources available to achieve your goals.

With her expert knowledge of the market place and competitive pricing coupled with exceptional negotiation skills, Jane is able to negotiate better prices for buyers and sellers and as a result has saved her clients *tens of thousands of dollars*, getting the process done quickly and with less issues and stress.

> **EXAMPLE:** *A recent buyer selected a home priced at $250,000. Jane put in an offer of $225,000 which was more appropriate for the market in that area, and the seller came back with an offer of $248,000. Though the back-and-forth negotiations didn't prove easy, she got the price down to $230,000 plus concessions saving her client $22,000, which represented a 1100% return on the buyer's investment of $2000.*

As a *fair, honest, and reputable* realtor, she always keeps you current, in the loop, and feeling safe by telling you exactly how it is. If a deal looks like it is falling apart and her clients get discouraged, she doesn't give up. Her *resiliency* keeps everything moving forward by trying out different approaches and solutions, *using fortitude, staying positive,* and *bouncing back*. Whether you are a seller or buyer, she helps you feel comfortable and stay positive even when obstacles occur.

> **EXAMPLE:** *When working with a bi-polar client, Jane helped appease her frustration when an issue with permits arose by refocusing her and working very closely with the attorney on her behalf. The house closed and the client was very thankful.*

Outcome-focused and *hardworking*, Jane is always there for her clients. Because she is *trusted, well-respected, and well-liked* in the industry, she "plays well" with other realtors who are more apt to do the things she needs them to do to help her clients, making the process go a lot *easier, quicker, and more smoothly*.

While other agents work primarily with sellers using a one-sided process, as a designated agent for both buyers and sellers, Janet's entire focus is on you. Being *positive and unbiased* with a *sense of humor*, she helps make the whole process *more pleasant, less stressful*, and the *fun and exciting experience* it should be.

> **EXAMPLE:** *When working with a divorced couple, she gained the confidence and trust of both parties, and neither felt she favored one over the other which resulted in a smooth process for both in the sale of their house.*

Jane is available to her clients on and off business hours and will return your calls the same day. And unlike most agents, she makes herself available during *every stage of the process* to look out for your best interests.

> **EXAMPLE:** *She doesn't just send the engineer out to appraise your home which is common practice, she is present to be sure the home is appraised correctly, understands problem areas that may require fixing, ensures that any required price adjustments are fair, and can generally save an additional 10% of the market value for her clients. Not many agents can or will do that.*

Having obtained *more training, certifications,* and *expertise* than most agents, Jane constantly keeps abreast of current market conditions that can affect her clients by taking real estate training classes and reading related books and articles on topics such as short sales, foreclosures, mortgages, and the like which helps her find more ways to help and benefit her clients.

With a high referral base from satisfied clients, Jane finds and sells single-family residential properties, condominiums, land, foreclosures, short sales, and apartment rentals.

She puts her real estate knowledge, resources, and connectivity to work for you which spans everything from client needs assessment, market value analysis, competitive pricing, and appraisals—to prequalifying buyers for mortgages and educating you on current real estate market conditions, certificates of title, real estate taxes, underwriters insurance, PITI, mortgage types, contract negotiations, and more.

She invites you to call her. You don't have to commit to anything up front as she doesn't sign on clients until she's walked you through a house or two and you first feel comfortable with her and the process. So there is no risk to you and you have everything to gain.

EXAMPLE: *When working with short sales (that is when the bank agrees to take less than what was originally paid for the house in lieu of the seller having to go into foreclosure), she works with attorneys who are very familiar with all the banks and highly skilled in getting approvals a lot quicker rather than having to wait 6 months to a year stalemating your entire house searching process.*

Today's market conditions represent extreme challenges for not only clients but for realtors as well. Many drop out of the field while others get disgruntled. But because Jane is an *optimistic* person who doesn't get discouraged, she will keep your process moving forward while communicating with you, the attorneys, appraisers, inspectors, engineers, mortgage brokers, and/or builders regularly to ensure everything is moving along smoothly.

Jane doesn't wait for opportunities to pop up for her clients; she works hard at connecting buyers with sellers and unearthing hidden buying or selling opportunities for them.

EXAMPLE: *She found an unlisted property for one of her clients within 2 months and sold their 2 homes within 6 months as opposed to the norm of 1 to 1.5 years in today's market.*

Jane is accessible, approachable, reliable, and accountable to each and every one of her clients. When times get rough, she will help empower, motivate, and inspire you to go forward and will put a smile on your face through her outgoing, entertaining, and playful nature. As a friendly, genuine, and impartial person, she is a good listener, and will try to help you achieve your goals in the very best way possible giving you the unbiased facts in a straightforward manner.

TAKE YOUR FIRST STEP: CONTACT JANE MURPHY at **000-000-000** or email her at **Xxxxxxx@Xxxxxxxxxx.com**.

BIOGRAPHY FOUNDATION #4

_____ *(Name)*

Your Slogan / Tagline

_____ *[Your full name]* **is a** _____, _____, **and** _____ *[your primary attributes]* [☐ leader | ☐ executive | ☐ manager | ☐ professional | ☐ other: _____] **who** _____ *[does what?].* **This includes** _____, _____, **and** _____ *[your primary core competencies / keywords].*

_____ *[Your first name]* **has** _____ *[#]* **years'** [☐ progressive | ☐ tenured | ☐ other: _____] **experience and** [☐ extensive | ☐ in-depth | ☐ proficient | ☐ working] **knowledge of** _____, _____, **and** _____ *[your secondary keywords].* **Expert in** _____, _____, **and** _____ *[your remaining keywords].* _____ *[name]* **is also proficient in/at** _____, _____, **and** _____ *[other functions].* **He/She is a(n)** _____, _____, **and** _____ *[other personal attributes].*

In his/her most current position as _____ *[title]* **at** _____ *[company],* **he/she was recruited to** _____ *[do what?].* **At the time of hire, the** [☐ firm | ☐ company | ☐ organization | ☐ institution | ☐ other: _____] **had/was** _____ *[original situation];* **it is now at** _____ *[current situation].* _____' *[Name]* **notable achievements include** _____, _____, **and** _____ *[your primary achievements that match your value proposition].*

At _____ *[previous employer],* _____ *[name]* _____ *[accomplished what?].* **There he/she served on the** _____ *[which?]* **Committee and** _____ *[accomplished what?].* _____ *[name]* [☐ developed | ☐ conducted | ☐ performed | ☐ other: _____] **the** [☐ Company's | ☐ Region's | ☐ Division's | ☐ Department's | ☐ other: _____] **first** _____ *[which?]* **Program for** _____ *[what purpose?]* **and** _____ *[what else?].*

Previously, _____ *[name]* **was** _____ *[title]* **at** _____ *[company],* **where he/she** [☐ developed | ☐ conducted | ☐ performed | ☐ other: _____] _____ *[what functions?].* **While serving on the** _____ *[which?]* **Committee, he/she created and implemented** _____ *[what?].* _____ *[Name]* **was selected as** _____ *[acting title]* **to perform** _____ *[what functions?].* **His/Her earlier career development involved** _____ *[what?]* **where he/she** _____ *[performed what?].*

Write a paragraph or two concerning your own unique value proposition and competitive edge: _____.

_____ *[Name]* **obtained his/her** _____ *[degree]* **Degree in** _____ *[major]* **from** _____ *[college or university].* **He/She is a member of** _____, _____, **and** _____ *[professional affiliations].*

_____ *[Name]* **can be reached at** _____ *[email]* _____ *[phone number]* [☐ **or visit his/her Web Portfolio at** _____ *(URL)].*

SAMPLE FOR A HIGHER EDUCATION LEADER

Marianne Jones **is a** strategic, innovative, **and** energetic higher-education leader **who** promotes continuous improvement to the quality of instruction at universities and colleges. **This includes** higher education specialist degree plan development, online program architecture, curriculum design, student assessment program creation, learning resource management, **and** student success coordination.

Marianne **has** 14 **years'** tenured **experience with** extensive **knowledge of** academic culture in multicultural instruction where she has served as Faculty Lead, Head of Academic Advising, and as subject matter expert to instructional staff, advisory committees, **and** students. **Expert in** on-site and online undergraduate and graduate program development, adult education, and Customer Relationship Management administration, Marianne **is also proficient at** time management, budget development, **and** planning. She is a resourceful, adaptable lifelong learner **and** team builder.

In her most current position as Mentor **at** ABC University, **she was recruited to** help create and facilitate the University's learning communities. **At the time of hire,** the University had 5000 students; the student body **is now at** 30,000+. Marianne consummated a 98% student graduation success rate by performing ongoing audits that align students' learning needs with assessments; achieved a high retention rate of the student body; helped increase the faculty team's Key Performance Indicators; significantly improved student learning outcomes and pass scores; and achieved "very satisfied" metrics and interdepartmental recognition.

At <u>DEF College, Marianne</u> **served on the** <u>Curriculum Design and Assessment</u> **Committee**. She <u>developed assessment measures and outcomes for each course taught that ensured alignment between performance metrics and learning outcomes. Marianne teaches Business, International Business, Consumer Behavior, and Marketing Research.</u>

Previously, <u>Marianne</u> **was** <u>Lead Faculty and/or Adjunct Faculty</u> **at** <u>GHI Institute, JKL School, and MNO Community College</u> **where she** <u>developed curriculum and taught Business, Finance, Management, and Marketing classes.</u> **While serving on the Committee** <u>for Accreditation,</u> **she created and implemented** <u>a Student Support Center.</u> **Her** **earlier career development involved** <u>store management</u> **where she** <u>managed the daily operations, customer service, human resources, budgeting, job scheduling,</u> **and** <u>training and development.</u>

<u>Marianne</u> **attained her** <u>MBA</u> **in** <u>General Management and Finance</u> **from** <u>PQR College,</u> **and her** <u>BA in Economics</u> **at** <u>STU University</u>. **She is a member of** <u>the Association of International Business.</u>

ADDITIONAL BIOGRAPHY PARAGRAPHS

_____ *[Your full name]* **is a** _____ *[title]* **who** [□ spearheads | □ champions | □ develops | □ establishes | □ performs | □ executes | □ other: _____] _____ *[type of]* [□ services | □ solutions | □ other: _____] **for his/her** [□ firm | □ clients | □ other: _____]. **He/She represents** [□ small | □ medium | □ large] [□ firms | □ businesses | □ individuals | □ other: _____] **in the** _____ , _____ , **and** _____ *[which?]* [□ industries | □ markets | □ professions | □ other: _____] **by providing** _____ *[type of]* **services including** _____ , _____ , **and** _____ *[services]*.

_____ *[First name]* **is a recognized expert in** _____ , _____ , **and** _____ *[primary areas of expertise]*. **With** _____ *[#]* **years of demonstrated experience in** _____ , _____ , **and** _____ *[additional areas of expertise]* **and proven success at** _____ , _____ , **and** _____ *[doing what well?]* **is a highly** [□ knowledgeable | □ responsive | □ creative | □ other: _____] _____ *[title]* **with** [□ vision | □ integrity | □ strategic insight | □ other attribute: _____].

_____ *[Name]* **is a** [□ innovative | □ strategic | □ energetic | □ other: _____] _____ *[title]* **who promotes continuous improvement in** _____ *[what?]*. **This includes** _____ , _____ , **and** _____ *[areas of expertise]*. **He/She is proficient in** _____ , _____ , **and** _____ *[programs or projects]* **to develop** _____ *[what?]* **that** [□ generates sales | □ procures new markets | □ maximizes profits | □ slashes costs | □ maximizes productivity | □ other benefit(s): _____]. _____ *[name]* **is expert in** _____ *[what areas?]* **from the ground up and is also proficient in** _____ , _____ , **and** _____ *[what areas?]*.

_____ *[Name]* **balances** _____ *[type of]* **experience with** _____ , _____ , **and** _____ *[type of]* [□ expertise | □ knowledge | □ other: _____] **to develop successful** _____ *[type of]* [□ programs | □ projects | □ products | □ solutions | □ other: _____] **that result in** _____ *[what benefits?]*. **His/Her** _____ , _____ , **and** _____ *[type of]* **abilities allow him/her to** _____ *[do what?]* **that help** _____ *[do what?]* **for** _____ *[whom or what?]*.

In his/her most current position as _____ *[title]* **at** _____ *[employer]*, **he/she was recruited to** _____ *[do what?]*. _____ *[Name]* **consummated a** _____ **%** *[percentage]* **success rate by** _____ *[doing what?]*. **Previously, he/she was** _____ *[title]* **at** _____ *[employer]* **where he/she** _____ *[did what?]*. **And at** _____ *[where?]*, **he/she was selected as** _____ *[function]* **where he/she** _____ *[accomplished what?]*. _____ **'s** *[Name]* **earlier career development involved** _____ , _____ , **and** _____ *[type of work]* **where he/she** _____ , _____ , **and** _____ *[did what?]*.

_____ *[Name]* **obtained his/her** _____ *[which?]* **Degree in** _____ *[major]* **from** _____ *[college or university]*, **and his/her** _____ *[which?]* **Degree in** _____ *[major]* **from** _____ *[college or university]*.

CREATE YOUR LINKED-IN PROFILE
For Use in Your Social Media

INTRODUCTION

 LinkedIn is hiring managers' social network of choice as most firms seek candidates to fill their open positions primarily through LinkedIn. All careerists and jobseekers should have a LinkedIn account. It can be written in the first person or third person. *(The LinkedIn Profile Samples below are written in the third person.)*

As in your Biography, your *LinkedIn Profile* should include your brand components. LinkedIn allows 2000 characters *(including spaces)* for your profile. The best way to create your LinkedIn profile is to start off with the *Personal Brand Biography* you just created and keep condensing down it until it is within the 2000-character limit. Or you can apply one of the Foundations below.

Here are four foundations you can use to create your profile. Samples follow each Foundation.

LINKED-IN PROFILE FOUNDATION #1

_____ *[Name]* **is the founder of** _____ *[Business Name],* **a** _____ *[type of]* **firm.** _____ *[Name]* _____ *[does what?]* **to meet the** _____ *[type of]* **needs of** _____ *[whom or what?].* **A(n)** _____ **and** _____ *[your attributes],* **he/she has** _____ *[accomplished what?].* _____ *[Name]* **strategically** _____ *[does what?]* **by** _____, _____, **and** _____ *[doing what well?].* **He/She** [□ performs | □ creates | □ develops | □ strategizes | □ other: _____] *[what?]* **by** _____ *[doing what?].* **His/Her** [□ industry-leading | □ expert | □ other: _____] _____ *[type of]* [□ expertise | □ knowledge | □ other: _____] **spans** _____, _____, _____, **and** _____ *[what areas?].*

SAMPLE FOR THE CAREER MANAGEMENT INDUSTRY LEADER *(See LinkedIn sample at end of this section.)*

Evelyn Salvador **is the founder of** Creative Image Builders, **a** Business and Personal Branding Strategy and Marketing **firm.** Evelyn fosters a comprehensive, innovative approach to meeting the business-building needs of companies and the career-development needs of the 21st century job seeker—both through successful branding. **A** visionary thought leader, **she has** championed the success of hundreds of businesses and thousands of job seekers since 1990.

Evelyn **strategically** markets businesses and individuals **by** identifying their benefits, defining their (business or personal) brand, creating their brand message, determining their value proposition, **and** capitalizing on their return on investment to their target audience (consumers and prospective employers, respectively) through innovative marketing communications.

She brands companies **by** creating successful websites, logos, brochures, direct mail pieces, and so on. **Her** industry-leading career development **expertise spans** resume writing, career coaching, job searching, web portfolio development, **and** positive online identity building.

LINKED-IN PROFILE FOUNDATION #2

_____ *[Name]* **balances** _____ *[type of]* **experience with** _____ *[what?]* [□ expertise | □ knowledge | □ education | □ other: _____] **to develop successful** _____ *[type of]* [□ products | □ campaigns | □ projects | □ other: _____] **that** [□ generate leads | □ increase sales | □ procure new target markets | □ maximize return on investment | □ catapult revenues | □ elevate productivity | □ decrease costs | □ other: _____]. **Coupled with his/her** [□ Master's | □ Bachelor's | □ Associate's] **Degrees in** _____ *[what?],* _____ *[#]* **years of successful** _____ *[type of]* **experience and** _____ **as well as** _____ *[what?]* **abilities allow him/her to help** _____ *[whom or what?].*

_____**'s** *[Name]* _____ *[which?]* **areas of expertise include** _____, _____, **and** _____ *[what areas?].* **Notable achievements include** _____, _____, **and** _____ *[state matching achievements].* [□ Client-focused | □ Solutions-oriented | □ Profitability-conscious | □ other attributes: _____], _____ *[name]* **believes that** _____ *[your beliefs]* **is the key to success. And that** _____, _____, **and** _____ *[what?]* **maximizes success.**

He/She is proficient in _____, _____, **and** _____ *[what programs?]* **that allows him/her to** _____ *[do what?].* _____ *[Name]* **has participated in** _____, _____, **and** _____ *[what areas?]* **and brings** [□ experience | □ enthusiasm | □ drive | □ other: _____] **to all of his/her** [□ projects | □ other: _____].

SAMPLE FOR THE MARKETING SPECIALIST

Kenshin Friedman **balances** marketing **experience with** sales, graphic design, and publishing expertise **to develop successful** online and print marketing campaigns **that** generate leads, procure new target markets, and maximize return on investment. **Coupled with his** dual Bachelor's **Degrees in** Marketing and Business Administration, nine **years of successful** marketing and sales **experience as well as** creative **abilities allow him to help** establish brand recognition, product visibility, and consumer awareness within highly competitive markets.

Kenshin's marketing and online advertising **areas of expertise include** SEO, SEM, PPC management, digital content management, brand management, social media management, **and** multiplatform advertising. **Notable achievements include** developing effective marketing collateral, creating strategic PowerPoint presentations, coordinating lead-generating events, and exceeding goals and expectations.

Client-focused and solutions-oriented, Kenshin **believes that** unearthing target audience needs and presenting product options that meet those needs **is the key to success. And that** networking, building strong client relationships and key account leadership solidifies long-term connections that **maximize that success!**

He is proficient in Adobe Photoshop, Illustrator, and InDesign; Microsoft PowerPoint and Excel; as well as SharePoint **that allows him to** creatively conceptualize and design unique marketing campaigns and materials. Kenshin **has participated in** trend research, analysis, tracking, and forecasting in the launch of new services **and brings** experience and enthusiasm **to all of his** projects.

LINKED-IN PROFILE FOUNDATION #3

As a _____ *[title]*, _____ *[name]* _____ *[does what?]*. **He/She works hard to** _____ *[do what?]* **in order to** achieve his/her [□ employers' | □ clients' | □ others: _____] **goals.**

With his/her expert knowledge of _____ *[what?]* **coupled with exceptional** _____, _____, **and** _____ *[your primary abilities]* **skills,** _____ *[name]* **is able to** _____ *[do what?]* **and as a result has** _____, _____, **and** _____ *[accomplished what?]*. **He/She keeps abreast of current** _____ *[type of]* **conditions that can affect his/her** [□ firm | □ clients | □ other: _____] **and stays on top of** _____ *[what areas?]*, **which helps him/her** _____ *[do what?]*.

Write a few sentences or paragraph concerning your own unique value proposition and competitive edge: _____. **Because** _____ *[name]* **is a(n)** _____ *[type of]* **person who** _____ *[does what?]*, **he/she will** _____ *[do what well?]*. _____ *[Name]* **doesn't wait for opportunities to present themselves; he/she** _____ *[does what well?]*.

_____ *[Name]* **is** [□ accessible | □ approachable | □ reliable | □ accountable | □ other attributes: _____] **to/for** _____ *[what?]*. **As a** [□ friendly | □ genuine | □ impartial | □ other attributes: _____] **person, he/she is** _____ *[attributes]* **and helps his/her** [□ firm | □ clients | □ other: _____] **achieve their goals by way of** _____ *[doing what?]*.

SAMPLE FOR THE REALTOR

As a Licensed Real Estate Salesperson and a Certified Buyers' Rep, Jane Murphy lists, markets, and sells more houses and finds more homes for buyers that match their needs than her average counterpart. **She works hard to** turn around sales or purchases more quickly and smoothly in the shortest timeframe using all resources available **in order to achieve her** clients' **goals.**

With her expert knowledge of the market place and competitive pricing **coupled with exceptional** negotiation **skills,** Jane **is able to** negotiate better prices for buyers and sellers **and as a result has** saved her clients tens of thousands of dollars, getting the process done quickly and with less issues and stress. **She keeps abreast of** current market **conditions that can affect her** clients **and stays on top of** short sales, foreclosures, and mortgage rates, **which helps her** find more ways to benefit her clients.

Today's market conditions represent extreme challenges for not only clients but for realtors as well. Many drop out of the field while others get disgruntled. **Because** Jane **is an** optimistic **person who** doesn't get discouraged, **she** will keep the process moving forward while communicating with her clients, the attorneys, appraisers, inspectors, engineers, mortgage brokers, and/or builders regularly to ensure everything is moving along smoothly. Jane **doesn't wait for opportunities** to pop up for her clients; **she** works hard at connecting buyers with sellers and unearthing hidden buying or selling opportunities for them.

Jane **is** accessible, approachable, reliable, and accountable **to** each and every one of her clients. When times get rough, she will help empower, motivate, and inspire you to go forward and will put a smile on your face through her outgoing, entertaining, and playful nature. **As a** friendly, genuine, and impartial **person, she is** a good listener **and helps her** clients achieve their goals in the very best way possible giving them the unbiased facts in a straight-forward manner.

LINKED-IN PROFILE FOUNDATION #4

I am a(n) _____, _____, and _____ *[your primary attributes]* [□ leader | □ executive | □ professional | □ other: _____] **who** _____ *[does what?].* **Including** _____, _____, _____, _____, **and** _____ *[your primary keywords / core competencies].*

With _____ *[#]* **years' experience in** _____, _____, **and** _____ *[your secondary keywords],* **I have served as** _____, _____, **and** _____ *[your various titles].* **I am expert in** _____, _____, **and** _____ *[what key areas?].*

As _____ *[your title or function]* **at** _____ *[company or organization],* **I was recruited to** _____ *[do what?]* **where I** _____, _____, **and** _____ *[accomplished what?]* **and achieved** _____ *[what?].*

At _____ *[company or organization],* **I** _____ *[performed what?].* **As** _____ *[title],* **I** _____, _____, **and** _____ *[accomplished what?].* **Serving on the** _____ *[which?]* **Committee, I developed** _____ *[what?].* **Previously, as** _____ *[title],* **I** _____, _____, **and** _____ *[accomplished what?].*

SAMPLE FOR THE HIGHER EDUCATION LEADER

I am a strategic, innovative, and energetic higher-education leader **who** promotes continuous improvement to the quality of instruction at universities and colleges. **Including** degree plan development, online program architecture, curriculum design, student assessment program creation, academic and international student advisement, learning resource management, and student success coordination.

With 14 **years' experience in** academic culture **and** multicultural instruction, **I have served as** Faculty Lead, Head of Academic Advising, Adjunct Faculty, **and** subject matter expert. **I am expert in** on-site and online undergraduate and graduate program development, adult education, and Customer Relationship Management administration.

As Mentor at ABC University, **I was recruited to** help create and facilitate the University's learning communities **where I** consummated a 98% student graduation success rate, helped increase the faculty team's Key Performance Indicators, significantly improved student learning outcomes, **and achieved** "very satisfied" metrics.

Serving on the Curriculum Design and Assessment **Committee**, I developed course assessment measures and co-championed the Department's Master of Science in Business plan. **Previously, as** Lead Faculty and Adjunct Faculty **at** various colleges, I devised curriculum and taught business, economics, and marketing courses and served on the Committee for Accreditation.

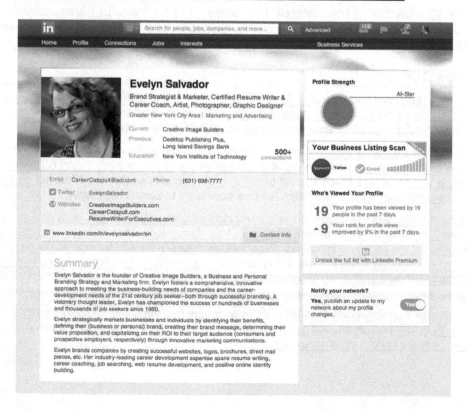

DEVELOP YOUR ELEVATOR PITCH
For Use in All of Your Networking & Interviews

INTRODUCTION

Your **Personal Brand Message** written in the form of an **Elevator Pitch** is what you would convey when you introduce yourself or discuss what you do while networking, at your interviews, and during other conversations. It serves as your standard response to the question, *"What do you do?"* or *"What can you tell me about yourself?"* and is best kept to within 30 to 60 seconds so it is easier for you to memorize and will catch your listener's attention. There is no "one size fits all" foundation suitable for everyone concerning the development of a brand message. However, guidelines, foundations, and samples follow that you can use as a guide to develop your own unique message.

PERSONAL BRAND "BEFORE AND AFTER" EXAMPLE

In the graphic that follows, take note of the **"KEY"** and where the five personal branding components are included in the brand message.

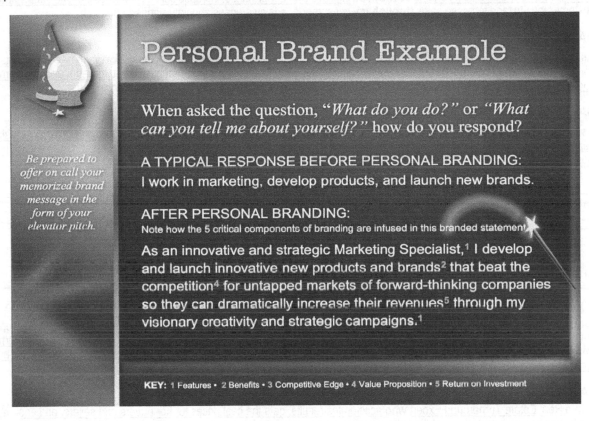

Personal Brand Example

Be prepared to offer on call your memorized brand message in the form of your elevator pitch.

When asked the question, *"What do you do?"* or *"What can you tell me about yourself?"* how do you respond?

A TYPICAL RESPONSE BEFORE PERSONAL BRANDING:
I work in marketing, develop products, and launch new brands.

AFTER PERSONAL BRANDING:
Note how the 5 critical components of branding are infused in this branded statement.

As an innovative and strategic Marketing Specialist,[1] I develop and launch innovative new products and brands[2] that beat the competition[4] for untapped markets of forward-thinking companies so they can dramatically increase their revenues[5] through my visionary creativity and strategic campaigns.[1]

KEY: 1 Features • 2 Benefits • 3 Competitive Edge • 4 Value Proposition • 5 Return on Investment

START DEVELOPING YOUR ELEVATOR PITCH

Now that you have all of the ingredients you need to write your Elevator Pitch, brainstorm all possible solutions that convey your brand; edit it until you are comfortable that it is accurate, includes all of your brand components, and presents you in the best of light. You can start with your **Personal Brand Biography** or **LinkedIn Profile** and condense it further, or take the lists you developed and sentences you wrote and join them, recreate them, and edit your message until you are satisfied. Make it memorable!

Then repeat it daily until you memorize it so you can use it over and over again whenever you network and go on interviews. Keep it handy on your person or desk to use during telephone conversations so you can read it until you start to memorize and own it. It will help empower you and your success!

ELEVATOR PITCH FOUNDATION #1

As a(n) _____ and _____ *[your primary attributes]* _____ *[job title]*, I _____ *[what you do, your features and benefits]* for _____ *[type of firms you provide benefits to]* **so they can** _____ *[what you help them achieve through your value proposition and ROI]* **through my** _____, _____, **and** _____ *[your competitive edge and/or attributes / features]*.

SAMPLE FOR A VICE PRESIDENT OF NEW BUSINESS DEVELOPMENT

As an innovative and strategic New Business Development Executive, **I** develop visionary products, increase market share, drive sales and revenues, and elevate product profitability **for** forward-thinking technology firms **so they can** deliver profits to shareholders **through my** strategic planning leadership and direction, new program creation, and business development initiatives.

SAMPLE FOR A CUSTOMER SERVICE MANAGER

As an experienced Customer Service Manager, **I** direct and oversee sales, customer service, merchandising, front end, and warehouse areas **for** Fortune 500 grocery chains **so they can** improve staff performance, increase service levels, streamline supply flow, elevate customer loyalty, and increase sales **through my** consumer-needs awareness and value-added approach.

SAMPLE FOR A COMPLIANCE OFFICER

As a proactive, quality-oriented Compliance Officer, **I** am an objective reviewer and evaluator **for** various departments of large corporations **so they can** be sure that all business activities are in compliance with regulatory requirements and company policies and procedures **through my** ability to identify potential risk areas and immediately resolve compliance issues.

SAMPLE FOR A PURCHASING AGENT

As a detail-oriented Purchasing Agent, **I** perform all facets of buying, merchandising, inventory control, and order processing **for** all departments of small to midsize businesses **so they can** successfully delivery products on time, increase purchasing service levels, and slash costs **through my** skillful contract negotiations and ability to manage and control inventory to meet the firms' needs.

ELEVATOR PITCH FOUNDATION #2

I am a _____ *[job title]*, **who** _____ *[does what?]* **with a** _____ *[type of]* **success rate of** _____ **%** *[percentage]*. **I do this by** _____ *[how accomplished]* **that includes** _____, _____, **and** _____ *[what areas?]*. **I am expert in/at** _____, _____, **and** _____ *[what areas?]*.

SAMPLE FOR THE CAREER MANAGEMENT INDUSTRY LEADER

I am a Business and Personal Brand Strategist, author, and award-winning career management industry leader **who** positions people in the top 2 percent in their industry. As such, they succeed a lot quicker and earn a lot more than their average counterpart. **I do this by** discovering and building their Personal Brand and leveraging it across marketing platforms in all of their print and online communications through creative design and marketing-savvy wordsmithing that compels hiring managers to seek them out.

SAMPLE FOR THE REALTOR

I am a Real Estate Turnaround Expert **who** accelerates results, gets the best prices for her buyers and sellers, and ensures the whole process runs smoothly—while making your house buying or selling experience enjoyable **with a** turnaround **success rate of** 95% for both my buyers and sellers.

SAMPLE FOR THE HIGHER EDUCATION LEADER

I am a higher-education leader **who** promotes continuous improvement to the quality of instruction at colleges and universities **with a** student graduation **success rate of** 98%. **I do this by** spearheading and launching new programs, plans, and curriculum design. **I am expert in** on-site and online undergraduate and graduate program development, adult education, affiliation agreements, and Customer Relationship Management.

ELEVATOR PITCH FOUNDATION #3

I balance _____ *[type of]* [□ experience | □ knowledge] **with** _____, _____, **and** _____ *[what?]* **expertise to develop successful** _____ *[what?]* [□ strategies | □ programs | □ products | □ plans | □ solutions | □ campaigns | □ other: _____] **that** _____, _____, **and** _____ *[does what?]*.

102

SAMPLE FOR THE MARKETING SPECIALIST

I **balance** marketing **experience with** sales, graphic design, **and** publishing **expertise to develop successful** online and print marketing campaign strategies and programs **that** generate leads, procure new target markets, **and** maximize return on investment for companies and clients alike.

ELEVATOR PITCH FOUNDATION #4

As a(n) _____ **and** _____ *[your primary attributes]* _____ *[job title]*, **I** [□ analyze | □ build | □ champion | □ conduct | □ conceptualize | □ configure | □ develop | □ design | □ direct | □ establish | □ implement | □ improve | □ launch | □ manage | □ maximize | □ oversee | □ perform | □ spearhead | □ strategize | □ structure | □ validate | □ other: _____] _____ *[what?]* **for** _____ *[whom or what?]* **that** _____ *[does what?]*, **thereby** _____ *[accomplishing what through your benefits and competitive edge?]* **and resulting in** _____ *[your value proposition]*.

SAMPLE FOR AN ARCHITECT / CONSTRUCTION MANAGER

As an innovative, detail-oriented Architect, **I** design and build highly complex multimillion-dollar commercial buildings and restoration sites **for** a leading national construction management firm **that** involves supervising up to 12 trades simultaneously, meeting all budgets, and coming in ahead of schedule **thereby** satisfying clients **and resulting in** obtaining referrals and escalating profits for my employer.

CREATE YOUR UNIQUE ELEVATOR PITCH

As mentioned earlier, developing your Personal Brand is the most thought-provoking part of all of the content contained in this Book; and since your brand message is critical to help position you in the top percentage of candidates in your field of expertise, take the time it needs to get it right. Your Elevator Pitch will be the first thing you say when meeting new contacts while networking and conducting your interviews, so you will want to ensure it is just the right message for you. It can also be included in your career marketing materials.

Answer the question, **"What do you do?"** or **"Tell me about yourself"** by brainstorming many different ways you can infuse your brand components into marketing-savvy sentences that sell your unique value. Jot down the first things that come to mind. Nothing is "wrong" at this stage. Construct a number of sentences or paragraphs as possible Elevator Pitches. Review each and combine and/or edit them to ensure it includes all of your brand components

Write out several possible brand messages, and perfect it until you feel you "own" it. Come back to it several times to edit it until you feel it is "right." In fact, as I often do when I craft resumes, circle back to it again after you complete the **Step-by-Step Resumes** process. Once you finalize It, double-check that it includes all of your brand components and start to memorize it. Keep it near your phone and/or computer at all times so you can use it as a script until you have memorized it.

Try Out Several Brand Messages for Your Elevator Pitch:

WRITE YOUR SLOGAN / TAG LINE
For Use in All of Your Career Marketing Materials

INTRODUCTION

A *Slogan*—or *Tag Line*—is a memorable, succinct phrase or motto that best sells you apart from your competition. Although optional, a Slogan is very beneficial to include in your resume as it states what you are good at and what you have to offer a prospective employer as soon as they view your resume. Your slogan should provide an idea of who you are or what you do in as few words as possible.

Add your Slogan to all of your career marketing materials including on your Resume, Cover Letter, Web Portfolio, LinkedIn Profile, all email and online messages, business cards, letterhead, blog, Career Portfolio, Interview Thank You Letters, and any other professional communications. In your resume, it is typically placed under your resume header centered in large italics.

Here you will create *Your Slogan / Tag Line.* It can be a condensed version of your Elevator Pitch or other catchy words that include your value proposition. The more catchy your Slogan, the easier it will be to remember. Using a well-defined, short Slogan can sell your value proposition to hiring managers right up front...before even reading your resume.

SAMPLE SLOGANS

- **CAREER MANAGEMENT INDUSTRY LEADER:** *"Positioning Candidates in the Top 2 Percent in their Field of Expertise"*
- **MARKETING SPECIALIST:** *"Balancing Marketing Experience with Sales, Graphic Design, and Publishing Expertise to Develop Successful Marketing Campaigns"*
- **REALTOR:** *"House turnaround expert who accelerates results, gets the best prices for her clients in competitive real estate markets, ensures the process goes smoothly, and makes the overall experience enjoyable"*
- **HIGHER EDUCATION EXECUTIVE:** *"Higher Education Leader Promoting Continuous Improvement to the Quality of Instruction with a 98% Student Graduation Success Rate."*
- **CONSTRUCTION MANAGER:** *"Bringing Projects in On Time and Within Budget...Every Time!"*
- **CREATIVE DIRECTOR:** *"Helping You Brand Your Clients Ahead of Their Competition"*
- **SALES MANAGER:** *"Meeting Challenges, Overcoming Obstacles, Selling Solutions, and Closing Sales"*
- **EXECUTIVE CHEF:** *"From Gourmet Appetizers to Fine Desserts"*
- **CHARTER PILOT:** *"Flying from the Caribbean to Mexico and Everywhere in Between"*
- **REGISTERED NURSE:** *"Providing Caring, Professional Medical Care to All Patients...from Infants to Geriatrics"*
- **ELEMENTARY TEACHER**: *"Creating a Trusting and Nurturing Learning Environment for All Students"*
- **HIGH SCHOOL TEACHER:** *"Helping Students Take Positive Steps Toward their Future"*
- **INFORMATION TECHNOLOGY PROFESSIONAL:** *"Providing complete IT solutions with dedication to service."*

WRITE YOUR SLOGAN

To write your own unique Slogan, start by culling out the critical keywords and phrases from your *Elevator Pitch* by moving around and editing the words until you come up with an impactful Slogan that exemplifies what you have to offer. Brainstorm a host of other short phrases that include your value proposition and/or some of your branding words. Edit and refine them. Try out a number of different phrases, condensing it to as few words as possible, until you feel your Slogan is just right for you.

CREATE YOUR PROFESSIONAL SUMMARY
For Your Resume

INTRODUCTION

Your *Professional Summary / Executive Profile*—the first section of your resume—differs somewhat from the *Elevator Pitch* and other personal branding formats you completed above, however, uses the same branding components you identified in the *Personal Brand Worksheet* you completed. Since your *Professional Summary* is an all-important encapsulated summary of your professional self and can determine whether or not your resume will be read, it should whet the appetite of the reader by showcasing the value you have to offer an employer.

Professional Summary Foundations (and corresponding samples) are provided below for you to include your unique information in order to construct a summary that showcase(s) your primary keywords, primary personal attributes, and brand components. Adjust sentences as they are applicable to your unique experience.

Note how each sample below and throughout this section that uses the same foundation is entirely different, and it is impossible to recognize that the same foundation was used to construct the *Professional Summary*.

PROFESSIONAL SUMMARY FOUNDATION #1

_____ *[#]* **years of** [□ progressive | □ tenured] _____ *[type of]* **experience in the** _____ *[which?]* **field** _____ *[doing what?]* **including** _____, _____, _____, **and** _____ *[your primary keywords].* **Proven proficiency in** _____, _____, _____, **and** _____ *[what areas?]* [□ with additional knowledge of _____ and _____ *(additional skill sets)].* [□ Clientele have included _____, _____, **and** _____ *(whom?)* | □ Interface directly with _____ *[whom?]* regarding _____ *[primary areas of expertise].*] **A(n)** _____ *[industry]* **professional with excellent** _____, _____, **and** _____ *[type of]* **skills** [□ and the ability to _____ *[do what well?]* | □ who delivers _____ *(your value proposition).*]

SAMPLE FOR A CREATIVE DIRECTOR / GRAPHIC DESIGNER

Three **years of** creative direction and graphic design **experience in the** advertising **field** designing successful advertising campaigns **including** client needs assessment, solutions strategizing, layout and design conceptualization, illustration, **and** photo retouching. **Proven proficiency in** creating logos, ads, brochures, **and** publications **with additional knowledge of** Website design and development. **Interface directly with** key advertising agencies and public relations firms **regarding** marketing, press coverage, publicity, and visual communications. **Clientele have included** Fortune 500 firms, industrial manufacturers, **and** small businesses. **An** advertising **professional with excellent** client relations, design, **and** problem-solving **skills who delivers** revenue-generating solutions for employers and clients alike.

SAMPLE FOR AN EXECUTIVE CHEF

Fourteen **years of** progressive **experience in** restaurant and hotel management in an Executive or Head Chef position **in the** culinary arts **field including** hiring and training sous chefs and cooks, menu planning and cooking, buying, catering, maintaining inventory, controlling and negotiating food costs, **and** delegating tasks. **Proven proficiency in** Continental and Italian culinary arts, butchering, **and** food decoration. **A** culinary management **professional with excellent** creativity and staff development **skills and the ability to** motivate staff to achieve the highest quality of culinary arts standards encompassing appetizers, entrees, and desserts resulting in high revenue returns.

SAMPLE FOR A SOCIAL WORKER

Eight **years of** tenured social work **experience** counseling adolescents at various cognitive and emotional levels in various settings **including** group homes, schools, **and** mental-health facilities. **Proven proficiency** in advocacy and linkage, casework, client needs assessments, goal planning, **and** life skills training **with knowledge of** housing coordination **and** referral servicing. **Clientele have included** emotionally disturbed, learning disabled, developmentally delayed, and depressed adolescents as well as those diagnosed with ADHD, bipolar disorder, schizophrenia, autism, cerebral palsy, **and** mental retardation. **A** mental health **professional with excellent** communications, advocacy, **and** troubleshooting **skills and the ability to** establish and build positive, solid relationships with clients, their families, associates, and all mental health professionals.

PROFESSIONAL SUMMARY FOUNDATION #2

A(n) _____ and _____ *[primary personal attributes]* _____ *[type of]* [□ professional | □ executive | □ manager] **experienced in** _____, _____, _____, **and** _____ *[primary skill areas]*. [□ **Fully versed in** _____, _____, **and** _____ *(secondary skill areas)* | □ Background encompasses the ability to _____ *(do what?)*]. **High degree of responsibility in** _____ *[what area?]*. [□ Demonstrated | □ Proven] **ability to work effectively both independently and as an integral part of a team effort to achieve** _____ *[what?]* **goals. A strong** _____ *[title / function]* **with a high degree of responsibility** [□ in _____ *(what?)* | □ who works well with _____ and _____ alike]. **Adept at handling** _____ *[what?]* **and developing proactive** _____ *[type of strategies, methods, procedures]*. [□ **Computer experience includes** _____, _____, **and** _____ *(programs)*.]

SAMPLE FOR A DATABASE MANAGER

A results-oriented Information Technology **professional experienced in** database installation, implementation, troubleshooting, and management, as well as office management and customer relations. **Fully versed in** tracking customer information, report generation, account management, estimate development, **and** project scheduling. **Demonstrated ability to work effectively both independently and as an integral part of a team effort to achieve** business **goals. A strong** problem-solver **with a high degree of responsibility** in tacking challenges with automated solutions.

SAMPLE FOR AN ACCOUNTING VICE PRESIDENT

A seasoned upper-level financial **executive with extensive experience** in accounting management. **Background encompasses the ability to** reduce overall costs while increasing levels of productivity and profitability. **Proven ability to** train and develop staff to exceed goals while raising morale. **Fully versed in** addressing and resolving client concerns and maintaining a positive rapport with all levels of internal and external clients. Analytically inclined problem-solver with leadership and management development skills. **Computer experience includes** Microsoft Word and Excel, Simply Accounting, Filemaker Pro, **and** ACCPAC.

SAMPLE FOR A SCHOOL PSYCHOLOGIST

A caring **and** patient mental-health **professional experienced in** psychology, early childhood intervention and evaluation, **and** testing gifted to multihandicapped children. **Fully versed in** psychological assessments, designing IEP goals, identifying and interpreting situations, counseling, running parent workshops, representing the school district at impartial hearings, **and** working with various clientele. **High degree of responsibility in** problem-solving with resolution follow up, client relations, **and** crisis intervention. **A strong** advocate who works well with staff, clients, and resource personnel alike. **Adept at handling** crises **and developing proactive** counseling plans to assist students in realizing their fullest potential.

PROFESSIONAL SUMMARY FOUNDATION #3

A(n) _____ *[attribute]* _____ *[title]* **with a** [□ distinctive | □ progressive] **career in** _____ **and** _____ *[primary targeted areas]* **management including** _____, _____, **and** _____ *[primary skill areas]* **with full responsibility for** _____ **and** _____ *[what?]*. **Diverse business spheres include** _____, _____, **and** _____ *[what environments?]*. **Broad-based experience encompasses** _____, _____, _____, **and** _____ *[primary keywords]*. **Recognized for the ability to** _____ *[do what well?]*. **A(n)** [□ effective | □ self-directed | □ motivated | □ other: _____] [□ leader | □ team builder | □ professional | □ executive | □ manager | □ other: _____] **with the ability to consistently achieve objectives. Computer experience includes** _____, _____, **and** _____ *[programs]*.

SAMPLE FOR A CHIEF FINANCIAL OFFICER

A results-oriented senior financial officer **with a distinctive career in** general and financial management **including** the direction and streamlining of corporate financial operations **with full responsibility for** financial reporting and cost reduction. **Diverse business spheres include** manufacturing, distribution, and entrepreneurial business startup. **Broad-based experience encompasses** business restructuring and reengineering, strategic planning, and cost containment. **Recognized for the ability to** coach and develop staff. **A self-directed and motivated executive with the ability to consistently achieve objectives. Computer experience includes** Microsoft Access, Excel, Word, Outlook, and Explorer; ACTI; Visual Manufacturing; Crystal Report Writer; **and** UNIX.

SAMPLE FOR AN INFORMATION TECHNOLOGY SALES & MARKETING EXECUTIVE

A proactive information technology **executive with a progressive career in** the high-tech industry and the electronic communications field **with full responsibility for** sales, marketing, advertising, **and** public relations functions. **Diverse business spheres include** the systems integration market place interfacing with distribution and manufacturing channels. **Broad-based experience encompasses** systems analysis, LAN-to-host connectivity, system component design, heterogeneous network solutions, **and** software customization. **Recognized for the ability to** stay on top of the high-tech industry and consistently increase profits. An effective problem-solver and staff motivator.

SAMPLE FOR A QUALITY ASSURANCE MANAGER

A seasoned Quality Assurance Manager **with a distinctive career in** quality assurance, operations, and front-line management **including** customer service, research and analysis, quality control, auditing, **and** personnel management. **Recognized for the ability to** manage multicounter operations, service agent productivity, **and** increase revenues. **An effective leader and team builder skilled in** training, developing, coaching, and motivating others **with the ability to consistently achieve objectives.**

PROFESSIONAL SUMMARY FOUNDATION #4

A(n) _____, _____ *[your primary attributes]* _____ *[title]* **with** _____ *[#]* **years of experience spanning all aspects of** _____, _____, **and** _____ *[your main core competencies].* **Extensive background in [**☐ managing | ☐ executing | ☐ performing | ☐ other: _____ **]** _____ *[what?]* **for this** _____ *[type of]* **firm including** [☐ commercial | ☐ residential | ☐ industrial | ☐ civil | ☐ municipal | ☐ other: _____ **]** [☐ design | ☐ design-and-build | ☐ construction | ☐ carpentry | ☐ installation | ☐ remodeling | ☐ repair | ☐ other: _____ **] projects including** _____, _____, **and** _____ *[project types].* **Adept at** _____ *[what functions?]* **including** _____, _____, **and** _____ *[what?].* **A solid knowledge of** _____, _____, **and** _____ *[what?]* **with exceptional [**☐ mechanical | ☐ mathematical | ☐ analytical | ☐ problem-solving | ☐ other: _____ **] skills. Consistent record of completing projects on time and within budget, while providing superior [**☐ workmanship | ☐ productivity | ☐ customer service | ☐ other: _____ **].**

SAMPLE FOR A PROJECT MANAGER

A results-oriented, profitability-conscious Project Manager **with** more than 12 **years of experience spanning all aspects of** project lifecycle management, trades coordination, labor relations management, **and** structural problem solving via action-driven leadership, direction, and support. **Extensive background in managing** major commercial construction **projects for this construction management firm** including high-rise buildings, universities, industrial plants, and retail malls. **Adept at** coordinating multiple subcontractors simultaneously and in developing tactical action plans that direct high-producing teams to overcome boundaries and successfully meet all challenges and goals

SAMPLE FOR AN ELECTRICIAN

A Licensed Electrician **with** 10 **years of experience spanning all aspects of** electrical installations, repairs, **and** maintenance for major civil and industrial **projects. Adept at** installing, testing, troubleshooting, and resolving all types of electrical **systems with a solid knowledge of** high-voltage electrical systems, high-tension distribution systems, above-ground conduits, **and** underground electrical services **with exceptional** mechanical and problem-solving **skills. Consistent record of completing projects on time and within budget, while providing superior** workmanship and customer service.

SAMPLE FOR A CONSTRUCTION LABORER

A trusted and dedicated Construction Laborer **with** seven **years of experience spanning all aspects of** carpentry, framing, floor-to-floor build-outs, steel reinforcement, drywall, tiling, trim work, roofing, **and** decking for residential construction **projects. Solid knowledge of** the use of all carpentry equipment, tools, **and** materials **with** high quality workmanship.

PROFESSIONAL SUMMARY FOUNDATION #5

_____ *[#]* **years of professional** _____ **and** _____ *[type of]* **experience in the** _____ *[which field or industry?]* **working for various** _____ *[type of]* [☐ facilities | ☐ firms | ☐ organizations | ☐ agencies | ☐ other: _____]. **Full knowledge of** _____, _____, **and** _____ *[primary skill areas].* **Proven ability to** _____, _____, _____, **and** _____ *[do what?].* **Highly skilled in** _____ **and** _____ *[additional skill areas].* [☐ Multiskilled _____ *[type of]* **professional who is** _____, _____, **and** _____ *(primary attributes).* | ☐ Attributes include _____, _____, **and** _____ *(primary attributes).]* **Proficient in** _____ **with knowledge of** _____ *[additional knowledge areas].*

SAMPLE FOR A MEDICAL BILLING & COLLECTIONS SPECIALIST

Twelve **years of professional** billing, collection, and supervisory **experience in the** medical **field working for various** multimodality **facilities. Full knowledge of** medical terminology and insurance laws as well as policies of Medicare, No-Fault, Workers' Compensation, HMOs, **and** third-party payers. **Highly skilled in** productivity improvement, quality assurance, research and analysis, bookkeeping, **and** general accounting. **Multiskilled** medical **professional who is** honest, hardworking, **and** detail-oriented with ability to work in a fast-paced environment, establish effective relationships, and work as a team player with patients, staff, and management. **Proficient in** Versyss, AccuMed, and Medic Vision systems **with knowledge of** ADS and Microsoft Word.

SAMPLE FOR A SECURITY DIRECTOR

Ten **years of experience in the** security and investigations **field. Full knowledge of** security investigations, employee and premises security, building integrity, product security, transporting of valuable items, bomb threat investigations, **and** handling volatile situations. **Proven ability in** managing personnel functions including scheduling, evaluations, **and** training. **Highly skilled in** making cost-effective recommendations regarding surveillance **and** detection equipment technology. **Attributes include** integrity, honesty, and ability to interact with all levels of management.

SAMPLE FOR A MOVIE SCREENING COORDINATOR

Three **years of professional** communications **experience in the** entertainment **industry. Full knowledge of** public relations, public speaking, and speech preparation. **Proven ability to** handle national and international special events coordination and movie screenings. **Highly skilled in** interpersonal communication and effective listening. **Attributes include** creativity, strong organization and conflict resolution skills, **and** outstanding public speaking abilities. **Ability to** take on difficult challenges and get things done in an impeccable manner while being deadline-conscious. **Proficient in** Excel, Kedit, SPSS, and SAS.

ADDITIONAL PROFESSIONAL SUMMARY SENTENCES

You can infuse or swap out some of these additional sentences, as relative, into your *"Professional Summary."*

☐ **A seasoned** _____ *[type of]* [☐ executive | ☐ professional | ☐ other: _____] **with extensive expertise in** _____ *[what field?].* **Background encompasses the ability to** _____ *[do what?].*

SAMPLE FOR A FINANCE EXECUTIVE

A seasoned upper-level financial executive **with extensive expertise in** accounting management. **Background encompasses the ability to** reduce overall costs while increasing levels of productivity and profitability.

☐ **Strong** _____ *[type of]* **ability,** _____ *[type of]* **knowledge,** _____ *[which?]* **skills, and** _____ *[features]* **with a good understanding of the** _____ *[field]* **business and company success goals.**

SAMPLE FOR A SALES ASSOCIATE

Strong sales **ability,** operational **knowledge,** merchandising **skills, and** work ethic **with a good understanding of the** retail business **and company success goals.**

☐ **Seasoned,** _____ **and** _____ *[attributes]* _____ *[job title]* **specializing in** _____ *[areas].*

SAMPLE FOR A TEACHER

Seasoned, energetic, **and** enthusiastic teacher **specializing in** developing innovative, interactive lesson plans utilizing the integration of technology and basic math principles.

☐ **A(n)** _____, _____, **and** _____ *[primary attributes]* **professional** _____ *[job title]* **offering substantial experience in** _____, _____, **and** _____ *[type of]* **settings.**

SAMPLE FOR A NURSE

A dedicated, compassionate, results-oriented **professional** Nurse **offering substantial experience in** shift management and patient care in acute-care **settings.**

☐ **Possess** [☐ excellent | ☐ in-depth | ☐ working] _____, _____, **and** _____ *[type of]* [☐ skills | ☐ knowledge | ☐ expertise] **coupled with the ability to** _____ *[do what?].* **Proven** _____ **and** _____ *[type of skills]* **adeptness and the ability to maintain superior levels of** _____ *[what?]* **under all types of circumstances.**

SAMPLE FOR A HEALTHCARE PROFESSIONAL

Possess excellent interpersonal, critical thinking, **and** assessment **skills coupled with the ability to** put individuals at ease. **Proven** planning **and** organizational **adeptness and the ability to maintain superior levels of** quality care **under all types of circumstances.**

CONTINUE TO EVOLVE, BUILD & ENHANCE YOUR BRAND

MANAGE YOUR BRAND

Managing your brand much the same way as a firm manages theirs is key to your success. And applying marketing techniques to help brand you in your field allows you to promote it successfully. (Your *Marketing Campaign* is addressed in *Step 7: Market Yourself!*)

Continue to Evolve, Build, and Enhance your Brand

Managing your brand much the same way a firm manages theirs is your key to success.

And applying marketing techniques to help brand you in your field allows you to manage it successfully.

12 methods you can use to strengthen your brand and become the best you can be:

1. Do what it takes to become an expert in your field.
2. Gain more knowledge, education, and experience.
3. Seek additional opportunities that can enhance your Personal Brand.
4. Maintain an up-to-date record of all of your accomplishments.
5. Create an outstanding Résumé and Cover Letter.
6. Network and promote yourself all the time.
7. Participate in LinkedIn, social media, and/or industry-specific groups and blogs.
8. Become the "go to" person in person and online.
9. Build ongoing relationships in person and online.
10. Monitor your online presence by Googling yourself *(in quotes)* monthly.
11. Update your Web Portfolio with your enhanced brand and additional achievements.
12. Redefine and strengthen your brand as it evolves.

PICK YOUR BRAND COLORS

Another way to build and enhance your brand is by selecting suitable colors that, to you, exemplify your personal brand. Pretty much any color or combination of (two or three) colors can be used to depict your brand. Professional colors, for example, are deep colors, such as navy, burgundy, dark green, and even deep purple. You can either select to use one of these colors for your brand colors or choose one of your own.

Think about colors you would create a logo or your marketing materials in (to use for your Web Portfolio or Twitter background, for example), would wear on your person (in the form of overall attire, a scarf, eyeglasses, a belt, tie, shoes, or even a hat), colors you would feel comfortable with surrounding yourself in, such as a purse or an attaché, your office accessories, or executive pen. If you select "loud" colors, such as chartreuse or bright orange, for example, suggest keeping them to a minimum in your attire, just enough to make a professional brand statement.

Then infuse your chosen brand colors into all of your career marketing materials. For example, you can make your resume header and headings in your brand color(s). The number one rule is to ensure consistency in your overall brand, so that when people see you or your

Next, select your resume bullets…

STEP 5

SELECT YOUR RESUME CLIPBULLETS™
FOR USE IN YOUR "PROFESSIONAL EXPERIENCE" SECTION

CONTENTS OF STEP 5

- [ ] Introduction
- [ ] Resume ClipBullet Introduction & Instructions
- [ ] Select Your Resume ClipBullets™ *(see list in Table of Contents)*

111

INTRODUCTION & INSTRUCTIONS

INTRODUCTION

Resume ClipBullets™ are prewritten, completely customizable bullet foundations you can place right into the *"Professional Experience"* section of your resume as job function and achievement bullets under your specific employers / job positions.

If you have not already done so, refer to the **Table of Contents** and check off all those functions you have handled. Then locate them in this chapter and select the bullet(s) under each category that best describes what you performed. Each bullet includes all of the necessary information required to complete it. Since all sentences (bullet foundations) are already written for you, simply find the most suitable bullet(s) within each section, select options, fill in the blanks, and put them directly into your resume. It's that easy!

Resume ClipBullet categories contains different types and levels of experience, possible achievements relative to that function, and a variety of ways to write similar information so you can use different bullets for various positions in your resume. Also, providing you with many possibilities also ensures no two resumes using this *Step-by-Step Resumes* process will ever be alike.

Bullets are written as **CAR** statements to include your **Challenge**, **Action**, and **Results**, wherever possible. If you have a specific achievement not mentioned, be sure to include it in your resume. The most important thing to keep in mind when compiling your resume is:

Don't just say what you did, state the challenge you were faced with, the actions you took to resolve it, how well you accomplished it, and the end results / benefits derived from your efforts.

INSTRUCTIONS

Resume ClipBullet categories are listed alphabetically. From the categories you identified under the **Table of Contents,** select functional and achievement options relative to your work, fill in the blanks, and change as appropriate to make all bullets true statements as to your own experience. When you complete this section, chances are you will have more bullets than you need. That's okay, as you will be editing them down in **Step 6: Pull Your Resume Together**. It's always better to have more than enough information to start with than to try to determine what else to include, such as in a standard template.

Each resume bullet contains a foundation **(in bold text)** and many applicable options from which to select. Bracketed *italics (in red, if you purchased the e-book version)* signifies instructional information. Since achievements are the most important part of your resume and everyone has different accomplishments, if you see a function that you performed well, be sure to include the benefits derived from your efforts.

SAMPLE BULLETS

Some Resume ClipBullets contain quite a number of options from which you can select to ensure all bases are covered. Here is such an example followed by various different bullets you can create with just this one foundation. When completing your bullets, if you find you have checked off a number of applicable options and the bullet is long, it is best to break it into two and slightly reword, as needed. Try not to exceed four lines per bullet wherever possible.

☐   [☐ Manage and oversee | ☐ Supervise] **all aspects of construction work including** [☐ reviewing project plans | ☐ preparing job estimates | ☐ estimating material and labor costs | ☐ securing competitive bids | ☐ selecting contractors and subcontractors | ☐ developing crew assignments and work schedules | ☐ coordinating projects with contractors | ☐ preparing work orders | ☐ ordering and setting up equipment | ☐ purchasing materials and supplies | ☐ directing and coordinating building construction | ☐ supervising a crew of _____ (#) | ☐ evaluating staff performance | ☐ inspecting work area | ☐ obtaining permits | ☐ mediating and resolving disputes | ☐ ensuring debris removal | ☐ providing technical construction assistance | ☐ preparing punch lists | ☐ overseeing inspection deadlines | ☐ negotiating and processing change orders | ☐ ensuring punch list item completion and customer satisfaction | ☐ coordinating concrete trucks | ☐ recommending land purchases to management | ☐ monitoring inventory and supply requests | ☐ ensuring safety practices | ☐ preparing accident reports | ☐ other: _____] **ensuring all jobs are completed in compliance with specifications and codes**.

SAMPLE COMPLETED BULLETS:

FOR A CONSTRUCTION PROJECT MANAGER:

- **Manage and oversee all aspects of construction work including** reviewing project plans, preparing job estimates, securing competitive bids, selecting subcontractors, coordinating construction, inspecting work, obtaining permits, preparing punch lists, and negotiating change orders, **ensuring all jobs are completed in compliance with specifications and codes**.

FOR A SUPERINTENDENT:

- **Supervise all aspects of construction work including** estimating material and labor costs, ordering and setting up equipment, developing work schedules, supervising a crew of 15, inspecting work area, ensuring debris removal, providing technical construction assistance, **ensuring all jobs are completed in compliance with specifications and codes**.

SELECT YOUR RESUME CLIPBULLETS™

Account Base Establishment & Maintenance

☐ **Successfully develop new and maintain existing** _____ *[type of]* **accounts for this** _____ *[type of]* **firm, selling** _____ *[type of]* **services to the** _____ *[what market?]* **and managing** _____ *[#]* **accounts simultaneously.**

☐ **Manage, coordinate, and service** _____ *[#]* _____ *[type of]* **accounts weekly, providing** _____ *[type of]* **client follow-up and advisement in the areas of** _____, _____, **and** _____ *[what areas?]*.

☐ **Promote and sell** _____ *[type of]* [☐ products | ☐ services] **via** _____, _____, **and** _____ *[what methods?]* **incorporating effective** [☐ product demonstrations | ☐ sales techniques | ☐ other: _____].

☐ **Successfully persuade new clients to make an investment in the future by** [☐ selling high-end projects | ☐ demonstrating the return on their investment | ☐ other methods: _____].

☐ **Sell large-dollar** [☐ products | ☐ services | ☐ projects | ☐ other: _____] **that provide a high return on investment for clients, resulting in** [☐ higher per-project sales | ☐ increased sales of $_____ (amount) | ☐ repeat business | ☐ referrals | ☐ other: _____].

☐ **Effectively manage up to** _____ *[#]* **accounts simultaneously for this** [☐ multimillion-dollar | ☐ $_____ *(revenues)*] _____ *[type of]* **firm selling** _____ *[type of]* **services to the** _____ *[what market?]*.

☐ **Develop** _____ *[type of]* **new accounts and maintain existing clients managing the overall service and profitability of** _____ *[#]* _____ *[type of]* **accounts consisting of** _____, _____, **and** _____ *[what market or industries?]* **for this** _____ *[type of firm]* **who is the** [☐ leading | ☐ forerunner in] _____ *[what area?]*.

☐ **Contact existing clients and solicit new prospects in the** _____ *[which?]* **market to** [☐ identify their requirements | ☐ discuss objectives | ☐ suggest approaches | ☐ negotiate details | ☐ provide costs | ☐ plan schedules and budgets | ☐ coordinate components | ☐ accept payments | ☐ other: _____] **for this** _____ *[type of]* **firm.**

ACHIEVEMENT SAMPLES:

☐ **Maintained a** _____% *[percentage]* **renewal ratio on newly acquired clients increasing** _____ *[type of]* **revenues by** _____% *[percentage]* **by** _____ *[doing what?]*.

☐ **Increased new business by opening a new market in** _____ *[what area?]* **despite heavy competition through** [☐ cold calling | ☐ telemarketing | ☐ getting to decision-makers | ☐ strong phone sales | ☐ knowing the competition, its advertising, and how it affects our business | ☐ other: _____].

☐ **Established payment schedules for** _____ *[#]* **accounts and decreased overdue** _____ *[type of]* **accounts receivables by** _____% *[percentage]* / $_____ *[amount]* **with tight control of accounts and strong follow-up.**

☐ **Established and maintained a new account base of** _____ *[#]* **via** _____, _____, **and** _____ *[which methods?]* **resulting in** _____ *[what benefits?]*.

☐ **Elevated profitability of account base from** _____% **to** _____% *[percentages]* **by** _____ *[what methods?]*.

☐ **Decreased overdue** _____ *[type of]* **accounts receivables** _____% *[percentage]* / $_____ *[amount]* **annually via** [☐ establishing payment schedules | ☐ collecting on _____ *[#]* outstanding accounts | ☐ executing tight control on all accounts | ☐ strong follow-up | ☐ other method: _____].

☐ **Through** [☐ client trust | ☐ relationship building | ☐ solutions selling | ☐ other method: _____] [☐ received many referrals | ☐ maintained loyal, enduring customer relationships | ☐ other benefit: _____]

☐ **Increased sales** $_____ *[amount]* **by successfully expanding** _____ *[type of]* **business into a previously unproductive territory.**

Account Planning, Coordination & Servicing

☐ **Lead and direct the company's consumer strategy and planning including** [☐ strategic development of client businesses | ☐ account planning process | ☐ consumer research | ☐ customer insight | ☐ implementation and analysis | ☐ intelligence support | ☐ other: _____] **ensuring** [☐ planning integrity, quality, and effectiveness | ☐ initiatives contribute to the strategic process | ☐ consistency with client needs and the company's goals | ☐ other: _____].

☐ **Serve as a liaison between the firm and** _____ *[type of]* **clients in the** [☐ sale | ☐ creation | ☐ development | ☐ other: _____] **of** _____ *[what?]*.

☐ **Coordinate and oversee the** _____ *[type of]* **efforts for this** $_____ *[revenues]* [☐ full-service] _____ *[type of]* **firm including** [☐ generating client leads | ☐ making presentations | ☐ assessing client needs | ☐ obtaining and closing sales | ☐ negotiating contracts | ☐ providing client support | ☐ other: _____].

☐ **Successfully manage all aspects of developing and implementing** _____ *[type of]* [☐ initiatives | ☐ tactics | ☐ other: _____] **from concept to completion on** _____ *[type of]* **projects including planning, coordination, execution, and monitoring.**

☐ **Maintain and support an efficient working environment for** _____ *[#]* **accounts including** [☐ daily servicing and support | ☐ account team assistance | ☐ project and presentation coordination | ☐ liaising between company and client | ☐ activity support | ☐ client relations | ☐ other: _____] **ensuring** [☐ execution of all assigned programs | ☐ support of day-to-day efforts | ☐ other: _____].

☐ **Provide** [☐ client account | ☐ customer service | ☐ administrative | ☐ other: _____] **support to** _____ *[#]* [☐ Account Executive(s) | ☐ Client Services Manager(s) | ☐ others: _____] **in the day-to-day administration of** _____ *[type of]* **initiatives including** [☐ participating in client meetings | ☐ reviewing vendor quotes | ☐ verifying production specifications | ☐ preparing project estimates and timelines | ☐ preparing account service-related documents and work-in-progress records | ☐ other: _____].

☐ **Work closely with the** _____ *[which?]* **Department(s) to** [☐ assess needs | ☐ provide complete turnkey projects | ☐ other: _____].

☐ **Provide** [☐ strategic | ☐ sound | ☐ innovative] **thought leadership to build the company's businesses inclusive of input on** [☐ information needs | ☐ planning processes | ☐ demographic data | ☐ consumer profiles | ☐ resources evaluation | ☐ other: _____].

☐ **Plan** _____ *[what?]* **strategies including** [☐ running qualitative research groups | ☐ analyzing market research statistics | ☐ researching and understanding the service | ☐ devising innovative ideas to reach target markets | ☐ other: _____].

☐ **Create the communication strategy for and drive the strategic direction of** _____ *[what?]* **and develop innovative ways to reach consumers for this** _____ *[type of]* **firm specializing in** _____ *[what?.*

☐ **Liaise with clients in** _____ *[which?]* **industries to** [☐ identify their goals | ☐ learn about the product or brand | ☐ determine their target audience | ☐ generate ideas | ☐ present conclusions | ☐ other: _____].

☐ **Apply a(n)** [☐ in-depth | ☐ comprehensive | ☐ proficient] **understanding of consumer behavior to solve** _____ *[type of]* **creative problems for** _____ *[types of]* **client accounts ensuring all work addresses and meets consumer preferences.**

ACHIEVEMENT SAMPLE:

☐ **Received progressive promotions from** [☐ Junior Account Planner | ☐ Assistant Account Planner | ☐ Account Planner | ☐ other title: _____] **to** [☐ Account Planner | ☐ Account Planning Supervisor | ☐ Account Planning Manager | ☐ Director of Account Planning | ☐ Executive Account Planner | ☐ other title: _____].

Achievement Samples – Construction Trades

See also "Construction Projects" and Achievements under specific areas of expertise.

ACHIEVEMENT SAMPLES:

☐ **Established a reputation for quality workmanship at competitive prices by** [☐ maintaining superior levels of craftsmanship | ☐ providing excellent customer service | ☐ other: _____].

☐ **Assisted in** _____ *[type of]* **installations and repairs of this** [_____ *[#]*-square foot _____ *[#]*-story] **building to ensure compliance with all** [☐ building | ☐ electrical | ☐ plumbing | ☐ fire safety | ☐ other: _____] **codes.**

☐ **Facilitated hands-on installation, maintenance, and/or repair of** [☐ commercial | ☐ domestic | ☐ industrial | ☐ other: _____] [☐ indoor | ☐ outdoor] _____ *[type of]* **systems including** _____, _____, **and** _____ *[what?]*.

☐ **Guided a** [☐ major | ☐ highly complex | ☐ technical | ☐ other: _____] _____ *[type of]* **project through to completion in accordance with the schedule and budget by** _____ *[doing what well?]*.

☐ **Mastered the use of** _____ *[what tools or methods?]* **including** _____, _____, **and** _____ *[what?]* **to accomplish** _____ *[what?]*.

☐ **Managed the completion of** _____ *[#]* _____ *[type of]* **jobs** [☐ monthly | ☐ annually] [☐ averaging $_____ to $_____ *(amounts)* | ☐ totaling $_____] **including** [☐ estimating job times, materials, and costs | ☐ selecting materials and hardware | ☐ preparing materials estimates | ☐ reviewing bids | ☐ ordering required job-related materials | ☐ scheduling jobs | ☐ inspecting completed jobs for code compliance | ☐ other: _____].

☐ **Handled on-site** _____ *[what functions?]* **while** [☐ company remained open for business | (☐ homeowners / ☐ employees) remained on premises | ☐ other: _____] **by** _____ *[doing what?]*, **which minimized the work impact so** [☐ business | ☐ home | ☐ facility | ☐ other: _____] **operations remained functional.**

☐ **Recommended and implemented** _____ *[type of]* **improvements to** _____ *[what?]*, **which helped facilitate** _____ *[what functions?]* **and resulted in** _____ *[what benefits?]*.

☐ **Participated in client consultations and overseeing** [☐ construction | ☐ design-and-build | ☐ development | ☐ other: _____] **of a** _____ *[project type]*. **Received commendations from** [☐ client | ☐ employer | ☐ other: _____] **for** [☐ professional expertise | ☐ dedication to job | ☐ a job well done | ☐ other: _____]. **(See "Testimonials.")** *[Note: Include a "Testimonials" section in resume.]*

☐ **Working with minimal supervision under tight deadlines on a** _____ *[type of]* **project, accomplished** _____ *[what?]*.

☐ **Involved in** [☐ managing | ☐ performing | ☐ coordinating | ☐ facilitating | ☐ other: _____] _____ *[what?]* **efforts that required** _____ *[what actions?]* **to meet** _____ *[what challenges?]* **and resulted in** _____ *[benefits]*.

☐ **Successfully turned around** _____ *[what challenge?]* **by** _____ *[doing what?]*, **which resulted in** _____ *[benefits]*.

☐ **Managed and coordinated** [☐ continuous | ☐ frequent] _____ *[type of]* **office space planning to accommodate** _____% *[percentage]* **employee growth in** _____ *[#]* **years. Required** [☐ locating | ☐ building | ☐ leasing | ☐ renovating | ☐ furnishing | other: _____] **offices within** _____ *[#]* **months of notice, including** [☐ telephone systems | ☐ equipment | ☐ furniture | ☐ other: _____].

☐ **Initiated and implemented** _____ *[type of]* **new programs that served to** _____ *[do what?]* **and resulted in** _____ *[what benefits?]*. **Program was executed company-wide and saved the firm $**_____ *[amount]* **annually.**

☐ **Organized company's move from a** _____ *[#]*-**square foot building in** _____ *[what town?]* **to a** _____ *[#]*- **square foot building** [☐ in the business section] **of** _____ *[what town?]*, **allowing the firm to** [☐ construct a front office | ☐ increase staff size | ☐ stock more supplies and materials | ☐ other: _____].

☐ [☐ **Developed and established** | ☐ **Recommended and implemented**] _____ *[type of]* [☐ **management**] [☐ **plans** | ☐ **standards** | ☐ **guidelines** | ☐ **policies** | ☐ **procedures** | ☐ **methods** | ☐ **other:** _____] **that maximized the effective use of** _____ *[what?]* **and supported the continuing improvement of** _____ *[which?]* **standards.**

☐ **Successfully met difficult challenges faced by** _____ *[what obstacles?]* **by** _____ *[doing what?]*, **which resulted in** _____ *[what benefits?]*.

☐ [☐ **Developed** | ☐ **established** | ☐ **performed**] **a "company first" in the area of** _____ *[what area?]* **by** _____ *[doing what?]*, **which resulted in** _____ *[what benefits?]*.

☐ **Gained extensive experience in** _____, _____, **and** _____ *[what areas or functions?]* **that helped facilitate** _____ *[what?]*.

Administrative Functions – Construction Trades

☐ **Coordinate and facilitate various** [☐ office management | ☐ general administration | ☐ facility management | ☐ human resources | ☐ general accounting | ☐ bookkeeping | ☐ payroll processing | ☐ purchasing | ☐ inventory management | ☐ other: _____] **functions for this** _____ *[type of]* **firm including** [☐ developing contracts | ☐ researching vendors | ☐ scheduling inspections | ☐ processing Town paperwork | ☐ verifying permit issuance | ☐ preparing closing statements | ☐ monitoring subcontracts and certificates of insurance | ☐ matching invoices to purchase orders and packing slips | ☐ entering Accounts Payable data | ☐ recording cash receipts | ☐ preparing deposits | ☐ generating _____ *(type of)* reports | ☐ other: _____].

☐ **Prepare and revise** [☐ construction contracts | ☐ subcontractor documents | ☐ bid comparisons | ☐ site visit field reports | ☐ owner change orders | ☐ cost reports | ☐ project correspondence | ☐ purchase orders | ☐ other: _____] **and other related documents for the project management team.**

☐ **Facilitate daily construction office administrative activities including** [☐ developing client proposals and estimates | ☐ preparing bids | ☐ generating material and equipment lists | ☐ preparing cost estimates | ☐ costing materials | ☐ purchasing supplies | ☐ writing contract specifications | ☐ preparing contract records and reports | ☐ issuing and evaluating contractor bids | ☐ negotiating contracts | ☐ scheduling jobs | ☐ hiring trades | ☐ coordinating jobs with (☐ engineers / ☐ architects / ☐ municipal officials / ☐ code officers / ☐ others: _____) | ☐ handling claims avoidance and dispute resolution | ☐ performing risk management | ☐ updating budget databases | ☐ maintaining legal obligations records | ☐ handling insurance needs | ☐ other: _____].

☐ **Provide** [☐ direct | ☐ a full-range of | ☐ general | ☐ all aspects of] _____ *[type of]* **administrative support to** _____ *[#]* [☐ Construction Manager | ☐ Project Managers | ☐ Executives | ☐ _____ *(which?)* Department staff | ☐ others: _____] **including** [☐ office management | ☐ appointment scheduling | ☐ executive calendar | ☐ switchboard operations | ☐ greeting visitors | ☐ keyboarding | ☐ document processing | ☐ bookkeeping | ☐ office supplies purchasing | ☐ travel arrangements | ☐ document filing | ☐ mail processing | ☐ correspondence | ☐ expense reporting | ☐ report generation and tracking | ☐ document scanning | ☐ meeting minutes | ☐ payroll processing | ☐ other: _____].

☐ **Track and review** _____ *[type of]* [☐ prequalification | ☐ contracts | ☐ authorizations | ☐ invoices | ☐ deliverables | ☐ correspondence | ☐ other: _____] **for Project Managers by** _____ *[doing what well?]*.

☐ **Perform a wide variety of administrative activities including** [☐ assisting with contractual initiatives | ☐ handling claims avoidance | ☐ updating budget databases | ☐ researching contractor claims and litigations | ☐ responding to inquiries relating to contract issues | ☐ handling data entry, filing, and copying | ☐ maintaining legal obligations records | ☐ other: _____].

☐ **Perform** [☐ materials costing | ☐ job estimating | ☐ contract negotiations | ☐ other: _____] **with** [☐ contractors | ☐ suppliers | ☐ others: _____] **of** _____ *[type of]* **jobs ranging $**_____ **to $**_____ *[amounts]*.

☐ **Review** [☐ construction schedules | ☐ job cost reports | ☐ payment requisitions | ☐ other: _____] **for** _____ *[purpose]* **and prepare and generate** [☐ monthly | ☐ weekly | ☐ periodic] **cost reports on** _____ *[type of]* **to** [☐ senior technical staff | ☐ senior management | ☐ project engineers | ☐ others: _____].

ACHIEVEMENT SAMPLES:

☐ **Increased** [☐ customer satisfaction | ☐ productivity | ☐ profits | ☐ other: _____] _____ **%** *[percentage]* **by** [☐ analyzing and costing proposals | ☐ determining profitability ratios | ☐ ensuring all jobs come in at _____ % *(percentage)* over cost | ☐ analyzing and trouble-shooting customer complaints | ☐ resolving problems | ☐ other methods: _____].

☐ **Generated** _____ *[#]* **new clients annually by conducting approximately** _____ *[#]* **telesales calls per day, resulting in increased revenue of $**_____ *[amount]*.

☐ **Applied knowledge of** [☐ specifications preparation | ☐ bid evaluations | ☐ bid awards | ☐ standard price and purchasing reference sources | ☐ modern purchasing methods and practices | ☐ government polices | ☐ other: _____] **in the procurement of** _____ *[what?]* **resulting in** _____ *[what achievement?]*.

☐ **Recommended and implemented** _____ *[type of]* [☐ solutions | ☐ improvements | ☐ other: _____] **that effectively addressed** _____ *[what?]* **and adhered to the Company's requirements** [☐ in accordance with all project timelines and budget | ☐ ensuring quality project standards | ☐ allowing for a smooth transition | ☐ other: _____].

☐ **Developed a "company first" in the area of** _____ *[what area?]* **by** _____ *[doing what?]*, **which resulted in** _____ *[what benefits?]*.

☐ **Successfully met difficult challenges faced by** _____ *[what obstacles?]* **by** _____ *[doing what?]*, **which resulted in** _____ *[what benefits?]*.

☐ **Increased sales $**_____ *[amount]* **by generating new and maintaining existing clientele through** [☐ phone contact | ☐ faxed broadcasts | ☐ telemarketing | ☐ strong follow-up | ☐ other: _____].

Administrative Functions – Office

☐ **Handle office and administrative functions that include** [document processing | general office administration | account servicing | data entry | client correspondence | daily customer service matters | payroll issues | filing | bookkeeping | other: _____] **for an office staff of** _____ *[#]*.

☐ **Facilitate various** [☐ operational aspects of | ☐ administrative support services for] **this $**_____ *[revenues]* _____ *[type of firm]*, **including** [☐ payroll processing | ☐ payroll issues resolution | ☐ 401K matters | ☐ data processing | ☐ correspondence | ☐ memoranda | ☐ records management | ☐ data processing | ☐ phone messages | ☐ mailings | ☐ materials distribution | ☐ records management | ☐ security | ☐ printing | ☐ computer troubleshooting |☐ other: _____].

☐ **Support** [☐ Construction Managers | ☐ executives | ☐ Project Managers | ☐ supervisors | ☐ others: _____] **in the areas of** [☐ fielding telephone calls | ☐ managing calendars | ☐ making travel, meeting and event arrangements | ☐ preparing reports and financial data | ☐ training and supervising support staff | ☐ monitoring budgets | ☐ receiving and directing visitors | ☐ creating spreadsheets and presentations | ☐ Internet research | ☐ data entry | ☐ vendor selections | ☐ supervising purchasing processes | ☐ processing expense reports | ☐ coordinating proposal submissions | ☐ planning meetings | ☐ preparing business correspondence | ☐ transcribing dictation | ☐ gathering documentation | ☐ compiling reports | ☐ coordinating schedules and activities | ☐ placing supply orders | ☐ tracking project progress | ☐ other: _____] **with** [☐ sensitivity to confidential matters | ☐ attention to detail | ☐ other: _____].

☐ **Handle** [☐ all | ☐ various] **administrative support services, including** [☐ inventory | ☐ purchasing | ☐ payroll | ☐ invoicing | ☐ other: _____] **for all** _____ *[#]* [☐ departments | ☐ offices | ☐ stores | ☐ other: _____] **ensuring accurate data entry of all information.**

☐ **Conduct office support by way of** [☐ fielding telephone calls | ☐ receiving and directing visitors | ☐ performing word processing | ☐ conducting Internet research | ☐ preparing spreadsheets | ☐ creating presentations | ☐ performing data entry | ☐ processing expense reports | ☐ maintaining departmental database | ☐ other: _____].

☐ **Coordinate and facilitate daily office administration activities for this** _____ *[type of]* **firm including** [☐ office management | ☐ general administration | ☐ human resources | ☐ payroll processing | ☐ other: _____] **for an office staff of** _____ *[#]*.

☐ [☐ **Supervise all** | ☐ **Handle various**] **administrative activities including** [☐ developing cost estimates | ☐ preparing budgets | ☐ coordinating projects with _____ *(whom)* | ☐ purchasing supplies | ☐ processing payroll | ☐ generating _____ *(type of)* reports | ☐ updating budget databases | ☐ other: _____] **keeping all records current and ensuring accuracy.**

☐ **Conduct various** [☐ administrative | ☐ office support] **functions including** [☐ fielding telephone calls | ☐ receiving and directing visitors | ☐ performing word processing | ☐ conducting Internet research | ☐ preparing spreadsheets | ☐ creating presentations | ☐ performing data entry | ☐ processing expense reports | ☐ tracking sales progress | ☐ filing | ☐ faxing | ☐ supporting executive assistants | ☐ filling in for receptionist | ☐ monitoring budgets | ☐ communicating with service providers | ☐ maintaining departmental database | ☐ supporting sales representatives | ☐ assisting with event planning | ☐ other: _____].

☐ **Systematically and accurately** [☐ file | ☐ classify | ☐ archive | ☐ retrieve | ☐ update | ☐ maintain | ☐ other: _____] **daily** [☐ account records | ☐ invoices | ☐ contracts | ☐ reports | ☐ client files | ☐ other documents: _____], **keeping on top of workload without accumulating a backlog.**

☐ **Prioritize workload and meet day-to-day functions with** [☐ impeccable timing | ☐ good business sense | ☐ professionalism | ☐ other: _____].

ACHIEVEMENT SAMPLES:

☐ **Coordinated and orchestrated** [☐ national conventions | ☐ trade shows | ☐ special events | ☐ conferences | ☐ other: _____], **resulting in** _____ *[what benefits?]*.

☐ **Prepared accurate bi-lingual translations from English to** [☐ Spanish | ☐ Italian | ☐ French | ☐ German | ☐ Polish | ☐ Russian | ☐ other: _____] **and vice versa within a timely fashion for** _____ *[whom or what?]*.

☐ [☐ **Developed and coordinated** | ☐ **Implemented and manage**] **the Company's** [☐ domestic | ☐ international] **travel policy, resulting in annual cost reductions of $**_____ *[amount]* **in** [☐ air travel | ☐ hotel rental | ☐ car rental | ☐ meal expenses | ☐ other: _____].

☐ **Configured, troubleshot, and resolved** [☐ hardware | ☐ software | ☐ other: _____] **problems; and provide technical assistance and troubleshooting on** [☐ computers | ☐ software | ☐ equipment | ☐ other: _____] **to** _____ *[whom?]*.

☐ **Keep on top of workload without accumulating backlog by** _____ *[doing what well?]*.

☐ **Developed and implemented a** _____ *[type of]* **change involving** _____ *[what?]*, **which resulted in** [☐ better inventory control | ☐ improved workflow | ☐ increased productivity | ☐ streamlined operations | ☐ other: _____].

Administrative Functions – Project Specific

See also "Project Management."

☐ **Oversee administrative support to the project management team in the areas of** _____, _____, **and** _____ *[which areas?]* **in setting project strategies and priorities**.

☐ **Perform quality control of reports prepared by** [☐ Architects | ☐ Engineers | ☐ Project Managers | ☐ others: _____] **including** _____, _____, **and** _____ *[type of reports]* **by** _____ *[doing what well?]*.

☐ **Manage and oversee all aspects of** _____ *[type of]* **projects including project** [☐ scope | ☐ initiation | ☐ planning | ☐ scheduling | ☐ budgeting | ☐ team selection | ☐ resource allocation | ☐ cost control | ☐ other: _____] **as well as** [☐ quality control | ☐ change management | ☐ system integration | ☐ other: _____] **keeping in line with all business objectives**.

☐ **Facilitate business management of this** _____ *[type of]* **firm including** [☐ leading and overseeing projects | ☐ prioritizing projects and balancing competing demands | ☐ reviewing contracts to verify legal requirements | ☐ translating requirements into effective legal solutions | ☐ establishing quality control procedures | ☐ developing revenue contracts | ☐ preparing specifications | ☐ performing inspections to facilitate quality assurance | ☐ identifying contractual problems or errors | ☐ quality testing materials | ☐ researching and writing legal and/or technical procedures | ☐ setting up and maintaining contract database | ☐ developing budgets and monitoring expenses | ☐ preparing inspection deficiency reports | ☐ recommending corrective actions | ☐ reviewing and approving cost estimates | ☐ approving contracting changes | ☐ holding meetings to discuss project progress processing documents | ☐ other: _____].

☐ **Initiate and implement** _____ *[type of]* [☐ policy formulation | ☐ procedure development | ☐ improvement methods] **in the areas of** [☐ safety | ☐ emergency measures | ☐ other: _____] **which served to improve** _____ *[what process?]*.

☐ **Review** [☐ construction schedules | ☐ job cost reports | ☐ payment requisitions | ☐ other: _____] **for** _____ *[purpose]* **and prepare and generate** [☐ monthly | ☐ weekly | ☐ periodic] **cost reports on** _____ *[type of projects]* **to** [☐ senior technical staff | ☐ senior management | ☐ project engineers | ☐ others: _____].

☐ **Apply expertise in** [☐ specifications preparation | ☐ bid evaluations | ☐ bid awards | ☐ standard price and purchasing reference sources | ☐ modern purchasing methods and practices | ☐ government polices | ☐ other: _____] **in the procurement of** _____ *[what?]* **resulting in** _____ *[benefits]*.

☐ [☐ Compose and update | ☐ Draft and edit] _____ *[type of]* [☐ contracts | ☐ agreements | ☐ technical material | (☐ company / ☐ department) policies and procedures | ☐ other: _____] **for** _____ *[purpose]*.

☐ **Perform** [☐ materials costing | ☐ job estimating | ☐ contract negotiations | ☐ other: _____] **with** [☐ contractors | ☐ suppliers | ☐ other: _____] **of** _____ *[type of]* **jobs ranging $**_____ **to $**_____ *[amounts]*.

☐ **Define, plan, and implement** _____ *[type of]* **projects including the** [☐ design | ☐ development | ☐ implementation | ☐ tracking | ☐ other: _____] **of those projects in support of the firm's business objectives.**

☐ **Accurately maintain up-to-date** [☐ job file records | ☐ project database information | ☐ project invoices | ☐ contractor's shop drawings | ☐ product data | ☐ field reports | ☐ other: _____] **and other records ensuring** _____ *[what?]*.

☐ **Accurately update and maintain** _____ *[type of]* [☐ documents | ☐ files | ☐ reports | ☐ other: _____] **according to** [☐ legal requirements | ☐ the firm's policies and procedures | ☐ other: _____].

☐ **Develop and maintain all** _____ *[type of]* [☐ systems | ☐ records | ☐ data | ☐ information | ☐ other: _____]; **and provide accurate periodic** [☐ progress | ☐ revenue | ☐ campaign | ☐ other: _____] **reports to** _____ *[whom?]*.

☐ **Review, approve, and implement** ☐ [legal | ☐ technical | ☐ other: _____] **documents to** [☐ ensure they conform to current standards and regulations | ☐ incorporate new developments | ☐ maintain optimal production | ☐ other purpose: _____].

☐ **Research, coordinate, document, edit, and periodically update the publication of** [☐ legal | ☐ policy and procedure | ☐ training | ☐ other: _____] **manuals and related** [☐ legal | ☐ technical | ☐ public information | ☐ user | ☐ other: _____] materials.

☐ **Document, implement, and monitor** _____ *[type of]* **quality assurance procedures ensuring their implementation on all projects including** [☐ client relationship management | ☐ contract drafting | ☐ legal document management | ☐ rights and clearances documentation | ☐ financial data verification | ☐ database updating | ☐ vendor compliance | ☐ project tracking | ☐ executive approval process | ☐ other: _____].

☐ **Process** [☐ customer invoices | ☐ correspondence | ☐ payments | ☐ other: _____] **in a timely manner.**

☐ **Coordinate new practices with** [☐ research and development | ☐ manufacturing | ☐ auditing | ☐ marketing | ☐ regulatory affairs | ☐ legal | ☐ other: _____] **personnel to** [☐ research existing practices | ☐ analyze auditing requirements | ☐ ensure compliance with all regulations | ☐ other: _____].

☐ **Work with the firm's** [☐ internal counsel | ☐ outside attorney] **to resolve** _____ *[type of]* **legal matters.**

ACHIEVEMENT SAMPLES: *See Achievement Samples under "Administrative Management & Leadership."*

Administrative Management & Leadership

See also "Business Management & Leadership," "Office Management & Supervision" and "Staff Management & Supervision."

☐ **Provide leadership and support to the** _____ *[which?]* **department(s) overseeing various** [☐ operational aspects of | ☐ administrative support services for] **this $**_____ *[revenues]* _____ *[type of firm]*, **covering** [☐ cost management | ☐ records management | ☐ research and analysis | ☐ procedures development | ☐ materials distribution | ☐ other: _____].

☐ **Oversee the administrative and office support services including** [☐ budget preparation | ☐ evaluation and reporting | ☐ contract negotiations | ☐ assignment of jobs | ☐ appointment scheduling | ☐ approval of time cards | ☐ supplies purchasing | ☐ material requisitions | ☐ recordkeeping | ☐ data entry | ☐ reception area | ☐ other: _____].

☐ **Facilitate business management of this** _____ *[type of]* **firm including** [☐ leading and overseeing projects | ☐ prioritizing projects and balancing competing demands | ☐ establishing quality control procedures | ☐ developing budgets and monitoring expenses | ☐ reviewing and approving cost estimates | ☐ holding meetings to discuss project progress processing documents | ☐ other: _____].

☐ **Direct office management and administrative activities that include** [☐ pricing strategies development | ☐ contract negotiations | ☐ claims avoidance | ☐ claims and litigations research | ☐ risk management | ☐ quality assurance methods development | ☐ research and analysis | ☐ _____ *(type of)* proposals and estimates | ☐ contractual initiatives | ☐ dispute resolution | ☐ grant applications submittal | ☐ employee interface | ☐ other: _____].

☐ **Manage and direct the firm's office and administrative functions, including** [☐ general office administration | ☐ payroll issues | ☐ data entry | ☐ document processing | ☐ inventory | ☐ purchasing | ☐ other: _____] **for an office staff of** _____ *[#]*.

☐ **Plan, set, and establish** _____ *[type of]* **administrative** [☐ goals | ☐ policies and procedures | ☐ objectives | ☐ budget projections | ☐ expense planning | ☐ other: _____].

☐ **Direct the day-to-day** _____ *[which?]* **administrative functions of this** [☐ multibillion-dollar | ☐ multimillion-dollar | ☐ $_____ (revenues)] _____ *[type of]* **firm including** _____, _____, **and** _____ *[which areas?]*.

☐ **Manage and oversee various** [☐ operational aspects of | ☐ administrative support services for] **this $_____** *[revenues]* _____ *[type of firm]*, **including** [☐ payroll | ☐ word processing | ☐ records management | ☐ data processing | ☐ materials distribution | ☐ security | ☐ computer troubleshooting | ☐ other: _____].

☐ **Serve on** _____ *[which?]* **Committee that** [☐ formulates | ☐ improves | ☐ recommends | ☐ prioritizes | ☐ coordinates | ☐ implements | ☐ establishes | ☐ tests | ☐ approves | ☐ monitors] _____ *[what?]* **for the purpose of** *[what outcome or benefits?]*.

☐ **Manage the coordination and facilitation of** [☐ office management | ☐ general administration | ☐ human resources | ☐ payroll processing | ☐ benefits administration | ☐ purchasing | ☐ inventory management and control | ☐ other: _____] **functions for this** _____ *[type of]* **firm.**

☐ **Supervise all** _____ *[type of]* **office administration activities including** [☐ budget preparation | ☐ the direction of trades work | ☐ assignment of jobs | ☐ verification and approval of material requisitions | ☐ approval of time cards | ☐ other: _____].

☐ [☐ **Direct and oversee** | ☐ **Supervise**] **all administrative support services, including** [☐ payroll | ☐ inventory | ☐ purchasing | ☐ other: _____] **for** _____ *[#]* [☐ departments | ☐ offices | ☐ other: _____] **requiring** [☐ accurate data entry of all information | ☐ determining ordering needs | ☐ other: _____].

☐ **Manage** [☐ office operations | ☐ administrative services | ☐ other: _____] **including** [☐ office space planning | ☐ procedures development | ☐ other: _____].

ACHIEVEMENT SAMPLES:

☐ **Assisted the** [☐ Executive Director | ☐ President | ☐ other title: _____] **in** [☐ evaluating | ☐ prioritizing | ☐ coordinating | ☐ developing | ☐ establishing | ☐ other: _____] **long-range** _____ *[type of]* **plans including** [☐ system-wide policies and standards | ☐ technology enhancements | ☐ other: _____].

☐ **Designed and executed** _____ *[type of]* [☐ administrative | ☐ operational | ☐ other: _____] **solutions that effectively addressed and adhered to the firm's requirements** [☐ in accordance with all project timelines and budget | ☐ verifying quality project standards | ☐ ensuring a smooth transition | ☐ other: _____].

☐ **Built a strong, supportive administrative team environment by exhibiting and modeling leadership skills in** [☐ communication | ☐ negotiation | ☐ problem-solving | ☐ obstacle tackling | ☐ other: _____].

☐ **Spearheaded and implemented a** _____ *[type of]* [☐ program | ☐ policy | ☐ procedure] **that** _____ *[did what?]*.

☐ **Championed** [☐ large-scale | ☐ complex | ☐ cross-organizational | ☐ other: _____] _____ *[type of]* [☐ administrative | ☐ operational] [☐ program | ☐ system | ☐ policy | ☐ procedures | ☐ solutions | ☐ implementation projects | ☐ other: _____] **involving** _____ *[what?]* **that** _____ *[accomplished what?]* **by** _____ *[doing what?]*.

☐ **Converted the firm's manual processing** _____ *[type of]* **office system to a functional** [☐ peer-to-peer] _____ *[type of]* **computerized** [☐ account database | ☐ billing | ☐ payroll | ☐ accounting | ☐ other: _____] [☐ system | ☐ environment] **increasing overall** [☐ productivity | ☐ efficiency | ☐ sales | ☐ other: _____] **increasing overall** [☐ productivity | ☐ efficiency | ☐ sales | ☐ other: _____].

☐ **Conceptualized, developed, and managed a $**_____ *[revenues]* _____ *[type of]* [☐ network | ☐ division | ☐ other: _____] **by** _____ *[doing what?]*, **resulting in it becoming the backbone of the company's growth from** _____ *[what size or measure?]* **to** _____ *[what size or measure?]*.

☐ **Assisted the** [☐ Executive Director | ☐ President | ☐ other title: _____] **in** [☐ evaluating | ☐ prioritizing | ☐ coordinating | ☐ developing | ☐ establishing | ☐ other: _____] **long-range** _____ *[type of]* **plans including** [☐ repair and improvement projects | ☐ building renewal plans | ☐ system-wide policies and standards | ☐ technology enhancements | ☐ other: _____].

☐ **Managed and implemented the firm's corporate** [☐ domestic | ☐ international] **travel policy, resulting in annual cost reductions of $**_____ *[amount]* **in** [☐ air travel | ☐ hotel rental | ☐ car rental | ☐ meal expenses | ☐ other: _____].

☐ **Organized company's move from a** _____ *[#]*-**square foot building in** _____ *[what town?]* **to a** _____ *[#]*- **square foot building** [☐ in the business section] **of** _____ *[what town?]*, **allowing the firm to** [☐ construct a front office | ☐ increase staff size | ☐ stock more supplies and materials | ☐ other: _____].

☐ **Managed and coordinated** [☐ continuous | ☐ frequent] _____ *[type of]* **office space planning to accommodate** _____% *[percentage]* **employee growth in** _____ *[#]* **years. Required** [☐ locating | ☐ building | ☐ leasing | ☐ renovating | ☐ furnishing | ☐ other: _____] **offices within** _____ *[#]* **months of notice, including** [☐ telephone systems | ☐ equipment | ☐ furniture | ☐ other: _____].

☐ **Spearheaded and implemented a** _____ *[type of]* [☐ program | ☐ policy | ☐ procedures] **that** [☐ maximized service and equipment utilization | ☐ other: _____] **by** _____ *[doing what?]*.

- ☐ **Designed and executed** _____ *[type of]* [☐ administrative | ☐ operational | ☐ other: _____] **solutions that effectively addressed and adhered to** [☐ firm's | ☐ clients'] **requirements** [☐ in accordance with all project timelines and budget | ☐ verifying quality project standards | ☐ ensuring a smooth transition | ☐ other: _____].

- ☐ [☐ **Developed and established** | ☐ **Recommended and implemented**] _____ *[type of]* [☐ management] [☐ plans | ☐ standards | ☐ guidelines | ☐ policies | ☐ procedures | ☐ methods | ☐ other: _____] **that maximized the effective use of** _____ *[what?]* **and supported the continuing improvement of** _____ *[which?]* **standards.**

- ☐ **Recruited as right hand to** _____ *[title]* **to save a once-profitable company from a then-floundering situation ($**_____ *[amount]* **loss on $**_____ *[amount]* **in sales) through effective** [☐ strategic and tactical efforts | ☐ other: _____] **resulting in its turnaround to $**_____ *[amount]* **profit on $**_____ *[amount]* **sales.**

- ☐ **Developed and implemented a** _____ *[type of]* **change involving** _____ *[what?]* **that resulted in** [☐ better inventory control | ☐ improved workflow | ☐ increased productivity | ☐ streamlined operations | ☐ other: _____] **in the areas of** _____, _____, **and** _____ *[what areas?].*

- ☐ **Built a strong, supportive administrative team environment by exhibiting and modeling leadership skills in** [☐ communication | ☐ negotiation | ☐ problem-solving | ☐ obstacle tackling | ☐ other: _____].

- ☐ **Involved in** [☐ managing | ☐ performing | ☐ coordinating | ☐ facilitating | ☐ other: _____] _____ *[what?]* **efforts that required** _____ *[what actions?]* **to meet** _____ *[what challenges?]* **and resulted in** _____ *[benefits].*

Awards & Recognition – Construction Trades

ACHIEVEMENT SAMPLES:

- ☐ **Starting as** [☐ Apprentice | ☐ Laborer | ☐ Carpenter | ☐ Superintendent | ☐ other: _____], **received promotions to** [☐ Labor Foreman | ☐ Lead Carpenter | ☐ General Foreman | ☐ Construction Superintendent | ☐ Project Manager | ☐ other: _____] **by learning the tools of the trade and exceeding expectations in the performance of** _____ *[list functions].*

- ☐ **Selected amongst** _____ *[#]* **other laborers to perform** _____, _____, **and** _____ *[which activities?]* **for** _____ *[purpose].*

- ☐ **Commended by** [☐ Project Manager | ☐ Site Foreman | ☐ Facility Manager | ☐ Building Operations Manager | ☐ Project Superintendent | ☐ _____ *(type of)* client | ☐ other: _____] **for** [☐ performance in the areas of _____, _____, **and** _____ *(which areas?)* | ☐ contributing to a safe workplace environment | ☐ other: _____] **by** [☐ providing strategic insights in the _____ *(what project or function?)* | ☐ identifying and reporting safety hazards | ☐ successfully completing _____ *(what?)* | ☐ other: _____].

- ☐ **Recipient of the "**_____**"** *[name of award]* **by** _____ *[whom?]* **for outstanding contributions in the areas of** _____, _____, **and** _____ *[which areas?].*

- ☐ **Commended by** _____ *[whom?]* **for** [☐ performance in the areas of _____, _____, **and** _____ *(which areas?)* | ☐ contributing to a safe workplace environment | ☐ other: _____] **by successfully completing** _____ *[what?].*

- ☐ **Selected amongst** _____ *[#]* [☐ other laborers | ☐ peers] **to** [☐ oversee | ☐ perform | ☐ facilitate | ☐ other: _____] _____, _____, **and** _____ *[which activities?]* **for** _____ *[what purpose?].*

- ☐ **Received** [(☐ excellent | ☐ high performing) evaluations from superiors | ☐ commendations from clients | ☐ congratulatory letters | ☐ recommendations | ☐ testimonials | ☐ other: _____] **for** [☐ precise workmanship | ☐ dependability | ☐ professional expertise | ☐ other: _____] **in the performance of** _____ *[what?].*

- ☐ **Selected to travel to** _____ *[where?]* **with company to** [☐ train crew | ☐ construct _____ *(what?)* | ☐ set up a repair facility | ☐ other: _____] **that involved** _____ *[what functions?]* **and resulted in** _____ *[what benefits?].*

- ☐ **Earned an outstanding reputation for knowledge and expertise** [☐ in the areas of _____, _____, **and** _____ *(which areas?)* | ☐ as trusted advisor to senior management | ☐ other: _____].

- ☐ **Received commendations from** [☐ client | ☐ employer | ☐ other: _____] **for** [☐ professional expertise | ☐ dedication to job | ☐ other: _____]. **(See "Testimonials.")** *[Note: Include a "Testimonials" section in resume.]*

- ☐ **Recruited as** _____ *[job title]*, **received promotions to** _____ *[job title]* **and** _____ *[job title]*, **by exceeding expectations in the performance of** _____, _____, **and** _____ *[list functions].*

- ☐ **Originally assigned as** _____ *[title]* **for** _____ *[type of work]*, **and within** _____ *[time period]* **received promotion to** _____ *[title].*

Bids & Proposals

See also "Purchasing," "Contract Negotiations," "Contracts Administration," and "Contracts Development & Review."

☐ **Direct and lead the review and evaluation of vendor** [☐ proposals | ☐ bids | ☐ specifications] **and selection of vendors with awards issued based on product** [☐ quality | ☐ value | ☐ source | ☐ usefulness | ☐ unique features and benefits | ☐ broad target market | ☐ copyrights | ☐ pricing | ☐ payment terms | ☐ delivery dates | ☐ shipping charges | ☐ packaging | ☐ final cost | ☐ other: _____] **for this** _____ *[type of]* **firm which services the** _____ *[which?]* **market.**

☐ **Review and evaluate bids and issue awards using** [☐ value analysis | ☐ lifecycle costing | ☐ weighted value procedures | ☐ value analysis | ☐ other: _____] **for** _____ *[what?].*

☐ **Obtain, review, and verify** _____ *[type of]* [☐ bids | ☐ plans | ☐ specifications | ☐ cost estimates | ☐ contracts | ☐ other: _____] **checking for compliance with** [☐ the firm's | ☐ clients' | ☐ department's] **requirements and** [☐ the Environmental Quality Act | ☐ Occupational Safety and Health Act | ☐ other: _____].

☐ **Determine** _____ *[type of]* [☐ requirements | ☐ methods of acquisition | ☐ material costs | ☐ other: _____], **prepare bid specifications, select vendors, and obtain written** [☐ bids | ☐ quotes | ☐ estimates] **on all** _____ *[what?].*

☐ **Conduct** [☐ vendor bids | ☐ comparative cost analyses | ☐ other: _____], **and make sound selections based on** [☐ quality | ☐ reliability | ☐ ability to meet required deadlines | ☐ other: _____] **for** _____ *[what?].*

☐ **Apply expertise in** [☐ specifications preparation | ☐ bid evaluations | ☐ bid awards | ☐ standard price and purchasing reference sources | ☐ modern purchasing methods and practices | ☐ government polices | ☐ other: _____] **in the procurement of** _____ *[what?]* **resulting in** _____ *[benefits].*

☐ **In ordering** _____ *[type of]* [☐ services | ☐ materials | ☐ supplies | ☐ equipment | ☐ tools | ☐ other: _____], **monitor and evaluate** [☐ vendor performance | ☐ price changes | ☐ back orders | ☐ other: _____], **correspond with vendors regarding** [☐ product | ☐ consumer | ☐ contract | ☐ other: _____] **problems, resolving any product delivery problems.**

☐ **Monitor and evaluate** [☐ vendor performance | ☐ price changes | ☐ back orders | ☐ other: _____]; **and correspond with vendors regarding any** [☐ product | ☐ consumer | ☐ contract | ☐ other: _____] **problems to work out solutions to the customers' satisfaction.**

☐ **Evaluate and interpret** _____ *[type of]* **product information, identify purchasing alternatives, prepare specifications, develop contracts, and initiate** _____ *[type of]* **purchasing transactions.**

☐ **Review and evaluate all vendor** [☐ proposals | ☐ bids | ☐ specifications]; **select appropriate vendors; and issue awards based on** [☐ quality | ☐ value | ☐ source | ☐ usefulness | ☐ features | ☐ benefits | ☐ pricing | ☐ payment terms | (☐ availability / ☐ delivery) dates | ☐ shipping charges | ☐ final costs | ☐ other: _____] **factors.**

☐ **Perform detailed reviews of** [☐ purchase orders | ☐ invoices | ☐ requisitions | ☐ job estimates | ☐ other: _____] **to ensure conformance with all policies and procedures and** _____ *[other requirements].*

☐ **Resolve** [☐ product delivery problems | ☐ vendor conflicts | ☐ other: _____] **regarding** [☐ undelivered shipments | ☐ shipment shortages | ☐ product defects | ☐ other: _____].

☐ **Determine** _____ *[type of]* [☐ requirements | ☐ methods of acquisition | ☐ material costs | ☐ other: _____], **prepare bid specifications, select vendors, and obtain written** [☐ bids | ☐ quotes | ☐ estimates] **on all** _____ *[what?].*

☐ **Conduct** [☐ vendor bids | ☐ comparative cost analyses | ☐ other: _____], **and make sound selections based on** [☐ quality | ☐ reliability | ☐ ability to meet required deadlines | ☐ other: _____] **for** _____ *[what?].*

☐ **Apply expertise in** [☐ specifications preparation | ☐ bid evaluations | ☐ bid awards | ☐ standard price and purchasing reference sources | ☐ modern purchasing methods and practices | ☐ government polices | ☐ other: _____] **in the procurement of** _____ *[what?]* **resulting in** _____ *[benefits].*

ACHIEVEMENT SAMPLES:

☐ **Increased margins** _____% *[percentage]* **by conducting** [☐ vendor | ☐ contractor | ☐ subcontractor] **searches for best quality and costs procuring** _____ *[which trades?]* **to** _____ *[do what?]* **for** _____ *[type of]* **projects.**

☐ **Prepared** [☐ commercial | ☐ residential | ☐ industrial | ☐ public works | ☐ other: _____] **construction cost estimates; interpreted commercial plans, contract drawings, and specifications; and obtained construction bids, selected contractors, and negotiated construction contracts on all** _____ *[type of]* **projects resulting in a savings of $**_____ *[amount].*

Billing / Invoicing

See "Client Billing."

Blueprint Reading, Interpreting & Updating

☐ **Read, interpret, and evaluate** _____ [type of] [☐ engineering | ☐ architectural] [☐ drawings | ☐ blueprints | ☐ diagrams | ☐ renderings | ☐ schematics | ☐ plans | ☐ specifications | ☐ other: _____] **for compliance with** _____ [which?] **codes.**

☐ **Review schematic drawings and construction details for** _____ [type of] **projects, make recommendations to modify as needed, and discuss** _____ [type of] **changes with clients before implementation.**

☐ **Interpret, review, and evaluate** _____ [type of] [☐ plans | ☐ specifications | ☐ drawings] **to** [☐ determine compatibility and adaptability with existing systems | ☐ ensure compliance with all codes | ☐ advise (☐ Project Engineer / ☐ Foreman / ☐ other: _____) on code requirements | ☐ other: _____]; **and modify blueprints to meet as-built specifications and dimensions.**

☐ **Interpret and update** [☐ blueprints | ☐ architectural drawings | ☐ plans | ☐ specifications | ☐ other: _____] **to reflect required changes made to** _____ [type of] **systems.**

☐ **Read** _____ [type of] **blueprints to unload the correct amount of** [☐ steel | ☐ wood | ☐ other materials: _____] **for various projects, arrange and lay out materials according to daily project needs, and** [☐ perform | ☐ oversee] **the construction of** _____ [type of work] **on schedule and within budget.**

☐ **Read and interpret** _____ [type of] [☐ blueprints | ☐ plans ☐ scale drawings | ☐ architectural details | ☐ other: _____] **regarding** [☐ design | ☐ specifications | ☐ materials | ☐ color | ☐ equipment | ☐ other: _____] **for the building of** _____ [what?], **and discuss changes with clients before implementing.**

☐ **Suggested design improvements to** _____ [what?], **which helped facilitate** _____ [what?] **and resulted in** _____ [what benefits?].

Budget Development & Expenditure Control

☐ **Perform** [☐ site evaluations | ☐ reports | ☐ construction budget estimates | ☐ schedules | ☐ other: _____] **of proposed** _____ [type of] **projects.**

☐ **Assist** [☐ Construction Project Manager | ☐ other: _____] **with preparation of** [☐ Request for Proposals | ☐ preliminary budgets | ☐ General Contractor bids | ☐ construction contracts | ☐ other: _____] **for new construction projects.**

☐ **Ensure** [☐ owner | ☐ contractor | ☐ other: _____] **contingencies are established and included within project budgets.**

☐ **Review and approve all** [☐ contracts | ☐ changes orders | ☐ applications | ☐ other: _____] **for** [☐ payment | ☐ invoices | ☐ project budgets | ☐ other: _____].

☐ **Develop, oversee, and monitor annual operating budgets and provide fiscal direction to the** _____ [which?] **Department(s) in the areas of** _____, _____, **and** _____ [which areas?].

☐ **Provide fiscal oversight for a $_____** [amount] _____ [which?] **budget to meet all** _____ [type of] **goals and objectives.**

☐ **Administer and monitor a $_____** [amount] _____ [which?] **budget, all** _____ [type of] **spending, and statistics on** _____ [what?]; **and approve** [☐ major expenditures | ☐ budget adjustments | ☐ other: _____] **ensuring spending is within budget and properly allocated.**

☐ **Develop and manage** _____ [type of] **budgets of $_____** [amount] [☐ monthly | ☐ annually | ☐ per project] **ensuring all expenditures remain within budgetary allotments and company guidelines.**

☐ **Estimate cost expenditures for future** _____ [type of] **project needs including evaluating** [☐ equipment life expectancy | ☐ equipment replacement costs | ☐ materials and supplies for anticipated projects | ☐ other: _____] **to ensure** _____ [what?].

☐ **Develop project budgets, monitor costs, and analyze expenses ensuring** [☐ all projects remain within budget | ☐ cost savings can be realized whenever possible to increase profitability | ☐ other: _____].

☐ **Prepare monthly budget variance analyses for all projections versus actual expenditures; and provide explanations to** _____ [whom?] **for any budgetary deviations.**

☐ [☐ Prepare | ☐ Assist in the preparation of] [☐ the firm's financial objectives | ☐ the annual budget | ☐ expenditure scheduling | ☐ variance analysis | ☐ corrective actions | ☐ other: _____] **for** _____ [what?].

☐ **Regularly monitor and review** _____ [type of] **project reports and status including reporting of** [☐ budget variances | ☐ schedule compliance | (☐ firm / ☐ division / ☐ departmental) performance indicators / ☐ other: _____].

☐ **Implement and oversee the departmental budget of $_____** [amount]; **and** [☐ review | ☐ monitor | ☐ approve] **all related expenses.**

☐ **Control _____** [which?] **expenses by** [☐ reviewing profit and loss statements | ☐ staying within budgets | ☐ cutting expenses where possible | ☐ other method(s): _____].

Building Inspections

See "Inspection & Compliance – Buildings & Structures."

Building Maintenance Scope

See also "Building Maintenance & Repair," "Preventive & Seasonal Maintenance," and "Carpentry / Construction Work."

☐ **Manage** [☐ a facility | ☐ a corporate | ☐ an industrial | ☐ other: _____] **maintenance team of _____** [#] [☐ superintendents | ☐ foremen | ☐ electricians | ☐ carpenters | ☐ maintenance workers | ☐ custodians | ☐ other: _____] **covering** [☐ two | ☐ three] **shifts of operation.**

☐ **Perform** [☐ building | ☐ facilities | ☐ grounds | ☐ other: _____] **maintenance functions for this _____** [type of] **firm including** [☐ construction | ☐ renovation | ☐ repair | ☐ remodel | ☐ other: _____] **projects ensuring they meet all** [☐ government | ☐ environmental | ☐ health | ☐ safety | ☐ security | ☐ other: _____] **standards.**

☐ **Conduct** [☐ facilities | ☐ building maintenance | ☐ grounds upkeep | ☐ space planning | ☐ remodel | ☐ other: _____] **projects for this _____** [#]**-square foot building with ground acreage of _____** [#] **and _____** [#] [☐ employees | ☐ work stations | ☐ offices | ☐ facilities | ☐ other: _____].

☐ **Maintain** [☐ buildings | ☐ facilities | ☐ grounds | ☐ other: _____] **in good repair including** [☐ heating | ☐ air conditioning | ☐ plumbing | ☐ electrical | ☐ wood | ☐ drywall | ☐ wall coverings | ☐ insulation | ☐ drop ceilings | ☐ painting | ☐ grading | ☐ underground utilities | ☐ drains | ☐ gutters | ☐ paving | ☐ other: _____].

☐ **Handle various** [☐ buildings | ☐ facilities | ☐ grounds | ☐ other: _____] **maintenance functions including** [☐ building maintenance and repair | ☐ office relocations | ☐ renovations | ☐ remodeling | ☐ roofing repairs | ☐ machinery maintenance and repair | ☐ regular and preventive maintenance | ☐ carpentry | ☐ electrical wiring | ☐ plumbing | ☐ HVAC systems | ☐ painting | ☐ custodial services | ☐ janitorial maintenance | ☐ groundskeeping | ☐ security systems | ☐ sprinkler systems | ☐ fire extinguisher and smoke alarm inspections | ☐ safety checks | ☐ boiler system | ☐ water system | ☐ heating system | ☐ cooling system | ☐ machinery maintenance and repair | ☐ other: _____].

☐ **Conduct the repair and maintenance of all** [☐ plumbing | ☐ electrical | ☐ HVAC | ☐ motors | ☐ appliances | ☐ fixtures | ☐ lights | ☐ ballasts | ☐ receptacles | ☐ switches | ☐ other: _____] **to** [☐ help improve the work environment | ☐ maintain proper operation of all equipment | ☐ maintain compliance with all OSHA and environmental regulations | ☐ other: _____].

☐ **Perform the** [☐ structural | ☐ mechanical | ☐ electrical | ☐ plumbing | ☐ other: _____] **aspects of _____** [type of] **building** [☐ design | ☐ utilization | ☐ space planning | ☐ construction | ☐ operation | ☐ maintenance | ☐ repair | ☐ remodel | ☐ other: _____] **projects ensuring that all work is performed in compliance with building codes, laws, and regulations.**

☐ **Apply** [☐ expert | ☐ proficient | ☐ working] knowledge of [☐ general principles and practices of building construction | ☐ building maintenance | ☐ physical plant operations | ☐ technical systems | ☐ building codes | ☐ ordinances | ☐ fire regulations | ☐ safety precautions | ☐ health and safety regulations | ☐ automated building control | ☐ indoor air quality | ☐ energy management systems | ☐ record-keeping techniques | ☐ other: _____] **to all aspects of building maintenance.**

☐ **Operate and maintain the company's fleet of _____** [#] [☐ lift trucks | ☐ pickup trucks | ☐ forklifts | ☐ hydraulic boom lifts | ☐ boom trucks | ☐ digger derricks | ☐ bucket trucks | ☐ other: _____].

ACHIEVEMENT SAMPLES: *See "Building Operations Projects," "Construction Projects," and various trades achievements.*

Building Maintenance & Repair

☐ **Coordinate all aspects of the physical workplace ensuring** [☐ the integration and coordination of business practices | ☐ work and people requirements | ☐ fulfilling maintenance and repairs | ☐ other: _____].

☐ **Assist the** [☐ Building Superintendent | ☐ Facilities Manager | ☐ other: _____] **in** [☐ evaluating | ☐ prioritizing | ☐ coordinating | ☐ developing | ☐ establishing] **long-range facility plans including** [☐ office relocations | ☐ repair and improvement projects | ☐ building renewal plans | ☐ system-wide policies and standards | ☐ regular, preventive, and seasonal maintenance | ☐ technical requirements | ☐ other: _____].

☐ **Perform skilled maintenance and repair of** _____ [type of] [☐ buildings | ☐ complexes | ☐ facilities] **in the areas of** _____, _____, **and** _____ [which areas?].

☐ **Handle** [☐ new construction | ☐ remodeling | ☐ repair | ☐ maintenance | ☐ leasing | ☐ space planning | ☐ other: _____] **projects of** _____ [what?] **that require** _____ [what actions?].

☐ **Provide building** [☐ maintenance | ☐ space planning | ☐ renovations | ☐ repairs | ☐ other: _____] **ensuring the physical, mechanical, and electrical aspects of the facility run smoothly including** [☐ examining facility for damage and leaks | ☐ maintaining building heating system and boilers | ☐ performing cooling system maintenance and repair | ☐ repairing water heaters | ☐ maintaining emergency generator | ☐ maintaining plumbing, electrical, and HVAC systems | ☐ performing carpentry work | ☐ maintaining sprinkler systems | ☐ checking security systems | ☐ performing groundskeeping | ☐ painting (☐ walls / ☐ furniture) | ☐ setting up sound systems | ☐ using specialized tools and equipment | ☐ replacing outlets and switches | ☐ ensuring vehicles are in safe operating condition | ☐ responding to emergency repair situations | ☐ installing lighting circuits | ☐ upgrading electrical wiring | ☐ repairing faucets and toilets | ☐ cutting, threading, and soldering piping | ☐ performing safety checks | ☐ repairing pumps | ☐ replacing seals, bearings, and couplings | ☐ other: _____].

☐ **Assist the** [☐ Foreman | ☐ Assistant Foreman | ☐ General Maintenance Foreman | ☐ other: _____] **in various administrative activities including** [☐ budget preparation | ☐ work direction | ☐ job assignments | ☐ material requisitions verification | ☐ time cards review | ☐ research and analysis | ☐ feasibility studies | ☐ other: _____].

☐ **On call 24 hours per day seven days a week, respond to emergency repair situations such as** _____ [what?] **by** _____ [doing what?] **resulting in** _____ [what benefits?].

☐ **Prepare recommendations to** _____ [whom?] **regarding** [☐ contractual defaults | ☐ time extensions | ☐ liquidated damages | ☐ other: _____].

☐ **Provide support and feedback to** [☐ Building Superintendent | ☐ Facilities Manager | ☐ other: _____] **regarding** [☐ maintenance | ☐ structural | ☐ mechanical | ☐ environmental | ☐ other: _____] **issues at the site**.

☐ **Helped improve the workplace and work environment by** _____ [doing what?], **which has resulted in** _____ [what benefits?].

☐ **Assisted Licensed Electrician in electrical installations and repairs of this** _____ [#]-square foot building to ensure plant is in compliance with all electrical codes.**

ACHIEVEMENT SAMPLES: *See "Building Operations Projects" and "Facility Management."*

Building Operations Management

See also "Building Operations Projects," "Facility Management," "Operations Management," and "Office Management."

☐ **Manage the day-to-day operations of** _____ [type of] **building including** [☐ reviewing project schedules | ☐ coordinating resources and materials | ☐ ordering supplies and equipment | ☐ identifying issues | ☐ troubleshooting and resolving problems | ☐ adhering to contract scope, specifications, and code | ☐ managing materials and inventory levels | ☐ accurately completing all assignment-related paperwork | ☐ other: _____].

☐ **Direct and oversee building operations and** _____ [type of] **construction projects for this** [☐ established | ☐ leading | ☐ national | ☐ other: _____] [☐ commercial construction firm | ☐ engineering and design consultancy | ☐ design(☐ -and-build) firm | ☐ construction management company | ☐ other: _____] **including** [☐ the application process | ☐ work oversight | ☐ operations budget | ☐ other: _____].

☐ **Manage the delivery of the** [☐ operations | ☐ facility maintenance | ☐ other: _____] **program, providing leadership to the** [☐ facilities | ☐ building maintenance | ☐ subcontractor | ☐ other: _____] **team(s) to ensure success.**

☐ **Plan, direct, and supervise all** _____ [type of] [☐ design | ☐ construction | ☐ fabrication | ☐ installation | ☐ repair | ☐ preventive maintenance | ☐ other: _____] **tasks required for** _____ [what?].

☐ **Direct day-to-day office operations of this** [☐ multibillion-dollar | ☐ multimillion-dollar | ☐ $_____] [☐ construction management | ☐ general-contracting | ☐ other: _____] **firm providing a full array of** _____ [type of] **services including the** [☐ design | ☐ construction | ☐ installation | ☐ risk management | ☐ security | ☐ building repair | ☐ maintenance | ☐ claims litigation | ☐ other: _____] **of** _____ [what?].

☐ **Act as liaison with customer and project staff to ensure positive customer relationships, job satisfaction, and service quality and to** [☐ properly identify and process scope changes | ☐ address and resolve any issues | ☐ communicate regarding project milestones | ☐ other: _____].

☐ **Working with** _____ [whom?], **develop, implement, and maintain** [☐ long-term | ☐ short-range] [☐ company | ☐ departmental | ☐ other: _____] [☐ plans | ☐ goals | ☐ objectives | ☐ projects | ☐ programs] **as well as operating policies and procedures.**

☐ **Regularly Communicate with** [☐ Project Manager | ☐ Superintendent | ☐ Maintenance Manager | ☐ general contractors | ☐ architects | ☐ engineers | ☐ crew | ☐ vendors | ☐ inspectors | ☐ others: _____] **regarding** [☐ production schedules | ☐ material and labor management | ☐ work production status | ☐ scope changes | ☐ back charges | ☐ change orders | ☐ other: _____].

☐ **Document reports and maintain up-to-date records of** [☐ individual's time | ☐ man hours expended on job orders | ☐ accidents and injuries | ☐ work progress | ☐ other: _____].

☐ **Assist the** [☐ Executive Director | ☐ Construction Vice President | ☐ other title: _____] **in** [☐ evaluating | ☐ prioritizing | ☐ coordinating | ☐ developing | ☐ establishing] **long-range** _____ [type of] **plans including** [☐ repair and improvement projects | ☐ building renewal plans | ☐ system-wide policies and standards | ☐ technical requirements | ☐ other: _____].

☐ **Review and approve all project-related** [☐ plans | ☐ specifications | ☐ cost estimates | ☐ change authorizations | ☐ pay requests | ☐ funds disbursements | ☐ other: _____].

☐ **Manage and oversee the company's** [☐ daily operations | ☐ day-to-day activities | ☐ support services | ☐ inventory | ☐ other: _____] **to maximize efficiency and** [☐ cut costs | ☐ strategize new ways to increase profitability | ☐ other: _____].

☐ **Lead and direct this** _____ [type of] **firm's operations to ensure maximum** [☐ productivity | ☐ efficiency | ☐ performance | ☐ profitability | ☐ other: _____] **through effective organizational** [☐ strategies | ☐ methods | ☐ policies | ☐ practices | ☐ procedures] **including supporting better** [☐ information flow | ☐ business processes | ☐ organizational planning | ☐ operational procedures | ☐ other: _____].

☐ **Plan, direct, and coordinate the firm's operations; improve performance, productivity, and profitability; and ensure smooth, efficient operations** [☐ that meets the needs and expectations of (☐ customers / ☐ clients) | ☐ in support of the firm's mission | ☐ through the implementation of effective _____ [type of] methods and strategies | ☐ other: _____].

☐ **Develop** _____ [type of] [☐ objectives | ☐ strategies | ☐ plans | ☐ programs | ☐ policies | ☐ procedures | ☐ methods | ☐ standards | ☐ cost/price models | ☐ other: _____] **for** _____ [what?] **that include** [☐ long-range (☐ objectives / ☐ forecasts / ☐ financial plans) | ☐ pricing strategy | ☐ marketing strategy | ☐ product-marketing strategies | ☐ advertising campaigns | ☐ sales promotions | ☐ other: _____] **that** [☐ increase the firm's efficiency and effectiveness | ☐ meet the organization's goals].

☐ **Guide and support** _____ [which?] [☐ Departments | ☐ teams] **to operate efficiently and meet the firm's goals covering** [☐ general business operations | ☐ recruitment | ☐ contract negotiations | ☐ budget matters | ☐ other: _____].

☐ **Apply** [☐ in-depth knowledge of | ☐ proficiency in] [☐ building codes and standards | ☐ structural and mechanical aspects of commercial buildings | ☐ safety and fire prevention methods and standards | ☐ other: _____] **in the development and execution of** _____ [what?].

☐ **Train and support** _____ [title(s)] **in** [☐ proper work methods | ☐ new equipment usage | ☐ safe practices | ☐ quality control methods | ☐ regulatory compliance | ☐ other: _____].

ACHIEVEMENT SAMPLES: *See "Building Operations Projects," "Facility Management," and "Construction Projects."*

Building Operations Projects

See also "Building Operations Management," "Facility Management – Functions," and "Construction Projects," as applicable.

☐ **Manage the completion of** _____ [#] _____ [type of] **jobs** [☐ weekly | ☐ monthly | ☐ annually] [☐ averaging $_____ to $_____ (amounts) | ☐ totaling $_____] including [☐ estimating job times, materials, and costs | ☐ selecting materials and hardware | ☐ preparing materials estimates | ☐ reviewing bids | ☐ ordering required job-related materials | scheduling jobs | ☐ inspecting completed jobs for code compliance | ☐ other: _____].

☐ **Define, plan, and implement** _____ [type of] **projects including the** [☐ design | ☐ development | ☐ implementation | ☐ tracking | ☐ other: _____] **of those projects in support of the firm's business objectives**.

☐ **Facilitate business management and inspection functions including** [☐ leading and overseeing projects | ☐ prioritizing projects and balancing competing demands | ☐ reviewing contracts to verify legal requirements | ☐ translating requirements into effective legal solutions | ☐ establishing quality control procedures | ☐ developing revenue contracts | ☐ preparing specifications | ☐ performing inspections to facilitate quality assurance | ☐ identifying contractual problems or errors | ☐ quality testing materials | ☐ researching and writing (☐ legal / ☐ technical) procedures | ☐ setting up and maintaining contract database | ☐ developing budgets and monitoring expenses | ☐ preparing inspection deficiency reports | ☐ recommending corrective actions | ☐ reviewing cost estimates | ☐ approving contracting changes | ☐ holding meetings to discuss project progress | ☐ processing documents | ☐ other: _____].

☐ **Manage and oversee all aspects of** _____ *[type of]* **facilities projects including** [☐ project scope | ☐ initiation | ☐ planning | ☐ scheduling | ☐ budgeting | ☐ team selection | ☐ resource allocation | ☐ quality control | ☐ cost control | ☐ other: _____] **keeping in line with all business objectives.**

ACHIEVEMENT SAMPLES:

☐ **Spearheaded** _____ *[#]*-**square foot** _____ *[type of]* **construction project within** _____ *[#]* [☐ weeks | ☐ months] —_____ *[time frame]* **ahead of schedule—by motivating trades to work additional shifts to meet required deadline.**

☐ **Played key role in establishing** _____ *[#]* [☐ new offices | ☐ relocations | ☐ expansions | ☐ leases | ☐ construction | ☐ other: _____] **to house** _____ *[what?].*

☐ **Coordinated and directed Company's headquarters move from** _____ *[city]* **to** _____ *[city]*, **moving** _____ *[#]* **employees on schedule. Estimated savings of $**_____ *[amount]* **over** _____ *[#]* **years.**

☐ **Championed** [☐ Executive Office | ☐ Headquarters | ☐ other: _____] **relocation from** _____ *[where?]* **to** _____ *[where?].* **Oversaw** [☐ Architect and Construction Contractor | ☐ furniture and equipment purchases | ☐ installation of new telephone system | ☐ other: _____]. **Recipient of** [☐ "President's Award" | ☐ other: _____] **plaque for** [☐ team excellence in the move | ☐ other: _____].

☐ **Managed and coordinated** [☐ continuous | ☐ frequent] _____ *[type of]* **office space planning to accommodate** _____ % *[percentage]* **employee growth in** _____ *[#]* **years. Required** [☐ locating | ☐ building | ☐ leasing | ☐ renovating | ☐ furnishing | ☐ other: _____] **offices within** _____ *[#]* **months of notice, including** [☐ telephone systems | ☐ equipment | ☐ furniture | ☐ other: _____].

☐ **Increased productivity** _____ **% (from** _____ **% to** _____ **%)** *[percentages]* **and saved $**_____ *[amount]* **in annual costs by** [☐ upgrading _____ *(type of)* (☐ systems / ☐ equipment) | ☐ initiating an outsourcing concept for _____ *(which?)* operations | ☐ other: _____], **which** _____ *[did what?].*

☐ **Reviewed and approved floor plans for** _____ *[#]* **new and expanding offices located in** _____ *[where?],* **and worked as liaison with** [☐ architects | ☐ contractors | ☐ building owners | ☐ others: _____].

☐ **Freed up costly warehouse space** _____ **%** *[percentage],* **by** [☐ reducing company-wide records retention | ☐ hiring a Records Retention Consultant to inspect all files | ☐ preparing a Records Retention Policy Manual | ☐ disposing of all unneeded records | ☐ eliminating the need to (☐ purchase / ☐ lease) additional storage space | ☐ other: _____].

☐ **Consolidated** _____ *[#]* **remote storage facilities into one warehouse facility for improved inventory control and accessibility. Reduced travel time to warehouse** _____ **% and saved $**_____ **annually.**

☐ **Facilitated** [☐ design | ☐ construction | ☐ lease negotiations | ☐ other: _____] **of** _____ *[#]* **facilities with a total square footage of** _____ *[#]* **resulting in** _____ *[what benefits?].*

Building Operations Projects Oversight

See also "Building Operations Projects."

☐ **Provide leadership, vision, and direction to a team of** _____ *[#]* **to initiate, plan, and** _____ *[type of]* **projects ranging from $**_____ **to $**_____ *[amounts]* **and resulting in** [☐ delivering bottom-line business value | ☐ business transformation | ☐ the translation of enterprise strategies into projects | ☐ increased productivity | ☐ other benefits: _____].

☐ **Coordinate and manage job preparations by** [☐ prioritizing work assignments | ☐ ordering required inventory | ☐ determining equipment needed | ☐ setting up each project with the correct tools, materials, and supplies | ☐ coordinating contracting trades | ☐ determining conditions and safety requirements | ☐ identifying required repairs and/or replacements | ☐ other: _____].

☐ **Project manage the assembly, build, and/or installation of** [☐ foundations | ☐ ceilings | ☐ flooring | ☐ carpeting | ☐ sheetrock | ☐ walls, partitions, and panels | ☐ cabinets | ☐ wall coverings | ☐ stairs | ☐ roofs | ☐ tiling | ☐ insulation and weather stripping | ☐ windows | ☐ door jambs and doors | ☐ retainer walls | ☐ trim work | ☐ platforms and podiums | ☐ railings, stair treads, nosings, and gratings | ☐ baseboard heating | ☐ garage doors | ☐ other: _____].

☐ **Work with** _____ *[which?]* **teams supporting** [☐ project managers | ☐ superintendents | ☐ plumbers | ☐ electricians | ☐ roofers | ☐ framers | ☐ finish carpenters | ☐ others: _____] [☐ in the preparation of building sites | ☐ throughout all project lifecycle phases | ☐ other: _____].

☐ **Develop** [☐ complex | ☐ extensive | ☐ detailed] _____ *[type of]* **building plan specifications to support the overall design and construction of** _____ *[what?].*

☐ **Manage and oversee all aspects of** _____ *[type of]* **projects including** [☐ project scope | ☐ initiation | ☐ planning | ☐ scheduling | ☐ budgeting | ☐ team selection | ☐ resource allocation | ☐ quality control | ☐ change management | ☐ cost control | ☐ system integration | ☐ other: _____] **keeping in line with all business objectives.**

☐ **Ensure** [☐ trucks arrive on time to pour concrete | ☐ laborers meet each day's scheduled workload | ☐ all materials are stored at the end of each day | ☐ all debris is cleared up | ☐ customer is satisfied with work | ☐ other: _____].

☐ **Manage and oversee various** _____ *[type of]* **job functions including** [☐ interpreting project blueprints and schematics | ☐ preparing job site | ☐ performing rough and finish carpentry | ☐ ensuring debris removal | ☐ maintaining machinery, tools, and equipment | ☐ ensuring safety practices | ☐ ensuring customer satisfaction | ☐ preparing punch lists and ensuring item completion | ☐ other: _____] **ensuring compliance with all codes and regulations and meeting required deadlines.**

☐ **Oversee a multitude of** _____ *[type of]* **carpentry work including** [☐ rough and finish carpentry | ☐ concrete forms setting | ☐ scaffolding erecting | ☐ tile installation | ☐ roof building and patching | ☐ flooring installations | ☐ stair building | ☐ insulation and weather stripping | ☐ siding installations | ☐ cabinet repair | ☐ partition installation | ☐ custom framing | ☐ wood and vinyl siding | ☐ conventional roofs | ☐ window replacements | ☐ door installations | ☐ other: _____] **according to blue print specifications.**

☐ **Provide technical** [☐ assistance | ☐ support | ☐ guidance | ☐ expertise | ☐ consultation | ☐ resolution] **on** _____ *[type of]* **issues** [☐ before | ☐ during | ☐ after] **the construction process.**

☐ **Apply an adapt knowledge of** [☐ construction methods | ☐ building codes | ☐ finish carpentry | ☐ tools, equipment, and materials | ☐ safety practices | ☐ building techniques | ☐ safety practices | ☐ building codes | ☐ electrical codes | ☐ plumbing codes | ☐ zoning regulations | ☐ other: _____] in all [☐ wood and metal framing | ☐ shingle and plywood roofing | ☐ wood and vinyl siding | ☐ masonry work | ☐ window and garage door replacement | ☐ home renovations | ☐ railroad ties | ☐ retainer walls | ☐ other: _____] **carpentry activities and ensure safety practices are followed.**

☐ **Provide support and feedback to** _____ *[whom?]* **regarding** [☐ structural | ☐ renovation | ☐ mechanical | ☐ environmental | ☐ other: _____] **issues at the building site.**

☐ **Define, plan, and implement** _____ *[type of]* **projects; and perform the** [☐ design | ☐ development | ☐ testing | ☐ implementation | ☐ tracking | ☐ reporting | ☐ other: _____] **of those projects in support of the** [firm's | clients'] **business objectives.**

☐ **Design and implement** _____ *[type of]* **solutions that effectively address and adhere to the Company's requirements** [☐ in accordance with all project timelines and budget | ☐ ensuring quality project standards and a smooth transition | ☐ other: _____].

ACHIEVEMENT SAMPLES:

☐ **Oversaw the completion of** _____ *[type of]* **project that included** [☐ estimating job costs | ☐ scheduling _____ *(type of)* work | ☐ ordering parts and materials | ☐ overseeing the installation process | ☐ managing a staff of _____ *(#)* | ☐ supervising quality control | ☐ billing clients | ☐ other: _____] [☐ meeting | ☐ exceeding] **aggressive timeframes.**

☐ **Coordinated all aspects of** _____ *[type of]* **projects with** [☐ clients | ☐ engineers | ☐ architects | ☐ municipal officials | ☐ county officials | ☐ code officers | ☐ others: _____] **ensuring compliance with all** [☐_____ *(which?)* codes | ☐ quality standards | ☐ work schedules | ☐ other: _____].

Building Maintenance Management

☐ **Manage** [☐ a facility | ☐ a corporate | ☐ an industrial | ☐ other: _____] **maintenance team of** _____ *[#]* [☐ superintendents | ☐ foremen | ☐ electricians | ☐ carpenters | ☐ maintenance workers | ☐ custodians | ☐ other: _____] **covering** [☐ two | ☐ three] **shifts of operation.**

☐ **Lead and direct** [☐ building | ☐ facilities | ☐ grounds | ☐ other: _____] **maintenance functions for this** _____ *[type of]* **firm including** [☐ construction | ☐ renovation | ☐ repair | ☐ remodel | ☐ other: _____] **projects ensuring they meet all** [☐ government | ☐ environmental | ☐ health | ☐ safety | ☐ security | ☐ other: _____] **standards.**

☐ **Oversee** [☐ facilities | ☐ building maintenance | ☐ grounds upkeep | ☐ space planning | ☐ remodel | ☐ other: _____] **projects for this** _____ *[#]*-**square foot building with ground acreage of** _____ *[#]* **and** _____ *[#]* [☐ employees | ☐ work stations | ☐ offices | ☐ facilities | ☐ other: _____].

☐ **Maintain** [☐ buildings | ☐ facilities | ☐ grounds | ☐ other: _____] **in good repair including** [☐ heating | ☐ air conditioning | ☐ plumbing | ☐ electrical | ☐ wood | ☐ drywall | ☐ wall coverings | ☐ insulation | ☐ drop ceilings | ☐ painting | ☐ grading | ☐ underground utilities | ☐ drains | ☐ gutters | ☐ paving | ☐ other: _____].

☐ **Supervise various** [☐ buildings | ☐ facilities | ☐ grounds | ☐ other: _____] **maintenance functions including** [☐ building maintenance and repair | ☐ office relocations | ☐ renovations | ☐ remodeling | ☐ roofing repairs | ☐ machinery maintenance and repair | ☐ regular and preventive maintenance | ☐ carpentry | ☐ electrical wiring | ☐ plumbing | ☐ HVAC systems | ☐ painting | ☐ custodial services | ☐ janitorial maintenance | ☐ groundskeeping | ☐ security systems | ☐ sprinkler systems | ☐ fire extinguisher and smoke alarm inspections | ☐ safety checks | ☐ boiler system | ☐ water system | ☐ heating system | ☐ cooling system | ☐ machinery maintenance and repair | ☐ other: _____].

☐ **Oversee** [☐ facility maintenance | ☐ contractors | ☐ subcontractors | ☐ others: _____] **in the repair and maintenance of all** [☐ plumbing | ☐ electrical | ☐ HVAC | ☐ motors | ☐ appliances | ☐ fixtures | ☐ lights | ☐ ballasts | ☐ receptacles | ☐ switches | ☐ other: _____] **to** [☐ help improve the work environment | ☐ maintain proper operation of all equipment | ☐ other: _____], **maintaining compliance with all** [☐ OSHA | ☐ environmental | ☐ other: _____] **regulations.**

☐ **Project manage the** [☐ structural | ☐ mechanical | ☐ electrical | ☐ plumbing | ☐ other: _____] **aspects of** _____ *[type of]* **building** [☐ design | ☐ utilization | ☐ space planning | ☐ construction | ☐ operation | ☐ maintenance | ☐ repair | ☐ remodel | ☐ other: _____] **ensuring all work is performed in compliance with building codes, laws, and regulations.**

☐ **Coordinate all aspects of the physical workplace ensuring** [☐ the integration and coordination of business practices | ☐ work and people requirements | ☐ fulfilling maintenance and repairs | ☐ other: _____].

☐ **Develop and establish long-range facility plans including** [☐ office relocations | ☐ repair and improvement projects | ☐ building renewal plans | ☐ system-wide policies and standards | ☐ regular, preventive, and seasonal maintenance | ☐ technical requirements | ☐ other: _____].

☐ **Lead and direct building** [☐ maintenance | ☐ space planning | ☐ renovations | ☐ repairs | ☐ other: _____] **ensuring the physical, mechanical, and electrical aspects of the facility run smoothly including** [☐ examining facility for damage and leaks | ☐ maintaining building heating system and boilers | ☐ overseeing cooling system maintenance and repair | ☐ maintaining emergency generator | ☐ maintaining plumbing, electrical, and HVAC systems | ☐ checking security systems | ☐ maintaining sprinkler systems | ☐ ensuring vehicles are in safe operating condition | ☐ other: _____].

Building Maintenance & Repair Oversight

☐ **Manage the installation, maintenance, and or replacement of electrical outlets and switches including** [☐ lighting circuits | ☐ new equipment power lines | ☐ fan motors | ☐ plant lighting | ☐ other: _____] **as needed.**

☐ **Supervise all plumbing functions including** [☐ cutting and threading pipe | ☐ soldering copper | ☐ installing PVC pipe | ☐ other: _____] **for** [☐ compressed air | ☐ potable water | ☐ cooling water | ☐ other: _____] **maintaining proper operation of all equipment.**

☐ **Maintain plant's heating system boilers, including cleaning** [☐ heads | ☐ flame sensor | ☐ igniter | ☐ other: _____].

☐ [☐ Perform | ☐ Manage] **cooling system maintenance and repair including** [☐ replacing burned out motors | ☐ cleaning blower cages | ☐ other: _____].

☐ **Maintain emergency** [☐ lighting system | ☐ generator] **and the proper operation of all equipment to ensure the** [☐ physical | ☐ mechanical | ☐ electrical | ☐ other: _____] **aspects of the facility run smoothly.**

☐ **Handle** [☐ new construction | ☐ remodeling | ☐ repair | ☐ maintenance | ☐ leasing | ☐ space planning | ☐ other: _____] **projects of** _____ *[what?]* **that require** _____ *[what actions?].*

☐ **Ensure all appliances are repaired and maintained including** [☐ gas and electric stoves and ovens | ☐ refrigerators | ☐ freezers | ☐ dishwashers | ☐ garbage disposals | ☐ microwaves | ☐ steam cookers | ☐ other: _____].

☐ **Maintain emergency** [☐ generator | ☐ lighting] **system through regular scheduled** [☐ maintenance | ☐ safety] [☐ checks | ☐ inspections].

☐ **Supervise the repair and/or replacement of broken** [☐ windows | ☐ doors | ☐ walls | ☐ ceilings | ☐ furniture | ☐ railings| ☐ stair treads | ☐ gratings | ☐ other: _____].

☐ **Oversee minor maintenance and repair of** [☐ construction vehicles | ☐ equipment | ☐ power tools | ☐ trucks | ☐ bulldozers | ☐ graders | ☐ cement mixers | ☐ welders | ☐ other: _____].

☐ **Direct the installation and/or repair of** [☐ faucets | ☐ toilets | ☐ urinals | ☐ other: _____] **and the cutting, threading, and/or soldering of** [☐ galvanized| ☐ black | ☐ copper | ☐ PVC] **pipe for** _____ *[what?].*

☐ **Ensure all** _____ *[type of]* **carpentry** [☐ machinery | ☐ tools | ☐ equipment | ☐ vehicles] **used by the trade are repaired and maintained.**

ACHIEVEMENT SAMPLE:

☐ **Managed the upgrade of electrical wiring of** _____ *[#]* **workstations, which required** _____ *[what?]* **and resulted in** _____ *[what benefits?].*

Business / Department Goals Setting

See also "Executive Functions" and "Cost Reductions," as applicable

- [ ] [☐ Establish | ☐ Assist in establishing] the [☐ division's | ☐ department's] _____ *[type of]* [☐ goals | ☐ action plans | ☐ project priorities | ☐ policies | ☐ procedures | ☐ guidelines | ☐ other: _____] **in** _____ *[what?]* **to support the firm's mission and objectives.**

- [ ] **Develop** [☐ short-term | ☐ long-range | ☐ short- and long-term] _____ *[type of]* [☐ plans | ☐ goals and objectives | ☐ other: _____] **encompassing** _____ *[type of]* [☐ research and analysis | ☐ program enhancements | ☐ operational effectiveness monitoring | ☐ budgetary requirements | ☐ financial support | ☐ resource generating | ☐ improvement changes | ☐ other: _____].

- [ ] **Devise and implement** [☐ one-year | ☐ multi-year | ☐ three-year | ☐ five-year | ☐ other: _____] **roadmap(s) for** _____ *[type of]* **initiatives encompassing** [☐ engaging stakeholders | ☐ cross-functional collaboration and support | ☐ relationship building | ☐ project execution | ☐ other: _____] **focusing on** _____ *[what areas?]*.

- [ ] **Ensure company and programs remain reputable, economically viable, and current by** [☐ providing a clear vision | ☐ proactive leadership | ☐ other: _____] **through strategically sound** [☐ mission statements | ☐ business plans | ☐ ongoing planning and implementation | ☐ other: _____] **that result in** [☐ sales increases of $_____ *(amount)* | ☐ other benefits: _____].

- [ ] **Develop and execute short- and long-term** [☐ company | ☐ division | ☐ departmental | ☐ other: _____] [☐ plans | ☐ objectives | ☐ projects | ☐ programs] **as well as its** _____ *[which?]* **operating policies and procedures**.

- [ ] **Develop and implement** _____ *[type of]* **business plans and set goals and objectives that support the firm's overall strategic vision by collaborating with** _____ *[whom?]* **in the** [☐ brainstorming of ideas | ☐ identifying of problems | ☐ evaluating of alternatives | ☐ implementing of effective solutions | ☐ evaluation of risk | ☐ other: _____].

- [ ] **Assist the** [☐ Chief Executive Officer | ☐ President | ☐ Board | ☐ Executive Vice President | ☐ Executive Director | ☐ Senior Vice President | ☐ Vice President of _____ *(type of)* | ☐ other: _____] **in** [☐ establishing | ☐ evaluating | ☐ prioritizing | ☐ coordinating | ☐ developing | ☐ other: _____] [☐ short-term plans | ☐ long-range goals | ☐ operating strategies | ☐ the firm's overall strategic vision | ☐ departmental goals | ☐ _____ *(which?)* action plans | ☐ other: _____] **to support business vision and corporate objectives**.

- [ ] **Co-develop the firm's overall strategy for** [☐ competitive | ☐ quality | ☐ cost-effective | ☐ visionary | ☐ other: _____] _____ *[type of]* [☐ projects | ☐ procedures | ☐ goals | ☐ products | ☐ services | ☐ other: _____].

- [ ] **Successfully support the business mission and goals of the firm by leading and managing the development and implementation of** _____ *[what initiatives?]* **to accomplish** _____ *[what?]*.

- [ ] **Assist in the preparation of** [☐ the firm's financial objectives | ☐ the annual budget | ☐ expenditure scheduling | ☐ variance analysis | ☐ corrective actions | ☐ other: _____] **for** _____ *[what?]*.

- [ ] **Lead and direct the** [☐ planning | ☐ setting | ☐ establishment] **of** _____ *[what?]* [☐ goals | ☐ policies | ☐ procedures | ☐ objectives | ☐ projections | ☐ strategies | ☐ other: _____].

- [ ] [☐ Establish | ☐ Lead the development of] **one-year tactical plans and** | [☐ five-year | ☐ three-year | ☐ multi-year | ☐ other: _____] [☐ enterprise | ☐ corporate | ☐ division | ☐ department | ☐ other: _____]**-level strategic plans** [☐ for supported _____ *(type of)* programs] **with alignment between the firm's strategic priorities** [☐ and learning] **investments.**

- [ ] [☐ Set | ☐ Partake in setting] **the firm's strategic goals and priorities, and establish** [☐ department standards and procedures | ☐ project management practices | ☐ other: _____] **that meet the organization's strategy including** _____, _____, **and** _____ *[what?]*.

- [ ] **Formulate and establish the** [☐ firm's | ☐ division's | ☐ department's] _____ *[which?]* [☐ goals and objectives | ☐ strategies and plans | ☐ standards and processes | ☐ policies and procedures | ☐ systems and guidelines | ☐ other: _____] **ensuring the highest standard of accuracy and efficiency.**

- [ ] **Working with** _____ *[whom?]*, **develop, implement, and maintain** [☐ long-term | ☐ short-range] [☐ company | ☐ division | ☐ departmental | ☐ other: _____] [☐ plans | ☐ goals | ☐ objectives | ☐ projects | ☐ programs] **as well as operating policies and procedures**.

- [ ] **Serve on** _____ *[which?]* **committee that** [☐ strategizes | ☐ formulates | ☐ plans | ☐ improves | ☐ recommends | ☐ prioritizes | ☐ coordinates | ☐ implements | ☐ establishes | ☐ tests | ☐ approves | ☐ monitors] _____ *[what?]*.

- [ ] [☐ Plan and set | ☐ Establish and Implement] _____ *[which?]* [☐ goals | ☐ policies | ☐ procedures | ☐ objectives | ☐ budget projections | ☐ expense planning | ☐ other: _____].

ACHIEVEMENT SAMPLES:

☐ **Assisted the** [☐ Executive Director | ☐ President | ☐ other title: _____] **in** [☐ evaluating | ☐ prioritizing | ☐ coordinating | ☐ developing | ☐ establishing | ☐ other: _____] **long-range** _____ *[type of]* **plans including** [☐ process improvements | ☐ building renewal plans | ☐ repair and improvement projects | ☐ system-wide policies and standards | ☐ technical requirements | ☐ other: _____].

Business Leadership

*See also "**Administrative Management & Leadership**," "**Executive Leadership**," and "**Office Management & Supervision**."*

☐ **Provide leadership and support to the** _____ *[which?]* **departments overseeing various** [☐ operational aspects of | ☐ administrative support services for] **this $** _____ *[revenues]* _____ *[type of firm]*, **including** [☐ payroll | ☐ data processing | ☐ materials distribution | ☐ records management | ☐ security | ☐ telecommunications | ☐ other: _____].

☐ **Lead and direct the administrative and office support services for this $** _____ *[revenues]* _____ *[type of]* **firm specializing in** _____ *[what?]* **including** [☐ budget preparation | ☐ inventory management and control | ☐ receivables monitoring and reporting | ☐ stock level control | ☐ evaluation and reporting | ☐ contract negotiations | ☐ assignment of jobs | ☐ maintenance activities | ☐ appointment scheduling | ☐ material requisitions | ☐ approval of time cards | ☐ supplies purchasing | ☐ accounting | ☐ invoicing | ☐ recordkeeping | ☐ data entry | ☐ reception area | ☐ mailroom | ☐ other: _____].

☐ **Direct the day-to-day operations of this** [☐ multibillion-dollar | ☐ multimillion-dollar | ☐ $_____ *(revenues)*] _____ *[type of]* **firm including** _____ , _____ , **and** _____ *[areas of primary responsibility]*.

☐ **Lead and oversee the** [☐ Office Manager | ☐ Administrator | ☐ others: _____] **in their interactions and negotiations with** [☐ clients | ☐ customers | ☐ vendors | ☐ others: _____] **facilitating** [☐ purchasing | ☐ customer service | ☐ troubleshooting | ☐ other: _____].

☐ **Plan, set, and establish** _____ *[type of]* **administrative** [☐ goals | ☐ policies and procedures | ☐ objectives | ☐ budget projections | ☐ expense planning | ☐ other: _____].

☐ **Direct and oversee the firm's administrative support services, including** [☐ inventory | ☐ purchasing | ☐ payroll | ☐ invoicing | ☐ other: _____] **for all** _____ *[#]* [☐ departments | ☐ offices | ☐ stores | ☐ other: _____] **requiring** [☐ calculating current stock | ☐ determining ordering needs | ☐ accurate data entry of all information | ☐ other: _____].

☐ **Compose and update** _____ *[type of]* [☐ contracts | ☐ agreements | ☐ technical material | (☐ company / ☐ department) policies and procedures | ☐ other: _____] **for** _____ *[purpose]*.

ACHIEVEMENT SAMPLES:

☐ **Championed** [☐ large-scale | ☐ complex | ☐ cross-organizational | ☐ other: _____] _____ *[type of]* [☐ administrative | ☐ operational] [☐ program | ☐ system | ☐ policy | ☐ procedures | ☐ solutions | ☐ implementation projects | ☐ other: _____] **involving** _____ *[what?]* **that** _____ *[accomplished what?]* **by** _____ *[doing what?]*.

☐ **Converted the firm's manual processing** _____ *[type of]* **office system to a functional** [☐ peer-to-peer] _____ *[type of]* **computerized** [☐ account database | ☐ billing | ☐ payroll | ☐ accounting | ☐ other: _____] [☐ system | ☐ environment] **increasing overall** [☐ productivity | ☐ efficiency | ☐ sales | ☐ other: _____] **increasing overall** [☐ productivity | ☐ efficiency | ☐ sales | ☐ other: _____].

☐ **Organized company's move from a** _____ *[#]*-**square foot building in** _____ *[what town?]* **to a** _____ *[#]*-**square foot building** [☐ in the business section] **of** _____ *[what town?]*, **allowing the firm to** [☐ construct a front office | ☐ increase staff size | ☐ stock more supplies and materials | ☐ other: _____].

☐ **Developed and established** _____ *[type of]* [☐ management] [☐ plans | ☐ standards | ☐ guidelines | ☐ policies | ☐ procedures | ☐ methods | ☐ other: _____] **that maximized the effective use of** _____ *[what?]* **and supported the continuing improvement of** _____ *[which?]* **standards.**

☐ **Spearheaded and implemented a** _____ *[type of]* [☐ program | ☐ policy | ☐ procedures] **that** [☐ maximized service and equipment utilization | ☐ other: _____] **by** _____ *[doing what?]*.

Business Management

☐ **Facilitate business management of this** _____ *[type of]* **firm including** [☐ leading and overseeing projects | ☐ prioritizing and balancing competing demands | ☐ reviewing contracts to verify legal requirements | ☐ establishing quality control procedures | ☐ developing revenue contracts | ☐ preparing specifications | ☐ performing inspections to facilitate quality assurance | ☐ quality testing materials | ☐ researching and writing (☐ legal / ☐ technical) procedures | ☐ setting up and maintaining contract database | ☐ developing budgets and monitoring expenses | ☐ preparing inspection deficiency reports | ☐ recommending corrective actions | ☐ reviewing and approving cost estimates | ☐ holding meetings to discuss project progress ☐ other: _____].

☐ **Manage the coordination and facilitation of** [☐ office management | ☐ general administration | ☐ facility management | ☐ human resources | ☐ general accounting | ☐ payroll processing | ☐ benefits administration | ☐ purchasing | ☐ inventory management and control | ☐ other: _____] **functions for this** _____ *[type of]* **firm.**

☐ **Plan, set, and establish** _____ *[type of]* **administrative** [☐ goals | ☐ policies and procedures | ☐ objectives | ☐ budget projections | ☐ expense planning | ☐ other: _____].

☐ **Manage the firm's administrative support services, including** [☐ inventory | ☐ purchasing | ☐ payroll | ☐ invoicing | ☐ other: _____] **for all** _____ *[#]* [☐ departments | ☐ offices | ☐ stores | ☐ other: _____] **requiring** [☐ calculating current stock | ☐ determining ordering needs | ☐ accurate data entry of all information | ☐ other: _____].

☐ **Oversee administrative support to the project management team in the areas of** _____, _____, **and** _____ *[which areas?]* **in setting project strategies and priorities.**

☐ **Manage** [☐ the office building | ☐ office operations | ☐ administrative services | ☐ other: _____] **including** [☐ office space planning | ☐ procedures development | ☐ account servicing | ☐ customer service | ☐ other: _____] **for this** [☐ leading | ☐ established | ☐ other: _____] _____ *[type of]* **firm.**

☐ [☐ **Compose and update** | ☐ **Draft and edit**] _____ *[type of]* [☐ contracts | ☐ agreements | ☐ technical material | (☐ company / ☐ department) policies and procedures | ☐ other: _____] **for** _____ *[purpose].*

☐ **Research, coordinate, document, edit, and periodically update the publication of** [☐ legal | ☐ policy and procedure | ☐ training | ☐ other: _____] **manuals and related** [☐ legal | ☐ technical | ☐ public information | ☐ user | ☐ other: _____] **materials.**

☐ **Coordinate new practices with** [☐ research and development | ☐ manufacturing | ☐ auditing | ☐ marketing | ☐ regulatory affairs | ☐ legal | ☐ other: _____] **personnel to** [☐ research existing practices | ☐ analyze auditing requirements | ☐ ensure compliance with all regulations | ☐ other: _____].

☐ **Define, plan, and implement** _____ *[type of]* **projects including the** [☐ design | ☐ development | ☐ implementation | ☐ tracking | ☐ other: _____] **of those projects in support of the firm's business objectives.**

ACHIEVEMENT SAMPLES:

☐ **Conceptualized, developed, and managed a $**_____ *[revenues]* _____ *[type of]* [☐ network | ☐ division | ☐ other: _____] **by** _____ *[doing what?],* **resulting in it becoming the backbone of the company's growth from** _____ *[what size or measure?]* **to** _____ *[what size or measure?].*

☐ **Assisted the** [☐ Executive Director | ☐ President | ☐ other title: _____] **in** [☐ evaluating | ☐ prioritizing | ☐ coordinating | ☐ developing | ☐ establishing | ☐ other: _____] **long-range** _____ *[type of]* **plans including** [☐ repair and improvement projects | ☐ building renewal plans | ☐ system-wide policies and standards | ☐ technology enhancements | ☐ other: _____].

☐ **Managed and coordinated** [☐ continuous | ☐ frequent] _____ *[type of]* **office space planning to accommodate** _____% *[percentage]* **employee growth in** _____ *[#]* **years. Required** [☐ locating | ☐ building | ☐ leasing | ☐ renovating | ☐ furnishing | ☐ other: _____] **offices within** _____ *[#]* **months of notice, including** [☐ telephone systems | ☐ equipment | ☐ furniture | ☐ other: _____].

☐ **Manage and implement the firm's corporate** [☐ domestic | ☐ international] **travel policy, resulting in annual cost reductions of $**_____ *[amount]* **in** [☐ air travel | ☐ hotel rental | ☐ car rental | ☐ meal expenses | ☐ other: _____].

☐ **Involved in** [☐ managing | ☐ performing | ☐ coordinating | ☐ facilitating | ☐ other: _____] _____ *[what?]* **efforts that required** _____ *[what actions?]* **to meet** _____ *[what challenges?]* **and resulted in** _____ *[benefits].*

☐ **Recommended and implemented** _____ *[type of]* [☐ management] [☐ plans | ☐ standards | ☐ guidelines | ☐ policies | ☐ procedures | ☐ methods | ☐ other: _____] **that maximized the effective use of** _____ *[what?]* **and supported the continuing improvement of** _____ *[which?]* **standards.**

☐ **Recruited as right hand to** _____ *[title]* **to save a once-profitable company from a then-floundering situation ($**_____ *[amount]* **loss on $**_____ *[amount]* **in sales) through effective** [☐ strategic and tactical efforts | ☐ other: _____] **resulting in its turnaround to $**_____ *[amount]* **profit on $**_____ *[amount]* **sales.**

CAD Drafting – General

*For all types of **CAD Drafting** and related functions, refer to the **ARCHITECTURE & ENGINEERING BOOK**.*

☐ **Prepare** _____ *[type of]* [☐ scale drawings | ☐ architectural renderings] **using** _____ *[which software?]* **computer-aided design and drafting that incorporate** [(☐ interior | ☐ exterior) elevations | ☐ design | ☐ specifications | ☐ materials | ☐ color | ☐ equipment | ☐ other: _____] **and discuss specifications with interior designers to ensure all objectives are accomplished within established time frames.**

☐ **Plan, design, and draft** _____ *[type of]* **client projects applying** [☐ expert | ☐ in-depth] **knowledge of** [☐ drafting | ☐ CAD programs | ☐ drafting devices | ☐ mathematics | ☐ zoning and building codes | ☐ building materials | ☐ other: _____].

☐ **Develop detailed visual guidelines that depict the technical details of** _____ *[type of]* [☐ structures | ☐ buildings | ☐ products | ☐ other: _____] **and include** [☐ specific dimensions | ☐ required materials | ☐ procedures and processes to be followed | ☐ other: _____] **for this $**_____ *[revenues]* [☐ drafting | ☐ engineering | ☐ architecture | ☐ construction management | ☐ other: _____] **firm**.

☐ **Draft to scale the technical details of** _____ *[what?]* **from** _____ *[type of]* [☐ architectural | ☐ engineering | ☐ surveyor | ☐ scientific | ☐ other: _____] [☐ drawings | ☐ rough sketches | ☐ specifications | ☐ codes | ☐ calculations | ☐ other: _____] **for** _____ *[whom or what?]*.

☐ **Create detailed** [☐ technical drawings | ☐ visual guidelines | ☐ plans] **for** [☐ construction workers | ☐ assemblers | ☐ others: _____] **to build** _____ *[type of]* [☐ structures | ☐ buildings | ☐ water systems | ☐ manufactured products | ☐ industrial machinery | ☐ machine parts | ☐ tools | ☐ pipelines | ☐ other: _____] **applying sound architectural standards for this $**_____ *[revenues]* _____ *[type of]* **firm**.

☐ **Draft** [☐ various | ☐ multiple | ☐ numerous] [☐ large-scale | ☐ moderate-size | ☐ highly complex | ☐ moderately complex | ☐ multisite | ☐ cross-organizational | ☐ other: _____] **projects for this** _____ *[type of]* **firm that** _____ *[does what?]* **for** _____ *[whom or what?]*.

☐ **Produce** [☐ working plans | ☐ profile drawings | ☐ base drawings | ☐ perspective drawings | ☐ overlays | ☐ maps | ☐ illustrations | ☐ other: _____] **of** _____ *[what?]*; **and prepare quantities and cost estimates using** [☐ AutoCAD | ☐ Land Development Desktop | ☐ WaterCAD | ☐ other: _____].

☐ **Draft CAD specifications for** _____ *[type of]* [☐ buildings | ☐ structures | ☐ other: _____] **to meet the** [☐ aesthetic | ☐ functional | ☐ safety | ☐ budgetary | ☐ project-timeline | ☐ other: _____] **goals of** [☐ commercial | ☐ residential | ☐ public works | ☐ other: _____] **clients ensuring compliance with all** [☐ building codes | ☐ zoning laws | ☐ fire regulations | ☐ OSHA | ☐ other: _____] **for this** _____ *[type of]* **firm**.

☐ **Create and design all aspects of** [☐ commercial sites | ☐ residential masterplan communities | ☐ other: _____] **applying an expert knowledge of** [☐ LDD (Land Development Desktop) | ☐ AutoCAD | ☐ MicroStation | ☐ other: _____] **software**.

☐ **Draft to scale the technical details of** _____ *[what?]* **from** [☐ drawings | ☐ rough sketches | ☐ specifications | ☐ codes | ☐ calculations | ☐ other: _____] **for** _____ *[what]*.

☐ **Provide hands-on CAD design of** _____ *[type of]* [☐ construction | ☐ renovation | ☐ new addition | ☐ restoration | ☐ grounds design | ☐ other: _____] **drawings for this** _____ *[type of]* **firm successfully meeting** _____ *[what?]* **drafting challenges**.

☐ **Apply extensive experience in AutoCAD and drafting standards in the preparation of** _____ *[type of]* **drawings consisting of** [☐ layouts | ☐ flow sheets | ☐ assemblies | ☐ isometrics | ☐ other: _____] **from** [☐ rough sketches | ☐ engineering and design information | ☐ other: _____].

CAD Drafting – Civil Projects

See also "CAD Drafting," "Architecture – General," "Architectural & Structural Engineering Functions," "Architectural Drawings & Renderings," and "Engineering Project Types," as applicable.

☐ **Prepare and/or update detailed** [☐ working plans | ☐ drawings | ☐ specifications | ☐ topographical and relief maps | ☐ cross-sections | ☐ profile sheets | ☐ other: _____] **from** [☐ field surveys | ☐ design notes | ☐ architectural sketches | ☐ other: _____] **according to specified dimensions for** [☐ major construction | ☐ civil engineering | ☐ roadway construction | ☐ land development | ☐ traffic | ☐ transportation | ☐ wastewater | ☐ survey | ☐ other: _____] **projects**.

☐ **Develop structural drawings for** [☐ land development | ☐ roadway | ☐ drainage | ☐ sewage | ☐ subdivision | ☐ other: _____] **projects for this $**_____ *[revenues]* **firm specializing in** [☐ private | ☐ commercial | ☐ retail | ☐ land-use | ☐ other: _____] **projects**.

☐ **Use** [☐ AutoCAD | ☐ Land Development Desktop (LDD) | ☐ MicroStation | ☐ other: _____] **for** [☐ earthwork | ☐ drainage | ☐ cut and fill | ☐ other: _____] **calculations to plot and draft** _____ *[type of]* [☐ civil | ☐ municipal | ☐ other: _____] **engineering projects**.

☐ **Provide drafting support and reports for** [☐ environmental investigative | ☐ groundwater modeling | ☐ other: _____] **for the purpose of** _____ *[what?]*.

☐ **Plot and draft to scale** [☐ profile sheets | ☐ cross-sections | ☐ three-dimensional views | ☐ sectional views | ☐ horizontal and vertical roadway alignment | ☐ units | ☐ parts of plans | ☐ maps | ☐ equipment | ☐ structures | ☐ other: _____] **for roadway** construction of [☐ highways | ☐ bridges | ☐ pipelines | ☐ water systems | ☐ sewage systems | ☐ drainage | ☐ flood control systems | ☐ parking lots | ☐ power systems | ☐ other: _____].

☐ **Perform a wide variety of** [☐ land development | ☐ roadway construction | ☐ civil engineering | ☐ other: _____] **drafting projects using leading-edge design tools including** _____, _____, **and** _____ *[tools used]*.

☐ **Prepare and letter** _____ *[type of]* **overlays showing topography of** _____ *[what?]*; **and make** [☐ prints | ☐ mylars | ☐ sepias | ☐ other: _____] **of** [☐ drawings | ☐ graphs | ☐ charts | ☐ records | ☐ other: _____] **for** _____ *[what?]*.

☐ **Working closely with ADOT on transportation projects, apply drafting principles and techniques when drafting** [☐ roadways | ☐ slopes | ☐ elevations | ☐ paving | ☐ drainage | ☐ grading | ☐ water and sewer calculations | ☐ other: _____] **toward the successful completion of** _____ *[what projects?]*.

CAD Drafting – Landscape Design

See also "Landscape Design."

☐ **Create CAD specifications for** _____ *[type of]* **landscapes to meet the** [☐ aesthetic | ☐ functional | ☐ safety | ☐ budgetary | ☐ project-timeline | ☐ other: _____] **goals of** [☐ residential | ☐ commercial | ☐ other: _____] **clients ensuring compliance with all** [☐ building codes | ☐ zoning laws | ☐ fire regulations | ☐ OSHA | ☐ other: _____].

☐ **Plan, design, and draft client landscape projects applying** [☐ expert | ☐ in-depth] **knowledge of** [☐ drafting | ☐ CAD programs | ☐ drafting devices | ☐ building materials | ☐ other: _____].

☐ **Develop detailed visual guidelines that depict the technical details of** _____ *[type of]* **landscape structures and include** [☐ specific dimensions | ☐ required materials | ☐ procedures and processes to be followed | ☐ other: _____] **for this** $_____ *[revenues]* [☐ landscape design | ☐ drafting | ☐ other: _____] **firm.**

☐ **Draft to scale the technical details of** _____ *[type of]* **landscapes from** _____ *[type of]* [☐ drawings | ☐ rough sketches | ☐ specifications | ☐ calculations | ☐ other: _____] **for** _____ *[whom or what?]*.

☐ **Create detailed** [☐ technical drawings | ☐ visual guidelines | ☐ plans] **to create** _____ *[type of]* [☐ structures | ☐ water systems | ☐ other: _____] **applying sound architectural standards.**

☐ **Draft** [☐ various | ☐ multiple] [☐ large-scale | ☐ moderate-size | ☐ highly complex | ☐ moderately complex | ☐ other: _____] **landscape projects for this** _____ *[type of]* **firm that** _____ *[does what?]* **for** _____ *[whom or what?]*.

☐ **Produce** [☐ working plans | ☐ profile drawings | ☐ base drawings | ☐ perspective drawings | ☐ overlays | ☐ maps | ☐ illustrations | ☐ other: _____] **of** _____ *[what?]*; **and prepare quantities and cost estimates using** [☐ AutoCAD | ☐ Land Development Desktop | ☐ WaterCAD | ☐ other: _____].

☐ **Prepare** _____ *[type of]* [☐ scale drawings | ☐ architectural renderings] **using** _____ *[which software?]* **computer-aided design and drafting that incorporate** [(☐ interior / ☐ exterior) elevations | ☐ design | ☐ specifications | ☐ materials | ☐ color | ☐ equipment | ☐ other: _____] **ensuring all objectives are accomplished within established time frames.**

☐ **Provide hands-on CAD design of** _____ *[type of]* **grounds** [☐ design | ☐ construction | ☐ renovation | ☐ restoration | ☐ other: _____] **drawings for this** _____ *[type of]* **firm successfully meeting** _____ *[what?]* **drafting challenges.**

☐ **Use** _____ *[type of]* [☐ computer-aided drafting systems | ☐ compasses | ☐ protractors | ☐ triangles | ☐ other: _____] **and other drafting tools and computations to draw angles and determine** [☐ scale | ☐ cost | ☐ distance | ☐ measurements | ☐ quantities of materials | ☐ other: _____] **and other data in drafting landscape designs.**

☐ **Use** _____ *[software program]* **to create** [☐ preliminary drawings | ☐ detailed sketches | ☐ schematic designs | ☐ plans | ☐ other: _____] **and to develop specifications for** _____ *[type of]* **landscape projects.**

☐ **Create and design all aspects of** _____ *[type of]* **landscape projects applying an expert knowledge of** [☐ LDD | ☐ AutoCAD | ☐ MicroStation | ☐ other: _____] **software.**

☐ **Provide hands-on CAD design of** _____ *[type of]* **grounds design drawings for this** _____ *[type of]* **landscaping company, successfully meeting all drafting challenges.**

☐ **Utilize** _____ *[type of]* **computer-assisted design software to produce detailed** [☐ sketches | ☐ preliminary drawings | ☐ architectural renderings | ☐ schematic designs | ☐ construction documents | ☐ specifications | ☐ plans | ☐ technical reports | ☐ correspondence | ☐ other: _____] **for** _____ *[what?]*.

☐ **Prepare** _____ *[type of]* **architectural renderings and presentations via computer-aided design and drafting (CADD) including interior and exterior elevations to clients for their review.**

☐ **Review, assess, and oversee various functions in the drafting process including** [☐ cost effectiveness | ☐ installation | ☐ processing efficiency | ☐ construction | ☐ repair | ☐ other: _____] **for** _____ *[what?]*.

Carpentry Labor Management & Supervision

See "Trades / Crew Supervision" and "Trades Coordination & Oversight."

Carpentry Projects

See also "Carpentry Projects Supervision" and "Construction Projects."

☐ **Perform a multitude of** _____ *[type of]* **carpentry work including** [☐ rough and finish carpentry | ☐ concrete forms setting | ☐ scaffolding erecting | ☐ tile installation | ☐ roof building and patching | ☐ flooring installations | ☐ stair building | ☐ insulation and weather stripping | ☐ siding installations | ☐ cabinet repair | ☐ partition installation | ☐ custom framing | ☐ wood and vinyl siding | ☐ conventional roofs | ☐ window replacements | ☐ door installations | ☐ other: _____] **according to blue print specifications**.

☐ **Ensure** [☐ trucks arrive on time to pour concrete | ☐ laborers meet each day's scheduled workload | ☐ all materials are stored at the end of each day | ☐ all debris is cleared up | ☐ customer is satisfied with work | ☐ other: _____].

☐ **Conduct hands-on** [☐ carpentry | ☐ masonry | ☐ concrete pouring | ☐ other: _____] **work in the areas of** _____, _____, **and** _____ *[type of work]*, **order materials, estimate projects, and lay out jobs for** _____ *[type of]* **projects ensuring all safety practices are followed on carpentry job sites.**

☐ **Construct, replace, repair, and/or install** [☐ windows | ☐ flooring | ☐ doors | ☐ walls | ☐ ceilings | ☐ door locks and closures | ☐ door jambs | ☐ drywall | ☐ railings | ☐ stair treads | ☐ partitions | ☐ ramps | ☐ fences | ☐ insulation | ☐ weather stripping | ☐ wall coverings | ceilings | ☐ plastic laminates | ☐ other: _____] **for this** _____ *[type of]* **firm**.

☐ **Set up prefabricated components including** [☐ frames | ☐ stairs | ☐ wall panels | ☐ other: _____] **to construct and build** _____, _____, **and** _____ *[what?]*.

☐ **Assemble, build, and/or install** [☐ foundations | ☐ ceilings | ☐ flooring | ☐ carpeting | ☐ sheetrock | ☐ walls, partitions, and panels | ☐ cabinets | ☐ wall coverings | ☐ stairs | ☐ roofs | ☐ tiling | ☐ insulation and weather stripping | ☐ windows | ☐ door jambs and doors | ☐ retainer walls | ☐ trim work | ☐ platforms and podiums | ☐ railings, stair treads, nosings, and gratings | ☐ baseboard heating | ☐ garage doors | ☐ other: _____].

☐ **Fit and install prefabricated** [☐ window frames | ☐ doorframes and doors | ☐ weather stripping | ☐ trim work | ☐ hardware | ☐ other: _____] **applying** [☐ sound-deadening | ☐ shock-absorbing | ☐ insulated | ☐ decorative | ☐ other: _____] **paneling to ceilings and walls resulting in successful** _____ *[type of]* **jobs**.

☐ **Handle various carpentry job functions including** [☐ interpreting project blueprints and schematics | ☐ preparing job site | ☐ performing rough and finish carpentry | ☐ ensuring debris removal | ☐ maintaining machinery, tools, and equipment | ☐ ensuring safety practices | ☐ unloading trucks with heavy equipment | ☐ ensuring customer satisfaction | ☐ operating (☐ forklifts / ☐ payloaders / ☐ cranes / ☐ bulldozers / ☐ other: _____) | ☐ preparing punch lists and ensuring item completion | ☐ other: _____] **ensuring compliance with all codes and regulations and meeting required deadlines.**

☐ **Develop** [☐ complex | ☐ extensive | ☐ detailed] _____ *[type of]* **building plan specifications to support the overall design and construction of** _____ *[what?]*.

☐ **Read blueprints to unload correct amounts of** [☐ steel | ☐ wood | ☐ other materials: _____] **for each project; arrange and lay out materials according to daily project needs; and oversee the construction of** [☐ window replacement | ☐ door layouts | ☐ walls | ☐ decks | ☐ roofing | ☐ other: _____] **on schedule, within budget.**

☐ **Working as a team,** [☐ unload trucks with heavy equipment and cranes | ☐ transport tools to job sites | ☐ set up daily materials and equipment | ☐ operate (☐ forklifts / ☐ payloaders / ☐ bulldozers) | ☐ tear down old construction | ☐ handle steel and concrete construction work | ☐ guide machinery to dig, clear, and backfill land | ☐ set up windows and doors for replacement | ☐ take accurate measurements for new construction | ☐ cut and connect PVC pipes from buildings to cesspool | ☐ other: _____] **ensuring customer satisfaction on all jobs.**

☐ **Cut, shape, and assemble** [☐ wood | ☐ steel | ☐ drywall | ☐ tiles | ☐ glass | ☐ plastic | ☐ fiberglass | ☐ other: _____], **and other materials for the construction of** [☐ buildings | ☐ highways | ☐ bridges | ☐ marinas | ☐ boats | ☐ other: _____], **and modify as needed to fit properly.**

☐ **Prepare recommendations to** _____ *[whom?]* **regarding** [☐ contractual defaults | ☐ time extensions | ☐ liquidated damages | ☐ other: _____].

☐ **Work with** _____ *[which?]* **teams supporting** [☐ project managers | ☐ superintendents | ☐ plumbers | ☐ electricians | ☐ roofers | ☐ framers | ☐ finish carpenters | ☐ others: _____] [☐ in the preparation of building sites | ☐ throughout all project lifecycle phases | ☐ other: _____].

☐ **Apply a thorough knowledge of** [☐ construction methods | ☐ building codes | ☐ finish carpentry | ☐ tools, equipment, and materials | ☐ safety practices | ☐ building techniques | ☐ other: _____] in all [☐ wood and metal framing | ☐ shingle and plywood roofing | ☐ wood and vinyl siding | ☐ masonry work | ☐ window and garage door replacement | ☐ home renovations | ☐ railroad ties | ☐ retainer walls | ☐ other: _____] **carpentry activities and ensure safety practices are followed**.

☐ **Provide support and feedback to** _____ *[whom?]* **regarding** [☐ structural | ☐ renovation | ☐ mechanical | ☐ environmental | ☐ other: _____] **issues at the site**.

ACHIEVEMENT SAMPLES: *See "Construction Projects."*

Carpentry Projects Supervision

Refer also to "Carpentry Supervision & Oversight," "Construction Projects," and individual trades positions, as applicable.

☐ **Supervise rough and finish carpentry work in all phases of construction including** [☐ pouring foundations | ☐ framing and sheetrocking | ☐ taping and spackling | ☐ other: _____] **and installing** [☐ windows | ☐ doors | ☐ flooring | ☐ tiling | ☐ ceilings | ☐ roofing | ☐ wall coverings | ☐ trim work | ☐ platforms | ☐ hardware | ☐ partitions | ☐ fences | ☐ ramps | ☐ insulation | ☐ other: _____].

☐ **Plan, coordinate, and oversee** [☐ rough | ☐ finish] **carpentry in the construction and** [☐ demolition | ☐ remodeling | ☐ renovation | ☐ assembly | ☐ repair | ☐ restoration | ☐ other: _____] of _____ *[type of]* **projects for this** _____ *[type of]* **firm**.

☐ **Manage multiple** [☐ large-scale | ☐ moderate-size | ☐ highly complex | ☐ moderately complex | ☐ multisite | ☐ cross-organizational | ☐ multiyear-timeline | ☐ multimonth-timeline | ☐ simultaneous | ☐ other: _____] **project rollouts from inception to successful completion for this** _____ *[type of]* **firm that** _____ *[does what?]* **for** _____ *[whom?]*.

☐ **Supervise** [☐ remodeling | ☐ renovations | ☐ finish carpentry | ☐ other: _____] **including installation of** [☐ custom framing | ☐ wood and vinyl siding | ☐ conventional roofs | ☐ window replacements | ☐ doors | ☐ tiling | ☐ countertops | ☐ other: _____] **according to blueprint specifications**.

☐ **Direct the construction and/or installation of** [☐ concrete forms | ☐ walls | ☐ doors | ☐ door jambs | ☐ roofs | ☐ floors | ☐ wall coverings | ☐ ceilings | ☐ paneling | ☐ plastic laminates | ☐ cabinets | ☐ platforms | ☐ partitions | ☐ hardware | ☐ podiums | ☐ partitions | ☐ fences | ☐ ramps | ☐ insulation | ☐ weather stripping | ☐ other: _____] **on** _____ *[type of]* **construction projects for this** _____ *[type of]* **firm**.

☐ **Supervise landscape installation functions including** [☐ grading | ☐ retainer walls | ☐ landscape borders | ☐ walkways | ☐ sprinkler systems | ☐ concrete masonry walls | ☐ soil thatching | ☐ tree and shrub plantings | ☐ others: _____].

☐ **Oversee maintenance and repair work including** [☐ windows | ☐ doors | ☐ walls | ☐ ceilings | ☐ furniture | ☐ railings / hand railings | ☐ stair treads | ☐ other: _____].

☐ **Direct the construction, replacement, repair, and/ or installation of** [☐ windows | ☐ flooring | ☐ doors | ☐ walls | ☐ ceilings | ☐ door locks and closures | ☐ door jambs | ☐ drywall | ☐ gratings | ☐ railings | ☐ stair treads | ☐ partitions | ☐ ramps | ☐ fences | ☐ insulation | ☐ weather stripping | ☐ other: _____].

☐ **Supervise** [☐ home construction | ☐ home improvement | ☐ interior renovation | ☐ room additions | ☐ finished attics and basements | ☐ other: _____] **including** [☐ framing | ☐ insulation | ☐ sheetrocking | ☐ taping and spackling | ☐ painting | ☐ flooring | ☐ tiling | ☐ roofing | ☐ landscaping | ☐ other: _____] **for individual clients**.

☐ **Oversee the concrete and steel reinforcement of** _____ *[type of]* **construction projects and the finishing of walls with** [☐ wood | ☐ structural metal | ☐ lath | ☐ plaster | ☐ other: _____] **materials meeting all project budgets and deadlines**.

☐ **Manage** [☐ home remodeling and renovations | ☐ various types of carpentry work | ☐ finish carpentry | ☐ other: _____] **including installation of** _____ , _____ , **and** _____ *[what?]* **according to blue print specifications**.

☐ **Prepare** [☐ job estimates | ☐ budgeting | ☐ other: _____] **with fair financial arrangements for customers and at good profits for company**.

☐ **Supervise the application of textured surfaces to** [☐ walls | ☐ ceilings | ☐ flooring | ☐ other: _____] **on** _____ *[type of]* **construction projects**.

ACHIEVEMENT SAMPLES: *See "Construction Projects."*

Carpentry Supervision & Oversight

See also "Carpentry Projects Supervision," "Project Management," "Trades / Crew Supervision," "Trades Coordination & Oversight," and various Carpentry and Construction categories.

☐ **Supervise and oversee _____** *[#]* **laborers in all phases of carpentry projects including** [☐ demolition | ☐ foundations | ☐ wall framing and partitions | ☐ insulation | ☐ sheet-rock installation| ☐ building and installing (☐ stairs / ☐ windows / ☐ doors / ☐ brattices) | ☐ taping and spackling | ☐ painting | ☐ trim work | ☐ flooring | ☐ tiling | ☐ ceilings | ☐ roofing | ☐ cabinet installations | ☐ masonry | ☐ welding | ☐ plumbing | ☐ electrical | ☐ HVAC | ☐ landscaping | ☐ other: _____].

☐ **Plan, coordinate, and supervise** [☐ rough | ☐ finish] **carpentry in the construction and** [☐ demolition | ☐ remodeling | ☐ renovation | ☐ assembly | ☐ repair | ☐ maintenance] **of** [☐ buildings | ☐ cabinets | ☐ roofs | ☐ furnishings | ☐ vinyl siding | ☐ other: _____] **for this $_____** *[revenues]* _____ *[type of]* **firm.**

☐ **Supervise the daily carpentry operations for this $_____** *[revenues]* _____ *[type of]* **firm including** [☐ blueprint reading | ☐ work scheduling | ☐ job site preparation | ☐ project management | ☐ building inspections | ☐ other: _____].

☐ **Lead all aspects of** [☐ carpentry | ☐ construction] **project lifecycles including** [☐ project scope | ☐ initiation | ☐ planning | ☐ scheduling | ☐ budgeting | ☐ contractor selection | ☐ resource allocation | ☐ risk assessment | ☐ quality control | ☐ change orders | ☐ cost control | ☐ punch lists | ☐ close-out billing | ☐ other: _____].

☐ **Oversee all aspects of carpentry work including** [☐ reviewing project plans | ☐ reading and interpreting blueprints | ☐ estimating time | ☐ preparing job estimates | ☐ estimating material and labor costs | ☐ securing competitive bids | ☐ selecting contractors and subcontractors | ☐ preparing work orders | ☐ developing crew assignments and work schedules | ☐ coordinating projects with contractors | ☐ preparing job sites | ☐ ordering and setting up equipment | ☐ purchasing materials and supplies | ☐ directing and coordinating building construction | ☐ supervising a crew of _____ *(#)* | ☐ performing rough and finish carpentry | ☐ evaluating staff performance | ☐ inspecting work area | ☐ obtaining permits | ☐ mediating and resolving disputes | ☐ ensuring debris removal | ☐ providing technical construction assistance | ☐ preparing punch lists | ☐ overseeing inspection deadlines | ☐ negotiating and processing change orders | ☐ ensuring punch list item completion and customer satisfaction | ☐ coordinating concrete trucks | ☐ recommending land purchases to management | ☐ monitoring inventory and supply requests | ☐ ensuring safety practices | ☐ preparing accident reports | ☐ other: _____] **ensuring all jobs are completed in compliance with specifications and codes.**

☐ **Supervise** [☐ home | ☐ office | ☐ commercial | ☐ industrial | ☐ public | ☐ other: _____] [☐ carpentry | ☐ construction | ☐ renovation] **for this** [☐ $_____ *(revenues)* | ☐ leading | ☐ established] _____ *[type of]* **general contractor, overseeing a _____** *[#]***-man crew and bringing jobs in on time and within budget.**

☐ **Manage a multitude of carpentry work including** [☐ setting concrete forms | ☐ erecting scaffolding | ☐ installing ceiling tiles | ☐ repairing cabinets | ☐ installing partitions | ☐ other: _____] **and perform finishing work for _____** *[type of]* **projects.**

☐ **Review schematic drawings and construction details for _____** *[type of]* **projects, interpret specifications, make recommendations to modify as needed, discuss changes with clients before implementation, and make field inspections.**

☐ **Plan and coordinate all activities of** [☐ small- | ☐ moderate- | ☐ large-] **scale _____** *[type of]* **carpentry projects in collaboration with** [☐ client reps | ☐ contractors | ☐ subcontractors] **for this _____** *[type of]* **firm that generates fiscal-year revenues of $_____** *[revenues].*

☐ **Coordinate and oversee** [☐ rough | ☐ finish] **carpentry in the construction and** [☐ demolition | ☐ remodeling | ☐ renovation | ☐ assembly | ☐ repair | ☐ restoration | ☐ other: _____] **of _____** *[type of]* **projects.**

☐ **Conceive, sketch, and design _____** *[type of]* **carpentry projects for _____** *[whom or what?]* **and prepare job estimates with fair financial arrangements for customers and at good profits for company.**

☐ **Prepare** [☐ site plans | ☐ planning applications | ☐ specifications | ☐ cost estimates | ☐ other: _____] **for land development of _____** *[what?]***; and coordinate proposed land features and structures.**

☐ **Order materials, estimate projects, and lay out jobs for this** [☐ residential | ☐ commercial | ☐ other: _____] **contractor specializing in _____** *[what?]* **ensuring** [☐ trucks arrive on time to pour concrete | ☐ laborers meet each day's scheduled workload | ☐ safety practices are followed on job sites | ☐ all materials are stored at the end of each day | ☐ all debris is cleared | ☐ customer satisfaction with work | ☐ other: _____].

☐ **Oversee rough and finish carpentry in the construction and/or installation of** [☐ buildings | ☐ houses | ☐ remodels | ☐ roofing | ☐ siding | ☐ cabinets | ☐ fencing | ☐ other: _____].

☐ **Obtain permits, estimate jobs, and hire and schedule trades acting as liaison with** [☐ building managers | ☐ inspectors | ☐ architects | ☐ engineers | ☐ others: _____].

☐ **Ensure all _____** *[type of]* **carpentry** [☐ machinery | ☐ tools | ☐ equipment | ☐ vehicles] **used by the trade are repaired and maintained.**

ACHIEVEMENT SAMPLES: *See "Construction Projects."*

Carpentry Work

Refer also to other related trades positions.

☐ **Handle** [☐ carpentry | ☐ construction] **projects from project start through completion including** [☐ client relations | ☐ construction drawings review | ☐ project initiation | ☐ trades coordination | ☐ change orders | ☐ cost control | ☐ punch lists | ☐ inspection | ☐ other: _____] **within the parameters of project cost, time, and quality**.

☐ **Work on several** [☐ demolition | ☐ construction | ☐ remodeling | ☐ renovation | ☐ restoration | ☐ repair | ☐ other: _____] **projects** [☐ some simultaneously] **with projects ranging from $_____ to $_____** *[amounts]* **including** [☐ commercial buildings | ☐ shopping malls | ☐ stores | ☐ restaurants | ☐ manufacturing plants | ☐ schools | ☐ colleges and universities | ☐ corporate offices | ☐ building lobbies | ☐ government agencies | ☐ houses | ☐ condominiums | ☐ apartment buildings | ☐ hospitals | ☐ laboratories | ☐ clean rooms | ☐ landmark restorations | ☐ highways | ☐ other: _____] **completing all projects on time and within budget.**

☐ **As** [☐ Lead Carpenter | ☐ General Contractor] perform [☐ home construction | ☐ home improvement | ☐ interior renovation | ☐ room additions | ☐ finished attics and basements | ☐ other: _____] **for individual clients including** [☐ framing | ☐ insulation | ☐ sheetrocking | ☐ taping and spackling | ☐ painting | ☐ flooring | ☐ tiling | ☐ roofing | ☐ other: _____] that result in _____ *[benefits]*.

☐ **Specializing in** [☐ demolition | ☐ carpentry | ☐ framing | ☐ sheetrocking | ☐ taping and spackling | ☐ flooring | ☐ painting | ☐ insulation | ☐ electrical | ☐ plumbing | ☐ tiling | ☐ trim work | ☐ ceilings | ☐ welding | ☐ roofing | ☐ masonry | ☐ other: _____] **perform** _____ *[type of]* [☐ large-scale | ☐ mid-size | ☐ highly complex | ☐ moderately complex | ☐ multisite | ☐ other: _____] **construction projects for** _____ *[whom?]* **resulting in** _____ *[what benefits?].*

☐ **Handle all aspects of remodeling** [☐ residential homes | ☐ commercial buildings | ☐ civil projects | ☐ other: _____] **including** _____, _____, **and** _____ *[type of renovations].*

☐ **Facilitate** [☐ home | ☐ office | ☐ commercial | ☐ industrial | ☐ public | ☐ other: _____] **carpentry projects for this** [☐ leading | ☐ established | ☐ other: _____] **general contractor, bringing all jobs in on time and within budget.**

☐ **Perform** [☐ residential | ☐ commercial | ☐ industrial | ☐ other: _____] [☐ new construction | ☐ remodeling | ☐ carpentry work | ☐ finish carpentry | ☐ other: _____] including installation of [☐ custom framing | ☐ wood/vinyl siding | ☐ conventional roofs | ☐ window replacements | ☐ doors | ☐ ceramic tile | ☐ other: _____] **according to blue print specifications.**

☐ **Involved in all aspects of** [☐ construction | ☐ carpentry] **including** [☐ reviewing project plans | ☐ reading and interpreting blueprints | ☐ estimating time | ☐ developing work schedules | ☐ preparing work orders | ☐ ordering and setting up equipment | ☐ purchasing supplies | ☐ preparing job sites | ☐ performing rough and finish carpentry | ☐ inspecting work areas | ☐ other: _____] **ensuring jobs are completed in compliance with all specifications and building codes.**

☐ **Work as a team with** _____ *[#]* **laborers in the construction and installation of** [☐ walls | ☐ doors | ☐ door jambs | ☐ roofs | ☐ floors | ☐ wall coverings | ☐ ceilings | ☐ partitions | ☐ fences | ☐ ramps | ☐ insulation | ☐ weather stripping | ☐ other: _____] **for this** _____ *[type of]* **firm.**

☐ **Perform hands-on rough and finish carpentry work including** [☐ pouring foundations | ☐ framing and sheet-rocking walls and partitions | ☐ taping and spackling | ☐ building stairs | ☐ installing windows | ☐ replacing doors | ☐ flooring | ☐ tiling | ☐ ceilings | ☐ painting | ☐ siding | ☐ roofs | ☐ ceilings | ☐ kitchen and bathroom cabinets | ☐ other: _____].

ACHIEVEMENT SAMPLES: *See "Construction Projects."*

Ceiling, Lathing, Insulation & Drywall Installation

See also "Carpentry / Construction Work" and other Carpentry / Construction Projects (specific).

☐ **Mount** [☐ drywall sheets | ☐ acoustical tiles | ☐ shock-absorbing materials | ☐ other: _____] **that reduce / reflect sound to ceilings and walls for** _____, _____, **and** _____ *[type of projects or companies].*

☐ **Prepare for** [☐ ceiling | ☐ drywall | ☐ other: _____] **installation jobs by first inspecting areas for** [☐ electrical wire | ☐ ductwork | ☐ piping | ☐ other: _____] **obstructions and** [☐ removing existing plaster, drywall, or paneling | ☐ measuring and marketing surfaces according to specifications | ☐ determining materials and installation methods | ☐ hanging dry lines to wall moldings to guide main runners | ☐ installing furring strips to framing to create flat, even surfaces | ☐ marking wall studs, light fixtures, and electrical boxes for ceiling joist locations | ☐ building and using T-braces for leverage and support to raise drywall panels | ☐ hanging and affixing drywall sheets | ☐ abutting tapered edges | ☐ taping and spackling | ☐ other: _____].

☐ **Fasten** [☐ metal | ☐ rockboard | ☐ wood | ☐ other: _____] **laths to inside framing of** [☐ walls | ☐ ceilings | ☐ partitions | ☐ other: _____] **of** *[type of]* [☐ commercial | ☐ residential | ☐ other: _____] **buildings working with** [☐ wire | ☐ metal mesh | ☐ rockboard lath | (☐ decorative / ☐ functional) tiling | ☐ other: _____] **using hand and power tools to** [☐ nail | ☐ screw | ☐ staple | ☐ wire-tie | ☐ other: _____] **lath directly to structural framework.**

☐ **Perform various** [☐ ceiling | ☐ lathing | ☐ drywall] **installation functions including** [☐ cutting and/or bending lath to fit openings and corners | ☐ fastening (☐ metal / ☐ rockboard) lath to (☐ framework / ☐ ceiling joists / ☐ partitions / ☐ concrete surfaces) | ☐ welding metal frame supports | ☐ fitting and fastening wallboards | ☐ cutting openings for outlets, plumbing, vents, and windows | ☐ adding decorative trim to doorways and windows | ☐ inspecting (☐ furrings / ☐ masonry) surfaces | ☐ installing tiling | ☐ sealing joints between tiles and walls | ☐ coordinating work with drywall finishers | ☐ installing insulation | ☐ filling cracks with sealing compound | ☐ installing metal casings around openings | ☐ other: _____.

☐ **Properly insulate** [☐ buildings | ☐ attics | ☐ exterior walls | ☐ ceilings | ☐ boilers | ☐ steam and hot water pipes | ☐ other: _____] **with** [☐ fiberglass | ☐ foam | ☐ cellulose | ☐ rock wool batt | ☐ other: _____] **insulation and** [☐ use wire meshes to spray foam insulation | ☐ wrap it with (☐ aluminum / ☐ plastic / ☐ canvas / ☐ other: _____) | ☐ screw sheet metal around insulated pipes | ☐ apply drywall and plaster | ☐ other: _____].

☐ **Apply** _____ *[type of]* **insulation to** _____ *[what?]* **using** [☐ stapling guns | ☐ power saws | ☐ compressor hose | ☐ trowels | ☐ brushes | ☐ knives | ☐ saws | ☐ pliers | ☐ tape | ☐ other: _____] **to keep seasonal air conditioning and heat in and vice versa, following all safety guidelines.**

☐ **Use** [☐ power saws to cut insulating materials | ☐ welding machines to join sheet metal and secure clamps | ☐ compressors to spray insulation | ☐ other: _____] **and** [☐ saws | ☐ compressor hose | ☐ trowels | ☐ brushes | ☐ knives | ☐ pliers | ☐ tape | ☐ stapling guns | ☐ other: _____] **to cut and secure insulation.**

☐ [☐ Oversee | ☐ Conduct] **drywall panel fastening to the framework of** _____ *[type of]* **buildings and prepare panels for painting by filling, taping, troweling, and finishing joints for** _____ *[what?].*

☐ **Specializing in drywall installations, perform** _____ *[type of]* **projects for** _____ *[whom?]* **including** [☐ fastening drywall panels to framework | ☐ taping and spackling | ☐ painting, filling, taping, troweling, and finishing joints | ☐ measuring, cutting, fitting, gluing, and screwing wallboard panels to framework | ☐ applying textured surfaces | ☐ other: _____].

☐ **Measure, cut, fit, glue and/or screw wallboard panels to wood and metal framework, cutting holes in panels for** [☐ windows | ☐ doors | ☐ electrical outlets | ☐ air-conditioning units | ☐ plumbing | ☐ other: _____] **and applying textured surfaces to** [☐ walls | ☐ ceilings | ☐ floors | ☐ other: _____] **using** [☐ trowels | ☐ brushes | ☐ spray guns | ☐ other: _____].

☐ **Use automatic taping tools and sand all treated areas on** [☐ large | ☐ midsize | ☐ variable] _____ *[type of]* **projects, ensuring smoothness perfection to match remaining wall surfaces.**

ACHIEVEMENT SAMPLES: *See also "Construction Projects."*

☐ **Increased productivity** _____ **%** *[percentage],* **slashed** _____ *[type of]* **project times, and decreased man hours from** _____ *[#]* [☐ hours | ☐ days] **to** _____ [☐ hours | ☐ days] **by using** [☐ ratcheting cargo jacks and telescopic paint roller handles to attach to beams and ladder treads to support sheetrock | ☐ other methods: _____] **allowing for one-person drywall ceiling installations.**

☐ **Reduced energy consumption** _____ **%** *[percentage]* **on** _____ *[type of]* **project by properly insulating** [☐ buildings | ☐ attics | ☐ exterior walls | ☐ ceilings | ☐ plaster walls | ☐ paneling | ☐ boilers | ☐ steam and hot water pipes | ☐ storage rooms | ☐ vats | ☐ tanks | ☐ other: _____] **with** [☐ fiberglass | ☐ foam | ☐ cellulose | ☐ rock wool | ☐ other: _____] **insulation protecting from weather conditions and damage.**

☐ **Completed drywall installation on various** _____ *[#]* [☐ room | ☐ square footage | ☐ other: _____] _____ *[type of]* [☐ demolition | ☐ construction | ☐ renovation | ☐ restoration | ☐ repair | ☐ other: _____] **projects ranging from** $_____ **to** $_____ *[amounts],* **completing all projects on time and within budget.**

Change Management

☐ **Strategize, plan, and develop change processes that inspire leaders and managers to drive and deliver** _____ *[type of]* **changes on time, on target, and on budget by** [☐ selecting appropriate Change Agents | ☐ identifying internal requirements | ☐ determining required resources | ☐ brainstorming possible roadblocks and implementation issues | ☐ examining external pressures | ☐ other: _____] **that drive change and increase** [☐ credibility | ☐ profitability | ☐ market share | ☐ customer satisfaction | ☐ productivity | ☐ efficiencies | ☐ work culture | ☐ momentum | ☐ opportunities | ☐ other: _____].

☐ **As the firm's** [☐ change management leader | ☐ change navigation planner | ☐ implementation planning and solutions architect | ☐ other: _____], **perform** [☐ strategy implementation | ☐ change management | ☐ other: _____] **covering** [☐ change navigation planning | ☐ business case development | ☐ business process improvement | ☐ process design and implementation |

☐ service delivery models) | ☐ job analysis and design | ☐ project management | ☐ job design | ☐ incentive programs | ☐ individual and team performance management | ☐ communications planning and execution | ☐ other: _____].

☐ **Coordinate and manage the development and execution of multiple** [☐ cross-organizational | ☐ cross-divisional | ☐ departmental] **change programs including** _____, _____, **and** _____ *[which programs?]* **that improve** [☐ individual | ☐ organizational] **performance company-wide in the areas of** _____, _____, **and** _____ *[which areas?]*.

☐ **Manage** [☐ large-scale] [☐ organizational change programs | ☐ company-wide change initiatives | ☐ training and development projects | ☐ human resource initiatives | ☐ other: _____] **that involve** [☐ strategic planning | ☐ organizational (☐ analysis / ☐ diagnoses / ☐ planning / ☐ problem-solving) | ☐ management coaching | ☐ team building | ☐ other: _____], **and design and implement associated training programs that meet operating goals and objectives.**

☐ **Influence, energize, and motivate team members to apply project management skills to help them** [☐ understand the impact of change | ☐ solve dynamic challenges | ☐ set realistic expectations | ☐ overcome resource problems | ☐ tackle political or bureaucratic obstacles | ☐ other: _____] **to bring projects to a successful delivery.**

☐ **Design and implement various** [☐ large-scale | ☐ other: _____] **Human Resource** _____ *[type of]* [☐ solutions | ☐ implementation projects | ☐ other: _____] **Involving** _____ *[what?]*.

Client Billing Scope

☐ [☐ Manage | ☐ Supervise | ☐ Prepare | ☐ Coordinate] **billing for a customer base of** _____ *[#]*, **keeping all records current and ensuring accuracy.**

☐ [☐ Conduct | ☐ Supervise] **computer entry of daily** [☐ billing | ☐ payments | ☐ recordkeeping | ☐ client communiqué | ☐ payroll | ☐ other: _____], **ensuring accurate data entry at all times.**

☐ **Perform data entry of** [☐ customer | ☐ contractual | ☐ sales | ☐ other: _____] **information, Including** _____, _____, **and** _____ **on** _____ *[name of]* **system.**

☐ **Accurately complete and verify data entry of** _____ *[#]* [☐ daily | ☐ weekly | ☐ monthly] **invoices using** [☐ QuickBooks | ☐ Excel | ☐ Quicken | ☐ other: _____].

☐ **Accurately complete and verify data entry of** _____ *[#]* **weekly invoices using** [☐ QuickBooks | ☐ Excel | ☐ Quicken | ☐ other: _____].

☐ **Process approximately** _____ *[#]* [☐ invoice pages | ☐ sales contracts | ☐ letters of credit | ☐ other: _____] **weekly compared to a norm of** _____ *[#]* **completing a five-day workload in only** _____ *[#]* **days.**

☐ **Keep track of all client billable hours and types of jobs performed, and calculate client fees based on dollar amounts to charge for each task for this** [☐ accounting | ☐ insurance | ☐ law | ☐ consulting | ☐ medical | ☐ other: _____] **firm.**

☐ **Compile accurate records of all** [☐ services rendered | ☐ goods sold | ☐ other: _____], **calculate amounts due, and post entries to** [*client* | ☐ customer | ☐ patron | ☐ patient | ☐ other: _____] **accounts.**

☐ **Prepare, verify and send client itemized** [☐ statements | ☐ invoices] **containing** [☐ dates of services provided | ☐ types and codes of services performed | ☐ credit terms | ☐ shipment dates | ☐ other: _____] **and total amounts due.**

☐ **Review** [☐ purchase orders | ☐ sales tickets | ☐ charge slips | ☐ other: _____] **to calculate customer amounts due taking into account any** [☐ discounts | ☐ special rates | ☐ credit terms | ☐ other: _____].

☐ **Research, troubleshoot, and resolve all billing errors, requiring** [☐ patience | ☐ diligence | ☐ ability to overcome frustration | ☐ other: _____] **when numbers frequently didn't balance.**

☐ **Charged with the responsibility of training newly hired employees due to** [☐ patience | ☐ high level of customer service | ☐ ability to make information clear | ☐ other: _____].

☐ **Create accurate** [☐ invoices | ☐ job estimates | ☐ other: _____] **by consulting rate books to determine** [☐ product | ☐ shipping | ☐ other: _____] **costs of** _____ *[what?]*.

☐ **Contact insurance companies to determine reimbursement amounts and advise** [☐ patients | ☐ clients | ☐ customers | ☐ patrons | ☐ other: _____] **of amounts due.**

☐ **Use** [☐ Quick Books | ☐ Quicken | ☐ Excel | ☐ other: _____] **to** [☐ post entries | ☐ calculate charges | ☐ prepare customer invoices | ☐ update client files | ☐ other: _____].

ACHIEVEMENT SAMPLE:

☐ **Created a** _____ *[type of]* [☐ filing | ☐ data entry | ☐ other: _____] [☐ system | ☐ procedure | ☐ program | ☐ other: _____], **which** resulted in _____ *[what benefits?]*.

Client Billing Functions

☐ **Coordinate and prepare** [☐ billing | ☐ bookkeeping | ☐ accounts payable | ☐ accounts receivable | ☐ general ledger | ☐ inventory | ☐ purchasing | ☐ other: _____] **for a customer base of** _____ *[#]*, **keeping all records current and ensuring their accuracy.**

☐ **Process approximately** _____ *[#]* [☐ invoice pages | ☐ sales contracts | ☐ letters of credit | ☐ other: _____] [☐ daily | ☐ weekly | ☐ monthly] **compared to a norm of** _____ *[#]* **completing a five-day workload in only** _____ *[#]* **days.**

☐ **Keep track of all client billable hours and types of jobs performed and calculate client fees based on dollar amounts to charge for each task.**

☐ **Prepare, verify and send client itemized** [☐ statements | ☐ invoices] **containing** [☐ dates of services provided | ☐ types and codes of services performed | ☐ credit terms | ☐ shipment dates | ☐ other: _____] **and total amounts due.**

☐ **Respond to customer questions and resolve all concerns relative to** [☐ invoice entries | ☐ billing errors | ☐ discrepancies | ☐ other: _____] **resulting in** [☐ customer satisfaction | ☐ decreased accounts receivables | ☐ customers paying their bills on time | ☐ other: _____].

☐ **Compile accurate records of all** [☐ services rendered | ☐ goods sold | ☐ other: _____], **calculate amounts due, and post entries to** [☐ client | ☐ customer | ☐ patron | ☐ other: _____] **accounts.**

☐ **Verify data entry of all customer information checking for errors before printing invoices and sending to customers.**

☐ **Review** [☐ purchase orders | ☐ sales tickets | ☐ charge slips | ☐ other: _____] **to calculate customer amounts due taking into account any** [☐ discounts | ☐ special rates | ☐ credit terms | ☐ other: _____].

☐ **Research, troubleshoot, and resolve all billing errors, requiring** [☐ patience | ☐ diligence | ☐ ability to overcome frustration | ☐ other: _____] **when numbers frequently didn't balance.**

☐ **Respond to customer questions and resolve all concerns relative to** [☐ invoice entries | ☐ billing errors | ☐ discrepancies | ☐ other: _____] **resulting in** [☐ customer satisfaction | ☐ decreased accounts receivables | ☐ customers paying their bills on time | ☐ other: _____].

☐ **Create accurate** [☐ invoices | ☐ job estimates | ☐ other: _____] **by consulting rate books to determine** [☐ product | ☐ shipping | ☐ other: _____] **costs of** _____ *[what?]*.

☐ **Use** [☐ Quick Books | ☐ Quicken | ☐ Excel | ☐ other: _____] **to** [☐ post entries | ☐ calculate charges | ☐ prepare customer invoices | ☐ update client files | ☐ other: _____].

☐ **Act as liaison with** _____ *[type of]* **companies for** _____ *[purpose]*.

Client Meeting & Strategizing – Construction

See also "Client Relations" and "Client Presentations & Proposals," and "Customer Service & Problem Resolution,"

☐ **Meet with potential** _____ *[type of]* **clients to** [☐ determine their design and construction needs | ☐ provide cost estimates | ☐ define requirements | ☐ demonstrate benefits of _____ *(what?)*] **in the design and build of** _____ *[what?]*.

☐ **Meet and strategize with** _____ *[type of]* **clients to determine the scope of their projects and related architectural design services required to build those projects including** [☐ assessing needs | ☐ identifying options | ☐ defining challenges | ☐ generating ideas | ☐ strategizing solutions | ☐ ascertaining budget | ☐ selling high-dollar projects | ☐ providing alternative methods | ☐ preparing job estimates | ☐ determining design direction | ☐ defining project scope | ☐ setting project timeframes | ☐ presenting proposals | ☐ providing technical advice | ☐ resolving challenges | ☐ delivering architectural drawings | ☐ other: _____].

☐ **Consult with clients to assess their** [☐ architectural | ☐ carpentry | ☐ electrical | ☐ plumbing | ☐ HVAC-R | ☐ other: _____] **needs, define their goals, and provide workable solutions for the** [☐ design | ☐ installation | ☐ construction | ☐ other: _____] **of** _____ *[what?]*.

☐ **Assess** [☐ business | ☐ client] **needs and translate** _____ *[type of]* **design and functional challenges into successful** _____ *[type of]* [☐ buildings | ☐ complexes | ☐ structures | ☐ systems | ☐ products | ☐ services | ☐ equipment | ☐ other: _____] **that reflects** [☐ clients' | ☐ firm's] **goals and objectives.**

☐ **Consult with client representatives to discuss** _____ *[type of]* [☐ design | ☐ construction | ☐ design-and-build] **project** [☐ objectives | ☐ scope | ☐ requirements | ☐ budget | ☐ other: _____] **required for proposed** _____ *[type of]* [☐ engineering | ☐ architectural | ☐ other: _____] **projects for the design and build of** _____ *[what?]*; **determine** _____ *[type of]* **requirements; and provide clients with various options.**

☐ **Meet and strategize with clients to assess their** _____ *[type of]* [☐ engineering | ☐ architectural | ☐ other: _____] **needs, define their goals, and provide workable solutions in the development of** _____ *[what?]* **complying with all** [☐ client goals and challenges | ☐ electrical codes | ☐ building codes | ☐ zoning laws | ☐ fire regulations | ☐ other: _____].

☐ **Identify, define, and document client priorities and translate those requirements into effective** _____ *[type of]* **design strategies and construction projects.**

☐ **Consult with clients on** [☐ the selection of building sites | ☐ the preparation of land-use studies | ☐ land development planning | ☐ energy saving measures | ☐ other: _____]; [☐ and conduct feasibility and/or environmental impact studies as needed].

Client Presentations & Proposals

See also "Client Meeting & Strategizing," "Client Relations," and "Customer Service."

☐ [☐ Create and generate | ☐ Review and approve] **detailed** _____ *[type of]* **client** [☐ presentations | ☐ proposals | ☐ cost estimates | ☐ project plans | ☐ contracts | ☐ other: _____] **based on clients' understanding and expectations so desired** _____ *[type of]* **solutions can be successfully implemented on time and within budget.**

☐ **Determine** [☐ internal | ☐ external] **client** _____ *[type of]* **goals and develop detailed** _____ *[type of]* [☐ project plans | ☐ proposals | ☐ presentations | ☐ other: _____] **for** _____ *[what?]* **that include all project** [☐ objectives | ☐ specifications | ☐ time frames | ☐ costs | ☐ budget | ☐ resource allocation | ☐ quality assurance | ☐ other: _____] **to ensure needs of all parties are met.**

☐ **Interface and work closely with** _____ *[whom?]* **in the** [☐ development of project strategies | ☐ identification of project scope | ☐ executing of project plans | ☐ determination of required materials and resources | ☐ coordination of resources | ☐ other: _____].

☐ **Define and document client priorities and translate those requirements into effective** _____ *[type of]* **solutions and strategies.**

☐ **Identify and define project scope and objectives with all** [☐ internal | ☐ external] **clients; and provide** [☐ project management | ☐ other: _____] **expertise in the development of** _____ *[type of]* [☐ project plans | ☐ proposals | ☐ presentations | ☐ other: _____].

☐ **Create and generate** _____ *[type of]* **client** [☐ presentations | ☐ publications | ☐ other: _____], **including** _____ *[type of]* [☐ newsletters | ☐ financials | ☐ manuals | ☐ reports | ☐ other: _____] **using** [☐ Microsoft (☐ PowerPoint / ☐ Publisher / ☐ Word) | ☐ Adobe InDesign | ☐QuarkXpress | ☐other: _____].

☐ **Use advanced word-processing functions such as** [☐ calculating tables | ☐ style galleries | ☐ columns | ☐ charts and graphs | ☐ headers and footers | ☐ mail merges | ☐ cross-referencing | ☐ borders and shading | ☐ other: _____] **to prepare** [☐ presentations | ☐ newsletters | ☐ brochures | ☐ sales materials | ☐ procedure manuals | ☐ training manuals | ☐ other: _____].

☐ **Use** _____ *[type of]* **software to create attractive** _____ *[type of]* [☐ presentations | (☐ company / ☐ product) brochures | ☐ flyers | ☐ direct mail pieces | ☐ other: _____] **for** [☐ prospective customers | ☐ management meetings | ☐ special events | ☐ other: _____].

☐ **Lay out, design, and produce** _____ *[what?]* **for** _____ *[whom?]* **that** [☐ creates a positive impression | ☐ increases value | ☐ achieves _____ *[what?]* | ☐ other: _____] **for company's high-end client projects.**

☐ **Deliver highly effective oral and visual sales presentations to a variety of** _____ *[type of]* **customers and attend industry trade shows to promote** _____ *[type of]* **company, products, and services resulting in** _____ *[benefits]*.

☐ **Handle** _____ *[what processes?]* **in the** [☐ creation | ☐ design | ☐ development | ☐ production | ☐ other: _____] **of various** _____ *[type of]* **projects, managing all phases—from concept to completion.**

Client Relations – Architecture & Construction

See also "Client Meeting & Strategizing," "Client Presentations & Proposals," "Customer Service," and "Billing."

☐ **Work with** [☐ Fortune ☐ 100 | ☐ 500 | ☐ 1000 | ☐ other: _____] **clients including** _____, _____, **and** _____ *[clients]* **to** [☐ understand their goals | ☐ identify their needs | ☐ conduct presentations | ☐ present proposals | ☐ help define strategy | ☐ provide technical advice | ☐ resolve challenges | ☐ solicit feedback | ☐ provide alternative solutions | ☐ communicate tradeoffs | ☐ establish a high level of trust | ☐ deliver client expectations | ☐ other: _____].

☐ **Collaborate with owners to maintain customer satisfaction by** [☐ listening to and interpreting their needs | ☐ paying careful attention to detail | ☐ making changes as needed | ☐ ensuring a 100% positive experience for all clients | ☐ other: _____].

☐ **Maintain direct client relationships and interact with** [☐ engineers | ☐ architects | ☐ contractors | ☐ subcontractors | ☐ urban planners | ☐ interior designers | ☐ landscape architects | ☐ zoning officials | ☐ inspectors | ☐ the town | ☐ other: _____] **and other professionals during the design and** [☐ construction | ☐ development | ☐ production] **process.**

☐ **Work with clients to maintain customer satisfaction by** [☐ listening to and interpreting their needs | ☐ paying careful attention to detail | ☐ making changes as needed | ☐ ensuring a 100% positive experience for all clients | ☐ other: _____].

☐ **Act as liaison with customer and project staff to ensure positive customer relationships, job satisfaction, and service quality and to** [☐ properly identify and process scope changes | ☐ address and resolve any issues | ☐ communicate regarding project milestones | ☐ other: _____].

☐ **Earned client respect and corporate recognition for providing exemplary care and ongoing support, service, and follow-up throughout all phases of** _____ *[type of]* **construction projects.**

☐ **As firm's primary client contact, evaluate the strengths and weaknesses of client** _____ *[which?]* **initiatives, determine whether they are adequately meeting clients' needs, and offer alternative creative solutions.**

☐ **Build long-term client relationships, maximizing** _____ *[what?]* **dollars, receiving repeat business and referrals by** _____ *[doing what?].*

ACHIEVEMENT SAMPLES:

☐ **Built strong, trusting, long-term client relationships, maximizing dollars and receiving repeat business and referrals by** [☐ ensuring customer needs are acknowledged, and addressed | ☐ promoting a partnership atmosphere | ☐ problem-solving challenges to the clients' satisfaction| ☐ demonstrating flexibility | ☐ clearly defining expectations | ☐ presenting alternative budget-friendly solutions | ☐ other: _____] **which resulted in** _____ *[what additional business or other benefits?].*

☐ **Earned client respect and corporate recognition for providing exemplary care and ongoing support, service, and follow-up throughout all phases of** _____ *[type of]* **projects.**

☐ **Actively maintained positive customer relationships to ensure satisfaction and service quality on all** [☐ service calls | ☐ projects | ☐ installations | ☐ repairs | ☐ other: _____] **by** [☐ relating to them in a professional and courteous manner | ☐ listening carefully to their concerns | ☐ responding to their questions or complaints | ☐ making satisfactory adjustments | ☐ escalating their requests to _____ *(whom?)* | ☐ other: _____].

☐ **Cultivated excellent client relations, resulting in a strong base of referral business and** _____ *[#]* **new accounts.**

Closeout Processing & Post Construction Services

See also "Inspections & Compliance" (various categories), as applicable.

☐ **Successfully complete and close out all** _____ *[type of]* [☐ design and] **construction projects, ensuring** [☐ verification of estimates | ☐ completion of all change orders and punch list items | ☐ all specifications and expected deliverables are met | ☐ client satisfaction with completed projects | ☐ receipt of client payment | ☐ all contractor disbursements are paid | ☐ other: _____].

☐ **Perform final project reviews for the construction close-out process, approve payment requests, and conduct building site inspections to ensure compliance with plans, specifications, and building codes.**

☐ **Conduct** [☐ post construction reviews | ☐ customer satisfaction surveys | ☐ project close-out documentation | ☐ approval of contractor invoices | ☐ records archival | ☐ other: _____] **for the administrative processing of all design-and-build project close-outs.**

☐ **Provide** _____ *[type of]* **postconstruction services and advice to clients to determine how well** [☐ architectural | ☐ engineering] [☐ design | ☐ construction] **is adapting to their needs, and make needed improvements.**

☐ **Review contractors' close-out administration ensuring all contractual requirements have been met, administer the completion and closeout process on all** _____ *[type of]* **projects, and review change orders** [☐ with (☐ Architects / ☐ Engineers / ☐ Project Managers / ☐ other: _____) | ☐ in accordance with the client's approval process | ☐ other: _____] **to ensure accuracy and job completion.**

Communications – Construction

See also "Interdisciplinary / Project Team Member" and "Work Collaboration" categories.

☐ **Conduct** _____ *[type of]* [☐ weekly | ☐ regular | ☐ intermittent | ☐ other: _____] [☐ preconstruction conferences | ☐ project meetings ☐ strategy sessions | ☐ teleconferences | ☐ other: _____] **to review** [☐ project progress | ☐ approval processes | ☐ lines of authority | ☐ other: _____] **ensuring** [☐ communication among all involved parties | ☐ projects remain on schedule and within budget | ☐ change orders are effected | ☐ disputes are amicably resolved | ☐ compliance with all building codes | ☐ other: _____].

☐ **Effectively facilitate across-the-board communication regarding** _____ *[type of]* **project scope, expected deliverables, and major milestones with** _____ *[whom?]* **and other involved parties** [☐ during all phases of the project lifecycle | ☐ from concept to completion | ☐ other: _____].

☐ **Communicate with and regularly keep** [☐ Project Manager | ☐ Superintendent | ☐ Maintenance Manager | ☐ crew | ☐ District Administrators | ☐ field representatives | ☐ general contractors | ☐ architects | ☐ engineers | ☐ vendors | ☐ inspectors | ☐ others: _____] **informed of** [☐ production schedule | ☐ material and labor management | ☐ work production status | ☐ scope changes | ☐ back charges | ☐ other: _____].

☐ **Effectively communicate with** [☐ all project team members | ☐ management | ☐ clients | ☐ others: _____] **and other involved parties regarding** _____ *[type of]* **project objectives, scope, expected deliverables, and milestones** [☐ during all project phases | ☐ from concept to completion | ☐ other: _____] **by** _____ *[doing what?]*.

☐ **Communicate with management staff, Architects, Engineers, subcontractors, and other involved parties regarding project scope, expected deliverables, and major milestones—from concept to completion.**

☐ **Determine appropriate recipient communication methods to ensure clear, effective, and up-to-date communications via** [☐ typed procedures | ☐ the firm's Intranet | ☐ formal memoranda | ☐ written reports | ☐ status meetings | ☐ continual direction | ☐ other: _____].

ACHIEVEMENT SAMPLES: *See also Achievements under "Project Management – General."*

☐ **Optimized communication between** [☐ engineers | ☐ architects | ☐ project management | ☐ other: _____], **and management staffs to more closely meet client needs by** _____ *[doing what?]*, **resulting in** [☐ projects that meet client needs 100% on target | ☐ fewer client changes | ☐ increased productivity | ☐ other benefits: _____].

☐ **Persuasively and clearly present information, respond to** _____ *[type of]* **questions, and facilitate across-the-board communication regarding** _____ *[type of]* **status on all** _____ *[which?]* **projects with** _____ *[whom?]*.

☐ **Optimized communication between** _____ *[whom?]* **and management staffs to more closely meet client needs by** _____ *[doing what?]*, **resulting in** [☐ projects that meet client needs | ☐ fewer client changes | ☐ increased productivity | ☐ other benefits: _____].

Compliance Investigations & Inspections

See "Inspections & Compliance."

Compliance – Safety & Responsibility for Others

See "Safety & Responsibility for Others."

Concrete Pouring, Setting & Finishing Labor

☐ **Set up** [☐ wood | ☐ plastic] **concrete forms, and spread, level, and finish poured concrete in segments at** _____ *[type of]* **construction sites, ensuring concrete is level and corners are finished off.**

☐ [☐ Construct | ☐ Fabricate | ☐ Install | ☐ Repair] [☐ concrete beams | ☐ columns | ☐ panels | ☐ structures | ☐ masonry | ☐ framework | ☐ roadways | ☐ driveways | ☐ sidewalks | ☐ bridges | ☐ parking lots | ☐ other: _____] **according to specifications for** _____ *[type of]* **jobs, conforming to all building codes.**

☐ **Set and align concrete forms to specified pitch and depth, direct the concrete casting, and check forms to ensure they are properly constructed for this** _____ *[type of]* **company.**

☐ **Install** [☐ steel plates | ☐ anchor bolts | ☐ door sills | ☐ _____ *(type of)* fixtures] **in poured concrete and** [☐ polish | ☐ stain | ☐ stamp | ☐ pattern | ☐ sprinkle colored (☐ marble / ☐ stone chips / ☐ powdered steel) to | ☐ other: _____] **surface to render an embedded** _____ *[type of]* **decorative finish.**

☐ **Spread, level, smooth, and finish concrete, using** [☐ pneumatic tampers | ☐ hand trowels | ☐ power trowels | ☐ edgers | ☐ jointers | ☐ hand screeds | ☐ power screeds | ☐ power vibrators | ☐ groovers | ☐ floats | ☐ bull floats | ☐ concrete saws | ☐ power tools | ☐ finishing spades | ☐ hoes | ☐ edging tools | ☐ polishing machines | ☐ surfacing machines | ☐ picks | ☐ shovels | ☐ brooms | ☐ rakes | ☐ levels | ☐ routers | ☐ sanders | ☐ calipers | ☐ other: _____] **applying hardening and sealing compounds to cure and waterproof surface.**

☐ **Perform general labor including** [☐ cleaning and preparing work sites | ☐ controlling passing traffic around work zones | ☐ measuring and marking layout areas | ☐ eliminating possible hazards | ☐ signaling construction equipment operators | ☐ compacting and leveling earth to grade specifications | ☐ safely operating concrete truck | ☐ facilitating concrete pouring | ☐ mixing cement | ☐ molding expansion joints and edges | ☐ identifying hazards | ☐ other: _____] **following all company policies and OSHA regulations.**

☐ **Assist** [☐ paving | ☐ construction] **crew with various activities including** [☐ loading and unloading materials | ☐ digging ditches or trenches | ☐ dumping trucks | ☐ backfilling excavations | ☐ building and clamping molds | ☐ spreading and leveling materials | ☐ shoveling and raking | ☐ running wheelbarrow | ☐ tearing down and cleaning forms when concrete is cured | ☐ other: _____].

☐ **Safely operate a concrete truck and deliver ready-mix concrete to** _____ *[type of]* **construction sites, recording sales and delivery information, keeping operator logs up to date in accordance with Department of Transportation (DOT) regulations, and maintaining delivery communication with Dispatcher.**

☐ **Apply** [☐ advanced | ☐ working] **knowledge of and experience in** [☐ blueprint reading | ☐ interpretation of plans and specifications | ☐ determining measurements and sizes | ☐ concrete formwork | ☐ concrete finishing | ☐ construction methods | ☐ concrete installation standards and procedures | ☐ concrete mixing procedures | ☐ surface finishing | ☐ concrete pile caps | ☐ heavy concrete columns | ☐ decorative concrete finishing | ☐ latex and epoxy applications | ☐ muriatic acid applications | ☐ chemical additives to speed up drying | ☐ concrete beams, columns, and panels fabrication | ☐ vertical face | ☐ pavement thickness | ☐ surface grout depth | ☐ safety policies and procedures | ☐ problem-solving | ☐ other: _____] **in performance of** _____ *[type of]* **jobs.**

☐ **Waterproof and/or restore** _____ *[type of]* **concrete surfaces using** _____ *[what?]* **applications and compounds.**

Concrete Pouring, Setting & Finishing Supervision & Oversight

☐ **Oversee the concrete and steel reinforcement of** [☐ residential | ☐ commercial | ☐ highway | ☐ other: _____] **construction projects and the finishing of** _____ *[type of]* **walls with** [☐ wood | ☐ structural metal | ☐ lath | ☐ plaster | ☐ other: _____] **materials meeting all project budgets and deadlines on or ahead of schedule.**

☐ **Plan, coordinate, and supervise the functions of** _____ *[#]* **concrete installers, finishers, and laborers for** _____ *[type of]* **jobs for this** _____ *[type of]* **firm.**

☐ **Supervise diverse** _____ *[type of]* **concrete projects including** [☐ foundation inspection and testing | ☐ structural fills / backfills | ☐ precise and cast-in-place concrete, grout, and mortar | ☐ reinforcing and structural steel | ☐ roofing | ☐ fireproofing | ☐ asphalt | ☐ other: _____].

☐ **Coordinate and direct project team crew activities in the areas of** [☐ scheduling | ☐ concrete preparation and pouring | ☐ building to specifications | ☐ concrete measurements | ☐ formwork | ☐ mixing | ☐ installation | ☐ application of chemical additives | ☐ surface finishing | ☐ problem troubleshooting | ☐ other: _____] **ensuring accurate measurements, quality of finished concrete projects, and compliance with all safety policies, practices, and procedures.**

☐ **Supervise and direct** _____ *[#]* **Concrete** [☐ Masons | ☐ Installers | ☐ Form Setters | ☐ Layers | ☐ Finishers | ☐ Smoothers | ☐ Laborers | ☐ Carpenters | ☐ Patchers | ☐ Grinder Operators | ☐ Curb Builders | ☐ Joint Setters | ☐ Joint Finishers | ☐ Stone Finishers | ☐ Material Testers | ☐ Floaters | ☐ Terrazzo Finishers | ☐ other: _____] [☐ as well as field supervisors and other contractors] **to ensure** [☐ efficient use of equipment and materials | ☐ correct elevation | ☐ all project objectives are met with quality | ☐ project is constructed in accordance with design, budget, and schedule | ☐ contractual performance of projects are met | ☐ other: _____].

☐ **Provide project management oversight in concrete operations including** [☐ quality control | ☐ monitoring labor budget | ☐ interpreting plans and specifications | ☐ ordering and maintaining sufficient supplies | ☐ inventory management and control | ☐ interviewing, hiring, and training (☐ employees / ☐ laborers) | ☐ equipment scheduling | ☐ identifying potential design or construction problems | ☐ clarifying discrepancies | ☐ administering Safety Program | ☐ scheduling equipment | ☐ monitoring how the weather affects the curing process | ☐ completing _____ *(type of)* paperwork | ☐ other: _____].

☐ **Manage and oversee project team crew activities in the areas of** [☐ scheduling | ☐ concrete preparation and pouring | ☐ building to specifications | ☐ concrete measurements | ☐ formwork | ☐ mixing | ☐ installation | ☐ application of chemical additives | ☐ surface finishing | ☐ problem troubleshooting | ☐ other: _____] **ensuring accurate measurements, quality of finished concrete projects, and compliance with all safety policies, practices, and procedures.**

☐ **Collaborate with other on-site labor teams including** _____ *[which?]* [☐ contractors | ☐ subcontractors | ☐ others: _____], **to resolve problems and ensure quality, safety, and support of** _____ *[type of]* **project objectives.**

Construction Leadership Scope

See also "Architectural Leadership & Direction," "Engineering Leadership," "Project Management Leadership," and "Executive Leadership & Direction," as applicable.

☐ **Provide senior management oversight in the start-up through completion of all** [☐ procurement | ☐ negotiation | ☐ demolition | ☐ design | ☐ construction | ☐ other: _____] **of** [☐ public works | ☐ civil | ☐ transportation | ☐ other: _____] **projects including** [☐ design-and-build | ☐ general contracting | ☐ construction management | ☐ other: _____] **of** _____ *[what?]* **essential to** [☐ transformation of communities | ☐ structural stability of transportation systems | ☐ other: _____].

☐ **Coordinate and oversee all** [☐ Architect | ☐ Project Manager | ☐ Engineer | ☐ other: _____] **team activities at a strategic level—from** [☐ procurement | ☐ demolition | ☐ construction | ☐ other: _____] **through to completion.**

☐ **Manage and oversee the** [☐ construction project | ☐ project delivery | ☐ field supervision | ☐ other: _____] **management team(s) in** [☐ strategy execution | ☐ design-and-build | ☐ financial management | ☐ procurement | ☐ resource acquisition | ☐ approval management | ☐ municipal permit attainment | ☐ quality assurance | ☐ safety | ☐ estimating | ☐ subcontracting | ☐ other: _____] **activities to develop, coordinate, and administer the design and construction of new and refurbished** _____ *[type of]* [☐ buildings | ☐ facilities | ☐ properties | ☐ other: _____].

☐ **Direct and oversee** [☐ strategic business planning | ☐ new business development | ☐ risk management | ☐ price/cost management | ☐ contract administration | ☐ teaming alliances | ☐ account management | ☐ personnel development | ☐ business management | ☐ other: _____].

☐ **Lead and direct the design and construction of** [☐ structural | ☐ architectural | ☐ civil | ☐ industrial | ☐ environmental | ☐ construction | ☐ transportation | ☐ water | ☐ geotechnical | ☐ electrical | ☐ agricultural | ☐ aeronautic | ☐ chemical | ☐ mechanical | ☐ electronics | ☐ biomedical | ☐ mining | ☐ petroleum | ☐ nuclear | ☐ geotechnical | ☐ other: _____] **engineering projects including** [☐ highways | ☐ roadways | ☐ buildings | ☐ airports | ☐ tunnels | ☐ water supply systems | ☐ sewage systems | ☐ bridges | ☐ other: _____] **for this $_____** *[revenues]* _____ *[type of]* [☐ engineering | ☐ architectural | ☐ design-and-build | ☐ construction management | ☐ other: _____] [☐ firm | ☐ government agency].

☐ **Provide executive oversight in the management and operations of the** _____ *[which?]* **departments for this $_____** *[revenues]* _____ *[type of]* **firm with** _____ *[#]* [☐ locations | ☐ employees | ☐ clients | ☐ other: _____] **including** [☐ the establishment of long-range goals | ☐ execution of operating plans | ☐ management of key customers | ☐ other: _____].

☐ **Manage and oversee all facets of this $_____** *[revenues]* [☐ commercial | ☐ civil | ☐ residential | ☐ other: _____] [☐ design-and-build | ☐ engineering | ☐ construction management | ☐ general contracting | ☐ other: _____] **firm coordinating projects with** [☐ engineers | ☐ architects | ☐ project managers | ☐ general contractors | ☐ subcontractors | ☐ business representatives | ☐ homeowners | ☐ other: _____].

☐ **Direct and oversee construction management functions including** [☐ strategic planning, design, and construction | ☐ capital improvement projects | ☐ client relationships | ☐ dispute resolution | ☐ proposed land developments | ☐ contract negotiations | ☐ construction timetables | ☐ construction cost estimating | ☐ construction submittals approval | ☐ recommendation of value-engineering and other cost saving opportunities spending versus budget monitoring | ☐ construction risk mitigation | ☐ other: _____] **to ensure quality control and compliance with all specifications and codes.**

☐ **Lead and direct the design and construction of** [☐ architectural | ☐ civil | ☐ industrial | ☐ structural | ☐ environmental | ☐ electrical | ☐ agricultural | ☐ materials | ☐ aeronautic | ☐ chemical | ☐ mechanical | ☐ electronics | ☐ biomedical | ☐ mining | ☐ petroleum | ☐ geotechnical | ☐ other: _____] **projects for this $_____** *[revenues]* _____ *[type of]* **firm.**

☐ **Facilitate** [☐ client contact | ☐ architectural design | ☐ site planning | ☐ project development | ☐ project coordination | ☐ engineering research and analysis | ☐ other: _____] **for the development and implementation of** _____ *[what?]* **ensuring compliance with all** [☐ building codes | ☐ zoning laws | ☐ fire regulations | ☐ health and safety regulations | ☐ cGMPs | ☐ other: _____] **for this** _____ *[type of]* **company.**

☐ **Provide construction management leadership and direction for all aspects of construction in the design and build of** _____ *[type of]* **projects for this $_____** *[revenues]* [☐ construction management | ☐ design-and-build | ☐ engineering | ☐ architectural | ☐ contracting | ☐ other: _____] **firm.**

☐ **Direct construction management operations for this $_____** *[revenues]* _____ *[type of]* **firm overseeing the** [☐ execution of final detailed construction project designs | ☐ verification of construction conceptual budgets | ☐ administration and archival of construction documents | ☐ other: _____].

☐ **Manage and oversee** [☐ trades supervision | ☐ construction inspection | ☐ quality control | ☐ building and safety codes enforcement | ☐ design guidelines and specifications standards development | ☐ other: _____].

☐ **Direct the construction of all** _____ *[type of]* **projects including the** [☐ review and/or modification of construction drawings | ☐ development of job estimates and budgets | ☐ securing of competitive bids | ☐ handling of contract negotiations | ☐ maintaining of client relationships | ☐ scheduling and coordination of trades | ☐ performing of on-site construction supervision | ☐ negotiation and processing of change orders | ☐ other: _____], **completing all projects on time and within budget.**

ACHIEVEMENT SAMPLES: See *"Achievement Examples," "Construction Projects,"* Achievements under *"Construction Leadership Functions," "Cost Reductions & Savings," "Employee Retention & Decreased Turnover," "Increased Account Base," "Increased Sales & Profitability," "Overcoming Obstacles,"* and *"Productivity Improvement."*

Construction Leadership Functions

See also "Executive Functions Scope" and "Team Leadership & Direction – Project Management Team."

☐ **Prepare and enforce all contracts and agreements in the design-and-build of** _____ *[type of]* **projects; and conduct building site inspections to ensure compliance in all areas.**

☐ **Perform senior-level construction planning activities in overseeing the management of** _____ *[type of]* **projects to ensure cost-effective, functional completed projects that consider** [☐ fiscal | ☐ legal | ☐ technical | ☐ demographic | ☐ economic | ☐ safety | ☐ other: _____] **aspects**.

☐ **Plan, design, and oversee construction and maintenance of** [☐ highways | ☐ roadways | ☐ buildings | ☐ airports | ☐ tunnels | ☐ water supply systems | ☐ sewage systems | ☐ bridges | ☐ other: _____] **civil engineering structures and facilities.**

☐ **Direct the** [☐ firm's | ☐ division's | ☐ department's] [☐ management practices | ☐ fiscal planning | ☐ other: _____] **to strategically** [☐ plan | ☐ design | ☐ formulate | ☐ spearhead | ☐ develop | ☐ administer | ☐ execute | ☐ implement | ☐ maintain] _____ *[what?]* **for the** [☐ location | ☐ design | ☐ construction | ☐ remodel | ☐ upkeep | ☐ operation | ☐ other: _____] **of all** _____ *[type of projects].*

☐ **Oversee commercial construction cost estimates and approve** _____ *[type of]* [☐ design | ☐ construction] [☐ bids | ☐ plans | ☐ specifications | ☐ cost estimates | ☐ contracts | ☐ other: _____] **checking for compliance with** [(☐ firm's / ☐ clients' / ☐ department's) requirements | ☐ construction methods | ☐ zoning and building codes | ☐ local ordinances | ☐ Environmental Quality Act | ☐ Occupational Safety and Health Act | ☐ other: _____].

☐ [☐ Set | ☐ Partake in setting] **the firm's strategic goals and priorities, and establish** [☐ project management practices | ☐ department standards and procedures | ☐ other: _____] **that meet the organization's strategy including** _____, _____, **and** _____ *[which practices?].*

☐ **Coordinate and oversee all** [☐ Engineer | ☐ Architect | ☐ Project Manager | ☐ other: _____] **team activities at a strategic level—from** [☐ procurement | ☐ demolition | ☐ design | ☐ construction | ☐ other: _____] **through to completion.**

☐ **Manage and oversee** [☐ client proposals | ☐ job estimates | ☐ project scheduling | ☐ budgeting | ☐ design | ☐ programming | ☐ quality management | ☐ client interface | ☐ project delivery management | ☐ field supervision activities | ☐ other: _____] **to ensure optimum client satisfaction and regulatory compliance for this** _____ *[type of]* **firm with a** [☐ staff | ☐ client base] **of** _____ *[#].*

☐ **Procure and manage** [☐ design | ☐ construction | ☐ other: _____] [☐ contractors | ☐ subcontractors] **on all directly managed** [☐ large commercial development | ☐ other type: _____] **projects—from inception to completion.**

☐ **Oversee and inspect** [☐ HVAC | ☐ mechanical | ☐ electrical | ☐ drywall | ☐ roofing | ☐ concrete | ☐ air conditioning | ☐ landscaping | ☐ other: _____] **contractor work in** [☐ commercial | ☐ civil | ☐ residential | ☐ government | ☐ roadway | ☐ bridge | ☐ hospital | ☐ hotel | ☐ resort | ☐ hospitality | ☐ school | ☐ prison | ☐ church | ☐ retail | ☐ mechanical | ☐ aviation | ☐ power | ☐ process | ☐ other: _____] **construction including** [☐ general contractors | ☐ design-and-build firms | ☐ home builders | ☐ real estate developers | ☐ hotel and resort developers | ☐ multifamily developers | ☐ retail developers | ☐ office developers | ☐ industrial developers | ☐ building products manufacturers | ☐ construction equipment manufacturers | ☐ others: _____].

☐ **Oversee regulatory inspections interfacing with** [☐ inspectors | ☐ municipal regulatory entities | ☐ others: _____] **to ensure** _____ *[what?].*

☐ **Perform on-site inspections of** [☐ buildings | ☐ highways | ☐ bridges | ☐ other: _____] **to** [☐ determine needed repairs | ☐ evaluate progress | ☐ comply with plans | ☐ ensure quality of construction | ☐ other: _____], **and meet with** [☐ Building | ☐ Department of Transportation | ☐ other: _____] **inspectors to ensure all work is performed satisfactorily.**

☐ **Manage and oversee** [☐ trades supervision | ☐ construction inspection | ☐ quality control | ☐ building and safety codes enforcement | ☐ design guidelines and specifications standards development | ☐ other: _____] **for the design and construction of** _____ *[type of]* [☐ buildings | ☐ structures | ☐ systems | ☐ other: _____].

☐ **Lead and oversee** [☐ construction inspection | ☐ quality control | ☐ building and safety codes enforcement | ☐ design guidelines and specifications standards development | ☐ other: _____].

☐ **Assume full accountability in establishing goals, providing direction, and implementing plans as well as supervising** [☐ office staff | ☐ accounting | ☐ project management | ☐ other: _____] **departments** [☐ and creating policy and procedure manuals for the company's daily operations | ☐ other: _____].

Construction Management

See also ***"Construction Projects"*** *and* ***"Project Management."***

☐ **Lead and direct all aspects of** _____ *[type of]* [☐ design | ☐ construction | ☐ design-and-build | ☐ other: _____] **projects to successful conclusion within tight time frames including** [☐ reviewing architectural plans | ☐ modifying construction drawings | ☐ negotiating contracts | ☐ determining staffing needs | ☐ selecting contractors and subcontractors | ☐ scheduling and coordinating all trades | ☐ purchasing materials | ☐ monitoring construction schedules | ☐ evaluating work progress | ☐ mediating and resolving disputes | ☐ negotiating and processing change orders | ☐ conducting on-site inspections | ☐ other: _____].

☐ **Effectively plan, manage, and lead** _____ *[type of]* **construction projects; and direct the activities of trades to ensure all projects are completed with high quality on time and within budget.**

☐ **Perform on-site construction supervision in all phases of construction—from demolition through completion—for various types of construction firms including** [☐ design-and-build | ☐ construction management | ☐ general contracting | ☐ commercial firms | ☐ the government | ☐ other: _____].

☐ **Oversee management of** [☐ residential | ☐ commercial | ☐ public works | ☐ other: _____] **construction projects including** [☐ commercial buildings | ☐ shopping malls | ☐ stores | ☐ restaurants | ☐ manufacturing plants | ☐ schools | ☐ colleges | ☐ corporate offices | ☐ building lobbies | ☐ state or government agencies | ☐ houses | ☐ condominiums | ☐ apartment buildings | ☐ hospitals | ☐ laboratories | ☐ clean rooms | ☐ landmark restorations | ☐ roads and highways | ☐ other: _____].

☐ **Provide** [☐ engineering | ☐ construction] **management leadership and direction in the design and build of** _____ *[type of]* **projects for this $_____** *[revenues]* [☐ construction management | ☐ engineering | ☐ architectural | ☐ contracting | ☐ other: _____] **firm.**

☐ **Direct the construction of all** _____ *[type of]* **projects including the** [☐ review and/or modification of construction drawings | ☐ development of job estimates and budgets | ☐ securing of competitive bids | ☐ handling of contract negotiations | ☐ maintaining of client relationships | ☐ scheduling and coordination of trades | ☐ performing of on-site construction supervision | ☐ negotiation and processing of change orders | ☐ other: _____], **completing all projects on time and within budget.**

☐ **Provide leadership and direction in the** [☐ concept | ☐ schematic design | ☐ site planning | ☐ construction | ☐ cost management | ☐ quantity control | ☐ other: _____] **of** [☐ interior spaces | ☐ exterior spaces | ☐ physical environments] **of** _____ *[type of]* **projects.**

☐ **Manage the construction of** [☐ structural | ☐ architectural | ☐ civil | ☐ other: _____] **construction projects including** _____, _____, **and** _____ *[type of]* **projects for this** [☐ architectural | ☐ design-and-build | ☐ construction management | ☐ engineering | ☐ other: _____] [☐ firm | ☐ government agency].

☐ **Draft** [☐ working plans | ☐ profile drawings | ☐ base drawings | ☐ perspective drawings | ☐ overlays | ☐ maps | ☐ illustrations | ☐ other: _____] **of** _____ *[what?]*; **and prepare quantities and cost estimates using** _____ *[software].*

☐ **Conceptualize design, and manage the construction of a wide variety of** [☐ buildings | ☐ complexes | ☐ structures] **including** [☐ commercial buildings | ☐ private and public buildings | ☐ residential houses | ☐ corporate offices | ☐ office space planning | ☐ shopping malls | ☐ stores | ☐ apartment complexes | ☐ condominiums | ☐ public schools | ☐ colleges and universities | ☐ manufacturing plants | ☐ hospitals | ☐ landmark restorations | ☐ building lobbies | ☐ clean rooms | ☐ other: _____] **with projects ranging from $_____ to $_____** *[amounts].*

☐ **Perform professional** [☐ architectural | ☐ project management | ☐ construction supervision | ☐ administrative | ☐ other: _____] **work involving the research, design, and construction of** _____ *[type of]* **projects ranging from $_____ to $_____** *[amounts]* **per project ensuring quality control, structural stability, and** _____ *[other?].*

☐ **Research and perform** _____ *[type of]* **studies to determine** [☐ the most effective use of space | ☐ functional and spatial requirements | ☐ required structural support | ☐ other: _____] **of** [☐ new structures | ☐ renovations | ☐ other: _____] **and** [☐ advise | ☐ consult with] **clients accordingly.**

☐ **Plan and oversee the design and construction of** _____ *[type of]* **client projects, applying knowledge of and expertise in** [☐ design | ☐ construction procedures | ☐ zoning and building codes | ☐ building materials | ☐ other: _____].

ACHIEVEMENT SAMPLES:

☐ **Spearheaded the construction of a** [☐_____ *(#)*-square foot | ☐_____ *(#)*-story | ☐ $_____ *(amount)*] _____ *[type of]* **project designed to** _____ *[do what?]* **for** _____ *[whom?]* **with a design challenge of** _____ *[what?]* **resulting in** _____ *[what?].*

☐ **Planned, managed, and led** _____ *[type of]* **construction projects with varying requirements; and directed all trade activities to ensure all projects were completed with high quality on time and within budget.**

☐ **Managed $_____** *[project cost]* _____ *[type of]* **project accommodating** _____ *[#]* [☐ employees | ☐ patrons | ☐ patients | ☐ other: _____] **within an aggressive** _____-*[#]* **month timeframe, completing projects** [☐ $_____ *(amount)* under budget | ☐ _____ *(#)* (☐ days / ☐ weeks) ahead of schedule | ☐ other achievement: _____].

☐ **Took over a $_____** *[project cost]* **problem-ridden** _____ *[type of]* **construction project that had** [☐ fallen behind schedule | ☐ exceeded cost estimates | ☐ other: _____] **by successfully spearheading the completion of** _____ *[which functions?]* **and passing all inspections.**

☐ **Oversaw the construction of** [☐ commercial buildings | ☐ private and public buildings | ☐ residential houses | ☐ corporate offices | ☐ office space planning | ☐ bridges | ☐ dams | ☐ shopping malls | ☐ stores | ☐ apartment complexes | ☐ condominiums | ☐ public schools | ☐ colleges and universities | ☐ manufacturing plants | ☐ hospitals | ☐ landmark restorations | ☐ building lobbies | ☐ clean rooms | ☐ other: _____] **with projects ranging from $_____ to $_____** *[amounts].*

☐ **Renovated this** _____ *[type of]* [☐ building | ☐ facility | ☐ other: _____] **involving coordination with** [☐ client | ☐ user group | ☐ engineer | ☐ trades | ☐ other: _____] **resulting in** _____ *[what benefits?]*.

☐ **Championed the completion of** [☐ multiple | ☐ highly complex | ☐ simultaneous | ☐ other: _____] _____ *[type of]* **construction projects within aggressive timeframes by** [☐ applying business intelligence strategy and technical solutions | ☐ establishing clear guidelines | ☐ performing frequent field inspections | ☐ immediately resolving and repairing inspection issues | ☐ addressing (☐ structural / ☐ environmental / ☐ other: _____) **challenges** | ☐ maintaining exceptional quality and safety standards | ☐ ensuring adherence to specifications | ☐ influencing trades to perform | ☐ strictly enforcing codes | ☐ other: _____].

☐ **Directed and oversaw** [☐ partial demolition | ☐ renovation | ☐ restoration | ☐ remodeling | ☐ construction] **of this** _____ *[type of]* **project while** [☐ company | ☐ stores | ☐ other: _____] **remained open for business acting as liaison with** [☐ client representative | ☐ store tenants | ☐ other: _____] **toward a successful completion** [☐ meeting | ☐ exceeding] [☐ business | ☐ mall management's | ☐ store owners' | ☐ others: _____] **and employer's expectations**.

☐ **Managed** [☐ new store construction | ☐ mall renovation while stores remained open for business | ☐ other: _____] **through to completion—meeting mall management's, store owners', and company's expectations and bringing project in** [☐ on time | ☐ _____ *(time frame)* ahead of schedule | ☐ within budget | ☐ $_____ *(amount)* under budget | ☐ other: _____].

☐ **Managed new construction and renovation of** _____ *[type of]* **sites, some simultaneously, with major construction and renovations successfully completed within** _____ *[time period]* **by** _____ *[doing what well?]*.

☐ **Led the** [☐ demolition | ☐ new construction | ☐ renovation] **of the following** _____ *[type of]* **sites:** _____ *[name]*, _____ *[town]*, _____ *[state]*; _____ *[name]*, _____ *[town]*, _____ *[state]*; **and** _____ *[name]*, _____ *[town]*, _____ *[state]* **to their successful completion**.

☐ **Formulated, implemented, and delivered successful** _____ *[type of]* **project execution processes that** [☐ achieved total project excellence | ☐ other: _____] **including** [☐ Construction Safety Management Systems | ☐ Behavioral Modification Processes | ☐ Contractor Evaluation Processes | ☐ other: _____].

☐ **Managed construction of** _____ *[project name]*, **taking over this** $_____ *[amount]* **project when Senior Project Manager became ill. Required delicate negotiations working closely with client rep through to successful completion. Received commendations for a job well done. (See "Testimonials.")** *Note: Add a "Testimonials" section to the end of your resume.*

☐ **Directed and oversaw mall** [☐ partial demolition | ☐ renovation | ☐ restoration | ☐ remodeling | ☐ construction] **while stores remained open for business acting as liaison with store tenants for a successful completion and** [☐ meeting | ☐ exceeding] **mall management's, store owners', and employer's expectations**.

☐ **Spearheaded the design and construction of a** [☐ _____ *(#)*-square foot | ☐ _____ *(#)*-story | ☐ $_____ *(amount)*] _____ *[type of]* **project designed to** _____ *[do what?]* **for** _____ *[whom?]* **with a design challenge of** _____ *[what?]* **resulting in** _____ *[what?]*.

☐ **Managed the** [☐ design | ☐ construction | ☐ trades supervision | ☐ administrative work | ☐ other: _____] **of** _____ / $_____ *[project name and cost]*, _____ / $_____ *[project name and cost]*, **and** _____ / $_____ *[project name and cost]* **with varying requirements ensuring all objectives were accomplished with high quality and within established time frames and budget**.

Construction Projects

See also Achievements under "Construction Leadership Functions."

ACHIEVEMENT SAMPLES:

☐ **Developed a** _____ *[#]*-**acre site for** _____ *[#]* **commercial buildings that encompassed** _____, _____, **and** _____ *[what processes?]*.

☐ **Handled on-site** _____ *[type of]* [☐ building | ☐ construction | ☐ installation | ☐ other: _____] **while** [☐ company remained open for business | ☐ homeowners remained on premises | ☐ other: _____] **by** _____ *[doing what?]*, **which minimized the work impact so** [☐ business operations remained functional | ☐ home remained livable].

☐ **Completed** _____ *[name of]* **project in record time and ahead of schedule; achieved by** [☐ organizing and planning daily workloads | ☐ getting the most productivity out of laborers | ☐ other: _____] **resulting in** [☐ company being awarded state bonuses | ☐ other achievement: _____].

☐ **Participated in a broad range of** _____ *[type of]* **construction projects involving** [☐ demolition | ☐ framing | ☐ sheetrocking | ☐ roofing | ☐ siding installation | ☐ site maintenance | ☐ materials transport | ☐ other: _____] **and general support of all phases of construction**.

☐ **Delivered all** _____ *[type of]* **projects on time and within budget by** [☐ performing quality workmanship | ☐ exceeding expectations | ☐ assuming additional responsibilities | ☐ working extended hours to meet project deadlines | other: _____].

☐ **Selected by** _____ *[whom?]* **to take over** _____ *[type of]* **project to smooth out conflicts. Accomplished [**☐ through firm negotiations and teamwork with client rep and all trades to put project back on track | ☐ by successfully completing project without compromising each other's responsibilities | ☐ by maintaining an excellent rapport with all | ☐ other: _____] **and receiving commendations from client and employer.**

☐ **Remodeled several [**☐ commercial | ☐ office space | ☐ residential | ☐ condominium | ☐ other: _____] **projects with project costs ranging $**_____ **to $**_____ *[amounts],* **performing all [**☐ estimating | ☐ negotiating | ☐ buyout | ☐ operations supervision | ☐ other: _____].

☐ **Built a** _____ *[#]*-**story,** _____ *[#]*-**acre** _____ *[type of]* **project with site work and construction cost at $**_____ *[amount].*

☐ **[**☐ Performed | ☐ Coordinated and directed] **the [**☐ demolition | ☐ construction | ☐ remodeling | ☐ renovation | ☐ restoration | ☐ other: _____] **of** _____ *[type of]* **building projects ranging from $**_____ **to $**_____ *[amounts]* **for this [**☐ multimillion-dollar | ☐ $_____] _____ *[type of]* **firm.**

☐ **Completed** _____ *[type of]* **job [**☐ $_____ *(amount)* under budget | ☐ _____ *[#]* (☐ days / ☐ weeks) ahead of schedule | ☐ other: _____] **by** _____ *[doing what well?].*

☐ **Performed design and construction administration of a** _____ *[#]*-[☐ floor | ☐ room | ☐ square foot | ☐ other: _____] _____ *[type of]* **project for** _____ *[whom?]* [☐ with a design challenge of _____ *(what?)* resulting in _____ *(what?)* | ☐ meeting clients' and company's expectations | ☐ other achievement: _____].

☐ **Renovated this** _____ *[type of]* **facility involving coordination with [**☐ client | ☐ user group | ☐ engineer | ☐ trades | ☐ other: _____] **resulting in a new design, which created** _____ *[what?].*

☐ **[**☐ Completed | ☐ Assisted in the completion] **of** _____ *[#]* _____ *[type of]* [☐ new construction | ☐ remodel | ☐ home improvement | ☐ HVAC | ☐ electrical | ☐ plumbing | ☐ landscaping | ☐ other: _____] **projects with budgets up to $**_____ *[amount].* **Projects ranged from** _____ *[type of small jobs]* **to** _____ *[type of large projects].*

☐ **Built** _____ *[type of]* [☐ homes | ☐ buildings | ☐ structures | ☐ other: _____] **valued at more than $**_____ *[amount]* **each, completing work on time and within budget while providing superior customer service.**

☐ **Saved** _____% *[percentage]* **on labor costs by completing a $**_____ *[project amount]* _____ *[type of]* **construction project** _____ *[time frame]* **ahead of schedule.**

☐ **Supervised all phases of** _____ *[type of]* **construction of** _____ *[type of]* **projects with varying requirements ensuring all objectives were accomplished with high quality and within established time frames and budget.**

☐ **Applying expertise in** _____ *[what?],* **led a [**☐ construction | ☐ carpentry | ☐ other: _____] **team of** _____ *[#]* _____ *[titles]* **in [**☐ building | ☐ installing | ☐ repairing | ☐ other: _____] _____ *[what?]* **for** _____ *[whom?]* **which resulted in** _____ *[what deliverables?].*

☐ **Built** _____ *[type of]* [☐ homes | ☐ buildings | ☐ structures | ☐ other: _____] **valued at $**_____ *[amount]* **each.**

☐ **Simultaneously managed** _____ *[#]* _____ *[type of]* [☐ design-and-build | ☐ construction | ☐ other: _____] **projects each averaging $**_____ *[amount],* **with project values totaling $**_____ **to $**_____ *[amount].*

☐ **Utilize expertise in [**☐ all aspects of structural, mechanical, and electrical construction | ☐ state and local building codes | ☐ commercial roofing specifications | ☐ asbestos abatement procedures | ☐ construction contract administration | ☐ other: _____] **to successfully [**☐ design and] **build** _____ *[what?].*

☐ **Coordinated and directed the [**☐ demolition | ☐ construction | ☐ remodeling | ☐ renovation | ☐ restoration | ☐ installation | ☐ repair | ☐ other: _____] **of** _____ *[type of]* **building projects ranging from $**_____ **to $**_____ *[amounts].*

☐ **Handled all aspects of remodeling [**☐ residential homes | ☐ commercial buildings | ☐ civil projects | ☐ other: _____] **including** _____, _____, **and** _____ *[type of renovations].*

☐ **Supervised new construction and renovation of** _____ *[type of]* **sites with major construction and renovations successfully completed on or ahead of schedule and within budget.**

☐ **Constructed** _____ *[type of]* **specialized [**☐ structures | ☐ buildings | ☐ projects | ☐ other: _____] **that** _____ *[did what?]* **while benefiting the [**☐ client | ☐ firm | ☐ other: _____] **by way of** _____ *[benefits].*

☐ **Gained valuable experience in [**☐ performance of carpentry functions | ☐ building industry operations and processes | ☐ other: _____] **as construction worker for full-service residential developer.**

Construction Supervision Scope

See also "Carpentry Supervision," "Project Management," "Construction Supervision Functions," and "General Contracting."

☐ **Provide construction supervision and direction for this** $_____ *[revenues]* [☐ construction management | ☐ contracting | ☐ other: _____] firm including [☐ reviewing plans | ☐ scheduling jobs | ☐ subbing out work | ☐ estimating projects | ☐ coordinating trades | ☐ purchasing materials | ☐ other: _____] **in all phases of construction.**

☐ **Supervise and oversee** [☐ home | ☐ office | ☐ other: _____] [☐ construction | ☐ renovation | ☐ carpentry] **activities for this** [$_____ *(revenues)* | ☐ multimillion-dollar | ☐ leading] **general contractor overseeing from one- to** _____ *[#]*-**man crews, bringing jobs in on time and within budget.**

☐ **Manage** [☐ residential | ☐ commercial | ☐ public works | ☐ other: _____] **construction projects including** [☐ single-family homes | ☐ multiple-family dwellings | ☐ condominiums | ☐ commercial buildings | ☐ shopping malls | ☐ stores | ☐ restaurants | ☐ manufacturing plants | ☐ schools | ☐ colleges | ☐ corporate offices | ☐ building lobbies | ☐ state or government agencies | ☐ hospitals | ☐ laboratories | ☐ clean rooms | ☐ landmark restorations | ☐ roads and highways | ☐ other: _____].

☐ **Plan, coordinate, and supervise the construction and** [☐ demolition | ☐ remodeling | ☐ renovation | ☐ assembly | ☐ repair | ☐ maintenance] of [☐ buildings | ☐ cabinets | ☐ roofs | ☐ furnishings | ☐ vinyl siding | ☐ other: _____] **for this** $_____ *[revenues]* _____ *[type of]* **firm.**

☐ **Coordinate and direct the** [☐ demolition | ☐ construction | ☐ remodeling | ☐ renovation | ☐ restoration | ☐ other: _____] of _____ *[type of]* **building projects ranging from** $_____ **to** $_____ *[amounts]* **for this** _____ *[type of]* **firm.**

☐ **Supervise all phases of construction from project start through completion including** [☐ reviewing construction drawings | ☐ developing job estimates and budgets | ☐ securing competitive bids | ☐ handling contract negotiations | ☐ maintaining direct client relationships | ☐ scheduling and coordinating all trades | ☐ performing on-site supervision | ☐ negotiating and processing change orders | ☐ other: _____] **completing all projects on time and within budget.**

☐ **Plan and coordinate all activities of** [☐ small- | ☐ medium- | ☐ large-] **scale client projects in collaboration with** [☐ client reps | ☐ architects | ☐ contractors | ☐ subcontractors | ☐ other: _____] **for this** _____ *[type of]* **firm with** _____ *[#]* [☐ locations | ☐ employees | ☐ other: _____] **that generates fiscal-year revenues of** $_____ *[revenues]*.

☐ **Lead and direct the daily construction operations for this** $_____ *[revenues]* _____ *[type of]* **firm including** [☐ blueprint reading | ☐ work scheduling | ☐ job site preparation | ☐ project management | ☐ building inspections | ☐ client close-out processing | ☐ other: _____].

☐ **Act as Superintendent on** _____ *[type of]* **construction projects including the** [☐ planning | ☐ directing | ☐ coordinating | ☐ supervising | ☐ other: _____] **of building construction.**

☐ **Supervise all aspects of project management—from planning to completion—**[☐ using standardized project management methodology | ☐ for multiple implementation projects | ☐ for projects that vary in scope and size | ☐ in support of firm's strategic visions | ☐ to support client objectives | ☐ in accordance with all project timelines and budget | ☐ other: _____].

☐ **Supervise rough and finish carpentry work including** [☐ setting concrete forms | ☐ pouring foundations | ☐ framing and sheetrocking walls and partitions | ☐ taping and spackling | ☐ building stairs | ☐ installing (☐ windows / ☐ doors / ☐ flooring / ☐ tiling / ☐ ceilings / ☐ roofs / ☐ wall coverings / ☐ trim work / ☐ platforms / ☐ podiums / ☐ partitions / ☐ fences / ☐ ramps / ☐ insulation / ☐ weather stripping / ☐ cabinets / ☐ baseboard heating / ☐ retainer walls / ☐ other: _____) | ☐ other: _____].

☐ **Oversee the concrete and steel reinforcement of** [☐ residential | ☐ commercial | ☐ other: _____] **construction projects and the finishing of walls with** [☐ wood | ☐ structural metal | ☐ lath | ☐ plaster | ☐ other: _____] **materials meeting all project budgets and deadlines usually ahead of schedule.**

☐ **Supervise** [☐ home construction | ☐ home improvement | ☐ interior renovation | ☐ room additions | ☐ finished attics and basements | ☐ other: _____] **for individual clients including** [☐ framing | ☐ insulation | ☐ sheetrocking | ☐ taping and spackling | ☐ painting | ☐ flooring | ☐ tiling | ☐ roofing | ☐ landscaping | ☐ other: _____].

☐ **Coordinate and supervise construction and** [☐ demolition | ☐ remodeling | ☐ renovation | ☐ assembly | ☐ repair | ☐ maintenance] **for** [☐ residential | ☐ commercial] **construction projects for this** $_____ *[revenues]* [☐ general contractor | ☐ construction management | ☐ other: _____] **firm.**

☐ **Supervise the construction of all** _____ *[type of]* **projects including the** [☐ review of construction drawings | ☐ development of job estimates and budgets | ☐ securing of competitive bids | ☐ handling of contract negotiations | ☐ maintaining of client relationships | ☐ scheduling and coordination of trades | ☐ performing of on-site construction supervision | ☐ negotiation and processing of change orders | ☐ other: _____], **completing all projects on time and within budget.**

☐ **Oversee** [☐ remodeling | ☐ renovations | ☐ carpentry work | ☐ finish carpentry | ☐ other: _____] **of the** _____ *[what project(s)?]* including installation of [☐ custom framing | ☐ siding | ☐ conventional roofs | ☐ window replacements | ☐ doors | ☐ ceramic tile | ☐ other: _____] **according to blueprint specifications**.

ACHIEVEMENT SAMPLES: *See "Construction Projects" and "General Contracting."*

Construction Supervision Functions

See also "Construction Supervision," "Inspections & Compliance," and "Carpentry / Construction Work."

☐ **Provide project management** [☐ coordination | ☐ consultation | ☐ supervision | ☐ review | ☐ other: _____] **during the construction phase of all projects.**

☐ **Involved in all phases of development, from initial client consultation through the entire construction process including** [☐ design | ☐ site selection | ☐ engineering | ☐ bidding process | ☐ field inspections | ☐ construction management | ☐ other: _____].

☐ **Supervise rough and finish carpentry in the construction and/or installation of** [☐ buildings | ☐ houses | ☐ remodels | ☐ roofing | ☐ siding | ☐ cabinets | ☐ fencing | ☐ other: _____].

☐ **Manage a multitude of carpentry work including** [☐ setting concrete forms | ☐ erecting scaffolding | ☐ installing ceiling tile | ☐ repairing cabinets | ☐ installing partitions | ☐ other: _____] **and perform finishing work for** _____ *[type of]* **projects**.

☐ **Obtain permits, estimate jobs, and hire and schedule trades acting as liaison with** [☐ building managers | ☐ inspectors | ☐ architects | ☐ others: _____].

☐ **Successfully plan and manage projects to achieve business objectives and fully use resource capabilities within the project parameters of cost, time, and quality which has resulted in** _____ *[what benefits?]*.

☐ **Oversee job operations and personnel management including** [☐ coordinating steel and concrete trades | ☐ scheduling laborers | ☐ managing construction | ☐ overseeing site materials and equipment set-up | ☐ other: _____].

☐ **Provide project management** [☐ coordination | ☐ consultation | ☐ supervision | ☐ review] **during construction phase of all projects.**

☐ **Prepare job estimates with fair financial arrangements for customers and at good profits for company.**

☐ **Apply a thorough knowledge of** [☐ construction methods | ☐ building codes | ☐ finish carpentry | ☐ tools, equipment, and materials | ☐ safety practices | ☐ building techniques | ☐ other: _____] **in all** [☐ wood and metal framing | ☐ shingle and plywood roofing | ☐ wood and vinyl siding | ☐ masonry work | ☐ window and garage door replacement | ☐ home renovations | ☐ girder manufacturing and installation | ☐ building decks | ☐ railroad ties | ☐ retainer walls | ☐ other: _____] **carpentry activities.**

☐ **Conduct hands-on carpentry and construction in the areas of** _____ *[type of work]*.

☐ **Provide technical assistance to laborers** [☐ in the areas of (☐ electrical / ☐ plumbing / ☐ carpentry / ☐ concrete construction / ☐ masonry / ☐ other: _____) | ☐ on projects involving _____ *(what?)* | ☐ other: _____].

☐ **Order materials, estimate projects, and lay out jobs for this** [☐ residential | ☐ commercial] **contractor specializing in** _____ *[what?]*.

☐ **Ensure** [☐ trucks arrive on time to pour concrete | ☐ laborers meet each day's scheduled workload | ☐ all materials are stored at the end of each day | ☐ all debris is cleared up | ☐ customer satisfaction with work | ☐ other: _____].

☐ **Ensure all safety practices are followed on carpentry job sites by** _____ *[doing what?]*.

☐ **Oversee the concrete and steel reinforcement of** _____ *[type of]* **construction projects and the finishing of walls with** [☐ wood | ☐ structural metal | ☐ lath | ☐ plaster | ☐ other: _____] **materials meeting all project budgets and deadlines.**

☐ **Manage the installation of** _____, _____, **and** _____ *[what?]* **according to blueprint specifications.**

☐ **Plan and coordinate** [☐ rough | ☐ finish] **carpentry in the construction and** [☐ demolition | ☐ remodeling | ☐ renovation | ☐ assembly | ☐ repair | ☐ maintenance] **of** [☐ buildings | ☐ cabinets | ☐ roofs | ☐ furnishings | ☐ siding | ☐ other: _____].

☐ **Conceive, sketch, and design** _____ *[type of]* **carpentry projects for** _____ *[whom or what?]*.

☐ **Meet with** [☐ Building | ☐ Department of Transportation (DOT) | ☐ other: _____] **Inspectors to ensure all work is performed satisfactorily.**

Construction Work / Labor

See "Carpentry / Construction Work."

Contract Administration

See also "Contracting Management" and "Policies & Procedures Development – Legal & Technical."

☐ **Manage and oversee all aspects of contract projects including** [☐ scope | ☐ initiation | ☐ planning | ☐ scheduling | ☐ budgeting | ☐ resource allocation | ☐ quality control | ☐ system integration | ☐ other: _____] **keeping in line with all business objectives**.

☐ **Provide** [☐ administrative | ☐ legal | ☐ other: _____] **support to the** [☐ Senior Contracts Manager | ☐ Director of Contracts | ☐ other title: _____] **in all contractual matters including** [☐ proposals development | ☐ pricing strategies | ☐ risk management | ☐ negotiations | ☐ contract management | ☐ other: _____].

☐ **Facilitate business management of this** _____ *[type of]* **firm including** [☐ leading and overseeing projects | ☐ reviewing contracts to verify legal requirements | ☐ translating requirements into effective legal solutions | ☐ setting up and maintaining contract database | ☐ establishing quality control procedures | ☐ developing revenue contracts | ☐ preparing specifications | ☐ identifying contractual problems or errors | ☐ researching and writing (☐ legal / ☐ technical / ☐ other: _____) procedures | ☐ recommending corrective actions | ☐ holding meetings to discuss project progress processing documents | ☐ other: _____].

☐ **Support the** _____ *[which?]* **contract of** _____ *[what?]* **by performing a** [☐ full range | ☐ wide variety] of [☐ commercial | ☐ governmental | ☐ other: _____] **contract administration functions—from proposal to contract completion**.

☐ **Perform various contract administrative functions including** [☐ assisting with contractual initiatives | ☐ developing pricing strategies | ☐ conducting research and analysis | ☐ preparing bids | ☐ performing contract negotiations | ☐ handling claims avoidance | ☐ researching contractor claims and litigations | ☐ responding to staff inquiries relating to contracts | ☐ performing risk management | ☐ incorporating quality assurance methods | ☐ developing client proposals and estimates | ☐ handling dispute resolution | ☐ developing and submitting grant applications | ☐ updating budget databases | ☐ preparing contract records and reports | ☐ handling data entry, filing, and copying | ☐ maintaining legal obligations records | ☐ interfacing with clients | ☐ document processing | ☐ other: _____].

☐ **Prepare recommendations to** _____ *[whom?]* **regarding** [☐ contractual defaults | ☐ time extensions | ☐ liquidated damages | ☐ other: _____].

☐ **Review, analyze, and approve** _____ *[type of]* [☐ proposals | ☐ estimates | ☐ agreements | ☐ contractual documents | ☐ other: _____] **and monitor performance to ensure conformance to** [☐ original proposals | ☐ contracts | ☐ legal requirements | ☐ regulations | ☐ customer specifications | ☐ other: _____].

☐ **Facilitate proposal development activities including** [☐ handling client interface | ☐ developing pricing strategies | ☐ preparing bids | ☐ developing proposal terms | ☐ interpreting contract terms and conditions | ☐ identifying risks and risk mitigation strategies | ☐ negotiating contracts | ☐ monitoring contract status | ☐ processing contract closeouts | ☐ other: _____].

☐ **Work with the firm's** [☐ internal counsel | ☐ outside attorney] **to resolve** _____ *[type of]* **legal matters**.

☐ **Provide support to** [☐ Project Managers | ☐ Engineers | ☐ Architects | ☐ Senior Contracts Manager | ☐ Director of Contracts | ☐ other: _____] **by** [☐ developing proposals | ☐ assisting with risk mitigation | ☐ preparing contracts | ☐ other: _____] **in a timely and professional fashion**.

☐ **Accurately update and maintain** _____ *[type of]* [☐ documents | ☐ files | ☐ reports | ☐ other: _____] **according to** [☐ legal requirements | ☐ the firm's policies and procedures | ☐ other: _____].

☐ **As the firm's primary** [☐ contractual | ☐ technical | ☐ legal] **resource hub, provide** [☐ expertise | ☐ advice | ☐ consultation] **to** [☐ staff | ☐ contractors | ☐ others: _____] **in the areas of** [☐ contractual guidelines | ☐ recommendations | ☐ appropriations | ☐ budgets | ☐ schedules | ☐ special projects | ☐ other: _____] **regarding** [☐ contract development | ☐ interpretation of contract documents | ☐ _____ *(type of)* procedures | ☐ related regulations | ☐ litigation of claims | ☐ other: _____].

☐ **Facilitate contract administrative functions including** [☐ document processing | ☐ account servicing | ☐ data entry | ☐ client correspondence | ☐ customer questions | ☐ contract filing | ☐ other: _____] **for an office staff of** _____ *[#]*.

☐ **Support the** _____ *[which?]* **contract of** _____ *[what?]* **by performing a** [☐ full range | ☐ wide variety] of [☐ commercial | ☐ governmental | ☐ other: _____] **contract administration functions—from proposal to contract completion**.

☐ [☐ Compose and update | ☐ Draft and edit] _____ *[type of]* [☐ contracts | ☐ agreements | ☐ technical material | (☐ company / ☐ department) policies and procedures | ☐ other: _____] **for** _____ *[purpose]*.

☐ **Facilitate** [☐ legal | ☐ administrative | ☐ logistical | ☐ other: _____] [☐ support | ☐ assistance | ☐ guidance] **to** _____ *[whom?]* **in the areas of** [☐ contractual issues | ☐ past performance factors | ☐ cost evaluations | ☐ proposal evaluations | ☐ preproposal conferences | ☐ other: _____] **of** _____ *[what?]*.

☐ **Document, implement, and monitor** _____ *[type of]* **quality assurance procedures ensuring their implementation on all projects including** [☐ contract drafting | ☐ legal document management | ☐ rights and clearances documentation | ☐ financial data verification | ☐ database updating | ☐ vendor compliance | ☐ project tracking | ☐ client relationship management | ☐ executive approval process | ☐ other: _____].

☐ **Handle various office administrative activities including** [☐ preparing contract records and reports | ☐ writing contract specifications | ☐ preparing cost estimates | ☐ costing materials | ☐ purchasing supplies | ☐ coordinating materials shipping | ☐ matching invoices to purchase orders and packing slips | ☐ issuing and evaluating bids | ☐ coordinating jobs with _____ *(whom)* | ☐ handling insurance needs | ☐ generating _____ *(type of)* reports | ☐ updating budget databases | ☐ handling data entry | ☐ other: _____].

Contract Development & Review

See also other Contracting categories.

☐ **Draft, review, and administer** _____ *[type of]* [☐ contractual documents | ☐ agreements | ☐ proposals | ☐ nondisclosure agreements | ☐ estimates | ☐ grant requests | ☐ service agreements | ☐ technical documents | ☐ license agreements | ☐ warrantees | ☐ guarantees ☐ teaming agreements | ☐ memoranda of understanding | ☐ government contracts | ☐ subcontractor agreements | ☐ amendments | ☐ provider agreements | ☐ real estate contracts | ☐ revenue contracts | ☐ estimates | ☐ amendments | ☐ other: _____] **with contracts ranging from $**_____**to $**_____ *[amounts].*

☐ **Write and execute** _____ *[type of]* **contracts for** _____ *[what?]* **that ensures compliance with all** [☐ corporate policies | ☐ client specifications | ☐ business requirements | ☐ legal requirements | ☐ codes and regulations | ☐ best practices | ☐ contract guidelines | ☐ bidding process procedures | ☐ Federal contract law | ☐ Service Contract Act | ☐ departmental practices | ☐ other: _____] **for this** _____ *[type of]* **firm.**

☐ **Draft, review, and edit** _____ *[type of]* [☐ contracts | ☐ agreements | ☐ legal documents | ☐ other: _____] **in conformance with** [☐ company policies | ☐ standard contract templates | ☐ other: _____] **to include** [☐ customer | ☐ product | ☐ services | ☐ terms | ☐ cost | ☐ product | ☐ other: _____] **information using** _____ *[what?].*

☐ **Document and execute** _____ *[type of]* [☐ contractual documents | ☐ license agreements | ☐ proposals | ☐ agreements | ☐ provider agreements | ☐ nondisclosure agreements | ☐ service agreements | ☐ government contracts | ☐ subcontractor agreements | ☐ real estate contracts | ☐ revenue contracts | ☐ estimates | ☐ amendments | ☐ guarantees | ☐ warrantees | ☐ other: _____] **for** _____ *[what?]* **in compliance with all** [☐ corporate policies | ☐ client specifications | ☐ business requirements | ☐ legal requirements | ☐ codes and regulations | ☐ best practices | ☐ contract guidelines | ☐ Federal contract law | ☐ Service Contract Act | ☐ other: _____].

☐ **Develop and negotiate** _____ *[type of]* **legal documents that include** [☐ services | ☐ terms | ☐ cost | ☐ materials | ☐ other: _____] **information in conformance with company policies and in support of major business initiatives.**

☐ **Prepare** [☐ client | ☐ architect | ☐ engineer | ☐ contractor | ☐ other: _____] **contracts ranging from $**_____ **to $**_____ *[amount]* **for** [☐ architectural plans for | ☐ design and build of | ☐ construction of] _____ *[what?].*

☐ **Review, approve, and execute** [☐ a wide range of] _____ *[type of]* [☐ contracts | ☐ contractual agreements | ☐ legal documents | ☐ agreements] **of** [☐ a complex nature | ☐ varying scope and complexity], **and document related** [☐ policies | ☐ procedures | ☐ processes | ☐ other: _____] **for** _____ *[what?].*

☐ **Document** _____ *[type of]* **agreements that meet** [☐ business | ☐ client | ☐ building code | ☐ legal | ☐ regulatory | ☐ audit | ☐ other: _____] **requirements with contracts ranging from $**_____ **to $**_____ *[amounts]* **for this** _____ *[type of]* **firm servicing** _____ *[which?]* **clientele base.**

☐ **Develop** _____ *[type of]* **revenue contracts for** _____ *[name of]* [☐ protocols | ☐ amendments] **from all** _____ *[type of]* **areas, making use of benchmarking cost data from the** _____ *[which?]* **database** [☐ provided | ☐ developed] **by** _____ *[whom?].*

ACHIEVEMENT SAMPLES: *See also Achievements under "Contract Negotiations."*

☐ **Reviewed and evaluated** [☐ monthly | ☐ quarterly | ☐ periodic | ☐ annual] _____ *[type of]* **compliance status reports insofar as compliance** [☐ planning | ☐ activity | ☐ efforts | ☐ investigations | ☐ assessments | ☐ risks | ☐ audits | ☐ actions taken | ☐ effectiveness | ☐ other: _____], **and determined** _____ *[type of]* **changes to improve compliance in the area of** _____ *[what?].*

☐ **Developed new** _____ *[type of]* **program to secure preferred and exclusive provider contracts with** _____ *[whom?]* **resulting in increased sales of $**_____.

☐ **Designed and implemented** _____ *[type of]* **solutions that effectively addressed and adhered to** [☐ the firm's | ☐ clients'] **requirements in the area(s) of** _____ *[area(s)]* [☐ in accordance with all project timelines and budget | ☐ ensuring quality project standards | ☐ ensuring a smooth transition | ☐ other: _____].

☐ **Secured** [☐ preferred provider agreements | ☐ wholesale distribution agreements | ☐ other: _____] **with** _____, _____, **and** _____ *[companies],* **by developing** _____ *[what?],* **positioning firm as the recognized leader in the sales of** _____ *[what?].*

☐ **Successfully coordinated and implemented** _____ *[type of]* **contracting projects with varying requirements completing all project phases with high quality and within established time frames and budget.**

☐ **Established win-win** _____ *[type of]* **contracts with** _____ *[whom?]* **and developed** _____ *[type of]* **project plans involving coordinating, scheduling, and managing jobs from start through completion.**

☐ **Effectively** [☐ planned | ☐ directed | ☐ coordinated | ☐ implemented] _____ *[type of]* **projects** [☐ and direct the activities of resources] **ensuring all objectives were accomplished with high quality and within established time frames and budget.**

Contract Functions

*See also other **Contracting** categories.*

☐ **As the firm's primary** [☐ contractual | ☐ technical | ☐ legal | ☐ other: _____] **resource hub, provide** [☐ expertise | ☐ advice | ☐ guidance | ☐ assistance | ☐ consultation] **to** [☐ project managers | ☐ staff | ☐ contractors | ☐ others: _____] **in the areas of** [☐ contractual guidelines | ☐ recommendations | ☐ appropriations | ☐ budgets | ☐ schedules | ☐ other: _____] **regarding** [☐ contract development | ☐ interpretation of contract documents | ☐ _____ *(type of)* procedures | ☐ related regulations | ☐ litigation of claims | ☐ other: _____].

☐ **Develop and establish** [☐ proposals | ☐ contract templates | ☐ legal standards | ☐ best practices | ☐ contract guidelines | ☐ subcontracting procedures | ☐ the contract review process | ☐ formal bidding process review procedures | ☐ other: _____]; **and ensure contracts consistency with all established terms and conditions.**

☐ **Handle various contract functions including** [☐ leading and overseeing contract projects | ☐ prioritizing projects and balancing competing demands | ☐ reviewing contracts to verify legal requirements | ☐ translating requirements into effective legal solutions | ☐ developing revenue contracts | ☐ preparing specifications | ☐ performing inspections to facilitate quality assurance | ☐ identifying contractual problems or errors | ☐ researching and writing legal procedures | ☐ setting up and maintaining contract database | ☐ developing budgets and monitoring expenses | ☐ preparing inspection deficiency reports | ☐ recommending corrective actions | ☐ reviewing and approving cost estimates | ☐ approving contracting changes | ☐ holding meetings to discuss project progress processing documents | ☐ other: _____].

☐ [☐ Prepare and execute | ☐ Assist in the preparation of] [☐ contract documents | ☐ prenegotiation objectives | ☐ source selection reports | ☐ price negotiation memoranda | ☐ draft briefings | ☐ draft correspondence | ☐ contract modifications | ☐ contract closeouts | ☐ other: _____] **for review and approval by** [☐ Contracting Officer | ☐ other: _____].

☐ **Facilitate** [☐ legal | ☐ administrative | ☐ logistical | ☐ other: _____] **support and guidance to** _____ *[whom?]* **in the areas of** [☐ contractual issues | ☐ past performance factors | ☐ cost evaluations | ☐ proposal evaluations | ☐ preproposal conferences | ☐ other: _____] **of** _____ *[what?]*.

☐ **Regularly review** _____ *[type of]* **contracts in the area(s) of** _____ *[what?]*, **make recommendations to senior management regarding** [☐ risks | ☐ issues | ☐ improvements | ☐ other: _____], **and implement** _____ *[what?]*.

☐ **Exercise** [☐ an in-depth | ☐ a proficient | ☐ a working] knowledge of contractual [☐ documents | ☐ language | ☐ types | ☐ terms | ☐ laws | ☐ regulations | ☐ practices | ☐ procedures | ☐ administration | ☐ other: _____] **in the preparation of** [☐ Subcontractor Agreements | ☐ Memoranda of Understanding | ☐ Nondisclosure Agreements | ☐ Teaming Agreements | ☐ government contracts | ☐ other: _____] **ensuring compliance with all** [☐ Federal Acquisition Regulations | ☐ Service Contract Act | ☐ zoning regulations | ☐ corporate policies | ☐ departmental practices | ☐ accounting principles | ☐ other: _____].

☐ **Apply expertise in and knowledge of** [☐ federal contracting law | ☐ contract terms | ☐ state and local building codes | ☐ Uniform Building Code | ☐ construction law | ☐ electrical and plumbing codes | ☐ fire and life safety codes | ☐ facility service contracts | ☐ license agreements | ☐ real estate leases | ☐ contract preparation and administration | ☐ contract negotiations | ☐ dispute resolution methods | ☐ architectural principles | ☐ construction requirements | ☐ other: _____] **in the** [☐ negotiation | ☐ documentation | ☐ evaluation | ☐ awarding | ☐ review | ☐ administration | ☐ other: _____] **of** [☐ construction] **contracts.**

☐ **Successfully** [☐ negotiate and manage | ☐ research, review, and process] _____ *[type of]* **revenue business contracts for** _____ *[what?]* **by** _____ *[doing what?]*.

☐ **Determine contract terms and conditions of all proposed product purchases and** _____ *[do what?]* **achieving** _____ *[what results?]*.

☐ **Calculate contractual** [☐ rental payment amounts | ☐ leasing options | ☐ one-time fees | ☐ other: _____] **to process payment vouchers for** _____ *[what?]*.

ACHIEVEMENT SAMPLES: *See also **"Contract Development & Review"** and **"Contract Negotiations."***

☐ [☐ Prepare and execute | ☐ Assist in the preparation of] [☐ contract documents | ☐ prenegotiation objectives | ☐ source selection reports | ☐ price negotiation memoranda | ☐ draft briefings | ☐ draft correspondence | ☐ contract modifications | ☐ contract closeouts | ☐ other: _____] **for review and approval by** [☐ Contracting Officer | ☐ other: _____].

☐ **Facilitate** [☐ legal | ☐ administrative | ☐ logistical | ☐ other: _____] **support and guidance to** _____ *[whom?]* **in the areas of** [☐ contractual issues | ☐ past performance factors | ☐ cost evaluations | ☐ proposal evaluations | ☐ preproposal conferences | ☐ other: _____] **of** _____ *[what?]*.

☐ **Exercise** [☐ an in-depth | ☐ a proficient | ☐ a working] **knowledge of contractual** [☐ documents | ☐ language | ☐ types | ☐ terms | ☐ laws | ☐ regulations | ☐ practices | ☐ procedures | ☐ administration | ☐ other: _____] **in the preparation of** [☐ Subcontractor Agreements | ☐ Memoranda of Understanding | ☐ Nondisclosure Agreements | ☐ Teaming Agreements | ☐ government contracts | ☐ other: _____] **ensuring compliance with all** [☐ Federal Acquisition Regulations | ☐ Service Contract Act | ☐ zoning regulations | ☐ corporate policies | ☐ departmental practices | ☐ accounting principles | ☐ other: _____].

☐ **Regularly review** _____ *[type of]* **contracts in the area(s) of** _____ *[what?]*, **make recommendations to senior management regarding** [☐ risks | ☐ issues | ☐ improvements | ☐ other: _____], **and implement** _____ *[what?]*.

☐ **Successfully** [☐ negotiate and manage | ☐ research, review, and process] _____ *[type of]* **revenue business contracts for** _____ *[what?]* **by** _____ *[doing what?]*.

☐ **Determine contract terms and conditions of all proposed product purchases and** _____ *[do what?]* **achieving** _____ *[what results?]*.

☐ **Calculate contractual** [☐ rental payment amounts | ☐ leasing options | ☐ one-time fees | ☐ other: _____] **to process payment vouchers for** _____ *[what?]*.

Contract Management

See also other Contracting categories.

☐ **Provide leadership, vision, and direction to a team of** _____ *[#]* **to initiate, plan, and execute** _____ *[type of]* [☐ contracts | ☐ projects] **ranging from $**_____ **to $**_____ *[amounts]* **and resulting in** [☐ delivering bottom-line business value | ☐ business transformation | ☐ new product offerings | ☐ the translation of enterprise strategies into projects | ☐ increased productivity | ☐ other benefits: _____].

☐ **Define, plan, and implement** _____ *[type of]* **projects; and direct and oversee the** [☐ design | ☐ development | ☐ testing | ☐ implementation | ☐ tracking | ☐ reporting | ☐ other: _____] **of those projects in support of** [☐ the firm's | ☐ clients'] **business objectives.**

☐ **Provide support to the** [☐ Senior Contracts Manager | ☐ Director of Contracts | ☐ _____ *(which?)* **departments** | ☐ other: _____] **in all contractual matters including** [☐ proposals development | ☐ pricing strategies | ☐ risk management | ☐ negotiations | ☐ contract management | ☐ other: _____] **in a timely and professional fashion.**

☐ **Review, analyze, and approve** _____ *[type of]* [☐ proposals | ☐ estimates | ☐ agreements | ☐ contractual documents | ☐ other: _____] **and monitor performance to ensure conformance to** [☐ original proposals | ☐ contracts | ☐ legal requirements | ☐ regulations | ☐ customer specifications | ☐ other: _____].

☐ **Direct and guide** _____ *[#]* **Contract Specialists and facilitate all office management functions including** [☐ financial records management | ☐ accounts payable and accounts receivable | ☐ quarterly taxes for accountant | ☐ client relationship management | ☐ estimating | ☐ contractor bids review | ☐ contract negotiations | ☐ project coordination | ☐ jobs scheduling | ☐ materials shipping | ☐ equipment purchasing (☐ and leasing) | ☐ payroll processing | ☐ equipment checks | ☐ company taxes | ☐ advertising campaigns to increase exposure | ☐ staff recruitment | ☐ payroll processing | ☐ other: _____].

☐ **Plan and coordinate all activities of** _____ *[type of]* **contracting projects for a wide range of clients in collaboration with** [☐ clients | ☐ vendors | ☐ senior management | ☐ other: _____].

ACHIEVEMENT SAMPLES: *See "Contract Development & Review" and "Contract Negotiations."*

Contract Negotiations – Architecture & Construction

See also other Contracting categories.

☐ **Successfully** [☐ negotiate and manage | ☐ research, review, and process] _____ *[type of]* **revenue business contracts for** _____ *[what?]* **by** _____ *[doing what?]*.

☐ **Negotiate fees and develop** _____ *[type of]* [☐ design | ☐ construction | ☐ repair | ☐ other: _____] **contracts with** [☐ architects | ☐ engineers | ☐ contractors | ☐ subcontractors | ☐ others: _____] **for** _____ *[what?]* **commensurate with project scope and budget.**

☐ [☐ Prepare, negotiate, and administer | ☐ Review, approve, and execute] [☐ a wide range of] _____ *[type of]* **Construction** [☐ contracts | ☐ contractual agreements | ☐ legal documents | ☐ agreements] **of** [☐ a complex nature | ☐ varying scope and complexity], **and document related** [☐ policies | ☐ procedures | ☐ processes | ☐ instructions | ☐ other: _____] **for same.**

☐ **Negotiate and document** _____ *[type of]* [☐ contracts | ☐ agreements] **that meet** [☐ business | ☐ client | ☐ legal | ☐ regulatory | ☐ audit | ☐ other: _____] [☐ requirements | ☐ needs] **with contracts ranging from $**_____ **to $**_____ *[amounts]* **for this $**_____ *[revenues]* _____ *[type of]* **firm servicing** _____ *[which?]* **clientele base.**

☐ **Prepare and negotiate** _____ *[type of]* **contracts with** _____ *[whom?]* **and determine contract terms and conditions.**

☐ [☐ Develop and negotiate | ☐ Review and approve] _____ *[type of]* [☐ contracts | ☐ contractual documents | ☐ agreements | ☐ proposals | ☐ amendments | ☐ legal documents | ☐ nondisclosure agreements | ☐ grant requests | ☐ license agreements | ☐ service agreements | ☐ technical documents | ☐ other: _____] **for** _____ *[what?]* **in support of major business initiatives.**

☐ **Negotiate fees and develop** _____ *[type of]* [☐ design | ☐ construction | ☐ repair | ☐ other: _____] **contracts with** [☐ architects | ☐ engineers | ☐ contractors | ☐ subcontractors | ☐ others: _____] **for** _____ *[what?]* **commensurate with project scope and budget.**

ACHIEVEMENT SAMPLES: *See also "Contract Development & Review."*

☐ **Led negotiations with** _____ *[whom?]* [☐ and investment bankers] **in acquiring company's most profitable** [☐ facility | ☐ plant | ☐ distribution center | ☐ branch | ☐ other: _____]. **With an appraised value versus purchase price of** _____ *[#]* **to one, profits exceeded acquisition costs in less than** _____ *[what time period?].*

☐ **Negotiated a $**_____ *[amount]* **contract with** _____ *[whom?],* **which served to** _____ *[purpose]* **and resulted in** _____ *[what was the win/win for the firm and the client?].*

☐ **Led negotiations with** _____ *[whom?]* **for long-term** _____ *[type of]* **agreements with forecasted savings of $**_____ *[amount]* **over a** _____ *[#]*-**year period.**

☐ **Saved the firm $**_____ *[amount]* **in the** [[☐ negotiation | ☐ litigation] **of** [☐ contractor | ☐ subcontractor | ☐ engineer | ☐ architect | ☐ other: _____] **claims ranging from $**_____ **to $**_____ *[amounts]* **which involved** [☐ interpreting legal documents | ☐ handling unforeseen conditions | ☐ other: _____] **and resulted in** _____ *[other benefits?].*

☐ **Negotiated and ratified** _____ *[#]* _____ *[type of]* **agreements with various** _____ *[type of]* **firms** [☐ nationwide | ☐ overseas | ☐ abroad], **resulting in** _____ *[benefits].*

☐ [☐ Managed | ☐ Performed] _____ *[type of]* **contract project rollouts from inception to successful implementation for this $**_____ *[revenues]* _____ *[type of]* **firm that** _____ *[does what?]* **for** _____ *[whom?].*

☐ **Played an integral role in obtaining a $**_____ **contract from** _____ *[whom?]* **to replace its current** _____ *[type of]* [☐ methodology | ☐ technology | ☐ products | ☐ other: _____] **with** _____ *[what?].*

☐ **Negotiated and wrote** [☐ client | ☐ architect | ☐ engineer | ☐ contractor | ☐ other: _____] _____ *[type of]* **contracts ranging from $**_____ **to $**_____ *[amounts]* **for** [☐ architectural plans for | ☐ the design and build of | ☐ construction of] _____ *[what?].*

Contractor / Subcontractor Influence & Collaboration

See also "Trades/Crew Supervision – All Trades" and "Trades Coordination & Oversight."

ACHIEVEMENT SAMPLES:

☐ **Built a strong, supportive contractor/subcontractor team environment by exhibiting and modeling leadership skills in** [☐ communication | ☐ negotiation | ☐ problem-solving | ☐ obstacle tackling | ☐ other: _____] **and** _____ *[doing what?].*

☐ **Challenge contractors in all trades to perform quality work on schedule and within budget by** _____ *[doing what well?].*

☐ **Influence all contractors to develop and maintain positive working relationships with all levels of** [☐ internal | ☐ external | ☐ internal and external] **management by** _____ *[doing what?].*

☐ **Collaborate with contractors and at all levels of the firm to** [☐ clarify scope | ☐ overcome obstacles | ☐ identify issues | ☐ solve problems | ☐ reach decisions | ☐ obtain solutions acceptance | ☐ guide projects to their successful completion | ☐ other: _____] **during the development and implementation of all projects.**

☐ **Influence, energize, and motivate contractors to bring projects to a successful delivery by** _____ *[doing what?].*

☐ **Gain contractor/subcontractor cooperation and commitment by** [☐ providing clear direction | ☐ soliciting feedback | ☐ serving as the primary resource hub | ☐ insisting on mutual support | ☐ sharing information | ☐ modeling professional behavior | ☐ building a collaborative environment | ☐ removing all obstacles to project success | ☐ other: _____].

☐ **Successfully produce results through others by** _____ *[doing what?].*

☐ **Persuaded crew to perform a clean job, ensuring all job site debris was removed before finishing. Accomplished through** [☐ peer pressure of others who were on task | ☐ other method: _____].

Cost Estimating – Architecture & Construction

☐ **Provide advice and input to** [☐ Architects | ☐ Engineers | ☐ CAD Designers | ☐ subcontractors | ☐ others: _____] **from project inception to completion on the financial feasibility of the design and construction of** _____ *[type of]* **projects ranging** $_____ **to** $_____ *[amounts]*.

☐ **Work with this** _____ *[type of]* **firm's** _____ *[which?]* **team to establish and/or confirm project budgets, prepare cost estimates, and serve as technical advisor to determine the financial success of** _____ *[type of]* **projects ranging** $_____ **to** $_____ *[amounts]*.

☐ **Determine the financial feasibility and return on investment of** _____ *[type of]* **projects along with** [☐ the image it will create | ☐ if it is responsive to the needs of (☐ its users / ☐ the community) | ☐ how well they will serve its intended purpose | ☐ other: _____] **for this** _____ *[type of]* **firm**.

☐ **Establish realistic construction capital costs on** _____ *[type of]* **projects by detailing cost planning and control to ensure projects are bid, documented, and completed in the most economical manner considering** [☐ quality | ☐ aesthetics | ☐ cost | ☐ location | ☐ image | ☐ practicality | ☐ functionality | ☐ timeliness | ☐ reliability | ☐ climate | ☐ user ability | ☐ future growth | ☐ other: _____].

☐ **By combining the functions of an economist, estimator, and accountant, use** [☐ engineering judgment | ☐ application of scientific principles and techniques | ☐ cost management principles | ☐ other: _____] **to focus on the feasibility and management of construction project costs and values.**

☐ **Accurately forecast project costs on** _____ *[type of]* **projects for this** [☐ multimillion-dollar | ☐ $_____] [☐ construction management | ☐ design-and-build | ☐ contracting | ☐ other: _____] **firm based on** _____ *[what factors or resources?]*.

☐ **Develop project cost information for** [☐ Project Engineers | ☐ Architects | ☐ Construction Managers | ☐ Facility Managers | ☐ Building Operations Managers | ☐ general contractors | ☐ business owners | ☐ corporate managers | ☐ others: _____] **required to** [☐ make bids for contracts | ☐ determine if a proposed project will be profitably feasible | ☐ other: _____], **considering all factors that influence costs including** [☐ materials | ☐ labor | ☐ equipment | ☐ location | ☐ special machinery | ☐ computer hardware and software | ☐ subcontracts | ☐ overhead | ☐ taxes | ☐ insurance | ☐ mark-up | ☐ other: _____].

☐ **Financially manage and control all** _____ *[type of]* **construction projects by reviewing project costs from inception through completion including** [☐ cost estimating | ☐ establishing realistic construction budgets | ☐ monitoring and managing costs from planning through completion | ☐ other: _____].

☐ **Monitor actual costs as the project develops against bid specifications including** [☐ plumbing | ☐ electrical work | ☐ excavation | ☐ concrete | ☐ masonry | ☐ other: _____] **to ensure project stays financially on track.**

☐ **Conduct preliminary cost estimation work including** [☐ reviewing preliminary drawings and specifications | ☐ making site visits of proposed projects | ☐ gathering information on availability of (☐ electricity / ☐ water / ☐ drainage / ☐ surface topography / ☐ other: _____) | ☐ determining seasonal weather conditions | ☐ recording all related information | ☐ other: _____].

☐ **Prepare quantity surveys and total project-cost summaries using** _____ *[type of software]* **detailing material costs, equipment needs, required crew size and labor costs, and sequence of operations; and submit bid proposals to** [☐ owner | ☐ architect | ☐ engineer | ☐ other: _____].

☐ **Attend** [☐ weekly | ☐ bi-monthly | ☐ periodic] **cost meetings to review** [☐ procurement | ☐ project | ☐ change orders | ☐ other: _____] **status with** [☐ contractors | ☐ project managers | ☐ engineering teams | ☐ management | ☐ others: _____].

☐ **Chair** [☐ weekly | ☐ bi-monthly | ☐ monthly] **schedule management meetings with** [☐ Project Managers | ☐ owner's representatives | ☐ contractors | ☐ others: _____] **to coordinate and report on project progress, address problem areas, and determine remedies to bring schedule progress back on track.**

☐ **Develop and monitor the** $_____ *[amount]* **construction budget including all project costs.** *(See "Budget Development and Expenditure Control" for additional bullets.)*

☐ **Review Construction Manager reports of total predicted costs, schedules, and variations to** [☐ proactively manage financial and physical aspects of all projects | ☐ accurately predict construction outcomes | ☐ assess risk | ☐ establish realistic capital costs of construction projects | ☐ assist project managers with handling changes and variations | ☐ other: _____].

☐ **Maximize and protect the firm's interest in the planning and completion of** _____ *[type of]* **projects enhancing the value of each project by** _____ *[doing what?]*.

☐ **Using an objective, unbiased approach, review and analyze** _____ *[what?]* **to determine the best course(s) of action regarding project cost estimations, cost control, profitability, and return on investment of** _____ *[type of]* **projects. Ensure all projects are completed within budget and meet all** [☐ performance | ☐ quality | ☐ other: _____] **standards.**

☐ **Coordinate** [☐ monthly | ☐ quarterly | ☐ year-end] **close requirements and prepare standard cost and gross margin variance analysis, reconciliation, and reporting.**

☐ **Use** _____ *[type of]* **control estimate and control schedules to** [☐ establish baselines | ☐ measure progress | ☐ track changes | ☐ predict cost overruns and schedule delays | ☐ provide information for management should intervention be required | ☐ other: _____] **on** _____ *[type of]* **projects.**

☐ **Collaborate with** _____ *[whom?]* **to optimize project planning, delivery, and operations.**

☐ **Establish project budgets ranging $**_____ **to $**_____ *[amounts]* **and baseline schedules for all** _____ *[type of]* **projects encompassing** _____ *[what?].*

☐ **Structure estimates and schedules based on** _____ *[type of]* **project** [☐ execution strategy | ☐ budget | ☐ other: _____], **test competitiveness of bids, and determine risk guidelines before authorizing project start.**

☐ **Predict final project costs and scheduling and identify possible variations from authorized baseline estimates and schedules by** _____ *[doing what?].*

ACHIEVEMENT SAMPLES: *See Achievements under "Cost Management."*

Cost Management – Architecture & Construction

See also "Cost Estimating," "Cost Reductions & Savings," "Increased Sales," and "Increased Revenues & Profits."

☐ **Provide detailed cost management services to/for** _____ *[whom or what?]* **involving** [☐ cost forecasting and reporting | ☐ invoice validation | ☐ change management | ☐ procurement management | ☐ project earned value analyses | ☐ other: _____].

☐ **Conduct analytical costing studies and provide** _____ *[#]* **alternative** _____ *[type of]* **solutions and/or selections based on proposed** _____ *[type of]* **projects to better utilize** _____ *[what?].*

☐ **Provide cost advice to** _____ *[whom?]* **on their proposed** _____ *[type of]* **projects during the early stages of development to assist in** [☐ determining project viability prior to design | ☐ preparing cost estimates | ☐ assessing the feasibility of undertaking the project | ☐ establishing a tentative budget | other: _____].

☐ **Use schematic drawings to conduct analytical costing studies and provide** _____ *[#]* **alternative design solutions / selections based on proposed** _____ *[type of]* **projects to better utilize** [☐ building size and shape | ☐ construction materials | ☐ other: _____].

☐ **Develop** _____ *[type of]* **cost estimates based on preliminary drawings supplied by** [☐ Architect | ☐ Engineer | ☐ CAD Drafter | ☐ outsourced firm | ☐ other: _____] **breaking down the cost of each functional construction element in its relationship to the whole to judge the economic viability of the entire project and make any needed changes.**

☐ **Undertake feasibility studies on the budget requirements of** _____ *[type of]* **construction projects to include** [☐ construction costs | ☐ operating and maintenance costs | ☐ site servicing | ☐ cash flows | ☐ other: _____] **by evaluating** [☐ market analysis | ☐ commercial returns | ☐ profitability | ☐ financing arrangements | ☐ land acquisition | ☐ revenue forecasts | ☐ other: _____].

☐ **Review all project costs to** [☐ analyze work progress | ☐ factor in amounts spent | ☐ determine reimbursable costs | ☐ track changes | ☐ summarize individual costs | ☐ predict total construction cost | ☐ other: _____].

☐ **Provide construction cost advice to** [☐ Architects | ☐ Engineers | ☐ CAD Drafters | ☐ other: _____] **on their proposed** _____ *[type of]* **projects during early stages of development to assist in determining project viability prior to design. Prepare cost estimates to assist in assessing the feasibility of undertaking the project and in establishing a tentative budget.**

☐ **Provide procurement services for** _____ *[type of]* [☐ construction | ☐ engineering | ☐ architectural | ☐ project management | ☐ other: _____] **services, including preparing Requests for Proposals (RFPs) and bid analysis.**

☐ **Conduct and prepare** [☐ Reserve Fund Studies | ☐ Cost-to-Complete Reports | ☐ Property Condition Reports | ☐ Insurance Replacement Cost Assessments | ☐ Risk Analysis | ☐ Bills of Quantities and Materials | ☐ Cost Control Estimates | ☐ Functional Cost Analysis | ☐ other: _____] **that include all costs related to** [☐ project management | ☐ project scheduling | ☐ construction management | ☐ related cash flows | ☐ mediation and arbitration | ☐ materials | ☐ other: _____].

ACHIEVEMENT SAMPLES:

☐ **Spearheaded a** _____ *[type of]* ***Cost Estimate System*** **whereby direct comparisons can be made between contractor price breakdowns and** _____ *[what else?].*

☐ Established and implemented a *Project Controls System (PCS)* for all capital projects based on their [☐ size | ☐ complexity | ☐ execution strategy | ☐ other: _____] **that encompassed** [☐ cost | ☐ planning | ☐ scheduling | ☐ change | ☐ other: _____] **management processes. The PCS** [☐ estimates project costs | ☐ monitors activities completion | ☐ reports schedule status | ☐ estimates change impact | ☐ predicts project outcomes | ☐ allows for corrective action | ☐ other: _____].

☐ Established and implemented the firm's *Project Change Management System* that identifies and reports on all variations from contract drawings and specifications and provides _____ [what?].

☐ Monitored and suggested changes to the _____ [which?] accounting [☐ policies | ☐ practices | ☐ systems] that drove improved analysis in the form of _____ [what?].

☐ Championed a _____ [type of] *Cost Estimate System* whereby direct comparisons can be made between contractor price breakdowns and _____ [what else?].

☐ Developed a _____ [type of] plan that manages project execution costs, schedules, and changes and _____ [benefited how?].

☐ Established and implemented the firm's *Project Change Management System* that identifies and reports on all variations from contract drawings and specifications and provides _____ [what?].

☐ Planned, organized, and defined the policies and procedures for all cost accounting activities including _____, _____, and _____ [which activities?].

☐ Drove _____ [type of] profit improvement activities that _____ [did what?].

☐ Established and implemented a *Project Controls System (PCS)* for all capital projects based on their [☐ size | ☐ complexity | ☐ execution strategy | ☐ other: _____] **that encompassed** [☐ cost | ☐ planning | ☐ scheduling | ☐ change | ☐ other: _____] **management processes. The PCS** [☐ estimates project costs | ☐ monitors activities completion | ☐ reports schedule status | ☐ estimates change impact | ☐ predicts project outcomes | ☐ allows for corrective action | ☐ other: _____].

☐ Established and implemented the firm's *Project Change Management System* that identifies and reports on _____ [what?] and provides _____ [what?].

☐ [☐ Established and implemented | ☐ Monitored and suggested changes to] the firm's Human Resource _____ [which?] [☐ policies | ☐ practices | ☐ systems] that drove improved analysis in the form of _____ [what?].

☐ Developed a _____ [type of] plan that manages project execution costs, schedules, and changes and _____ [benefited how?].

☐ Planned, organized, and defined the policies and procedures for all cost accounting activities including _____, _____, and _____ [which activities?].

Cost Reduction Programs Development

☐ Reduced total [☐ operating expenses | ☐ overhead costs] [☐ by _____% (percentage) | ☐ in excess of $_____ (amount)] annually by establishing a _____ [type of] initiative to _____ [do what?].

☐ [☐ Recommended | ☐ Developed] and implemented a cost-effective method to _____ [do what?], which improved _____ [what process?] and reduced operating expenses $_____ [amount] / _____% [percentage].

☐ Successfully cut _____ [which?] costs $_____ [amount] and increased revenues $_____ [amount] annually by [☐ introducing | ☐ implementing] a new _____ [type of] [☐ concept | ☐ cost-reduction method | ☐ other: _____].

☐ Created and implemented a successful _____ [type of] program to [☐ cut down the workload | ☐ reduce overtime | ☐ increase productivity | ☐ streamline operations | ☐ cut _____ (which?) expenses | ☐ other: _____], which has resulted in _____ [what benefits?].

☐ Spearheaded a _____ [type of] cost-reduction program by [☐ evaluating business bottlenecks and turning them into assets | ☐ other method: _____].

☐ Saved $_____ [amount] annually by implementing a cost-effective _____ [type of] [☐ policy | ☐ procedure | ☐ program | ☐ campaign | ☐ method | ☐ other: _____], which improved _____ [what process?].

☐ Reduced total [☐ operating expenses | ☐ overhead costs] [☐ _____% (percentage) | ☐ in excess of $_____ (amount)] annually by establishing a _____ [type of] initiative to _____ [do what?].

☐ **Saved employer $_____ annually through skillful research and negotiation of cost-effective _____** [what methods?].

☐ **Decreased overdue receivables _____%** [percentage] **/ $_____** [amount] **with tight control of accounts and strong follow-up.**

Cost Reductions & Savings – General

See also "Cost Management," "Purchasing," and various "Cost Reductions & Savings" categories, as applicable.

ACHIEVEMENT SAMPLES:

☐ **Developed and implemented a cost-effective method to _____** [do what?] **that improved _____** [what process?] **and reduced _____** [which?] **[☐ payroll | ☐ compensation | ☐ overtime | ☐ employee benefits | ☐ operating | ☐ overhead | ☐ other: _____] expenses by $_____** [amount] **/ _____%** [percentage].

☐ **Created and implemented a successful _____** [type of] **program to [☐ cut down the workload | ☐ reduce overtime | ☐ increase productivity | ☐ streamline operations | ☐ reduce expenses | ☐ other: _____], resulting in a savings of $_____** [amount].

☐ **Generated a cost savings of $_____** [amount] **in _____** [what?] **by [☐ spearheading | ☐ developing and implementing | ☐ recommending | ☐ other: _____] a _____** [type of] **business [☐ forecasting | ☐ analysis | ☐ other: _____] model that _____** [does what?] **by way of _____** [what?].

☐ **Reduced total [☐ operating expenses | ☐ overhead costs] [☐ by _____%** (percentage) **| ☐ in excess of $_____** (amount)**] annually by establishing a(n) _____** [type of] **initiative to _____** [do what?].

☐ **Decreased _____** [which?] **costs $_____** [amount] **/ _____%** [percentage] **[☐ annually] by [☐ spearheading cost-reduction methods in _____** (what?) **| ☐ establishing _____** (what?) **standards | ☐ coming in under budget in _____** (what area?) **| ☐ training all employees on _____** (what?) **| ☐ implementing cutting-edge solutions in _____** (what?) **| ☐ anticipating and proactively meeting (☐ clients' / ☐ the firm's) needs | ☐ using state-of-the-art technology to _____** (accomplish what?) **| ☐ bringing payroll in line with budget | ☐ developing a more efficient _____** (what?) **process | ☐ eliminating the need for _____** (what process?) **| ☐ selecting more cost-effective vendors | ☐ other: _____].**

☐ **Successfully cut _____** [which?] **costs $_____** [amount] **and increased revenues $_____** [amount] **annually by [☐ introducing | ☐ implementing] a new _____** [type of] **[☐ concept | ☐ cost-reduction method | ☐ other: _____] to _____** [do what?] **in _____** [#] **[☐ offices | ☐ locations | ☐ departments].**

☐ **Cut company _____** [which?] **costs $_____** [amount] **/ _____%** [percentage] **and increased revenues $_____** [amount] **annually by introducing the _____** [what?] **[☐ concept | ☐ program | ☐ procedure] and [☐ eliminating the need for _____** (what process?) **| ☐ demonstrating how information technology can be used as a competitive edge | ☐ other: _____], which resulted in _____** [additional benefits?].

☐ **Spearheaded a _____** [type of] **cost-reduction program that _____** [does what?] **by [☐ evaluating business bottlenecks and turning them into assets | ☐ other method: _____], which involved _____** [what actions?].

☐ **Designed and executed business forecasting and analysis models that generated a cost savings of _____%** [percentage] **/ $_____** [amount] **after executing a new _____** [type of] **[☐ training | ☐ production | ☐ other: _____] program that _____** [does what?].

☐ **Saved $_____** [amount] **annually and increased customer satisfaction level from _____%** [percentage] **to _____%** [percentage] **at a value of $_____** [amount] **by [☐ establishing a state-of-the-art _____** (type of) **program | ☐ reducing staff by _____** (#) **without affecting production levels | ☐ other: _____].**

☐ **[☐ Recommended | ☐ Developed] and implemented a cost-effective method to _____** [do what?], **which improved _____** [what process?] **and reduced operating expenses by $_____ / _____%** [amount and/or percentage].

☐ **Saved $_____** [amount] **in [☐ production time | ☐ supplies | ☐ equipment | ☐ other: _____] costs by _____** [doing what?].

☐ **Reduced company costs by coming in $_____** [amount] **under budget in _____** [what area?] **by _____** [doing what?].

Cost Reductions & Savings – Construction

See also "Cost Reductions & Savings – General."

ACHIEVEMENT SAMPLES:

☐ **Saved $_____** [amount] **by [☐ coming in under budget on _____** (project) **| ☐ reconfiguring _____** (type of) **space without reconstruction | ☐ resolving a complex _____** (type of) **problem quickly | ☐ implementing a cost-effective _____** (type of) **method to _____** (do what?) **| ☐ other: _____] resulting in _____** [what benefits?].

☐ **Cut lost tools costs down to a minimum by assigning the job of "Tool Counter" to a different person every week, saving company $_____** *[amount]* **annually.**

☐ **Decreased** _____ *[which?]* **costs $_____** [☐ through selection of more cost-effective vendors | ☐ training all employees on product features and benefits | ☐ other: _____].

☐ **Reduced labor costs $_____** *[amount]* **and increased profitability $_____** *[amount]* [☐ using direct field labor in lieu of subcontractors on smaller projects | ☐ hiring more effective crews for specific assignments | ☐ assigning laborers to handle simple tasks and freeing up mechanics to work on more technical issues | ☐ purchasing company-owned equipment in lieu of rentals | ☐ other achievement: _____].

☐ **Reduced** _____ *[which?]* **fees by $_____** *[amount]* **annually by spearheading the construction of a** _____ *[type of]* **facility for** _____ *[purpose],* **which resulted in** _____ *[what benefit?].*

Cost Reductions & Savings – Overhead / Operations

See also "Cost Reductions & Savings – General" and "Cost Management."

ACHIEVEMENT SAMPLES:

☐ **Reduced overhead costs $_____** *[amount]* **annually by** [☐ purchasing company-owned equipment | ☐ keeping operations running smoothly | ☐ giving 100% to the job | ☐ implementing a bidding process | ☐ successfully negotiating down costs | ☐ focusing on a commitment to excellence | ☐ other: _____].

☐ **Spearheaded a** _____ *[type of]* **cost-reduction program that** _____ *[does what?]* **by** [☐ evaluating business bottlenecks and turning them into assets | ☐ other method: _____] **which saved $_____** *[amount]* **annually.**

☐ **Slashed** _____ *[type of]* **overhead costs $_____** *[amount]* | _____% *[percentage]* **annually by** [☐ anticipating and proactively meeting the firm's needs | ☐ implementing employee bonus programs with salaries based on their production | ☐ acquiring newer technology to meet the facility's needs | ☐ updating computers | ☐ implementing a more efficient network | ☐ evaluating and enhancing the operational effectiveness of _____ *(which?)* (☐ systems / ☐ hardware / ☐ software) |☐ other: _____] **resulting in** [☐ staff exhibiting a genuine mental sharpness | ☐ fewer job-related errors | ☐ better attendance | ☐ higher team spirit | ☐ decreased turnover | ☐ increased production | ☐ other: _____].

☐ **Reduced total** [☐ operating expenses | ☐ overhead costs] [☐ by _____% *(percentage)* | ☐ in excess of $_____ *(amount)*] **annually by establishing a** _____ *[type of]* **initiative to** _____ *[do what?].*

☐ **Successfully cut** [☐ operating expenses | ☐ overhead costs | ☐ other: _____] **$_____** *[amount]* **by** [☐ introducing a new _____ *(type of)* concept | ☐ establishing a _____ *(type of)* initiative that _____ *[does what?]* | ☐ implementing cost-reduction methods | ☐ improving employee morale | ☐ reducing turnover and training costs | ☐ other achievement: _____].

☐ **Lowered total** [☐ operating expenses | ☐ overhead costs | ☐ controllable expenses | ☐ other: _____] **$_____** / _____% *[amount]* [☐ annually | ☐ over previous year] **by** [establishing a _____ *(type of)* initiative to _____ *(do what?)* |☐ implementing improved (☐ security | ☐ safety awareness programs) | ☐ other: _____].

☐ **Implemented a cost-effective method to** _____ *[do what?],* **which improved** _____ *[what process?]* **and reduced operating expenses by $_____** | _____% *[dollars and percentage].*

Cost Reductions & Savings – Payroll & Overtime

See also "Cost Reductions & Savings – General."

ACHIEVEMENT SAMPLES:

☐ **Decreased** [☐ overtime | ☐ payroll costs | ☐ contractor expenses | ☐ other: _____] **$_____** **by** [☐ scheduling employees to match their skills | ☐ developing troubleshooting programs to address quality issues | ☐ developing a scheduling program with a limited staff that met both the Company's and employees' needs | ☐ implementing vendor checks | ☐ structuring daily work schedules | ☐ other: _____] **resulting in** [☐ less absenteeism | ☐ decreased turnover | ☐ better customer servicing | ☐ other: _____].

☐ **Created and implemented a successful** _____ *[type of]* **program that** [☐ reduced (☐ workload / ☐ overtime) $_____ *(amount)* | ☐ increased productivity _____% *(amount)* | ☐ streamlined operations | ☐ cut expenses | ☐ other: _____].

☐ **Eliminated $_____** *[amount]* **in extraneous payroll costs by** [☐ reviewing employees' performance on a(n) (☐ weekly / ☐ monthly / ☐ annual) basis | ☐ terminating employees who were not meeting established performance levels | ☐ other: _____].

☐ **Slashed** [☐ payroll | ☐ overtime] **expenses $_____** *[amount]* **annually by** [☐ improving employee morale | ☐ reducing turnover rate | ☐ decreasing training costs | ☐ bringing payroll in line with budget | ☐ introducing a new _____ *(type of)* concept | ☐ implementing cost-reduction methods | ☐ evaluating business bottlenecks and turning them into assets | ☐ implementing a comprehensive scheduling program with a limited staff which met both the Company's and employees' needs, resulting in (☐ less absenteeism / ☐ better customer servicing) | ☐ other method: _____].

☐ **Cut** [☐ payroll | ☐ benefits | ☐ other: _____] **costs** _____% *[percentage]* **while maintaining** [☐ personnel | ☐ store | ☐ employee benefit | ☐ other: _____] **coverage by** [☐ splitting full-time positions amongst _____ *(#)* other stores in district | ☐ hiring part-time help in lieu of filling open full-time positions | ☐ other method(s): _____].

☐ **Saved $**_____ *[amount]* **annually to the bottom line by reducing payroll expenses while simultaneously increasing productivity levels** _____% *[percentage]* **from an already low** _____% *[percentage]* **the prior year** [☐ despite union raises during this period].

☐ **Decreased overtime $**_____ *[amount]* **by** [☐ implementing (☐ vendor checks / ☐ nightly walk-throughs) to track and determine daily work schedules | ☐ other method: _____].

☐ **Successfully decreased payroll expenses $**_____ *[amount]* **annually by** [☐ improving employee morale | ☐ reducing turnover and training costs | ☐ bringing payroll in line with budget | ☐ introducing a new _____ *(type of)* concept | ☐ implementing cost-reduction methods | ☐ evaluating business bottlenecks and turning them into assets | ☐ other method: _____].

☐ **Developed and implemented new employee** [☐ compensation | ☐ incentive | ☐ other: _____] **plans decreasing payroll by** _____% *[percentage]* **and elevating revenues from new business by** _____% *[percentage]*.

Cost Reductions & Savings – Technology Upgrades

See also "Technology Upgrades & Enhancements" and "Cost Reductions & Savings – General."

☐ **Cut costs $**_____ *[amount]* **and increased revenues $**_____ *[amount]* **annually by** [☐ updating _____ *(type of)* (☐ hardware / ☐ software) | ☐ using information technology as a competitive edge | ☐ other: _____], **which resulted in** _____ *[what other benefits?]*.

☐ **Decreased** _____ *[type of]* **costs** _____% *[percentage]* **by** [☐ anticipating clients' needs | ☐ using state-of-the-art technology | ☐ implementing cutting-edge solutions | ☐ other achievement: _____].

☐ **Achieved an annual savings of $**_____ *[amount]* **in** _____ *[which?]* **costs and dramatically improved** _____ *[what?]* **by** [☐ upgrading | ☐ purchasing | ☐ installing | ☐ other: _____] _____ *[type of]* **equipment.**

☐ **Saved $**_____ *[amount]* **annually by** [☐ evaluating and enhancing the operational effectiveness of _____ *(type of)* (☐ systems / ☐ hardware / ☐ software) | ☐ acquiring newer technology to meet the organization's needs | ☐ other method: _____], **which resulted in** _____ *[what benefits?]*.

☐ **Reduced** _____ *[type of]* **overhead costs $**_____ *[amount]* **/** _____% *[percentage]* **annually by** [☐ anticipating and proactively meeting the firm's needs | ☐ updating computers | ☐ implementing a more efficient network | ☐ establishing (☐ high-speed network capability / ☐ ISDN teleconferencing / ☐ effective cost-reduction methods) | ☐ reducing turnover | ☐ other: _____].

☐ **Wrote** [☐ support documentation for computer requisitions | ☐ recommendations for (☐ hardware / ☐ software) purchases | ☐ other: _____] **to link together multiple areas with similar needs, translating end user needs into system requirements, and saving the** [☐ firm | ☐ department | ☐ division | ☐ other: _____] **$**_____ *[amount]* **in** _____ *[what areas?]*.

☐ **Dramatically improved** _____ *[what?]* **by** [☐ upgrading | ☐ purchasing | ☐ other: _____] _____ *[type of]* **equipment, which resulted in an annual savings of $**_____ *[amount]* **in production costs.**

Crew Supervision

See "Trades Coordination & Oversight" and/or "Staff Management & Supervision."

Custodial / Janitorial Services

See also "Custodial / Janitorial Services Management & Supervision," "Grounds Maintenance Projects & Functions," and "Landscaping & Groundskeeping," as applicable.

☐ **Perform intensive cleaning, sanitation, maintenance, and repair work in all assigned areas for this** _____ *[type of]* **firm including all** [☐ floors | ☐ walls | ☐ woodwork | ☐ windows | ☐ draperies | ☐ shades | ☐ fire extinguishers | ☐ windows | ☐ desks and furniture | ☐ light fixtures | ☐ glass items | ☐ other: _____].

☐ **Update and maintain all custodial records and reports for** [☐ requisitions | ☐ supplies and equipment purchases | ☐ product use | ☐ equipment catalogs | ☐ grounds maintenance | ☐ others: _____].

☐ **Facilitate a number of custodial services for the interior** [☐ and exterior] **of this** _____ [type of] **company including** [☐ building cleaning coordination | ☐ facility cleaning | ☐ repair and remodel work | ☐ new product evaluations | ☐ record maintenance | ☐ facilities inspections | ☐ custodial equipment maintenance | ☐ supplies ordering | ☐ record and report updates | ☐ snow removal activities | ☐ garbage removal | ☐ other: _____] **ensuring all sanitation and safety levels meet licensing and inspection agency standards.**

☐ **Report to the** [☐ Custodial Supervisor | ☐ Lead Custodian | ☐ other: _____] **any found damage or repair needs required to the** [☐ premises | ☐ property | ☐ facilities | ☐ grounds | ☐ equipment | ☐ furniture | ☐ fixtures | ☐ other: _____], **fire hazards, and any findings that may pose a health or safety danger to staff or visitors.**

☐ **Perform heavy-duty** [☐ cleaning | ☐ washing | ☐ scrubbing | ☐ sweeping | ☐ mopping | ☐ shampooing | ☐ vacuuming | ☐ sanitizing | ☐ dusting | ☐ buffing | ☐ disinfecting | ☐ sanding | ☐ stripping | ☐ polishing | ☐ waxing | ☐ sealing | ☐ other: _____] **of** _____, _____, **and** _____ [what?] **as well as** [☐ floor finishing | ☐ waste and debris removal | ☐ snow and ice removal | ☐ landscape cutting, watering, and fertilizing | ☐ graffiti removal | ☐ equipment maintenance and repair | ☐ equipment parts replacement | ☐ dispensers refilling | ☐ other: _____], **always ensuring building areas are locked and secure.**

☐ **Facilitate the** [☐ moving of furniture or appliances | ☐ setting up of ladders and scaffolding | ☐ setting up of bleachers, tables, and/or chairs | ☐ preparing audio/visual equipment | ☐ providing direction for patron events | ☐ other: _____] **as needed, ensuring all facilities operate smoothly in the process.**

Custodial / Janitorial Services Management & Supervision

See also "Custodial / Janitorial Services."

☐ **Manage and oversee the intensive cleaning, sanitation, maintenance, and repair work of** _____ [#] **building(s) including** [☐ administrative offices | ☐ lavatories | ☐ other: _____].

☐ **Plan and organize custodial services ensuring the** _____ [type of] **building(s) is/are cleaned in compliance with all Federal and State health and safety codes.**

☐ **Supervise, oversee, and schedule the custodial cleaning of** _____ [type of] **building(s) on a daily basis, ensuring staff and public safety at all times.**

☐ **Supervise** _____ [#] **employees in the cleaning and maintenance of** _____ [#] _____ [type of] **building(s)** [☐ and grounds].

☐ **Hire, train, develop, and evaluate performance of the custodial staff of** _____ [#] **including training employees on operation, repair and preventive maintenance of** [☐ cleaning | ☐ HVAC | ☐ electrical | ☐ plumbing | ☐ other: _____] **systems and equipment.**

☐ **Inspect and assess facilities, and schedule and oversee all required maintenance and repair work ensuring building(s) is/are cleaned, repaired, and documented in compliance with all Federal and State Health and Safety Codes and Infection-Control Standards.**

☐ **Supervise custodial services including** [☐ preparing custodial care plans | ☐ establishing work priorities | ☐ coordinating work schedules | ☐ determining assignments | ☐ monitoring staff work habits | ☐ implementing quality assurance programs | ☐ training staff on proper care and use of custodial equipment | ☐ other: _____] **ensuring optimum work quality, productivity levels, quality assurance, and safety practices and adherence to established departmental policies and procedures.**

☐ **Oversee all custodial services including** [☐ equipment and supplies specifications development | ☐ facility cleaning plans and schedules development | ☐ problem resolution | ☐ new product evaluations based on jobs performed | ☐ file maintenance of custodial requisitions, purchases, and inventory | ☐ product and equipment catalogs maintenance | ☐ facilities inspections | ☐ repair and remodel work planning and scheduling | ☐ building cleaning scheduling and coordination | ☐ custodial equipment maintenance | ☐ supplies ordering and replenishing | ☐ cleaning supplies requisitions | ☐ record and report updates | ☐ policies and procedures development | ☐ other: _____] **ensuring all sanitation and safety levels meet licensing and inspecting agencies' standards.**

☐ **Manage the daily activities of custodial services including** [☐ personnel assignment | ☐ work allocation | ☐ training and development | ☐ quality assurance | ☐ problem resolution | ☐ supplies purchasing | ☐ inventory control | ☐ other: _____].

☐ **Assist** _____ [whom?] **in the development of** [☐ custodial policies and procedures | ☐ quality assurance programs | ☐ annual budget planning process | ☐ supplies and equipment specifications | ☐ other: _____] **to ensure** [☐ all functions are performed safely and correctly | ☐ ample supplies are always available | ☐ other: _____].

☐ **Apply** [☐ an in-depth] **knowledge of custodial-management-related activities including** [☐ safety regulations | ☐ infection control standards | ☐ planning and scheduling techniques | ☐ prioritizing work assignment scheduling | ☐ custodial methods, materials, and equipment | ☐ annual budget planning process | ☐ custodial work inspections | ☐ cleaning agents and possible reactions | ☐ custodial safety practices | ☐ sanitation and infection control | ☐ quality of work consistency | ☐ department equipment care and maintenance | ☐ equipment and supplies ordering | ☐ inventory control | ☐ job cost estimating | ☐ budget preparation | ☐ fiscal management | ☐ custodial work training methods | ☐ cost-cutting procedures | ☐ work order reviews | ☐ records maintenance | ☐ other: _____] **in the management of custodial services.**

☐ **Provide administrative management in the areas of** [☐ staff interviewing and hiring | ☐ orienting new custodial employees | ☐ setting work priorities | ☐ determining custodial assignments | ☐ evaluating performance | ☐ setting quality assurance and safety standards | ☐ conducting staff meetings | ☐ monitoring custodial services expenditures | ☐ recommending new or revised policies and operating procedures | ☐ other: _____].

Customer Complaints & Problem Resolution

☐ **Successfully handle and resolve customer problems through effective** [☐ customer service | ☐ teamwork | ☐ troubleshooting | ☐ patience | ☐ other: _____] **and by implementing a** _____ *[type of]* **philosophy.**

☐ **Research, evaluate, and resolve customer complaints to their satisfaction by applying effective** [☐ listening skills | ☐ problem-solving techniques | ☐ mediating skills | ☐ other: _____] [☐ via an ear for understanding their point of view | ☐ by balancing customer satisfaction without "giving away the store" | ☐ other: _____].

☐ **Working with a wide range of clientele, resolve difficult problems and/or discrepancies in a** [☐ diplomatic | ☐ patient | ☐ calm | ☐ friendly | ☐ courteous | ☐ positive | ☐ knowledgeable | ☐ professional | ☐ caring] **manner and by keeping composure during peak periods by** [☐ tackling each situation as it arises | ☐ remaining calm | ☐ soliciting and obtaining help from peers making short-staff situations transparent to customers | ☐ other methods: _____].

☐ **Obtain customer satisfaction through** [☐ quick resolution of customer issues regarding (☐ pricing / ☐ signing / ☐ company policies / ☐ returns) | ☐ other: _____] **ensuring the quality of customer service delivered meets high standards of excellence by** [☐ monitoring and evaluating staff's progress | ☐ other means: _____].

☐ **Handle and resolve all customer complaints, resolving time-sensitive issues in an expedient manner by using effective** [☐ listening skills | ☐ problem-solving techniques | ☐ mediating skills | ☐ other: _____] **and** [☐ lending an ear for understanding their point of view | ☐ troubleshooting the problem | ☐ balancing customer satisfaction without "giving away the store" | ☐ other means: _____].

☐ **Keep composure during peak times by** [☐ tackling each situation as it arises | ☐ remaining calm | ☐ soliciting and obtaining help from peers to make short-staff situations transparent to customers | ☐ other methods: _____].

☐ **Appease dissatisfied customers and turn them into satisfied consumers through** [☐ effective listening | ☐ patience | ☐ a caring manner | ☐ understanding | ☐ other methods: _____].

☐ **Handle and resolve** [☐ customer complaints | ☐ difficult issues] **by** [☐ utilizing effective problem-solving techniques and mediating skills | ☐ other method: _____].

☐ **Successfully handle customer service before and after sale by implementing a** _____ *[type of]* **philosophy.**

☐ **Handle customer complaints via** [☐ effective listening skills | ☐ an ear for understanding their point of view | ☐ balance customer satisfaction with not "giving away the store" | ☐ other: _____].

☐ **Handle all customer complaints by successfully appeasing dissatisfied customers and turning them into satisfied clients through** [☐ effective listening | ☐ patience | ☐ understanding | ☐ a caring manner | ☐ other methods: _____].

☐ **Troubleshoot, research, evaluate, and resolve customer inquiries and complaints to their satisfaction by using effective** [☐ listening skills | ☐ problem-solving techniques | ☐ mediating skills | ☐ understanding | ☐ other: _____].

☐ **Handle and resolve all** [☐ customer | ☐ staff | ☐ other: _____] **complaints, resolving time-sensitive issues in an expedient manner to the** [customer's | ☐ staff's | ☐ company's | ☐ other: _____] **satisfaction.**

☐ **Successfully resolve** [☐ customer account problems | ☐ conflicts with employees | ☐ account discrepancies | ☐ other: _____] **through effective** [☐ customer service | ☐ teamwork | ☐ troubleshooting | ☐ patience | ☐ other: _____].

ACHIEVEMENT SAMPLES:

☐ **Tackled and resolved customer** [☐ problems | ☐ complaints | ☐ account discrepancies | ☐ other: _____] **through** [☐ effective customer service | ☐ teamwork | ☐ troubleshooting | ☐ patience | ☐ a caring manner | ☐ other methods: _____] **and** [☐ an ear for understanding their point of view | ☐ balancing customer satisfaction with not "giving away the store" | ☐ by implementing a _____ *(type of)* philosophy | ☐ other: _____], **thereby appeasing dissatisfied customers and turning them into satisfied clients.**

☐ **Successfully** [☐ developed | ☐ resurrected | ☐ implemented] **a $_____** *[amount]* **project bringing it to fruition through** [☐ field research | ☐ tactical marketing | ☐ market, competition, product, and pricing awareness | ☐ other: _____]. **Company profited $_____** *[revenues]*—**earmarking this as the first of the high budget projects it would undertake.**

☐ **Received** [☐ many | ☐ _____ (#)] [☐ client | ☐ customer] **commendations** [☐ regarding staff performance | ☐ due to (☐ having a positive attitude / ☐ being efficient / ☐ a quest for excellence / ☐ going beyond the expected / ☐ other trait: _____], **resulting in** [☐ more satisfied customers | ☐ an increased account base | ☐ repeat business | ☐ referrals | ☐ other: _____] **for company.**

Customer Service

See also "Customer Service Management," "Customer Complaints & Problem Resolution," "Client Meeting & Strategizing," and "Client Relations."

☐ **Identify, define, and document client needs and priorities as well as** [☐ options | ☐ risks | ☐ costs | ☐ benefits | ☐ alternative solutions | ☐ other: _____] **and translate requirements into effective** _____ *[type of]* **solutions.**

☐ **Interface with and assist** _____ *[type of]* **customers by** [☐ providing information | ☐ answering all project-related questions | ☐ offering solutions that meet their needs | ☐ processing and expediting their requests | ☐ resolving customer complaints | ☐ handling client billing | ☐ checking project scheduling | ☐ providing follow-up and advisement | ☐ other: _____].

☐ **Provide customers with** [☐ advice | ☐ professional help | ☐ consultation | ☐ other: _____] **in** _____ *[what functions?]* **for this** $_____ *[revenues]* _____ *[type of]* **firm with** _____ *[#]* [☐ locations | ☐ employees | ☐ accounts].

☐ **Handle various customer service functions including** [☐ preparing orders | ☐ facilitating customer orders | ☐ answering inquiries | ☐ solving credit problems | ☐ resolving customer complaints | ☐ handling client billing | ☐ other: _____] **ensuring all interactions leave a positive impression by being** [☐ courteous | ☐ professional | ☐ helpful | ☐ other: _____] **to all visitors and callers.**

☐ **Maintain high levels of customer satisfaction by** [☐ listening to and interpreting their needs | ☐ paying careful attention to detail | ☐ providing solution selling | ☐ offering alternative options | ☐ upselling higher-end services | ☐ other: _____].

☐ **Convert customer desires into needs by** _____ *[doing what?]*, **achieving** [☐ increased sales | ☐ repeat business | ☐ referrals | ☐ other achievement: _____] **for company.**

☐ **Handle** [☐ heavy | ☐ moderate] **telephone contact with** [☐ clients | ☐ suppliers | ☐ vendors | ☐ other: _____] **in a professional manner, always ensuring appropriate follow-through within a** _____ *[#]*-[☐ hour | ☐ minute] **timeframe.**

☐ **Assist customers with** _____ *[type of]* **inquiries in person and via** [☐ phone | ☐ e-mail | ☐ fax] **by** _____ *[methods]*.

☐ **Greet and direct all customers in a professional manner, assisting them with** _____ , _____ , **and** _____ *[what areas?]* **while promoting company and going above and beyond to fulfill customer needs.**

☐ **Screen and service all** [☐ internal | ☐ external | ☐ internal and outside] **calls in a professional manner, ensuring all callers get the help they need with** [☐ confidentiality | ☐ courtesy | ☐ follow-up | ☐ other: _____].

ACHIEVEMENT SAMPLES: *See also "Customer Service & Satisfaction Levels Improvement," "Customer Service Management," and "Customer Complaints & Problem Resolution."*

☐ **Through direct, consumer-sensitive approach and** _____ *[other method]*, **increased** [☐ customer loyalty | ☐ repeat business | ☐ referrals | ☐ sales | ☐ other: _____] **from** _____ *[#]* **to** _____ *[#]*.

☐ **Regularly obtain customer satisfaction through** [☐ quick resolution of customer issues regarding (☐ pricing / ☐ signing / ☐ company policies / ☐ returns) | ☐ other: _____] **ensuring the quality of customer service delivered meets high standards of excellence by** [☐ monitoring and evaluating staff's progress | ☐ other means: _____].

☐ **Tackled and resolved customer** [☐ problems | ☐ complaints | ☐ account discrepancies | ☐ other: _____] **through** [☐ effective customer service | ☐ teamwork | ☐ troubleshooting | ☐ patience | ☐ a caring manner | ☐ other methods: _____] **and** [☐ an ear for understanding their point of view | ☐ balancing customer satisfaction with not "giving away the store" | ☐ by implementing a _____ *(type of)* philosophy | ☐ other: _____], **thereby appeasing dissatisfied customers and turning them into satisfied clients.**

☐ **Identified and implemented** [☐ cross-sell | ☐ upsell | ☐ add-on | ☐ other: _____] **opportunities, including** _____ **and** _____ **by** [☐ providing employee incentives | ☐ other method: _____], **resulting in** _____ *[what benefit?]*.

☐ **Received** [☐ many | ☐ _____ (#)] [☐ client | ☐ customer] **commendations** [☐ regarding (☐ staff performance / ☐ product availability / ☐ overall store satisfaction / ☐ other: _____) | ☐ due to (☐ having a positive attitude / ☐ being efficient / ☐ a quest for excellence / ☐ going beyond the expected / ☐ other trait: _____)], **resulting in** [☐ more satisfied customers | ☐ an increased account base | ☐ repeat business | ☐ referrals | ☐ other: _____] **for company.**

☐ **Obtain customer satisfaction through** [☐ quick resolution of customer issues regarding (☐ pricing / ☐ signing / ☐ company policies / ☐ returns) | ☐ other: _____] **ensuring the quality of customer service delivered meets high standards of excellence by** [☐ monitoring and evaluating staff's progress | ☐ other means: _____].

☐ **Regularly obtain customer satisfaction through** [☐ quick resolution of customer issues regarding pricing, signing, company policies, and returns | ☐ fast and friendly check lines | ☐ other: _____] **ensuring the quality of customer service delivered meets high standards of excellence by** [☐ monitoring and evaluating staff's progress | ☐ other means: _____].

Customer Service Management

See also **"Customer Service"** *categories.*

☐ [☐ **Manage and oversee** | ☐ **Facilitate**] **all facets of customer service—from handling inquiries and assisting customers with their purchasing decisions to resolving problems with difficult customers using effective problem-solving techniques—resulting in superior customer service for this** $_____ *[revenues]* _____ *[type of]* **company with** _____ *[#]* [☐ **stores** | ☐ **locations** | ☐ **employees** | ☐ **accounts**] **that sells** _____ *[what?]* **to** _____ *[type of]* **consumers.**

☐ [☐ **Manage and oversee** | ☐ **Supervise**] [☐ **customer service operations** | ☐ **the distribution center** | ☐ **purchasing** | ☐ **other:** _____] **of this** _____ *[type of]* **firm that provides** _____ *[type of]* [☐ **products** | ☐ **services**] **to the** _____ *[which?]* **market.**

☐ **Lead and direct the** [☐ customer service operations | ☐ total sales support | ☐ other: _____] **of** [☐ this recognized world standard setter for] _____ *[type of]* [☐ **services** | ☐ **projects** | ☐ **other:** _____] **previously averaging** $_____ *[amount]* **per sale, and with redirection placing the company in the** $_____ *[amount]* **per-sale market.**

☐ **Oversee customer service of this** _____ *[type of]* **firm that provides** _____ *[type of]* **services to the** _____ *[which?]* **market including providing customers with** [☐ advice | ☐ professional help | ☐ consultation | ☐ other: _____] **in** _____ *[what functions?]*.

☐ **Monitor, track, and review** [☐ service | ☐ productivity | ☐ product promotions | ☐ cash control | ☐ inventory control | ☐ auditing | ☐ training | ☐ other: _____] **ensuring compliance with all store policies, procedures, and standards.**

☐ **Work closely with** _____ *[whom?]* **to address** [☐ business needs | ☐ client solutions] **in the development of** [☐ project plans | ☐ systems design | ☐ other: _____] **to meet those needs**.

ACHIEVEMENT SAMPLES: *See also "Customer Service – General," "Customer Service & Satisfaction Levels Improvement," and "Customer Complaints & Problem Resolution."*

☐ **Spearheaded cost-effective, high quality** _____ *[type of]* [☐ customer service | ☐ sales support] **program(s) that resulted in increased** [☐ annual sales of $_____ *(amount)* | ☐ customer satisfaction levels of _____ % *(percentage)* | ☐ other: _____].

☐ **Successfully** [☐ developed | ☐ resurrected | ☐ implemented] **a** $_____ *[amount]* [☐ product | ☐ service | ☐ project] **bringing it to fruition through** [☐ field research | ☐ tactical marketing | ☐ market, competition, product, and pricing awareness | ☐ other: _____]. **Company profited** $_____ *[revenues]*—**earmarking this as the first of the high budget projects it would undertake.**

☐ **Organized a** [☐ hodgepodge order-as-you-need-it supply system | ☐ other area: _____] **by focusing on centralization, resulting in** [☐ a streamlined supply flow | ☐ more on-time deliveries | ☐ elimination of panic order situations | ☐ other: _____].

☐ **Spearheaded cost-effective, high quality** _____ *[type of]* [☐ customer service | ☐ sales support | ☐ other: _____] **program(s) that resulted in increased** [☐ annual sales of $_____ *(amount)* | ☐ customer satisfaction levels of _____ % *(percentage)* | ☐ other: _____].

☐ **Developed and implemented a new** _____ *[name of]* **Customer Service Program that** _____ *[program purpose]* **resulting in** $_____ *[amount]* **in new business.**

☐ **Identified and implemented** [☐ cross-sell | ☐ upsell | ☐ add-on | ☐ other: _____] **opportunities, including** _____ **and** _____ **by** [☐ providing employee incentives | ☐ other method: _____], **resulting in** _____ *[what benefit?]*.

Customer Service & Satisfaction Levels Improvement

See also "Customer Service – General," "Customer Service – Management," "Customer Complaints & Problem Resolution," and "Increased Account Base."

ACHIEVEMENT SAMPLES:

☐ **Increased customer loyalty by** [☐ designing creative promotional pieces | ☐ providing a direct consumer-sensitive approach | ☐ tackling difficult challenges | ☐ meeting client goals head-on / other: _____].

☐ **Spearheaded cost-effective, high quality** _____ *[type of]* [☐ customer service | ☐ sales support | ☐ other: _____] **program(s) that resulted in increased** [☐ annual sales of $_____ *(amount)* | ☐ customer satisfaction levels of _____ % *(percentage)* | ☐ other: _____].

☐ **Elevated levels of client satisfaction by** _____**%** [percentage] **by** [☐ providing knowledgeable service in a friendly manner | ☐ researching and resolving customer complaints in a timely fashion | ☐ other: _____].

☐ **Successfully achieved a** [☐ 100% | ☐ other: _____%] [percentage] **customer satisfaction rate by** [☐ providing superior customer service | ☐ completing all projects on time and within budget | ☐ answering all project-related questions | ☐ offering solutions | ☐ rectifying customer complaints and problems as they arose | ☐ resolving time-sensitive issues in an expedient manner | ☐ using effective problem-solving techniques | ☐ successfully appeasing dissatisfied customers and turning them into satisfied clients | ☐ using effective listening skills | ☐ accomplishing goal to turn every customer into a satisfied customer | ☐ other: _____].

☐ **Recommended and oversaw** _____ [what?] **to appeal to new client base including** [☐ creating and implementing product changes | ☐ other: _____] **resulting in increased customer service levels of** _____% [percentage] **and profitability of $**_____ [amount].

☐ **Increased customer satisfaction level from** _____% **to** _____% [percentages] **at a value of $**_____ [amount] **annually by** [☐ establishing a state-of-the-art _____ (type of) program | ☐ reducing staff by _____ (#) without affecting production levels | ☐ other: _____].

☐ **Through direct, consumer-sensitive approach and** _____ [other method], **increased** [☐ customer loyalty | ☐ repeat business | ☐ referrals | ☐ sales | ☐ other: _____].

☐ **Fostered good business relationships with all** [☐ clients | ☐ customers | ☐ referral sources | ☐ vendors | ☐ other: _____] **by** [☐ successfully meeting their needs | ☐ being above board with all communications | ☐ other: _____], **which increased** _____ [which?] **service levels from** _____% **to** _____% [percentages].

☐ **Conceptualized and developed seamless, cost-effective customer service strategies, such as** _____, _____, **and** _____ [type of strategies], **resulting in** _____ [what benefits?].

Drywall Installation

See "Ceiling, Lathing, Insulation & Drywall Installation" and "Carpentry Work."

Electrical Engineering Scope

See also "Electrical Engineering – Management" as well as "Engineering Functions – General," "Architecture" categories, "CAD Drafting," "Engineering Projects," and "Inspections & Compliance."

☐ **Perform electrical engineering design and development involving the** [☐ research | ☐ design | ☐ redesign | ☐ fabrication | ☐ construction | ☐ installation | ☐ maintenance | ☐ other: _____] **of** _____ [type of] **engineering projects ranging from $**_____ **to $**_____ [amounts] **per project, ensuring application of best practices.**

☐ **Provide** [☐ electrical engineering design expertise | ☐ project development services | ☐ other: _____] **in** [☐ writing specifications | ☐ developing effective solutions | ☐ creating PCB layouts | ☐ evaluating tradeoffs | ☐ testing | ☐ other: _____] **to** _____ [whom?] **in the development and implementation of** _____ [what?] **for this** _____ [type of] **firm.**

☐ **Perform** _____ [type of] **electrical** [☐ systems | ☐ equipment] **engineering work for the** [☐ design | ☐ redesign | ☐ installation | ☐ operation | ☐ maintenance | ☐ research | ☐ production | ☐ manufacture | ☐ other: _____] **of** _____ [what?] **ensuring application of best practices for this $**_____ [revenues] _____ [type of] **firm.**

☐ **Develop specifications for the installation of** [☐ voltage transformers | ☐ overhead cables | ☐ underground cables | ☐ _____ (type of) electrical equipment | ☐ other: _____] **for conducting electrical energy from high-voltage distribution lines to consumers.**

☐ **Estimate the time and cost of all components to manufacture electrical engineering** _____ [type of] **projects ranging from $**_____ **to $**_____ [project cost range].

☐ **Conduct** [☐ complex] **engineering work including the** [☐ design | ☐ development | ☐ testing | ☐ debugging | ☐ troubleshooting | ☐ other: _____] **of electrical** [☐ systems | ☐ equipment | ☐ products | ☐ other: _____] **applying current research principles and techniques.**

☐ **Design, develop, install, test, and validate** _____ [type of] **electrical** [☐ systems | ☐ equipment | ☐ products | ☐ components | ☐ parts | ☐ assemblies | ☐ subassemblies | ☐ other: _____] **for** _____ [what?], **and prepare associated electrical** [☐ plans | ☐ drawings | ☐ specifications | ☐ proposals | ☐ instructions | ☐ other: _____] **using standard engineering principles and practices.**

☐ **Collaborate with** [☐ Engineering Manager | ☐ Architects | ☐ Project Managers | ☐ other engineering groups | ☐ others: _____] **regarding effective design** [☐ concepts | ☐ philosophies | ☐ approaches] **that solve dynamic** _____ [type of] **electrical challenges and ensure engineering criteria is suitable for proposed applications.**

☐ **Lead and direct the design and installation of** _____ *[type of]* **electronic engineering projects for this $**_____ *[revenues]* _____ *[type of]* **firm servicing** _____ *[type of]* **clients ensuring on-time and within-budget deliverables**.

☐ **Facilitate electrical engineering work for the** [☐ design | ☐ redesign | ☐ installation | ☐ operation | ☐ maintenance | ☐ other: _____] _____ *[type of]* **engineering projects ranging from $**_____ **to $**_____ *[amounts]* **per project ensuring application of best practices**.

☐ **Conduct electrical** [☐ systems | ☐ equipment] **engineering work for the** [☐ design | ☐ redesign | ☐ manufacture | ☐ installation | ☐ operation | ☐ maintenance | ☐ other: _____] **of** _____ *[what?]* **ensuring application of best practices**.

☐ [☐ Design | ☐ Redesign | ☐ Manufacture | ☐ Install | ☐ Maintain | ☐ Test | ☐ other: _____] **electrical systems and equipment including** _____ , _____ , **and** _____ *[systems or equipment]* **for this** _____ *[type of]* **firm**.

☐ **Design and develop** _____ *[type of]* **electrical** [☐ control systems | ☐ equipment | ☐ product | ☐ other: _____] **specifications and design functionality focusing on** [☐ safety | ☐ reliability | ☐ quality | ☐ economy | ☐ sustainability | ☐ other: _____] **by** [☐ using research techniques to validate design theory | ☐ integrating high-level, functional requirements | ☐ developing test documents | ☐ integrating testing parts and systems | ☐ other: _____].

☐ **Develop, maintain, and/or modify electrical system designs for** [☐ cable systems | (☐ exterior / ☐ interior) lighting | ☐ voltage transformers | ☐ fuel systems | ☐ proximity systems | ☐ cargo systems | ☐ power (☐ generation / ☐ distribution / ☐ conversion) | ☐ other: _____] **based on customer needs, Company standards, and regulatory requirements**.

☐ **Develop, test, and manufacture** _____ *[type of]* **electrical** [☐ systems | ☐ equipment | ☐ other: _____] **including** _____ , _____ , **and** _____ *[what?]* **for this $**_____ *[revenues]* _____ *[type of]* **firm**.

☐ **Create, test, and oversee the** [☐ development | ☐ installation | ☐ other: _____] **of** _____ *[type of]* **electrical** [☐ systems | ☐ wiring | ☐ equipment | ☐ other: _____] **including** _____ , _____ , **and** _____ *[what?]*.

☐ **Lead and direct electrical functions for** _____ *[type of]* **public works projects including** [☐ repairing underground conduits | ☐ trimming trees for wire clearance | ☐ operating underground cable locators to find, and updating maps to include, cable locations and underground faults | ☐ operating (☐ pickup trucks / ☐ digger derricks / ☐ bucket trucks / ☐ other: _____)].

☐ **Develop, maintain, and/or modify electrical system designs for** [☐ cable systems | (☐ exterior | ☐ interior) lighting | ☐ voltage transformers | ☐ fuel systems | ☐ proximity systems | ☐ cargo systems | ☐ power (☐ generation | ☐ distribution | ☐ conversion) | ☐ other: _____] **based on customer needs, Company standards, and regulatory requirements**.

☐ **Plan, direct, prioritize, schedule, and oversee** _____ *[#]* _____ *[titles]* **in the technical engineering aspects of all** _____ *[type of]* **electrical work and services for** _____ *[what?]* **ensuring project deliverables within schedule constraints**.

ACHIEVEMENT SAMPLES:

☐ **Performed electrical engineering design and development involving the** [☐ research | ☐ design | ☐ construction | ☐ other: _____] **of** _____ *[type of]* **engineering projects ranging from $**_____ **to $**_____ *[amounts]*.

☐ **Optimized plant operations** _____ **%** *[percentage]* **by providing** _____ *[type of]* **automated electrical** [☐ solutions | ☐ services | ☐ products] **through the development of efficient** _____ *[type of]* [☐ lighting | ☐ cable | ☐ proximity | ☐ fuel | ☐ cargo | ☐ power | ☐ circuit | ☐ petroleum | ☐ petrochemical | ☐ other: _____] [☐ electronic | ☐ electrical] **system and equipment designs for** _____ *[what?]* **including** [☐ gas-engine | ☐ motor | ☐ gas-turbine | ☐ steam-turbine | ☐ electric-motor] **driven** [☐ reciprocating compressors | ☐ generators | ☐ mechanical drives | ☐ ☐ control systems | ☐ instrumentation | ☐ other: _____].

☐ **Optimized plant operations by providing automated electrical** [☐ solutions | ☐ services | ☐ products] **through the development of efficient** _____ *[type of]* [☐ lighting | ☐ cable | ☐ proximity | ☐ fuel | ☐ cargo | ☐ power | ☐ circuit | ☐ petroleum | ☐ petrochemical | ☐ other: _____] **electrical system and equipment designs for** _____ *[what?]* **including** [☐ gas-engine | ☐ motor | ☐ gas-turbine | ☐ steam-turbine | ☐ electric-motor] **driven** [☐ reciprocating compressors | ☐ generators | ☐ mechanical drives | ☐ control systems | ☐ instrumentation | ☐ other: _____].

☐ **Performed electrical engineering design and development involving the** [☐ research | ☐ design | ☐ construction | ☐ other: _____] **of** _____ *[type of]* **engineering projects ranging from $**_____ **to $**_____ *[amounts]* **per project**.

Electrical Engineering Management

See also "Electrical Engineering – General."

☐ **Plan and supervise all phases of** _____ *[type of]* **electrical wiring projects in** [☐ commercial | ☐ residential | ☐ industrial | ☐ public works | ☐ other: _____] **settings including repairing and maintaining electrical** [☐ systems | ☐ motors | ☐ devices | ☐ control panels | ☐ conduit | ☐ switches | ☐ other: _____] **for this** _____ *[type of]* **firm**.

☐ **Project Manage the** [☐ installation | ☐ repair | ☐ rewiring | ☐ testing | ☐ inspection | ☐ troubleshooting | ☐ diagnosis | ☐ replacement | ☐ maintenance | ☐ servicing | ☐ other: _____ **of** [☐ electrical | ☐ lighting | ☐ climate control | ☐ conduit | ☐ motor control | ☐ telecommunications | ☐ security | ☐ intercom | ☐ signaling | ☐ computer | ☐ fire alarm | ☐ industrial | ☐ digital | ☐ pneumatic tube | ☐ energy management | ☐ public address | ☐ other: _____ **systems for this** [☐ multimillion-dollar | ☐ $_____] [☐ electrical contractor | ☐ industrial plant | ☐ public services company | ☐ other: _____].

☐ **Provide electrician oversight in the installation of** _____ *[type of]* **electrical** [☐ systems | ☐ equipment | ☐ components | ☐ instruments | ☐ apparatus | ☐ accessories | ☐ other: _____] **including** [☐ electronic controls | ☐ motors | ☐ starters | ☐ switches | ☐ fixtures | ☐ fuses | ☐ other: _____].

☐ **Lead and direct the installation and repair of electrical equipment used for** [☐ lighting | ☐ power circuits | ☐ automatically controlled circuits | ☐ elevators | ☐ conveyors | ☐ other: _____] **including** [☐ generators | ☐ conduits | ☐ transformers | ☐ programmable controllers | ☐ motor controllers | ☐ AC & DC motors | ☐ circuit breakers | ☐ heating units | ☐ pull boxes | ☐ switches | ☐ transmission equipment | ☐ other: _____].

☐ **Oversee** _____ *[#]* **electricians and coordinate trades work in the installation of electrical equipment for** [☐ lighting systems | ☐ power circuits | ☐ automatically controlled circuits | ☐ elevators | ☐ conveyors | ☐ other: _____] **including** [☐ generators | ☐ conduits | ☐ transformers | ☐ programmable controllers | ☐ motor controllers | ☐ AC & DC motors | ☐ circuit breakers | ☐ heating units | ☐ pull boxes | ☐ switches | ☐ switchboards | ☐ transmission equipment | ☐ lighting circuits | ☐ new equipment power lines | ☐ fan motors | ☐ plant lighting | ☐ other: _____] **to ensure all electrical codes and principles are followed**.

☐ **Supervise and coordinate electrical work involved in the** [☐ installation | ☐ construction | ☐ remodeling | ☐ alteration | ☐ maintenance | ☐ service | ☐ repair | ☐ other: _____] **of** [☐ public works | ☐ residential | ☐ industrial | ☐ commercial] [☐ electrical | ☐ electronic | ☐ climate control | ☐ security | ☐ communications | ☐ computer | ☐ fire alarm | ☐ other: _____] [☐ systems | ☐ equipment | ☐ componentry | ☐ instruments | ☐ devices | ☐ apparatus].

☐ **Facilitate electrician oversight in the** [☐ installation | ☐ repair | ☐ rewiring | ☐ testing | ☐ inspection | ☐ troubleshooting | ☐ diagnosis | ☐ replacement | ☐ maintenance | ☐ servicing] **of** [☐ electrical | ☐ lighting | ☐ climate control | ☐ conduit | ☐ motor control | ☐ security | ☐ communications | ☐ intercom | ☐ signaling | ☐ bus bar | ☐ computer | ☐ fire alarm | ☐ industrial | ☐ digital | ☐ pneumatic tube | ☐ energy management | ☐ public address | ☐ other: _____] **systems covering** [☐ electronic controls | ☐ motors | ☐ starters | ☐ switches | ☐ fixtures | ☐ fuses | ☐ coax cables | ☐ wiring | ☐ lighting fixtures | ☐ electrical panels | ☐ cables | ☐ outlets | ☐ other: _____].

☐ **Oversee the installation and repair of various** [☐ domestic | ☐ industrial | ☐ commercial] **systems including** [☐ electrical | ☐ lighting | ☐ climate control | ☐ conduit | ☐ security | ☐ communications | ☐ signaling | ☐ computer | ☐ fire alarm | ☐ other: _____] **for** _____ *[type of]* [☐ buildings |☐ grounds | ☐ equipment | ☐ other: _____].

☐ **Direct and manage the installation and repair of** [☐ domestic | ☐ industrial | ☐ commercial] [☐ electrical | ☐ lighting | ☐ climate control | ☐ conduit | ☐ security | ☐ communications | ☐ signaling | ☐ computer | ☐ fire alarm | ☐ other: _____] [☐ systems | ☐ equipment | ☐ components | ☐ devices] **for** _____ *[type of]* [☐ buildings | ☐ grounds | ☐ equipment | ☐ other: _____].

☐ **Oversee and direct the installation, maintenance, and repair of** [☐ electrical equipment | ☐ electronic controls | ☐ other: _____] **used for** [☐ light | ☐ power circuits | ☐ automatically controlled circuits | ☐ elevators | ☐ conveyors | ☐ other: _____] **including** [☐ generators | ☐ conduits | ☐ transformers | ☐ programmable controllers | ☐ motor controllers | ☐ AC & DC motors | ☐ circuit breakers | ☐ heating units | ☐ pull boxes | ☐ switches | ☐ switchboards | ☐ transmission equipment | ☐ other: _____].

☐ **Oversee the installation, testing, and/or repair of** _____ *[type of]* [☐ electrical systems | ☐ public works electrical equipment, overhead lines, and poles | ☐ telecommunications wiring and cable | ☐ lighting systems | ☐ electronic controllers | ☐ intercom systems | ☐ climate control systems | ☐ fire alarm systems | ☐ low-voltage switching systems | ☐ high-voltage building panels | ☐ computer coax cables | ☐ conduit, conductors, and junction boxes | ☐ fuse boxes and circuit breakers | ☐ motors, transformers, and generators | ☐ security systems | ☐ signaling systems | ☐ lighting systems | ☐ equipment | ☐ other: _____] **on** _____ *[type of]* **projects**.

☐ **Investigate technical problems and establish** [☐ procedures | ☐ corrective actions | ☐ other: _____] **to avoid recurrences**.

Electrical Engineering Projects & Functions

See also other "Electrical Engineering" categories, as well as "Engineering Functions – General," "Architecture" categories, "CAD Drafting," "Engineering Projects," and "Inspections & Compliance."

☐ **Read and interpret** [☐ schematics | ☐ diagrams | ☐ diagnostic computer programs] **as well as information generated from** [☐ analyzers | ☐ oscilloscopes | ☐ multi-meters | ☐ other: _____] **for the purpose of** _____ *[what purpose?]*.

☐ **Estimate the time and cost of all components to manufacture electrical engineering** _____ *[type of]* **projects ranging from $_____ to $_____** *[project cost range]*.

☐ **Perform electrical engineering functions including** [☐ design and develop electrical (☐ control systems / ☐ components) | ☐ prepare dimensions | ☐ plot and draft (☐ working plans / ☐ sketches / ☐ thumbnails / ☐ detailed drawings / ☐ profile sheets / ☐ cross-sections / ☐ 3D and sectional views / ☐ topographical overlays / ☐ other: _____) | ☐ create client presentations | ☐ estimate drafting project time and costs | ☐ provide technical assistance | ☐ prepare contract change orders | ☐ inspect projects for compliance | ☐ define issues | ☐ perform evaluations | ☐ generate parts specifications | ☐ conduct status meetings | ☐ ensure quality control | ☐ oversee and monitor installation | ☐ troubleshoot breakdowns | ☐ control process efficiency | ☐ other: _____].

☐ **Collaborate with** [☐ Engineering Manager | ☐ Architects | ☐ Project Managers | ☐ other engineering groups | ☐ others: _____] **regarding effective design** [☐ concepts | ☐ philosophies | ☐ approaches] **that solve dynamic** _____ *[type of]* **electrical challenges and ensure engineering criteria are suitable for proposed applications.**

☐ **Develop project specifications, test theoretical designs, and prepare specification details for** _____ *[what products?]*, **which result in** _____ *[benefits]*.

☐ **Perform various electrical engineering functions including** [☐ design and develop electrical (☐ control systems / ☐ components) | ☐ draft (☐ working plans / ☐ sketches / ☐ thumbnails / ☐ detailed drawings) | ☐ prepare dimensions | ☐ plot and draft (☐ profile sheets / ☐ cross-sections / ☐ 3D and sectional views / ☐ other: _____) | ☐ create client presentations | ☐ plot topographical overlays | ☐ estimate drafting project time and costs | ☐ direct and coordinate manufacturing | ☐ provide technical assistance | ☐ conduct inspections | ☐ prepare contract change orders | ☐ inspect projects for compliance | ☐ define issues | ☐ work closely with specialists | ☐ perform assessments and evaluations | ☐ generate parts specifications | ☐ conduct simulation testing | ☐ consult with interdisciplinary teams | ☐ devise new approaches to solve problems | ☐ plan and conduct conferences and meetings | ☐ ensure quality control | ☐ monitor product quality | ☐ oversee and monitor (☐ installation / ☐ production) | ☐ troubleshoot breakdowns | ☐ control process efficiency | ☐ test manufactured products | ☐ other: _____].

☐ **Plan, direct, prioritize, schedule, and oversee** _____ *[#]* _____ *[titles]* **in the technical engineering aspects of** _____ *[type of]* **electrical work for** _____ *[what?]* **ensuring project deliverables within schedule constraints.**

☐ **Evaluate** [☐ new | ☐ existing] **design specifications and component reliability, and select the best methods and techniques for obtaining the best possible solutions to meet** _____ *[type of]* **challenges.**

☐ **Manage and oversee various electrical functions including** [☐ developing specifications | ☐ completing work orders | ☐ estimating job time and materials | ☐ preparing cost estimates | ☐ handling subcontractor contract negotiations | ☐ meeting with clients | ☐ calculating electrical equipment requirements | ☐ ordering electrical parts and supplies | ☐ ensuring quality control standards | ☐ keeping abreast of equipment improvements | ☐ training Electricians in the installation and repair of electrical systems | ☐ evaluating performance criteria | ☐ ensuring component safety | ☐ inspecting and testing electrical equipment | ☐ other: _____].

☐ **Plan, conduct, and coordinate** _____ *[type of]* **engineering** [☐ analyses | ☐ tests | ☐ validations | ☐ other: _____], **and prepare detailed** [☐ reports | ☐ summaries] **regarding results.**

☐ **Use computer-aided design applications including** [☐ AutoCAD | ☐ Pro Engineering | ☐ OrCAD Capture and Layout | ☐ VHDL | ☐ ViewLogic | ☐ Spice | ☐ other: _____] **and** _____ *[type of]* **test equipment in the design of** _____ *[what?]*.

☐ **Develop specifications for the installation of** [☐ voltage transformers | ☐ overhead cables | ☐ underground cables | ☐ _____ *(type of)* electrical equipment | ☐ other: _____] **for conducting electrical energy from high-voltage distribution lines to consumers.**

ACHIEVEMENT SAMPLES: *See Achievements under "Electrical Scope."*

Electrical Scope

See also other Electrical and Electrician categories as well as "Equipment, Tools & Testing Devices – Electrician," "Inspections & Compliance – Electrical," and "Maintenance & Repair Projects."

☐ **Install, maintain, service, and repair** _____ *[type of]* **electrical** [☐ systems | ☐ equipment | ☐ components | ☐ instruments | ☐ apparatus | ☐ accessories | ☐ other: _____] **including** [☐ electrical equipment | ☐ electronic controllers | ☐ motors | ☐ starters | ☐ switches | ☐ fixtures | ☐ fuse boxes | ☐ coax cables | ☐ wiring | ☐ circuit breakers | ☐ lighting fixtures | ☐ electrical panels | ☐ cables | ☐ outlets | ☐ switches | ☐ pumps | ☐ fans | ☐ transformers | ☐ generators | ☐ other: _____] **for this** _____ *[type of]* **firm.**

☐ **Install, maintain, repair, and/or replace** [☐ air compressors | ☐ steam boilers | ☐ pump seals, bearings, and couplings | ☐ gas boilers | ☐ electric boilers | ☐ water heaters | ☐ steam lines | ☐ heat return lines | ☐ main water lines | ☐ roof drains | ☐ motors | ☐ blower cages | ☐ electrical outlets | ☐ switches | ☐ lighting circuits | ☐ power lines | ☐ fan motors | ☐ plant lighting | ☐ windows | ☐ doors | ☐ walls | ☐ ceilings | ☐ furniture | ☐ railings | ☐ stair treads | ☐ gratings | ☐ faucets | ☐ toilets | ☐ urinals | ☐ other: _____] **of** [☐ heating | ☐ cooling | ☐ ventilating | ☐ refrigeration | ☐ other: _____] **systems for** _____ *[what or whom?]*.

☐ **Serve as** [☐ journeyman electrician | ☐ apprentice | ☐ electrician | ☐ master electrician | ☐ lead electrician | ☐ other: _____] **on** _____ *[#]* [☐ new home construction | ☐ commercial | ☐ other: _____] **projects.**

☐ **Perform** [☐ installation | ☐ servicing | ☐ repair | ☐ rewiring | ☐ testing | ☐ inspection | ☐ troubleshooting | ☐ diagnosis | ☐ replacement | ☐ maintenance] **of** [☐ electrical | ☐ lighting | ☐ climate control | ☐ conduit | ☐ motor control | ☐ security | ☐ communications | ☐ intercom | ☐ signaling | ☐ bus bar | ☐ computer | ☐ fire alarm | ☐ industrial | ☐ digital | ☐ pneumatic tube | ☐ energy management | ☐ public address | ☐ other: _____] **systems for this $_____** *[revenues]* [☐ electrician firm | ☐ general contractor | ☐ other: _____].

☐ **Perform** [☐ highly skilled | ☐ journeyman-level | ☐ apprentice-level | ☐ Master Electrician level] installation, repair, and trouble–shooting work of [☐ domestic | ☐ industrial | ☐ commercial] [☐ electrical | ☐ lighting | ☐ climate control | ☐ conduit | ☐ security | ☐ communications | ☐ signaling | ☐ computer | ☐ fire alarm | ☐ other: _____] [☐ systems | ☐ equipment | ☐ componentry | ☐ devices | ☐ other: _____] **for** _____ *[type of]* [☐ buildings | ☐ grounds | ☐ equipment | ☐ other: _____].

☐ **Install and repair** [☐ electrical equipment | ☐ electronic controls | ☐ other: _____] **used for** [☐ light | ☐ power circuits | ☐ automatically controlled circuits | ☐ elevators | ☐ conveyors | ☐ other: _____] **including** [☐ generators | ☐ conduits | ☐ transformers | ☐ programmable controllers | ☐ motor controllers | ☐ AC & DC motors | ☐ circuit breakers | ☐ heating units | ☐ pull boxes | ☐ switches | ☐ switchboards | ☐ transmission equipment | ☐ other: _____].

☐ **Inspect, service, troubleshoot, and repair** _____ *[type of]* **electrical systems for** _____ *[what?]* **ensuring compliance with all electrical and building codes, safety regulations, and customer specifications.**

☐ **Conduct** [☐ high-voltage | ☐ low-voltage | ☐ fiber optic | ☐ specialized | ☐ other: _____] **electrical work involved in the** [☐ installation | ☐ construction | ☐ remodeling | ☐ alteration | ☐ service | ☐ repair | ☐ other: _____] of [☐ public works | ☐ residential | ☐ industrial | ☐ commercial] [☐ electrical | ☐ climate control | ☐ security | ☐ communications | ☐ computer | ☐ fire alarm | ☐ other: _____] [☐ systems | ☐ equipment | ☐ components | ☐ instruments | ☐ devices | ☐ apparatus].

☐ **Install, repair, overhaul, and/or reconfigure** _____ *[type of]* [☐ alternating | ☐ direct current | ☐ other: _____] **electrical equipment, and maintain up-to-date documentation.**

ACHIEVEMENT SAMPLES:

☐ **Facilitated electrical wiring and Installation for** _____ *[type of]* [☐ commercial | ☐ residential | ☐ other: _____] **construction projects, including** [☐ new construction | ☐ retrofits | ☐ remodels | ☐ reconfigurations | ☐ plant expansions | ☐ other: _____].

☐ [☐ Performed | ☐ Assisted in] **the complete** [☐ wiring | ☐ rewiring | ☐ reconfiguration | ☐ other: _____] of _____ *[what building, plant, or project?]*, **which included** [☐ estimating job costs | ☐ scheduling electrical work | ☐ ordering parts and materials | ☐ overseeing the installation process | ☐ managing a staff of _____ (#) (☐ apprentices / ☐ electricians) | ☐ supervising quality control | ☐ ensuring electrical code compliance | ☐ billing clients | ☐ other: _____].

☐ **Completely re-wired a** _____ *[#]*-**year-old,** _____ *[#]*-**story** _____ *[type of]* **house, including** [☐ removing (☐ insulation / ☐ copper fittings) | ☐ installing _____ (#) ground faults | ☐ adding _____ (#) outlets | ☐ other: _____] **resulting in** _____ *[what benefits?]*.

☐ **Developed specifications for the installation of** [☐ voltage transformers | ☐ overhead cables | ☐ underground cables | ☐ _____ *(type of)* electrical equipment | ☐ other: _____] **for conducting electrical energy from high-voltage distribution lines to consumers.**

☐ **Saved** [☐ the facility | ☐ clients] $_____ *[amount]* **annually by implementing** _____ *[type of]* **energy-efficient solutions that** _____ *[did what?]*.

☐ **Reviewed and upgraded** _____ *[type of]* **electrical systems including** _____ *[what?]* **by performing** _____ *[what functions?]* **ensuring electrical compatibility and compliance with all electrical codes, resulting in** _____ *[benefits]*.

☐ **Installed, tested, and repaired** _____ *[type of]* [☐ electrical systems | ☐ electronic controllers | ☐ public works electrical equipment, overhead lines, and poles | ☐ telecommunications wiring and cable | ☐ lighting systems | ☐ intercom systems | ☐ climate control systems | ☐ fire alarm systems | ☐ low-voltage switching systems | ☐ high-voltage building panels | ☐ computer coax cables | ☐ conduit, conductors, and junction boxes | ☐ fuse boxes and circuit breakers | ☐ receptacles and switches | ☐ motors, transformers, and generators | ☐ security systems | ☐ signaling systems | ☐ bus bar | ☐ outlet boxes | ☐ receptacles | ☐ lighting systems | ☐ connectors | ☐ equipment | ☐ other: _____] **on** _____ *[type of]* **projects and hook up** [☐ primary | ☐ secondary] **power lines for** _____ *[purpose]*.

☐ **Performed the upgrade of electrical wiring of** _____ *[#]* _____ *[type of]* **workstations, which required** _____ *[what?]* **and resulted in** _____ *[what benefits?]*.

☐ **Gained extensive experience in** [☐ electrical installations, repairs, and overhauls | ☐ complex troubleshooting and problem resolution | ☐ interpreting and following schematic diagrams, blueprints, and specifications | ☐ mastering the use of testing instruments | ☐ other: _____].

☐ **Designed and developed** _____ *[type of]* **electrical equipment that** _____ *[does what?]*, **resulting in** _____ *[what benefits?]*.

Electrical Inspections & Compliance

Refer to "Inspections & Compliance – Electrical."

Electrical Installations

See also other "Electrical" and "Electrician" categories as well as "Equipment, Tools & Testing Devices – Electrician," "Inspections & Compliance – Electrical," and "Maintenance & Repair Projects."

☐ **Read, interpret, and lay out** _____ *[type of]* **electrical work from** [☐ complex] ☐ electrical blueprints | ☐ schematic drawings | ☐ circuit diagrams | ☐ plans | ☐ specifications | ☐ manuals | ☐ written instructions | ☐ verbal instructions | ☐ other: _____ **following safety regulations, customer specifications, and company policies to** [☐ plan installation procedures | ☐ determine installation locations | ☐ install electrical equipment | ☐ other: _____].

☐ **Lay** [☐ inside | ☐ outside | ☐ underground | ☐ above-ground] [☐ conduit | ☐ electrical services | ☐ specialized electrical (☐ equipment / ☐ machinery) | ☐ conductors | (☐ single- / ☐ double- / ☐ triple-) phase electric cables | ☐ primary power lines | ☐ secondary service laterals | ☐ other: _____] **for** _____ *[what?]*.

☐ **Install complete electrical service on** [☐ new | ☐ existing] **construction in** [☐ upscale residential homes | ☐ apartment complexes | ☐ commercial buildings | ☐ public works projects | ☐ other: _____].

☐ **Facilitate installation of electrical** [☐ conduit | ☐ circuit breakers | ☐ switches | ☐ outlet boxes | ☐ cables | ☐ transformers | ☐ other: _____], **ensuring compliance with electrical code and OSHA practices**.

☐ **Install and maintain public works** [☐ electrical equipment | ☐ overhead lines | ☐ poles | ☐ other: _____] **used for the operation and control of** [☐ street lights | ☐ traffic signals | ☐ pumps | ☐ other: _____].

☐ **Conduct** [☐ high-voltage | ☐ low-voltage | ☐ fiber optic | ☐ specialized | ☐ other: _____] **electrical work involved in the** [☐ installation | ☐ construction | ☐ remodeling | ☐ alteration | ☐ maintenance | ☐ service | ☐ repair | ☐ other: _____] **of** [☐ public works | ☐ residential | ☐ industrial | ☐ commercial] [☐ electrical | ☐ electronic | ☐ climate control | ☐ security | ☐ communications | ☐ computer | ☐ fire alarm | ☐ other: _____] [☐ systems | ☐ equipment | ☐ componentry | ☐ instruments | ☐ devices | ☐ apparatus].

☐ **Assemble, install, and check** [☐ electrical | ☐ plumbing | ☐ mechanical | ☐ structural | ☐ other: _____] [☐ equipment | ☐ components | ☐ accessories | ☐ other: _____] **using hand and power tools**.

☐ **Install and test** _____ , _____ , **and** _____ *[what?]* **used for** _____ *[type of]* [☐ generators | ☐ conduits | ☐ transformers | ☐ controllers | ☐ motors | ☐ equipment | ☐ other: _____].

☐ **Install, operate, and test** [☐ commercial | ☐ industrial | ☐ residential | ☐ public works] **electrical** [☐ systems | ☐ equipment | ☐ components | ☐ other: _____] **ensuring correct** [☐ loads | ☐ amps | ☐ voltage | ☐ other: _____].

☐ **Install low-voltage wiring for** [☐ security systems | ☐ fire alarms | ☐ video systems | ☐ telephones | ☐ other: _____].

ACHIEVEMENT SAMPLES: *See Achievements under "Electrical Scope."*

Electrical Maintenance & Repair Work

See also other "Electrical" and "Electrician" categories as well as "Equipment, Tools & Testing Devices – Electrician," "Inspections & Compliance – Electrical," and "Maintenance & Repair Projects."

☐ **Troubleshoot, diagnose, repair, and/or replace defective** [☐ parts | ☐ wiring | ☐ componentry | ☐ other: _____] **associated with** [☐ motors | ☐ starters | ☐ switches | ☐ pumps | ☐ fans | ☐ controls | ☐ fuse boxes | ☐ circuit breakers | ☐ electronic controllers | ☐ transformers | ☐ generators | ☐ other: _____] **for** _____ *[type of]* [☐ high-voltage | ☐ low-voltage | ☐ variable frequency | ☐ wiring | ☐ other: _____] [☐ systems | ☐ electrical equipment | ☐ machinery | ☐ other: _____].

☐ **Monitor, troubleshoot, and repair** [☐ electrical | ☐ electronic] **control circuits, identify any safety or operational problems, and immediately resolve them**.

☐ **Perform maintenance and repair work on** _____ *[type of]* **electrical** [☐ wiring | ☐ equipment | ☐ motor controls | ☐ instruments | ☐ other: _____] **including** [☐ servicing | ☐ testing | ☐ inspecting | ☐ calibrating | ☐ replacing | ☐ lubricating | ☐ regulating | ☐ fine-tuning | ☐ other: _____] **for** _____ *[what?]*.

☐ **Conduct electrical maintenance and repair work and regular and preventive maintenance checks on** _____ *[what?]* **in compliance with all electrical codes and regulations**.

☐ **Service and maintain all types of** [☐ electrical | ☐ electronic] [☐ systems | ☐ equipment | ☐ components | ☐ instruments | ☐ apparatus | ☐ accessories | ☐ other: _____] **for** _____ *[what?]* **including** [☐ electronic controls | ☐ motors | ☐ starters | ☐ switches | ☐ fixtures | ☐ pumps | ☐ fans | ☐ controls | ☐ fuse boxes | ☐ circuit breakers | ☐ transformers | ☐ other: _____].

- [ ] **Troubleshoot, diagnose, repair, and test electrical problems in the facility's** [☐ power distribution | ☐ electrical equipment | ☐ instrument and control wiring | ☐ lighting systems | ☐ other: _____].

- [ ] **Facilitate** [☐ electrical | ☐ electronic] **repair of** _____ *[type of]* [☐ generators | ☐ air conditioning units | ☐ air compressors | ☐ water pumps | ☐ water heaters | ☐ motors | ☐ elevators | ☐ other: _____] **in compliance with all codes.**

- [ ] **Conduct troubleshooting and diagnostic work on** _____ *[type of]* [☐ electrical | ☐ electronic] **equipment including** [☐ lighting | ☐ climate control | ☐ conduit | ☐ motor control | ☐ security | ☐ communications | ☐ intercom | ☐ signaling | ☐ bus bar | ☐ computer | ☐ fire alarm | ☐ industrial | ☐ digital | ☐ pneumatic tube | ☐ energy management | ☐ public address | ☐ other: _____] **systems.**

- [ ] **Troubleshoot, maintain, and repair** [☐ electrical | ☐ electronic] [☐ equipment | ☐ motor controls | ☐ other: _____] **ensuring all** _____ *[type of]* **systems and equipment operate efficiently and all repairs are performed in a timely, professional manner.**

- [ ] **Use various methods and techniques to troubleshoot, isolate, diagnose, and repair defects and/or malfunctions in** [☐ high-voltage circuits | ☐ distribution systems | ☐ electrical controls | ☐ programmable logic controllers | ☐ motor control centers | ☐ cable runs | ☐ motors | ☐ _____ *(type of)* electrical equipment | ☐ wiring | ☐ switches | ☐ other: _____].

ACHIEVEMENT SAMPLES: *See Achievements under "Electrical Scope."*

Electrical Projects & Functions

See also other "Electrical" and "Electrician" categories as well as "Equipment, Tools & Testing Devices – Electrician," "Inspections & Compliance – Electrical," and "Maintenance & Repair Projects."

- [ ] **Maintain emergency** [☐ lighting system | ☐ generator | ☐ other: _____] **and the proper operation of all equipment through regular scheduled** [☐ maintenance checks | ☐ safety inspections] **to ensure the** [☐ physical | ☐ mechanical | ☐ electrical | ☐ other: _____] **aspects of the facility run smoothly.**

- [ ] **Facilitate various electrical functions for** _____ *[type of]* **public works projects including** [☐ repairing underground conduits | ☐ trimming trees for wire clearance | ☐ operating underground cable locators to find, and updating maps to include, cable locations and underground faults | ☐ operating (☐ pickup trucks / ☐ digger derricks / ☐ bucket trucks / ☐ other: _____].

- [ ] **Operate and maintain a** _____ *[#]*-**volt** [☐ high-tension | ☐ other: _____] **distribution systems including** _____ *[what functions?]*.

- [ ] **Ensure that** [☐ buildings | ☐ facilities | ☐ grounds | ☐ employees | ☐ customers and others] **are safe and secure by** [☐ following safe work procedures | ☐ exercising a high degree of awareness | ☐ complying with all safety codes | ☐ other: _____] **and applying** [☐ an expert | ☐ a proficient | ☐ a working] **knowledge of** [☐ National Electric Code | ☐ electrical standards and practices | ☐ materials and tools of the electrical trade | ☐ occupational hazards | ☐ safety precautions | ☐ other: _____] **in performing all electrician functions.**

- [ ] **Handle administrative functions including** [☐ responding to emergency customer callbacks | ☐ completing work orders | ☐ preparing maintenance logs | ☐ ensuring quality control standards are met | ☐ keeping abreast of equipment improvements | ☐ training other Electricians in the installation and repair of electrical systems | ☐ other: _____].

- [ ] **Follow electrical** [☐ blueprints | ☐ schematic drawings | ☐ circuit diagrams | ☐ plans | ☐ other: _____] **to determine** [☐ circuit locations | ☐ outlets | ☐ load centers | ☐ panel boards | ☐ other: _____] **in the installation and repair of** _____ *[what?]*.

- [ ] **Perform** [☐ highly-specialized | ☐ complex | ☐ routine] **electrical work for** _____ *[#]* [☐ clients | ☐ departments | ☐ buildings | ☐ other: _____] **in the areas of** [☐ heating | ☐ refrigeration | ☐ generators | ☐ motors | ☐ fire alarms | ☐ other: _____].

- [ ] **Facilitate** [☐ large-scale | ☐ complex] _____ *[type of]* **electrical projects for** [☐ commercial | ☐ residential | ☐ industrial | ☐ other: _____] **clients.**

- [ ] **Perform** _____ *[type of]* [☐ control wiring | ☐ welding | ☐ fabrication | ☐ other: _____] **of** _____ *[what?]* **facility electrical systems and other electrical and mechanical work.**

ACHIEVEMENT SAMPLES: *See Achievements under "Electrical Scope."*

Electrical – Testing

See "Inspections & Compliance – Electrical."

Electrical – Tools & Equipment Usage

See "Equipment, Tools & Testing Devices – Electrical."

Electrician Management Scope

See also other "Electrical" and "Electrician" categories as well as "Equipment, Tools & Testing Devices – Electrician," "Inspections & Compliance – Electrical," and "Maintenance & Repair Projects."

☐ **Plan and supervise all phases of** _____ *[type of]* **electrical wiring projects in** [☐ commercial | ☐ residential | ☐ industrial | ☐ public works | ☐ other: _____] **settings including repairing and maintaining** [☐ electrical | ☐ electronic] [☐ systems | ☐ motors | ☐ devices | ☐ control panels | ☐ conduit | ☐ switches | ☐ other: _____] **for this** _____ *[type of]* **firm**.

☐ **Provide electrician oversight in the installation, maintenance, and servicing of** _____ *[type of]* **electrical** [☐ systems | ☐ equipment | ☐ components | ☐ instruments | ☐ apparatus | ☐ accessories | ☐ other: _____] **including** [☐ electronic controls | ☐ motors | ☐ starters | ☐ switches | ☐ fixtures | ☐ fuses | ☐ other: _____].

☐ **Provide decisive leadership and clear direction in all phases of** [☐ large-scale | ☐ complex] _____ *[type of]* **electrical projects for** [☐ commercial | ☐ residential | ☐ industrial | ☐ other: _____] **clients overseeing a top-performing team of** _____ *[#]* **electricians**.

☐ **Manage and oversee the** [☐ installation | ☐ repair | ☐ rewiring | ☐ testing | ☐ inspection | ☐ troubleshooting | ☐ diagnosis | ☐ replacement | ☐ maintenance | ☐ servicing | ☐ other: _____] **of** [☐ electrical | ☐ lighting | ☐ climate control | ☐ conduit | ☐ motor control | ☐ telecommunications | ☐ security | ☐ intercom | ☐ signaling | ☐ computer | ☐ fire alarm | ☐ industrial | ☐ digital | ☐ pneumatic tube | ☐ energy management | ☐ public address | ☐ other: _____] **systems for this** [☐ multimillion-dollar | ☐ $_____] [☐ electrical contractor | ☐ industrial plant | ☐ public services company | ☐ other: _____].

☐ **Lead and direct the installation, maintenance, and repair of** [☐ electrical equipment | ☐ electronic controls | ☐ other: _____] **used for** [☐ lighting | ☐ power circuits | ☐ automatically controlled circuits | ☐ elevators | ☐ conveyors | ☐ other: _____] **including** [☐ generators | ☐ conduits | ☐ transformers | ☐ programmable controllers | ☐ motor controllers | ☐ AC & DC motors | ☐ circuit breakers | ☐ heating units | ☐ pull boxes | ☐ switches | ☐ transmission equipment | ☐ other: _____].

☐ **Monitor and oversee** [☐ electrical installations | ☐ instrument and control wiring | ☐ control center wiring | ☐ other: _____], **ensuring all equipment and installations meet electrical code.**

☐ **Provide** [☐ highly skilled | ☐ Master Electrician level] **installation, repair, and troubleshooting oversight of** [☐ domestic | ☐ industrial | ☐ commercial] [☐ electrical | ☐ lighting | ☐ climate control | ☐ conduit | ☐ security | ☐ communications | ☐ signaling | ☐ computer | ☐ fire alarm | ☐ other: _____] [☐ systems | ☐ equipment | ☐ componentry | ☐ devices] **for** _____ *[type of]* [☐ buildings | ☐ grounds | ☐ equipment | ☐ other: _____].

☐ **Supervise all electrical work involved in the** [☐ installation | ☐ construction | ☐ remodeling | ☐ alteration | ☐ maintenance | ☐ service | ☐ repair | ☐ other: _____] **of** [☐ public works | ☐ residential | ☐ industrial | ☐ commercial] [☐ electrical | ☐ electronic | ☐ climate control | ☐ security | ☐ communications | ☐ computer | ☐ fire alarm | ☐ other: _____] [☐ systems | ☐ equipment | ☐ components | ☐ instruments | ☐ devices | ☐ apparatus].

☐ **Oversee and direct the installation, maintenance, and repair of** [☐ electrical equipment | ☐ electronic controls | ☐ other: _____] **used for** [☐ light | ☐ power circuits | ☐ automatically controlled circuits | ☐ elevators | ☐ conveyors | ☐ other: _____] including [☐ generators | ☐ conduits | ☐ transformers | ☐ programmable controllers | ☐ motor controllers | ☐ AC & DC motors | ☐ circuit breakers | ☐ heating units | ☐ pull boxes | ☐ switches | ☐ switchboards | ☐ transmission equipment | ☐ other: _____].

ACHIEVEMENT SAMPLES: *See Achievements under "Electrical Scope."*

Electrician Management Functions

See also other "Electrical" and "Electrician" categories as well as "Equipment, Tools & Testing Devices – Electrician," "Inspections & Compliance – Electrical," and "Maintenance & Repair Projects."

☐ **Inspect Electrician work to evaluate and ensure compliance with electrical codes, quality work performance, and** [☐ electrical compatibility | ☐ component safety | ☐ operating problems are resolved | ☐ performance criteria | ☐ other: _____].

☐ **Oversee the installation and repair of various** [☐ domestic | ☐ industrial | ☐ commercial] systems including [☐ electrical | ☐ lighting | ☐ climate control | ☐ conduit | ☐ security | ☐ communications | ☐ signaling | ☐ computer | ☐ fire alarm | ☐ other: _____] **for** _____ *[type of]* [☐ buildings |☐ grounds | ☐ equipment | ☐ other: _____].

☐ **Supervise and coordinate electrical work involved in the** [☐ installation | ☐ construction | ☐ remodeling | ☐ alteration | ☐ maintenance | ☐ service | ☐ repair | ☐ other: _____] **of** [☐ public works | ☐ residential | ☐ industrial | ☐ commercial] [☐ electrical | ☐ electronic | ☐ climate control | ☐ security | ☐ communications | ☐ computer | ☐ fire alarm | ☐ other: _____] [☐ systems | ☐ equipment | ☐ componentry | ☐ instruments | ☐ devices | ☐ apparatus].

☐ **Test, troubleshoot, and diagnose electrical** [☐ circuits | ☐ equipment | ☐ installations | ☐ machinery | ☐ components | ☐ devices | ☐ other: _____] **of** [☐ safety equipment | ☐ emergency lighting | ☐ generators | ☐ other: _____] **to locate and correct** _____ *[type of]* **problems and ensure compliance with all electrical codes.**

☐ **Assist Electricians with the installation, testing, and repair of** _____ *[type of]* [☐ electrical systems | ☐ electronic controllers | ☐ public works electrical equipment, overhead lines, and poles | ☐ telecommunications wiring and cable | ☐ lighting systems | ☐ intercom systems | ☐ climate control systems | ☐ fire alarm systems | ☐ low-voltage switching systems | ☐ high-voltage building panels | ☐ computer coax cables | ☐ conduit, conductors, and junction boxes | ☐ fuse boxes and circuit breakers | ☐ motors, transformers, and generators | ☐ security systems | ☐ signaling systems | ☐ lighting systems | ☐ equipment | ☐ other: _____] **on** _____ *[type of]* **projects.**

☐ **Lead and direct electrical functions for** _____ *[type of]* **public works projects including** [☐ repairing underground conduits | ☐ trimming trees for wire clearance | ☐ operating underground cable locators to find, and updating maps to include, cable locations and underground faults | ☐ operating (☐ pickup trucks / ☐ digger derricks / ☐ bucket trucks / ☐ other: _____)].

☐ **Manage the inspection, servicing, and repair of** _____ *[type of]* **electrical systems for** _____ *[what?]* **ensuring compliance with all electrical codes, safety regulations, customer specifications, and company policies.**

☐ **Inspect, test, and calibrate** _____ *[type of]* [☐ electrical devices | ☐ equipment | ☐ structures | ☐ materials | ☐ other: _____] **to identify and solve** _____ *[type of]* **problems or defects using specialized electrical testing equipment.**

☐ **Manage and oversee electrical and administrative functions including** [☐ responding to emergency customer callbacks | ☐ completing work orders | ☐ developing maintenance schedules | ☐ estimating job time and materials | ☐ preparing cost estimates | ☐ handling subcontractor contract negotiations | ☐ meeting with clients | ☐ calculating electrical equipment requirements | ☐ ordering electrical parts and supplies | ☐ coordinating materials shipping | ☐ documenting maintenance logs | ☐ ensuring quality control standards are met | ☐ keeping abreast of equipment improvements | ☐ training Electricians in the installation and repair of electrical systems | ☐ documenting performance standards | ☐ interpreting electrical circuit diagrams | ☐ evaluating performance criteria | ☐ ensuring component safety | ☐ inspecting and testing electrical equipment | ☐ developing specifications | ☐ handling inventory management and control | ☐ other: _____].

☐ **Maintain emergency** [☐ lighting system | ☐ generator | ☐ other: _____] **and the proper operation of all equipment to ensure the** [☐ physical | ☐ mechanical | ☐ electrical | ☐ other: _____] **aspects of the facility run smoothly.**

☐ **Direct and manage the installation and repair of** [☐ domestic | ☐ industrial | ☐ commercial] [☐ electrical | ☐ lighting | ☐ climate control | ☐ conduit | ☐ security | ☐ communications | ☐ signaling | ☐ computer | ☐ fire alarm | ☐ other: _____] [☐ systems | ☐ equipment | ☐ components | ☐ devices] **for** _____ *[type of]* [☐ buildings | ☐ grounds | ☐ equipment | ☐ other: _____].

☐ **Manage and oversee electrical maintenance and repair work and regular and preventive maintenance checks on** _____ *[what?]* **to ensure compliance with all electrical codes and regulations.**

ACHIEVEMENT SAMPLES: *See Achievements under "Electrical – General."*

Electrician Supervision

See also "Staff Management & Supervision," "Team Leadership & Direction," and/or "Trades/Crew Supervision," as applicable.

☐ **Supervise the day-to-day activities of** _____ *[#]* [☐ Electricians | ☐ Mechanics | ☐ Apprentices | ☐ other: _____] **in their performance of** _____, _____, **and** _____ *[what functions?].*

☐ **Lead, guide, and train** _____ *[#]* **Electricians in the installation and maintenance of electronic controls for** [☐ construction | ☐ maintenance | ☐ other: _____] **business equipment applying and meeting all electrical principles and codes.**

☐ **Schedule and supervise** _____ *[#]* **Electricians in the inspection, maintenance, troubleshooting, and repair of** _____ *[type of]* **electrical systems for** _____ *[what?]* **ensuring compliance with all codes and specifications.**

☐ **Guide and support Electricians in their troubleshooting and diagnosing of** _____ *[type of]* [☐ electrical | ☐ lighting | ☐ climate control | ☐ conduit | ☐ motor control | ☐ security | ☐ communications | ☐ intercom | ☐ signaling | ☐ bus bar | ☐ computer | ☐ fire alarm | ☐ industrial | ☐ digital | ☐ pneumatic tube | ☐ energy management | ☐ public address | ☐ other: _____] **systems.**

☐ **Oversee** _____ *[#]* **electricians and coordinate trades work in the installation of** [☐ electrical equipment | ☐ electronic controls | ☐ electrical outlets and switches | ☐ other: _____] **for** [☐ lighting systems | ☐ power circuits | ☐ automatically controlled circuits | ☐ elevators | ☐ conveyors | ☐ other: _____] **including** [☐ generators | ☐ conduits | ☐ transformers | ☐ programmable controllers | ☐ motor controllers | ☐ AC & DC motors | ☐ circuit breakers | ☐ heating units | ☐ pull boxes | ☐ switches | ☐ switchboards | ☐ transmission equipment | ☐ lighting circuits | ☐ new equipment power lines | ☐ fan motors | ☐ plant lighting | ☐ other: _____] **to ensure all electrical codes and principles are followed.**

☐ **Supervise and oversee Electrician performance of** [☐ highly-specialized | ☐ complex | ☐ routine | ☐ other: _____] **electrical work for** _____ *[#]* [☐ clients | ☐ departments | ☐ buildings | ☐ other: _____] **in the areas of** [☐ heating | ☐ refrigeration | ☐ generator equipment | ☐ motors | ☐ fire alarms | ☐ other: _____] **ensuring quality control.**

☐ **Oversee electricians in the installation and maintenance of electronic controls for** [☐ construction | ☐ maintenance | ☐ other: _____] **business equipment and machinery applying all electrical principles and meeting codes**.

☐ **Facilitate electrician oversight in the** [☐ installation | ☐ repair | ☐ rewiring | ☐ testing | ☐ inspection | ☐ troubleshooting | ☐ diagnosis | ☐ replacement | ☐ maintenance | ☐ servicing] **of** [☐ electrical | ☐ lighting | ☐ climate control | ☐ conduit | ☐ motor control | ☐ security | ☐ communications | ☐ intercom | ☐ signaling | ☐ bus bar | ☐ computer | ☐ fire alarm | ☐ industrial | ☐ digital | ☐ pneumatic tube | ☐ energy management | ☐ public address | ☐ other: _____] **systems covering** [☐ electronic controls | ☐ motors | ☐ starters | ☐ switches | ☐ fixtures | ☐ fuses | ☐ coax cables | ☐ wiring | ☐ lighting fixtures | ☐ electrical panels | ☐ cables | ☐ outlets | ☐ other: _____].

☐ **Oversee** _____ [#] **electricians in the installation, maintenance, and servicing of** _____ [type of] **electrical** [☐ systems | ☐ equipment | ☐ components | ☐ instruments | ☐ apparatus | ☐ accessories | ☐ other: _____] **including** [☐ electronic controls | ☐ motors | ☐ starters | ☐ switches | ☐ fixtures | ☐ fuses | ☐ other: _____].

ACHIEVEMENT SAMPLES: *See Achievements under "Electrical Scope."*

Electrician Tools & Testing Devices

See "Equipment Tools & Testing Devices – Electrical."

Employee Retention & Decreased Turnover

ACHIEVEMENT SAMPLES:

☐ **Improved** [☐ executive | ☐ management | ☐ employee | ☐ labor] **retention by** [☐ recruiting top talent | ☐ building loyal employee-employer relationships | ☐ allowing for job flexibility | ☐ improving overall communications | ☐ fostering strong internal relationships | ☐ offering recognition and appreciation | ☐ following through on promises | ☐ increasing decision-making authority and accountability | ☐ empowering subordinates to succeed | ☐ adding meaning to employee career challenges | ☐ other: _____]* **through the development and execution of** [☐ a formal employee retention program | ☐ direct report surveys | ☐ other program: _____] **company-wide**. *Ideas generated from Hornberger Management Company human resource surveys.*

☐ **Increased morale and minimized turnover through** [☐ mutual respect | ☐ honesty | ☐ effective two-way communication | ☐ other: _____], **which provided a healthy and positive environment that allowed employees to succeed and the company to grow.**

☐ **Minimized turnover** _____% [percentage] [☐ achieving the lowest employee turnover rate in the (☐ firm's | ☐ department's) history] **by** [☐ implementing proactive hiring policies | ☐ facilitating ongoing training and development programs | ☐ improving employee morale and staff loyalty | ☐ creating a positive and proactive atmosphere | ☐ developing reachable but challenging goals | ☐ elevating employee satisfaction with their jobs | ☐ treating all employees fairly | ☐ providing equal opportunity for promotion | ☐ other: _____].

☐ **Decreased employee turnover** _____% (from _____% to _____%) [percentages] **by** _____ [doing what?], **which resulted in** _____ [what additional benefits?].

☐ **Retained** _____% [percentage] **of recruited** [☐ employees | ☐ management staff] **and minimized turnover** _____% [percentage] [☐ achieving the lowest employee turnover rate in the (☐ firm's / ☐ department's) history] **by** [☐ implementing proactive (☐ recruitment policies / ☐ succession planning programs / ☐ other: _____) | ☐ facilitating ongoing training and development programs | ☐ improving employee morale and staff loyalty | ☐ creating a positive and proactive atmosphere | ☐ developing reachable but challenging goals | ☐ elevating employee satisfaction with their jobs | ☐ allowing all employees to feel they have a stake in the firm | ☐ promoting top-notch staff | ☐ other: _____].

☐ **Maximized** [☐ employee morale | ☐ productivity | ☐ other: _____] **and improved job turnover rate by** [☐ effectively using employee skills and talents | ☐ providing training opportunities to enhance employees' skills | ☐ elevating employee satisfaction with their jobs | ☐ other: _____].

☐ **Achieved the lowest employee turnover rate in the firm's history by implementing** [☐ proactive hiring policies | ☐ ongoing training and development programs | ☐ other achievement: _____].

☐ **Maintain one of the lowest employee turnover ratios of** _____% [percentage] **in the** [☐ district | ☐ region | ☐ department | ☐ company | ☐ other: _____] **due to the implementation of** [☐ proactive hiring and training policies | ☐ ongoing training and development | ☐ effective mentoring | ☐ productivity monitoring | ☐ other achievement: _____].

☐ **Through effective use of** _____ [what initiatives?], **increased employee morale and minimized turnover, which resulted in** [☐ an extremely low turnover rate for the industry | ☐ an employee turnover ratio of _____% (percentage) | ☐ an annual cost savings of $_____ (amount) | ☐ other benefits: _____].

☐ **Improved** [☐ employee morale | ☐ productivity | ☐ job turnover rate | ☐ other: _____] **by** [☐ effectively using employee skills and talents | ☐ providing training opportunities to enhance employees' skills | ☐ elevating employee satisfaction with their jobs | ☐ other: _____].

☐ **Minimized turnover** _____ **%** [percentage] **by increasing** [☐ employee morale | ☐ staff loyalty | ☐ other: _____] **by** [☐ using morale-building techniques | ☐ creating a positive and proactive atmosphere | ☐ developing reachable but challenging goals | ☐ treating all employees fairly | ☐ providing equal opportunity for promotion | ☐ enforcing company guidelines | ☐ other: _____].

Environmental, Safety & Health Management Compliance

See also "Safety & Responsibility for Others."

☐ **Manage and oversee the firm's environmental, safety, and health activities including** _____ , _____ , **and** _____ [which activities?] **to ensure compliance with the** [☐ Occupational Safety and Health Act (OSHA) | ☐ Environmental, Safety, and Health Management Policy (ES&HMP) | ☐ Environmental Management System (EMS) | ☐ Resource Conservation and Recovery Act (RCRA) | ☐ Environmental Protection Act (EPA) | ☐ Clean Air Act (CAA) | ☐ Clean Water Act (CWA) | ☐ Safe Drinking Water Act (SDWA) | ☐ Superfund Amendments and Reauthorization Act (SARA) | ☐ National Ambient Air Quality Standard (NAAQS) | ☐ Toxic Substances Control Act (TSCA) | ☐ Comprehensive Environmental Response, Compensation, and Liability Act (CERCLA) | ☐ Code of Federal Regulations (CFR) | ☐ National Emission Standards for Hazardous Air Pollutants (NESHAP) | ☐ other: _____].

☐ **Coordinate and oversee field investigations that review and evaluate** _____ [type of] **activities related to** [☐ department buildings | ☐ equipment operations | ☐ work procedures | ☐ other: _____] **to ensure compliance with all safety practices and standards.**

☐ [☐ Administer | ☐ Co-administer] **the firm's Health and Safety Program by** [☐ writing and updating the Employee Safety Manual | ☐ ensuring compliance with current OSHA requirements | ☐ preparing health and safety staff bulletins | ☐ serving on the firm's Health and Safety Committee | ☐ scheduling and planning employee Wellness Training Programs | ☐ other: _____].

☐ **Manage daily environmental compliance issues, interpret applicable regulations, and provide regulatory support to** _____ [whom?] **ensuring** [☐ plant | ☐ site | ☐ process | ☐ operational | ☐ other: _____] **compliance with state, local, and federal requirements.**

☐ **Promote** [☐ environmental | ☐ health | ☐ project | ☐ worksite | ☐ other: _____] **safety and health by** _____ [doing or applying what?].

☐ **Review, evaluate, and Interpret** [☐ proposed] [☐ air- | ☐ water- | ☐ soil- | ☐ other: _____] **related environmental** [☐ regulations | ☐ EPA documentation | ☐ compliance requirements | ☐ other: _____] **for** [☐ environmental | ☐ industrial | ☐ financial | ☐ public | ☐ other: _____] **impact on** _____ [what?] **and interact with** [☐ federal | ☐ state | ☐ local] **regulators to resolve compliance issues.**

☐ **Implement and maintain Title V compliance for** _____ [what?] **by way of** _____ [doing what?].

☐ [☐ Establish | ☐ Update] **the firm's** [☐ compliance | ☐ operational] **processes, report questionable activities, investigate complaints, resolve incidents, and audit the performance of its** [☐ Compliance Program | ☐ Environmental, Safety, and Health Management Policy | ☐ other: _____].

☐ **Review and interpret** _____ [type of] **environmental regulations, anticipate new regulations, and apply environmental principles to** _____ [type of] **operations to minimize their impact on operations and ensure compliance with all regulations.**

☐ **Manage this** _____ [type of] **firm's environmental compliance issues in the areas of** _____ , _____ , **and** _____ [areas].

☐ **Notify** [☐ senior management | ☐ Corporate Compliance | ☐ Compliance Officer | ☐ other: _____] **of** [☐ audit findings | ☐ areas of compliance vulnerability | ☐ associated risk | ☐ unresolved compliance issues | ☐ status of compliance efforts | ☐ other: _____] **involving potential** [☐ regulatory issues | ☐ safety hazards | ☐ environmental concerns | ☐ _____ (type of) exposures | ☐ job-related accidents | ☐ personal injuries | ☐ potential work-related illnesses | ☐ other: _____].

☐ **Compile, set up, and review** _____ [type of] **databases for tracking** [☐ permit compliance | ☐ record keeping requirements | ☐ other: _____].

ACHIEVEMENT SAMPLES:

☐ **Developed and administered** he **firm's Health and Safety Program by** [☐ ensuring compliance with current OSHA requirements | ☐ preparing health and safety staff bulletins | ☐ serving on the firm's Health and Safety Committee | ☐ updating the Employee Safety Manual | ☐ scheduling and planning employee Wellness Training Programs | ☐ conducting safety meetings | ☐ other: _____].

☐ **Maintain optimum** [☐ company | ☐ facility | ☐ building] **safety and security by** [☐ overseeing supply orders | ☐ ensuring accounting reconciliation | ☐ minimizing materials theft | ☐ filing theft reports | ☐ other: _____] **and implementing safety procedures in accordance with** [☐ OSHA | ☐ other: _____] **regulations.**

☐ **Developed and delivered Safety Management Systems for major** _____ *[type of]* [☐ construction projects | ☐ turnaround ventures | ☐ other: _____] **ensuring all client requirements, governmental regulations, and company procedures were met.**

☐ **Achieved safety performance levels to** _____ *[what level?]* **from previous incident rate of** _____ *[what level?]* **by** _____ *[doing what?]*, **ensuring overall business and personnel safety and security.**

☐ **Decreased controllable expenses by $**_____ *[amount]* **over previous year by implementing improved** _____ *[type of]* [☐ safety programs | ☐ security programs | ☐ safety awareness | ☐ other: _____] **that** _____ *[does what?]*, **resulting in** _____ *[what benefits?]*.

☐ **Recommended and implemented** _____ *[type of]* **safety features that reduced** _____ *[whose?]* **exposure to** [☐ chemical | ☐ physical | ☐ biological | ☐ other: _____] **hazards in support of the firm's environmental goals.**

☐ **Performed environmental compliance in the areas of** [☐ wastewater treatment operations and testing | ☐ storm-water testing and permitting | ☐ well testing monitoring | ☐ yearly stack testing | ☐ hazardous waste removal | ☐ solid waste storage | ☐ materials recycling program | ☐ dust collector performance evaluations | ☐ continuous emissions monitoring | ☐ other: _____], **resolving** _____ *[type of]* **issues by** _____ *[doing what?]*.

☐ **Evaluated hazardous conditions in** _____ *[what?]* **and developed** _____ *[type of]* **hazard control methods that ensure compliance with all environmental, health, and safety regulations in the design and development of** _____ *[what?]*.

☐ **Designed and developed** _____ *[what?]* **projects that considered the impact on the environment by** _____ *[doing what?]*.

☐ **Developed, implemented, and provided training on** [☐ environmental | ☐ health | ☐ safety | ☐ other: _____] **procedures insofar as tracking the compliance status of** _____ *[what?]*.

☐ **Performed environmental compliance management and oversight at** _____ *[#]* _____ *[type of]* **facilities including the** [☐ review of federal, state, and local (☐ regulations | ☐ submittals) | ☐ involvement with _____ *(type of)* systems design | ☐ other: _____].

☐ **Coordinated and oversaw field investigations that review and evaluate** _____ *[type of]* **activities related to** [☐ department buildings | ☐ equipment operations | ☐ work procedures | ☐ other: _____] **to ensure compliance with all safety practices and standards.**

Equipment, Tools & Testing Devices – General

See also "Heavy Equipment Operations" and other "Equipment, Tools & Testing Devices" categories.

☐ **Operate and maintain all** _____ *[trade]* **equipment, machinery, and tools including** _____, _____, **and** _____ *[equipment]* **to ensure safe operating condition, abiding by all safety rules and precautions.**

☐ **Provide production management oversight to a staff of** _____ *[#]* **in the set-up and operation of** _____ *[type of]* **equipment to produce** _____ *[what?]*.

☐ **Lead and direct the operation of** _____ *[type of]* [☐ heavy] **equipment used to** [☐ produce | ☐ develop | ☐ manufacture | ☐ test | ☐ other: _____] _____ *[what?]*.

☐ [☐ Manage and oversee | ☐ Set up and operate] _____ *[type of]* **equipment for the** [☐ construction | ☐ production | ☐ installation | ☐ other: _____] **of** _____ *[what?]*.

☐ **Follow safety precautions using protective equipment around exposure to** [☐ extreme temperatures | ☐ toxic chemicals | ☐ biohazardous materials | ☐ smoke and fumes | ☐ other: _____].

☐ **Ensure all equipment is maintained in optimum running condition including** _____, _____, **and** _____ *[types of equipment]*.

☐ **Safely use and maintain various** [☐ electrical | ☐ plumbing | ☐ welding | ☐ other: _____] [☐ hand and power tools | ☐ testing instruments | ☐ measuring devices | ☐ conduit bending and threading equipment | ☐ drills | ☐ hoists | ☐ other: _____] **associated with the trade.**

☐ **Troubleshoot, diagnose, repair, adjust, and maintain all** _____ *[type of]* **equipment to ensure optimum running condition; and troubleshoot and repair** _____ *[type of]* **computer malfunctions.**

☐ **Operate** _____ *[type of]*-**related equipment including** [☐ hand and power tools | ☐ measurement tools | ☐ wire and cable winches | ☐ knock-out punches | ☐ PVC benders | ☐ hydraulic pipe benders | ☐ pipe cutters | ☐ pipe threaders | ☐ grinders | ☐ sand blasters | ☐ bead blasters | ☐ drill presses | ☐ cement cutters | ☐ cutting torches | ☐ jackhammers | ☐ electric drills and hacksaws | ☐ skill saws | ☐ portable generators | ☐ portable compressors | ☐ other: _____], **conforming to all safety codes.**

☐ **Use various instruments, equipment, and devices during the inspection process including** [☐ survey instruments | ☐ metering devices | ☐ test equipment | ☐ tape measures | ☐ concrete strength measurers | ☐ other: _____].

☐ **Perform** [☐ preventive | ☐ routine | ☐ periodic | ☐ other: _____] **cleaning and maintenance of** _____ *[type of]* **equipment on** _____, _____, **and** _____ *[what?]*.

☐ **Ensure all** _____ *[type of]* [☐ machinery | ☐ tools | ☐ equipment | ☐ vehicles | ☐ other: _____] **used in the** _____ *[which?]* **trade are repaired and maintained.**

☐ **Operate all tools and equipment following safety methods and precautions; and maintain equipment to ensure safe operating condition.**

☐ **Maintain all office equipment, including** [☐ multiline telephone systems | ☐ computers | ☐ photocopiers | ☐ postal stamp machines | ☐ telex machines | ☐ fax machines | ☐ others: _____].

☐ [☐ Oversee | ☐ Perform] **minor maintenance and repair on** [☐ construction vehicles | ☐ equipment | ☐ power tools | ☐ trucks | ☐ bulldozers | ☐ graders | ☐ cement mixers | ☐ welders | ☐ other: _____].

☐ **Maintain the proper operation of all** _____ *[type of]* **equipment to ensure the physical, mechanical, and electrical aspects of the facility run smoothly.**

ACHIEVEMENT SAMPLES:

☐ **Due to clear focusing and quick decoding abilities, learned to operate** _____ *[type of]* **machines after one time on-the-job instruction.**

☐ **Brought** _____ *[type of]* [☐ equipment | ☐ machinery] **downtime to** _____% *[percentage]* **by ensuring** [☐ all workers had parts available when needed | ☐ other achievement: _____].

☐ **Mastered the use of testing devices and measuring instruments including** [☐ voltmeters | ☐ thermometers | ☐ manometers | ☐ pressure gauges | ☐ ammeters | ☐ ohmmeters | ☐ testing lamps | ☐ other: _____] **to check** [☐ airflow | ☐ refrigerant pressure | ☐ electrical circuits | ☐ burners | ☐ other: _____] **and various tools** [☐ metal snips | ☐ electric drills | ☐ pipe cutters and benders | ☐ measurement gauges | ☐ acetylene torches | ☐ other: _____] **to service** [☐ refrigerant lines | ☐ air ducts | ☐ other: _____].

☐ **By purchasing and using a variety of** _____ *[type of]* **machines including** _____, _____, **and** _____ *[which?]*, **able to serve a wide variety of customers handling their** _____ *[type of]* **needs.**

☐ **Configured, troubleshot, and resolved** _____ *[type of]* **equipment problems and provided technical assistance and troubleshooting on** _____ *[what?]*.

☐ **Developed a preventive maintenance schedule for all** _____ *[type of]* **equipment that encompasses** _____ *[what?]*.

☐ **Purchased and implemented** _____ *[type of]* **equipment that** [☐ allows the integration of various _____ *(type of)* technologies | ☐ helped the firm service all _____ *(type of)* markets | ☐ other: _____].

Equipment, Tools & Testing Devices – Carpentry / Construction

See also other "Equipment, Tools & Testing Devices" categories.

☐ **Safely operate and maintain various types of heavy equipment including** [☐ 18-wheel semi-trucks | ☐ A-frame mowers | ☐ backhoes | ☐ backup trucks | ☐ bulldozers | ☐ bush hogs | ☐ catch basin cleaners | ☐ concrete mixers | ☐ concrete pavers | ☐ cranes | ☐ distributors | ☐ draglines | ☐ dump trucks | ☐ electric dollies | ☐ excavators | ☐ forklifts | ☐ front-end loaders | ☐ grinders | ☐ heavy dump trucks (with ☐ plows / ☐ wings / ☐ spreaders) | ☐ hoists | ☐ hydraulic equipment | ☐ lane closure trucks | ☐ large rollers | ☐ loaders | ☐ motor graders | ☐ orange peelers | ☐ patch rollers | ☐ payloaders | ☐ pilot cars | ☐ planers | ☐ plow trucks | ☐ pneumatic asphalt tampers | ☐ post pounders | ☐ power shovels | ☐ scaffolding | ☐ seeders | ☐ sewer cleaners | (☐ single-blade / ☐ wing) plows | ☐ semi-truck trailers | ☐ sprayers | ☐ snowplows | ☐ stump grinders | ☐ sweepers | ☐ tractor mowers | ☐ tractors | ☐ trench diggers | ☐ wideners | ☐ wrecking balls | ☐ other: _____] **with an excellent safety record.**

☐ **Operate various hand and power tools including** [☐ air compressors | ☐ axes | ☐ brush hooks | ☐ bush axes | ☐ chainsaws | ☐ compressor hose | ☐ hammers | ☐ hand shovels | ☐ mattocks | ☐ mechanical soil compactors | ☐ picks | ☐ power saws | ☐ post hole diggers | ☐ rakes | ☐ sledge hammers | ☐ stapling guns | ☐ trowels | ☐ welding machines | ☐ other: _____] **in accordance with workplace safety practices.**

☐ **Use** [☐ glass cutters | ☐ glazing knives | ☐ power saws | ☐ suction cups | ☐ drills | ☐ grinders | ☐ other: _____] **to lay out, cut, install, and weatherproof** _____ *[type of]* [☐ windows | ☐ glass doors | ☐ tempered glass | ☐ laminated glass panels | ☐ skylights | ☐ sun rooms | ☐ bath and shower enclosures | ☐ table tops | ☐ room dividers | ☐ metal framework extrusions | ☐ windshields | ☐ other: _____] **for various** _____ *[type of]* **projects ranging $**_____ **to $**_____ *[amounts]*.

☐ **Perform** [☐ carpentry | ☐ masonry | ☐ concrete pouring | ☐ other: _____] **using** _____, _____, **and** _____ *[type of]* **tools and equipment ensuring all safety practices are followed on job sites.**

☐ **Operate heavy plow truck to keep major arteries of** _____ *[territory]* **open and passable for traffic flow during snow and ice conditions and inclement weather ensuring caution around electrical wires, gas lines, and cable lines.**

☐ **Operate all** _____ *[type of]* **equipment including** [☐ hand and power tools | ☐ measurement tools | ☐ grinders | ☐ sand blasters | ☐ drill presses | ☐ cement cutters | ☐ cutting torches | ☐ jackhammers | ☐ electric drills | ☐ hacksaws | ☐ skill saws | ☐ other: _____]**, conforming to all safety codes.**

☐ **Use** [☐ knee kickers | ☐ carpet shears | ☐ loop pile cutters | ☐ heat irons | ☐ hammers | ☐ staple guns | ☐ carpet knives | ☐ drills | ☐ rubber mallets | ☐ wall trimmers | ☐ power stretchers | ☐ rollers | ☐ trowels | ☐ sanding machines | ☐ machine saw | ☐ power wet saw | ☐ other: _____] **to install** _____ *[type of]* **floor coverings.**

☐ **Measure, cut, fit, glue and/or screw wallboard panels to wood and metal framework, cutting holes in panels for** [☐ windows | ☐ doors | ☐ electrical outlets | ☐ air-conditioning units | ☐ plumbing | ☐ other: _____] **and applying textured surfaces to** [☐ walls | ☐ ceilings | ☐ floors | ☐ other: _____] **using** [☐ trowels | ☐ brushes | ☐ spray guns | ☐ other: _____].

ACHIEVEMENT SAMPLES:

☐ **Reduced equipment downtime** _____ **%** *[percentage]* **by** [☐ cleaning and maintaining all equipment after each use | ☐ repairing machinery | ☐ following preventive maintenance schedules | ☐ meeting scheduled timeframes | ☐ being alert and operating all machinery properly | ☐ other: _____] **thereby** [☐ extending equipment life | ☐ reducing company costs | ☐ minimizing property damage | ☐ keeping the public safe | ☐ other: _____].

Equipment, Tools & Testing Devices – Electrical

See also other "Equipment, Tools & Testing Devices" categories.

☐ **Safely use and maintain all** [☐ electrical | ☐ electronics | ☐ Electrician's] [☐ hand and power tools | ☐ testing instruments | ☐ drills | ☐ measuring devices | ☐ conduit bending and threading equipment | ☐ hoists | ☐ other: _____] **associated with the trade.**

☐ **Use all electrician-related equipment including** [☐ hand and power tools | ☐ measurement tools | ☐ wire and cable winches | ☐ knock-out punches | ☐ PVC benders | ☐ hydraulic pipe benders | ☐ pipe cutters | ☐ pipe threaders | ☐ grinders | ☐ sand blasters | ☐ bead blasters | ☐ drill presses | ☐ cement cutters | ☐ cutting torches | ☐ jackhammers | ☐ electric drills and hacksaws | ☐ skill saws | ☐ other: _____], **conforming to all safety codes.**

☐ **Operate and use all** [☐ electrical | ☐ electrical | ☐ other: _____] **machinery and equipment including** [☐ hand and power tools | ☐ pipe benders | ☐ propane torches | ☐ welding equipment | ☐ sewer rooters | ☐ other: _____] **in a safe manner according to established safety precautions.**

☐ **Troubleshoot, diagnose, repair, adjust, and maintain all electrical equipment and machinery to ensure optimum running condition and safety including** [☐ hand and power tools | ☐ pipe benders | ☐ propane torches | ☐ welding equipment | ☐ forklifts | ☐ other: _____].

☐ **Operate and maintain the company's fleet of** _____ *[#]* [☐ lift trucks | ☐ pickup trucks | ☐ forklifts | ☐ hydraulic boom lifts | ☐ boom trucks | ☐ digger derricks | ☐ bucket trucks | ☐ other: _____].

☐ **Use specialized testing equipment and measurement tools to test, install, and/or repair electrical circuits and equipment including** [☐ ampmeters | ☐ ohmmeters | ☐ oscilloscopes | ☐ voltmeters | ☐ volt-ohm meters | ☐ test lamps | ☐ cable locating meters | ☐ fault locators | ☐ Megger meters | ☐ other: _____] **to check** [☐ circuits | ☐ other: _____] **for** [☐ proper connections | ☐ electrical compatibility | ☐ component safety | ☐ functionality | ☐ proper operation | ☐ other: _____].

☐ **Operate all** [☐ electrical | ☐ electrical | ☐ other: _____] **tools and equipment following safety techniques and precautions, and maintain equipment to ensure safe operating condition by abiding by all safety rules.**

☐ **Handle various electrical functions for** _____ *[type of]* **public works projects including** [☐ repairing underground conduits | ☐ trimming trees for wire clearance | ☐ operating underground cable locators to find, and updating maps to include, cable locations and underground faults | ☐ operating (☐ pickup trucks / ☐ digger derricks | ☐ bucket trucks | ☐ other: _____].

☐ **Operate and maintain** _____ *[#]*-**volt** [☐ high-tension | ☐ other: _____] **distribution systems including** _____ *[what functions?]*.

Equipment, Tools & Testing Devices – HVAC / HVAC-R

See also other "Equipment, Tools & Testing Devices" categories.

☐ **Service** [☐ refrigerant lines | ☐ air ducts | ☐ other: _____] **using various hand and power tools of the trade including** [☐ pipe cutters and benders | ☐ measurement gauges | ☐ acetylene torches | ☐ metal snips | ☐ electric drills | ☐ other: _____].

☐ **Operate and use all HVAC machinery and equipment including** [☐ hand and power tools | ☐ pipe benders | ☐ propane torches | ☐ welding equipment | ☐ sewer rooters | ☐ other: _____] **in a safe manner according to established safety precautions.**

☐ **Use a variety of testing devices including** [☐ voltmeters | ☐ thermometers | ☐ manometers | ☐ pressure gauges | ☐ other: _____] **to check** [☐ airflow | ☐ refrigerant pressure | ☐ electrical circuits | ☐ burners | ☐ other: _____]; **and various tools including** [☐ metal snips | ☐ electric drills | ☐ pipe cutters and benders | ☐ measurement gauges | ☐ acetylene torches | ☐ other: _____] **to service refrigerant lines and air ducts.**

☐ **Ensure proper** [☐ furnace | ☐ heating equipment | ☐ other: _____] **system functioning using combustion test equipment including** [☐ carbon dioxide testers | ☐ oxygen testers | ☐ other: _____] **and** _____ *[other methods]* **resulting in** _____ *[what benefits?].*

☐ **Troubleshoot, diagnose, repair, adjust, and maintain all HVAC equipment to ensure optimal running condition and safety including** [☐ hand and power tools | ☐ pipe benders | ☐ propane torches | ☐ welding equipment | ☐ sewer rooters | ☐ forklifts | ☐ trenchers | ☐ backhoes | ☐ other: _____].

☐ **Operate all** [☐ HVAC | ☐ plumbing | ☐ other: _____] [☐ tools | ☐ machinery | ☐ equipment] **following safety techniques and precautions, and maintain equipment to ensure safe operating condition.**

☐ **Perform** [☐ preventive | ☐ routine | ☐ periodic | ☐ other: _____] **cleaning and maintenance of all plumbing equipment including** [☐ hand and power tools | ☐ pipe benders | ☐ propane torches | ☐ welding equipment | ☐ sewer rooters | ☐ other: _____].

Equipment, Tools & Testing Devices – Landscaping & Masonry

See also other "Equipment, Tools & Testing Devices" categories.

☐ **Set up, operate, repair, and/or maintain all** [☐ landscaping | ☐ groundskeeping | ☐ masonry] **equipment** [☐ and vehicles] **including** [☐ backhoes | ☐ boom trucks | ☐ bulldozers | ☐ cement mixers | ☐ compressors | ☐ cranes | ☐ crawlers | ☐ dozers | ☐ dump bodies | ☐ force-feed loaders | ☐ forklifts | ☐ front loaders | ☐ gear cutting machines | ☐ graders | ☐ heavy dump trucks | ☐ hoists | ☐ hook lift hoists | ☐ hook lifts | ☐ hydraulic excavators | ☐ mowers | ☐ municipal dump bodies | ☐ orange peelers | ☐ paving equipment | ☐ payloaders | ☐ pick-up trucks | ☐ piggy-back forklifts | ☐ platforms | ☐ plow trucks | | ☐ rear loaders | ☐ road milling machines | ☐ roadrangers | ☐ roll-offs | ☐ roof mowers | ☐ sewer jets | ☐ side loaders | ☐ snow plows | ☐ spreaders | ☐ steam rollers | ☐ street sweepers | ☐ tiger mowers | ☐ tractors | ☐ trenchers | ☐ truck loaders | ☐ other: _____].

☐ **Use hand tools and power equipment including** [☐ shovels | ☐ rakes | ☐ electric clippers | ☐ sod cutters | ☐ saws | ☐ pruning saws | ☐ chain saws | ☐ hedge and brush trimmers | ☐ axes | ☐ snow blowers | ☐ other: _____] **to ensure the proper upkeep and repair of** _____ *[what?].*

☐ **Ensure all employees use correct operational procedures for all groundskeeping** [☐ tools | ☐ machinery | ☐ equipment | ☐ vehicles | ☐ other: _____] **and that all safety practices are followed.**

☐ **Use** [☐ chisels | ☐ diamond blade saws | ☐ mallets | ☐ trowels | ☐ crowbars | ☐ other: _____] **to form masonry materials and build** _____ *[type of]* **projects.**

☐ **Follow safety practices in** [☐ operating equipment and power tools | ☐ mixing and using landscape chemicals | ☐ other: _____].

☐ **Use** [☐ truck-mounted lifts | ☐ power pruners | ☐ handsaws | ☐ shears | ☐ pruning hooks | ☐ clippers | ☐ other: _____] **to trim trees and shrubs; and fill tree cavities to promote healing and prevent deterioration.**

☐ **Working closely with related trades to create** _____ *[type of]* **structures, precisely align all** [☐ stones | ☐ bricks | ☐ pavers | ☐ edgers | ☐ other: _____] **with wedges, plumblines, levels, and brackets to ensure a precision fit and attractive finish using chisels, diamond blade saws, mallets, trowels, and crowbars.**

Equipment, Tools & Testing Devices – Plumbing

See also other "Equipment, Tools & Testing Devices" categories.

☐ **Service** _____ *[what?]* **using various hand and power tools of the trade including** [☐ pipe cutters and benders | ☐ measurement gauges | ☐ acetylene torches | ☐ metal snips | ☐ electric drills | ☐ other: _____].

☐ **Ensure proper** [☐ furnace | ☐ heating equipment | ☐ other: _____] **system functioning using combustion test equipment including** [☐ carbon dioxide testers | ☐ oxygen testers | ☐ other: _____] **and** _____ *[other methods]* **resulting in** _____ *[what benefits?].*

☐ **Troubleshoot, diagnose, repair, adjust, and maintain all plumbing equipment and machinery to ensure optimum running condition and safety including** [☐ hand and power tools | ☐ pipe benders | ☐ propane torches | ☐ welding equipment | ☐ sewer rooters | ☐ forklifts | ☐ trenchers | ☐ backhoes | ☐ other: _____].

☐ **Repair and maintain** _____ *[type of]* **plumbing** [☐ tools | ☐ equipment | ☐ other: _____] **used in the trade including** _____ *[what?].*

☐ **Safely operate and use various plumbing machinery and equipment including** [☐ hand and power tools | ☐ pipe benders | ☐ propane torches | ☐ welding equipment | ☐ sewer rooters | ☐ other: _____].

☐ **Operate all plumbing tools and equipment following safety techniques and precautions, and maintain equipment to ensure safe operating condition by abiding by all safety rules.**

Equipment, Tools & Testing Devices – Welding / Steamfitting

See also other "Equipment, Tools & Testing Devices" categories.

☐ **Operate and maintain various steamfitting machinery and equipment including** [☐ metal forming equipment | ☐ centrifugal chiller and steam absorption machines | ☐ drill presses | ☐ metal-removing machines | ☐ milling machines | ☐ gear cutting machines | ☐ CNC machines | ☐ Atlas machines | ☐ other: _____] **and other heavy equipment a safe manner and according to established safety precautions.**

☐ **Use** _____ *[type of]* **precision instruments and operate** [☐ metal-removing machines | ☐ metal-forming equipment | ☐ drill presses | ☐ _____ *(type of)* welding devices | ☐ other: _____] **and** [☐ milling | ☐ gear cutting | ☐ CNC | ☐ Atlas | ☐ centrifugal chiller | ☐ steam absorption | ☐ other: _____] **to** [☐ fabricate | ☐ fit | ☐ assemble | ☐ manufacture | ☐ repair | ☐ other: _____] _____ *[type of]* [☐ parts | ☐ equipment | ☐ other: _____] **working from** [☐ blueprints | ☐ plans | ☐ diagrams | ☐ specifications] **to determine dimensions, tolerances, and work layout.**

☐ **Handle all aspects of torch cutting using precision-measuring instruments including** [☐ protractors | ☐ micrometers | ☐ vernier calipers | ☐ other: _____] **welding in various positions including** [☐ flat | ☐ horizontal | ☐ vertical | ☐ overhead | ☐ other: _____].

☐ **Keep fleet of trucks in running condition by ensuring** [☐ hydraulics pistons and seals and hopper blades are all in excellent working order | ☐ hydraulic oil and pressure is at right levels at all times | ☐ other: _____].

☐ **Perform** [☐ torch cutting | ☐ joint welding | ☐ other: _____] **for** _____ *[what?]* **including** [☐ groove | ☐ bead | ☐ edge | ☐ plug | ☐ slot | ☐ fillet | ☐ arc-seam | ☐ other: _____] **using precision-measuring instruments including** [☐ protractors | ☐ micrometers | ☐ venire calipers | ☐ other: _____].

☐ **Operate and** [☐ troubleshoot | ☐ diagnose | ☐ repair | ☐ adjust | ☐ maintain] **all** [☐ electrical | ☐ plumbing | ☐ other: _____] **equipment and machinery to ensure optimum running condition and safety including** [☐ hand and power tools | ☐ pipe benders | ☐ propane torches | ☐ welding equipment | ☐ sewer rooters | ☐ forklifts | ☐ other: _____].

☐ **Ensure proper** _____ *[type of]* **system functioning using combustion test equipment including** [☐ carbon dioxide testers | ☐ oxygen testers | ☐ other: _____] **and** _____ *[other methods]* **for** _____ *[what?].*

☐ **Service** _____ *[what?]* **using hand and power tools of the trade including** [☐ pipe cutters | ☐ benders | ☐ measurement gauges | ☐ acetylene torches | ☐ metal snips | ☐ electric drills | ☐ other: _____].

☐ **Troubleshoot, diagnose, repair, adjust, and maintain all welding equipment and machinery to ensure optimum running condition and safety including** _____, _____, **and** _____ *[which equipment or what functions?].*

☐ **Follow safety precautions using protective equipment around exposure to** [☐ extreme temperatures | ☐ toxic chemicals | ☐ explosive gases | ☐ biohazardous materials | ☐ helium | ☐ oxygen | ☐ acetylene | ☐ smoke and fumes | ☐ grease | ☐ other: _____].

Estimating

See "Cost Estimating."

Executive Leadership Scope

See also other "Executive Leadership" categories as well as "Team Leadership & Direction."

☐ **Direct and lead the** _____, _____, **and** _____ *[which?]* **activities of this** _____ *[type of]* **firm with** _____ *[#]* [☐ locations | ☐ employees] **including** [☐ program development | ☐ establishment of best practices | ☐ other: _____] **ensuring compliance with all state and federal regulations.**

☐ **Plan, direct, and implement all aspects of the** _____ *[which?]* [☐ Division(s) | ☐ Departments | ☐ Region | ☐ Territory | ☐ other: _____] **of this** [☐ multimillion-dollar | ☐ $_____ *(revenues)*] _____ *[type of]* **firm including** _____, _____, **and** _____ *[which areas?].*

☐ **Direct the** _____ [which?] **division, including** _____ [#] **direct reports and** _____ [#] **indirect reports of this** $_____ [revenues] _____ [type of] **firm specializing in** _____ [type of products or services].

☐ **Lead and direct the** _____ [which?] **management team(s) in** [☐ strategy execution | ☐ financial management | ☐ procurement | ☐ resource acquisition | ☐ quality assurance | ☐ safety | ☐ other: _____] **activities to develop, coordinate, and administer** _____ [what?].

☐ **Provide executive oversight in the management and operations of the** _____ [which?] [☐ Division(s) | ☐ Department(s)] **for this** $_____ [revenues] _____ [type of] **firm with** _____ [#] [☐ locations | ☐ employees | ☐ clients | ☐ other: _____] **including** [☐ the establishment of long-range goals | ☐ execution of operating plans | ☐ development of operating budgets | ☐ management of key customers | ☐ other: _____].

☐ **Direct day-to-day** [☐ corporate affairs | ☐ operations | ☐ other: _____] **of this** _____ [type of] **firm with annual revenues in excess of** $_____ [revenues], **including** _____, _____, **and** _____ [primary activities].

☐ **Jointly with** _____ [whom?], [☐ plan and direct | ☐ manage and administer] **all facets of the firm's** _____ [which?] [☐ Division(s) | ☐ Departments | ☐ Region | ☐ Territory | ☐ other: _____] **operations and support activities in the areas of** _____, _____, **and** _____ [what areas?].

☐ **Oversee and manage all facets of** _____ [what?] **for this recognized** [☐ national | ☐ world] **leader in** _____ [what?] **including** _____, _____, **and** _____ [primary responsibilities].

☐ **Manage and direct overall** _____ [what area(s)?] **for the** _____ [which?] **Division of this** $_____ [revenues] _____ [type of] **firm that specializes in the** _____ [which?] **market by** [☐ establishing personal contacts with Fortune 100/500 companies | ☐ other method: _____].

☐ **Design, administer, and implement corporate-level** _____ [type of] **initiatives that support the firm's business mission and objectives including** _____, _____, **and** _____ [areas], **which drove** _____ [what benefits?].

☐ **Direct and oversee** [☐ worldwide | ☐ nationwide | ☐ regional | ☐ other: _____] _____ [type of] **activities including** _____, _____, **and** _____ [what activities?] **and the strategic direction of** _____ [what?], **taking the** [☐ company | ☐ division | ☐ other: _____] **from** $_____ **to** $_____ [amount] **in annual sales.**

☐ **Facilitate senior-level management and oversight of the** _____ [which?] **operations for this** $_____ [revenues] _____ [type of] **firm with** _____ [#] [☐ locations | ☐ employees | ☐ clients | ☐ other: _____] **including** [☐ the establishment of long-range goals | ☐ execution of operating plans | ☐ management of key customers | ☐ other: _____].

☐ **Lead and direct** _____ [which?] [☐ Division(s) | ☐ Departments | ☐ Region | ☐ Territory | ☐ other: _____] **including** [☐ employment | ☐ compensation | ☐ salary administration | ☐ employee benefits | ☐ training and development | ☐ employee relations | ☐ other: _____] **for this** $_____ [revenues] _____ [type of] **firm.**

☐ **Manage the functional areas of** [☐ corporate affairs | ☐ procurement and asset utilization | ☐ ethics and compliance | ☐ business conduct policies and practices | ☐ regulatory and legal standards | ☐ corporate governance systems | ☐ safety and health promotion | ☐ other: _____].

ACHIEVEMENT SAMPLES: _Refer to areas of expertise for specific achievements in those areas._

Executive Leadership General Functions

See also "Executive Leadership Scope."

☐ **Direct and lead the** _____, _____, **and** _____ [which?] **activities of this** _____ [type of] **firm with** _____ [#] [☐ locations | ☐ employees] **including** [☐ program development | ☐ establishment of best practices | ☐ other: _____] **ensuring compliance with all state and federal regulations.**

☐ **Drive strategic innovation in** _____, _____, **and** _____ [what areas?] **across all** [☐ divisions | ☐ departments | ☐ units | ☐ stores | ☐ other: _____]; **and create alignment with** _____ [what?] **toward optimum business success for this** [☐ multimillion-dollar | ☐ $_____ (revenues)] _____ [type of] **firm with** _____ [#] [☐ employees | ☐ locations] [☐ worldwide | ☐ nationwide].

☐ **Strategize, plan, and direct the development, implementation, and operation of the** _____ [which?] [☐ Division's | ☐ Department's | ☐ Region's | ☐ Territory's | ☐ other: _____] _____ [type of] [☐ systems | ☐ policies | ☐ procedures | ☐ other: _____], **and advise and assist** [☐ division heads | ☐ department managers | ☐ others: _____] **regarding** _____ [which?] **matters.**

☐ **Champion large-scale** _____ [type of] [☐ organizational programs | ☐ company-wide initiatives | ☐ other: _____] **that involved** [☐ strategic planning | ☐ analysis, diagnosis, and solution development and deployment | ☐ other: _____], **and designed and implemented associated** _____ [type of] **programs that met operating goals and objectives.**

☐ **Mentor and coach** _____ *[which?]* [☐ division heads | ☐ department managers | ☐ other: _____] **in the development and implementation of operating** [☐ goals | ☐ practices | ☐ procedures | ☐ budget | ☐ other: _____], **and participation in the firm's** [☐ business planning | ☐ policy development | ☐ solutions delivery | ☐ other: _____].

☐ **Develop, oversee, and monitor annual operating budgets and provide fiscal direction to the** _____ *[which?]* [☐ Division(s) | ☐ Departments | ☐ Region | ☐ Territory | ☐ other: _____] **in the areas of** _____, _____, **and** _____ *[areas]*.

☐ **Ensure compliance with all applicable** [☐ Federal and state | ☐ civil rights | ☐ Affirmative Action | ☐ Equal Employment Opportunity | ☐ Americans with Disabilities Act | ☐ Rehabilitation Act | ☐ other: _____] **laws and regulations relating to** [☐ employment | ☐ personnel management | ☐ labor relations | ☐ other: _____].

☐ **Facilitate leadership team meetings with** _____ *[whom?]* **to collaborate on** [☐ organizational development | ☐ leadership development | ☐ talent assessment | ☐ performance management | ☐ change management | ☐ employee engagement | ☐ succession management | ☐ other: _____] **strategies, challenges, and opportunities through** [☐ strategic thought leadership | ☐ knowledge transfer | ☐ objective and robust analysis | ☐ project delivery excellence | ☐ other: _____] **focusing on** _____, _____, **and** _____ *[what areas?]*.

☐ **Provide** [☐ strategic leadership | ☐ tactical direction | ☐ practical management | ☐ other: _____] **to uphold the firm's corporate physical security and safety of its** [☐ assets | ☐ facilities | ☐ intellectual property | ☐ computer systems | ☐ employees | ☐ other: _____] **and related areas including** [☐ loss prevention | ☐ fraud prevention | ☐ privacy | ☐ digital security | ☐ business continuity planning | ☐ other: _____].

☐ **Motivate and coach** _____ *[which?]* **business leaders in the areas of** _____, _____, **and** _____ *[areas]* **ensuring** [☐ business goals are translated into actionable performance objectives | ☐ development programs impact critical business and leadership issues | ☐ accountability for results | ☐ other: _____].

☐ **Provide** _____ *[type of]* **advice to** [☐ firm | ☐ agency | ☐ division | ☐ district | ☐ department] **on all** _____ *[type of]* **matters to** [☐ facilitate the operation of the company | ☐ establish operating objectives | ☐ achieve strategic priorities | ☐ direct short- and long-range plans | ☐ provide fiscal and operational data | ☐ coordinate activities | ☐ address concerns | ☐ exchange information | ☐ other: _____].

☐ **Direct and oversee all aspects of** _____, _____, **and** _____ *[areas or projects]* **including** [☐ mergers and acquisitions | ☐ joint venture development | ☐ extensive support programs | ☐ other: _____] **for this** _____ *[type of]* **firm specializing in** _____ *[what?]*.

☐ [☐ Spearhead | ☐ Co-develop] **the firm's** _____ *[type of]* [☐ programs | ☐ systems | ☐ polices | ☐ procedures | ☐ standards | ☐ guidelines | ☐ initiatives | ☐ other: _____] **that involve** _____ *[what actions?]* **and result in** _____ *[what benefits?]*.

☐ **Direct and operate this** _____ *[type of]* **firm's** _____, _____, **and** _____ *[which?]* **activities including establishment and maintenance of** _____, _____, **and** _____ *[what?]*.

ACHIEVEMENT SAMPLES: *Refer to areas of expertise for specific achievements in those areas.*

Executive Leadership Strategy Development & Deployment

See also "Business Goals Setting" and "Executive Leadership Scope."

☐ **Drive the vision and strategy behind this** _____ *[type of]* **firm's** _____ *[which?]* **Division(s) and related** [☐ research and analysis | ☐ presentations | ☐ project prioritization | ☐ planning | ☐ conceptualization | ☐ assessments | ☐ quality control | ☐ other: _____] **functions of** _____ *[type of]* **projects ensuring the firm's overall compliance with** _____ *[what regulations or standards?]*.

☐ **Direct and guide the** _____ *[which?]* **Division Heads in support of** _____ *[what?]* **strategy development applying an in-depth knowledge of** [☐ organizational change systems | ☐ performance management | ☐ other: _____].

☐ **Lead and direct the Strategic Business Unit (SBU) strategy by** [☐ building key stakeholder relationships | ☐ enhancing and increasing the capability of senior leaders and managers | ☐ devising solutions that influence cross-functional strategy alignment | ☐ building and integrating strategic frameworks that drive sound decisions | ☐ other: _____] **to attract, grow, and retain superior talent that meets business goals and employee career aspirations.**

☐ **Perform senior-level** _____ *[type of]* **planning and strategizing activities in overseeing the management of** _____ *[type of]* [☐ programs | ☐ projects | ☐ initiatives] **to ensure cost-effectiveness and functionality and considers all** [☐ fiscal | ☐ legal | ☐ technical | ☐ demographic | ☐ economic | ☐ safety | ☐ other: _____] **aspects.**

☐ **Lead and direct the** _____ *[which?]* [☐ Division(s) | ☐ Departments | ☐ Region | ☐ Territory | ☐ other: _____] **strategy by** [☐ building key stakeholder relationships | ☐ enhancing and increasing the capability of senior leaders | ☐ devising solutions that influence cross-functional strategy alignment | ☐ establishing succession planning strategies ☐ other: _____] **to attract, grow, and retain superior talent.**

☐ **Drive the planning and execution of** _____ *[which?]* **strategies including developing and cultivating** [☐ internal and external relationships | ☐ superior management talent | ☐ other: _____] **that supports** [☐ a diverse talent pipeline | ☐ the execution of business strategy | ☐ other: _____] **to** [☐ add value to the organization | ☐ meet the firm's mission and goals | ☐ achieve long-term business success | ☐ other: _____].

☐ **Direct the** [☐ firm's | ☐ division's | ☐ department's] [☐ management practices | ☐ fiscal planning | ☐ other: _____] **to strategically** [☐ spearhead | ☐ plan and strategize | ☐ design and execute | ☐ formulate and coordinate | ☐ develop and administer | ☐ implement and maintain] _____ *[what?]* **for the** [☐ operation | ☐ upkeep | ☐ other: _____] **of** _____ *[what?]*.

☐ **Plan, direct, and monitor the development and implementation of the firm's diverse** _____ *[which?]* [☐ strategies | ☐ operations | ☐ programs | ☐ initiatives | ☐ projects | ☐ policies | ☐ procedures | ☐ other: _____] **including** _____ , _____ , **and** _____ *[what?]* **in response to the** [☐ firm's | ☐ agency's | ☐ organization's | ☐ department's] **needs.**

ACHIEVEMENT SAMPLES:

☐ **Planned, developed, and implemented resource-generating strategies that resulted in identifying and securing** _____ *[type of]* [☐ revenue sources | ☐ funding in the amount of $_____ *(amount)* **from** _____ *[whom?]* **for the firm, which resulted in** [☐ building | ☐ developing ☐ implementing | ☐ other: _____] _____ *[what?]*.

☐ **Designed and implemented** _____ *[type of]* **solutions that effectively addressed and adhered to** [☐ firm's | ☐ clients'] **requirements** [☐ in accordance with all project timelines and budget | ☐ ensuring quality project standards | ☐ allowing for a smooth transition | ☐ other: _____].

Facilities & Plant Inspections & Compliance

See "Inspections & Compliance – Facilities & Plants."

Facility Management Scope

See also "Facility Management Functions," "Building Operations Management," "Inspections & Compliance – Facilities & Plants" and "Inspections & Compliance – General."

☐ **Manage** _____ *[#]* **buildings and** _____ *[#]-***acre grounds for this** _____ *[type of]* **firm including overseeing** [☐ construction | ☐ renovation | ☐ repair | ☐ remodel | ☐ maintenance | ☐ other: _____] **projects to ensure they meet** [☐ government | ☐ environmental | ☐ health | ☐ safety | ☐ security | ☐ environmental | ☐ other: _____] **standards.**

☐ **Direct and oversee the** [☐ facilities | ☐ building maintenance | ☐ grounds upkeep | ☐ space planning | ☐ remodel projects | ☐ other: _____] **of this** _____ *[#]-***square foot building with ground acreage of** _____ *[#]* **and** _____ *[#]* [☐ employees | ☐ work stations | ☐ offices | ☐ facilities].

☐ **Direct architectural** [☐ design | ☐ planning | ☐ review | ☐ management] **of** [☐ construction | ☐ remodeling | ☐ maintenance] **projects for** [☐ commercial | ☐ department | ☐ other: _____] **buildings and facilities of this** _____ *[type of]* **firm.**

☐ **Manage and oversee this** _____ *[type of]* **plant's facilities handling all aspects of** [☐ office administration | ☐ facilities management | ☐ construction oversight | ☐ purchasing | ☐ lease negotiations | ☐ space planning | ☐ budget preparation | ☐ executive expense analysis | ☐ other: _____].

☐ **Direct the day-to-day operations of this** _____ *[type of]* **facility including** [☐ client meeting | ☐ needs assessment | ☐ estimating | ☐ proposal development | ☐ bidding | ☐ work orders | ☐ budgeting | ☐ project prioritizing | ☐ timelines | ☐ scheduling | ☐ site inspections | ☐ equipment and supplies purchasing | ☐ sales and marketing | ☐ payroll processing | ☐ company taxes | ☐ preventive maintenance | ☐ trades coordination | ☐ other: _____] **ensuring all projects are completed on time and professionally and job sites are left clean of debris to increase safety and customer satisfaction.**

☐ **Check and evaluate the** [☐ physical | ☐ mechanical | ☐ structural | ☐ other: _____] **aspects of facilities to ensure everything is operating in a safe, functional, and proper manner.**

☐ **Manage and maintain Executive Office facilities consisting of** _____ *[#]* **floors and** _____ *[#]* **square feet, with responsibility for Executive Office Facility budget of** $_____ *[amount]*.

☐ **Manage, coordinate, and oversee all aspects of** [☐ building maintenance | ☐ project planning | ☐ facility function | ☐ environmental factors | ☐ lease management | ☐ architectural planning and design | ☐ real estate purchases and sales | ☐ space planning | ☐ renovations | ☐ other: _____] **for this** _____ *[type of]* **company.**

☐ **Oversee the** [☐ structural | ☐ mechanical | ☐ electrical | ☐ plumbing | ☐ other: _____] **aspects of** _____ *[type of]* **building** [☐ design | ☐ utilization | ☐ space planning | ☐ construction | ☐ operation | ☐ maintenance | ☐ repair | ☐ remodel | ☐ other: _____] **projects ensuring that all work is performed in compliance with building codes, laws, and regulations.**

☐ **Manage various** [☐ building | ☐ facility | ☐ grounds] **maintenance functions including** [☐ building maintenance and repair | ☐ office relocations | ☐ renovations | ☐ remodeling | ☐ roofing repairs | ☐ machinery maintenance and repair | ☐ regular and preventive maintenance | ☐ carpentry | ☐ electrical wiring | ☐ plumbing | ☐ HVAC systems | ☐ painting | ☐ custodial services | ☐ janitorial maintenance | ☐ groundskeeping | ☐ security systems | ☐ sprinkler systems | ☐ fire extinguisher and smoke alarm inspections | ☐ safety checks | ☐ boiler system | ☐ water system | ☐ heating system | ☐ cooling system | ☐ other: _____].

☐ **Direct and review** [☐ grounds | ☐ facilities | ☐ other: _____] **improvement projects including the** [☐ development of building plan specifications | ☐ inspection of facilities under construction or renovation | ☐ review of contractors' progress schedules | ☐ other: _____].

☐ [☐ **As an independent subcontractor,**] **work as a team to assist and support management in directing all building** [☐ construction | ☐ maintenance | ☐ improvement | ☐ repair | ☐ remodel | ☐ other: _____] **work; and monitor facilities to ensure they are safe, secure, and well maintained.**

☐ **Successfully balance managing facility operations and coordinating all aspects of the physical workplace with** [☐ overseeing | ☐ performing] [☐ carpentry | ☐ maintenance and repair | ☐ groundskeeping | ☐ other: _____] **functions by** _____ *[doing what?].*

☐ **Direct all aspects of** [☐ multiple | ☐ simultaneous] _____ *[type of]* [☐ construction | ☐ facility | ☐ other: _____] **management projects including** [☐ budgeting | ☐ subcontractor selection | ☐ trades scheduling | ☐ materials acquisition | ☐ design revisions | ☐ client satisfaction | ☐ inspections | ☐ other: _____].

ACHIEVEMENT SAMPLES: *See also "Achievement Examples – General," "Building Operations Projects," "Construction Projects," "Cost Reductions & Savings," "Overcoming Obstacles," and "Productivity Improvement."*

☐ **Significantly improved operating conditions of the building's** _____ *[what machinery?]* **by implementing and rigidly following a regular maintenance schedule which proved critical to the successful and continuous operation of Company's production equipment.**

☐ **Involved in** [☐ managing | ☐ performing] _____ *[which?]* **relocation efforts that required** _____ *[what actions?]* **to meet** _____ *[what challenges?]* **and resulted in** _____ *[what benefits?].*

☐ **Improved operating conditions of** [☐ buildings | ☐ plants | ☐ structures | ☐ machinery | ☐ equipment | ☐ other: _____] **by** [☐ championing a _____ *(type of)* program that _____ *(does what?)* | ☐ implementing and rigidly following a preventive maintenance schedule | ☐ modifying machinery to run more efficiently | ☐ other: _____], **which resulted in** [☐ eliminating shutdowns by maintaining all equipment in optimum operating condition | ☐ other: _____].

☐ **Made recommendations for the** [☐ maintenance | ☐ upgrade | ☐ remodel | ☐ other: _____] **of** _____ *[which?]* **physical facilities; and prepared comprehensive** _____ *[type of]* **reports to support these recommendations, which resulted in** _____ *[what benefits?].*

☐ **Totally eliminated need for equipment shutdowns by** [☐ maintaining air compressors and boilers in optimum operating condition at all times | ☐ performing regularly scheduled maintenance checks | ☐ changing oil and filters as needed | ☐ other: _____].

☐ **Reduced air compressor downtime from an average of** _____ *[#]* **machine(s) per** [☐ day | ☐ week | ☐ other: _____] **to once every** _____ *[#]* [☐ weeks | ☐ months] **by** [☐ contributing to a new air piping layout | ☐ setting up and maintaining a Preventative Maintenance Program | ☐ other: _____].

☐ **Improved operating conditions of** _____ *[type of]* **machinery by paying close attention to detail in performing and planning** _____ *[type of]* **jobs.**

☐ **Converted building heat from steam to hot water, installing heat exchangers and blower units, resulting in lowering the company's fuel bills by $**_____ *[amount]* **annually.**

☐ **Modified** _____ *[type of]* [☐ equipment | ☐ machinery | ☐ other: _____] **to run more efficiently through a team effort approach.**

☐ **Reorganized and inventoried machine and repair parts, saving** _____ *[#]* **hours in prep time by** _____ *[doing what?].*

☐ **Helped improve the workplace and work environment by** _____ *[doing what?],* **which has resulted in** _____ *[benefits].*

Facility Management Functions

See also "Facility Management – General," "Building Operations Management," and "Inspections & Compliance – Facilities & Plants."

☐ **Maintain** [☐ buildings | ☐ facilities | ☐ grounds | ☐ machinery | ☐ other: _____] **in good repair including** [☐ heating | ☐ air conditioning | ☐ plumbing | ☐ electrical | ☐ drywall | ☐ wall coverings | ☐ insulation | ☐ drop ceilings | ☐ painting | ☐ grading | ☐ underground utilities | ☐ drains | ☐ gutters | ☐ paving | ☐ other: _____].

☐ **Evaluate, prioritize, and coordinate short- and long-range facility plans including** [☐ repair and improvement projects | ☐ building renewal plans | ☐ system-wide policies and standards | ☐ technical requirements | ☐ other: _____].

☐ **Successfully balance managing facility operations and coordinating all aspects of the physical workplace with overseeing carpentry, maintenance, groundskeeping, and** _____ *[other?]* **functions in an exemplary manner by** _____ *[doing what well?]*.

☐ **Handle** [☐ new construction | ☐ remodeling | ☐ repair | ☐ maintenance | ☐ leasing | ☐ space planning | ☐ other: _____] **projects of** _____ *[what?]* **that require** _____ *[what actions?]*.

☐ **Apply** [☐ expert | ☐ proficient | ☐ working] **knowledge of** [☐ general principles and practices of building construction | ☐ building maintenance | ☐ physical plant operations | ☐ technical systems | ☐ bid specification | ☐ inspection methods | ☐ building codes | ☐ ordinances | ☐ fire regulations | ☐ safety precautions | ☐ health and safety regulations | ☐ principles of contract law | ☐ automated building control | ☐ indoor air quality requirements | ☐ energy management systems | ☐ recordkeeping techniques | ☐ other: _____] **to all aspects of facility management.**

☐ **Perform various business-related facility management functions including** [☐ managing and overseeing all aspects of facilities projects | ☐ coordinating department proposals | ☐ directing architectural design and planning | ☐ handling lease negotiations and management | ☐ overseeing construction and remodeling | ☐ coordinating janitorial maintenance and custodial services | ☐ maintaining compliance with all OSHA and environmental regulations | ☐ ensuring facility is safe, secure, and well maintained | ☐ coordinating all aspects of the physical workplace | ☐ analyzing and overseeing the physical and mechanical aspects of the facility | ☐ ensuring facility runs smoothly at all times | ☐ examining facility for damage and overseeing repairs | ☐ developing project plans and overseeing planning | ☐ setting up preventive maintenance schedules | ☐ developing budgets and monitoring expenses | ☐ conducting feasibility studies | ☐ developing safety and security solutions | ☐ conducting research and analysis | ☐ approving cost estimates | ☐ writing maintenance and administrative reports | ☐ following up on security reports | ☐ other: _____]. *(See also "Administrative Management" and "Office Management.")*

☐ **Plan and direct skilled maintenance and repair of** _____ *[type of]* [☐ buildings | ☐ complexes | ☐ facilities] **in the areas of** _____ *[which areas?]*.

☐ **Prepare recommendations to** _____ *[whom?]* **regarding** [☐ contractual defaults | ☐ time extensions | ☐ liquidated damages | ☐ other: _____].

☐ **Manage a multitude of facility** [☐ installation | ☐ construction | ☐ maintenance | ☐ repair | ☐ other: _____] **functions including** [☐ ensure proper operation of boiler, water heater, furnace, and refrigeration | ☐ maintain plumbing, electrical, and HVAC systems | ☐ maintain the facility and grounds | ☐ maintain sprinkler systems | ☐ supervise machinery maintenance and repair | ☐ evaluate equipment life expectancy | ☐ replace equipment when needed | ☐ handle environmental factors | ☐ plan and design office spaces | ☐ direct architectural design and planning | ☐ project manage all renovations | ☐ determine project deadlines | ☐ spearhead corporate office relocations | ☐ initiate and implement policies and procedures | ☐ purchase furniture and equipment | ☐ serve as technical advisor | ☐ negotiate contracts | ☐ review and approve space requests | ☐ inspect proposed space leasing sites and direct space planning | ☐ determine critical maintenance priorities | ☐ conduct facility surveys | ☐ procure contracting services | ☐ review contractor work and inspect for compliance | ☐ project future needs | ☐ estimate material needs | ☐ supervise skilled trades staff | ☐ ensure vehicles are in safe operating condition | ☐ monitor security systems | ☐ handle real estate (☐ purchases / ☐ sales) | ☐ evacuate staff in emergencies | ☐ manage energy conservation programs | ☐ other: _____].

☐ **Coordinate all aspects of the physical workplace ensuring** [☐ the integration and coordination of business practices | ☐ work and people requirements | ☐ architecture | ☐ other: _____].

☐ **Conduct** _____ *[type of]* [☐ research and analysis | ☐ feasibility studies | ☐ other: _____] **for** _____ *[purpose]* **resulting in** _____ *[what benefits?]*.

☐ **Provide** [☐ building maintenance | ☐ space planning | ☐ renovations | ☐ other: _____] **for** _____ *[type of]* **projects.**

☐ **Oversee and inspect** [☐ new construction | ☐ remodeling | ☐ repair | ☐ maintenance | ☐ leasing | ☐ space planning | ☐ other: _____] **projects of** _____ *[what?]* **that require** _____ *[what actions?]*.

ACHIEVEMENT SAMPLES: See *"Facility Management,"* Achievements under *"Building Operations Projects," "General Contracting Projects & Functions,"* and *"Construction Projects."*

Flooring Projects & Functions

See also "Carpentry/Construction Work Functions" and all Carpentry/Construction Projects (specific).

☐ **Lay** [☐ wood | ☐ tile | ☐ carpet | ☐ other: _____] **floor coverings according to blueprints in** [☐ homes | ☐ corporate offices | ☐ building lobbies | ☐ schools | ☐ colleges | ☐ apartment buildings | ☐ hospitals | ☐ manufacturing plants | ☐ shopping malls | ☐ stores | ☐ restaurants | ☐ other: _____] **with professional results.**

☐ **Install** _____ *[type of]* **floor covering materials for** [☐ decorative | ☐ sound deadening | ☐ shock absorbing | | ☐ air-tight | ☐ heat insulating | ☐ other: _____] **purposes to meet client needs.**

☐ **Closely inspect all floor surfaces prior to installation and correct** _____ *[type of]* **imperfections to ensure a smooth foundation before installing** _____ *[type of]* **floor coverings.**

☐ **Prepare for floor installations by** [☐ measuring floor areas | ☐ planning layouts and seam placements around traffic patterns and stairs | ☐ installing tackless strips and padded cushions | ☐ other: _____] **ensuring all seams are joined evenly for best appearance, maximum wear, and a professional job. Finish with moldings that match client's décor.**

☐ **Accurately cut, trim, apply, and set** [☐ marble tile | ☐ slabs | ☐ other: _____] **to floors, walls, and ceilings ensuring all tiles are laid evenly and polished to a high luster according to specified designs for a uniform appearance.**

☐ **Use** [☐ knee kickers | ☐ carpet shears | ☐ loop pile cutters | ☐ heat irons | ☐ hammers | ☐ staple guns | ☐ carpet knives | ☐ drills | ☐ rubber mallets | ☐ wall trimmers | ☐ power stretchers | ☐ rollers | ☐ trowels | ☐ sanding machines | ☐ machine saw | ☐ power wet saw | ☐ tile cutters | ☐ other: _____] **to install** _____ *[type of]* **floor coverings.**

ACHIEVEMENT SAMPLES: *See "Construction Projects."*

General Contracting

See also "Construction Projects."

☐ **Direct day-to-day operations of this general contracting firm providing a full array of construction services including** [☐ demolition | ☐ floor-to-floor buildouts | ☐ metal stud framing | ☐ bathroom, kitchen, and tile installations | ☐ drywall | ☐ HVAC | ☐ plumbing | ☐ electrical | ☐ acoustical ceilings | ☐ millwork | ☐ masonry | ☐ other: _____] **and other general contracting work to** _____ *[type of]* **clients.**

☐ **Manage and oversee all facets of operations for this general contracting firm with** _____ *[#]* [☐ employees | ☐ clients | ☐ locations] **and annual revenues in excess of $**_____ *[amount].*

☐ **Manage the day-to-day operations of this** _____ *[type of]* **firm including** [☐ client meeting | ☐ needs assessment | ☐ estimating | ☐ proposal development | ☐ bidding | ☐ work orders | ☐ budgeting | ☐ project prioritizing | ☐ timelines | ☐ scheduling | ☐ site inspections | ☐ equipment and supplies purchasing | ☐ sales and marketing | ☐ payroll processing | ☐ company taxes | ☐ preventive maintenance | ☐ trades coordination | ☐ other: _____] **ensuring all projects are completed on time and professionally and job sites are left clean of debris to increase safety and customer satisfaction.**

☐ **Direct all facets of operations including** [☐ sales and marketing | ☐ estimating | ☐ budgeting | ☐ design | ☐ construction | ☐ other: _____] **efforts for this** [☐ commercial and residential | ☐ roofing | ☐ painting | ☐ other: _____] **general contracting firm.**

☐ **Oversee the daily operations of** _____ *[type of]* **job sites including** [☐ reviewing project schedules | ☐ coordinating resources and materials | ☐ managing and scheduling crew | ☐ generating task tools and material lists | ☐ ordering materials | ☐ supervising installations | ☐ collaborating with other trades | ☐ identifying issues | ☐ troubleshooting and resolving problems | ☐ adherence to contract scope, specifications, and code | ☐ managing materials and inventory levels | ☐ facilitating technical and milestone communication | (☐ coordinating / ☐ developing) electrical maintenance programs | ☐ accurately completing all assignment-related paperwork | ☐ other: _____].

☐ **Assess each project's needs, provide clients with proposals and estimates, work out accurate timelines, sub out and supervise construction, set up and coordinate crews for all trades, perform site inspections, and complete all** _____ *[type of]* **customer projects in a timely and efficient manner.**

☐ **Plan, direct, and supervise all** _____ *[type of]* [☐ design | ☐ construction | ☐ fabrication | ☐ installation | ☐ repair | ☐ other: _____] **tasks required for** _____ *[what?].*

☐ **Oversee job site protection and safety during all construction projects by** [☐ protecting all (☐ furniture / ☐ decks / ☐ windows / ☐ driveways / ☐ bushes / ☐ other: _____) | ☐ ensuring no damage to site | ☐ keeping jobs neat and clean of debris on an ongoing basis | ☐ other: _____].

☐ **Effectively negotiate and manage** _____ *[type of]* **contract services and ensure that services are provided by all trades in accordance with contract specifications, codes, and company standards.** *(See also "Contract Negotiations.")*

☐ **Facilitate** _____ *[which trade?]* **management functions including** [☐ reviewing and evaluating specifications | ☐ coordinating bid selections | ☐ estimating project time, materials, and costs | ☐ preparing estimates | ☐ negotiating contracts | ☐ writing purchase requests | ☐ evaluating subcontractor bids | ☐ prioritizing work assignments | ☐ scheduling jobs | ☐ supervising various trades | ☐ setting up projects with materials | ☐ determining safety requirements | ☐ coordinating materials shipping | ☐ purchasing or leasing equipment | ☐ preparing cost estimates | ☐ ensuring safety practices | ☐ maintaining tools and equipment | ☐ ordering equipment | ☐ obtaining required permits | ☐ making on-site visits | ☐ inspecting work for compliance with codes | ☐ training staff | ☐ handling inventory control | ☐ coordinating projects with (☐ engineers / ☐ architects) | ☐ monitoring equipment | ☐ other: _____].

☐ **Perform computer layout and design services using** _____ *[software program]* **to meet** _____ *[type of]* **client needs on** _____ *[kind of]* **projects.**

☐ **Document reports and maintain up-to-date records of** [☐ individual's time | ☐ man hours expended on job orders | ☐ accidents and injuries | ☐ work progress | ☐ other: _____].

☐ **Actively maintain positive customer relationships to ensure satisfaction and service quality on all** [☐ service calls | ☐ projects | ☐ installations | ☐ repairs | ☐ other: _____] **by** [☐ relating to them in a professional and courteous manner | ☐ listening carefully to their concerns | ☐ responding to their questions or complaints | ☐ making satisfactory adjustments | ☐ escalating their requests to _____ *(whom?)* | ☐ other: _____].

☐ **Maintain the upkeep of all** _____ *[type of]* **equipment and tools including** _____, _____, **and** _____ *[equipment].*

ACHIEVEMENT SAMPLES: *See also "Achievement Examples," "Construction Projects," "Increased Sales & Profitability," and all other achievement categories.*

☐ **Working with other subcontractors, built** _____ *[#]* [☐ new homes | ☐ extensions | ☐ finished basements | ☐ attics | ☐ custom-built kitchens | ☐ remodeled bathrooms | ☐ other: _____] **including** _____, _____, **and** _____ *[projects]* **ranging $**_____ **to $**_____ *[amounts].*

☐ **Established a reputation for quality workmanship at competitive prices by** [☐ maintaining superior levels of craftsmanship | ☐ ensuring excellent customer service | ☐ providing after job follow-up | ☐ other: _____].

Glazier Projects & Functions

See also "Carpentry / Construction Work."

☐ [☐ Direct and manage | ☐ Supervise | ☐ Handle] [☐ small to large | ☐ multiple | ☐ complex | ☐ other: _____] _____ *[type of]* [☐ residential | ☐ commercial | ☐ other: _____] **glazing projects, handling the full project scope—from contract award through closeout for this** [☐ commercial glazing company | ☐ contractor | ☐ other: _____].

☐ **Supervise and oversee the work of** _____ *[#]* **commercial glaziers upholding a high quality of work standards and ensuring the completion of successful projects on time and within budget.**

☐ **Lay out, cut, install, and weatherproof** _____ *[type of]* [☐ windows | ☐ glass doors | ☐ tempered glass | ☐ glass panels | ☐ blast resistant windows | ☐ skylights | ☐ doors | ☐ entrance enclosures | ☐ sun rooms | ☐ storefronts | ☐ shower enclosures | ☐ aluminum curtain walls | ☐ backsplashes | ☐ display cases | ☐ table tops | ☐ decorative room dividers | ☐ security windows | ☐ metal framework extrusions | ☐ windshields | ☐ aluminum storefronts | ☐ glass railing systems | ☐ mirrors | ☐ other: _____] **using** [☐ glass cutters | ☐ glazing knives | ☐ power saws | ☐ suction cups | ☐ drills | ☐ grinders | ☐ other: _____] **for various** _____ *[type of]* **projects ranging $**_____ **to $**_____ *[amounts].*

☐ **Coordinate and collaborate with** _____ *[which?]* **trades in the installation of** _____ *[type of]* **glass projects for** [☐ commercial | ☐ residential | ☐ automotive | ☐ other: _____] **clients** [☐ using precision-cutting methods | ☐ cutting glass panes manually | ☐ spreading glazing compound around molding edges | ☐ trimming excess material | ☐ other: _____] **for a perfect fit and polished, professional look.**

☐ **Work closely with** [☐ plastics | ☐ granite | ☐ marble | ☐ steel | ☐ aluminum | ☐ other: _____] **laborers to** [☐ install | ☐ replace] **glass and** [☐ mount sashes | ☐ install frames | ☐ attach locks, hinges, rubber gaskets, and moldings | ☐ other: _____] **resulting in a** [☐ professional look | ☐ unique design | ☐ decorative finish | ☐ other: _____].

☐ **Inspect and monitor work to ensure quality installation, compliance, and customer satisfaction according to** [☐ contractual obligations | ☐ manufacturer's installation instructions | ☐ industry standards | ☐ estimated manhours and benchmarks | ☐ safety program | ☐ other: _____].

☐ **Apply** [☐ working | ☐ proficient] **knowledge and experience in** [☐ the glass industry | ☐ reading and interpreting blueprints and instructions | ☐ calculating figures including area, circumference, and volume | ☐ measuring and cutting glass to size or pattern | ☐ installing frames | ☐ insulating glass | ☐ using (☐ sanding / ☐ beveling / ☐ polishing) machines | ☐ other: _____].

☐ **Communicate with** [☐ customers | ☐ Project Manager | ☐ Superintendent | ☐ Shop Foreman | ☐ Estimator | ☐ Glaziers | ☐ draftsmen | ☐ vendors | ☐ Architects | ☐ General Contractor | ☐ co-workers | ☐ others: _____] **regarding** [☐ project scope and requirements | ☐ setting and managing expectations | ☐ project specifications | ☐ project scheduling | ☐ daily work schedules | ☐ materials lead time | ☐ equipment requirements | ☐ material deliveries | ☐ project progress | ☐ labor coordination with other contractors | ☐ scope changes | ☐ risks and liabilities | ☐ quality | ☐ production | ☐ other: _____] **throughout project stages—taking project from inception through completion.**

☐ **Handle various project-related administrative functions including** [☐ reviewing and verifying project drawings | ☐ interpreting specifications | ☐ securing material quotes | ☐ negotiating vendor pricing | ☐ estimating project costs | ☐ preparing bid proposals | ☐ issuing purchase orders | ☐ determining equipment costs | ☐ reviewing and approving project contracts | ☐ ordering and scheduling materials | ☐ documenting project progress and conditions | ☐ maintaining accurate progress records | ☐ photographing progress and results | ☐ approving invoices for payment | ☐ managing shop drawing process | ☐ closeout processing | ☐ processing change orders | ☐ closeout processing | ☐ records management | ☐ other: _____].

ACHIEVEMENT SAMPLES: *See "Construction Projects."*

Grievance Investigations & Dispute Resolution

See also "Equal Employment Opportunity Compliance," "Union Leadership," and "Union Functions."

☐ **Investigate and resolve** [☐ discrimination complaints | ☐ Equal Employment Opportunity (EEO) matters | ☐ Affirmative Action grievances | ☐ civil rights infractions | ☐ staff disputes | ☐ staff misconduct | ☐ policy infractions | ☐ violations of corporate practices | ☐ other: _____], **perform statistical analyses** [☐ reports of findings | ☐ EEO statistical reports | ☐ other: _____], **and/or negotiate settlements.**

☐ **Advise and counsel** [☐ employees | ☐ labor] **and management to prevent and/or resolve disputes over** [☐ employee | ☐ labor] **relation's issues including** [☐ contractual agreements | ☐ labor agreements | ☐ other: _____] **to avoid costly litigation, strikes, or other disruptions.**

☐ **Coordinate and oversee field investigations that review and evaluate** _____ *[type of]* **activities related to** [☐ department buildings | ☐ equipment operations | ☐ work procedures | ☐ other: _____] **to ensure compliance with all safety practices and standards.**

☐ **Confer with** [☐ employees | ☐ employee representatives | ☐ union representatives | ☐ management | ☐ _____ *(which?)* government agencies | ☐ others: _____] **to resolve** _____ *[type of]* [☐ problems | ☐ grievances | ☐ discipline issues | ☐ other: _____] **and negotiate solutions and/or settlements.**

☐ **Conduct** [☐ confidential fact-finding investigations | ☐ grievance management | ☐ other: _____] **on** _____ *[what matters or issues?]*, **examine corporate practices to determine violations, prepare reports of findings, and provide** [☐ mediation | ☐ guidance | ☐ advice] **as warranted.**

☐ [☐ Research and analyze | ☐ Investigate] **Human Resource** [☐ management | ☐ organization] [☐ problems | ☐ issues | ☐ grievances | ☐ other: _____] **and formulate** _____ *[type of]* [☐ reports | ☐ recommendations | ☐ settlements | ☐ other: _____], **which have produced** _____ *[what results?]*.

☐ **For all complaints and violations that warrant a grievance, attempt to resolve disputes prior to pursuing them under the grievance process by speaking with all involved parties, management, and any witnesses and** _____ *[doing what?]*.

☐ **Process all stages of grievances, arbitrations, and appeals including** [☐ investigations | ☐ witness preparation | ☐ exhibits | ☐ position papers | ☐ filing | ☐ other: _____].

☐ **Investigate and resolve any and all reported violations of the firm's compliance program and work with** _____ *[whom?]* **to handle violations promptly, accurately, and consistently.**

☐ **Thoroughly investigate all problems carefully, calmly resolve disputes, and advise members as to their rights in** _____ *[type of]* **matters to ensure** [☐ members are properly represented | ☐ management gives serious consideration to legitimate complaints | ☐ other: _____].

☐ **Present** _____ *[type of]* [☐ employee | ☐ labor] **grievances to the** [☐ management team | ☐ designated labor relations staff member | ☐ other: _____] **meeting all** [☐ grievance filing | ☐ bargain requests | ☐ Unfair Labor Practice filings | ☐ other: _____] **deadlines.**

☐ **Review all involved** [☐ jobs and classifications | ☐ job descriptions | ☐ work area and equipment | ☐ pay rates and computation methods | ☐ seniority list and names and addresses of all involved | ☐ previous settlement and arbitration history | ☐ past practice information | ☐ government acts and laws | ☐ safety codes | ☐ workers' compensation regulations | ☐ collective agreement | ☐ company rules and policies | ☐ other: _____].

☐ **Arbitrate and decide disputes that bind both** [☐ employees | ☐ labor] **and management to specific terms and conditions of** [☐ employees | ☐ labor] **contracts.**

ACHIEVEMENT SAMPLES:

☐ [☐ Settled | ☐ Closed out] _____ *[#]* **potentially significant lawsuits involving** _____ *[what?]* **and amounting to** $_____ *[amount]* **for under** $_____ *[amount]* [☐ by offering buy-out packages | ☐ through effective attorney negotiations | ☐ other: _____].

☐ **Disengaged teamsters' organization effort of the** _____ *[which?]* [☐ union | ☐ center | ☐ division | ☐ department | ☐ unit | ☐ other: _____] **by** _____ *[doing what?].*

Grounds Maintenance Projects & Functions

See also "Custodian / Janitorial Services."

☐ **Provide** [☐ large-scale] **weekly** [☐ grounds | ☐ landscape] **maintenance services for** _____ *[#]* **properties including** _____ *[which properties?].*

☐ **Provide** [☐ all | ☐ various] **aspects of grounds maintenance services for** _____ *[whom or what?]* **including** [☐ lawn mowing | ☐ leaf removal | ☐ tree trimming | ☐ weed control | ☐ fertilizing | ☐ insect control | ☐ pest elimination | ☐ flower gardening | ☐ shrub pruning | ☐ horticulture | ☐ grading | ☐ seeding | ☐ detaching | ☐ aerating | ☐ planting | ☐ plant damage care | ☐ snow removal | ☐ other: _____].

☐ **Oversee the complete upkeep of the** _____ *[which?]* **grounds to maximize property potential and aesthetics.**

☐ **Maintain** _____ *[what?]* **grounds including all** [☐ mowing | ☐ edging | ☐ trimming | ☐ fertilizing | ☐ gardening | ☐ pruning | ☐ grading | ☐ seeding | ☐ aerating | ☐ planting | ☐ transplanting | ☐ irrigating | ☐ raking | ☐ mulching | ☐ weeding | ☐ painting | ☐ troubleshooting | ☐ other: _____] **services and activities for** _____ *[whom or what?].*

☐ **Handle specialized** [☐ landscaping | ☐ grounds maintenance] **work at this** _____ *[type of]* **firm including** [☐ thatching soil | ☐ planting new grass | ☐ pruning bushes | ☐ mowing lawns | ☐ mulching gardens | ☐ pulling weeds | ☐ raking leaves | ☐ eliminating pests | ☐ watering acreage | ☐ other: _____].

Heavy Equipment Operations

☐ **Coordinate and direct crews in the execution of all** [☐ construction | ☐ road-building | ☐ earth moving | ☐ asphalt batching and paving | ☐ concrete batch plant operations | ☐ concrete paving | ☐ transit mixer operation | ☐ quarrying | ☐ water well | ☐ other: _____] **assignments and operations.**

☐ **Operate and maintain** _____ *[type of]* **heavy construction equipment to** [☐ demolish and rebuild | ☐ build | ☐ construct | ☐ pave] _____ *[type of]* [☐ structures | ☐ foundations | ☐ highways | ☐ roads | ☐ bridges | ☐ buildings | ☐ retaining walls | ☐ outdoor areas | ☐ piers | ☐ streets | ☐ other: _____] **requiring** [☐ rebuilding | ☐ restructuring | ☐ other: _____] **for this** [☐ construction company | ☐ heavy equipment contractor | ☐ public works department | ☐ other: _____].

☐ **As a(n)** [☐ Equipment Operator | ☐ Heavy Equipment Operator | ☐ Operating Engineer | ☐ Back Hoe Operator | ☐ Loader Operator | ☐ Motor Grader Operator | ☐ Track Hoe Operator | ☐ Excavator Operator | ☐ Grader Operator | ☐ other: _____], **safely operate various types of heavy construction equipment including** [☐ bulldozers | ☐ compressors | ☐ crawler tractors | ☐ derricks | ☐ dump trucks | ☐ front-end loaders | ☐ graders | ☐ motor graders | ☐ pile drivers | ☐ power cranes | ☐ pumps | ☐ road graders | ☐ scrapers | ☐ tracked loaders | ☐ trench excavator | ☐ tractors | ☐ truck loaders | ☐ trucks | ☐ other: _____] **to** [☐ excavate, backfill, and grade earth | ☐ compact soil | ☐ grade curves and shoulders | ☐ locate underground services | ☐ erect structures | ☐ pour concrete | ☐ clear brush and tree stumps | ☐ load and move (☐ dirt / ☐ sand / ☐ boulders / ☐ rocks / ☐ coal / ☐ cargo / ☐ refuse) | ☐ other: _____] **to specifications, complying with all safety protocols.**

☐ **Spread, level, and compact** [☐ asphalt | ☐ concrete | ☐ other: _____] **for** [☐ highway construction | ☐ community roads | ☐ parking lots | ☐ driveways | ☐ other: _____] **using** [☐ asphalt spreaders | ☐ concrete paving machines | ☐ tamping equipment | ☐ other: _____].

☐ **Conduct preoperational checks on** _____ *[type of]* [☐ mobile | ☐ stationary] [☐ equipment | ☐ machinery] **prior to use and clean and lubricate equipment and maintain** _____ *[type of]* [☐ records | ☐ reports].

☐ **Apply** [☐ hands-on | ☐ working | ☐ proficient] **knowledge of** _____ *[type of]* [☐ equipment | ☐ machines | ☐ controls | ☐ attachments | ☐ materials | ☐ methods | ☐ tools | ☐ other: _____] **involved in the** [☐ demolition | ☐ construction | ☐ repair | ☐ other: _____] **of** [☐ buildings | ☐ houses | ☐ structures | ☐ other: _____].

☐ **Apply** [☐ basic | ☐ in-depth] **knowledge of** [☐ soil composition and conformation | ☐ terrain features | ☐ equipment attachments | ☐ other: _____] **to determine proper approaches and attachments according to surface and subsurface conditions.**

☐ **Handle various labor functions to prepare for** _____ *[type of]* [☐ building | ☐ demolition | ☐ excavation | ☐ heavy construction | ☐ highway | ☐ other: _____] **projects including** [☐ reviewing plans and specifications | ☐ cleaning and preparing sites | ☐ clearing up debris | ☐ erecting scaffolding | ☐ digging trenches | ☐ setting up braces | ☐ removing hazardous materials | ☐ eliminating obstacles and hazards | ☐ loading and unloading building materials and machinery | ☐ positioning and dismantling concrete forms | ☐ positioning and aligning structural components | ☐ digging trenches | ☐ leveling and compacting earth to grade specifications | ☐ signaling equipment operators | ☐ other: _____].

☐ **Operate heavy dredging equipment to** [☐ reclaim earth fill | ☐ determine excavation depth | ☐ excavate waterways | ☐ remove sand, rock, and gravel | ☐ deepen waterways | ☐ other: _____] **from** [☐ harbors | ☐ lakes | ☐ rivers | ☐ streams] **to** [☐ restore wetlands | ☐ reclaim land | (☐ create / ☐ maintain) beaches | ☐ other: _____].

☐ **Deploy and operate heavy equipment including** [☐ boom trucks | ☐ boom / digger trucks | ☐ cranes | ☐ bucket trucks | ☐ 5th wheel tractors | ☐ 2-ton line trucks | ☐ other: _____] **for work on** [☐ high-voltage transmissions | ☐ low-voltage lighting systems | ☐ distribution powerlines | ☐ other: _____] **for** [☐ highways and streets | ☐ traffic signal systems | ☐ airport runways | ☐ taxiways | ☐ athletic field lighting | ☐ conducting energy between generating stations, substations, and consumers | ☐ other: _____].

Highway & Bridge Maintenance

See also "Highway & Bridge Maintenance Management."

☐ **Work on a wide range of highway projects including** [☐ picking up roadside litter | ☐ repairing ditches and other drainage structures | ☐ repairing highway signs | ☐ cleaning roadway signs and markers | ☐ acting as flag person | ☐ closing lanes | ☐ sealing road patches and cracks | ☐ removing undergrowth from highway rights of ways | ☐ working on traffic control using traffic cones and flares | ☐ sweeping, shoveling, and raking asphalt | ☐ plowing snow | ☐ hauling garbage | ☐ other: _____].

☐ **Certified on** _____ *[what?]*, **operate highway maintenance equipment and machinery including** _____ *[which machinery?]* **for** _____ *[purpose]*.

☐ **Haul, dump, and/or spread** [☐ sand | ☐ salt | ☐ gravel | ☐ asphalt | ☐ clay | ☐ chlorides | ☐ other: _____] **to** [☐ abate ice | ☐ fill washouts | ☐ repair road shoulders | ☐ repair joints | ☐ patch broken pavement | ☐ other: _____].

☐ [☐ Maintain | ☐ Improve | ☐ Construct | ☐ Repair | ☐ Clean | ☐ other: _____] [☐ highways | ☐ roadways | ☐ right-of-ways | ☐ bridges | ☐ other: _____] **including** [☐ cutting brush and grass | ☐ excavating and grading ditches | ☐ digging channels | ☐ applying chemicals to vegetation | ☐ performing traffic control | ☐ patching and sealing pavement | ☐ handling drainage work | ☐ hauling trash | ☐ performing emergency response | ☐ conducting snow and ice control | ☐ assisting stranded motorists | ☐ inspecting and repairing drainage systems | ☐ making minor equipment repairs | ☐ loading and unloading freight | ☐ emptying litter barrels | ☐ controlling graffiti | ☐ other: _____].

☐ **Help maintain the integrity of state highways by performing various roadway, roadside, and structural maintenance activities including** _____, _____, **and** _____ *[what functions?]*.

☐ **Under the direction of the** [☐ Zone Manager | ☐ Project Manager | ☐ other: _____], **manage and direct a team of** _____ *[#]* **bridge crew members in their bridge maintenance and repair functions.**

☐ **Stripe roadways throughout the** _____ *[state, county, township, or region]* **operating center, edge-line, and automatic-skip-line controls and ensuring correct longitude and transverse pavement markings are first measured and tested in order to provide proper traffic control and safety.**

☐ **Erect, install, or/or repair** [☐ guardrails | ☐ road shoulders | ☐ highway lighting | ☐ highway markers | ☐ warning signals | ☐ berms | ☐ other: _____] **using** _____ *[type of hand and power tools]*.

☐ [☐ Install and repair | ☐ Supervise the installation and repair of] **highway and roadway** [☐ signs | ☐ fences | ☐ guardrails | ☐ drainage structures | ☐ other: _____].

☐ **Remove debris and litter from** [☐ paved surfaces | ☐ roadways | ☐ catch basins | ☐ drain structures | ☐ rock and mud slides | ☐ culverts | ☐ drop inlets | ☐ ditches | ☐ other: _____].

☐ **Conduct physically demanding labor in the areas of** [☐ cleaning and reshaping ditches | ☐ erecting signs | ☐ performing landscaping activities | ☐ other: _____].

☐ **Respond to 24/7 emergency callouts within** [☐ 30 minutes | ☐ one hour | ☐ other: _____] **to perform emergency clean-up of** [☐ snow and ice removal | ☐ downed trees | ☐ storm debris clean-up | ☐ other: _____].

☐ **Perform snow and ice clearance using** [☐ single-blade | ☐ wing] **plows and applying** [☐ chlorides | ☐ salt | ☐ other: _____] **in** _____ *[what areas?]*.

ACHIEVEMENT SAMPLES: *See "Highway & Bridge Maintenance Management" and "Construction Projects."*

Highway & Bridge Maintenance Management

See also "Highway & Bridge Maintenance."

☐ **Plan, direct, and supervise** [☐ a crew of _____ *(#)* | ☐ multiple crews] **engaged in** [☐ new | ☐ reconstruction] **highway work including** [☐ clearing | ☐ filling | ☐ grading | ☐ laying | ☐ other: _____] **of new surfaces**.

☐ **Manage and oversee various highway maintenance activities including** [☐ traffic control | ☐ highway inspection and repair | ☐ preventative maintenance | ☐ herbicide and pesticide application | ☐ roadway right of way maintenance during emergencies | ☐ excessive foliage removal in right-of-way areas | ☐ following up on road complaints | ☐ other: _____] **for the** _____ *[state]* **Department of Transportation (DOT)**.

☐ **Supervise a crew of** _____ *(#)* **in** **bridge maintenance work including the** [☐ repair | ☐ construction] **of** _____ *[type of]* **bridge-building structures and** [☐ bridge opening machinery | ☐ engine generator sets | ☐ routine maintenance | ☐ other: _____] **to ensure efficient and dependable bridge operations including all electrical and mechanical systems**.

☐ **Supervise inspections and repairs on damaged bridge** [☐ components | ☐ guardrails | ☐ pavement | ☐ barrier walls | ☐ overpass structures | ☐ drainage structures | ☐ signs | ☐ delineators | ☐ lighting | ☐ fencing | ☐ other: _____].

☐ **Supervise maintenance crew work including** [☐ flagging motorists | ☐ diverting traffic around work areas | ☐ removing debris and litter from roadways | ☐ controlling snow and ice | ☐ spreading (☐ sand / ☐ salt / ☐ gravel) | ☐ erecting guardrails | ☐ installing sign and warning signals | repairing highway lighting | ☐ mowing grass | ☐ operating heavy machinery | ☐ driving trucks to transport crews and equipment to work sites | ☐ preventive maintenance of heavy equipment | ☐ other: _____] **and other physical maintenance work**.

☐ **Oversee** [☐ bridge and work zone inspections | ☐ repair functions | ☐ bridge cleaning | ☐ traffic control functions | ☐ preventive maintenance and repairs | ☐ concrete repairs | ☐ vegetative activities | ☐ debris cleaning around structures | ☐ snow removal | ☐ other: _____] **to ensure bridge safety, proper traffic control, and compliance with all safety and environmental regulations as well as** [☐ proper methods | ☐ quality control | ☐ timely project completion | ☐ other: _____].

☐ **Supervise a** [☐ district-wide | ☐ maintenance patrol | ☐ other: _____] [☐ highway | ☐ bridge | ☐ other: _____] **maintenance crew of** _____ *[#]* **in their performance of** _____, _____, **and** _____ *[what functions?]*.

☐ **Supervise and oversee** [☐ pavement care | ☐ roadside shoulder restoration and repairs | ☐ equipment deliveries | ☐ snow removal operations | ☐ other: _____] **ensuring environmental compliance in all areas**.

☐ **Maintain** [☐ local | ☐ interstate | ☐ country | ☐ township] **highways and adjacent right-of-way properties including** [☐ roadways | ☐ municipal roads | ☐ rural roads | ☐ airport runways | ☐ other: _____] **through** [☐ road repair | ☐ brush removal | ☐ tree trimming and pruning | ☐ litter removal | ☐ snow and ice containment | ☐ fence and guard rail repair | ☐ other: _____].

☐ **Work closely with the** [☐ Department of Transportation (DOT) | ☐ State Police | ☐ Traffic Management Center | ☐ government officials | ☐ private entities | ☐ the public | ☐ others: _____] **in the areas of** _____, _____, **and** _____ *[which areas?]* **to minimize traffic flow interruptions and ensure public safety is maintained**.

☐ **Oversee the** _____ *[which?]* **maintenance section to provide for safe driving thoroughfare within** _____ *[what?]* **area(s) covering** _____ *[#]* **miles of highways and roadways by ensuring the maintenance of all roads, structures, and rights-of-way**.

☐ **Ensure all incident responses to highway emergencies are handled timely and professionally**.

☐ **Inspect** [☐ construction | ☐ maintenance | ☐ repair] **of** _____ *[type of]* [☐ highway | ☐ bridge | ☐ other: _____] **projects to determine and order the materials and equipment needed for** _____ *[what?]* **in order to maximize production and ensure highest standards of performance**.

☐ **Supervise and coordinate maintenance crew activities in the installation and repair of** [☐ traffic signals | ☐ signs | ☐ traffic islands | ☐ barriers | ☐ other: _____].

ACHIEVEMENT SAMPLES: *See also "Construction Projects."*

☐ **Facilitated restoration and repair of** _____ *[which?]* **roadway surfaces which helped maintain the integrity of state** [☐ highways | ☐ bridges | ☐ other: _____]. **Performed roadway, roadside, and structural maintenance activities keeping** [☐ pavement surfaces | ☐ shoulders | ☐ clear zones | ☐ roadways | ☐ other: _____] **in good repair**.

☐ **As part of the** _____ *[which?]* **Committee, evaluated the** *Safety and Accident Prevention Program* **and recommended** _____ *[what?]*, **which helped improve the state's DOTs safety rating from** _____ *[previous rating]* **to** _____ *[current rating]* **by** _____ *[doing what?]* **and reduced risk in the area(s) of** _____ *[which area(s)?]*.

☐ **By promoting and practicing a culture of safety**, [(☐ reduced / ☐ eliminated) accidents and injuries | ☐ other achievements: _____].

☐ **Recipient of** [☐ "Highway Safety" | ☐ "Snow Fighter" | ☐ other: "_____"] **Award** _____ *[#]* **consecutive years for** [☐ having no accidents | ☐ reducing company liability | ☐ work at Ground Zero | ☐ other: _____].

☐ **Often requested by** _____ *[whom?]* **to** _____ *[perform what?]* **due to** [☐ my safety precautions | ☐ diligent highway work oversight | ☐ other: _____].

☐ **Received** [☐ excellent | ☐ above average] **performance evaluations for** [☐ safety measures | ☐ damage control methods | ☐ machinery knowledge | ☐ diligence in completing _____ *(what?)* | ☐ other achievements: _____].

Human Resources

☐ **Oversee personnel management functions including** [☐ new hire selections | ☐ training and development | ☐ performance ratings | ☐ commendatory and disciplinary actions | ☐ promotions | ☐ demotions | ☐ transfers | ☐ terminations | ☐ other: _____] **to** [☐ optimize staffing needs | ☐ maintain work force productivity | ☐ ensure quality workmanship ☐ other: _____].

☐ **Manage and oversee** [☐ human resource | ☐ equal employment opportunity | ☐ affirmative action | ☐ health benefits | ☐ other: _____] **policies, procedures, services, and activities for this** _____ *[type of]* **firm with** _____ *[#]* **employees**.

☐ **Direct and oversee the firm's** [☐ recruitment | ☐ training | ☐ affirmative action | ☐ career development | ☐ compensation | ☐ salary administration | ☐ employee benefits | ☐ other: _____] **activities including establishment and maintenance of** [☐ employee records and systems | ☐ employee incentive programs | ☐ department safety program | ☐ retirement program | ☐ employee rating system | ☐ retirement program | ☐ insurance benefits | ☐ Social Security | ☐ other: _____].

☐ **Manage the firm's Human Resources functions including establishing, administering, and maintaining** [☐ personnel | ☐ insurance benefits | ☐ Social Security | ☐ retirement | ☐ employee rating system | ☐ other: _____] **records and advising and assisting department managers in personnel matters.**

☐ **Develop, administer, and update the firm's Human Resource** [☐ policies and procedures | ☐ objectives | ☐ short- and long-range planning | ☐ other: _____] **as well as HR projects and programs.**

☐ [☐ Plan and develop | ☐ Coordinate and implement | ☐ Administer] **all day-to-day human resource activities including** [☐ equal employment opportunity | ☐ affirmative action | ☐ civil rights | ☐ outreach | ☐ health benefits | ☐ salary administration | ☐ training and development | ☐ other: _____] **services and activities for this** _____ *[type of]* **firm with** _____ *[#]* **employees.**

☐ **Oversee the update and maintenance of the firm's** [☐ automated | ☐ manual] [☐ personnel | ☐ compensation | ☐ safety | ☐ benefits | ☐ Workers' Compensation | ☐ OSHA | ☐ other: _____] **records for** _____ *[#]* **employees including employee** [☐ job titles | ☐ earnings | ☐ tax withholding | ☐ benefits | ☐ plan change requests | ☐ promotions | ☐ absences | ☐ vacations | ☐ performance evaluations | ☐ awards and commendations | ☐ other: _____].

☐ **Manage and administer all facets of the firm's Human Resource services and support activities including** [☐ recruiting services | ☐ HR policies and procedures | ☐ salary administration | ☐ benefits programs | ☐ change management | ☐ strategy implementation | ☐ management consulting | ☐ training and development | ☐ staff services | ☐ other: _____].

☐ **Provide human resource services in various areas including** [☐ outreach | ☐ interviewing | ☐ applicant selection | ☐ recruitment | ☐ civil rights | ☐ affirmative action | ☐ job classifications | ☐ performance evaluations | ☐ test preparation | ☐ other: _____].

☐ **Facilitate various Human Resource functions including** [☐ preparation of vacancy announcements | ☐ distribution of job postings | ☐ applicant screening and interviewing | ☐ selecting and hiring employees | ☐ delegating and overseeing jobs | ☐ appraising performance | ☐ authorizing vacation and sick leave | ☐ updating personnel records | ☐ rewarding and disciplining employees | ☐ resolving staff problems | ☐ other: _____] **to ensure staffing needs and maintain workforce productivity.**

☐ **Coordinate, organize, and schedule** [☐ job classification studies | ☐ pay and benefit surveys | ☐ classified ads | ☐ applicant screening and testing | ☐ new employee paperwork processing | ☐ compensation | ☐ 401k plan administration | ☐ the firm's Health and Safety Program | ☐ drug tests | ☐ physical examinations | ☐ orientation sessions | ☐ other: _____].

☐ **Maintain all employee records with** [☐ dates of hire | ☐ compensation | ☐ benefits | ☐ leave records | ☐ other: _____] **and other pertinent personnel data, and prepare and file employer reports to** [☐ government agencies | ☐ insurance companies | ☐ union | ☐ other: _____].

☐ **Plan, organize, and conduct** _____ *[type of]* **job** [☐ analysis | ☐ classification] **studies and** [☐ evaluate jobs using _____ *(what?)* methodology | ☐ recommend position classifications | ☐ create job descriptions and salary grades | ☐ other: _____].

ACHIEVEMENT SAMPLES:

☐ **Championed** [☐ organizational change programs | ☐ company-wide change initiatives | ☐ training and development projects | ☐ human resource initiatives | ☐ other: _____] **that involved** [☐ strategic planning | ☐ organizational (☐ analysis / ☐ diagnoses / ☐ planning / ☐ problem-solving) | ☐ management coaching | ☐ team building | ☐ other: _____], **and designed and implemented associated training programs that met operating goals and objectives.**

☐ **Spearheaded the firm's centralized Human Resource** _____ *[type of]* [☐ system | ☐ polices |☐ procedures | ☐ standards | ☐ program | ☐ guidelines | ☐ methods | ☐ initiatives | ☐ other: _____], **which involved** _____ *[what actions?]* **and resulted in** _____ *[what benefits?].*

☐ **Formulated and established the firm's Human Resources** [☐ policies and procedures | ☐ goals and objectives | ☐ strategies and plans | ☐ standards and processes | ☐ systems and guidelines | ☐ other: _____] **ensuring the highest standard of accuracy and efficiency.**

☐ **Designed** _____ *[type of]* **HR procedures that required** [☐ performing research | ☐ facilitating investigations | ☐ gathering information | ☐ conducting data analysis | ☐ analyzing job data | ☐ determining examination plans | ☐ developing examinations | ☐ ensuring content validity of exams | ☐ developing reports exams | ☐ other: _____] **and resulted in** _____ *[what benefits?].*

☐ [☐ Co-developed | ☐ Designed and implemented] **the firm's** [☐ Human Resource Policies and Procedures | ☐ Employee Handbook | ☐ Retirement Program | ☐ Training and Development initiatives | ☐ recruitment procedures | ☐ employee relations policy administration | ☐ other: _____], **providing consistency of Human Resource policies, procedures, and practices.**

☐ **Reduced Unemployment Insurance by** _____ *[doing what?]* **producing a** _____% *[percentage]* **savings in** [☐ the first year | ☐ other time period: _____].

☐ [☐ Bid | ☐ Rebid | ☐ Outsourced] **the firm's** [☐ payroll services | ☐ employee benefits programs | ☐ other: _____] **including** [☐ medical | ☐ dental | ☐ life insurance | ☐ short-term disability | ☐ long-term disability | ☐ workers compensation | ☐ other: _____] **services resulting in** [☐ an annual savings of $_____ *(amount)* | ☐ a reduction of _____% *(percentage)* | ☐ other: _____].

☐ **Updated the firm's** [☐ personnel | ☐ compensation | ☐ safety | ☐ benefits | ☐ Workers' Compensation | ☐ other: _____] **records for** _____ *[#]* **employees including** [☐ employee information | ☐ job titles | ☐ earnings | ☐ tax withholdings | ☐ health insurance benefits | ☐ life insurance coverage | ☐ benefits plan change requests | ☐ promotions | ☐ absences | ☐ vacations | ☐ performance evaluations | ☐ employee awards and commendations | ☐ management reports | ☐ other: _____].

HVAC / HVAC-R Scope

See also other "HVAC/HVAC-R" categories, as applicable.

☐ **Conduct** [☐ journey- | ☐ apprentice- | ☐ masters- | ☐ other: _____] **level** [☐ installation | ☐ maintenance | ☐ servicing |☐ repair] of HVAC systems for this $_____ *[revenues]* _____ *[type of]* **firm that services** _____ *[type of]* **clientele.**

☐ **Install, repair, and service** [☐ heating and air conditioning systems | ☐ industrial and commercial refrigerant systems | ☐ other: _____] **to ensure control of temperature, humidity, and air quality in** _____ *[type of]* **buildings for this** [☐ HVAC firm | ☐ contracting company | ☐ manufacturer | ☐ wholesaler | ☐ school district | ☐ other: _____].

☐ **Service and repair climate-control equipment in** [☐ residential homes | ☐ office buildings | ☐ stores | ☐ malls | ☐ schools | ☐ hospitals | ☐ restaurants | ☐ factories | ☐ other: _____].

☐ **Handle air conditioning installations and repair for** [☐ commercial | ☐ industrial | ☐ residential] **customers including** [☐ rooftop installations | ☐ attic duct work | ☐ condenser connections | ☐ charging systems with Freon | ☐ other: _____] **for this** $_____ *[revenues]* _____ *[type of]* **firm.**

☐ [☐ Conduct | ☐ Supervise] **all** [☐ HVAC | ☐ HVAC-R | ☐ mechanical systems | ☐ other: _____] **related activities including** [☐ preventive maintenance | ☐ heating and cooling equipment inspections | ☐ duct airflow readings | ☐ HVAC systems balancing | ☐ fuel system components maintenance | ☐ building and automation systems monitoring | ☐ production and injection systems repair | ☐ water treatment tests | ☐ firing and fuel ratio controls upkeep | ☐ other: _____].

☐ **Troubleshoot, diagnose, repair, and/or adjust** [☐ oil burner | ☐ gas burner | ☐ hot water | ☐ refrigeration | ☐ other: _____] **systems to ensure they are operating efficiently by checking and testing** [☐ thermostats | ☐ blowers | ☐ burners | ☐ nozzles | ☐ controls | ☐ other: _____], **and other components.**

☐ **Install, service, replace, and/or repair** [☐ air conditioning units | ☐ HVAC control systems | ☐ air conditioning compressors | ☐ chillers | ☐ air distribution equipment | ☐ variable speed equipment | ☐ air handlers | ☐ forced air systems | ☐ furnaces | ☐ boilers | ☐ water heaters | ☐ heat pumps | ☐ split systems | ☐ rooftop units | ☐ electrical circuits | ☐ air movement equipment | ☐ electric motors | ☐ evaporative coolers | ☐ cooling towers | ☐ fire control systems | ☐ exhaust systems | ☐ pneumatic controls | ☐ air filters | ☐ pumps | ☐ duct work | ☐ grills | ☐ piping | ☐ blowers | ☐ shafts | ☐ bearings | ☐ coils | ☐ dampers | ☐ diffusers | ☐ package units | ☐ other: _____] **of various makes and models including** [☐ American Standard | ☐ Bryant | ☐ Carrier | ☐ Coleman | ☐ Frigidaire | ☐ Honeywell | ☐ Johnson Controls | ☐ Liebert | _____ | ☐ Lennox | ☐ Luxaire | ☐ Maytag | ☐ McQuay |

☐ Rheem | ☐ Ruud | ☐ Seibe | ☐ Siemens | ☐ Tappan | ☐ Thermo King | ☐ Toshiba | ☐ Trane | ☐ Westinghouse | ☐ York | ☐ others: _____] **consisting of** [☐ one to five | ☐ 5 to 20 | ☐ 20 to 50 | ☐ other: _____] **tons.**

☐ **Handle approximately** _____ *[#]* **HVAC jobs** [☐ weekly | ☐ monthly | ☐ annually] [☐ averaging $_____ to $_____ | ☐ totaling $_____] **including** [☐ estimating job times and costs | ☐ selecting materials | ☐ preparing materials estimates | ☐ reviewing bids | ☐ ordering job-related materials | ☐ scheduling jobs | ☐ performing HVAC functions | ☐ inspecting completed jobs | ☐ other: _____].

☐ **Working as apprentice with** [☐ owner of (☐ small / ☐ large) proprietorship | ☐ Plumbing Foreman | ☐ other: _____], **acquired skills necessary to perform** [☐ oil burner | ☐ gas burner | ☐ air conditioning refrigeration | ☐ other: _____] [☐ installation | ☐ servicing] **within** _____ *[timeframe].*

☐ **Install, service, and repair** [☐ industrial | ☐ commercial] **refrigeration systems and equipment including** [☐ motors | ☐ condensing units | ☐ compressors | ☐ evaporators | ☐ piping | ☐ other: _____] **following** [☐ design specifications | ☐ blueprints | ☐ manufacturers' instructions | ☐ other: _____].

ACHIEVEMENT SAMPLES: *See "HVAC / HVAC-R Projects & Functions" and "Construction Projects."*

HVAC / HVAC-R Installations

See also other "HVAC/HVAC-R" categories, as applicable.

☐ **Install and service** [☐ HVAC | ☐ HVAC-R control | ☐ central air conditioning | (☐ gas / ☐ electric / ☐ solid fuel) heating systems | ☐ solar panels | ☐ commercial refrigerant | ☐ pneumatic HVAC control | ☐ digital HVAC | ☐ natural gas and water piping | ☐ production and injection | ☐ pneumatic piping | ☐ water supply | ☐ air distribution and balance | ☐ auxiliary control | ☐ forced air | ☐ other: _____] **systems for** _____ *[what?]* **in accordance with blueprint specifications.**

☐ **Handle air conditioning installations and repair for** [☐ commercial | ☐ industrial | ☐ residential] **customers including** [☐ rooftop installations | ☐ attic duct work | ☐ connecting condensers | ☐ charging systems with Freon | ☐ other: _____], **testing all units for proper installation and operation.**

☐ [☐ Coordinate HVAC jobs with | ☐ Perform the functions of] [☐ Sheet Metal Workers | ☐ Electricians | ☐ Plumbers | ☐ Pipe Fitters | ☐ Pipe Layers | ☐ Steamfitters | ☐ Boilermakers | ☐ other: _____] **in the installation and servicing of** _____ *[type of]* [☐ cooling | ☐ heating | ☐ other: _____] **systems including** _____ *[what functions?].*

☐ **Oversee the installation and replacement of heating and cooling systems including** [☐ air conditioning units | ☐ HVAC control systems | ☐ air conditioning compressors | ☐ chillers | ☐ air distribution equipment | ☐ variable speed equipment | ☐ air handlers | ☐ forced air systems | ☐ furnaces | ☐ boilers | ☐ water heaters | ☐ heat pumps | ☐ split systems | ☐ rooftop units | ☐ electrical circuits | ☐ air movement equipment | ☐ electric motors | ☐ evaporative coolers | ☐ cooling towers | ☐ fire control systems | ☐ exhaust systems | ☐ pneumatic controls | ☐ air filters | ☐ pumps | ☐ duct work | ☐ grills | ☐ piping | ☐ blowers | ☐ shafts | ☐ bearings | ☐ coils | ☐ dampers | ☐ diffusers | ☐ package units | ☐ other: _____] **of various makes and models.**

☐ **Facilitate the installation and servicing of** [☐ central air-conditioning systems | ☐ fuel and water supply lines | ☐ air ducts | ☐ vents | ☐ pumps | ☐ fuel lines | ☐ water supply lines | ☐ air compressors | ☐ steam boilers | ☐ pump seals, bearings, and couplings | ☐ solar panels | ☐ other: _____], **connect wiring and controls to** [☐ ductwork | ☐ refrigerant lines | ☐ electrical wiring | ☐ other: _____]; **charge systems with refrigerant;, and test for proper operation.**

ACHIEVEMENT SAMPLES: *See "HVAC/HVAC-R Projects & Functions" and "Construction Projects."*

HVAC / HVAC-R Maintenance & Repair Work

See also "Maintenance & Repair Projects," "Equipment, Tools & Testing Devices – HVAC / HVAC-R," and other HVAC categories.

☐ **Diagnose, repair, and test the performance of** [☐ mechanical | ☐ electrical] **components throughout HVAC systems, including** [☐ motors | ☐ compressors | ☐ condensing units | ☐ evaporators | ☐ piping | ☐ metal and fiberglass ducts | ☐ pumps | ☐ fans | ☐ thermostats | ☐ other: _____] **and other components.**

☐ **Working as apprentice with** [☐ owner of small proprietorship | ☐ Plumbing Foreman | ☐ other: _____], **acquired skills to perform** [☐ oil burner | ☐ gas burner | ☐ air conditioning | ☐ other: _____] **servicing within** _____ *[#]* **months.**

☐ **Repair and service** [☐ heating and air conditioning systems | ☐ industrial and commercial refrigerant systems | ☐ other: _____] **to ensure control of temperature, humidity, and air quality in** [☐ residential | ☐ commercial | ☐ industrial | ☐ manufacturing | ☐ other: _____] **buildings for this** [☐ HVAC firm | ☐ contracting company | ☐ manufacturer | ☐ wholesaler | ☐ school district | ☐ other: _____].

☐ **Monitor and maintain** [☐ firing and fuel ratio controls | ☐ fuel system components | ☐ heat exchangers and sand traps | ☐ heat exchange equipment | ☐ feed and return water pumps | ☐ other: _____].

☐ **Service and repair climate-control equipment in** [☐ residential homes | ☐ office buildings | ☐ stores | ☐ schools | ☐ hospitals | ☐ restaurants | ☐ factories | ☐ other: _____].

☐ **Identify and correct** _____ *[type of]* **problems of** _____ *[type of]* **systems through the use of** _____ *[what methods, tools, or equipment?].*

☐ **Troubleshoot, dismantle, optimize, and repair** [☐ heating | ☐ cooling | ☐ ventilating | ☐ refrigeration | ☐ other: _____] **systems including** [☐ oil burners | ☐ gas boilers | ☐ electric boilers | ☐ water heaters | ☐ steam lines | ☐ heat return lines | ☐ main water lines | ☐ roof drains | ☐ electromechanical equipment | ☐ chillers | ☐ vacuum pumps | ☐ water pumps | ☐ air compressors | ☐ fans | ☐ other: _____] **to ensure they are operating efficiently by checking and testing** [☐ thermostats | ☐ blowers | ☐ burners | ☐ nozzles | ☐ controls | ☐ other: _____] **and other components.**

☐ **Perform cooling system maintenance and repair including** [☐ replacing burned out motors | ☐ cleaning blower cages | ☐ other: _____].

☐ **Complete inspection and maintenance work by** [☐ overhauling compressors | ☐ replacing filters and ducts | ☐ other: _____] **to ensure its efficient** [☐ HVAC | ☐ HVAC-R] **operation.**

☐ **Successfully complete all** _____ *[type of]* **HVAC repair work orders consisting of** _____ *[type of]* **work** [☐ ahead of schedule | ☐ within required timeframes] **by** _____ *[doing what well?].*

☐ **Maintain plant's heating system boilers including cleaning** [☐ heads | ☐ flame sensor | ☐ igniter | ☐ other: _____] **and repair as needed all** [☐ leaks | ☐ broken pipes | ☐ other: _____], **maintaining accurate records of all** [☐ labor hours | ☐ materials used | ☐ other: _____].

☐ **Diagnose, service, and adjust oil burner systems to ensure they are operating efficiently by checking and testing** [☐ thermostats | ☐ blowers | ☐ burners | ☐ nozzles | ☐ controls | ☐ other: _____], **and other components.**

☐ **Prevent the release of chlorofluorocarbon and hydro chlorofluorocarbon refrigerants in air-conditioning and refrigeration systems from entering the ozone layer by** [☐ ensuring there are no system leaks | ☐ venting refrigerant into cylinders | ☐ other manner: _____].

☐ **Apply an expert working knowledge of** [☐ electrical | ☐ electronic | ☐ mechanical] [☐ heating | ☐ ventilation | ☐ air conditioning | ☐ refrigeration] [☐ theory | ☐ methods | ☐ practices | ☐ other: _____] **in the** [☐ troubleshooting and repair of electrical control systems | ☐ design of (☐ centrifugal / ☐ reciprocal) compressors | ☐ operation of pneumatic control systems | ☐ maintenance of steam condensate return traps, pumps, and compressors | ☐ other: _____] **to operate, maintain, and repair HVAC systems.**

☐ **Maintain and repair all kitchen appliances including** [☐ gas and electric stoves and ovens | ☐ refrigerators | ☐ freezers | ☐ dishwashers | ☐ garbage disposals | ☐ microwaves | ☐ steam cookers | ☐ sinks | ☐ faucets | ☐ valves | ☐ other: _____].

☐ **Complete inspection and maintenance work by** [☐ overhauling compressors | ☐ replacing filters and ducts | ☐ other: _____] **to ensure its efficient** [☐ HVAC | ☐ HVAC-R] **operation.**

ACHIEVEMENT SAMPLES: *See "HVAC/HVAC-R Projects & Functions" and "Construction Projects."*

HVAC / HVAC-R Management

See also "HVAC / HVAC-R Work," "Plumbing Management Scope," "Trades/Crew Supervision – All Trades," "Inspections & Compliance – Trades," "Contractor/Subcontractor Influence & Collaboration," "Work Collaboration," and other HVAC categories.

☐ **Manage and lead the installation and servicing of** [☐ heating and air conditioning systems | ☐ refrigeration systems | ☐ industrial and commercial refrigerant systems | ☐ fuel supply lines | ☐ water supply and drain lines | ☐ steam lines | ☐ water heaters | (☐ gas / ☐ electric / ☐ open flame) boilers | ☐ pipes, faucets, and valves | ☐ specialty items | ☐ other: _____] **and test units to ensure proper control of temperature, humidity, and air quality in** [☐ residential | ☐ commercial | ☐ industrial | ☐ other: _____] **buildings.**

☐ **Provide a full array of** [☐ plumbing | ☐ HVAC | ☐ refrigeration | ☐ steamfitting | ☐ welding | ☐ carpentry | ☐ other: _____] **services including** [(☐ plumbing / ☐ electrical / ☐ general contracting) work | (☐ bathroom / ☐ kitchen / ☐ tile) installations | ☐ other: _____] **for this** [☐ HVAC | ☐ general contracting | ☐ construction | ☐ other: _____] **firm.**

☐ **Oversee and supervise air conditioning installations and repair for** [☐ commercial | ☐ industrial | ☐ residential] **customers including** _____ *[what functions?]* **for this $**_____ *[revenues]* _____ *[type of]* **firm.**

☐ **Direct day-to-day operations of this** [☐ HVAC | ☐ plumbing | ☐ general contracting | ☐ construction | ☐ other: _____] **firm providing a full array of** [☐ HVAC | ☐ plumbing | ☐ steamfitting | ☐ carpentry | ☐ other: _____] **services including** [☐ bathroom and kitchen installation | ☐ plumbing, electrical, and general contracting work | ☐ other: _____].

☐ **Supervise and perform the installation, maintenance, repair, and/or replacement of all required HVAC** [☐ equipment | ☐ systems | ☐ pipes | ☐ fixtures | ☐ valves | ☐ pumps | ☐ other: _____] **to** [☐ set up | ☐ operate | ☐ maintain] **the**

[□ water distribution | □ heating and cooling | □ other: _____] **system(s) and related equipment of** _____ *[what?]*.

☐ **Lead and direct approximately** _____ *[#]* **HVAC jobs** [□ weekly | □ monthly | □ annually] [□ averaging $_____ to $_____ *(amounts)* | □ totaling $_____ *(amount)*] **including** [□ estimating job times and costs | □ selecting materials | □ preparing materials estimates | □ reviewing bids | □ ordering required job-related materials | □ scheduling jobs | □ performing HVAC functions | □ inspecting completed jobs | □ other: _____].

☐ **Supervise all** [□ HVAC | □ HVAC-R | □ mechanical systems | □ other: _____] **related activities including** [□ preventive maintenance | □ heating and cooling equipment inspections | □ duct airflow readings | □ HVAC systems balancing | □ fuel system components maintenance | □ building and automation systems monitoring | □ production and injection systems repair | □ water treatment tests | □ firing and fuel ratio controls upkeep | □ other: _____].

☐ **Supervise and oversee** _____ *[#]* **HVAC Technicians in the service and repair of climate-control equipment in** [□ residential homes | □ office buildings | □ stores | □ schools | □ hospitals | □ restaurants | □ factories | □ hotels □ other: _____].

☐ **Provide leadership and direction to** _____ *[#]* **HVAC Technicians in the installation and maintenance of** [□ central air conditioning systems | □ fuel and water supply lines | □ gas | □ oil | □ electric | (□ solid-fuel / □ multiple-fuel) heating | □ other: _____]; **and test units for proper installation and operation ensuring compliance with** [□ blueprints | □ specifications].

☐ **Supervise** [□ journey- | □ apprentice- | □ masters-] **level** [□ installation | □ maintenance | □ servicing | □ repair] **of HVAC systems for this** $_____ *[revenues]* _____ *[type of]* **firm that services** _____ *[type of]* **clientele**.

☐ **Direct the HVAC** [□ installation | □ replacement | □ maintenance | □ repair | □ administrative | □ other: _____] **operations including all aspects of plumbing required in** [□ new construction | □ remodel | □ maintenance | □ repair | □ other: _____] **jobs for this** $_____ *[revenues]* _____ *[type of]* **firm**.

☐ **Supervise HVAC** [□ installation | □ replacement | □ repair | □ other: _____] **functions including all aspects of plumbing required in** [□ new construction | □ remodel | □ maintenance | □ other: _____] **jobs on** _____ *[type of]* **projects**.

☐ [□ **Lead and direct**] [□ **Supervise and perform**] **the installation, maintenance, repair, and/or replacement of all required HVAC** [□ equipment | □ systems | □ pipes | □ fixtures | □ valves | □ pumps | □ other: _____] **to** [□ set up | □ operate | □ maintain] **the** [□ water distribution | □ heating and cooling | □ other: _____] **system(s) and related equipment of** _____ *[what?]*.

☐ **Oversee the installation, maintenance, and servicing of** [□ heating and air conditioning systems | □ industrial and commercial refrigerant systems | □ other: _____] **to ensure control of temperature, humidity, and air quality in** [□ residential | □ commercial | □ industrial | □ manufacturing | □ other: _____] **buildings for this** _____ *[type of]* **firm**.

☐ **Review and evaluate HVAC** [□ plans | □ specifications | □ drawings] **and other** [□ blueprints | □ diagrams | □ schematics | □ specifications] **to** [□ determine compatibility and adaptability with existing systems | □ ensure compliance with all codes | □ advise (□ Project Engineer / □ HVAC Foreman / □ Lead Plumber / □ other: _____) on code requirements | □ other: _____]; **and modify blueprints to meet as-built specifications and dimensions**.

ACHIEVEMENT SAMPLES: *See "HVAC/HVAC-R Projects & Functions" and "Construction Projects."*

HVAC / HVAC-R Monitoring & Testing

See "Inspections & Compliance – HVAC / HVAC-R" and "Equipment, Tools & Testing Devices – HVAC/HVAC-R."

HVAC / HVAC-R Projects & Functions, Other

See "Maintenance & Repair Projects" as well as other HVAC / HVAC-R categories.

☐ **Specializing in the** [□ installation | □ maintenance | □ service | □ repair] **of** [□ heating | □ cooling | □ refrigeration | □ other: _____] **equipment, perform** _____, _____, **and** _____ *[which?]* **functions required for** _____ *[what?]*.

☐ [□ **On call 24 hours a day, seven days a week** | □ _____ *(#)* **days a week**] **to respond to customer emergency callbacks within a** _____ *[#]*-**mile radius and** _____ *[#]*-**hour turnaround**.

☐ **Prepare for all HVAC jobs by** [□ prioritizing work assignments | □ ordering required materials | □ determining equipment needed | □ setting up each project with the correct tools, materials, and supplies | □ coordinating contracting vendors/trades | □ determining conditions and safety requirements | □ identifying required repairs and/or replacements | □ other: _____].

☐ **Apply** [□ expert | □ proficient | □ basic] **working knowledge of** [□ electrical | □ electronic | □ mechanical] [□ heating | □ ventilation | □ air conditioning | □ refrigeration] [□ theory | □ methods | □ practices | □ other: _____] **in the** [□ troubleshooting and repair of electrical control systems | □ design of (□ centrifugal / □ reciprocal) compressors | □ operation of pneumatic control systems | □ maintenance of steam condensate return traps, pumps, and compressors | □ other: _____] **to install, maintain, and repair HVAC systems**.

☐ **Handle various HVAC-related plumbing functions including** [☐ cutting and threading pipe | ☐ soldering copper | ☐ installing PVC pipe | ☐ other: _____] **for** [☐ compressed air | ☐ potable water | ☐ cooling water | ☐ other: _____] **maintaining proper operation of all equipment.**

☐ **Interpret and update** [☐ blueprints | ☐ architectural drawings | ☐ plans | ☐ specifications | ☐ other: _____] **to reflect required changes made to HVAC systems.**

☐ **Connect refrigeration equipment to** [☐ refrigerant lines | ☐ ductwork | ☐ electrical power source | ☐ other: _____], **charge with refrigerant, test systems, and program controls.**

☐ **Prevent release of chlorofluorocarbon and hydro chlorofluorocarbon refrigerants in** [☐ air conditioning | ☐ refrigeration] **systems from depleting the ozone layer and protect against ultraviolet radiation by** [☐ ensuring there are no system leaks | ☐ using care to recover and conserve refrigerants | ☐ venting refrigerant into cylinders | ☐ recycling it for reuse | ☐ other methods: _____].

☐ **Coordinate all aspects of HVAC projects with** [☐ clients | ☐ engineers | ☐ architects | ☐ municipal officials | ☐ county officials | ☐ code officers | ☐ others: _____] **ensuring compliance with all** [☐ plumbing codes | ☐ quality standards | ☐ work schedules | ☐ other: _____].

☐ **Perform a number of additional HVAC activities including** [☐ inspecting heating and cooling equipment | ☐ conducting water treatment tests | ☐ operating high-pressure steam boilers | ☐ replacing filters and ducts | ☐ testing and maintaining generators | ☐ troubleshooting chiller operations | ☐ running wire and installing outlet boxes | ☐ checking fans, piping, gauges, and indicator lights | ☐ welding and repairing brazing pipes | ☐ diagnosing and repairing heating and hot water problems | ☐ overhauling compressors | ☐ operating microprocessor fan controls | ☐ performing attic duct work | ☐ charging refrigerant systems with Freon | ☐ performing roof-top installations | ☐ programming energy management equipment | ☐ analyzing water treatment and adjusting chemicals for chill water and heating systems | ☐ monitoring building and automation systems for HVAC and fire hazards | ☐ other: _____].

ACHIEVEMENT SAMPLES:

☐ **Significantly increased production and efficiency** _____% *[percentage]* **by renovating a** _____ *[#]*-**foot-long** _____ *[type of]* **furnace with new** [☐ control room | ☐ structural work | ☐ refractory | ☐ burners | ☐ blowers | ☐ ductwork | ☐ gas trains | ☐ other: _____].

☐ **Installed** _____ *[type of]* [☐ HVAC | ☐ HVAC-R] **systems including** _____, _____, **and** _____ *[which systems?]* **to provide** [☐ gas heaters for freeze protection | ☐ fresh-air supply for control rooms | ☐ furnace waste heat for pipe drying | ☐ infrared tube heaters for curing rooms | ☐ other: _____].

Increased Account Base

See also "Increased Sales" and "Increased Revenue & Profitability."

ACHIEVEMENT SAMPLES:

☐ **Elevated** [☐ customer base | ☐ new business | ☐ referrals] **by** _____ *[#]* / _____% *[percentage]* **over previous year(s) by** [☐ developing (☐ dynamic presentations / ☐ unique concepts / ☐ innovative ideas) | ☐ providing clients with superior service and opportunities | ☐ developing a strong rapport with satisfied clients | ☐ concentrating on higher-end sales | ☐ increasing loyalty of existing customer base | ☐ gaining increased referrals | ☐ problem-solving customer problems | ☐ other means: _____].

☐ **Successfully persuaded new clients to make an investment in the future by** [☐ selling high-end projects | ☐ presenting value proposition | ☐ demonstrating the return on their investment | ☐ educating consumers on _____ *(what?)* | ☐ other: _____].

☐ **Expanded firm's account base by** [☐ delivering (☐ fresh / ☐ unique) design concepts | ☐ finding new talent to help develop those concepts | ☐ creating innovative client proposals | ☐ developing dynamic presentation layouts | ☐ increasing loyalty of existing client base | ☐ problem-solving customer challenges | ☐ other methods: _____]

☐ **Brought in multiple, high-volume** _____ *[type of]* **clients generating $**_____ **in new business by** _____ *[how you accomplished this].*

☐ **Instrumental in reviving** _____ *[what account?]* **via** [☐ strong customer rapport | ☐ follow-up techniques | ☐ diligent service | ☐ other: _____].

☐ **Procured the nation's** _____ *[#]* **largest** _____ *[type of]* **company as a client via** [☐ thorough research | ☐ professional persistence | ☐ dedication to my goal | ☐ persuasive marketing materials | ☐ convincing phone campaign | ☐ other: _____] **resulting in increased annual income of** _____% *[percentage]* / $_____ *[amount].*

☐ **Through** [☐ client trust | ☐ relationship building | ☐ other method: _____] [☐ received many referrals | ☐ maintained loyal, enduring customer relationships | ☐ increased account base | ☐ other benefit: _____].

☐ **Increased profitability of account base from** _____% **to** _____% *[percentages]* **by** _____ *[what methods?].*

☐ **Configured, proposed, and closed sale of** _____ *[what?]* **for** _____ *[what or whom?]*, **resulting in $**_____ **in increased sales.**

☐ **Increased account base** _____ *[#]* / _____ **%** *[percentage]*—**from** _____ *[#]* **to** _____ *[#]* **accounts—by** [☐ concentrating on higher-end sales | ☐ increasing loyalty of existing client base | ☐ obtaining repeat customers | ☐ problem-solving customer challenges | ☐ other: _____].

☐ **Successfully solicit and obtain new business through** [☐ networking with _____ *(whom?)* | ☐ client referrals | ☐ advertising in _____ *(what publication?)* | ☐ canvassing | ☐ other means: _____].

☐ **Created large-dollar projects bringing return on investment for clients and higher sales for firm, resulting in** [☐ higher per-project sales | ☐ repeat business | ☐ referrals | ☐ other: _____].

☐ **Through** [☐ client trust | ☐ relationship building | ☐ creative initiatives | ☐ other method: _____] [☐ received many referrals | ☐ maintained loyal, enduring customer relationships | ☐ increased profitability of account base by _____% | ☐ other benefit: _____].

☐ **Increased existing business by** [☐ assessing and servicing client needs | ☐ working within their budgets | ☐ meeting all deadlines | ☐ other methods: _____].

☐ **Brought in multiple, high-volume** _____ *[type of]* **clients generating $**_____ *[amount]* **in new business by** _____ *[how you accomplished this].*

☐ **Generated annual sales of $**_____ **through** [☐ attractive visual presentations | ☐ attaining referrals through word of mouth from satisfied clients | ☐ other: _____].

Increased Customer Service Levels

See *"Customer Service & Satisfaction Levels Improvement."*

Increased Market Share

ACHIEVEMENT SAMPLES:

☐ **Drove market share** _____ **%** *[percentage]* / **$**_____ *[amount]* **in** _____ *[what area?]* **by** [☐ performing feasibility studies | ☐ researching and analyzing historic activities | ☐ determining new markets in the _____ *[which?]* region | ☐ adding new _____ *[type of]* (☐ products / ☐ services) | ☐ creating a _____ *[type of]* program designed to _____ *(do what?)* | ☐ promoting (☐ coordinating products / ☐ add-on sales) | ☐ brainstorming with long-time (☐ employees / ☐ customers / ☐ distributors) | ☐ strategizing successful marketing plans | ☐ structuring profitable but user-friendly pricing | ☐ other: _____].

☐ **Grew a previously untapped** _____ *[type of]* **market in the** _____ *[what?]* **area, increasing sales of** _____ *[what items?]* **by $**_____ **annually.**

☐ **Increased market share** _____ **%** *[percentage]* / **$**_____ *[amount]* **in the** _____ *[which?]* **market, bringing annual sales to $**_____ **by** [☐ recruiting a talented staff | ☐ providing training | ☐ other: _____], **allowing company to be more service-oriented.**

☐ **Prospected and developed untouched new territory including** _____, _____, **and** _____ [☐ Fortune (☐ 100 / ☐ 500 / ☐ 1000) | ☐ other: _____] **companies by** [☐ setting up trade shows | ☐ hiring and training a winning sales management staff | ☐ other: _____].

☐ **Elevated market share by converting numerous competitive accounts via** [☐ buy-backs | ☐ sell-downs | ☐ other: _____], **developing a strong pattern of repeat sales and customers though** [☐ loyal customer service | ☐ persistent follow-up | ☐ other: _____].

☐ **Positioned firm as a market leader in** _____ *[what?]* **to the** _____ *[which?]* **market by** _____ *[doing what?]*, **which derived** _____ *[what benefits?].*

☐ **Successfully** [☐ managed | ☐ fulfilled] **mission to develop Company into a major full-service** _____ *[type of]* [☐ wholesaler | ☐ distributor | ☐ retailer | ☐ manufacturer | ☐ other: _____] **by penetrating the** _____ *[which?]* **marketplace.**

☐ **Prospected and developed untouched new territory including** _____, _____, **and** _____ [☐ Fortune (☐ 100 / ☐ 500) companies] **by** [☐ setting up trade shows | ☐ hiring and training a winning creative staff | ☐ other: _____].

☐ **Increased sales of products and services to the** _____ *[which?]* **market while positioning firm as a market leader in** _____ *[what discipline?].*

☐ [☐ Researched and studied _____ (what?) | ☐ Visited various _____ (what?)] **in major markets throughout the** [☐ **U.S.** | ☐ **region** | ☐ **district** | ☐ **other:** _____] **to** [☐ **gain new product development ideas** | ☐ **participate in international trade shows** | ☐ **other:** _____] **promoting company's** _____ [type of] **products to** _____ [which?] **consumers**.

☐ **Positioned firm as number** _____ [#] **in the** _____ [which?] **industry through successful** [☐ **corporate communications** | ☐ **promotional** | ☐ **brand management** | ☐ **media relations** | ☐ **sales support** | ☐ **public relations** | ☐ **other:** _____] **strategies.**

☐ **Spearheaded company's entrance into the** _____ [type of] **market environment through successful development of** _____ [what methods?].

☐ **By creating a** _____ [type of] **program that enabled** _____ [what?], **increased annual sales in the** _____ [which?] **marketplace by** _____% (from $_____ to $_____ [amounts]) **and profits from $_____ to $_____** [amounts].

☐ **Increased annual sales in the** _____ **marketplace by** _____% [from $_____ to $_____] [percentages] **and profits from $_____ to $_____** [amounts] **by creating a** _____ [type of] **program that enabled** _____ [what benefits?].

☐ **Rapidly established company's national presence in the** _____ [which?] **marketplace by** _____ [achievements that promoted presence].

☐ **Secured preferred-provider arrangements with** _____, _____, **and** _____ [companies], **allowing company to become the recognized leader in the sales of** _____ [type of] **products**.

Increased Revenue & Profitability

See also "Cost Reductions & Savings."

ACHIEVEMENT SAMPLES:

☐ **Drove profitability $_____** [amount] **/ _____%** [percentage] **by** [☐ analyzing and costing proposals | ☐ determining profitability ratios | ☐ working with more creditworthy clientele | ☐ analyzing and troubleshooting customer complaints | ☐ resolving problems quickly | ☐ providing product ability analyses | ☐ acquiring a niche market for _____ (type of) | ☐ other methods: _____].

☐ **Drove revenues _____%** [percentage] [☐ **annually**] **through the acquisition of a** [☐ contract from _____ (where?) | ☐ foreclosed development and turning it into a profitable venture in less than _____ (timeframe) | ☐ other: _____].

☐ **Raised overall business from $_____ to $_____** [amounts] **in revenue in a** _____ [#]**-year period by implementing a** _____ [type of] **program involving** [☐ all aspects of quality production | ☐ other: _____].

☐ **Increased profits $_____** [amount] **and improved customer service _____%** [percentage] **by effectively** [☐ leading continuous improvement | ☐ planning production activities | ☐ establishing production priorities | ☐ managing cost performance | ☐ forecasting demand / soliciting and welcoming customer feedback | ☐ building a positive production team environment | ☐ meeting commitments | ☐ shortening life cycles | ☐ integrating leaner business processes | ☐ forecasting budgets | ☐ executing distribution | ☐ improving customer satisfaction | ☐ meeting operation targets | ☐ minimizing risk and errors | ☐ improving product quality | ☐ meeting daily productivity and quality requirements | ☐ maintaining profit loss control | ☐ other: _____].

☐ **Planned, developed, and implemented resource-generating strategies that resulted in identifying and securing** _____ [type of] [☐ **revenue sources** | ☐ **funding in the amount of $_____**] **from** _____ [whom?] **for the firm, which resulted in** [☐ **building** | ☐ **developing** | ☐ **other:** _____] _____ [what?].

☐ **Drove** _____ [type of] **profit improvement activities by** _____ [doing what?], **which resulted in** _____ [benefits].

☐ **Designed and implemented** _____ [type of] **solutions that effectively addressed and adhered to** _____ [type of] **requirements in the area(s) of** _____ [area(s)] [☐ **in accordance with all project timelines and budget** | ☐ **ensuring quality project standards** | ☐ **ensuring a smooth transition** | ☐ **other:** _____].

☐ **Maximized return on investment by purchasing** _____ [type of] [☐ **computers** | ☐ **programs** | ☐ **materials** | ☐ **other:** _____] **to produce** _____ [what?] **more effectively and in less time**.

☐ **Steadily increased revenues annually by** [☐ developing strong networking contacts in the community | ☐ advertising in local print media | ☐ networking at local Chambers of Commerce | ☐ providing discounts on customer referrals | ☐ other: _____].

☐ **Build revenue by** [☐ increasing sales and profits $_____ (amount) | ☐ controlling expenses | ☐ ensuring a consistent, quality experience for customers | ☐ other: _____].

☐ **Elevated profitability $_____** [amount] **and reduced labor costs by $_____** [amount] **by purchasing** _____ [type of] **state-of-the-art** [☐ equipment | ☐ tools | ☐ materials | ☐ other: _____].

☐ **Recruited as right hand to** _____ [title] **to save a once-profitable company from a then-floundering situation** [☐ $_____ (amount) **loss on** $_____ (amount) **in sales**] **through effective** [☐ strategic and tactical efforts | ☐ other: _____] **resulting in its turnaround to** $_____ [amount] **profit on** $_____ [amount] **sales.**

Increased Sales – Construction

See also "Increased Account Base" and "Cost Reductions & Savings."

ACHIEVEMENT SAMPLES:

☐ **Established a reputation for quality workmanship at competitive prices by** [☐ maintaining superior levels of craftsmanship | ☐ providing excellent customer service | ☐ meeting or exceeding customer needs, challenges, and demands | ☐ other: _____] **which resulted in** _____ [what measurable benefits?].

☐ **Eliminated potential liability for client and increased contract amount by** $_____ [amount] **by recommending** _____ [what?] **which resulted in** _____ [what client and firm benefits?].

☐ **Increased sales** $_____ [amount] **by working with a network of** _____ [which?] **trade professionals to increase exposure throughout the** _____ [which?] **industry and keeping informed of current and future** _____ [type of] **projects resulting in** _____ [what benefits?].

☐ **Spearheaded the** _____ [type of] **initiative to** _____ [do what?] **which realized increased** [☐ sales | ☐ profits | ☐ corporate gains | ☐ market share | ☐ other: _____] **of** $_____ [amount] **/** _____ % [percentage] **in** _____ [what areas?].

☐ **Elevated** [☐ annual] **sales** $_____ [amount] **/** _____ % [percentage] **in** _____ [timeframe] **by** [☐ designing and implementing successful _____ (type of) promotions | ☐ selling trust | ☐ educating consumers | ☐ changing management culture | ☐ creating a marketing portfolio containing photographs and letters of recommendation from previous clients | ☐ obtaining many repeat clients | ☐ elevating referral business by developing a strong rapport with satisfied clients | ☐ ensuring persistent follow-up | ☐ providing loyal customer service | ☐ promoting coordinating services ☐ presenting creative presentations | ☐ attending trade shows | ☐ networking | ☐ promoting a consumer-sensitive approach | ☐ promoting add-on | ☐ other method(s): _____].

☐ **Catapulted sales** $_____ [amount] **by** _____ [doing what?] **which received** [☐ significant business for the firm | ☐ rave reviews from clients | ☐ other: _____] **and resulted in** _____ [what?].

☐ **Brought company from an original staff of** _____ [#] **to a staff of** _____ [#], **with sales increases of** $_____ (amount) **after** _____ [timeframe]. **Accomplished through** [☐ increased marketing | ☐ added services | ☐ increased sales coverage | ☐ providing ancillary support departments with a turnkey approach | ☐ other: _____].

☐ **Contributed to the firm's increased sales and growth in the area(s) of** _____ [what areas?] **by successfully** _____ [doing what?].

☐ **Elevated sales with a** _____ [#]**-year compounded annual growth of** _____ % [percentage] **and net income with a** _____ [#]**-year compounded annual growth of** _____ % [percentage] **through effective use of** _____ [methods].

☐ **Increased sales** $_____ [amount] **by working with a network of** _____ [which?] **trade professionals to increase exposure throughout the** _____ [which?] **industry and keeping informed of current and future** _____ [type of] **projects resulting in** _____ [what benefits?].

☐ **Eliminated potential liability for client and increased contract amount by** $_____ [amount] **by recommending** _____ [what?] **which resulted in** _____ [what client and firm benefits?].

☐ **Elevated sales with a** _____ [#]**-year compounded annual growth of** _____ % [percentage] **and net income with a** _____ [#]**-year compounded annual growth of** _____ % [percentage] **through effective use of** _____ [methods].

Information Technology – Equipment & Software Acquisition

See also "Cost Reductions & Savings – Technology Upgrades" and "Purchasing."

☐ **Direct the** [☐ acquisition | ☐ allocation | ☐ other: _____] **of** _____ [type of] [☐ equipment | ☐ services | ☐ support | ☐ other: _____] **including** _____ , _____ , **and** _____ [what?].

☐ **Order and distribute all** _____ [type of] [☐ hardware | ☐ software | ☐ equipment] **including** _____ , _____ , **and** _____ [which products?] **for** [☐ the firm | ☐ clients].

☐ **Purchase, load, and install** _____ [type of] [☐ software packages | ☐ peripheral components] **for the firm's** _____ [type of] **computers including** [☐ operating systems | ☐ word processing | ☐ spreadsheet programs | ☐ other: _____] **onto workstation PCs.**

☐ **Select and purchase compatible** _____ *[type of]* [☐ software | ☐ hardware | ☐ peripherals] **for** _____ *[what purpose?]* **ensuring ongoing price and service comparisons.**

☐ **Approve pricing of equipment components to ensure** [☐ best quality | ☐ pricing | ☐ delivery schedules | ☐ other: _____], **and ensure timely delivery of all** [☐ supplies | ☐ merchandise | ☐ materials | ☐ computer equipment | ☐ phone systems | ☐ office machinery | ☐ other: _____].

☐ **Serve as liaison with vendors handling** [☐ purchasing | ☐ merchandise buying | ☐ customer service | ☐ delivery troubleshooting | ☐ other: _____].

☐ **Conduct** [☐ vendor bids | ☐ comparative cost analyses | ☐ other: _____], **and make sound selections based on** [☐ product quality | ☐ vendor reliability | ☐ ability to meet required deadlines | ☐ other: _____] **for** _____ *[what?]*.

☐ **Perform hardware and software purchasing management including** [☐ creating purchase orders | ☐ negotiating pricing | ☐ placing blanket orders | ☐ expediting open orders | ☐ handing high-volume buying | ☐ ensuring follow-up | ☐ troubleshooting delivery problems | ☐ maintaining up-to-date client and vendor records | ☐ preparing weekly inventory reports | ☐ other: _____].

☐ **Ensure up-to-date client and vendor records using** _____ *[type of program]*.

☐ **Purchase, inspect, and store** _____ *[type of]* [☐ product | ☐ merchandise | ☐ supplies | ☐ materials | ☐ other: _____] **and ensure proper storage and disposal of** [☐ chemical waste | ☐ hazardous materials | ☐ other: _____].

☐ **Purchase** _____ *[type of]* [☐ equipment | ☐ products | ☐ supplies | ☐ other: _____] **from** _____ *[where purchased]*, **and ensure successful delivery.**

☐ **Act as liaison with** [☐ system | ☐ software] **developers to gain a full understanding of the** [☐ operating system | ☐ applications] **for which documentation is to be prepared.**

☐ **Continually research** _____ *[type of]* [☐ hardware | ☐ software | ☐ other: _____] **upgrades to provide state-of-the-art** _____ *[type of]* **tools needed for** _____ *[what?]* **so the** [☐ agency | ☐ firm | ☐ other: _____] **stays on the cutting edge of technology to meet** [☐ client | ☐ user | ☐ staff | ☐ other: _____] _____ *[type of]* **needs.**

☐ **Keep abreast of all technical updates and enhancements affecting the system and applications, update** [☐ training | ☐ technical] **manuals accordingly, and disseminate to staff in the form of effective** _____ *[type of]* **training workshops.**

ACHIEVEMENT SAMPLES: *See also Achievements under other **"Information Technology"** categories.*

☐ **Wrote** [☐ support documentation for computer requisitions | ☐ recommendations for (☐ hardware / ☐ software) purchases | ☐ other: _____], **translating end user needs into system requirements, saving firm $**_____ *[amount]* **by linking together multiple areas with similar needs and resulting in** _____ *[what benefits?]*.

☐ **Researched and evaluated computer hardware and software requirements against current productivity levels, and made recommendations for** _____ *[type of]* [☐ hardware | ☐ software] **upgrading which saved $**_____ *[amount]* **annually and** _____ *[did what?]*.

Information Technology – Equipment & Software Installation & Configuration

*See also **"Information Technology – Testing & Troubleshooting."***

☐ **Configure, implement, debug, and support** _____ *[type of]* [☐ hardware components | ☐ computer systems | ☐ peripheral | ☐ applications | ☐ system updates and enhancements | ☐ software upgrades and fixes | ☐ peripheral components] **including** [☐ servers | ☐ CPUs | ☐ desktops | ☐ laptops | ☐ handheld devices | ☐ virus protection software | ☐ back-up software | ☐ monitors | ☐ motherboards | ☐ RAM | ☐ keyboards | ☐ printers | ☐ disk drives | ☐ CD and DVD readers and writers | ☐ other: _____] [☐ at user workstations | ☐ on clients' premises | ☐ other: _____].

☐ **Install, configure, test, troubleshoot, and maintain** _____ *[type of]* [☐ hardware | ☐ software] **products including** _____ , _____ , **and** _____ *[what?]*.

☐ **Set up and support** _____ *[type of]* [☐ computer systems | ☐ applications] **including** [☐ system updates and enhancements | ☐ software upgrades and fixes | ☐ virus protection software | ☐ back-up software | ☐ other: _____], **configuring software to individual systems.**

☐ **Analyze, plan, design, and/or install new personal computer systems, and upgrade existing** _____ *[type of]* [☐ hardware | ☐ software] **for** _____ *[what?]*.

☐ **Provide** [☐ expertise | ☐ guidance | ☐ support] **in** [☐ installing | ☐ configuring | ☐ troubleshooting | ☐ upgrading] [☐ personal computer | ☐ network] **hardware and software as well as** [☐ file server | ☐ cabling | ☐ network operating systems | ☐ other: _____] **in a** [☐ PC | ☐ Windows | ☐ Macintosh | ☐ LAN | ☐ WAN | ☐ other: _____] **environment.**

☐ **Coordinate** [☐ hardware | ☐ software] **updates from vendors, monitoring all** [☐ maintenance agreements | ☐ warranties | ☐ site licenses | ☐ other: _____].

☐ **Implement and support** _____ *[type of]* [☐ computer systems | ☐ applications] **including** [☐ system updates and enhancements | ☐ software upgrades and fixes | ☐ virus protection software | ☐ back-up software | ☐ other: _____], **configuring software to individual systems.**

☐ **Supervise the troubleshooting, isolation, and analysis of network problems to** [☐ maintain service levels | ☐ ensure timely recovery of services when experiencing downtime | ☐ other: _____].

☐ **Perform** [☐ installation | ☐ configuration | ☐ integration] **of** [☐ system fixes | ☐ software updates | ☐ multiple generations of Microsoft Windows | ☐ custom applications | ☐ other: _____].

☐ **Monitor** [☐ problem | ☐ change | ☐ other: _____] **activities and coordinate** [☐ staff | ☐ client | ☐ vendor] **involvement to ensure effective implementation of** [☐ new | ☐ enhanced] **systems and resolution of user problems.**

☐ **Provide** [☐ expertise | ☐ guidance | ☐ support] **in** [☐ installing | ☐ configuring | ☐ troubleshooting | ☐ upgrading] **hardware and software as well as** [☐ file server | ☐ cabling | ☐ network operating systems | ☐ other: _____] **in a** [☐ Windows | ☐ Macintosh | ☐ other: _____] **environment.**

☐ **Reporting to** [☐ Help Desk Manager | ☐ Technical Support Officer | ☐ PC Support Manager | ☐ LAN/WAN Manager | ☐ Customer Service Administrator | ☐ other: _____], *[analyze / plan / design / install]* **new personal computer systems and upgrade existing** [☐ hardware | ☐ software].

☐ **Set up, test, and operationally sustain** _____ *[type of]* [computer systems / applications] **including** [☐ diagnosing | ☐ repairing | ☐ replacing | ☐ decommissioning | ☐ other: _____] _____ *[what?]*.

☐ **Set up, configure, debug, and support** _____ *[type of]* [hardware / peripheral] **components including** [☐ CPUs | ☐ PC desktops | ☐ laptops | ☐ handheld devices | ☐ servers | ☐ monitors | ☐ motherboards | ☐ RAM | ☐ keyboards | ☐ printers | ☐ disk drives | ☐ CD and DVD readers and writers | ☐ other: _____] [☐ at user workstations | ☐ on clients' premises | ☐ other: _____].

Inspections & Compliance – General

See also "Inspections & Compliance" in other areas.

☐ **Make periodic visits during the** _____ *[type of]* [☐ construction | ☐ installation | ☐ repair | ☐ other: _____] **process to monitor compliance with codes, specifications, and regulations including** [☐ initial inspections before foundation is poured | ☐ completed foundations | ☐ first phase of construction | ☐ follow-up inspections during the construction phase | ☐ final comprehensive inspection upon project completion | ☐ other: _____] **conducting** _____ *[what?]* **during closeout processing.**

☐ **Provide guidance on applicable** _____ *[type of]* **codes and requirements to** [☐ architects | ☐ engineers | ☐ contractors | ☐ developers | ☐ owners | ☐ governmental officials | ☐ the general public | ☐ other: _____] **and other interested parties.**

☐ **Perform** _____ *[type of]* **inspection functions including** [☐ inspecting approved plans and specifications | ☐ testing (☐ new installations / ☐ alternations) of _____ *(what?)* | ☐ interpreting laws, regulations, and codes to particular situations | ☐ writing code violation notices | ☐ gathering code violation evidence | ☐ testifying at hearings | ☐ preparing reports | ☐ determining work priorities of lower-level Inspectors | ☐ performing accident investigations | ☐ evaluating complaints | ☐ other: _____].

☐ **Conduct various** _____ *[type of]* **inspection functions to ensure compliance in all areas including** [☐ reviewing plans to verify code requirements | ☐ identifying construction problems or design errors | ☐ quality testing construction materials | ☐ conducting energy audits | ☐ issuing stop-work orders | ☐ notifying contractors of defective work | ☐ recommending corrective action | ☐ resolving construction personnel disputes | ☐ conducting preventive maintenance | ☐ negotiating plan changes with architects | ☐ holding meetings to discuss project progress | ☐ maintaining work logs and reports | ☐ other: _____].

☐ **Monitor** _____ *[type of]* **the** [☐ construction | ☐ installation | ☐ repair | ☐ other: _____] **progress through on-site field inspections and review to ensure conformance to** [☐ design specifications | ☐ cost estimates | ☐ time schedules | ☐ other: _____] **and to** [☐ quality test materials | ☐ identify problems | ☐ recommend corrective actions | ☐ other: _____] **and immediately** [☐ resolve | ☐ refer] **any problems.**

☐ **Investigate and resolve any and all reported violations of the firm's compliance program and work with** _____ *[whom?]* **to handle violations promptly, accurately, and consistently.**

☐ **Assist** [☐ Plan Examiner | ☐ Foreman | ☐ Project Superintendent | ☐ Building Inspector | ☐ other: _____] **in conducting** _____ *[type of]* **site inspections to determine** [☐ building code and life-safety compliance | ☐ handicap accessibility | ☐ conformance with plans, specifications and state laws | ☐ compliance with all r codes and regulations | ☐ other: _____].

☐ [☐ Prepare and submit | ☐ Review and approve] _____ *[type of]* **records and reports including** _____ *[type of]* [☐ plans | ☐ plan review documentation | ☐ inspection reports | ☐ permit forms | ☐ permits | ☐ other: _____].

☐ **Perform** [☐ initial | ☐ incremental | ☐ follow-up | ☐ final | ☐ periodic] **worksite inspections of the** [☐ construction | ☐ installation | ☐ remodeling | ☐ repair | ☐ maintenance | ☐ other: _____ **of** [☐ commercial | ☐ residential | ☐ civil | ☐ other: _____] _____ *[type of]* [☐ structures | ☐ buildings | ☐ projects] **through each phase of construction to ensure code and contract compliance.**

☐ **Interact and communicate with** [☐ inspectors | ☐ contractors | ☐ plumbers | ☐ electricians | ☐ HVAC contractors | ☐ owner representatives | ☐ architects | ☐ engineers | ☐ governmental officials | ☐ the general public | ☐ other: _____] **to discuss** _____ *[which?]* **code requirements.**

☐ **Perform final project inspections of all completed work during the construction close-out process, approve payment requests, conduct building site inspections, and** _____ *[other?]* **to ensure compliance with plans, specifications, and building codes.**

☐ **Check** [☐ plans | ☐ specifications | ☐ other: _____] **for compliance with** [☐ Building Code | ☐ other: _____] **and approve and issue consents on** _____ *[what?].*

☐ **Track and monitor** _____ *[type of]* [☐ job | ☐ installation | ☐ construction | ☐ project | ☐ design-and-build | ☐ other: _____] **progress by conducting on-site inspections to ensure conformance to** [☐ design specifications | ☐ cost estimates | ☐ contracts | ☐ building codes | ☐ zoning regulations | ☐ time schedules | ☐ electrical codes | ☐ plumbing codes | ☐ other: _____] **and** [☐ resolve | ☐ refer] **any problems.**

☐ **Ensure quality compliance with all** [☐ engineering contracts | ☐ state and local regulations | ☐ electrical codes | ☐ building codes | ☐ zoning laws | ☐ fire regulations | ☐ plumbing codes | ☐ life-safety codes | other: _____] **and other ordinances.**

☐ **Inspect and monitor** [☐ new construction | ☐ installations | ☐ alternations | ☐ other: _____] **of** _____ *[type of]* [☐ private | ☐ public | ☐ other: _____] **construction sites to ensure adherence to and enforce all safety standards, building codes, and specifications.**

☐ **Perform compliance-related activities including building** [☐ inspections | ☐ consents | ☐ investigations | ☐ issues | ☐ resolutions | ☐ compliance schedules | ☐ other: _____] **that comply with all statutory obligations.**

☐ **Research, evaluate, and resolve** [☐ complex | ☐ sensitive] **customer** [☐ service issues | ☐ complaints] **as they relate to** [☐ commercial buildings | ☐ residential homes | ☐ building construction and code compliance | ☐ other: _____].

☐ **Track and monitor** _____ *[type of]* **compliance actions through** _____ *[type of]* **inspections, and review to ensure conformance to** _____ *[which?]* **regulations.**

Inspections & Compliance – Buildings & Structures

See also "Inspections & Compliance – General" and "Inspections & Compliance – Facilities & Plants."

☐ **Inspect** [☐ new | ☐ existing] [☐ commercial | ☐ residential] **buildings including** _____ *[type of projects]* **during various stages of** [☐ construction | ☐ remodeling | ☐ repair] **recommend modifications, and enforce compliance with all applicable codes, ordinances, and regulations.**

☐ **Facilitate site inspections of** _____ *[type of]* **projects in collaboration with** [☐ Project Manager | ☐ Project Superintendent | ☐ Foreman | ☐ Building Inspector | ☐ other: _____] **to determine** [☐ building code and life-safety compliance | ☐ conformance with plans, design specifications, and state laws | ☐ handicap accessibility | ☐ other: _____] **and ensure quality compliance with all** [☐ construction contracts | ☐ Uniform Building Code (UBC) | ☐ Federal regulations | ☐ state and local building codes | ☐ International Code Council (ICC) | ☐ zoning laws | ☐ fire regulations | ☐ electrical codes | ☐ plumbing codes | ☐ life-safety codes | ☐ ANSI | ☐ handicap accessibility | ☐ asbestos removal requirements | ☐ other: _____].

☐ **Monitor building construction progress through on-site field inspection and review to ensure conformance to** [☐ design specifications | ☐ cost estimates | ☐ time schedules | ☐ building codes | ☐ other: _____].

☐ **Conduct on-site building inspections to ensure contractors and subcontractors are following design specs and codes, using specified materials, meeting quality work standards and deadlines, and** _____ *[other?]* **to determine** [☐ building code and life-safety compliance | ☐ handicap accessibility | ☐ conformance with state laws | ☐ compliance with client specifications | ☐ other: _____].

☐ **Check** [☐ plans | ☐ specifications | ☐ other: _____] **for compliance with** [☐ Building Code | ☐ other: _____] **and approve and issue consents on** _____ *[what?].*

☐ **Perform** [☐ initial | ☐ incremental | ☐ follow-up | ☐ final | ☐ periodic] **worksite inspections throughout the construction process to inspect the** [☐ soil conditions | ☐ excavation and fill operations | ☐ positioning and depth of footings | ☐ concrete forms and foundations | ☐ asphalt paving | ☐ grading operations | ☐ workmanship quality | ☐ structural safety | ☐ other: _____]; **and to monitor compliance with specifications and codes.**

☐ **Inspect commercial** [☐ buildings | ☐ facilities | ☐ structures | ☐ other: _____] **to identify required** [☐ repairs | ☐ maintenance | ☐ improvement | ☐ disaster-related damage | ☐ other: _____] **to meet current** [☐ building and safety codes | ☐ zoning ordinances | ☐ land use permits | ☐ other: _____] **including** [☐ fire escapes | ☐ signage | ☐ equipment | ☐ other: _____].

☐ **Jointly with the Construction** [☐ Foreman | ☐ Superintendent | ☐ Project Manager | ☐ Engineer | ☐ other: _____], **facilitate on-site inspections of** _____ *[type of]* [☐ buildings | ☐ structures | ☐ grading | ☐ footings | ☐ other: _____] **while** [☐ construction | ☐ remodeling | ☐ maintenance] **work is in process to ensure compliance with approved specifications and enforce all applicable building codes, ordinances, and regulations.**

☐ **Perform on-site building inspections to ensure contractors and subcontractors are following design specs and codes, using specified materials, meeting quality work standards and deadlines, and** _____ *[other?]* **to determine** [☐ building code and life-safety compliance | ☐ handicap accessibility | ☐ conformance with state laws | ☐ compliance with client specifications | ☐ other: _____].

☐ **Apply an expert working knowledge of** [☐ construction methods and materials | ☐ building codes and standards | ☐ other: _____] **in the review and inspection of** _____ *[what?]* **using** _____ *[type of]* [☐ survey instruments | ☐ metering devices | ☐ test equipment | ☐ other: _____] **in the inspection process.**

☐ **Inspect the** [☐ construction | ☐ repair] **of** [☐ buildings | ☐ structures | ☐ highways | ☐ sewer systems | ☐ water systems | ☐ bridges | ☐ land development | ☐ other: _____] **and other structures to ensure compliance with** [☐ state and local building codes | ☐ zoning laws and regulations | ☐ contract specifications | ☐ fire regulations | ☐ electrical codes | ☐ plumbing codes | ☐ life-safety codes | ☐ OSHA standards | ☐ Environmental Health and Safety Standards | ☐ energy conservation requirements | ☐ asbestos abatement requirements | ☐ other: _____].

☐ **Perform work-site inspections of building projects to determine** [☐ building code and life-safety compliance | ☐ handicap accessibility | ☐ conformance with plans, specifications, and state and county laws | ☐ correct asbestos removal | ☐ other: _____] **and to** [☐ quality test construction materials | ☐ identify construction problems | ☐ notify (☐ Construction Foreman / ☐ Project Manager / ☐ others: _____) of defective contractor work | ☐ recommend corrective action | ☐ other: _____].

Inspections & Compliance – Electrical

See also "Inspections & Compliance – General."

☐ **Inspect Electrician work to evaluate and ensure compliance with electrical codes, quality work performance, and** [☐ electrical compatibility | ☐ component safety | ☐ operating problems are resolved | ☐ performance criteria | ☐ other: _____].

☐ **Inspect and troubleshoot** _____ *[type of]* **electrical** [☐ systems | ☐ structures | ☐ installations | ☐ components | ☐ wiring | ☐ equipment | ☐ materials | ☐ other: _____] **for** _____ *[what?]* **ensuring compliance with all** [☐ electrical codes | ☐ building codes | ☐ safety regulations | ☐ customer specifications | ☐ company policies | ☐ other: _____].

☐ **Inspect, maintain, troubleshoot, and repair** _____ *[type of]* **electrical systems for** _____ *[what?]* **ensuring compliance with all** [☐ electrical codes | ☐ building codes | ☐ safety regulations | ☐ customer specifications | ☐ company policies | ☐ other: _____].

☐ **Perform** [☐ first-piece inspections | ☐ in-process inspections | ☐ final inspections | ☐ inspections of all production phases | ☐ other: _____], **ensuring compliance with all regulations, state and federal laws, and manufacturing specs.**

☐ **Oversee** _____ *[type of]* **electrical installations and repairs to ensure all procedures are followed with quality control and deadlines in mind by** [☐ taking hourly production counts | ☐ handling mechanical difficulties | ☐ overseeing quality control personnel's functions | ☐ other: _____].

☐ **Visit worksites to examine** [☐ new | ☐ existing] _____ *[type of]* [☐ structures | ☐ electrical wiring | ☐ HVAC systems | ☐ mechanical equipment | ☐ other: _____] **and other** [☐ systems | ☐ components] **and recommend necessary repair.**

☐ **Conduct site inspections to determine** [☐ electrical, building code, and life-safety compliance | ☐ compliance with state laws | ☐ conformance to client specifications | ☐ other: _____].

☐ **Test, troubleshoot, and diagnose electrical** [☐ circuits | ☐ equipment | ☐ installations | ☐ machinery | ☐ components | ☐ devices | ☐ other: _____] **of** [☐ safety equipment | ☐ emergency lighting | ☐ generators | ☐ other: _____] **to locate and correct** _____ *[type of]* **problems and ensure compliance with all electrical codes.**

☐ **Check** _____ *[what?]* **for** [☐ accurate assembly and installation | ☐ proper operation | ☐ control | ☐ safety | ☐ faulty wires | ☐ defects | ☐ loose connections | ☐ other: _____] **to identify any required** [☐ repairs | ☐ maintenance | ☐ improvement | ☐ other: _____] **in order to meet current** [☐ electrical codes | ☐ building codes | ☐ safety regulations | ☐ OSHA and environmental regulations | ☐ other: _____].

☐ **Perform** [☐ initial | ☐ incremental | ☐ follow-up | ☐ final | ☐ periodic] **worksite inspections of all electrical engineering projects throughout the installation process to ensure contractors are following** [☐ design specs | ☐ electrical code | ☐ contract specifications | ☐ other: _____] **and** [☐ meeting quality work standards and deadlines | ☐ using specified materials | ☐ other: _____].

☐ **Ensure quality compliance with all** [☐ engineering contracts | ☐ electrical codes | ☐ building codes | ☐ zoning laws | ☐ fire regulations | ☐ plumbing codes | ☐ life-safety codes | ☐ other: _____].

☐ **Conduct** _____ *[type of]* **inspections of all** [☐ generators | ☐ conduits | ☐ transformers | ☐ programmable controllers | ☐ motor controllers | ☐ AC & DC motors | ☐ circuit breakers | ☐ heating units | ☐ pull boxes | ☐ switches | ☐ switchboards | ☐ transmission equipment | ☐ other: _____] **to ensure** [☐ all systems are running smoothly | ☐ compliance with all OSHA and environmental regulations | ☐ other: _____].

☐ **Inspect, test, and calibrate** _____ *[type of]* **electrical systems and components to identify and solve** _____ *[type of]* **problems or defects using specialized electrical testing equipment.**

☐ **Ensure proper safety precautions and regulations are observed during all electrical installations and repairs by** _____ *[doing what?]* **to prevent physical injury to self and others.**

☐ **Conduct** [☐ initial | ☐ incremental | ☐ follow-up | ☐ final | ☐ periodic] **worksite inspections throughout the development process to inspect** _____ *[what?]* **and to monitor compliance with all** [☐ contract specifications | ☐ electrical codes | ☐ other: _____].

☐ **Test and troubleshoot** _____ *[type of]* [☐ assemblies | ☐ systems | ☐ communication cables | ☐ hardware | ☐ software products | ☐ operating system | ☐ other: _____] **to** [☐ isolate faults | ☐ ensure the integration of design supports | ☐ other: _____] **and** [☐ resolve malfunctions using (☐ analogue | ☐ digital | ☐ video circuits | ☐ logic systems | ☐ other: _____) applications | ☐ replace parts as required to maintain optimum online condition of network | other: _____].

☐ **Monitor development progress through on-site field inspection and review to ensure conformance to** [☐ design specifications | ☐ cost estimates | ☐ time schedules | ☐ building codes | ☐ other: _____] **and immediately resolve any problems.**

☐ **Inspect the installation of all** _____ *[type of]* **electrical components of** _____ *[what?]* **including** _____ *[which components?].*

☐ **Perform all aspects of** [☐ functional | ☐ operational | ☐ other: _____] **testing and troubleshooting including** [☐ calibration | ☐ alignments | ☐ acceptance | ☐ other: _____], **collect relevant data, write test and discrepancy reports, and prepare rework instructions as required.**

☐ [☐ Develop | ☐ Use] **various test documentation including** [☐ blueprints | ☐ block diagrams | ☐ schematics | ☐ specifications | ☐ other: _____] **to conform to established test procedures and provide direction on all rework or repair required.**

☐ **Operate** _____ *[type of]* **test equipment to perform functional and operational testing of** _____ *[what?]* **to ensure the highest quality of services at all times.**

☐ **Conduct testing, troubleshooting, and repair of** [☐ systems | ☐ electronic equipment | ☐ electromechanical components | ☐ assemblies | ☐ subassemblies | ☐ other: _____] **to ensure conformance to product specifications.**

ACHIEVEMENT SAMPLES:

☐ **Designed and implemented** _____ *[type of]* **testing** [☐ requirements | ☐ methods | ☐ programs | ☐ guides | ☐ other: _____] **that** _____ *[does what?]* **for new product development projects resulting in** _____ *[what benefits?].*

☐ **Conducted testing of** _____ *[type of]* **boards and handled electronic parts with an acceptance rate of** _____% *[percentage]* **where a** _____% *[percentage]* **failure rate was accepted as the norm.**

☐ **Troubleshoot and pinpoint problems faster than the norm due to** [☐ math | ☐ electronics | ☐ other: _____] **expertise and ability to grasp concepts quickly.**

☐ **Investigated** _____ *[type of]* **technical problems on** _____ *[what?]* **and established** [☐ procedures | ☐ corrective actions | ☐ other: _____] **to avoid recurrences.**

Inspections & Compliance – Enforcement

See also "Inspections & Compliance – General."

☐ **Perform inspection and enforcement activities of** _____ *[type of]* [☐ commercial | ☐ residential | ☐ industrial | ☐ public | ☐ other: _____] **building sites for which a building permit is required to ensure contractors and subcontractors are following design specs, using specified materials, working in compliance with all building codes and ordinances, and meeting quality work standards.**

☐ **Impartially determine and firmly enforce compliance with all regulations and specifications during the inspection process, communicating with** [☐ contractors | ☐ project architects | ☐ superintendents | ☐ other: _____] **during all construction phases.**

☐ **Issue violation compliance notices to** _____ *[whom?]* **and maintain accurate, chronological history records for legal recourse as required.**

☐ **Gather evidence and prepare** _____ *[type of]* **inspection reports on all** _____ *[type of]* **violations and assist local municipalities in the enforcement of building codes.**

☐ **Identify defective work and any nonconformance with required** [☐ materials | ☐ permits | ☐ other: _____]; **investigate** [☐ building code | ☐ housing code | ☐ zoning laws | ☐ other: _____] **violations; and recommend corrective actions to resolve problems within a specified time period.**

☐ **Maintain all** _____ *[type of]* **inspection activity files including** [☐ plans | ☐ blueprints | ☐ site layouts | ☐ specifications | ☐ construction methods | ☐ findings | ☐ compliance reports | ☐ photographs | ☐ testing data | ☐ hazardous conditions | ☐ abatement reports | ☐ corrections of violations | ☐ correspondence | ☐ other: _____] **on all active projects.**

☐ **Perform compliance-related activities including building** [☐ inspections | ☐ consents | ☐ investigations | ☐ issues | ☐ resolutions | ☐ compliance schedules | ☐ other: _____] **that comply with all statutory obligations.**

☐ **Log, route, monitor, and process all incoming** _____ *[type of]* **plans and respond to** [☐ homeowners | ☐ owner's representatives | ☐ architects | ☐ contractors | ☐ builders | ☐ others: _____] **regarding any code or related questions, keeping track of all construction inspection activities and status.**

☐ **Coordinate and monitor the status of all inspection activities including** [☐ keeping track of permits | ☐ taking photographs | ☐ accurately recording project details | ☐ maintaining work logs | ☐ writing and filing reports | ☐ other: _____]; **notify** [☐ contractors | ☐ project architects | ☐ superintendents | ☐ others: _____] **when there are code or ordinance violations; and specify time periods to correct problems.**

☐ **Enforce applicable provisions of all** [☐ town | ☐ city | ☐ state | ☐ federal] [☐ regulations | ☐ codes | ☐ ordinances | ☐ specifications] **with emphasis on** [☐ structural construction | ☐ fire and life safety | ☐ handicap access to buildings | ☐ plumbing | ☐ gas | ☐ electrical installation | ☐ grading | ☐ other: _____] **issuing stop-work orders when specified time periods have elapsed without the necessary corrective actions taken.**

☐ **Ensure quality control and compliance during the final construction phase by** _____ *[doing what?]* **to ensure buildings and structures are suited to the engineering and environmental demands of the site.**

☐ **Facilitate** _____ *[type of]* **on-site inspections to determine** [☐ building code and life-safety compliance | ☐ conformance with plans, specifications, and state laws | ☐ other: _____] **and enforce quality compliance with all** [☐ construction contracts | ☐ Uniform Building Code (UBC) | ☐ Federal regulations | ☐ state and local building codes | ☐ International Code Council (ICC) | ☐ zoning laws | ☐ fire regulations | ☐ electrical codes | ☐ plumbing codes | ☐ life-safety codes | ☐ ANSI | ☐ other: _____] **and other ordinances.**

☐ **Detected** _____ *[type of]* **defective work on various** _____ *[type of]* **projects that involved** _____ *[what?]* **and required** _____ *[what?]* **thereby saving** _____ *[what from happening?].*

☐ **Accurately record all** [☐ project | ☐ inspection] **details; and prepare** _____ *[type of]* **reports using** _____ *[which?]* **program(s), to include** [☐ project progress | ☐ inspection deficiencies | ☐ construction conditions | ☐ detected violations | ☐ enforcement actions | ☐ court rulings | ☐ other: _____].

☐ **Conduct** _____ *[type of]* [☐ inspections | ☐ enforcement activities] **of the** [☐ construction | ☐ remodeling | ☐ repair | ☐ maintenance | ☐ other: _____] **of** [☐ commercial | ☐ residential | ☐ civil | ☐ other: _____] **structures through each phase of construction to ensure code and contract compliance.**

Inspections & Compliance – Facilities & Plants

See also "Inspections & Compliance – General" and "Inspections & Compliance – Buildings & Structures."

☐ **Inspect facilities for** [☐ maintenance and repair needs | ☐ fire, safety, and health hazards | ☐ safe and efficient operation | ☐ other: _____] **including** [☐ boilers | ☐ heaters | ☐ chillers | ☐ furnace | ☐ fans | ☐ filters | ☐ plumbing | ☐ electrical | ☐ HVAC | ☐ motors | ☐ appliances | ☐ fixtures | ☐ lights | ☐ ballasts | ☐ receptacles | ☐ switches | ☐ fire extinguishers | ☐ alarm systems | ☐ air compressors | ☐ steam boilers | ☐ pump seals | ☐ bearings | ☐ couplings | ☐ other: _____].

☐ **Conduct facility and grounds inspections of all** [☐ plumbing | ☐ electrical | ☐ HVAC | ☐ motors | ☐ appliances | ☐ fixtures | ☐ other: _____] **to ensure** [☐ all systems are running smoothly | ☐ compliance with all OSHA and environmental regulations | ☐ all facilities, grounds, and people are safe and secure | ☐ other: _____] **by** _____ *[doing what?].*

☐ **Inspect and evaluate the** [☐ physical | ☐ mechanical | ☐ structural | ☐ other: _____] **aspects of facilities to ensure everything is operating in a safe, functional, and proper manner, checking for** _____, _____, **and** _____ *[what aspects?].*

☐ **Check and evaluate the** [☐ physical | ☐ mechanical | ☐ structural | ☐ other: _____] **aspects of** _____ *[#]* [☐ buildings | ☐ facilities | ☐ offices | ☐ other: _____] **to identify required** [☐ repairs | ☐ maintenance | ☐ improvement | ☐ other: _____] **in order to meet current** [☐ building and safety codes | ☐ OSHA and environmental regulations | ☐ other: _____] **and ensure everything is operating in a safe, functional, and proper manner.**

☐ **Inspect water and steam systems for proper operation of** [☐ boiler | ☐ water heater | ☐ furnace | ☐ refrigeration | ☐ other: _____] **ensuring systems have no leaks and all machinery is functioning properly.**

☐ **Assist the** [☐ Foreman | ☐ Project Superintendent | ☐ Building Inspector | ☐ other: _____] **in conducting site inspections to determine** [☐ building code and life-safety compliance | ☐ handicap accessibility | ☐ conformance with plans, specifications, and state laws | ☐ compliance with specifications | ☐ other: _____].

☐ **Track and monitor** _____ *[type of]* [☐ installation | ☐ construction | ☐ manufacture | ☐ other: _____] **progress through** _____ *[type of]* **inspections, and review to ensure conformance to** [☐ specifications | ☐ cost estimates | ☐ time schedules | ☐ contracts | ☐ codes | ☐ other: _____] **and immediately** [☐ resolve | ☐ refer] **any problems.**

☐ **Inspect, maintain, troubleshoot, and repair** _____ *[type of]* **electrical systems for** _____ *[what?]* **ensuring compliance with all** [☐ electrical codes | ☐ building codes | ☐ plumbing codes | ☐ safety regulations | ☐ customer specifications | ☐ company policies | ☐ other: _____].

☐ **Ensure that all** [☐ buildings | ☐ facilities | ☐ grounds | ☐ employees | ☐ customers and others | ☐ other: _____] **are safe and secure by inspecting** _____ *[doing what?].*

☐ **Examine building interior(s) and exterior(s) for any damage or operating difficulties and schedule necessary repairs as required to ensure** [☐ all systems are running smoothly | ☐ compliance with all OSHA and environmental regulations | ☐ other: _____].

☐ **Review and approve all** _____ *[type of]* **building plans to determine whether they** [☐ comply with building and electrical codes and standards | ☐ are suitable for the engineering demands of the site | ☐ are environmentally-friendly | ☐ do not pose any risk to adjoining buildings | ☐ other: _____].

☐ **Conduct** [☐ initial | ☐ incremental | ☐ follow-up | ☐ final | ☐ periodic] _____ *[type of]* **inspections throughout the project lifecycle process to inspect** _____ *[what?]* **and monitor compliance with** _____ *[what?].*

☐ **Inspect** _____ *[type of]* [☐ systems | ☐ facilities | ☐ other: _____] **for** [☐ proper operation | ☐ any damage | ☐ malfunction | ☐ operating difficulties | ☐ leaks | ☐ other: _____] **and oversee needed repairs to ensure** [☐ quality compliance | ☐ everything is functioning a safe and proper manner | ☐ other: _____].

☐ **Review and approve facility and grounds inspection reports to ensure all** [☐ plumbing | ☐ electrical | ☐ HVAC | ☐ water | ☐ steam | ☐ heating | ☐ cooling | ☐ other: _____] **systems are** [☐ running smoothly | ☐ safe and secure | ☐ in proper operating condition | ☐ in compliance with all OSHA and environmental regulations | ☐ meet building codes | ☐ other: _____].

☐ **Check** _____ *[what?]* **to identify required** [☐ repairs | ☐ maintenance | ☐ improvement | ☐ other: _____] **to meet current codes, and ensure** _____ *[what?]* **is safe and secure by** _____ *[doing what?].*

Inspections & Compliance – HVAC / HVAC-R

See also "Inspections & Compliance – General."

☐ **Inspect and test** [☐ mechanical | ☐ electrical | ☐ electronic | ☐ pneumatic | ☐ other: _____] **components of** [☐ heating | ☐ air conditioning | ☐ refrigeration | ☐ ventilation | ☐ other: _____] **systems including** [☐ motors | ☐ compressors | (☐ metal / ☐ fiberglass) ducts | ☐ pipes | ☐ pumps | ☐ fans | ☐ switches | ☐ thermostats | ☐ other: _____] **for** _____ *[type of]* **clients.**

☐ **Test the performance of** [☐ mechanical | ☐ electrical | ☐ other: _____] **components throughout HVAC systems, including** [☐ motors | ☐ compressors | ☐ condensing units | ☐ evaporators | ☐ piping | ☐ metal and fiberglass ducts | ☐ pumps | ☐ fans | ☐ thermostats | ☐ other: _____] **and other components, and make required repairs.**

☐ **Monitor, test, and maintain** [☐ emergency electrical equipment | ☐ generators | ☐ battery-operated lighting] **and appliances such as** [☐ coolers | ☐ freezers | ☐ refrigerators | ☐ washers | ☐ dryers | ☐ dishwashers | ☐ ice machines | ☐ other: _____].

☐ **Test and diagnose problems related to the repair of** _____ *[type of]* [☐ HVAC systems | ☐ control devices | ☐ other: _____] **including** _____ *[what?].*

☐ **Inspect and monitor** [☐ feed and return water pumps | ☐ internal and external boiler components | ☐ sump pumps | ☐ chemical pumps | ☐ water softeners | ☐ heat exchangers | (☐ pneumatic / ☐ automatic) piping systems | ☐ sand traps | ☐ check valves | ☐ related electrical systems | ☐ other: _____] **for proper operation and safety, and make necessary repairs as warranted.**

☐ **Test the performance of** [☐ mechanical | ☐ electrical] **components throughout HVAC systems, including** [☐ motors | ☐ compressors | ☐ condensing units | ☐ evaporators | ☐ piping | ☐ ducts | ☐ pumps | ☐ fans | ☐ thermostats | ☐ other: _____] **and other components, and make required repairs.**

☐ **Monitor and adjust** [☐ water heaters | ☐ boilers | ☐ heating pipes | ☐ pneumatic valves | ☐ mixing valves | ☐ pumps | ☐ pump seals | ☐ steam traps | ☐ bearing assembles | ☐ backflow devices | ☐ dampers | ☐ coils | ☐ fans | ☐ heat exchangers | ☐ air handlers | ☐ water softeners | ☐ sump and chemical pumps | ☐ geothermal pumps | ☐ thermostats | ☐ boiler components | ☐ thermostats | ☐ valves | ☐ faucets | ☐ flush valves | ☐ sinks | ☐ fountains | ☐ toilets | ☐ urinals | ☐ other: _____].

☐ **Complete inspection and maintenance work by** [☐ overhauling compressors | ☐ replacing filters and ducts | ☐ other: _____] **to ensure its efficient** [☐ HVAC | ☐ HVAC-R] **operation.**

☐ **Monitor, balance, and control the temperature, humidity, and air quality of** [☐ heating | ☐ air conditioning | ☐ other: _____] **systems in** [☐ residential | ☐ commercial | ☐ industrial | ☐ other: _____] **buildings by performing** _____ *[functions].*

☐ **Pressure test all** _____ *[type of]* **pipes, assess** [☐ leakage | ☐ breakage | ☐ rust | ☐ damage | ☐ other: _____] **problems, identify plumbing malfunction sources, and perform required** _____ *[type of]* **plumbing repairs within specified timeframes.**

☐ **Prevent the release of chlorofluorocarbon and hydro chlorofluorocarbon refrigerants in air-conditioning and refrigeration systems from entering the ozone layer by** [☐ ensuring there are no system leaks | ☐ venting refrigerant into cylinders | ☐ other manner: _____].

☐ **Apply an expert working knowledge of** [☐ electrical | ☐ electronic | ☐ mechanical] [☐ heating | ☐ ventilation | ☐ air conditioning | ☐ refrigeration] [☐ theory | ☐ methods | ☐ practices | ☐ other: _____] **in the** [☐ troubleshooting and repair of electrical control systems | ☐ design of (☐ centrifugal / ☐ reciprocal) compressors | ☐ operation of pneumatic control systems | ☐ maintenance of steam condensate return traps, pumps, and compressors | ☐ other: _____] **to operate, maintain, and repair HVAC systems.**

Inspections & Compliance – Landscape & Masonry

See also "Inspections & Compliance – General."

☐ **Inspect excavation and fill operations including** [☐ grading operations | ☐ placement of forms for concrete | ☐ concrete mixing and pouring | ☐ poured foundations | ☐ asphalt paving | ☐ reinforced concrete structures | ☐ ditching and dredging operations | ☐ other: _____].

☐ **Conduct initial, incremental, follow-up, and final comprehensive worksite inspections throughout the construction process to inspect the** [☐ soil conditions | ☐ excavation and fill operations | ☐ positioning and depth of footings | ☐ concrete forms and foundations | ☐ asphalt paving | ☐ grading operations | ☐ workmanship quality | ☐ structural safety | ☐ other: _____] **and to monitor compliance with all contract specifications, building codes, and regulations.**

☐ **Perform on-site inspections of** _____ *[what?]* **for compliance with regulations and enforce state and local mandates and zoning regulations, as required.**

Inspections & Compliance – Plumbing

See also "Inspections & Compliance – General."

☐ **Reporting to** [☐ the Chief Plumbing Inspector | ☐ other title: _____], **examine and test** [☐ new | ☐ existing | ☐ new and existing] **plumbing systems of** _____ *[type of]* **projects for this** [☐ city agency | ☐ county agency | ☐ plumbing firm | ☐ other: _____], **reporting and informing owners of any national, state, county, and/or city plumbing code violations.**

☐ **Inspect and test all phases of** [☐ plumbing | ☐ heating | ☐ ventilating | ☐ cooling | ☐ energy management | ☐ control | ☐ other: _____] **system installations** [☐ and repairs] **by** [☐ making frequent on-site visits | ☐ using _____ *(type of)* control software | ☐ verifying temperature controls | ☐ ensuring its efficiency | ☐ recommending the adjustment of (☐ mixed / ☐ return / ☐ discharge) air | ☐ performing combustion analyses | ☐ other methods: _____] **to ensure they are properly installed and comply with all national, state, county, and city codes.**

☐ **Inspect** [☐ plumbing | ☐ sewer line | ☐ gas | ☐ other: _____] **system and equipment installations in** [☐ new | ☐ existing | ☐ new and existing] _____ *[type of]* [☐ buildings | ☐ structures | ☐ businesses | ☐ homes | ☐ schools | ☐ retail stores | ☐ other: _____] **including** [☐ hot water systems | ☐ domestic water systems | ☐ sanitary plumbing systems | ☐ water heaters | ☐ gas piping | ☐ cesspools | ☐ septic tanks | ☐ sewer lines | ☐ wet and dry sandpipes | ☐ fire sprinkler systems | ☐ lawn sprinkler systems | ☐ other: _____] **for** [☐ quality | ☐ tank capacity | ☐ pressure | ☐ leakage | ☐ size and type of pipes and fittings | ☐ any hazardous conditions | ☐ other: _____] **to ensure compliance with plans and specifications, plumbing code, and safety and health standards.**

☐ **Review, verify, and approve applications for** [☐ plumbing | ☐ gas | ☐ sewage | ☐ other: _____] **installation permits to determine compliance with code requirements.**

☐ **Pressure test all** _____ *[type of]* **pipes, assess** [☐ leakage | ☐ breakage | ☐ rust | ☐ damage | ☐ other: _____] **problems, identify plumbing malfunction sources, and perform required** _____ *[type of]* **plumbing repairs within specified timeframes.**

☐ **Handle various plumbing inspection functions including** [☐ reviewing (☐ proposed) construction plans | ☐ conducting testing | ☐ evaluating (☐ buildings / ☐ construction sites) | ☐ issuing permits | ☐ writing reports | ☐ making recommendations | ☐ investigating complaints | ☐ other: _____] **to determine compliance with all plumbing laws, regulations, and codes.**

☐ **Perform** _____ *[type of]* **plumbing [**☐ installations **|** ☐ repairs **|** ☐ alterations **|** ☐ inspections **|** ☐ other: _____**] ensuring all [**☐ new plumbing **|** ☐ plumbing alterations **|** ☐ drainage installations **|** ☐ other: _____**] in** _____ *[type of]* **[**☐ public **|** ☐ private**] buildings are in compliance with all codes, laws, and regulations.**

☐ **Functioning as a [**☐ lead **|** ☐ senior**] inspector, perform a full range of plumbing inspection functions including [**☐ inspecting approved plans and specifications **|** ☐ testing (☐ new installations / ☐ alternations) of plumbing systems **|** ☐ interpreting laws, regulations, and codes to particular situations **|** ☐ checking (☐ piping size / ☐ connections / ☐ trap seals / ☐ cleanouts / ☐ use of materials, devices, fixtures, and equipment / ☐ other: _____) **|** ☐ verifying plumbers are properly licensed **|** ☐ writing code violation notices **|** ☐ gathering code violation evidence **|** ☐ testifying at hearings **|** ☐ preparing reports **|** ☐ determining work priorities of lower-level Plumbing Inspectors **|** ☐ performing accident investigations **|** ☐ evaluating complaints **|** ☐ other: _____**].**

☐ **Apply [**☐ in-depth **|** ☐ proficient **|** ☐ working**] knowledge of [**☐ the plumbing trade **|** ☐ plumbing codes, laws, rules, and regulations **|** ☐ plumbing practices and processes **|** ☐ investigative procedures and methods **|** ☐ plumbing inspection techniques **|** ☐ occupational hazards and safety precautions **|** ☐ plumbing tools, equipment, and materials **|** ☐ other: _____**] in performing plumbing inspections and testing.**

Inspections & Compliance – Public Works / Civil Projects

See also "Inspections & Compliance – General."

☐ **Ensure that [**☐ Federal **|** ☐ state **|** ☐ local**] government construction of [**☐ reinforced concrete **|** ☐ water systems **|** ☐ sewer systems **|** ☐ highways **|** ☐ streets **|** ☐ bridges **|** ☐ dams **|** ☐ ditches **|** ☐ dredging operations **|** ☐ other: _____**] conforms to detailed contract specifications.**

☐ **Inspect the [**☐ construction **|** ☐ repair**] of [**☐ buildings **|** ☐ structures **|** ☐ highways **|** ☐ sewer systems **|** ☐ water systems **|** ☐ bridges **|** ☐ land development **|** ☐ other: _____**] and other structures to ensure compliance with [**☐ state and local building codes **|** ☐ zoning laws and regulations **|** ☐ detailed contract specifications **|** ☐ fire regulations **|** ☐ electrical codes **|** ☐ plumbing codes **|** ☐ life-safety codes **|** ☐ OSHA standards **|** ☐ Environmental Health and Safety Standards **|** ☐ energy conservation requirements **|** ☐ asbestos abatement requirements **|** ☐ other: _____**].**

☐ **Facilitate engineering [**☐ building **|** ☐ structural **|** ☐ other: _____**] consultation and inspections of [**☐ elevators **|** ☐ escalators **|** ☐ fire sprinklers **|** ☐ alarms **|** ☐ smoke control systems **|** ☐ building contents **|** ☐ mechanical equipment **|** ☐ fire exits **|** ☐ conveying devices **|** ☐ handicap access **|** ☐ other: _____**].**

☐ **Perform on-site inspections of [**☐ highways **|** ☐ bridges **|** ☐ equipment **|** ☐ other: _____**] projects to [**☐ determine needed repairs **|** ☐ evaluate progress **|** ☐ comply with plans **|** ☐ ensure quality of construction **|** ☐ other: _____**].**

☐ **Examine [**☐ buildings **|** ☐ highways and streets **|** ☐ sewer and water systems **|** ☐ bridges **|** ☐ other: _____**] for their structural quality and safety to ensure [**☐ construction **|** ☐ repair **|** ☐ other: _____**] conforms to all contract specifications, building codes and ordinances, and zoning regulations.**

☐ **Manage daily environmental compliance issues, interpret applicable regulations, and provide regulatory support to** _____ *[whom?]* **ensuring [**☐ plant **|** ☐ site **|** ☐ process **|** ☐ operational **|** ☐ other: _____**] compliance with state, local, and federal requirements.**

☐ **Check and evaluate the [**☐ physical **|** ☐ mechanical **|** ☐ structural **|** ☐ other: _____**] aspects of facilities to ensure everything is operating in a safe, functional, and proper manner.**

Inspections & Compliance – Recordkeeping

☐ **Log, route, monitor, and process all incoming** _____ *[type of]* **plans and respond to [**☐ homeowners **|** ☐ owner's representatives **|** ☐ architects **|** ☐ contractors **|** ☐ builders **|** ☐ others: _____**] regarding any code or related questions, keeping track of all construction inspection activities and status.**

☐ **Accurately record all [**☐ project **|** ☐ inspection**] details; and prepare** _____ *[type of]* **reports using** _____ *[which?]* **program(s), to include [**☐ project progress **|** ☐ inspection deficiencies **|** ☐ construction conditions **|** ☐ detected violations **|** ☐ enforcement actions **|** ☐ court rulings **|** ☐ other: _____**].**

☐ **Maintain all** _____ *[type of]* **inspection activity files including [**☐ plans **|** ☐ blueprints **|** ☐ site layouts **|** ☐ specifications **|** ☐ construction methods **|** ☐ findings **|** ☐ compliance reports **|** ☐ photographs **|** ☐ testing data **|** ☐ hazardous conditions **|** ☐ abatement reports **|** ☐ corrections of violations **|** ☐ correspondence **|** ☐ other: _____**] on all active projects.**

☐ **Gather evidence and prepare** _____ *[type of]* **inspection reports on all** _____ *[type of]* **violations and assist local municipalities in the enforcement of building codes.**

Inspections & Compliance – Residential Projects

See also "Inspections & Compliance – General."

☐ **Perform engineering inspections on all** [☐ newly built | ☐ previously owned | ☐ remodeled] **home** [☐ structures | ☐ systems | ☐ components | ☐ other: _____] **including their electrical, plumbing, heating, and/or cooling systems; and report findings to home** [☐ buyers | ☐ owners].

☐ **Examine building interior and exterior for** [☐ damage | ☐ malfunction | ☐ leaks | ☐ operating difficulties | ☐ other: _____], **and make necessary repairs as required, such as** _____ *[type of repairs].*

☐ **Check** _____, _____, **and** _____, *[what?]* **to identify required** [☐ repairs | ☐ maintenance | ☐ improvement | ☐ other: _____] **to meet current** _____ *[what?].*

☐ **Represent** [☐ building owners | ☐ insurance companies | ☐ financial institutions | ☐ others: _____] **to ensure that** _____ *[type of]* **residential work is performed and completed according to design specifications.**

☐ **Inspect previously occupied** _____ *[type of]* **homes for code compliance, verify legal data, and authorize** [☐ permits | ☐ Certificates of Occupancy | ☐ other: _____] **for approved areas.**

Inspections & Compliance – Trades Work (General)

See also "Inspections & Compliance – General."

☐ **Facilitate** [☐ plumbing | ☐ electrical | ☐ HVAC | ☐ welding | ☐ carpentry | ☐ other: _____] **inspections to ensure compliance with all relevant** [☐ building | ☐ safety | ☐ plumbing | ☐ electrical | ☐ other: _____] **codes, standards, and** [☐ specifications | ☐ contracts | ☐ regulations | ☐ policies | ☐ standards | ☐ other: _____] **including relevant aspects of** [☐ OSHA | ☐ EPA | ☐ MSDS | ☐ ADA | ☐ other: _____].

☐ **Monitor installation of** _____ *[type of]* [☐ plumbing | ☐ electrical wiring | ☐ equipment | ☐ appliances | ☐ other: _____] **to ensure installation is performed in compliance with all applicable codes and regulations.**

☐ **Track and monitor** _____ *[type of]* **progress through** [☐ grounds | ☐ top-out | ☐ finish] [☐ phases of construction | ☐ plumbing inspections], **and review to ensure conformance to** [☐ specifications | ☐ cost estimates | ☐ time schedules | ☐ contracts | ☐ codes | ☐ other: _____] **and immediately** [☐ resolve | ☐ refer] **any problems.**

☐ **Examine the construction, installation, and functioning of all** [☐ concrete structures | ☐ framing | ☐ insulation | ☐ electrical wiring | ☐ plumbing fixtures, traps, and systems | ☐ water supply systems | ☐ water distribution systems | ☐ irrigation systems | ☐ drainage systems | ☐ waste and vent lines | ☐ HVAC equipment | ☐ security systems | ☐ smoke control systems | ☐ alarm systems | ☐ fire sprinklers | ☐ fire protection equipment | ☐ disposal systems | ☐ gas and oil piping | ☐ gasoline and butane tanks | ☐ escalators | ☐ elevators | ☐ asbestos abatement | ☐ roofing systems | ☐ fire exits | ☐ other: _____] **to ensure adherence to all related codes and standards.**

☐ **Inspect and monitor** [☐ new construction | ☐ installations | ☐ alternations | ☐ other: _____] **of** _____ *[type of]* [☐ private | ☐ public | ☐ other: _____] **construction sites to ensure adherence to and enforce all safety standards, building codes, and specifications.**

☐ **Manage and oversee inspection and compliance functions including** [☐ reviewing plans to verify code requirements | ☐ overseeing construction projects | ☐ performing on-site construction inspections | ☐ identifying construction problems | ☐ quality testing construction materials | ☐ notifying foremen and contractors of defective work | ☐ recommending corrective actions | ☐ resolving construction personnel disputes | ☐ conducting preventive maintenance | ☐ negotiating plan changes with architects | ☐ holding meetings to discuss project progress | ☐ other: _____].

☐ **Facilitate on-site inspections of** [☐ building | ☐ highway | ☐ bridge | ☐ equipment | ☐ other: _____] **projects to** [☐ determine needed repairs | ☐ evaluate progress | ☐ comply with plans | ☐ ensure quality of construction | ☐ other: _____].

☐ **Visit worksites to examine** [☐ new | ☐ existing | ☐ other: _____] _____ *[type of]* [☐ structures | ☐ electrical wiring | ☐ lighting | ☐ HVAC systems | ☐ mechanical equipment | ☐ plumbing systems | ☐ other: _____] **and other** [☐ systems | ☐ components] **and recommend any necessary repair.**

☐ **Conduct** [☐ initial | ☐ incremental | ☐ follow-up | ☐ periodic | ☐ final] _____ *[type of]* **inspections throughout the** [☐ plumbing | ☐ electrical | ☐ HVAC | ☐ other: _____] **installation and repair process to inspect** _____ *[what?]* **and monitor compliance with all related codes.**

☐ **Inspect the** [☐ demolition | ☐ carpentry | ☐ framing | ☐ sheetrocking | ☐ taping and spackling | ☐ flooring | ☐ painting | ☐ insulation | ☐ electrical | ☐ plumbing | ☐ HVAC | ☐ tiling | ☐ trim work | ☐ ceilings | ☐ welding | ☐ roofing | ☐ masonry | ☐ landscaping | ☐ other: _____] **perform** _____ *[type of]* [☐ large-scale | ☐ moderate-size | ☐ highly complex | ☐ moderately complex | ☐ multisite | ☐ other: _____] **construction projects for** _____ *[whom?]* **resulting in** _____ *[what benefits?].*

☐ **Inspect the installation of all** _____ *[type of]* **components of** _____ *[what?]* **including** _____, _____, **and** _____ *[which components?]*.

☐ **Use various instruments, equipment, and devices during the inspection process including** [☐ survey instruments | ☐ metering devices | ☐ test equipment | ☐ tape measures | ☐ concrete strength measurers | ☐ other: _____].

☐ **Conduct on-site inspections of** [☐ buildings | ☐ structures | ☐ grading | ☐ footings | ☐ other: _____] **while** [☐ construction | ☐ remodeling | ☐ maintenance] **work is in process to ensure compliance with approved specifications; and enforce all applicable building codes, ordinances, and regulations**.

Inspections Recordkeeping

☐ **Log, route, monitor, and process all incoming** _____ *[type of]* **plans and respond to** [☐ architects | ☐ contractors | ☐ builders | ☐ others: _____] **regarding any code or related questions, keeping track of all construction inspection activities and status**.

☐ **Accurately record all** [☐ project | ☐ inspection] **details; and prepare** _____ *[type of]* **reports using** _____ *[which?]* **program(s), to include** [☐ project progress | ☐ inspection deficiencies | ☐ construction conditions | ☐ detected violations | ☐ enforcement actions | ☐ court rulings | ☐ other: _____].

☐ **Maintain all** _____ *[type of]* **inspection activity files including** [☐ plans | ☐ blueprints | ☐ site layouts | ☐ specifications | ☐ construction methods | ☐ findings | ☐ compliance reports | ☐ photographs | ☐ testing data | ☐ hazardous conditions | ☐ abatement reports | ☐ corrections of violations | ☐ correspondence | ☐ other: _____] **on all active projects**.

☐ **Gather evidence and prepare** _____ *[type of]* **inspection reports on all** _____ *[type of]* **violations and assist local municipalities in the enforcement of building codes**.

Insulation Functions & Projects

See "Ceiling, Lathing, Insulation & Drywall Installation" as well as "Carpentry / Construction Work."

Interaction & Liaison – Strategic Level

See also "Work Coordination" and "Interdisciplinary/Project Team Member."

☐ **Interact and liaise with** [☐ architects | ☐ engineers | ☐ contractors | ☐ subcontractors | ☐ project management staff | ☐ building officials | ☐ other: _____] **to ensure that** [☐ construction | ☐ demolition | ☐ remodel | ☐ alteration | ☐ other: _____] **work is within parameters identified by the firm and in compliance with** _____ *[what?]* **and all building codes**.

☐ **Oversee staff interactions with** [☐ building officials | ☐ contractors | ☐ contractor reimbursement agencies | ☐ Accounts Payable | ☐ departmental service coordinators | ☐ others: _____] **to** [☐ maintain productive working relationships with _____ *(type of)* agencies | ☐ schedule construction | ☐ facilitate final inspections | ☐ ensure proper handling and receipt of payments | ☐ other: _____].

☐ **Serve as principal liaison with** [☐ architects | ☐ human resources | ☐ purchasing officers | ☐ legal | ☐ others: _____] **in** [☐ selecting contractors | ☐ handling documentation | ☐ executing legal actions | ☐ other: _____] **related to** [☐ design | ☐ new construction | ☐ project management | ☐ facility improvement issues | ☐ other: _____] **issues**.

☐ **Collaborate with** _____ *[whom?]* **to ensure that** _____ *[type of]* **work is within parameters identified by the firm and in compliance with all building codes and client specifications**.

☐ **Liaise with owners to maintain customer satisfaction by** [☐ listening to and interpreting their needs | ☐ giving careful attention to detail | ☐ other: _____].

☐ **Liaise and interface regularly with** [☐ architects | ☐ engineers | ☐ contractors | ☐ subcontractors | ☐ project management staff | ☐ departmental management | ☐ governmental regulators | ☐ outside agencies | ☐ vendors | ☐ other: _____] **to** [☐ determine project scope | ☐ develop project plans | ☐ review feedback on project goals and timelines | ☐ schedule projects | ☐ identify and problem solve issues | ☐ manage construction | ☐ track projects | ☐ other: _____] **in various project phases**.

Interdisciplinary / Project Team Member

See also "Work Coordination" and "Team Leadership & Direction."

☐ **Participate in** [☐ interdisciplinary | ☐ multidisciplinary | ☐ interagency | ☐ other: _____] **team meetings with** _____, _____, **and** _____ *[whom?]* **working together** [☐ for the benefit of | ☐ to meet | ☐ to ensure] _____ *[what goals?]* **and communicate milestones, commitments, and achievements**.

☐ **Actively participate in meetings with the interdisciplinary team consisting of** _____, _____, **and** _____ *[whom?]* **in the development and monitoring of** _____ *[type of]* **goals and to provide progress update reports.**

☐ **Serve on a project team of** _____ *[#]* **including** _____ *[whom?]* **that defines, plans, and implements new** _____ *[type of]* **projects; and perform the** [☐ design | ☐ development | ☐ deployment | ☐ other: _____] **of those projects in support of the** [☐ firm's | ☐ clients'] **objectives.**

☐ **As a member of the** _____ *[which?]* [☐ interdisciplinary | ☐ multidisciplinary | ☐ interagency] **team** [☐ develop | ☐ implement | ☐ track | ☐ assess | ☐ modify | ☐ other: _____] _____ *[type of]* [☐ programs | ☐ plans] **to** [☐ resolve _____ *(type of)* problems and challenges | ☐ write _____ *(what?)* reports | ☐ other: _____] **concerning** _____ *[type of]* **complex projects**.

☐ **Work collaboratively in a team environment with** _____ *[whom?]* [☐ while leading multiple projects | ☐ adapting to frequently changing priorities | ☐ demonstrating a strong commitment to improvement | ☐ other: _____].

☐ **Participate as a member of a project team of** _____ *[#]* **to** [☐ prepare and distribute project schedules | ☐ provide support | ☐ communicate project status | ☐ resolve issues | ☐ other: _____] **that meet schedule requirements** .

☐ **In collaboration with the** _____ *[what team?]* [☐ create accurate project estimates | ☐ prepare schedules | ☐ allocate resources | ☐ other: _____] **that support company-wide projects and maintain project management practices.**

ACHIEVEMENT SAMPLES:

☐ **As a member of the** _____ *[which?]* **team, presented** _____ *[type of]* **ideas, made** _____ *[what?]* **recommendations, and developed** _____ *[type of]* **plans designed to** _____ *[do what?]*.

Inventory Audits

See also "Inventory Management & Control," "Purchasing," and "Recordkeeping."

☐ **Make sound decisions regarding** [☐ establishment of audit objectives | ☐ scope of investigations needed | ☐ depth of audit testing required | ☐ significance of audit issues | ☐ corrective remedies required | ☐ recommended means to obtain compliance | ☐ disposition of audit results | ☐ other: _____].

☐ **Execute thorough, independent internal** [☐ appraisals | ☐ audits | ☐ investigations | ☐ quality assurance reviews] **of the firm's inventory management and control** [☐ policies | ☐ procedures | ☐ standards | ☐ systems] **effectiveness.**

☐ **Perform** [☐ daily | ☐ weekly | ☐ monthly] **inventory** [☐ counts | ☐ analysis | ☐ audits] **of** _____ *[type of]* [☐ products | ☐ merchandise | ☐ goods | ☐ supplies | ☐ materials | ☐ other: _____] **to determine any discrepancies, quickly resolve any inventory issues, and ensure sufficient in-house** [☐ stock | ☐ systems | ☐ programs | ☐ other: _____] **are adequate to meet** [☐ the firm's | ☐ the Division's | ☐ client | ☐ others: _____] **needs.**

☐ **Conduct** [☐ general | ☐ special | ☐ independent | ☐ other: _____] **inventory audits to evaluate the accuracy of all inventory records including** [☐ shipments | ☐ deliveries | ☐ warehousing | ☐ storekeeping | ☐ recordkeeping | ☐ fulfillment | ☐ replenishment | ☐ purchase orders | ☐ invoices | ☐ receipts | ☐ bills of lading | ☐ other: _____] **including performing** [☐ physical inventory inspections | ☐ procedures review | ☐ internal controls | ☐ shipping and receiving processes | ☐ security controls efficiency | ☐ irregularities investigations | ☐ other: _____] **to ensure** [☐ transaction accuracy | ☐ compliance with applicable laws and established policies and procedures | ☐ the safeguarding of assets | ☐ other: _____].

☐ **Verify the accuracy of the company's inventory records, checking for any** [☐ discrepancies | ☐ mismanagement | ☐ security breaches | ☐ system risks | ☐ fraud | ☐ illegal activities | ☐ other: _____] **which has resulted in** _____ *[findings]*.

☐ **Audit the** [☐ firm's | ☐ Department's] **inventory records including** [☐ shipments | ☐ deliveries | ☐ warehousing | ☐ storekeeping | ☐ recordkeeping | ☐ purchase orders | ☐ invoices | ☐ receipts | ☐ logs | ☐ other: _____].

☐ **Conduct inventory audits covering all areas of inventory management and control including** [☐ conducting physical inventories | ☐ examining documents | ☐ analyzing and interpreting data | ☐ conducting transaction reviews | ☐ investigating questionable items | ☐ conducting cost analyses | ☐ identifying errors | ☐ preparing reports | ☐ communicate findings | ☐ making recommendations | ☐ following up on audits | ☐ other: _____].

☐ **Conduct comprehensive audits of inventory records including** [☐ performing physical inventory counts | ☐ developing audit findings | ☐ reviewing work papers | ☐ conducting negotiations | ☐ editing drafts | ☐ preparing final audit reports | ☐ other: _____].

☐ **Apply auditing principles and practices and sound decision-making in the** [☐ audit plans preparation | ☐ exposure assessment | ☐ risk identification | ☐ evidence gathering | ☐ conclusions documentation | ☐ other: _____].

☐ **Recommended** _____ *[type of]* **automated controls to ensure** [☐ data integrity | ☐ system reliability | ☐ other: _____] **which has brought about** [☐ positive changes in | ☐ a resultant savings of $_____] **in** _____ *[what areas?]*.

☐ **Review and evaluate efficiency of the firm's inventory operations, effectiveness of policies, and compliance with procedures and regulations for this** _____ *[type of]* **firm with** _____ *[#]* [☐ **locations** | ☐ **employees**].

☐ **Formulate and document appropriate required actions and effectively complete all audit activities by** [☐ using a variety of data analysis techniques | ☐ incorporating the type and quantity of information and evidence needed | ☐ analyzing processes within the context of audit objectives | ☐ executing innovative approaches | ☐ identifying areas for improvement | ☐ performing subsequent audits | ☐ ensuring corrective measures have been taken | ☐ auditing financial statements | ☐ other: _____].

Inventory Management & Control

See also ***"Purchasing"*** *and* ***"Recordkeeping."***

☐ **Order sufficient** _____ *[type of]* [☐ materials | ☐ supplies | ☐ products | ☐ goods | ☐ other: _____] **in accordance with project needs and the firm's** [☐ inventory usage cycles | ☐ project requirements | ☐ quality initiatives | ☐ established procedures | ☐ other: _____] **while effectively balancing physical storage and usage demands.**

☐ **Manage and control inventory on a** [☐ daily | ☐ weekly | ☐ monthly] **basis including** [☐ purchasing, inspecting, and storing materials and supplies | ☐ managing and overseeing the purchase and distribution of tools and equipment | ☐ ordering sufficient products and supplies to meet demand | ☐ conducting audits to determine any discrepancies and resolving inventory issues | ☐ ensuring a continuous and adequate supply of materials, tools, and equipment at all times | ☐ other: _____].

☐ **Ensure the inventory of all** _____ *[type of]* [☐ equipment | ☐ tools | ☐ supplies | ☐ raw materials | ☐ merchandise | ☐ furniture | ☐ other: _____] **is sufficient to meet** [☐ the firm's | ☐ clients'] **needs for all** _____ *[type of]* **projects.**

☐ **Perform** [☐ daily | ☐ weekly | ☐ monthly] **inventory** [☐ counts | ☐ analysis | ☐ audits | ☐ other: _____] **to determine any discrepancies and resolve any inventory issues.**

☐ **Direct and lead the** [☐ acquisition | ☐ purchase | ☐ distribution | ☐ control | ☐ sale | ☐ transfer | ☐ disposition] **of** [☐ reusable | ☐ recyclable] [☐ property | ☐ furniture | ☐ equipment | ☐ supplies | ☐ goods | ☐ product | ☐ merchandise | ☐ materials | ☐ other: _____] **in compliance with** [☐ the firm's established policies and procedures | ☐ federal and state regulations | ☐ other: _____].

☐ **Receive and inspect all** _____ *[type of]* [☐ equipment | ☐ supplies | ☐ materials | ☐ goods | ☐ merchandise | ☐ furniture | ☐ other: _____] **and evaluate their condition.**

☐ **Manage and oversee the** [☐ purchase | ☐ distribution | ☐ control] **of** _____ *[type of]* [☐ supplies | ☐ materials | ☐ tools | ☐ equipment | ☐ other: _____] **to ensure a continuous and adequate supply is maintained to meet current and future usage requirements.**

☐ **Direct and lead the** [☐ inventory control | ☐ receiving | ☐ storage | ☐ other: _____] **staff responsible for inventory** [☐ planning | ☐ management | ☐ control | ☐ replenishment | ☐ distribution | ☐ scheduling | ☐ other: _____] **of tools, materials, and equipment totaling $** _____ *[amount].*

☐ **Conduct physical inventories of** _____ *[what?]* **and other materials to ensure sufficient supply on hand to meet demand requirements.**

☐ **Maintain effective physical inventory control of** [☐ receiving | ☐ shipping | ☐ storage | ☐ warehousing | ☐ distribution | ☐ other: _____] **by** _____ *[doing what?]*; **and ensure adequate product inventory to meet the firm's needs.**

☐ **Manage inventory control up to $** _____ *[amount],* **and dispose of destroyed merchandise.**

☐ **Ensure a continuous and adequate supply of** _____ *[type of]* [☐ tools | ☐ equipment | ☐ supplies | ☐ materials | ☐ other: _____] **is maintained meet current and future usage requirements.**

☐ **Facilitate inventory control of all** _____ *[type of]* [☐ product | ☐ goods | ☐ supplies | ☐ materials | ☐ other: _____], **ensuring sufficient in-house stock to meet** [☐ the firm's | ☐ client] **needs.**

☐ **Maintain inventory control of all** _____ *[type of]* [☐ product | ☐ merchandise | ☐ goods | ☐ supplies | ☐ materials | ☐ other: _____], **ensuring sufficient in-house stock to meet** [☐ the firm's | ☐ client] **needs.**

☐ [☐ **Receive and**] **Inspect all** _____ *[type of]* [☐ furniture | ☐ equipment | ☐ supplies | ☐ goods | ☐ merchandise | ☐ materials | ☐ other: _____] **and evaluate their condition.**

☐ **Oversee inventory control for all aspects of this $** _____ *[revenues]* **store inventory including** _____, _____, **and** _____ *[what major inventory or merchandise?].*

☐ **Perform** [☐ daily | ☐ weekly | ☐ monthly] **inventory** [☐ counts | ☐ analysis | ☐ audits] **to determine any discrepancies and quickly resolve any and all inventory issues.**

☐ **Update and maintain records of the** [☐ receipt | ☐ inspection | ☐ distribution | ☐ transporting | ☐ warehousing | ☐ other: _____] **of all** [☐ property | ☐ furniture | ☐ equipment | ☐ supplies | ☐ goods | ☐ product | ☐ merchandise | ☐ materials |

☐ other: _____] **acquisitions and dispositions.**

ACHIEVEMENT SAMPLES:

☐ **Spearheaded a/an** _____ *[type of]* **inventory control** [☐ program | ☐ management system | ☐ strategies | ☐ other: _____] **for improving the firm's** [☐ operating efficiency | ☐ service levels | ☐ storage capacity by $_____ *(amount)* | ☐ waste management by _____% *(percentage)* | ☐ other: _____] **while reducing** [☐ inventory levels | ☐ operating costs | ☐ waste | ☐ other: _____].

☐ **Developed, implemented, and maintain an automated inventory control program utilizing** _____ *[name of]* **software, which provided real time information on** [☐ product costs | ☐ usage | ☐ transfers | ☐ monthly overages and shortages | ☐ previous month comparisons | ☐ balances | ☐ other: _____].

☐ **Increased inventory turns by** [☐ working with merchants to set the merchandise for pallet type quantities | ☐ other method: _____].

☐ **Developed, implemented, manage, and control the firm's annual inventory** [☐ control procedures | ☐ budget | ☐ business plan | ☐ other: _____].

Job Preparation – Construction

☐ **Prepare for all** _____ *[type of]* **jobs by** [☐ prioritizing work assignments | ☐ ordering required inventory | ☐ determining equipment needed | ☐ setting up each project with the correct tools, materials, and supplies | ☐ coordinating contracting trades | ☐ determining conditions and safety requirements | ☐ identifying required repairs and/or replacements | ☐ other: _____].

☐ [☐ Lay out | ☐ Draft | ☐ Evaluate] [☐ engineering proposals | ☐ shop drawings | ☐ technical devices | ☐ parts specifications | ☐ other: _____] **depicting the fabrication, construction, and assembly of** _____ *[what?]* **ensuring** [☐ sound electrical engineering practice | ☐ compliance with all electrical codes | ☐ conformance with established (☐ safety / ☐ design) criteria].

☐ **Handle** [☐ estimating | ☐ contract negotiations | ☐ other: _____] **with** [☐ contractors | ☐ subcontractors | ☐ suppliers | ☐ other: _____] **involving** _____ *[what?]*.

☐ **Apply an adapt knowledge of** _____ *[which?]* **trade** [☐ tools, equipment, and materials | ☐ safety practices | ☐ building codes | ☐ electrical codes | ☐ plumbing codes | ☐ zoning regulations | ☐ other: _____] **related to the installation, maintenance, and repair of** _____ *[what?]*.

☐ **Provide technical** [☐ assistance | ☐ support | ☐ guidance | ☐ expertise | ☐ consultation | ☐ resolution] **on** _____ *[type of]* **issues** [☐ before | ☐ during | ☐ after] **the construction process.**

☐ **Apply provisions of all** [☐ building codes | ☐ electrical codes | ☐ safety standards and regulations | ☐ fire codes | ☐ other: _____] **in the** _____ *[which?]* **trade to** _____ *[type of]* **projects.**

☐ **Coordinated all aspects of** _____ *[type of]* **projects with** [☐ clients | ☐ engineers | ☐ architects | ☐ municipal officials | ☐ county officials | ☐ code officers | ☐ others: _____] **ensuring compliance with all** [☐_____ *(which?)* codes | ☐ quality standards | ☐ work schedules | ☐ other: _____].

ACHIEVEMENT SAMPLES:

☐ **Performed the complete** _____ *[what building, plant, or other project?]*, **which included** [☐ estimating job costs | ☐ scheduling _____ *(type of)* work | ☐ ordering parts and materials | ☐ overseeing the installation process | ☐ managing a staff of _____ *(#)* _____ *(titles)* | ☐ supervising quality control | ☐ billing clients | ☐ other: _____] [☐ meeting | ☐ exceeding] **aggressive timeframes.**

☐ **Coordinated all aspects of** _____ *[type of]* **projects with** [☐ clients | ☐ engineers | ☐ architects | ☐ municipal officials | ☐ county officials | ☐ code officers | ☐ others: _____] **ensuring compliance with all** [☐_____ *(which?)* codes | ☐ quality standards | ☐ work schedules | ☐ other: _____].

Labor Relations

See also "Grievance Investigations & Dispute Resolution," "Union Functions," and "Union Leadership."

☐ **Lead and direct labor relations across the organization involving** [☐ aligning Human Resource strategies with business strategies | ☐ developing staffing strategies | ☐ spearheading internal investigative procedures | ☐ streamlining and enhancing staffing systems | ☐ developing Human Resource programs / ☐ minimizing risk and legal exposure | ☐ managing (☐ workforce reductions / ☐ company structures / ☐ organizational changes / ☐ communication channels / ☐ other: _____) | ☐ monitoring the Affirmative Action Program (AAP) | ☐ other: _____] **ensuring compliance with all federal, state, and local regulations.**

☐ **Manage and oversee** [☐ developing and building hiring processes for _____ *(what?)* levels | ☐ tracking reporting and analyses |

☐ developing training (☐ courses / ☐ materials) | ☐ presenting information on regulatory changes | ☐ executing Human Resource programs | ☐ streamlining and standardizing Human Resource policies and practices | ☐ developing Human Resource to be more effective in managing human capital | ☐ successful completion of government agency compliance review | ☐ other: _____].

☐ **Provide labor relations** [☐ consultation | ☐ counsel | ☐ guidance | ☐ coaching | ☐ support] **services to** [☐ Department Managers | ☐ Field Managers | ☐ others: _____] **on** [☐ performance management | ☐ employee conduct handling | ☐ problem resolution | ☐ performance review process | ☐ progressive discipline | ☐ policy interpretation | ☐ documentation preparation | ☐ complex, difficult, and emotional issues | ☐ labor law interpretations | ☐ company procedures | ☐ personnel practices | ☐ employment laws | ☐ other: _____] **delivering effective solutions that drive performance.**

☐ **Supervise and oversee staffing administration for this** _____ *[type of]* **firm with** _____ *[#]* **employees covering** [☐ sourcing | ☐ recruiting | ☐ relocation | ☐ internship | ☐ immigration | ☐ other: _____] **initiatives and processes, ensuring compliance with all state and federal employment and discrimination regulations**.

☐ **Facilitate labor relations support to** _____ *[type of]* **staff to** [☐ answer questions regarding company Human Resources policies | ☐ resolve workplace and grievance issues | ☐ mediate employee and supervisor differences | ☐ provide administrative support | ☐ other: _____] **ensuring the equitable application of the firm's policies and procedures and adherence to regulations.**

☐ **Serve as** [☐ Employee Relations Subject Matter Expert | ☐ member of the Employee Relations Solutions Team | ☐ central point of Human Resources contact | ☐ Department representative | ☐ other: _____] **for employee relation issues and concerns covering** [☐ human resources assistance | ☐ complaint investigations | ☐ job eliminations | ☐ corrective actions | ☐ risk-related issues | ☐ other: _____] **to deliver** [☐ timely | ☐ high-quality | ☐ effective | ☐ relevant] **employee relations solutions and follow-up.**

☐ **Coach and advise managers regarding labor relations matters across the organization including** [☐ progressive discipline | ☐ corrective actions | ☐ performance issues | ☐ other: _____] **ensuring** [☐ clarity of messages delivered to employees | ☐ a consistent and aligned approach | ☐ other: _____].

☐ **Facilitate various labor relations functions including** [☐ participating in progressive discipline meetings | ☐ preparing and presenting presentations on employee relations issues | ☐ responding to personnel policy and procedure inquiries | ☐ recommending needed training for managers, supervisors, and staff | ☐ preparing employee relations documentation | ☐ participating in exit interviews | ☐ monitoring (☐ Complaint Tracking / ☐ Employee Relations Case Management / ☐ other: _____) system | ☐ responding to unemployment filings | ☐ following up on correspondence | ☐ participating in department-specific performance improvement initiatives | ☐ other: _____] **maintaining a positive labor relations environment and ensuring compliance with all regulatory requirements.**

☐ **Respond to and resolve employee** [☐ grievances | ☐ discrimination charges | ☐ unemployment filings | ☐ legal hearings | ☐ record-related subpoenas | ☐ other: _____] **by way of** _____ *[methods you use or actions you take]*.

☐ **Build and maintain a positive employee relations environment by** [☐ enabling management capability | ☐ professionally handling employee (☐ claims / ☐ issues / ☐ cases) | ☐ enhancing staffing systems | ☐ overseeing managers' employee relations activities | ☐ other means: _____].

☐ **Conduct fact-finding** [☐ interviews | ☐ investigations | (☐ internal / ☐ external) audits | ☐ other: _____], **analyze data and interpret findings,** [☐ prepare employment claims documentation | ☐ rack (☐ absences / ☐ disciplinary actions / ☐ performance management / ☐ organizational changes / ☐ other: _____) | ☐ identify training trends | ☐ other: _____].

☐ **Work with** [☐ in-house legal counsel | ☐ Human Resources team | ☐ other: _____] **to conduct** [☐ proactive] [☐ internal investigations | ☐ self-audits | ☐ Affirmative Action compliance analyses | ☐ others: _____] **regarding** [☐ internal complaints | ☐ violation allegations of (☐ company policies / ☐ employee grievances / ☐ working conditions / ☐ code of conduct / ☐ disciplinary actions / ☐ other: _____) | ☐ conflict resolution | ☐ other: _____] **promoting an environment that supports diversity.**

☐ **As the company's** [☐ point of contact | ☐ subject matter expert | ☐ subject resource] **on** [☐ employee relations issues | ☐ Affirmative Action regulations and requirements | ☐ other: _____] **for** _____ *[#]* **personnel,** [☐ discuss and resolve employee concerns | ☐ provide needed training and development services | ☐ actively participate in department performance improvement initiatives | ☐ counsel with supervisors and employees regarding performance and disciplinary matters | ☐ help employees find resolution to their concerns | ☐ provide the best employee options regarding company policies and procedures | ☐ other: _____].

☐ [☐ Develop | ☐ Recommend] _____ *[type of]* **action plans that** _____ *[accomplish what?]* **based on identified** _____ *[type of]* **trends.**

☐ **Provide Employee Relations support in the areas of** [☐ terminations review and processing | ☐ separation agreements completion | ☐ electronic file maintenance | ☐ grievance procedure administration | ☐ recordkeeping compliance | ☐ labor agreements interpretation | ☐ data analysis | ☐ workforce training facilitation | ☐ conflict resolution | ☐ contract negotiations | ☐ other: _____] **as well as** [☐ conducting labor relations investigations | ☐ promoting direct communication and positive rapport | ☐ performance management monitoring | ☐ addressing job performance issues | ☐ responding to employee relation issues | ☐ reviewing liability reports | ☐ other: _____].

Landscape Design

See also "CAD Design," "Trades Coordination & Oversight – Landscape Projects," and "Trades Coordination & Oversight – Masonry Projects."

☐ **Manage and oversee all aspects of this landscape design firm including** [☐ sales | ☐ customer service | ☐ installations | ☐ contract negotiations | ☐ account servicing | ☐ administration | ☐ cash management | ☐ client and financial database | ☐ hiring, training, and scheduling employees | ☐ budgeting | ☐ other: _____].

☐ **Design and install attractive, functional landscape areas including building and/or installing** [☐ sidewalks | ☐ walkways | ☐ retainer walls | ☐ decks | ☐ porches | ☐ patios | ☐ terraces | ☐ arbors | ☐ gazebos | ☐ pools | ☐ cabanas | ☐ fountains | ☐ fences | ☐ planters | ☐ benches | ☐ parking lots | ☐ sprinkler systems | ☐ lighting | ☐ flower beds | ☐ borders | ☐ other: _____].

☐ **Provide full-service landscape design services to** [☐ commercial | ☐ residential | ☐ public] **clients for** [☐ residential buildings | ☐ custom homes | ☐ office buildings | ☐ shopping malls | ☐ hotels | ☐ stores | ☐ other: _____].

☐ **Manage daily activities of a landscaping design team of** _____ *[#]* **coordinating all functions for** _____ *[#]* _____ *[type of]* **accounts including** _____ *[type of accounts]* **ensuring all work is completed according to landscaping plans and schedules.**

☐ **Design** [☐ indoor | ☐ outdoor] [☐ garden areas | ☐ tree groves | ☐ other: _____] **in** [☐ commercial | ☐ public] **facilities including** [☐ botanical gardens | ☐ parks | ☐ shopping malls | ☐ hotels | ☐ other: _____].

☐ **Work with** _____ *[which?]* **trades to coordinate the design and installation of** [☐ walkways | ☐ terraces | ☐ patios | ☐ decks | ☐ other: _____] **to create** [☐ functional | ☐ aesthetic | ☐ homogenous | ☐ attractive | ☐ pleasant | ☐ other: _____] **environments for** _____ *[whom or what?]*.

☐ **Provide** [☐ large-scale | ☐ intricate | ☐ complex | ☐ other: _____] **landscape design services for** _____ *[#]* [☐ commercial | ☐ residential | ☐ public] **properties including** [☐ condominiums | ☐ apartment complexes | ☐ residential properties | ☐ commercial grounds | ☐ public facilities | ☐ parks | ☐ shopping centers | ☐ golf courses | ☐ botanical gardens | ☐ nurseries | ☐ garden centers | ☐ banks | ☐ factories | ☐ school grounds | ☐ public parking lots | ☐ train stations | ☐ club houses | ☐ hotels | ☐ athletic fields | ☐ college campuses | ☐ large estates | ☐ highways and roadways | ☐ communities | ☐ other: _____].

☐ **Use** _____ *[type of]* **landscaping methods to develop attractive, functional landscape designs including** [☐ ensuring required soil conditions | ☐ grading property | ☐ planting new gardens | ☐ constructing terraces | ☐ installing walkways | ☐ building cabanas | ☐ other: _____].

☐ **Create detailed specifications for multiple** [☐ large-scale | ☐ moderate-size | ☐ highly complex | ☐ moderately complex | ☐ other: _____] **landscape projects with varying requirements ensuring all objectives are accomplished within established time frames.**

☐ **Plan, design, and direct the installation of** _____ *[#]* **acres of** _____ *[type of]* **landscapes for** _____ *[whom or what?]* **covering all aspects of** _____ *[what?]* **including** [☐ installing landscaped areas | ☐ building walkways, terraces, patios, decks | ☐ grading property | ☐ installing lighting | ☐ planting new gardens | ☐ maintaining swimming pools | ☐ controlling weeds, disease, and insect infestation | ☐ other: _____].

ACHIEVEMENT SAMPLES: *See also "Construction Projects."*

☐ **Designed and installed** _____ *[type of]* **unique landscaped areas for** _____ *[whom or what?]* **by** _____ *[doing what?]*.

☐ **Simultaneously drafted detailed landscaping plans and specifications for the following sites:** _____ *[name]*, _____ *[town]*, _____ *[state]*; _____ *[name]*, _____ *[town]*, _____ *[state]*; **and** _____ *[name]*, _____ *[town]*, _____ *[state]*, **resulting in their successful completion.**

☐ **Apply an in-depth knowledge of** [☐ site environments | ☐ plant types | ☐ nutritional requirements | ☐ soil preparation | ☐ ground covers | ☐ other: _____] **in** [☐ identifying best planting methods | ☐ adjusting soil pH | ☐ determining fertilizer applications | ☐ other: _____].

☐ **Created and installed a detailed landscape plan of** _____ *[what?]* **that involved** _____ *[what?]* **with a design challenge of** _____ *[what?]* **resulting in** _____ *[what achievements?]*.

Landscape Installation

See also "Landscaping / Groundskeeping Projects & Functions," "Masonry Projects & Functions," "Inspections & Compliance – Landscape & Masonry" and "Construction Projects," as applicable.

☐ **Supervise the installation of** [☐ retainer walls | ☐ flower beds | ☐ landscape borders | ☐ walkways | ☐ sprinkler systems | ☐ concrete masonry wall units | ☐ other: _____] **including** [☐ grading | ☐ planting | ☐ sod laying | ☐ transplanting | ☐ trimming | ☐ masonry | ☐ other: _____] **of** [☐ lawns | ☐ flowers | ☐ plants | ☐ shrubbery | ☐ shade and ornamental trees | ☐ annuals | ☐ perennials | ☐ other: _____] **taking into account** [☐ sun exposure | ☐ shading | ☐ existing soil | ☐ other: _____] **conditions**.

☐ **Manage and oversee all landscaping installations including** [☐ property grading | ☐ retainer walls | ☐ walkways | ☐ pathways | ☐ patios | ☐ new garden plantings | ☐ irrigation systems | ☐ other: _____].

☐ **Oversee the installation of** _____ *[type of]* **landscapes that** [☐ achieve pleasant and functional outdoor environments | ☐ increase property values | ☐ create a positive first impression | ☐ establish a tranquil mood | ☐ other: _____] **of** _____ *[what?]*.

☐ **Minimize landscape installation impact so** [☐ business | ☐ home] **operations can still be functional by** _____ *[doing what?]*.

☐ **Plan, organize, coordinate, and direct landscaping activities including** [☐ planting trees, shrubs, flowers | ☐ maintaining lawns | ☐ applying fertilizers and pesticides | ☐ other: _____] **to meet contract specifications**.

☐ **Handle** _____ *[type of]* **specialized landscaping work at this** _____ *[type of]* **firm including** [☐ planting new grass | ☐ pruning bushes | ☐ mulching gardens | ☐ other: _____].

☐ **Install and maintain sprinkler systems including** [☐ sprinkler system layout and design | ☐ installation | ☐ testing | ☐ other: _____] **ensuring complete customer satisfaction**.

☐ **Plant and transplant** [☐ trees | ☐ shrubs | ☐ sod | ☐ plants | ☐ flowers | ☐ bulbs | ☐ annuals | ☐ perennials | ☐ other: _____] **by** [☐ correcting soil conditions to allow proper drainage | ☐ using the appropriate grasses | ☐ other: _____] **to ensure proper growth and prevent disease and spoilage**.

☐ **Review client** _____ *[type of]* **landscaping contracts to determine required services, equipment, methods, materials, and labor**.

☐ **Plan and install** _____ *[type of]* **irrigation systems, making efficient use of the system to cover all grounds by effectively** _____ *[doing what well?]*.

Landscape Management

See also "Landscaping / Groundskeeping Projects & Functions," "Landscape Design," "Masonry Projects & Functions," "Inspections & Compliance – Landscape & Masonry," "Trades/Crew Supervision," "Trades Coordination & Oversight – Landscaping & Masonry," and "Construction Projects."

☐ **Plan, organize, coordinate, and direct** [☐ landscaping | ☐ groundskeeping | ☐ lawn service] **activities including** ☐ planting trees, shrubs, flowers | ☐ maintaining lawns | ☐ applying fertilizers and pesticides | ☐ other: _____] **to meet contract specifications**.

☐ **Manage and oversee all aspects of this** _____ *[type of]* **landscaping business including** [☐ sales | ☐ customer service | ☐ installations | ☐ maintenance | ☐ account servicing | ☐ administration | ☐ cash management | ☐ client and financial database | ☐ hiring, training, and scheduling employees | ☐ equipment maintenance | ☐ budgeting | ☐ other: _____].

☐ **Supervise the installation of** [☐ retainer walls | ☐ flower beds | ☐ landscape borders | ☐ walkways | ☐ sprinkler systems | ☐ concrete masonry wall units | ☐ other: _____] **including** [☐ grading | ☐ planting | ☐ sod laying | ☐ transplanting | ☐ trimming | ☐ masonry | ☐ other: _____] **of** [☐ lawns | ☐ flowers | ☐ plants | ☐ shrubbery | ☐ shade and ornamental trees | ☐ annuals | ☐ perennials | ☐ other: _____] **taking into account** [☐ sun exposure | ☐ shading | ☐ existing soil | ☐ other: _____] **conditions**.

☐ **Schedule and supervise the daily operations and landscaping activities of a crew of** _____ *[#]*; **and oversee the complete upkeep of the** _____ *[which?]* **grounds for this** _____ *[type of]* [☐ landscaping | ☐ groundskeeping | ☐ lawn maintenance | ☐ general contracting | ☐ public services | ☐ other: _____] **company**.

☐ **Supervise all** [☐ landscaping | ☐ grounds maintenance | ☐ other: _____] **activities including the installation of** [☐ structural wall panels | ☐ retainer walls | ☐ pathways | ☐ patios | ☐ decks | ☐ firebrick linings | ☐ refractory tile | ☐ soaking pits | ☐ other: _____] **and the application of** [☐ marble | ☐ granite | ☐ limestone | ☐ concrete block | ☐ marble chips | ☐ brick veneer | ☐ tile | ☐ other: _____] **and other masonry projects**.

☐ **Direct the installation of** _____ *[#]* **acres of** _____ *[type of]* **landscapes for** _____ *[whom or what?]* **covering all aspects of** _____ *[what?]* **including** [☐ installing landscaped areas | ☐ building walkways, terraces, patios, decks | ☐ grading property | ☐ installing lighting | ☐ planting new gardens | ☐ maintaining swimming pools | ☐ controlling weeds, disease, and insect infestation | ☐ other: _____].

☐ **Manage all aspects of grounds maintenance services including** [☐ lawn mowing | ☐ leaf removal | ☐ tree trimming | ☐ weed control | ☐ fertilizing | ☐ insect control | ☐ pest elimination | ☐ flower gardening | ☐ shrub pruning | ☐ horticulture | ☐ grading | ☐ seeding | ☐ detaching | ☐ aerating | ☐ planting | ☐ plant damage care | ☐ snow removal | ☐ other: _____].

☐ **Manage a landscaping team of** _____ *[#]* **including hiring, training, scheduling, and evaluating crew; and supervise and coordinate daily crew operations for this** _____ *[type of]* **firm.**

☐ **Manage and oversee all** [☐ landscaping | ☐ landscaping installations | ☐ grounds maintenance] including [☐ lawn | ☐ shrub | ☐ flower] acreage care for _____ *[what?]* **including** [☐ building retainer walls | ☐ constructing pathways | ☐ installing patios | ☐ other: _____].

☐ **Provide decisive leadership and clear direction in all phases of** [☐ large-scale | ☐ complex] _____ *[type of]* **projects for** [☐ residential | ☐ commercial | ☐ industrial | ☐ other: _____] **clients overseeing a top-performing team of** _____ *[#]* **landscapers.**

☐ **Direct and schedule landscape crew's functions and oversee the complete upkeep of the** _____ *[which?]* **grounds for this** _____ *[type of]* **firm with** _____ *[#]* **clients to maximize property potential and aesthetics.**

☐ **Supervise and coordinate the activities of a crew of** _____ *[#]* [☐ skilled | ☐ semi-skilled | ☐ unskilled] [☐ Landscape Laborers | ☐ Greenhouse Workers | ☐ Park Caretakers | ☐ Nursery Workers | ☐ other: _____] **in the grounds upkeep of** _____ *[what?].*

☐ **Oversee and supervise the** _____ *[type of]* **activities of a team of** _____ *[#]* **skilled** [☐ Landscape Architects | ☐ Ornamental Horticulturists | ☐ Park Naturalists | ☐ other: _____] **in the design and installation of** _____ *[what?].*

☐ **Manage daily activities of a landscaping team of** _____ *[#]* **coordinating all** [☐ landscaping | ☐ grounds maintenance | ☐ horticulture | ☐ other: _____] **work functions for** _____ *[#]* [☐ commercial | ☐ residential | ☐ public] **accounts including** _____ *[type of accounts]* **ensuring all work is completed according to landscaping plans and schedules.**

☐ **Coordinate landscaping and masonry functions with other trades in the design and installation of** _____ *[what?].*

☐ **Direct concrete casting and supervise** _____ *[#]* **laborers who spread, level, float, and smooth concrete, create joints, and trowel surfaces to ensure wedges, plumblines, levels, and brackets create a precision fit and attractive finish.**

☐ **Review client contracts to determine required services, equipment, methods, materials, and labor and make project determinations based on** _____ *[what?].*

☐ **Plan, organize, and coordinate landscaping and masonry activities including** [☐ planting trees, shrubs, and flowers | ☐ installing lawns | ☐ applying fertilizers and pesticides | ☐ other: _____] **to meet** [☐ client needs | ☐ contract specifications].

☐ **Schedule and supervise the daily operations and all landscaping activities of a crew of** _____ *[#]*; **and oversee the complete upkeep of the** _____ *[which?]* **grounds.**

ACHIEVEMENT SAMPLES: *See "Construction Projects."*

Landscape Equipment Operation & Maintenance

See "Equipment, Machinery, Tools & Testing Devices – Landscaping & Masonry."

Landscape Projects Oversight

See also "Landscaping/Groundskeeping Projects & Functions," "Landscape Design," "Masonry Projects & Functions," "Inspections & Compliance – Landscape & Masonry," "Trades/Crew Supervision," "Trades Coordination & Oversight – Landscaping & Masonry," and "Construction Projects."

☐ **Oversee landscaping and masonry trades in their landscape work for** [☐ commercial | ☐ residential | ☐ public] _____ *[type of]* **properties including** [☐ condominiums | ☐ apartment complexes | ☐ residential properties | ☐ commercial grounds | ☐ public facilities | ☐ parks | ☐ shopping centers | ☐ golf courses | ☐ botanical gardens | ☐ nurseries | ☐ garden centers | ☐ banks | ☐ factories | ☐ school grounds | ☐ parking lots | ☐ train stations | ☐ club houses | ☐ hotels | ☐ athletic fields | ☐ cemeteries | ☐ college campuses | ☐ large estates | ☐ highways and roadways | ☐ communities | ☐ other: _____].

☐ **Inspect** [☐ lawns | ☐ trees | ☐ shrubs | ☐ plants | ☐ crops | ☐ other: _____] **for** [☐ disease | ☐ insect | ☐ pest | ☐ other: _____] **problems and apply** [☐ fertilizers | ☐ insecticides | ☐ pesticides | ☐ herbicides | ☐ fungicides | ☐ _____ *(type of)* chemicals] **to** [☐ eradicate weeds | ☐ stimulate growth | ☐ eliminate insect infestation | ☐ rid of pests | ☐ other: _____] **resulting in** _____ *[what outcome?].*

☐ **Oversee the performance of various landscaping functions including installing** [☐ landscaped areas | ☐ sod | ☐ retainer walls | ☐ terraces | ☐ patios | ☐ decks and porches | ☐ flower beds | ☐ botanical crops | ☐ landscape borders | ☐ walkways | ☐ sprinkler systems | ☐ concrete masonry wall units | ☐ lighting | ☐ irrigation systems | ☐ shade and ornamental trees | ☐ annuals | ☐ perennials | ☐ other: _____] **and** [☐ grading | ☐ planting | ☐ transplanting | ☐ trimming | ☐ thatching | ☐ seeding | ☐ raking | ☐ masonry | ☐ other: _____] **lawns.**

☐ **Coordinate landscaping and masonry functions with other trades in the design and installation of** _____ *[what?]*.

Landscaping & Greenskeeping Scope

See also "Landscape Management," "Landscape Design," and "Masonry Projects & Functions."

☐ **Tend to the landscaping needs of** _____ *[type of]* **clients'** [☐ private homes | ☐ businesses | ☐ other: _____] **by maintaining** [☐ lawns | ☐ trees | ☐ shrubbery | ☐ gardens | ☐ leaf removal | ☐ weed control | ☐ other: _____].

☐ **Provide** [☐ all | ☐ various] **aspects of commercial** [☐ grounds | ☐ landscape | ☐ masonry | ☐ other: _____] **maintenance services for** _____ *[whom or what?]* **including** [☐ lawn mowing | ☐ leaf removal | ☐ tree trimming | ☐ weed control | ☐ fertilizing | ☐ insect control | ☐ pest elimination | ☐ flower gardening | ☐ shrub pruning | ☐ horticulture | ☐ grading | ☐ seeding | ☐ dethatching | ☐ aerating | ☐ planting | ☐ plant damage care | ☐ snow removal | ☐ other: _____].

☐ **Maintain** _____ *[what?]* **grounds including all** [☐ mowing | ☐ edging | ☐ trimming | ☐ fertilizing | ☐ gardening | ☐ pruning | ☐ grading | ☐ seeding | ☐ dethatching | ☐ aerating | ☐ planting | ☐ transplanting | ☐ irrigating | ☐ harvesting | ☐ raking | ☐ mulching | ☐ weeding | ☐ painting | ☐ troubleshooting | ☐ other: _____] **services and activities for** _____ *[what?]*.

☐ **Provided customer service for this** [☐ local nursery | ☐ garden center | ☐ other: _____] **with an in-house landscaping contractor.**

☐ **Handle specialized** _____ *[type of]* [☐ landscaping | ☐ grounds maintenance] **work at this** _____ *[type of]* **firm including** [☐ thatching soil | ☐ planting new grass | ☐ pruning bushes | ☐ mowing lawns | ☐ mulching gardens | ☐ pulling weeds | ☐ raking leaves | ☐ eliminating pests | ☐ watering acreage | ☐ other: _____].

☐ **Plan, design, install, and maintain** _____ *[type of]* **landscapes for** _____ *[whom or what?]* **covering all aspects of** _____ *[what?]*.

☐ **Provide full-service landscape maintenance services to** [☐ residential | ☐ commercial] **clients for** [☐ residential buildings | ☐ office buildings | ☐ shopping malls | ☐ hotels | ☐ other: _____].

☐ **Keep** [☐ natural | ☐ artificial] **turf fields in top condition by** [☐ correcting soil conditions to allow proper drainage | ☐ using the appropriate grasses | ☐ disinfecting synthetic turf after each use | ☐ other: _____] **to prevent** [☐ disease | ☐ bacteria | ☐ spoilage | ☐ other: _____] [☐ and ensure proper growth].

☐ **Care for and maintain** [☐ indoor | ☐ outdoor] [☐ gardens | ☐ trees | ☐ plantings | ☐ other: _____] **in** [☐ commercial | ☐ public] **facilities including** _____ , _____ , **and** _____ *[type of facilities]*.

☐ **Provide** [☐ large-scale] **weekly** [☐ grounds | ☐ landscape | ☐ greenskeeping | ☐ other: _____] **maintenance services for** _____ *[#]* [☐ commercial | ☐ residential | ☐ public] **properties including** [☐ condominiums | ☐ apartment complexes | ☐ residential properties | ☐ commercial facilities | ☐ parks | ☐ shopping centers | ☐ golf courses | ☐ parks | ☐ picnic areas | ☐ botanical gardens | ☐ nurseries | ☐ garden centers | ☐ banks | ☐ factories | ☐ school grounds | ☐ public parking lots | ☐ train stations | ☐ club houses | ☐ hotels | ☐ public facilities | ☐ athletic fields | ☐ recreational facilities | ☐ cemeteries | ☐ colleges | ☐ university campuses | ☐ cemeteries | ☐ memorial gardens | ☐ large estates | ☐ highways | ☐ roadways | ☐ communities | ☐ country clubs | ☐ playgrounds | ☐ other public spaces | ☐ other: _____].

☐ **Install and maintain** _____ *[type of]* **landscapes for** _____ *[whom?]* **covering all aspects of** _____ *[what?]*.

☐ **Identify and resolve** [☐ plant | ☐ crop | ☐ lawn | ☐ shrub | ☐ tree] **damage by successfully** _____ *[doing what well?]*.

Landscaping & Greenskeeping Projects & Functions

☐ **Review client contracts to determine required services, equipment, methods, materials, and labor and make project determinations based on** _____ *[what?]*.

☐ **Perform various landscaping functions including installing** [☐ landscaped areas | ☐ sod | ☐ retainer walls | ☐ terraces | ☐ patios | ☐ decks and porches | ☐ flower beds | ☐ botanical crops | ☐ landscape borders | ☐ walkways | ☐ sprinkler systems | ☐ concrete masonry wall units | ☐ lighting | ☐ irrigation systems | ☐ shade and ornamental trees | ☐ annuals | ☐ perennials | ☐ other: _____] **and** [☐ grading | ☐ planting | ☐ transplanting | ☐ trimming | ☐ thatching | ☐ seeding | ☐ raking | ☐ masonry | ☐ other: _____] **lawns.**

☐ **Handle** [☐ landscaping | ☐ landscaping installations | ☐ grounds maintenance] **including** [☐ lawn | ☐ shrub | ☐ flower | ☐ other: _____] **acreage care for** _____ *[what?]* **including** [☐ building retainer walls | ☐ constructing pathways | ☐ installing patios | ☐ other: _____] **taking into account** [☐ sun exposure | ☐ shading | ☐ existing soil | ☐ other: _____] **conditions**.

☐ **Plan, organize, and coordinate** [☐ landscaping | ☐ groundskeeping | ☐ lawn service | ☐ masonry | ☐ other: _____] **activities including** [☐ planting trees, shrubs, and flowers | ☐ maintaining lawns | ☐ applying fertilizers and pesticides | ☐ other: _____] **to meet** [☐ client needs | ☐ contract specifications].

☐ **Perform** [☐ landscaping | ☐ grounds maintenance | ☐ other: _____] **activities functions including** [☐ installations | ☐ maintenance | ☐ administration | ☐ hiring, training, and scheduling employees | ☐ equipment maintenance | ☐ budgeting | ☐ other: _____] **of** _____ [what?].

☐ **Oversee the complete upkeep of the** _____ [which?] **grounds to maximize property potential and aesthetics including** [☐ dethatching and aerating (☐ lawns / ☐ fields / ☐ grounds) | ☐ transplanting trees and shrubs | ☐ pruning shrubs | ☐ trimming trees | ☐ mulching planting areas | ☐ cutting away dead branches | ☐ fertilizing flowering plants and lawns | ☐ identifying and resolving plant damage | ☐ mowing and edging lawns | ☐ repairing sidewalks and parking lots | ☐ applying pesticides, herbicides, fungicides, and insecticides | ☐ clearing snow from walkways and parking lots | ☐ raking and mulching leaves | ☐ ensuring required soil composition | ☐ disinfecting synthetic turf | ☐ recommending new plantings | ☐ painting outdoor furniture and structures | ☐ maintaining swimming pools | ☐ controlling weeds, disease, and insect infestation | ☐ other: _____].

☐ **Transport and plant** [☐ trees | ☐ shrubs | ☐ sod | ☐ plants | ☐ flowers | ☐ bulbs | ☐ other: _____]; **and water lawn and gardens to maintain the upkeep of** _____ [what?].

☐ **Provide** [☐ large-scale] **weekly** [☐ grounds | ☐ landscape] **maintenance services for** _____ [#] **properties including** _____ [properties].

☐ **Perform various greenskeeping functions for** _____ [whom or what?] **including** [☐ mowing lawns | ☐ pruning shrubs and trees | ☐ planting flowers | ☐ disinfecting synthetic turf | ☐ removing debris | ☐ applying fertilizers and pesticides | ☐ relocating putting green holes | ☐ covering ground with artificial turf | ☐ planting botanical gardens | ☐ painting outdoor structures and furniture | ☐ removing snow | ☐ other: _____] **to** [☐ eliminate uneven turf wear | ☐ add visual interest | ☐ make a positive aesthetic impression | ☐ other: _____].

☐ **Handle greenskeeping maintenance activities during the growing season for** _____ [type of] **clients on a regular basis including** [☐ mowing | ☐ edging | ☐ trimming | ☐ raking | ☐ fertilizing | ☐ dethatching | ☐ aerating | ☐ mulching | ☐ other: _____] [☐ fields | ☐ greens | ☐ grounds | ☐ acreage].

☐ **Schedule and supervise the daily operations and all landscaping activities of a crew of** _____ [#]; **and oversee the complete upkeep of the** _____ [which?] **grounds**.

☐ **Inspect** [☐ lawns | ☐ trees | ☐ shrubs | ☐ plants | ☐ crops | ☐ other: _____] **for** [☐ disease | ☐ insect | ☐ pest | ☐ other: _____] **problems and apply** [☐ fertilizers | ☐ insecticides | ☐ pesticides | ☐ herbicides | ☐ fungicides | ☐ _____ (type of) chemicals] **to** [☐ eradicate weeds | ☐ stimulate growth | ☐ eliminate insect infestation | ☐ rid of pests | ☐ other: _____] **resulting in** _____ [what outcome?].

☐ **Trim trees and shrubs to remove dead and excess branches in and around** [☐ parks | ☐ highways | ☐ roads | ☐ sidewalks | ☐ facilities | ☐ utilities | ☐ golf courses | ☐ private residences | ☐ other: _____] **to** [☐ improve the appearance and health of trees | ☐ maintain rights-of-way | ☐ clear power lines | ☐ other: _____].

☐ **Direct and schedule employees' functions and oversee the complete upkeep of the** _____ [which?] **grounds to maximize property potential and aesthetics.**

☐ **Mix and apply** [☐ fertilizers | ☐ insecticides | ☐ pesticides | ☐ herbicides | ☐ fungicides | ☐ _____ (type of) chemicals] **to** [☐ lawns | ☐ trees | ☐ shrubs | ☐ flowering plants | ☐ crops | ☐ herb gardens | ☐ other: _____] **using** [☐ sprayers | ☐ applicators | ☐ handlers | ☐ other: _____] **on a** [☐ seasonal | ☐ bi-monthly | ☐ periodic | ☐ other: _____] **basis**.

Maintenance & Repair Projects

See "Preventive & Seasonal Maintenance," "Facility Management," and position-related Maintenance and Repair Work of various trades (Electrical, HVAC, Plumbing, Welding, Landscaping, Masonry).

Management – General

See areas of specialization for primary management functions and achievements.

☐ **Manage the daily operations of the** _____ [which?] [☐ Department | ☐ Center | ☐ unit | ☐ office] **and all related services critical to** _____ [what?] **including** _____, _____, **and** _____ [areas].

☐ **Provide specialized** _____ [type of] [☐ consultation | ☐ leadership and guidance | ☐ technical direction and support | ☐ other: _____] **to a** _____ [which?] **staff of** _____ [#] **in the areas of** _____, _____, **and** _____ [what areas?].

- ☐ [☐ Plan and develop | ☐ Coordinate and implement | ☐ Administer and quality control | ☐ Other: _____] **day-to-day** _____ *[which?]* **activities for this** _____ *[type of]* **firm with** _____ *[#]* **employees.**

- ☐ **Direct and guide a** _____ *[which?]* **staff of** _____ *[#]* **in the development and maintenance of** _____, _____, **and** _____ *[what?]*.

- ☐ **Partake in the development, implementation, and update of** _____ *[what?]* [☐ short-and long-range planning | ☐ establishment of goals and objectives | ☐ policies and procedures development | ☐ new _____ *(type of)* program development | ☐ enhancement of integrated _____ *(type of)* services | ☐ records establishment and maintenance | ☐ other: _____].

- ☐ **Lead and direct a wide range of** _____ *[which?]* **functions including the** [☐ planning | ☐ organizing | ☐ coordinating | ☐ developing | ☐ facilitating | ☐ other: _____] **of** _____ *[what?]*.

- ☐ **Manage and oversee the** _____ *[which?]* **operations and key functions including** _____, _____, **and** _____ *[what areas?]* **to provide comprehensive** _____ *[type of]* **services to** _____ *[whom?]*.

- ☐ **Serve as a key member of the firm's** _____ *[which?]* **management team accountable for developing** _____ *[type of]* **strategies and plans that serve to** _____, _____, **and** _____ *[do what?]*.

- ☐ **Direct and coordinate the organization's** _____ *[which?]* [☐ Department | ☐ Center | ☐ unit | ☐ office] **including** _____, _____, **and** _____ *[what functions or activities?]*.

- ☐ **Serving as** _____ *[title]*, **perform management and administrative support to the** _____ *[which?]* [☐ Department | ☐ Director | ☐ Manager] **in the areas of planning, coordinating, developing, and/or reviewing** _____ *[what?]*.

- ☐ [☐ Manage and administer | ☐ Coordinate and oversee] **all facets of the firm's** _____ *[which?]* **Department** [☐ services | ☐ support activities | ☐ operations] **including** _____, _____, **and** _____ *[what areas?]*.

- ☐ **Implement and oversee the operation of** _____ *[which?]* **Department's** [☐ systems | ☐ policies | ☐ procedures] **in** _____, _____, **and** _____ *[what areas?]*.

- ☐ **Develop, administer, and update the firm's** _____ *[which?]* [☐ policies and procedures | ☐ objectives | ☐ short- and long-range planning | ☐ five-year road map | ☐ other: _____].

- ☐ **Provide leadership, vision, and direction to a team of** _____ *[#]* _____ *[which?]* **Specialists to initiate, plan, and implement** _____ *[type of]* **projects that result in** _____ *[what benefits?]*.

- ☐ **Manage and administer all facets of the firm's** _____ *[which?]* [☐ services | ☐ support activities | ☐ operations | ☐ other: _____] **including** _____, _____, **and** _____ *[what areas?]*.

- ☐ **Identify, define, and document** _____ *[which?]* **priorities, as well as** [☐ options | ☐ costs | ☐ benefits | ☐ milestones | ☐ other: _____] **and translate requirements into effective** _____ *[type of]* **solutions.**

ACHIEVEMENT SAMPLES:

- ☐ [☐ Co-developed | ☐ Designed and implemented] **the firm's** _____ *[type of]* [☐ Policies and Procedures | ☐ initiatives | ☐ programs | ☐ work simplification methods | ☐ other: _____], **which benefited the firm by way of** _____ *[how?]*.

- ☐ **Contributed to the success of this** _____ *[type of]* **firm by** _____ *[doing what?]*.

- ☐ **Recommended and implemented** _____ *[type of]* **improvements to** _____ *[what?]*, **which helped facilitate** _____ *[what functions?]* **and resulted in** _____ *[what benefits?]*.

- ☐ **Involved in managing and coordinating** _____ *[what?]* **efforts that required** _____ *[what actions?]* **to meet** _____ *[what challenges?]* **and resulted in** _____ *[benefits]*.

- ☐ **Run efficient** _____ *[type of]* **business through** [☐ proper staffing and scheduling | ☐ improving staff morale and efficiency | ☐ ensuring quality work in all areas | ☐ other: _____].

Masonry Projects & Functions

See also "Landscape Installation," "Landscaping / Groundskeeping Projects & Functions," "Equipment, Tools & Testing Devices – Landscaping & Masonry," and "Inspections & Compliance – Landscape & Masonry."

- ☐ **Design and build attractive landscape designs including** [☐ walkways | ☐ sidewalks | ☐ patios | ☐ roadways | ☐ flooring | ☐ concrete surfaces | ☐ exposed aggregate walls | ☐ concrete beams | ☐ columns | ☐ panels | ☐ other: _____] **for this** [☐ masonry | ☐ landscaping | ☐ general contracting | ☐ other: _____] **firm that services** [☐ residential | ☐ commercial | ☐ other: _____] **clients.**

- ☐ **Design, cut, and lay out different masonry shapes and effects, such as** _____ *[what?]* **for various** _____ *[type of]* **projects, which result in** _____ *[what client or employer benefits?]*.

☐ **Use a variety of masonry techniques to build creative and functional projects, such as** [☐ colorizing concrete for a decorative finish | ☐ polishing and sealing masonry surfaces to prevent breakage, separation, and chipping | ☐ installing decorative interlocking pavers and edging materials | ☐ staggering blocks to create unique designs | ☐ creating ornate stone walls | ☐ designing and installing decorative patios and steps | ☐ embedding gravel chips for a pebble finish | ☐ brushing surfaces for a coarse, nonskid finish | ☐ creating unique finishes by applying _____ *(what?)* | ☐ using various masonry materials that create contrast and visual interest | ☐ other: _____].

☐ **Specialize in installing** [☐ structural wall panels | ☐ firebrick linings in industrial furnaces | ☐ refractory tile in boilers and furnaces | ☐ soaking pits in industrial establishments | ☐ other: _____] **using** [☐ marble | ☐ granite | ☐ limestone | ☐ concrete block | ☐ marble chips | ☐ brick veneer | ☐ tile | ☐ glass | ☐ other: _____] **and other masonry materials**.

☐ **Lay out, cut, and install a variety of interlocking pavers and edging materials to create decorative** [☐ landscape designs | ☐ walkways | ☐ paths | ☐ driveways | ☐ patios | ☐ panels | ☐ playgrounds | ☐ steps | ☐ other: _____] **for** _____ *[whom or what?]*.

☐ **Build** _____ *[type of]* **structures with precision and uniformity by** [☐ aligning masonry materials with wedges, plumb lines, levels, and brackets for a precision fit | ☐ using the corner lead and corner pole methods | ☐ other technique: _____] **depending on job complexity and blueprint specifications.**

☐ **Install** _____ *[type of]* [(☐ structural / ☐ insulated / ☐ other: _____) wall panels | ☐ exposed aggregate and retainer walls | ☐ roadways | ☐ driveways | ☐ walkways | ☐ paths | ☐ playgrounds | ☐ stone walls | ☐ ornate exteriors | ☐ concrete beams and columns | ☐ other: _____].

☐ **Working closely with related trades to create** _____ *[type of]* **structures, ensure the precise alignment of all** [☐ stones | ☐ bricks | ☐ pavers | ☐ edgers | ☐ other: _____] **with wedges, plumblines, levels, and brackets for a precision fit and attractive finish using chisels, diamond blade saws, mallets, trowels, and crowbars.**

☐ **Create and install decorative, durable** _____ *[type of]* **masonry** [☐ surfaces | ☐ structures | ☐ other: _____] **with varying complexity for** _____ *[type of]* **clients including** [☐ stone walls | ☐ masonry walkways | ☐ structural wall panels | ☐ concrete foundations | ☐ ornate exteriors | ☐ roadways | ☐ driveways | ☐ other: _____] **on** [☐ high-rise buildings | ☐ office buildings | ☐ residential homes | ☐ lobbies | ☐ other: _____] **by** _____ *[doing what?]*.

☐ **Build solid, level concrete** [☐ foundations | ☐ panels | ☐ other: _____] **creating joints and** [☐ blending marble chip mixtures into cement | ☐ grinding terrazzo | ☐ embedding gravel chips for a pebble finish | ☐ using colored concrete for a decorative finish | ☐ laying pavers | ☐ installing edging materials | ☐ other: _____] **and** [☐ cleaning | ☐ polishing | ☐ sealing | ☐ brushing | ☐ other: _____] **surfaces, taking necessary preventive measures to prevent defects from occurring.**

☐ **Repair cracks and imperfections in** [☐ walls | ☐ walkways | ☐ flooring | ☐ partitions | ☐ fireplaces | ☐ chimneys | ☐ parking lots | ☐ other: _____].

☐ **Perform concrete demolition, installation, and repair functions including** [☐ removing existing pavement | ☐ grading soil | ☐ installing and compacting base material | ☐ accurately setting and aligning concrete forms | ☐ casting concrete | ☐ spreading, leveling, floating, and smoothing concrete | ☐ building solid, level concrete foundations | ☐ using corner lead and corner pole methods | ☐ troweling surface and creating joints | ☐ monitoring how the wind, heat, and cold affect concrete curing to prevent defects | ☐ laying pavers | ☐ grinding terrazzo | ☐ filling spaces with sand | ☐ installing edging materials | ☐ cleaning, polishing, and sealing surfaces | ☐ repairing cracks | ☐ other: _____] **on** _____ *[type of]* **projects.**

☐ **Accurately set and align concrete forms; direct concrete casting; and supervise laborers to spread, level, float, and smooth concrete; create joints; and trowel surfaces.**

New Business Development

See also "Increased Account Base" and "Increased Revenue & Profitability."

☐ **Manage and direct New Business Development for this** _____ *[type of]* **firm that specializes in selling** _____ *[what?]* **to** _____ *[which?]* **market(s) including** _____, _____, **and** _____ *[type of clients]*.

☐ **Lead and direct this** _____ *[type of]* **firm's** [☐ new business development | ☐ sales | ☐ marketing | ☐ other: _____] **program(s) including assignment of** [☐ sales territories | ☐ goal setting | ☐ sales training programs establishment | ☐ other: _____].

☐ **Plan, direct, and coordinate new business development initiatives through effective** [☐ sales goals development | ☐ sales planning | ☐ promotional campaigns | ☐ market surveys | ☐ other: _____] **ensuring** [☐ product profitability | ☐ market share | ☐ return on investment | ☐ profit growth | ☐ company expansion | ☐ achievement of all sales objectives | ☐ other: _____].

- ☐ **Direct and lead all aspects of** [☐ new business development | ☐ sales and marketing | ☐ strategic planning | ☐ new program development | ☐ brand management | ☐ client relations | ☐ other: _____], **including** [☐ mergers and acquisitions | ☐ joint venture development | ☐ extensive _____ *(type of)* support programs | ☐ vendor relations | ☐ other: _____].

- ☐ **Actively and successfully explore new business-development opportunities to expand growth potential by** _____ *[doing what?]*, **resulting in** _____ *[benefit]*.

- ☐ **Direct the** [☐ New Business Development | ☐ Sales and Marketing | ☐ other: _____] **Division including** _____ *[#]* **direct reports and** _____ *[#]* **indirect reports of this** [☐ multimillion-dollar | ☐ $_____ *(revenues)*] _____ *[type of]* **firm specializing in** _____ *[what?]*.

- ☐ **Manage and coordinate all** [☐ new business development efforts | ☐ advertising projects | ☐ marketing campaigns | ☐ promotional programs | ☐ creative planning | ☐ account servicing | ☐ other: _____], **including** _____, _____, **and** _____ **of the** _____ *[which?]* **market.**

- ☐ **Direct and oversee** [☐ worldwide | ☐ nationwide | ☐ regional | ☐ local] **new business development activities, including** [☐ advertising campaigns | ☐ trade shows | ☐ direct-mail efforts | ☐ other: _____] **and the strategic direction of products, taking the** [☐ firm | ☐ division | ☐ region | ☐ department] **from $_____ to $_____** *[amounts]* **in annual sales.**

- ☐ **Manage all major** [☐ wholesalers | ☐ distributors | ☐ buying groups | ☐ vendors | ☐ other: _____] **providing** [☐ new product proposals | ☐ promotional presentations | ☐ motivational seminars | ☐ ride-alongs | ☐ other: _____], **and resulting in increased sales of $_____ .**

- ☐ **Directly network and sell to CIOs and CFOs of** [☐ middle to large] _____ *[type of]* **corporations servicing Fortune** [☐ 100 | ☐ 500 | ☐ 1000] **companies including** _____, _____, **and** _____ *[if not a breach of confidentiality]*.

ACHIEVEMENT SAMPLES: *See also Achievements under "New Business Development Management."*

- ☐ **Spearheaded proactive business development of** _____ *[what?]* **with concentration in the** _____ *[which?]* **regions that resulted in** _____ **and** _____ *[benefits]*.

- ☐ **Prospected and developed new business $_____** *[amount]* **and expanded client base in the area(s) of** _____ *[area(s)]* **while managing existing account base, including** _____, _____, **and** _____ [☐ Fortune ☐ 100 | ☐ 500 | ☐ 1000 companies] **by** _____ *[doing what?]*.

- ☐ **Championed** [☐ growth of business | ☐ proactive business development] **by building client relationships based on** [☐ honesty | ☐ integrity | ☐ trust | ☐ knowledge | ☐ other: _____] **and resulting in stronger and lasting relationships.**

- ☐ **Devised and implemented various new business-development initiatives, including** _____, _____, **and** _____, *[which initiatives?]* **resulting in annual sales increases of $_____ and** _____ *[other benefits]*.

- ☐ **Successfully** [☐ managed | ☐ fulfilled] **mission to develop Company into a major full-service** _____ *[type of]* [☐ wholesaler | ☐ distributor | ☐ retailer | ☐ manufacturer | ☐ other: _____] **by penetrating the** _____ *[which?]* **marketplace.**

- ☐ **Devised and implemented various new business-development initiatives, including** _____, _____, **and** _____, *[explain]* **resulting in annual sales increases of $_____** *[amount]* **and** _____ *[other benefits]*.

- ☐ **Generated $_____** *[amount]* **of new business within** [☐ first year | ☐ other: _____] **for a** _____ *[type of]* **client, which spearheaded the company's expansion into** _____ *[what arena?]*.

- ☐ **Qualified sales leads and generated new business from** [☐ direct mail | ☐ website | ☐ advertising campaigns | ☐ industry trade shows | ☐ other methods: _____].

- ☐ **Played an integral role in obtaining a $_____** *[amount]* **contract from** _____ *[whom?]* **to replace their current** _____ *[type of contract]* **with** _____ *[what?]* **resulting in** _____ *[what benefits?]*.

- ☐ **Increased sales $_____** *[amount]* **and account base** _____% *[percentage]* **through** _____ *[type of]* **new business development initiatives including** _____ *[what did you put in place?]*.

- ☐ **Aided in developing new** [☐ internal | ☐ external] **business opportunities at national level by** _____ *[how accomplished]*.

- ☐ **Networked and set up a referral base of** _____ *[#]* _____ *[type of]* **customers, developing proposals at a fair price to win over clients from competition.**

- ☐ **Created and presented** _____ *[type of]* **proposals, conducted contract negotiations, and developed** [☐ multimillion-dollar | ☐ $_____ *(amount)*] [☐ marketing | ☐ sales | ☐ other: _____] [☐ budgets | ☐ initiatives | ☐ programs].

- ☐ **Built a rapport with** _____ *[whom?]*, **which allowed** _____ *[what?]* **and resulted in new business.**

- ☐ **Solicited** [☐ wholesalers | ☐ distributors | ☐ businesses | ☐ consumers | ☐ homeowners | ☐ other: _____] **for** _____ *[what?]* **and signed on** _____ *[#]* **customers by** [☐ exhibiting a positive attitude | ☐ handling the rejection process well | ☐ overcoming obstacles | ☐ in-depth product knowledge | ☐ other: _____].

☐ **Prospected and developed untouched new territory, handled exiting account base including** _____, _____, **and** _____ [☐ Fortune (☐ 100 / ☐ 500 / ☐ 1000)] **companies, set up trade shows, and hired and trained new Sales Associates.**

☐ **Utilized point-of-sale material to increase consumer awareness and sales, which resulted in** _____ *[what measurable benefits?].*

☐ **Solicited new business and generated** [☐ leads | ☐ sales] **via** [☐ door-to-door sales | ☐ telemarketing | ☐ cold calling | ☐ coupon booklets | ☐ tickets | ☐ products | ☐ other: _____].

☐ **Actively and successfully explored new business-development opportunities that expanded growth potential by** _____ *[doing what?],* **resulting in** _____ *[benefit].*

☐ **Gained $**_____ *[amount]* **in new business through** [☐ effective sales techniques | ☐ handling all customer associations in a positive, professional manner | ☐ building a rapport | ☐ calling on professionals in the community | ☐ other: _____].

New Business, Division & Department Start-up – Architecture & Construction

See also "New Business Development Initiatives," "Increased Account Base," and "Increased Revenue & Profitability."

ACHIEVEMENT SAMPLES:

☐ [☐ Founded | ☐ Co-founded] **company from the ground up to a** [☐ leading] **full service** [☐ design-and-build | ☐ construction management | ☐ general contracting | ☐ other: _____] **firm with** [☐ a staff of _____ *(#)* | ☐ _____ *(#)* locations | ☐ $_____ *(amount)* in annual sales | ☐ other: _____].

☐ **Developed, built, and operate a startup** _____ *[type of]* **firm culminating in** _____ *[#]* **locations with** _____ *[#]* **employees, and resulting in annual revenues of $**_____ *[revenues]* **over a(n)** _____ *[#]*-**year period.**

☐ **Championed the development of a successful** _____ *[type of]* **company from the ground up to $**_____ *[amount]* **in annual sales by** [☐ creating _____ *(which?)* Division(s) | ☐ hiring talented management staff | ☐ networking and building an account base of _____ *(#)* | ☐ other: _____].

☐ **Built company from start-up to a client base of** _____ *[#],* **by networking with** _____ *[whom?]* **resulting in** [☐ steady work | ☐ increased annual profits of _____% *(percentage)* | ☐ repeat business | ☐ many referrals from satisfied customers | ☐ other: _____].

☐ **Started up a new** _____ *[name of]* **group** _____ *[doing what?]* **which resulted in** [☐ growing client base by $_____ *(amount)* | _____% *(percentage)* | ☐ revenues of $_____ *(amount)* | ☐ other achievement: _____] **through effective** _____ *[what actions?]* **efforts.**

☐ **Grew Company from $**_____ **to $**_____ *[amounts]* **in** [☐ sales | ☐ revenues] **to one of the** [☐ leading | ☐ top | ☐ most profitable | ☐ most successful | ☐ recognized | ☐ other: _____] _____ *[type of]* **firms in the industry through effective** [☐ corporate communications | ☐ promotional | ☐ brand management | ☐ media relations | ☐ sales support | ☐ public relations | ☐ other: _____] **strategies.**

☐ [☐ Started up | ☐ Revamped | ☐ Turned around] **the** _____ *[which?]* [☐ Division | ☐ Department(s)] **of the firm that entailed** _____ *[what actions?]* **and resulted in** _____ *[what benefits?].*

☐ **Founded the firm from the ground up to $**_____ **in annual sales by** [☐ networking and building an account base of _____ *(#)* | ☐ hiring talented department heads | ☐ improving quality of the _____ *(which?)* lines | ☐ targeting the _____ *(which?)* market | ☐ building strong relationships with _____ *(whom?)].*

☐ **Created** _____ *[which?]* **Departments which entailed** _____ *[what actions?]* **and resulted in** _____ *[benefits].*

Office Management & Supervision – General

See also "Administrative" categories, "Management – General," "Operations Management," and "Staff Management & Supervision – Office Support Staff."

☐ **Coordinate, delegate, and oversee the day-to-day** _____ *[type of]* [☐ operations | ☐ tasks] **of the** _____ *[which?]* [☐ division | ☐ department | ☐ team] **including** _____, _____, **and** _____ *[what areas?]* **to ensure** _____ *[what?]* **for this $**_____ *[revenues]* _____ *[type of]* **firm with** _____ *[#]* [☐ locations | ☐ employees | ☐ customers | ☐ other: _____].

☐ **Manage and oversee the overall** [☐ office administration | ☐ administrative management | ☐ payroll | ☐ purchasing | ☐ inter-company supply | ☐ other: _____] **operations including** [☐ _____ *(#)* facilities | ☐ reception area | ☐ other: _____] **with an operational budget of $**_____ *[amount]* **and an office staff of** _____ *[#].*

☐ **Facilitate** [☐ general office administration | ☐ payroll issues | ☐ health insurance | ☐ 401K matters | ☐ other: _____] **for**
    ☐ **Coordinate, delegate, and oversee the day-to-day** _____ *[type of]* [☐ operations | ☐ tasks] **of the** _____ *[which?]*
[☐ division | ☐ department | ☐ unit | ☐ store | ☐ team] **including** _____ , _____ , **and** _____ *[what areas?]* **to
ensure** _____ *[what?]* **for this $** _____ *[revenues]* _____ *[type of]* **firm with** _____ *[#]* [☐ locations |
☐ branches | ☐ employees | ☐ accounts | ☐ customers | ☐ other: _____].

☐ **Provide an administrative management role in** [☐ departmental communications | ☐ document preparation and organization |
☐ systems development and implementation | ☐ database management | ☐ correspondence preparation | ☐ calendar upkeep |
☐ telephone support | ☐ other: _____].

☐ **Manage the** [☐ operational aspects | ☐ administrative support services ☐ other: _____] **of this** _____ *[type of]* **office
including** [☐ recruitment | ☐ administration | ☐ payroll | ☐ compensation | ☐ accounting | ☐ accounts payable | ☐ reconciliation |
☐ materials distribution | ☐ printing | ☐ security | ☐ records management | ☐ computer troubleshooting | ☐ other: _____].

☐ **Oversee various** [☐ administrative | ☐ office support] **functions including** [☐ fielding telephone calls | ☐ receiving and directing visitors
| ☐ conducting Internet research | ☐ preparing spreadsheets | ☐ creating presentations | ☐ performing data entry | ☐ processing
expense reports | ☐ tracking sales progress | ☐ monitoring budgets | ☐ communicating with service providers | ☐ maintaining
departmental database | ☐ other: _____].

☐ **Working with** _____ *[whom?]*, **develop, implement, and maintain** [☐ long-term | ☐ short-range] [☐ company | ☐ departmental
| ☐ other: _____] [☐ plans | ☐ goals | ☐ objectives | ☐ projects | ☐ programs] **as well as operating policies and procedures.**

☐ **Coordinate and oversee all facets of** _____ *[what?]*—**from** _____ *[what functions?]* **to** _____ *[what functions?]*
for this [☐ multimillion-dollar | ☐ $ _____ *[amount]*] _____ *[type of]* **firm with** _____ *[#]* [☐ stores | ☐ locations
| ☐ employees | ☐ accounts].

☐ **Monitor, track, and review** [☐ service | ☐ productivity | ☐ product promotions | ☐ cash control | ☐ inventory control | ☐ auditing |
☐ training | ☐ other: _____] **compliance with all** [☐ company | ☐ store | ☐ departmental] **policies, procedures, and standards.**

Operations Management

See also "Building Operations Management" and related categories, as applicable.

☐ **Manage and oversee the company's** [☐ daily operations | ☐ day-to-day activities | ☐ General Ledger | ☐ financial and budget
activities | ☐ payroll systems | ☐ time accounting | ☐ support services | ☐ inventory | ☐ other: _____] **to maximize efficiency
and** [☐ cut costs | ☐ strategize new ways to increase profitability | ☐ other: _____].

☐ **Lead and direct this** _____ *[type of]* [☐ firm's | ☐ department's] **operations to ensure maximum** [☐ productivity | ☐ efficiency
| ☐ performance | ☐ profitability | ☐ other: _____] **through effective organizational** [☐ strategies | ☐ methods | ☐ policies
| ☐ practices ☐ procedures] **including supporting better** [☐ information flow | ☐ business processes | ☐ organizational planning
| ☐ operational procedures | ☐ other: _____].

☐ **Provide strategic leadership for the firm's** [☐ financial | ☐ risk | ☐ budget | ☐ human resources | ☐ sales | ☐ marketing |
☐ customer service | ☐ logistics | ☐ production | ☐ support services | ☐ resource | ☐ training and development | ☐ information
processing | ☐ support services | ☐ communications | ☐ purchasing | ☐ administrative | ☐ other: _____] **management
functions inclusive of** [☐ operational strategizing | ☐ objectives establishment | ☐ policy formulation | ☐ resources control |
☐ information recording | ☐ work planning and prioritizing | ☐ other: _____] **geared toward operational excellence.**

☐ **Manage and increase the efficiency and effectiveness of the company's support services including** [☐ Finance | ☐ Human
Resources | ☐ Information Technology | ☐ Sales | ☐ Marketing | ☐ other: _____] **including its operational systems,
processes, and policies by driving strategic management initiatives that contribute to long-term operational excellence.**

☐ **Plan, direct, and coordinate the firm's operations; improve performance, productivity, and profitability; and ensure smooth,
efficient operations** [☐ that meets the needs and expectations of (☐ customers / ☐ clients) | ☐ in support of the firm's mission |
☐ through the implementation of effective _____ *[type of]* methods and strategies | ☐ other: _____].

☐ **Develop** _____ *[type of]* [☐ objectives | ☐ strategies | ☐ plans | ☐ programs | ☐ policies | ☐ procedures | ☐ methods |
☐ standards | ☐ cost/price models | ☐ other: _____] **for** _____ *[what?]* **that include** [☐ long-range (☐ objectives
/ ☐ forecasts / ☐ financial plans) | ☐ pricing strategy | ☐ marketing strategy | ☐ product-marketing strategies | ☐ advertising campaigns
| ☐ sales promotions | ☐ other: _____] **that** [☐ increase the firm's efficiency and effectiveness | ☐ meet the organization's goals].

☐ **Increase effectiveness and efficiency of all support services through improvements to** [☐ Finance | ☐ Human Resources |
☐ Information Technology | ☐ other: _____] **systems and processes by spearheading strategic management initiatives
that contribute to long-term operational excellence.**

☐ **Guide and support** _____ *[which?]* [☐ Departments | ☐ teams] **to operate efficiently and meet the firm's goals covering**
[☐ general business operations | ☐ recruitment | ☐ contract negotiations | ☐ budget matters | ☐ other: _____].

☐ **Direct and coordinate the firm's financial and budget activities to** [☐ maximize investments | ☐ increase efficiency | ☐ fund operations | ☐ other: _____].

☐ **Plan, develop, and manage the firm's annual** _____ *[which?]* [☐ program ☐ organizational] **budget(s) to include** [☐ financial performance assessments and forecasts | ☐ short- and long-term financial and managerial reporting | ☐ accounts receivable and payable processing | ☐ payroll management | ☐ invoicing | ☐ check disbursements | ☐ fiscal document organization | ☐ generation of year-end reports | ☐ monthly activity reconciliations | ☐ tax-related requirements fulfillment | ☐ other: _____].

☐ **Examine the firm's** [☐ operating practices and procedures | ☐ internal programs | ☐ other: _____] **including** [☐ operational records | ☐ management reports | ☐ financial statements | ☐ budgetary information | ☐ expense reports | ☐ sales and activity reports | ☐ sales trends | ☐ performance data | ☐ other: _____] **to** [☐ perform (☐ financial / ☐ cost-benefit) analysis | ☐ measure productivity and goal achievement | ☐ perform quality control | ☐ Identify underlying principles | ☐ track and measure staff performance | ☐ determine areas requiring (cost reduction / program improvement) | ☐ improve profitability | ☐ other function(s): _____].

☐ **Monitor, evaluate, and improve efficiency of support services by** [☐ planning and supporting sales and marketing activities | ☐ facilitating coordination and communication between support functions | ☐ other: _____].

ACHIEVEMENTS:

☐ **Established** _____ *[type of]* [☐ organizational structures | ☐ departmental policies | ☐ goals and objectives | ☐ procedures | ☐ other: _____] **that** _____ *[accomplished what?]*.

☐ **Assessed the value, importance, and/or quality of various operational** [☐ policies | ☐ functions | ☐ resources | ☐ other: _____], **and** [☐ spearheaded new | ☐ formulated suggestions on] _____ *[type of]* [☐ strategies | ☐ plans | ☐ applications | ☐ ideas | ☐ systems | ☐ products | ☐ other: _____] **that resulted in** [☐ making optimum use of resources | ☐ adjusting prices on (☐ goods / ☐ services) sold | ☐ achieving growth and sustaining long-term profitability | ☐ efficiently and effectively providing needed services while staying within budgetary limits | ☐ other benefit: _____].

☐ **Reduced company costs $**_____ *[amount]* **and streamlined operations by** [☐ spearheading highly efficient operating procedures through the research and analysis of [☐ operating costs | ☐ sales | ☐ business practices | ☐ other: _____].

☐ **Planned and implemented effective** _____ *[type of]* **operational** [☐ strategies | ☐ processes | ☐ policies] **that** [☐ maximized output | ☐ contributed to the financial wellbeing of the company | ☐ ensured smooth operations | | ☐ supported organizational goals | ☐ achieved the firm's operational objectives | ☐ other: _____].

☐ **Decreased inventory adjustments by** _____% *[percentage]* **by** [☐ incorporating audit trails into inventory process | ☐ other: _____].

☐ **Increased profitability** _____% *[percentage]* **by devising policies that** [☐ raised awareness of P&L effects of (☐ costs / ☐ sales / ☐ credits / ☐ inventory charges / ☐ other: _____) | ☐ other method: _____].

Overcoming Obstacles

ACHIEVEMENT SAMPLES:

☐ **Assigned to take over the** _____ *[which?]* **project to smooth out conflicts. Handled through firm negotiations and teamwork with client rep and all trades to put project back on track.**

☐ **Turned around a mismanaged** _____ *[type of]* **project; accomplished** [☐ through firm negotiations and teamwork with client rep and all trades to put project back on track | ☐ by successfully completing project without compromising each other's responsibilities | ☐ by maintaining an excellent rapport | ☐ other: _____] **and receiving commendations from client and employer.**

☐ **Successfully turned around** _____ *[what challenge?]* **by** _____ *[doing what?]*, **which resulted in** _____ *[what benefit?]*.

☐ **Effectively met difficult** _____ *[type of]* **challenge(s)** [☐ faced by _____ *(what obstacles?)* | to _____ *(do what?)* | ☐ other: _____] **by** _____ *[doing what?]*, **which resulted in** _____ *[what benefits?]*.

☐ **Faced with the challenge of** _____ *[what?]*, **successfully turned around a** _____ *[type of]* **project; accomplished by** _____ *[what means?]* **and receiving commendations from** [☐ senior management | ☐ client | ☐ employer | ☐ other: _____].

☐ **Acquired skills to build** _____ *[#]* **clean rooms for** _____ *[whom?]* **within** _____ *[#]* [☐ weeks | ☐ months] **on the job—which was essential as** _____ *[#]* **clean rooms were needed for** [☐ the return of an in-orbit Space Shuttle Mission to continue experiments conducted in space | ☐ other: _____].

☐ **Consistently met** [☐ project quality | ☐ timeline | ☐ safety | ☐ code | ☐ client | ☐ other: _____] **requirements despite** _____ *[type of]* **challenges and obstacles including** _____, _____, **and** _____ *[type of challenges]* **by** _____ *[doing what well?]*.

☐ **Resolved** [☐_____ *(type of)* problems | ☐ conflicts with employees | ☐ other: _____] **through effective** [☐ influential skills | ☐ customer service | ☐ teamwork | ☐ other: _____].

Painting Projects & Functions

See also "General Contracting," "Carpentry/Construction Functions & Projects,"
"Carpentry / Construction Work Scope," and "Equipment, Tools & Testing Devices," as applicable.

☐ [☐ Supervise | ☐ Perform] **approximately** _____ *[#]* **painting jobs per** [☐ week | ☐ month] **ranging from $**_____ **to $**_____ *[amounts]* **for** _____ *[type of]* **clients**.

☐ **Plan, organize, and** [☐ supervise | ☐ facilitate] **surface preparation and application of** [☐ paint | ☐ stain | ☐ varnish | ☐ other: _____] **products on** [☐ interiors | ☐ exteriors] **of** [☐ residential homes | ☐ commercial buildings | ☐ other: _____] **for this** _____ *[type of]* [☐ contracting firm | ☐ agency | ☐ other: _____].

☐ **Meet with prospective clients requiring painting work to** [☐ define project parameters | ☐ advise on surface effect(s) | ☐ determine suitable paint and stain products | ☐ estimate project time | ☐ estimate material and labor costs | ☐ provide job estimates | ☐ other: _____].

☐ **Provide decisive leadership and clear direction in all phases of** [☐ large-scale | ☐ complex] _____ *[type of]* **painting and staining projects for** [☐ residential | ☐ commercial | ☐ industrial | ☐ other: _____] **clients overseeing a top-performing team of** _____ *[#]* **painters**.

☐ **Prepare the surfaces of all** _____ *[type of]* **painting jobs by removing dirt, mold, and any peeling paint; patching cracks and holes; and protecting areas by taping trim and using drop cloths; and preventing damage to location to ensure a professional outcome.**

☐ **Apply an in-depth knowledge of all types of painting** [☐ equipment | ☐ materials | ☐ techniques | ☐ safety techniques | ☐ other: _____] **in the preparation, application, and completion of** _____ *[type of]* **painting, staining, varnishing projects**.

☐ **Mix, match, and color coordinate various paints and stains using** [☐ tinting bases | ☐ liquid color | ☐ primers | ☐ other: _____] **for application on** _____ *[type of]* **projects using** [☐ power sprayers | ☐ rollers | ☐ brushes | ☐ and _____ *(type of)* equipment].

☐ **Maintain brushes, rollers, trays, sprayers, compressors, and related equipment; store paints and stains and inventories for future use; complete work orders and logs.**

☐ **Supervise journey-level painters, monitor painting projects to ensure effective and productive work, and troubleshoot and problem-solve any project or customer concerns by** [☐ listening carefully to their needs | ☐ immediately rectifying problems | ☐ offering alternative solutions | ☐ other methods: _____].

☐ **Coordinate painting work with other contractors to ensure it is completed according to agreement and complies with standards.**

☐ **Handle a variety of painting and other projects including** [☐ hanging wallpaper | ☐ staining furniture | ☐ painting stripes in _____ *(which?)* (☐ parking lots / ☐ football fields / ☐ gym floors / ☐ other: _____) | ☐ other: _____] **completing all projects on time.**

ACHIEVEMENT SAMPLES:

☐ **Increased revenues** _____ **%** *[percentage]* **by** [☐ obtaining a solid referral business with a reputation for excellent work | ☐ developing targeted advertising campaigns | ☐ creating a website | ☐ dropping off flyers in local communities | ☐ other: _____].

☐ **Successfully achieved a 100% customer satisfaction rate by** [☐ achieving company's number one goal to turn every customer into a satisfied customer | ☐ completing all projects on time and within budget | ☐ other method: _____].

☐ **Steadily increased revenues annually by** [☐ developing strong networking contacts in the real estate community | ☐ advertising in local print media | ☐ networking at local Chambers of Commerce | ☐ providing discounts on customer referrals | ☐ other: _____].

☐ **Established a reputation for quality workmanship at competitive prices by** [☐ maintaining superior levels of craftsmanship | ☐ providing excellent customer service | ☐ other: _____].

☐ **Increased safety and customer satisfaction by** [☐ providing professional painting services | ☐ ensuring end-of-day clean up and debris removal from all work areas and sites | ☐ other: _____].

Plumbing Scope

See also "Plumbing Projects," "HVAC/HVAC-R Scope," "Welding/Steamfitting Functions,"
and "Work Collaboration & Coordination – Plumbing Projects."

☐ **Facilitate hands-on installation, maintenance, and repair of** [☐ commercial | ☐ domestic | ☐ industrial | ☐ other: _____] [☐ indoor | ☐ outdoor | ☐ indoor and outdoor] **plumbing systems including** _____, _____, **and** _____ *[what?]*.

☐ **Install, maintain, and/or repair** _____ *[type of]* [☐ plumbing systems | ☐ heating and cooling systems | ☐ refrigeration systems | ☐ water supply and drain lines | ☐ steam lines | ☐ roof drains | ☐ water heaters | (☐ gas / ☐ electric / ☐ open flame) boilers | ☐ fire sprinkler systems | ☐ sewer lines | ☐ storm drains | ☐ cesspools | ☐ septic tanks | ☐ pipes, faucets, valves, fixtures, and fittings | ☐ specialty plumbing items | ☐ other: _____].

☐ **Perform** [☐ journeyman | ☐ apprentice | ☐ master] **-level plumbing installation, maintenance, and repair of** _____, _____, **and** _____ *[what?]* **following all current plumbing practices and techniques for the trade and ensuring compliance with all plumbing codes for this $**_____ *[revenues]* _____ *[type of]* **firm.**

☐ **Handle approximately** _____ *[#]* **plumbing jobs** [☐ daily | ☐ weekly | ☐ monthly | ☐ annually] [☐ averaging $_____ to $_____ *(amounts)* | ☐ totaling $_____] **including** [☐ estimating job times, materials, and costs | ☐ selecting materials and hardware | ☐ preparing materials estimates | ☐ reviewing materials bids | ☐ ordering required job-related materials | ☐ scheduling jobs | ☐ performing plumbing functions | ☐ inspecting completed plumbing jobs for code compliance | ☐ other: _____].

☐ **Perform hands-on installation, maintenance, and/or repair of** [☐ commercial | ☐ domestic | ☐ industrial | ☐ other: _____] [☐ indoor | ☐ outdoor] **plumbing systems including** _____, _____, **and** _____ *[what?]*.

☐ **Assemble, install, and test** _____ *[type of]* **plumbing** [☐ equipment | ☐ pipes | ☐ fittings | ☐ fixtures | ☐ pumps | ☐ motors | ☐ other: _____] **of** [☐ heating | ☐ cooling | ☐ ventilation ☐ drainage | ☐ sprinkler | ☐ gas | ☐ water supply | ☐ sewer | ☐ other: _____] **systems ensuring compliance with all plumbing codes, specifications, and timeframes.**

☐ **Install and maintain all** _____ *[type of]* [☐ plumbing | ☐ fittings | ☐ fixtures | ☐ other: _____] **in accordance with the Uniform Plumbing Code including** [☐ cutting | ☐ fitting | ☐ connecting | ☐ installing | ☐ maintaining | ☐ repairing] _____ *[type of]* **plumbing piping for** _____ *[what or whom?]*.

☐ **Install, repair, and service** [☐ heating and air conditioning systems | ☐ industrial and commercial refrigerant systems | ☐ other: _____] **to ensure control of temperature, humidity, and air quality in** [☐ residential | ☐ commercial | ☐ industrial | ☐ manufacturing | ☐ other: _____] **buildings for this** [☐ HVAC firm | ☐ plumbing contractor | ☐ general contractor | ☐ manufacturer | ☐ wholesaler | ☐ other: _____].

☐ **Following** [☐ isometric drawings | ☐ architectural plans | ☐ building code specifications | ☐ other: _____], **install appropriate** [☐ piping | ☐ valves | ☐ fittings | ☐ fixtures | ☐ pumps | ☐ other: _____] **on** [☐ gas | ☐ water | ☐ waste | ☐ other: _____] **piping within specified timeframes.**

Plumbing Functions

☐ **Facilitate all plumbing activities required in the installation, maintenance, and/or repair of** _____ *[what projects?]* **including** _____, _____, **and** _____ *[which functions?]*.

☐ **Prepare for all plumbing jobs by** [☐ prioritizing work assignments | ☐ ordering required inventory | ☐ determining equipment needed | ☐ setting up each project with the correct tools, materials, and supplies | ☐ coordinating contracting trades | ☐ determining conditions and safety requirements | ☐ identifying required repairs and/or replacements | ☐ other: _____].

☐ **Maintain and repair as needed all** [☐ leaks | ☐ broken pipes | ☐ other: _____] **of** _____, _____, **and** _____ *[what?]*, **maintaining accurate records of all** [☐ labor hours | ☐ materials used | ☐ other: _____].

☐ **Assist** [☐ plumbing | ☐ electrical | ☐ maintenance | ☐ carpentry | ☐ crafts | ☐ other: _____] **staff(s) in performing the** [☐ assembly | ☐ installation | ☐ repair | ☐ maintenance | ☐ monitoring | ☐ testing | ☐ upkeep | ☐ other: _____] **of** _____ *[what?]*.

☐ **Supervise the installation and/or repair of** _____ *[what?]* **and the cutting, threading, and/or soldering of** [☐ galvanized | ☐ copper | ☐ PVC] **pipe for** _____, _____, **and** _____ *[types of jobs]*.

☐ **Conduct a variety of plumbing functions including** [☐ cutting and threading _____ *(type of)* pipes | ☐ winterizing piping (☐ and sprinkler) systems | ☐ installing (☐ waste / ☐ gas) pipes and pipe fittings | ☐ repairing drain systems | ☐ dismantling and repairing plumbing devices | ☐ plumbing kitchen facilities | ☐ inspecting piping systems | ☐ installing and servicing HVAC systems | ☐ inspecting piping systems | ☐ replacing steam lines and roof drains | ☐ winterizing (☐ piping / ☐ sprinkler) systems | ☐ dismantling and repairing plumbing devices | ☐ unclogging sewer and cesspool lines | ☐ responding to client emergency situations | ☐ other: _____] **for** _____ *[what or whom?]*.

☐ **Handle various plumbing functions including** [☐ cutting and threading pipe | ☐ soldering copper | ☐ installing PVC pipe | ☐ other: _____] **for** [☐ compressed air | ☐ potable water | ☐ cooling water | ☐ other: _____] **maintaining proper operation of all equipment.**

☐ [☐ Assemble and install | ☐ Monitor and adjust | ☐ Repair, replace, and maintain] **various types of** [☐ water heaters | ☐ boilers | ☐ heating pipes | ☐ pneumatic valves | ☐ mixing valves | ☐ pumps | ☐ pump seals | ☐ steam traps | ☐ bearing assembles |

☐   □ backflow devices | □ dampers | □ univents | □ coils | □ fans | □ heat exchangers | □ air handlers | □ thermostats | □ valves | □ faucets | □ flush valves | □ sinks | □ fountains | □ toilets | □ urinals | □ other: _____].

☐   **Accomplish** _____ *[type of]* **plumbing projects using design** [□ drawings | □ specifications | □ diagrams | □ other: _____].

☐   **Control and maintain the** [□ heating | □ ventilating | □ cooling | □ systems] **of** _____ *[what?]* **by** [□ monitoring equipment | □ inspecting energy management systems | □ using _____ *(type of)* control software | □ making frequent on-site visits to check computer programming | □ verifying temperature controls | □ adjusting temperatures | □ maximizing the efficiency of control systems | □ adjusting (□ mixed / □ return / □ discharge) air | □ performing combustion analyses | □ other methods: _____].

☐   **Apply plumbing knowledge of** [□ tools, materials, and equipment of the trade | □ National plumbing code | □ time and materials estimating | □ building plans and blueprint interpreting | □ other: _____] **in performing** _____ *[which?]* **plumbing jobs.**

Plumbing Maintenance & Repair

☐   **Repair and/or replace** [□ gas boilers | □ electric boilers | □ water heaters | □ steam lines | □ heat return lines | □ main water lines | □ roof drains | □ other: _____] **of** [□ heating | □ cooling | □ ventilating | □ refrigeration | □ other: _____] **systems for** _____ *[what or whom?].*

☐   **Pressure test all** _____ *[type of]* **pipes, assess** [□ leakage | □ breakage | □ rust | □ damage | □ other: _____] **problems, identify plumbing malfunction sources, and perform required** _____ *[type of]* **plumbing repairs within specified timeframes.**

☐   **Successfully complete all** _____ *[type of]* **plumbing repair work orders consisting of** _____ *[type of]* **work** [□ ahead of schedule | □ within required timeframes] **by** _____ *[doing what?].*

☐   **Maintain and repair as needed all** [□ leaks | □ broken pipes | □ other: _____] **of** _____ , _____ , _____ , **and** _____ *[what?],* **maintaining accurate records of all** [□ labor hours | □ materials used | □ other: _____].

☐   **Assess and detect any and all plumbing repairs required on** _____ *[type of]* [□ systems | □ buildings | □ facilities | □ grounds | □ equipment | □ other: _____] **and repair as needed following standard inspection procedures.**

☐   **Install, maintain, and/or repair** [□ air compressors | □ steam boilers | □ pump seals, bearings, and couplings | □ other: _____] **for** _____ *[what?].*

☐   **Perform cooling system maintenance and repair including** [□ replacing burned out motors | □ cleaning blower cages | □ other: _____].

☐   **Maintain emergency** [□ lighting system | □ generator] **and the proper operation of all equipment to ensure the** [□ physical | □ mechanical | □ electrical | □ other: _____] **aspects of the facility run smoothly.**

☐   **Repair and maintain all kitchen appliances including** [□ gas and electric stoves and ovens | □ refrigerators | □ freezers | □ dishwashers | □ garbage disposals | □ microwaves | □ steam cookers | □ sinks | □ faucets | □ valves | □ other: _____].

☐   **Install and repair** [□ faucets | □ toilets | □ urinals | □ other: _____] **and cut, thread, and/or solder** [□ galvanized | □ black | □ copper | □ PVC] **pipe for** _____ *[what?].*

☐   **Maintain plant's heating system boilers, including cleaning** [□ heads | □ flame sensor | □ igniter | □ other: _____] **as needed.**

Plumbing Management

See also "Plumbing Projects," "Plumbing Scope," "HVAC/HVAC-R Management Scope," and "Inspections & Compliance," and "Trades/Crew Supervision," as applicable.

☐   **Direct day-to-day plumbing operations of this** [□ plumbing | □ general contracting | □ construction | □ other: _____] **firm providing a full array of** [□ plumbing | □ HVAC | □ steamfitting | □ other: _____] **services including the installation and repair of** [□ water heaters | □ steam lines | □ roof drains | □ water distributors | □ sewer lines | □ storm drains | □ cesspools | □ septic tanks | □ specialty plumbing items | □ sprinkler lines | □ drainage | □ water supply and drain lines | □ gas, electric, open flame boilers | pipes, faucets, valves, fixtures, and fittings | □ other: _____].

☐   **Oversee the installation of all required plumbing** [□ equipment | □ systems | □ pipes | □ fixtures | □ valves | □ pumps | □ other: _____] **to** [□ set up | □ operate | □ maintain] **the** [□ water distribution | □ drainage | □ heating and cooling | □ sewage collection | □ sprinkler | □ other: _____] **system(s) and related equipment of** _____ *[what?].*

☐ **Manage and oversee the installation, maintenance, and repair of** [☐ plumbing | ☐ heating | ☐ cooling | ☐ ventilating | ☐ refrigeration | ☐ water supply | ☐ sewer | ☐ fire | ☐ sprinkler | ☐ other: _____] **systems including** [☐ drain lines | ☐ steam lines | ☐ roof drains | ☐ water heaters | (☐ gas / ☐ electric / ☐ open flame) ☐ boilers | ☐ storm drains | ☐ cesspools | ☐ septic tanks | ☐ pipes, faucets, valves, fixtures, and fittings | ☐ specialty plumbing items | ☐ other: _____].

☐ **Direct and supervise the plumbing** [☐ installation | ☐ replacement | ☐ maintenance | ☐ repair] **work required in** [☐ new construction | ☐ remodel | ☐ other: _____] **jobs for this** [☐ plumbing | ☐ general contracting | ☐ construction | ☐ other: _____] **firm.**

☐ **Manage the completion of approximately** _____ *[#]* **plumbing jobs** [☐ daily | ☐ weekly | ☐ monthly | ☐ annually] **averaging $**_____ **to $**_____ *[average job amount]* **and handle** [☐ estimating of job times, materials, and costs | ☐ reviewing materials bids | ☐ ordering materials and hardware | ☐ scheduling jobs | ☐ performing plumbing functions | ☐ inspecting completed jobs for code compliance | ☐ other: _____].

☐ **Provide a full array of** [☐ plumbing | ☐ HVAC | ☐ refrigeration | ☐ steamfitting | ☐ welding | ☐ carpentry | ☐ other: _____] **services including** [(☐ plumbing / ☐ electrical / ☐ general contracting) work | (☐ bathroom / ☐ kitchen / ☐ tile) installations | ☐ other: _____] **for this** [☐ plumbing | ☐ general contracting | ☐ other: _____] **company.**

☐ **Control and maintain the** [☐ heating | ☐ ventilating | ☐ cooling | ☐ systems] of _____ *[what?]* **by** [☐ monitoring equipment | ☐ inspecting energy management systems | ☐ using _____ *(type of)* control software | ☐ making frequent on-site visits to check computer programming | ☐ verifying temperature controls | ☐ adjusting temperatures | ☐ maximizing the efficiency of control systems | ☐ adjusting (☐ mixed / ☐ return / ☐ discharge) air | ☐ performing combustion analyses | ☐ other methods: _____].

☐ **Lead and direct the installation, maintenance, repair, and/or replacement of all required plumbing** [☐ equipment | ☐ systems | ☐ pipes | ☐ fixtures | ☐ valves | ☐ pumps | ☐ other: _____] **to** [☐ set up | ☐ operate | ☐ maintain] **the** [☐ water distribution | ☐ drainage | ☐ heating and cooling | ☐ sewage collection | ☐ sprinkler | ☐ other: _____] **system(s) and related equipment.**

☐ **Supervise all plumbing activities required in the installation, maintenance, and/or repair of** _____ *[what?]* **including** _____ , _____ , **and** _____ *[which functions?].*

☐ **Lead and direct a variety of plumbing activities including** [☐ cutting and threading _____ *(type of)* pipes | ☐ winterizing piping (☐ and sprinkler) systems | ☐ soldering copper | ☐ installing PVC piping | ☐ installing (☐ waste / ☐ gas) pipes and pipe fittings | ☐ repairing drain systems | ☐ dismantling and repairing plumbing devices | ☐ plumbing kitchen facilities | ☐ inspecting piping systems | ☐ responding to client emergency situations | ☐ other: _____] **for** _____ *[what or whom?].*

☐ **Maintain plant's heating and cooling systems including cleaning boiler** [☐ heads | ☐ flame sensor | ☐ igniter | ☐ other: _____] **and** [☐ replacing burned out motors | ☐ cleaning blower cages | ☐ other: _____].

☐ **Facilitate plumbing management functions including** [☐ reviewing and evaluating plumbing specifications | ☐ coordinating bid selections | ☐ estimating project time, materials, and costs | ☐ preparing estimates | ☐ negotiating contracts | ☐ writing purchase requests | ☐ evaluating subcontractor bids | ☐ prioritizing work assignments | ☐ scheduling jobs | ☐ supervising various trades | ☐ setting up projects with materials | ☐ determining safety requirements | ☐ coordinating materials shipping | ☐ purchasing or leasing equipment | ☐ preparing cost estimates | ☐ ensuring plumbing safety practices | ☐ maintaining plumbing tools and equipment | ☐ ordering and maintaining plumbing parts | ☐ obtaining required permits | ☐ making on-site visits | ☐ inspecting work for compliance with codes | ☐ maintaining plumbing tools and equipment | ☐ training staff in plumbing techniques | ☐ handling inventory management and control | ☐ coordinating projects with (☐ engineers / ☐ architects) | ☐ monitoring equipment | ☐ other: _____].

☐ **Oversee the repair and maintenance of all** [☐ plumbing | ☐ electrical | ☐ HVAC | ☐ motors | ☐ appliances | ☐ fixtures | ☐ lights | ☐ ballasts | ☐ receptacles | ☐ switches | ☐ other: _____] **to** [☐ help improve the work environment | ☐ maintain proper operation of all equipment | ☐ maintain compliance with all OSHA and environmental regulations | ☐ other: _____].

☐ **Perform** [☐ machining | ☐ rigging | ☐ industrial pipefitting | ☐ other: _____] **for** _____ *[what?].*

☐ **Coordinate and oversee the installation of** [☐ plumbing | ☐ heating | ☐ cooling | ☐ ventilating | ☐ refrigeration | ☐ water supply | ☐ sewer | ☐ fire | ☐ sprinkler | ☐ other: _____] **systems including** [☐ drain lines | ☐ steam lines | ☐ roof drains | ☐ water heaters | (☐ gas / ☐ electric / ☐ open flame) boilers | ☐ storm drains | ☐ cesspools | ☐ septic tanks | ☐ pipes, faucets, valves, fixtures, and fittings | ☐ specialty plumbing items | ☐ other: _____].

☐ **Coordinate with other trades and oversee plumbing installations in** [☐ new construction | ☐ remodel | ☐ restoration | ☐ other: _____] **of** _____ *[type of]* **projects.**

ACHIEVEMENT SAMPLES:

☐ **Increased plumbing sales** _____ **% by** [☐ creating a marketing portfolio containing photographs and letters of recommendation from previous clients | ☐ other means: _____].

☐ **Successfully met difficult** _____ *[type of]* **plumbing challenges faced by** _____ *[what obstacles?]* **by** _____ *[doing what?],* **which resulted in** _____ *[what benefits?].*

☐ **Elevated plumbing referral business by** [☐ developing a strong rapport with satisfied clients | ☐ other means: _____].

☐ **Increased** _____ *[type of]* **plumbing productivity by** [☐ resolving issues and concerns | ☐ upholding company standards | ☐ creating a fair and equitable environment | ☐ maintaining inventory control | ☐ effective time management | ☐ other: _____].

☐ **Created and implemented a successful** _____ *[type of]* **plumbing program to** [☐ cut down the workload | ☐ increase sales | ☐ reduce overtime | ☐ increase productivity | ☐ streamline operations | ☐ cut expenses | ☐ other: _____], **which has resulted in** _____ *[what benefits?]*.

☐ **Utilize** _____ *[type of]* [☐ methods | ☐ techniques | ☐ attributes | ☐ skills | ☐ other: _____] **to maintain a productive, quality-producing plumbing staff, which has resulted in** _____ *[what benefits?]*.

☐ **Increased plumbing productivity** _____ **% by** [☐ resolving issues and concerns | ☐ upholding company standards | ☐ creating a fair and equitable environment | ☐ maintaining inventory control | ☐ effective time management | ☐ other: _____] **which resulted in** _____ *[benefits to company]*.

Plumbing Projects

See also "Plumbing Functions," "Plumbing Scope," "HVAC/HVAC-R Scope,"
and "Welding/Steamfitting Functions & Projects."

☐ **Perform the installation, maintenance, repair, and/or replacement of all required** _____ *[type of]* **plumbing** [☐ equipment | ☐ systems | ☐ pipes | ☐ fixtures | ☐ valves | ☐ pumps | ☐ other: _____] **to** [☐ set up | ☐ operate | ☐ maintain] **the** [☐ water distribution | ☐ drainage | ☐ heating and cooling | ☐ sewage collection | ☐ sprinkler | ☐ other: _____] **system(s) and related equipment of** _____ *[what?]*.

☐ **Ensure all appliances are properly maintained including** [☐ gas and electric stoves and ovens | ☐ refrigerators | ☐ freezers | ☐ dishwashers | ☐ garbage disposals | ☐ microwaves | ☐ steam cookers | ☐ other: _____].

☐ **Install** [☐ industrial plumbing | ☐ PVC piping | ☐ pipes, fittings, valves and fixtures | ☐ sewer lines, septic tanks, and storm drains | ☐ gas lines | ☐ kitchen and bathroom plumbing | ☐ fire sprinkler systems | ☐ water supply and drain lines | ☐ gas and electric heaters, steam lines, and/or chlorine gas feeders | ☐ waste or gas pipes and pipe fittings | ☐ open flame boilers and water heaters | ☐ other: _____] **for** _____ *[whom or what?]*.

☐ **Repair** [☐ industrial | ☐ residential | ☐ commercial | ☐ other: _____] **plumbing systems including** [☐ leaks and broken pipes | ☐ drain systems | ☐ plumbing, sprinkler, and/or drain systems | ☐ water heaters, boilers, and steam controls | ☐ faucets and valves | ☐ HVAC heat return and main water lines | ☐ industrial | ☐ residential plumbing systems | ☐ circulating pumps | ☐ swimming pool filtration pumps | ☐ soda ash and chlorine gas feeders | ☐ other: _____] **for** _____ *[whom or what?]*.

☐ **Facilitate all plumbing activities required in the installation and maintenance of in-ground pools including installing and/or repairing swimming pool** [☐ circulation pumps | ☐ filtration pumps | ☐ mixing valves | ☐ pumps | ☐ filters | ☐ underwater lighting | ☐ chlorine gas feeders | ☐ soda ash feeders | ☐ other: _____].

☐ **Maintain plant's heating system boilers, including cleaning** [☐ heads | ☐ flame sensor | ☐ igniter | ☐ other: _____].

☐ **Control and maintain the** [☐ heating | ☐ ventilating | ☐ cooling | ☐ other: _____] **systems of** _____ *[what?]* **by** [☐ monitoring equipment | ☐ inspecting energy management systems | ☐ using _____ *(type of)* control software | ☐ making frequent on-site visits to ensure quality control | ☐ verifying temperature controls | ☐ adjusting temperatures | ☐ maximizing the efficiency of control systems | ☐ adjusting (☐ mixed / ☐ return / ☐ discharge) air | ☐ performing combustion analyses | ☐ other: _____].

☐ [☐ Assemble and install | ☐ Monitor and adjust | ☐ Repair, replace, and maintain] [☐ water heaters | ☐ boilers | ☐ heating pipes | ☐ pneumatic valves | ☐ mixing valves | ☐ pumps | ☐ pump seals | ☐ steam traps | ☐ bearing assembles | ☐ backflow devices | ☐ dampers | ☐ univents | ☐ coils | ☐ fans | ☐ heat exchangers | ☐ air handlers | ☐ thermostats | ☐ valves | ☐ faucets | ☐ flush valves | ☐ sinks | ☐ fountains | ☐ toilets | ☐ urinals | ☐ other: _____].

ACHIEVEMENT SAMPLES:

☐ **Facilitated all plumbing activities required in the installation and maintenance of in-ground pools including installing and/or repairing swimming pool** [☐ circulation pumps | ☐ filtration pumps | ☐ mixing valves | ☐ pumps | ☐ filters | ☐ underwater lighting | ☐ chlorine gas feeders | ☐ soda ash feeders | ☐ other: _____].

Plumbing Tools, Equipment & Testing Devices

See "Equipment, Tools & Testing Devices – Plumbing."

Preventive & Seasonal Maintenance

See also "Facility Management Functions" as well as trades-related "Maintenance and Repair Work"
(Electrical, HVAC, Plumbing, Welding / Steamfitting, Landscaping, Masonry).

☐ **Facilitate** [☐ regular | ☐ routine | ☐ weekly | ☐ monthly | ☐ periodic | ☐ other: _____] **preventive maintenance schedules on all** _____ *[what?]*, **and handle required maintenance and repair, as needed.**

☐ **Conduct regular and preventive maintenance checks on** _____ *[what?]* **ensuring** [☐ buildings | ☐ systems | ☐ machinery | ☐ equipment | ☐ appliances | ☐ vehicles | ☐ other: _____] **are in safe operating condition at all times.**

☐ **Perform preventive maintenance on** _____ *[what?]* **and repair and/or replace** _____, _____, **and** _____ *[which?]* **components of** _____ *[type of]* [☐ equipment | ☐ systems | ☐ other: _____] **as required.**

☐ **Facilitate** [☐ preventive | ☐ routine | ☐ periodic | ☐ seasonal | ☐ other: _____] **cleaning and maintenance of all** _____ *[type of]* **equipment including** [☐ hand and power tools | ☐ pipe benders | ☐ propane torches | ☐ welding equipment | ☐ sewer rooters | ☐ other: _____].

☐ **Perform seasonal furnace maintenance and repair work including** [☐ inspecting the system | ☐ servicing and adjusting burners and blowers | ☐ replacing filters and ducts | ☐ overhauling compressors | ☐ checking thermostat, burner nozzles, and controls | ☐ other: _____].

☐ **Conduct** [☐ seasonal overhauls | ☐ seasonal transitions | ☐ winterizing | ☐ other: _____] **of** _____ *[type of]* **systems to and from heating and cooling, ensuring** [☐ a comfortable air and temperature balance | ☐ other: _____] **throughout the four seasons.**

☐ **Conduct** [☐ preventive | ☐ routine | ☐ periodic] **maintenance, adjustments, and repair work on all** [☐ pneumatically | ☐ digitally | ☐ other: _____] **controlled** [☐ HVAC | ☐ boiler | ☐ fire | ☐ air distribution equipment | ☐ hot and chilled water distribution | ☐ variable volume | ☐ other: _____] **systems to keep the system(s) operating efficiently.**

☐ **Assess and detect any and all** _____ *[type of]* **repairs required on** _____ *[type of]* [☐ systems | ☐ buildings | ☐ facilities | ☐ grounds | ☐ equipment | ☐ other: _____] **and repair as needed following standard inspection procedures.**

☐ **Successfully complete all** _____ *[type of]* **repair work orders consisting of** _____ *[type of]* **work** [☐ ahead of schedule | ☐ within required timeframes] **by** _____ *[doing what?]*.

☐ **Oversee installation, operation, maintenance, and/or repair of** _____ *[type of]* [☐ machines | ☐ tools | ☐ engines | ☐ other: _____] **and other equipment including centralized** [☐ heat | ☐ gas | ☐ water | ☐ steam | ☐ other: _____] **systems.**

☐ **Maintain and repair as needed all** _____ *[what?]* **of** _____, _____, **and** _____ *[what?]*, **maintaining accurate records of all** [☐ labor hours | ☐ materials used | ☐ other: _____].

☐ [☐ Manage and oversee | ☐ Perform] _____ *[type of]* **maintenance and repair including** _____, _____, **and** _____ *[functions]*.

ACHIEVEMENT SAMPLES

☐ **Assisted in establishing** _____ *[type of]* **preventive maintenance programs for** _____ *[what?]* **that included** _____ *[what requirements?]*.

☐ **Significantly improved operating conditions of the building's** _____, _____, **and** _____ *[what functions?]* **by rigidly following a regular maintenance schedule, which proved critical to the successful and continuous operation of** _____ *[what?]*.

☐ **Developed and established** _____ *[type of]* **preventive maintenance programs for** _____ *[what?]* **that incorporated** _____ *[what?]* **and resulted in** _____ *[what benefits?]*.

Productivity Improvement

See also "Process Improvement."

ACHIEVEMENT SAMPLES:

☐ **Focusing on** _____ *[#]* **targeted areas of improvement per month, look for opportunities to improve performance, which resulted in** _____ *[what benefits?]*.

☐ **Spearheaded the corporate-wide initiative to** _____ *[do what?]*, **which realized production gains of** _____ **%** *[percentage]* **with no additional labor expenses by** _____ *[how?]*.

☐ **Drove overall improvements in** _____ *[what?]* **performance efficiency via effective** [☐ capacity planning | ☐ schedule management | ☐ operations streamlining in _____ *(what areas?)* | ☐ _____ *(type of)* cost-cutting process improvements | ☐ other: _____] **that** _____ *[did what?]*.

☐ **Catapulted** _____ *[type of]* **productivity** _____ **%** *[percentage]* **and company profits $**_____ *[amount]* **by** [☐ educating laborers on smart, productive work methods | ☐ expecting employees to work to their full potential | ☐ not accepting mediocrity | ☐ ensuring all staff fully understood their assigned jobs | ☐ resolving issues and concerns | ☐ upholding company standards | ☐ creating a fair and equitable environment | ☐ maintaining inventory control | ☐ effective time management | ☐ other: _____].

☐ **Increased daily production from** _____ *[what level?]* **to** _____ *[what level?]* **without raising overhead by** _____ *[doing what?]* **while monitoring project deliverables and maintaining compliance with all government regulations, engineering drawings, and customer requirements.**

☐ **Created forecasting and troubleshooting procedures in the areas of** _____, _____, **and** _____ *[what areas?]* **to identify and rectify** _____ *[type of]* **problem areas, which resulted in** _____ *[benefit to company]*.

☐ **Increased productivity** _____ **%** *[percentage]* **and saved $**_____ *[amount]* **in annual costs by initiating an outsourcing** _____ *[type of]* **concept for** _____ *[which?]* **operations that** _____ *[accomplished what?]*.

☐ **Significantly enhanced productivity by spearheading** _____ *[what initiative?]* **that resulted in** _____ *[benefits]*.

☐ **Developed and implemented** _____ *[type of]* **operational systems, which improved productivity** _____ **%** *[percentage]* **and increased profitability** _____ **%** *[percentage]*. **Accomplished by** [☐ streamlining operations | ☐ increased training and development | ☐ building a strong support system amongst staff | ☐ other: _____].

☐ **Totally eliminated need for equipment shutdowns by** [☐ maintaining air compressors and boilers in optimum operating condition at all times | ☐ performing regularly scheduled maintenance checks | ☐ changing oil and filters as needed | ☐ other: _____].

☐ **Created and implemented a successful** _____ *[type of]* **program to** [☐ cut down the workload | ☐ increase sales | ☐ reduce overtime | ☐ increase productivity | ☐ streamline operations | ☐ cut expenses | ☐ other: _____], **which has resulted in** _____ *[what benefits?]*.

☐ **Increased** _____ *[type of]* **productivity** _____ **%** *[percentages]* **(from** _____ **% to** _____ **%)** *[percentages]* **by** [☐ using smart, productive work methods | ☐ resolving _____ *(type of)* issues and concerns | ☐ upholding company standards | ☐ creating a fair and equitable environment | ☐ maintaining inventory control | ☐ effective time management | ☐ focusing on a commitment to excellence | ☐ giving 100% to the job | ☐ upgrading _____ *(type of)* (☐ systems | ☐ equipment) | ☐ initiating an outsourcing concept for _____ *(which?)* operations | ☐ other: _____], **which resulted in** _____ *[benefits]*.

☐ **Utilize** _____ *[type of]* [☐ methods | ☐ techniques | ☐ skills | ☐ other: _____] **to maintain a productive, quality-producing staff, which has resulted in** _____ *[what benefits?]*.

☐ **Increased productivity** _____ **%** *[percentage]* **by** _____ *[doing what?]*, **which resulted in** _____ *[benefits]*.

Project Development & Initiation

See also "Product Development," "Project Planning & Coordination," "Project Prioritization & Demand Balancing," and "Project Time Tracking," as applicable.

☐ **Assess and identify** [☐ client needs | ☐ project resources | ☐ materials | ☐ contractor requirements | ☐ other: _____] **and translate business strategies and requirements into** [☐ functional | ☐ technical | ☐ other: _____] **specifications that reflect** [☐ client | ☐ firm's] **values, diversity, and vision and meet project objectives and deliverables.**

☐ **Determine best implementation strategy, approaches, and methodology to set projects in motion and obtain expected deliverables by** _____ *[doing what?]*.

☐ **Formulate and define project plans that consider project** [☐ strategy | ☐ scope | ☐ goals | ☐ objectives | ☐ deliverables | ☐ needs identification | ☐ costs | ☐ required skill sets | ☐ tasks | ☐ resource allocations | ☐ work assignments | ☐ scheduling | ☐ technical scope | ☐ timeline check points | ☐ other: _____] **using project management planning and scheduling techniques.**

☐ **Assess business needs and translate business strategies and requirements into** [☐ functional | ☐ technical] **specifications that reflect** [☐ client | ☐ firm's] **values, diversity, and vision.**

☐ **Translate new product development strategies and goals into specific project plans using** _____ *[what methods?]* **and resulting in** [☐ effective solutions | ☐ successful project completions | ☐ other: _____].

☐ **Identify, define, and document** _____ *[type of]* **priorities, as well as** [☐ options | ☐ risks | ☐ costs | ☐ benefits | ☐ milestones | ☐ solutions | ☐ other: _____] **and translate requirements into effective** _____ *[type of]* **projects.**

☐ **Assess and evaluate** _____ *[what?]* **in collaboration with** _____ *[whom?]* **to determine detailed business requirements in the design and implementation of** _____ *[what?]*.

☐ **Successfully plan and manage** _____ *[type of]* **projects to achieve business objectives; and utilize resource capabilities within project parameters of scope, cost, time, and quality.**

☐ **Organize, schedule and manage all** _____ *[type of]* **projects with sensitivity to client deadlines and project requirements.**

☐ **Determine client needs and ensure end products meet** [☐ client specifications | ☐ technical standards | ☐ regulatory compliance | ☐ other: _____].

☐ **Determine best implementation** [☐ strategy | ☐ approaches | ☐ methodology] **to set** _____ *[type of]* **projects in motion and obtain expected deliverables by** _____ *[doing what?]*.

ACHIEVEMENT SAMPLES: *See also Achievements under "Project Management – General."*

☐ **Sourced, built, and directed the activities of a project team of** _____ *[#]* **with the necessary skill sets to take** _____ *[type of]* **projects from inception through completion.**

☐ **Developed new** _____ *[type of]* **approaches by** [☐ refining existing theories | ☐ blending creativity, problem-solving, and technical skills | ☐ employing benefits of leading edge technology | ☐ other: _____] **that resulted in** [☐ seizing new opportunities | ☐ achieving and sustaining business success | ☐ increasing productivity by _____% *(percentage)* | ☐ decreasing costs by $_____ *(amount)* | ☐ other benefit: _____].

☐ **Organized various** _____ *[type of]* **projects including** [☐ coordinating schedules | ☐ organizing activities | ☐ ordering supplies and services | ☐ tracking progress and results | ☐ other: _____].

☐ **Addressed** _____ *[which?]* **business** [☐ strategies | ☐ goals | ☐ other: _____] **in the project** [☐ development | ☐ initiation | ☐ execution | ☐ other: _____] **stage(s) of** _____ *[what?]* **and determined the best implementation and execution approaches to set projects in motion and obtain expected deliverables.**

☐ **Identified and defined** _____ *[which?]* **priorities, as well as** [☐ options | ☐ risks | ☐ costs | ☐ benefits | ☐ milestones | ☐ alternative solutions | ☐ other: _____] **and translated requirements into effective** _____ *[type of]* **design-and-build projects.**

☐ **Defined, planned, and implemented** _____ *[type of]* **projects including the** [☐ design | ☐ development | ☐ implementation | ☐ tracking | ☐ other: _____] **of those projects in support of the firm's business objectives.**

Project Lifecycle Management – Construction

See also "Project Development & Initiation," "Project Planning & Coordination," "Project Prioritization & Demand Balancing," and "Project Time Tracking," as applicable.

☐ **Lead all aspects of construction project management** [☐ for multiple construction projects | ☐ for projects that vary in scope and size | ☐ to support client objectives | ☐ in accordance with all project timelines and budget ☐ in support of firm's strategic vision | ☐ other: _____] **considering all key components of project lifecycle (scope, time, cost, quality, and resources) in the initiation and coordination of all design projects.**

☐ **Direct and oversee** [☐ trades supervision | ☐ construction inspection | ☐ building and safety codes enforcement | ☐ quality control | ☐ other: _____].

☐ **Effectively plan, manage, and lead** _____ *[type of]* **construction projects; and direct the activities of trades to ensure all projects are completed with high quality on time and within budget.**

☐ **Manage and oversee all aspects of** _____ *[type of]* **construction project lifecycles including** [☐ planning | ☐ project scope | ☐ budgeting | ☐ project initiation | ☐ contractor selection | ☐ scheduling | ☐ budgeting | ☐ resource allocation | ☐ risk assessment | ☐ quality control | ☐ change orders | ☐ cost control | ☐ punch lists | ☐ close-out billing | ☐ other: _____].

☐ **Consider all key components of project management (scope, time, cost, quality, resources, communication, issues, risk, changes, integration) ensuring compliance with all standard project management methodologies in the** [☐ development of new | ☐ leveraging of existing] _____ *[type of]* **practices by** _____ *[doing what?]*.

☐ **Direct and oversee all aspects of project management—from planning to completion—**[☐ using standardized project management methodology | ☐ for projects that vary in scope and size | ☐ in support of firm's strategic visions | ☐ for multiple implementation projects | ☐ to support client objectives | ☐ in accordance with all project timelines and budget].

☐ **Manage and direct all aspects of** _____ *[type of]* **project lifecycles including** [☐ project scope | ☐ initiation | ☐ planning | ☐ risk assessment | ☐ scheduling | ☐ budgeting | ☐ resource allocation | ☐ quality control | ☐ change orders | ☐ cost control | ☐ other: _____].

☐ **Provide project management** [☐ coordination | ☐ consultation | ☐ supervision | ☐ guidance] **during the** _____ *[which?]* **phase of all** _____ *[type of]* **projects**.

☐ **Formulate and define project plans that consider project** [☐ strategy | ☐ scope | ☐ goals | ☐ objectives | ☐ deliverables | ☐ needs identification | ☐ costs | ☐ required skill sets | ☐ tasks | ☐ resource allocations | ☐ work assignments | ☐ scheduling | ☐ technical scope | ☐ timeline check points | ☐ other: _____] **using project management planning and scheduling techniques.**

☐ **Manage and oversee all aspects of** _____ *[type of]* **projects including project** [☐ scope | ☐ initiation | ☐ planning | ☐ scheduling | ☐ budgeting | ☐ team selection | ☐ resource allocation | ☐ cost control | ☐ other: _____] **as well as** [☐ quality control | ☐ change management | ☐ system integration | ☐ other: _____] **keeping in line with all business objectives.**

☐ **Manage and oversee** _____ *[type of]* **project lifecycles including** [☐ project scope | ☐ initiation | ☐ planning | ☐ scheduling | ☐ budgeting | ☐ resource allocation | ☐ risk assessment | ☐ quality control | ☐ change orders | ☐ cost control | ☐ other: _____].

☐ **Lead all aspects of project management** [☐ for multiple projects | ☐ for projects that vary in scope and size | ☐ to support client objectives | ☐ in accordance with all project timelines and budget | ☐ other: _____] **considering all key components of project management (scope, time, cost, quality, and resources) in the initiation and coordination of all** _____ *[type of]* **projects.**

☐ **Successfully manage** _____ *[type of]* **construction projects and utilize resource capabilities within the project parameters of cost, time, and quality which has resulted in** _____ *[what firm or client benefits?]*

ACHIEVEMENT SAMPLES:

☐ **Planned and coordinated all activities of** [☐ small- | ☐ medium- | ☐ large-] **scale client** _____ *[type of]* **projects for a wide range of** _____ *[type of]* **clients in collaboration with** [☐ client reps | ☐ contractors | ☐ subcontractors | ☐ other: _____] **for this** _____ *[type of]* **firm with** _____ *[#]* [☐ locations | ☐ employees | ☐ other: _____] **that generates fiscal-year revenues of $**_____ *[revenues]*.

☐ **Structured and developed** _____ *[type of]* **client project plans** [☐ following client-specific project management methodology | ☐ other methods: _____] **resulting in** _____ *[what benefits?]*.

☐ **Oversaw close-out administration on a** [☐ large | ☐ complex | ☐ multisite | ☐ other: _____] _____ *[type of]* **project ensuring all contractual requirements were met, change orders were reviewed and approved, and closeout processing was completed, which involved meeting with** [☐ Architects | ☐ Engineers | ☐ Project Managers | ☐ others: _____] **to ensure accuracy and successful deliverables.**

Project Management

☐ **Oversee the management of** _____ *[type of]* **projects to ensure cost-effective, functional completed projects that consider** [☐ fiscal | ☐ legal | ☐ technical | ☐ demographic | ☐ economic | ☐ safety | ☐ other: _____] **aspects.**

☐ **Proactively manage, lead, and guide** [☐ cross-functional | ☐ multilevel | ☐ other: _____] _____ *[which?]* **teams to ensure** _____, _____, **and** _____ *[what?]*.

☐ **Manage all phases of** _____ *[type of]* **projects from project start through completion including** [☐ developing job estimates and budgets | ☐ securing competitive bids | ☐ handling contract negotiations | ☐ maintaining direct client relationships | ☐ other: _____] **completing all projects on time and within budget.**

☐ **Facilitate direct project management** [☐ coordination | ☐ consultation | ☐ supervision | ☐ review] **during development phase of all projects.**

☐ **Lead a team of** _____ *[#]* _____ *[titles]* **providing support for project** [☐ management | ☐ execution | ☐ communication | ☐ logistics | ☐ other: _____] **of** _____ *[type of]* **programs ensuring** [☐ team meets or exceeds all goals and objectives | ☐ the firm meets its stated growth objectives | ☐ other: _____].

☐ **Provide project management leadership and direction for this $**_____ *[revenues]* _____ *[type of]* **firm including** _____, _____, **and** _____ *[what areas?]* **and supervising all phases of** _____ *[type of]* **projects.**

☐ **Design and implement various** [☐ large-scale] _____ *[type of]* [☐ solutions | ☐ implementation projects | ☐ other: _____] **that effectively address and adhere to** [☐ firm's | ☐ clients'] **requirements** [☐ in accordance with all project timelines and budget | ☐ ensuring quality project standards | ☐ ensuring a smooth transition | ☐ other: _____].

☐ **Manage the development and maintenance of project-related** _____ *[type of]* **plans and operating strategies associated with the design and execution of** _____ *[what?]*.

☐ **Prepare detailed and timely** [☐ project schedules | ☐ budgets | ☐ status reports | ☐ other: _____] **for all** _____ *[type of]* **projects** [☐ averaging | ☐ up to] $_____ *[amount]* **with an annual return on investment of $**_____ *[amount]*.

☐ **Effectively** [☐ plan | ☐ direct | ☐ coordinate | ☐ implement] _____ *[type of]* **projects** [☐ and direct the activities of resources] **to ensure all objectives are accomplished with high quality and within established time frames and budget.**

☐ **Strategize, plan, and coordinate the activities of** _____ *[type of]* **projects in collaboration with** _____ *[whom?]* **for this** _____ *[type of]* **firm with** _____ *[#]* [☐ locations | ☐ employees | ☐ other: _____] **that generates fiscal-year revenues of $_____** *[revenues]*.

☐ **Plan, supervise, and lead** _____ *[type of]* **projects with varying requirements to ensure all projects are completed with high quality and within established time frames and budget.**

☐ **Plan and coordinate all activities of** _____ *[type of]* **projects for a wide range of clients in collaboration with** [☐ clients | ☐ vendors | ☐ senior management | ☐ other: _____].

☐ **Manage multiple** [☐ multimillion-dollar | ☐ large-scale | ☐ moderate-size | ☐ highly complex | ☐ moderately complex | ☐ multisite | ☐ cross-organizational | ☐ multiyear-timeline | ☐ multimonth timeline | ☐ simultaneous | ☐ other: _____] _____ *[type of]* **project rollouts from inception to successful completion.**

☐ **Manage and oversee all aspects of** _____ *[type of]* **projects including** [☐ project scope | ☐ initiation | ☐ planning | ☐ scheduling | ☐ budgeting | ☐ team selection | ☐ resource allocation | ☐ quality control | ☐ change management | ☐ cost control | ☐ system integration | ☐ other: _____] **keeping in line with all business objectives.**

☐ **Define, plan, and implement** _____ *[type of]* **projects; and perform the** [☐ design | ☐ development | ☐ testing | ☐ implementation | ☐ tracking | ☐ reporting | ☐ other: _____] **of those projects in support of the** [☐ firm's | ☐ clients'] **business objectives.**

☐ **Design and implement** _____ *[type of]* **solutions that effectively address and adhere to** [☐ firm's | ☐ clients'] **requirements** [☐ in accordance with all project timelines and budget | ☐ ensuring quality project standards | ☐ and ensure a smooth transition | ☐ other: _____].

☐ **Effectively develop teamwork within** [☐ the department | ☐ other company departments | ☐ other: _____] **by successfully** _____ *[doing what?]*.

ACHIEVEMENT SAMPLES:

☐ **Designed and implemented** _____ *[type of]* **structured resource management processes including** [☐ organizational charts | ☐ standardized roles | ☐ job description database | ☐ generic acquisition forms | ☐ tracking and reporting formats | ☐ skill set profiles | ☐ other: _____] **for all project resources that resulted in** _____ *[what benefits?]*.

☐ **Determined best implementation strategy, approaches, and methodology of** _____ *[what?]* **to set projects in motion and successfully obtain expected deliverables by** _____ *[doing what?]*.

☐ **Formulated and defined project** _____ *[type of]* **plans that consider project** [☐ design | ☐ scope | ☐ goals | ☐ costs | ☐ deliverables | ☐ task requirements | ☐ resource allocations | ☐ work assignments | ☐ scheduling | ☐ risk identification | ☐ timeline check points | ☐ project monitoring | ☐ other: _____] **using project management planning and scheduling techniques.**

☐ **Championed** _____ *[type of]* **solutions that effectively addressed and adhered to** [☐ firm's | ☐ clients'] **requirements** [☐ in accordance with all project timelines and budget | ☐ ensuring quality project standards | ☐ allowing for a smooth transition | ☐ other: _____].

☐ **Developed a** _____ *[type of]* **plan that manages project execution costs, schedules, and changes and** _____ *[benefited how?]*.

☐ **Directed and oversaw all aspects of** [☐ complex | ☐ multiple | ☐ large-scale | ☐ other: _____] _____ *[type of]* **projects including** _____ *[what?]* **and consistently delivered all projects on time and within budget.**

☐ **Oversaw the management of** _____ *[type of]* **projects ranging $_____ to $_____** *[project costs]* **and involving** _____ *[what?]*.

☐ **Significantly improved** [☐ cost efficiency | ☐ profitability | ☐ client satisfaction | ☐ other: _____] **and enhanced project outcomes by** [☐ by leveraging _____ *(type of)* experience | ☐ evaluating methods | ☐ implementing _____ *(type of)* quality control programs that _____ *(did what?)* | ☐ optimizing plans | ☐ other: _____].

☐ **Managed multiple** [☐ multimillion-dollar | ☐ large-scale | ☐ moderate-size | ☐ highly complex | ☐ moderately complex | ☐ multisite | ☐ cross-organizational | ☐ multiyear-timeline | ☐ multimonth-timeline | ☐ simultaneous | ☐ other: _____] **project rollouts from inception to successful completion.**

☐ **Successfully planned, managed, and led the development and implementation of** _____ *[type of]* **projects with varying requirements ensuring all objectives were accomplished with high quality and within established time frames and budget.**

☐ **Helped improve the workplace and work environment by way of** _____ *[doing what?]*, **benefiting** _____ *[whom?]* **through** _____ *[what means?]*.

☐ **Analyzed, interpreted, and met the unique** _____ *[which?]* **needs of** _____ *[type of]* **project and performed** _____ *[what?]*, **successfully applying** _____ *[what?]* **expertise.**

☐ **Gained** _____ [type of] **project cooperation and commitment from** _____ [whom?] **by** [☐ providing clear direction | ☐ soliciting feedback | ☐ serving as the primary resource hub | ☐ insisting on mutual support | ☐ sharing information | ☐ modeling professional behavior | ☐ building a collaborative environment | ☐ removing all obstacles to project success | ☐ other: _____]

☐ **Supervised and oversaw** _____ [#]_____ [type of] **projects averaging $**_____ [amount] **each, with** [☐ property values | ☐ other: _____] **totaling $**_____ **to $**_____ [amounts] **annually**.

☐ **Championed the development and implementation of the** _____ [type of] [☐ program | ☐ project | ☐ initiative | ☐ other: _____] **that** _____ [accomplished what?] **and** _____ [benefited how?].

☐ **Successfully completed** _____ [type of] **projects within** _____ [time period] **by** _____ [doing what well?].

☐ **Effectively facilitate across-the-board communication regarding** _____ [type of] **project scope, expected deliverables, and major milestones with** _____ [whom?] **and other involved parties** [☐ during all phases of the project lifecycle | ☐ from concept to completion | ☐ other: _____].

☐ **Keep all** _____ [which?] **team members informed about project scope, status, issues, and expected deliverables by** [☐ establishing effective means of communication | ☐ providing clear, concise, and complete written and verbal communication | ☐ adapting communication style to meet end user needs | ☐ other: _____].

☐ **Conduct** _____ [type of] [☐ weekly | ☐ regular | ☐ intermittent | ☐ other: _____] [☐ project meetings ☐ strategy sessions | ☐ teleconferences | ☐ other: _____] **to review** _____ [type of] **project progress ensuring** [☐ communication among all involved parties | ☐ projects remain on schedule and within budget | ☐ other: _____].

☐ **Ensure** _____ [which?] [☐ department members | ☐ senior management | ☐ project team | ☐ others: _____] **and others are informed of projects' objectives, scope, tasks, milestones, and expected deliverables by** _____ [doing what?].

☐ **Completed** _____ [name of] **project in record time and ahead of schedule; achieved by** [☐ getting the most productivity out of laborers | ☐ organizing and planning daily workloads | ☐ other: _____] **resulting in** [☐ company being awarded state bonuses | ☐ other achievement: _____].

☐ **Develop various** _____ [type of] **project status formats for presentation to different audiences, such as** [☐ work session details | ☐ client status reports | ☐ executive report cards | ☐ budget reports | ☐ meeting minutes | ☐ other: _____].

Project Management Leadership

☐ **Lead and direct all aspects of** _____ [type of] **projects including** [☐ project scope | ☐ initiation | ☐ planning | ☐ scheduling | ☐ budgeting | ☐ team selection | ☐ resource allocation | ☐ quality control | ☐ cost control | ☐ other: _____] **keeping in line with all business objectives**.

☐ **Provide** [☐ senior management oversight | ☐ leadership and direction] **in the start-up through completion of all** _____ [type of] **projects including** _____, _____, **and** _____ [what?] **essential to** _____ [what?] **for this** $_____ [revenues] _____ [type of] **firm**.

☐ **Provide leadership, vision, and direction to a team of** _____ [#] **to initiate, plan, and** _____ [type of] **projects ranging from $**_____ **to $**_____ [amounts] **and resulting in** [☐ delivering bottom-line business value | ☐ business transformation | ☐ the translation of enterprise strategies into projects | ☐ increased productivity | ☐ other benefits: _____].

☐ **Direct and oversee all aspects of** _____ [type of] **project management—from planning and coordination to implementation and delivery—**[☐ using standardized project management methodology | ☐ for multiple implementation projects | ☐ for projects that vary in scope and size | ☐ in support of firm's strategic visions | ☐ to support client objectives | ☐ in accordance with all project timelines and budget | ☐ other: _____].

☐ **Define, plan, and implement** _____ [type of] [☐ projects | ☐ solutions | ☐ programs] **and perform the** [☐ planning | ☐ development | ☐ testing | ☐ implementation | ☐ tracking | ☐ reporting | ☐ other: _____] **of those projects in support of the firm's business objectives**.

☐ **Provide leadership, vision, and direction to a project management team of** _____ [#] **in the initiation, planning, and execution of** _____ [type of] **projects—from project start through completion**.

☐ **Review all project costs to** [☐ analyze work progress | ☐ factor in amounts spent | ☐ determine reimbursable costs | ☐ track changes | ☐ summarize individual costs | ☐ predict total cost | ☐ other: _____].

☐ **Develop project budgets, monitor costs, and analyze expenses ensuring all projects remain within budget. Realized a cost savings of $**_____ [amount] **that increased profitability in the area of** _____ [which area?] **by** _____ [doing what?].

☐ **Oversee the management of** _____ [type of] **projects to ensure cost-effective, functional completed projects that consider** [☐ fiscal | ☐ legal | ☐ technical | ☐ demographic | ☐ economic | ☐ safety | ☐ other: _____] **aspects**.

☐ **Lead a project team of** _____ *[#]* **Project Managers in the development and implementation of high quality, cost-effective** [☐ business | ☐ information systems | ☐ other: _____] **solutions that successfully address the firm's requirements and ensure appropriate project implementation** [☐ company-wide | ☐ division-wide | ☐ interdepartmentally | ☐ other: _____].

☐ **Plan, coordinate, and implement** _____ *[type of]* **special projects including** [☐_____ *(type of)* **programs** | ☐ special events | ☐ media involvement | ☐ publication advertising | ☐ other: _____].

☐ **Design and implement** _____ *[type of]* **communications solutions that effectively address and adhere the firm's business requirements** [☐ in accordance with all project timelines and budget | ☐ ensuring quality project standards / other: _____].

☐ **Proactively manage** [☐ innovative | ☐ on-time | ☐ on-budget] **deliverables by** [☐ recruiting, leading, and inspiring a winning team | ☐ improving development process | ☐ anticipating and solving problems | ☐ negotiating risks and conflicts | ☐ other: _____].

ACHIEVEMENT SAMPLES: *See Achievements under "Project Management – General."*

Project Management Projects – Construction

See also "Construction Projects," "Project Management – General" and various other "Project Management" categories, as applicable.

☐ **Prepare detailed and timely** [☐ project schedules | ☐ budgets | ☐ status reports | ☐ other: _____] **for all client** _____ *[type of]* **projects** [☐ averaging | ☐ up to] $_____ *[amount]* **with an annual return on investment of** $_____ *[amount]*.

☐ **Effectively plan, manage, and lead** _____ *[type of]* **construction projects; and direct the activities of trades to ensure all projects are completed with high quality on time and within budget.**

☐ **Manage all construction activities including** [☐ client presentations | ☐ site logistics plans development and implementation | ☐ submittal review and approval | ☐ subcontractor coordination and scheduling | ☐ on-site quality assurance and quality control | ☐ on-site safety management | ☐ field conflicts resolution | ☐ project closeout processing | ☐ other: _____].

☐ **Provide** [☐ consultation | ☐ guidance | ☐ recommendations] **for** [☐ new building sites | ☐ building changes | ☐ other: _____] **for** _____ *[what?]*.

☐ **Plan, supervise, and lead the construction of** _____ *[type of]* **projects with varying requirements; and direct the activities of** _____ *[which?]* **trades to ensure all projects are completed with high quality and within established time frames and budget.**

☐ **Strategize, plan, and coordinate the activities of** [☐ small- | ☐ medium- | ☐ large-] **scale client projects for a wide range of** _____ *[type of]* **clients in collaboration with** [☐ client reps | ☐ contractors | ☐ subcontractors | ☐ other: _____] **for this** _____ *[type of]* **firm with** _____ *[#]* [☐ locations | ☐ employees | ☐ other: _____] **that generates fiscal-year revenues of** $_____ *[revenues]*.

☐ **Manage multiple** [☐ multimillion-dollar | ☐ large-scale | ☐ moderate-size | ☐ highly complex | ☐ moderately complex | ☐ multisite | ☐ cross-organizational | ☐ multiyear-timeline | ☐ multimonth timeline | ☐ simultaneous | ☐ other: _____] _____ *[type of]* **project rollouts from inception to successful completion.**

☐ **Oversee job operations and personnel management including** [☐ coordinating steel and concrete trades | ☐ scheduling laborers | ☐ managing construction | ☐ overseeing site materials and equipment set-up | ☐ other: _____].

☐ **Obtain permits, estimate jobs, and hire and schedule trades acting as liaison with** [☐ building managers | ☐ union delegates | ☐ architects | ☐ engineers | ☐ others: _____].

☐ **Direct the** _____ *[type of]* **projects of all** _____ *[type of]* **projects including the** [☐ review and/or modification of drawings | ☐ development of job estimates and budgets | ☐ securing of competitive bids | ☐ handling of contract negotiations | ☐ maintaining of client relationships | ☐ scheduling and coordination of trades | ☐ performing of on-site supervision | ☐ negotiation and processing of change orders | ☐ other: _____], **completing all projects on time and within budget.**

☐ **Oversee the management of** [☐ residential | ☐ commercial | ☐ public works | ☐ other: _____] **construction projects including** [☐ commercial buildings | ☐ shopping malls | ☐ stores | ☐ restaurants | ☐ manufacturing plants | ☐ schools | ☐ colleges | ☐ corporate offices | ☐ building lobbies | ☐ state or government agencies | ☐ houses | ☐ condominiums | ☐ apartment buildings | ☐ hospitals | ☐ laboratories | ☐ clean rooms | ☐ landmark restorations | ☐ roads and highways | ☐ other: _____].

☐ **Supervise the work of** [☐ Architects | ☐ Engineers | ☐ Drafters | ☐ others: _____] **in the preparation of** [☐ master plans | ☐ architectural renderings | ☐ cost estimates | ☐ specifications | ☐ construction drawings | ☐ other: _____] **in the completion of design projects.**

☐ **Manage and oversee** [☐ trades supervision | ☐ construction inspection | ☐ quality control | ☐ building and safety codes enforcement | ☐ design guidelines and specifications standards development | ☐ other: _____] **to ensure quality compliance with all** [☐ construction contracts | ☐ state and local building codes | ☐ Uniform Building Code | ☐ zoning laws | ☐ fire regulations | ☐ electrical codes | ☐ plumbing codes | ☐ life-safety codes | ☐ other: _____] **and other ordinances.**

☐ **Monitor construction progress through on-site field inspection and review to ensure conformance to** [☐ design specifications | ☐ cost estimates | ☐ time schedules | ☐ building codes | ☐ other: _____] **and immediately resolve any problems**.

☐ **Supervise and oversee all aspects of** [☐ construction project | ☐ product development | ☐ other: _____] **project lifecycles including** [☐ project scope | ☐ initiation | ☐ planning | ☐ scheduling | ☐ budgeting | ☐ contractor selection | ☐ resource allocation | ☐ risk assessment | ☐ quality control | ☐ change orders | ☐ cost control | ☐ other: _____].

☐ **Manage and direct** [☐ trades supervision | ☐ construction | ☐ inspection | ☐ quality control | ☐ building and safety codes enforcement | ☐ design guidelines and specifications standards development | ☐ other: _____].

ACHIEVEMENT SAMPLES: *See also Achievements under "Project Management."*

☐ **Successfully coordinated and supported various design-and-build projects with multiple interaction points and deadlines by** [☐ integrating effective communications | ☐ increasing productivity | ☐ other: _____].

☐ **Provided** _____ *[type of]* [☐ architectural design | ☐ project development services | ☐ environmental technical information | ☐ other: _____] **to** _____ *[whom?]* **in the development and implementation of long-range** _____ *[type of]* **development plans**.

Project Management Support – Construction

See also "Project Team Management Leadership" and "Interdisciplinary / Project Team Member."

☐ **Support project management staff in the processing and tracking of** _____ *[type of]* **projects in the areas of** [☐ pay application processing | ☐ issues management | ☐ project auditing | ☐ meeting coordination | ☐ project filing | ☐ data entry | ☐ communications | ☐ other: _____] **for all** [☐ new construction | ☐ renovations | ☐ remodels | ☐ other: _____].

☐ **As the firm's Field representative on** _____ *[type of]* **projects, observe construction work for conformance with drawings and specifications and** _____ *[what else?]*.

☐ **Provide technical support to** [☐ construction laborers | ☐ production workers | ☐ manufacturing staff | ☐ end users groups | ☐ client representatives | ☐ other: _____] **in the area(s) of** [☐ design | ☐ construction | ☐ installation | ☐ testing | ☐ maintenance | ☐ servicing | ☐ other: _____].

☐ **Provide administrative support to the project management team in the areas of** _____, _____, **and** _____ *[areas]* **using** [☐ initiative | ☐ discretion | ☐ independent judgment | ☐ other: _____] **in setting priorities and carrying out assignments for this established** [☐ commercial construction | ☐ engineering and design | ☐ design-and-build | ☐ construction management | ☐ general contracting | ☐ other: _____] **firm**.

☐ [☐ **Prepare and revise** | ☐ **Oversee the preparation and revisions of**] [☐ construction contracts | ☐ subcontractor documents | ☐ bid comparisons | ☐ site visit field reports | ☐ owner change orders | ☐ cost reports | ☐ project correspondence | ☐ purchase orders | ☐ other: _____] **and other related documents for the project management team**.

☐ **Facilitate project-related administrative functions including** [☐ reviewing contract specifications | ☐ preparing cost estimates | ☐ compiling material lists | ☐ soliciting and evaluating contractor bids | (☐ making / ☐ recommending) bid selections | ☐ planning and coordinating projects | ☐ developing preventive maintenance schedules | ☐ recording work and materials | ☐ writing inspection deficiency reports | ☐ estimating repair and maintenance costs | ☐ preparing work orders | ☐ writing purchase requests | ☐ ordering parts | ☐ maintaining logs | ☐ preparing records and reports | ☐ other: _____] **for** _____ *[type of]* **projects**.

☐ **Review and approve all project-related** [☐ plans | ☐ specifications | ☐ cost estimates | ☐ change authorizations | ☐ pay requests | ☐ funds disbursements | ☐ other: _____].

☐ **In support of** _____ *[#]* **Project Managers, process and track** _____ *[type of]* **projects in the areas of** [☐ pay application processing | ☐ issues management | ☐ project auditing | ☐ meeting coordination | ☐ project filing | ☐ data entry | ☐ communications | ☐ other: _____] **for all** [☐ new construction | ☐ renovations | ☐ remodels | ☐ other: _____] **within the** _____ *[which?]* **industry**.

☐ **Expedite subcontractor documentation and reporting requirements and enter and maintain all** [☐ subcontractor data in ERP system | ☐ other: _____].

☐ **Coordinate and manage** [☐ drawings | ☐ submittals | ☐ Request for Quote (RFQ) process | ☐ Requests for Information (RFI) | ☐ purchase order tracking | ☐ job meetings | ☐ customer interactions | ☐ other: _____].

☐ **Perform a wide variety of administrative activities including** [☐ assisting with contractual initiatives | ☐ handling claims avoidance | ☐ updating budget databases | ☐ researching contractor claims and litigations | ☐ responding to staff inquiries relating to contract issues | ☐ handling data entry, filing, and copying | ☐ maintaining legal obligations records | ☐ other: _____].

☐ **Work closely with the firm's** [☐ Project Managers | ☐ Architects | ☐ Engineers | ☐ technical staff | ☐ others: _____] **in** the coordination and performance of construction administration services, including _____, _____, and _____ [what functions?] on _____ [type of] projects.

☐ Track and review _____ [type of] [☐ prequalification | ☐ contracts | ☐ authorizations | ☐ invoices | ☐ deliverables | ☐ correspondence | ☐ other: _____] for Project Managers by _____ [doing what?].

☐ Jointly with the [☐ Project Manager | ☐ Site Manager | ☐ Construction Department | ☐ other: _____] review and ensure the accuracy of all [☐ project invoices | ☐ contractor requests for payment | ☐ change requests | ☐ subcontractor (☐ invoices / ☐ certificates / ☐ insurance requirements) | ☐ other: _____].

☐ Administer [☐ Change Order Management | ☐ Claim Management | ☐ other: _____] and [☐ review change orders | ☐ negotiate subcontractor closeout | ☐ finalize subcontract documents | ☐ identify risk and minimize consequences | ☐ coordinate approval process | ☐ maintain change order logs | ☐ other: _____] on all _____ [type of] projects.

ACHIEVEMENT SAMPLES: *See Achievements under "Project Management."*

Project Planning & Coordination – Construction

See also "Project Development & Initiation," "Project Lifecycle Management," "Project Management Support," "Project Prioritization & Demand Balancing."

☐ Identify, define, and document client needs and priorities, as well as [☐ options | ☐ risks | ☐ costs | ☐ benefits | ☐ alternative solutions | ☐ other: _____] and translate requirements into effective _____ [type of] system layouts and installations.

☐ Collaborated in the selection of _____ [type of] building sites including [☐ directing site selection | ☐ preparing land-use studies | ☐ developing planning | ☐ considering environmental impact | ☐ infusing energy efficient methods | ☐ other: _____].

☐ Plan and coordinate all activities of [☐ small- | ☐ medium- | ☐ large-] scale [☐ client | ☐ in-house] projects _____ [type of] [☐ for a wide range of _____ (type of) clients] in collaboration with [☐ department representatives | ☐ architect | ☐ contractors | ☐ client reps | ☐ contractors | ☐ subcontractors | ☐ others: _____] for this _____ [type of] firm.

☐ Partake in the project planning, development, and initiation stages by [☐ collaborating and coordinating _____ (what?) with _____ (whom?) | ☐ applying project planning and scheduling methodology | ☐ formulating and defining project plans | ☐ performing _____ (what activities?) | ☐ other: _____].

☐ Oversee the management of _____ [type of] projects to ensure cost-effective, functional completed projects that consider [☐ fiscal | ☐ legal | ☐ technical | ☐ demographic | ☐ economic | ☐ safety | ☐ other: _____] aspects.

☐ [☐ Manage | ☐ Perform | ☐ Facilitate] various [☐ multimillion-dollar | ☐ large-scale | ☐ moderate-size | ☐ highly complex | ☐ moderately complex | ☐ multisite | ☐ simultaneous] project types including [☐ new construction | ☐ remodeling | ☐ renovation | ☐ restoration | ☐ maintenance and repair | ☐ demolition | ☐ installation | ☐ other: _____] of _____ [what?].

☐ Read, review, and approve all _____ [type of] project plans and specifications to determine whether they [☐ comply with building code requirements | ☐ conform to electrical codes and standards | ☐ are suitable for the engineering demands of the site | ☐ are environmentally-friendly | ☐ do not pose any risk to staff | ☐ are fire and life safe | ☐ other: _____].

☐ Structure and develop client project plans following client-specific project management methodology resulting in _____ [what benefits?].

☐ Consult with [☐ architect | ☐ department representatives | ☐ others: _____] to discuss project [☐ scope | ☐ objectives | ☐ requirements | ☐ budget | ☐ other: _____] required for proposed _____ [type of] projects.

☐ Assess business needs and translate design and functional challenges into successful _____ [type of] [☐ buildings | ☐ complexes | ☐ facilities | ☐ other: _____] that reflect the firm's goals and objectives.

☐ Ensure project plans are developed to deliver implementation within realistic scope, schedule, cost, and quality by _____ [doing what?].

☐ Determine [☐ best implementation strategy, approaches, and methodology | ☐ required staffing skill sets | ☐ other: _____]; define project team roles and responsibilities; and develop project-specific job descriptions for _____ [#] [☐ Project Managers | ☐ team members | ☐ others: _____] to set engineering projects in motion and obtain expected deliverables

☐ Confer with _____ [whom?] on [☐ proposed construction activities | ☐ land development planning | ☐ energy saving measures | ☐ the negotiation of plan changes to alleviate potential building problems | ☐ project progress | ☐ other: _____].

☐ Assess and identify [☐ project resources | ☐ staffing requirements | ☐ system changes | ☐ training needs | ☐ other: _____] to meet project objectives and deliverables of _____ [type of] projects.

☐ Formulate and define project plans that consider project [☐ design | ☐ scope | ☐ goals | ☐ deliverables | ☐ costs | ☐ task requirements | ☐ resource allocations | ☐ work assignments | ☐ scheduling | ☐ risk identification | ☐ timeline check points | ☐ project monitoring | ☐ other: _____] using project management planning and scheduling techniques.

☐ [☐ Manage and oversee | ☐ Perform] **approximately** _____ *[#]* **of** _____ *[type of]* **projects** [☐ weekly | ☐ monthly | ☐ annually] **ranging $**_____ **to $**_____ *[amounts].*

☐ **Source, build, and direct the activities of a project team of** _____ *[#]* **with the necessary skill sets to take** _____ *[type of]* **projects from inception through implementation and delivery.**

☐ **Prepare detailed and timely** [☐ project schedules | ☐ budgets | ☐ status reports | ☐ other: _____] **for all** _____ *[type of]* **projects averaging $**_____ *[amount]* **with an annual return on investment of $**_____ *[amount].*

ACHIEVEMENT SAMPLES: *See Achievements under "Project Management."*

Project Prioritization & Demand Balancing

See also "Project Development & Initiation," "Project Lifecycle Management," "Project Planning & Coordination," and "Project Resources & Staffing Requirements," as applicable.

☐ **Review, prioritize, rank, and balance incoming project requests with competing demands and/or differing needs (relative to scope, time, cost, and quality) by** _____ *[doing what?].*

☐ **Prioritize and balance competing project demands of internal clients by** [☐ listening to and understanding departmental needs | ☐ weighing short- and long-term benefits against other groups' needs | ☐ building strong relationships with functional managers and understanding their priorities | ☐ identifying user requirements versus available time and resources | ☐ selecting projects with greatest organizational impact | ☐ designing cross-functional solutions with shared business vision | ☐ other: _____].

☐ **Rank and prioritize incoming project requests based on** _____ *[what criteria?].*

☐ **Evaluate feasibility and rank proposals of all projects based on established criteria by** [☐ analyzing project requests | ☐ establishing project scope | ☐ determining required services | ☐ other: _____].

☐ **Balance project load between high-revenue projects and those that are** [☐ community-service oriented | ☐ smaller in scale | ☐ other: _____] **by** _____ *[doing what?].*

ACHIEVEMENT SAMPLES:

☐ **Simultaneously managed and tackled dynamic** _____ *[type of]* **projects in varying stages by successfully** [☐ tackling change management | ☐ facilitating conflict resolution | ☐ increasing productivity and performance | ☐ other: _____].

☐ **Negotiated within and across business lines on** [☐ project strategy | ☐ functional impact | ☐ project deliverables | ☐ other: _____] **towards the successful implementation of** _____ *[type of]* **design-and-build projects.**

☐ **Tackled the obstacle of a** _____ *[type of]* **situation with conflicting needs and requirements through** [☐ professionalism | ☐ tact | ☐ respect | ☐ commitment follow-through | ☐ other: _____] **resulting in** _____ *[benefits].*

☐ **Successfully coordinated and supported various** _____ *[type of]* **projects with multiple interaction points and deadlines by** [☐ integrating effective communications | ☐ increasing productivity | ☐ other: _____].

Project Resources & Staffing Requirements

☐ **Assess and** [☐ identify | ☐ recommend] [☐ project resources | ☐ staffing requirements | ☐ system changes | ☐ training needs | ☐ other: _____] **to meet project objectives and deliverables of** _____ *[type of]* **projects.**

☐ **Determine required staffing skill sets, define project team roles and responsibilities, and develop project-specific job descriptions for** _____ *[#]* [☐ project managers | ☐ team members | ☐ others: _____].

☐ **Review and approve the resource acquisition plan identifying the required resource mix of** [☐ existing employees | ☐ new hires | ☐ outside consultants | ☐ outsourced resources | ☐ redeployments | ☐ vendors | ☐ other: _____] **to accomplish specific project objectives.**

☐ **Design and implement structured resource management processes including** [☐ organizational charts | ☐ standardized roles | ☐ job description database | ☐ generic acquisition forms | ☐ tracking and reporting formats | ☐ skill set profiles | ☐ other: _____] **for all project resources.**

☐ **Source, build, and direct the activities of a project team of** _____ *[#]* **with the necessary skill sets to take** _____ *[type of]* **projects from inception through launch.**

☐ [☐ Direct | ☐ Supervise] **the administrative processing for all new employees including** [☐ payroll | ☐ orientation | ☐ benefits | ☐ training | ☐ other: _____].

Project Tracking & Reporting

See also "Client Billing," "Recordkeeping," and "Report Generation & Review."

☐ **Track all time spent on each project, and detail project-time breakdowns achieving an average of _____ %** *[percentage]* **billable capacity against project budgets for all projects.**

☐ **Regularly monitor and review _____** *[type of]* **project reports and status including reporting of** [☐ budget variances | ☐ schedule compliance | (☐ firm / ☐ division / ☐ departmental) performance indicators | ☐ other: _____].

☐ **Use** [☐ Microsoft Project | ☐ Project Central | ☐ Primavera Project Management | ☐ SAP Project Management | ☐ other: _____] **software to establish project timelines, phases, activities, milestones, dependencies, and resource requirements in compliance with the** [☐ firm's | ☐ clients'] **strategic direction.**

☐ **Provide timely and accurate project status through effective** [☐ progress and variance tracking | ☐ risk and issues mitigation | ☐ other: _____] **throughout project lifecycles.**

☐ **Track projects and produce various status reports and documents including** [☐ project work plans | ☐ process documents | ☐ business requirements | ☐ budget analyses | ☐ functional documents | ☐ risk management plan | ☐ project deliverables | ☐ schedules | ☐ monthly management reports | ☐ meeting minutes | ☐ solution recommendations | ☐ test plans | ☐ reference guides | ☐ financial reports | ☐ other: _____].

☐ **Provide** [☐ daily | ☐ weekly | ☐ bi-weekly | ☐ monthly] **project tracking and reporting of all** [☐ tasks | ☐ activities | ☐ time | ☐ costs | ☐ controls | ☐ documentation | ☐ follow-up | ☐ other: _____] **in compliance with project methodology and standards for project reporting and documentation.**

☐ **Review and provide feedback and direction on status reports including** [☐ identifying and resolving potential time and cost slippages | ☐ actual work costs versus budgeted costs | ☐ issues resolution | ☐ task completion status | ☐ other: _____].

☐ **Track project success on a** [☐ daily | ☐ weekly | ☐ bi-monthly | ☐ monthly] **basis using project performance metrics; monitor project results against technical specifications; and produce detailed, intuitive project control reports including _____, _____, and _____** *[what reports?].*

☐ **Facilitate milestone management oversight and project control in all timeline areas to ensure all project management** [☐ phases | ☐ controls | ☐ progress] **are in compliance with project management methodology and expected deliverables.**

☐ **Develop, produce, and deliver timely, clear reports on** [☐ project timelines | ☐ resource supply and demand | ☐ utilization analysis | ☐ cost tracking | ☐ work change orders | ☐ earned value | ☐ issues identification | ☐ test cases | ☐ project closures | ☐ other: _____] **which provide accurate, real-time project status.**

☐ [☐ Implement | ☐ Update] **required** [☐ forms | ☐ project reports | ☐ other: _____] **critical to the success of _____** *[type of]* **projects including** [☐ preliminary budgets | ☐ schedules | ☐ progress | ☐ committed costs | ☐ site visit reports | ☐ completion costs | ☐ other: _____].

☐ **Communicate any** [☐ schedule changes | ☐ current project progress | ☐ other: _____] **with** [☐ Construction Manager | ☐ all departments | ☐ other: _____].

☐ **Coordinate** [☐ preconstruction | ☐ site kick-off | ☐ other: _____] **meetings with** [☐ vendors | ☐ General Contractors | ☐ others: _____] **for compliance with document requirements.**

ACHIEVEMENT SAMPLES:

☐ **Prepared, initiated, and deliver accurate and detailed client** [☐ contract billing | ☐ support documentation | ☐ project hours logs | ☐ actual resource utilization | ☐ expense reports | ☐ actual versus projected budget records | ☐ overage justification | ☐ other: _____] **obtaining client payment for services and deliverables within a _____** *[what?]* **timeframe as opposed to _____** *[previous timeframe].*

Purchasing

See also "Inventory Management & Control" and "Recordkeeping."

☐ **Purchase, inspect, and store all _____** *[type of]* [☐ materials | ☐ supplies | ☐ merchandise | ☐ goods | ☐ products | ☐ equipment | ☐ tools | ☐ machinery | ☐ other: _____] **at the best prices and quality ensuring** [☐ successful delivery to _____ *(where?)* | ☐ timely delivery schedules | ☐ all criteria are met | ☐ research value analysis criteria on all product purchases | ☐ correct storage | ☐ proper disposal of chemical waste and hazardous materials | ☐ other: _____].

☐ **Analyze and calculate all bids using various methods including** [☐ life-cycle costing | ☐ weighted value | ☐ value analysis | ☐ other methods: _____] **ensuring _____** *[what criteria?].*

☐ **Determine all** [☐ product requirements | ☐ methods of acquisition | ☐ other: _____], **prepare bid specifications, select vendors, and obtain written** [☐ bids | ☐ quotes | ☐ estimates] **on all purchases averaging $_____ to $_____** *[amounts]*.

☐ **Perform various purchasing functions including** [☐ preparing specifications | ☐ determining bidding conditions and documents | ☐ preparing purchase orders | ☐ negotiating pricing | ☐ selecting vendors | ☐ awarding contracts | ☐ performing lifecycle costing | ☐ authorizing procurement | ☐ placing blanket orders | ☐ expediting open orders | ☐ handing high-volume buying | ☐ ensuring follow-up | ☐ troubleshooting delivery problems | ☐ processing internal stock numbers | ☐ maintaining up-to-date client and vendor records | ☐ preparing weekly inventory reports | ☐ updating the incoming shipment log | ☐ other: _____].

☐ **Research the cost and value of all** _____ *[type of]* [☐ products | ☐ supplies | ☐ services | ☐ materials | ☐ equipment | ☐ other: _____] **for** [☐ department | ☐ company-wide | ☐ district | ☐ other: _____] **use; and negotiate and prepare vendor contracts.**

☐ **Monitor** [☐ production schedules | ☐ flow of merchandise and its components from vendor to company | ☐ inventory reports | ☐ other: _____].

☐ **Apply value-analysis criteria to** _____ *[type of]* [☐ products | ☐ supplies | ☐ services | ☐ materials | ☐ equipment | ☐ other: _____] **analyzing the** [☐ quality | ☐ price | ☐ delivery | ☐ shipping charges | ☐ lifecycle costing | ☐ final costs | ☐ maintenance costs | ☐ other: _____].

☐ **Locate, select, and purchase** _____ *[type of]* [☐ materials | ☐ equipment | ☐ tools | ☐ furniture | ☐ telephones | ☐ office equipment | ☐ other: _____] **for** _____ *[what?]* **considering** [☐ least cost | ☐ most reliable sources | ☐ best quality | ☐ ability to meet deadlines | ☐ trade licensing requirements | ☐ other: _____].

☐ **Consult with manufacturers' representatives regarding** [☐ products | ☐ cost | ☐ quantities | ☐ trade policies | ☐ replacement policies | ☐ other: _____] **to select and approve the purchase of** [☐ construction materials | ☐ equipment | ☐ tools | ☐ furniture | ☐ telephones | ☐ office equipment | ☐ other: _____].

☐ **Directly interface with** [☐ vendors | ☐ clients | ☐ state and federal agencies | ☐ others: _____] **regarding the purchasing of products for best price and quality, maximizing the firm's return on investment.**

☐ **Coordinate the purchasing of all production materials including** _____ *[type of]* [☐ equipment | ☐ tooling | ☐ fixtures | ☐ components | ☐ parts | ☐ supplies | ☐ other: _____] **at the best prices and quality by** _____ *[doing what?]*

☐ **Order sufficient** [☐ product | ☐ supplies | ☐ goods | ☐ merchandise | ☐ materials | ☐ other: _____] **in accordance with the firm's** [☐ inventory usage cycles | ☐ quality initiatives | ☐ established procedures | ☐ other: _____] **while effectively balancing physical storage and usage demands.**

☐ **Negotiate, execute, and administer all purchase orders for** [☐ company and its various subsidiaries | ☐ materials required in the production of _____ *(what?)* | ☐ other: _____].

☐ **Conduct** [☐ vendor bids | ☐ comparative cost analyses | ☐ other: _____], **and make sound selections based on** [☐ product quality | ☐ vendor reliability | ☐ ability to meet required deadlines | ☐ other: _____] **for** _____ *[what?]*.

☐ **Perform various purchasing functions for the** [☐ production | ☐ manufacturing | ☐ other: _____] **of** _____ *[what?]* **including** [☐ creating purchase orders | ☐ negotiating pricing | ☐ placing blanket orders | ☐ expediting open orders | ☐ handing high-volume buying | ☐ ensuring follow-up | ☐ troubleshooting delivery problems | ☐ maintaining up-to-date client and vendor records | ☐ preparing weekly inventory reports | ☐ other: _____].

☐ **Approve pricing of manufacturing components to ensure** [☐ best quality | ☐ pricing | ☐ delivery schedules | ☐ other: _____], **and ensure timely delivery of all** _____ *[type of]* [☐ parts | ☐ components | ☐ equipment | ☐ other: _____].

☐ **Purchase** _____ *[type of]* [☐ products | ☐ materials | ☐ supplies | ☐ equipment | ☐ other: _____] **from** _____ *[where purchased]*; **ensuring successful delivery.**

☐ **Serve as liaison with vendors and** _____ *[other types of companies]* **handling** [☐ purchasing | ☐ merchandise buying and/or selling | ☐ customer service | ☐ delivery troubleshooting | ☐ other: _____].

☐ **Handle new and existing** _____ *[type of]* **customers** _____ *[type of]* **purchases averaging** _____ *[#]* | $_____ *(amount)* [☐ weekly | ☐ monthly | ☐ annually].

☐ **By utilizing effective** [☐ inventory level monitoring | ☐ purchasing requirements | ☐ other: _____], **created consistent** _____**% annual service levels, resulting in** [☐ enhanced company credibility | ☐ a following in the community | ☐ other benefits: _____].

ACHIEVEMENT SAMPLES:

☐ **Increased purchasing annual service levels from** _____**% to** _____**%** *[percentages]* **efficiency through various regimented disciplines including** [☐ inventory level monitoring | ☐ client and vendor interface and follow-up | ☐ enhanced computer purchasing programs to monitor inventory levels | ☐ frequent product line reviews | ☐ other: _____] **resulting in** _____ *[benefits]*.

☐ **Conducted** _____ *[type of]* **research to identify best vendor selections by performing** [☐ value analysis | ☐ lifecycle costing] **on all** [☐ materials | ☐ equipment | ☐ products | ☐ supplies | ☐ services | ☐ other: _____] **for** _____ *[what?]*.

☐ **Saved $**_____ **in the negotiation and purchase of** _____ *[what]* **by obtaining product information from various sources and** [☐ reviewing literature | ☐ checking competitor pricing | ☐ consulting with sales reps | ☐ visiting trade shows | ☐ attending product demonstrations | ☐ other: _____].

☐ **Prepared $**_____ **in purchase orders** [☐ monthly | ☐ quarterly | ☐ annually | ☐ other: _____] **for** _____ *[type of]* [☐ supplies | ☐ materials | ☐ machinery | ☐ equipment | ☐ tools | ☐ parts | ☐ accessories | ☐ other: _____] **for** _____ *[what?]* **ensuring** [☐ verification of all specifications | ☐ pricing and availability of merchandise | ☐ other: _____].

☐ **Process in excess of** _____ *[#]* [☐ pounds | ☐ pieces | ☐ packages | ☐ yards | ☐ other measure: _____] **per week, with yearly profits of $**_____ , *[amount]* **surpassing competitors by $**_____ *[amount]*.

☐ **Saved the firm $**_____ *[amount]* **in extraneous costs by applying value-analysis criteria to** _____ *[type of]* [☐ supplies | ☐ services | ☐ materials | ☐ equipment | ☐ other: _____] **analyzing the** [☐ quality | ☐ price | ☐ delivery | ☐ shipping charges | ☐ lifecycle costing | ☐ final costs | ☐ maintenance costs | ☐ other: _____].

☐ **Slashed purchasing costs $**_____ **by determining the best** [☐ acquisition | ☐ procurement | ☐ buying | ☐ other: _____] **methods in the purchase of** _____ *[type of]* **equipment and supplies, preparing specifications, selecting vendors, and awarding contracts for** _____ *[what?]*.

☐ **As a persuasive negotiator, overcame** [☐ sales pitches | ☐ objections | ☐ other: _____] **to save on purchasing costs and meet the needs of company by way of** _____ *[what methods?]*.

☐ **Working in a fast-paced, high-pressure environment, handle high-volume purchasing with effective follow-through ensuring all** [☐ governmental regulations | ☐ company policies | ☐ other: _____] **are met.**

☐ **Reduced purchasing costs in excess of $**_____ **annually by establishing a** _____ *[what negotiation or initiative?]* **to** _____ *[do what?]*.

Quality Assurance & Quality Control – Construction

☐ **Ensure compliance with all building codes, ordinances, laws, and regulations including** [☐ contract specifications | ☐ zoning regulations | ☐ Uniform Building Code (UBC) | ☐ International Code Council (ICC) | ☐ electrical codes | ☐ fire regulations | ☐ plumbing codes | ☐ life-safety codes | ☐ environmental safety codes | ☐ ANSI | ☐ Federal regulations | ☐ state and local building codes | ☐ Title I | ☐ Title II | ☐ Title III | ☐ Title IV | ☐ Title V | ☐ other: _____].

☐ **Oversee quality control and compliance of** _____ *[which?]* **trades in their installation of** [☐ commercial | ☐ industrial | ☐ residential | ☐ other: _____] _____ *[type of]* **systems.**

☐ **By** _____ *[doing what?]*, **ensured all contractors and subcontractors followed design specs, used specified materials, followed code, and met quality work standards and deadlines.**

☐ **Conduct** [☐ weekly | ☐ monthly | ☐ periodic] **meetings with** [☐ Project Managers | ☐ contractors | ☐ subcontractors | ☐ others: _____] **to identify ways to improve** [☐ workmanship | ☐ productivity | ☐ competitive edge | ☐ other: _____].

☐ **Ensure quality workmanship in all trade areas covering** [☐ project specifications | ☐ expected deliverables | ☐ timely completion | ☐ other: _____] **making sound decisions regarding** [☐ corrective actions required | ☐ recommended means to obtain compliance | ☐ other: _____].

☐ **Manage and oversee quality assurance activities including** [☐ project scheduling | ☐ milestone establishment | ☐ resource scheduling | ☐ project monitoring | ☐ progress reporting | ☐ regulatory requirements compliance | ☐ other: _____] **for** _____ *[what?]* **ensuring compliance with all codes and regulations.**

☐ **Facilitate project control in the areas of** _____ , _____ , **and** _____ *[which areas?]* **to ensure all project management phases and progress are in compliance with project management methodology and expected deliverables.**

☐ **Develop, coordinate, and execute** _____ *[type of]* **quality assurance** [☐ plans | ☐ procedures | ☐ programs] **and** [☐ corrective | ☐ preventive] **actions to support interdisciplinary project teams in the construction of** _____ *[what?]*.

☐ **Identify and resolve quality issues by** [☐ applying sound problem-solving methodologies | ☐ improving quality issues awareness | ☐ supporting quality (☐ goals / ☐ priorities / ☐ disciplines / ☐ practices) | ☐ other: _____].

☐ **Direct and lead a broad range of** _____ *[type of]* **activities including** [☐ strategy development | ☐ direction setting | ☐ project planning, coordination, scheduling, tracking, and reporting | ☐ quality assurance standards development | ☐ other: _____] **to attain business goals.**

Recordkeeping – General

See also "Client Billing," "Project Time Tracking," and "Report Generation & Review."

☐ **Perform computer entry of daily** [☐ billing | ☐ payments | ☐ recordkeeping | ☐ client communiqué | ☐ other: _____], **ensuring** [☐ accurate data entry | ☐ all client records are current and accurate | ☐ other: _____].

☐ **Maintain up-to-date records of** [☐ man hours expended on job orders | ☐ employee time | ☐ accidents and injuries | ☐ work progress | ☐ other: _____].

☐ **Accurately complete and verify data entry of** _____ *[#]* **weekly invoices using** [☐ QuickBooks | ☐ Quicken | ☐ Excel | ☐ Microsoft Word | ☐ other program: _____]

☐ **Update project records** [☐ and generate reports] **that include** [☐ project time tracking | ☐ client billing | ☐ job history files | ☐ cost breakdowns | ☐ material requisitions | ☐ equipment specifications | ☐ maintenance history | ☐ work orders | ☐ other: _____].

☐ **Handle financial recordkeeping of all** [☐ purchases | ☐ supplies | ☐ monthly billing | ☐ budget monitoring | ☐ financial transaction processing | ☐ other process: _____] **for** _____ *[#]* **accounts.**

☐ **Facilitate all monthly billing for** _____ *[#]* **accounts with recordkeeping of all purchases and supplies per account using** _____ *[what program or method?].*

☐ **Update and maintain records of the** [☐ receipt | ☐ inspection | ☐ distribution | ☐ transporting | ☐ warehousing | ☐ other: _____] **of all** [☐ supplies | ☐ goods | ☐ product | ☐ merchandise | ☐ materials | ☐ property | ☐ furniture | ☐ equipment | ☐ other: _____] **acquisitions and dispositions.**

☐ **Prepare** _____ *[type of]* [☐ records | ☐ reports] **for** _____ *[type of]* [☐ bids | ☐ specifications | ☐ cost breakdowns | ☐ material and equipment inventory | ☐ orders | ☐ other: _____].

☐ **Keep accurate, up-to-date** [☐ purchasing | ☐ merchandising | ☐ buying | ☐ inventory | ☐ other: _____] **records of all** _____ *[type of]* **items purchased including** [☐ costs | ☐ quantities | ☐ delivery | ☐ distribution | ☐ product performance | ☐ inventory levels | (☐ materials / ☐ supplies) usage | ☐ other: _____].

☐ **Update and maintain records of the** [☐ receipt | ☐ inspection | ☐ distribution | ☐ transporting | ☐ warehousing | ☐ other: _____] **of all** [☐ property | ☐ furniture | ☐ equipment | ☐ supplies | ☐ goods | ☐ merchandise | ☐ materials | ☐ other: _____] **acquisitions and dispositions.**

☐ **Maintain up-to-date client and vendor records of** _____ *[#]* **accounts using** _____ *[what program?].*

☐ **Review and approve all production records including** [☐ job orders | ☐ job tickets | ☐ customer invoices | ☐ production logs | ☐ meter reports | ☐ stock inventories | ☐ equipment time and supplies usage | ☐ inventory records | ☐ sales reports | ☐ budgets | ☐ financial reports | ☐ cash receipts | ☐ bank deposits | ☐ other: _____].

☐ **Accurately maintain up-to-date** _____ *[type of]* [☐ documents | ☐ files | ☐ reports | ☐ records | ☐ data | ☐ information | ☐ other: _____] **including** [☐ job file records | ☐ project database information | ☐ project invoices | ☐ product data | ☐ field reports | ☐ other: _____] **according to** [☐ legal requirements | ☐ the firm's policies and procedures | ☐ other: _____].

☐ **Prepare and maintain** _____ *[type of]* [☐ preventive maintenance | ☐ history | ☐ work order | ☐ material requisition | ☐ scope of work | ☐ project status | ☐ other: _____] [records | ☐ reports | ☐ documentation | ☐ schedules | ☐ manuals] **and submit to** _____ *[whom?]* **on a** [☐ weekly | ☐ monthly | ☐ other: _____] **basis.**

ACHIEVEMENT SAMPLES:

☐ **Set up and maintained** _____ *[type of]* [☐ preventive maintenance | ☐ history | ☐ work order | ☐ material requisition | ☐ scope of work | ☐ project status | ☐ other: _____] [☐ records | ☐ reports | ☐ documentation | ☐ schedules | ☐ manuals] **and provided accurate periodic** [☐ progress | ☐ revenue | ☐ other: _____] **reports to** _____ *[whom?].*

☐ **Developed the** _____ *[type of]* [☐ system | ☐ records | ☐ data | ☐ information | ☐ other: _____] **that provides accurate periodic** [☐ progress | ☐ revenue | ☐ campaign | ☐ other: _____] **reports to** _____ *[whom?].*

☐ **Assisted** _____ *[whom?]* **by preparing** _____ *[type of]* [☐ records | ☐ reports] **for** _____ *[type of]* [☐ bids | ☐ cost breakdowns | ☐ material and equipment inventory | ☐ orders | ☐ other: _____], **which benefited by way of** _____ *[what?].*

Recordkeeping – Project Management

☐ **Update project records** [☐ and generate reports] **that include** [☐ project time tracking | ☐ client billing | ☐ job history files | ☐ cost breakdowns | ☐ material requisitions | ☐ equipment specifications | ☐ maintenance history | ☐ work orders | ☐ other: _____].

☐ **Prepare and maintain** _____ [type of] [☐ scope of work | ☐ project status | ☐ history | ☐ work order | ☐ requisition | ☐ other: _____] [☐ records | ☐ reports | ☐ documentation | ☐ schedules] and submit to _____ [whom?] **on a** [☐ weekly | ☐ monthly | ☐ other: _____] **basis.**

☐ **Manage the update and maintenance of** _____ [which?] **project management records including the** [☐ receipt | ☐ inspection | ☐ distribution | ☐ transporting | ☐ other: _____] **of all** [☐ equipment | ☐ supplies | ☐ materials | ☐ other: _____] **acquisitions and dispositions.**

☐ **Prepare** _____ [type of] [☐ records | ☐ reports] **for** _____ [type of] [☐ bids | ☐ specifications | ☐ cost breakdowns | ☐ material and equipment inventory | ☐ orders | ☐ other: _____].

☐ **Review and approve all** _____ [type of] **records including** [☐ job orders | ☐ job tickets | ☐ customer invoices | ☐ stock inventories | ☐ equipment time and supplies usage | ☐ inventory records | ☐ sales reports | ☐ budgets | ☐ financial reports | ☐ cash receipts | ☐ bank deposits | ☐ other: _____].

☐ **Maintain up-to-date records of** [☐ man hours expended on projects | ☐ employee time | ☐ accidents and injuries | ☐ work progress | ☐ other: _____].

☐ **Update and maintain records of the** [☐ receipt | ☐ inspection | ☐ distribution | ☐ transporting | ☐ warehousing | ☐ other: _____] **of all** [☐ supplies | ☐ goods | ☐ product | ☐ merchandise | ☐ materials | ☐ property | ☐ furniture | ☐ equipment | ☐ other: _____] **acquisitions and dispositions.**

☐ **Perform computer entry of daily** [☐ recordkeeping | ☐ billing | ☐ payments | ☐ client communiqué | ☐ other: _____], **ensuring** [☐ accurate data entry | ☐ all client records are current and accurate | ☐ other: _____].

☐ **Keep accurate, up-to-date project management records of all** _____ [type of] **items purchased including** [☐ costs | ☐ quantities | ☐ delivery | ☐ inventory levels | (☐ materials / ☐ supplies) usage | ☐ other: _____].

☐ **Accurately maintain up-to-date** _____ [type of] [☐ documents | ☐ files | ☐ reports | ☐ records | ☐ data | ☐ information | ☐ other: _____] **including** [☐ job file records | ☐ project database information | ☐ project invoices | ☐ product data | ☐ field reports | ☐ other: _____] **according to** [☐ legal requirements | ☐ the firm's policies and procedures | ☐ other: _____].

☐ [☐ Accurately complete | ☐ Review and verify] **data entry of** _____ [#] **weekly invoices using** [☐ QuickBooks | ☐ Quicken | ☐ Excel | ☐ Microsoft Word | ☐ other program: _____]

☐ **Handle financial recordkeeping of all** [☐ purchases | ☐ supplies | ☐ billing | ☐ budget monitoring | ☐ financial transaction processing | ☐ other process: _____] **for** _____ [#] **accounts.**

☐ **Perform quality control of reports prepared by** [☐ Architects | ☐ Engineers | ☐ Project Managers | ☐ others: _____] **including** _____, _____, **and** _____ [type of reports] **and** _____ [do what?].

☐ **Accurately maintain up-to-date** [☐ job file records | ☐ project database information | ☐ project invoices | ☐ contractor's shop drawings | ☐ product data | ☐ field reports | ☐ other: _____] **and other records ensuring** _____ [what?].

☐ **Develop and maintain all** _____ [type of] [☐ systems | ☐ records | ☐ data | ☐ information | ☐ other: _____]; **and provide accurate periodic** [☐ progress | ☐ revenue | ☐ other: _____] **reports to** _____ [whom?].

ACHIEVEMENT SAMPLES:

☐ **Set up and maintained** _____ [type of] [☐ scope of work | ☐ project status | ☐ work order | ☐ material requisition | ☐ other: _____] [☐ records | ☐ reports | ☐ documentation | ☐ schedules] **and provided accurate period progress reports to** _____ [whom?].

☐ **Developed the** _____ [type of] [☐ system | ☐ records | ☐ data | ☐ information | ☐ other: _____] **that provides accurate periodic** [☐ progress | ☐ revenue | ☐ campaign | ☐ other: _____] **reports to** _____ [whom?].

☐ **Assisted** _____ [whom?] **by preparing** _____ [type of] [☐ records | ☐ reports] **for** _____ [type of] [☐ bids | ☐ cost breakdowns | ☐ material and equipment inventory | ☐ orders | ☐ other: _____].

☐ **Devised, executed, and maintain the** _____ [type of] [☐ records | ☐ data | ☐ information | ☐ other: _____] **and provide accurate periodic** [☐ progress |☐ revenue | ☐ other: _____] **reports to** _____ [whom?].

Recordkeeping Management

See also "Inventory Management & Control."

☐ **Manage the update and maintenance of** _____ *[which?]* **records including the** [☐ receipt | ☐ inspection | ☐ distribution | ☐ transporting | ☐ warehousing | ☐ other: _____ **] of all** [☐ equipment | ☐ supplies | ☐ goods | ☐ product | ☐ merchandise | ☐ materials | ☐ other: _____ **] acquisitions and dispositions.**

☐ **Manage and oversee the firm's inventory recordkeeping to ensure accurate, up-to-date** [☐ inventory | ☐ purchasing | ☐ buying | ☐ invoicing | ☐ other: _____ **] records of all** _____ *[type of]* **items purchased including** [☐ costs | ☐ quantities | ☐ delivery | ☐ distribution | ☐ product performance | ☐ inventory levels | (☐ materials / ☐ supplies) usage | ☐ other: _____].

☐ **Ensure all** [☐ property | ☐ supplies | ☐ goods | ☐ product | ☐ merchandise | ☐ materials | ☐ furniture | ☐ equipment | ☐ other: _____ **] acquisition and disposition records are up to date, including** [☐ receipts | ☐ inspections | ☐ distribution | ☐ transporting | ☐ warehousing | ☐ other: _____].

☐ **Manage the firm's financial recordkeeping of** [☐ inventory | ☐ purchasing | ☐ merchandising | ☐ buying | ☐ billing | ☐ other: _____ **] including** _____ *[what functions?]*.

☐ **Supervise and oversee computer entry of daily** [☐ receipts | ☐ billing | ☐ invoicing | ☐ payments | ☐ recordkeeping | ☐ client communiqué | ☐ other: _____], **ensuring** [☐ accurate data entry at all times | ☐ all client records are current and accurate | ☐ other: _____].

☐ **Review and verify data entry of** _____ *[#]* **weekly invoices using** [☐ QuickBooks | ☐ Quicken | ☐ Excel | ☐ Microsoft Word | ☐ other: _____].

☐ **Review and approve all** _____ *[type of]* **records including** [☐ job orders | ☐ job tickets | ☐ customer invoices | ☐ stock inventories | ☐ equipment time and supplies usage | ☐ inventory records | ☐ sales reports | ☐ budgets | ☐ financial reports | ☐ cash receipts | ☐ bank deposits | ☐ other: _____].

☐ **Oversee all recordkeeping of** [☐ purchases and supplies | ☐ monthly billing | ☐ budget monitoring | ☐ financial transaction processing | ☐ other process: _____ **] for** _____ *[#]* **accounts.**

☐ **Manage and oversee monthly billing for** _____ *[#]* **accounts with recordkeeping of all purchases and supplies per account using** _____ *[program or method]*.

Recruitment / Employment – General

See also "Recruitment – Human Resources."

☐ **Oversee all facets of staff hiring, training and development, scheduling and terminations for** _____ *[#]* **employees.**

☐ **Interview, recruit,** [☐ schedule | ☐ train | ☐ develop] **a top-tier** _____ *[type of]* **staff, selecting and assigning recruits based on their ability to** _____ *[do what well?]* **and ensuring compliance with all Equal Employment Opportunity (EEO), affirmative action, Americans with Disabilities Act guidelines and laws, and the firm's human resources policies and procedures.**

☐ **Run efficient** _____ *[type of]* **business through** [☐ proper staffing and scheduling | ☐ improving staff morale and efficiency | ☐ ensuring quality work in all areas | ☐ other: _____].

☐ **Recruit, train, manage, and evaluate the performance of all** _____ *[which?]* **staff, including** _____, _____, **and** _____ *[job titles]*.

☐ **Investigate the backgrounds of potential employees by** [☐ researching applicant's resumes | ☐ interviewing references | ☐ other methods: _____ **] resulting in** [☐ recruiting talented _____ (titles) employees | ☐ producing a high volume of quality work | ☐ other: _____].

☐ **Obtain** _____ *[type of]* **qualitative background information from** [☐ educational | ☐ employment | ☐ military | ☐ other: _____ **] references and sources to make informed hiring decisions.**

☐ **Hire, direct, train, and evaluate a supervisory staff of** _____ *[#]* **and oversee a construction team of** _____ *[#]* **including** [☐ planning | ☐ scheduling | ☐ performance appraisals | ☐ employee incentives | ☐ disciplinary actions | ☐ problem resolution | ☐ other: _____].

☐ **Maintain employee records with** [☐ dates of hire | ☐ compensation | ☐ benefits | ☐ leave records | ☐ other: _____ **] and other pertinent personnel data, and prepare and file employer reports to** [☐ government agencies | ☐ insurance companies | ☐ union | ☐ other: _____].

☐ **Direct field and office project management** [☐ recruiting | ☐ training and development | ☐ performance evaluations | ☐ compensation reviews | ☐ payroll administration | ☐ other: _____].

☐ **Recruit and hire the most qualified** [☐ laborers | ☐ professional staff | ☐ management team | ☐ other: _____] **to meet the firm's needs and develop trained** [☐ personnel | ☐ workers | ☐ staff] **by** _____ *[methods used]*.

Report Generation & Review – Construction

See also "Client Billing" and "Project Time Tracking," as applicable.

☐ **Prepare** _____ *[type of]* [☐ records | ☐ reports] **for** _____ *[type of]* [(☐ job / ☐ client) history files | ☐ construction bids | ☐ architectural drawings | ☐ specifications | ☐ cost breakdowns | ☐ material and equipment (☐ inventory | ☐ orders | ☐ specifications) | ☐ other: _____].

☐ **Direct and lead** _____ *[type of]* **research and analysis including** [☐ planning | ☐ evaluation and assessment | ☐ concept and design | ☐ coordination | ☐ development | ☐ simulation | ☐ testing | ☐ construction | ☐ production | ☐ implementation | ☐ quality control | ☐ supervision | ☐ maintenance | ☐ other: _____] **of** _____ *[what?]*.

☐ **Perform quality control of reports prepared by** [☐ Architects | ☐ Engineers | ☐ Project Managers | ☐ others: _____] **including** _____, _____, **and** _____ *[type of reports]* **by** _____ *[doing what?]*.

☐ **Accurately record all** [☐ project | ☐ inspection | ☐ other: _____] **details; and prepare** _____ *[type of]* **reports using** _____ *(which?)* **program(s), to include** [☐ project progress | ☐ inspection deficiencies | ☐ work conditions | ☐ detected violations | ☐ other: _____].

☐ **Maintain** _____ *[type of]* **reports, and follow up with** _____ *[which?]* [☐ departments | ☐ divisions | ☐ writers | ☐ other: _____] **to ensure timely submission of** _____ *[type of]* **items**.

☐ **Prepare** _____ *[type of]* [☐ records | ☐ reports] **for** _____ *[type of]* [☐ job files | ☐ client history files | ☐ bids | ☐ cost breakdowns | ☐ material and equipment | ☐ other: _____].

☐ **Accurately record all** _____ *[type of]* **details; and prepare** _____ *[type of]* **reports using** _____ *(which?)* **program(s), to include** _____ *[what?]*.

☐ **Oversee the** [☐ preparation | ☐ analysis | ☐ negotiation | ☐ review] **of** [☐ contracts | ☐ invoices | ☐ estimates | ☐ billing | ☐ other: _____] **related to the** [☐ purchase | ☐ sale ☐ other: _____] **of** [☐ equipment | ☐ materials | ☐ supplies | ☐ products | ☐ services | ☐ other: _____].

☐ **Facilitate distribution of** [☐ financial statements | ☐ journal entries | ☐ articles | ☐ publications | ☐ other: _____] **and oversee the** [☐ compilation | ☐ coordination | ☐ accuracy | ☐ other: _____] **of all** _____ *[what data?]*.

☐ **Regularly monitor and review** _____ *[type of]* **project reports and status including reporting of** [☐ budget variances | ☐ schedule compliance | (☐ firm / ☐ division / ☐ departmental) performance indicators | ☐ other: _____].

☐ **Prepare** _____ *[type of]* **reports detailing the progress of all** _____ *[type of]* **projects, addressing any related problems, and making sound recommendations to solve them.**

☐ **Interpret and evaluate** [☐ legal | ☐ contractual | ☐ practical | ☐ complex | ☐ engineering | ☐ other: _____] _____ *[type of]* [☐ data | ☐ problems | ☐ information], **and furnish** _____ *[type of]* **recommended solutions for** _____ *[what?]* **to** _____ *[whom?]*.

ACHIEVEMENT SAMPLES:

☐ **Made recommendations for** _____ *[what?]*; **and prepared comprehensive** _____ *[type of]* **reports to support these recommendations**.

☐ **Developed a(n)** _____ *[type of]* [☐ invoice | ☐ report | ☐ billing chart | ☐ template | ☐ form | ☐ other: _____] **to record** _____ *[what?]* **superceding the manual method and saving the company $**_____ *[amount]* **in the area of** _____ *[what area?]*.

☐ **Prepared and maintain** _____ *[type of]* [☐ history | ☐ work order | ☐ scope of work | ☐ compliance | ☐ project status | ☐ material requisition | ☐ preventive maintenance | ☐ other: _____] [☐ records | ☐ reports | ☐ documentation | ☐ schedules | ☐ manuals | ☐ other: _____] **and submit to** _____ *[whom?]* **on a** [☐ weekly | ☐ monthly | ☐ other: _____] **basis**.

☐ **Assessed compliance findings via** _____ *[type of]* **compliance reports, and followed up with** _____ *[which?]* [☐ departmental | ☐ divisional | ☐ other: _____] **managers to ensure compliance with** _____ *[what?]*.

☐ **Developed a** _____ *[type of]* **compliance report that records** _____ *[what information?]* **and supplies** _____ *[what?]* **to** _____ *[whom?]*.

Roofing Functions & Projects

See also "Carpentry / Construction Work Functions."

☐ [☐ Manage | ☐ Perform] _____ *[type of]* **roofing construction projects for** [☐ general commercial construction | ☐ residential homes | ☐ decks and porches | ☐ sunrooms | ☐ cabanas | ☐ other: _____] **according to company's established policies, procedures, and guidelines and in compliance with all codes.**

☐ **Plan and direct roofing surveys of** _____ *[what?]* **to determine** _____ *[type of]* **maintenance and new roof requirements**.

☐ **Apply** [☐ proficiency in | ☐ considerable knowledge of | ☐ other: _____] **various** [☐ commercial | ☐ residential | ☐ other: _____] **roofing systems, materials, and installation methods;** [☐ state and local building codes | ☐ Uniform Building Code | ☐ electrical codes | ☐ plumbing codes | ☐ other: _____]; **and** [☐ construction site development | ☐ commercial construction | ☐ demolition | ☐ other: _____] **procedures in the installation of** _____ *[type of]* **roofs**.

☐ **[☐ Direct | ☐ Facilitate] [☐ large-scale | ☐ mid-size | ☐ other: _____]** _____ *[type of]* **commercial roofing projects ensuring all quality standards are followed and all work is completed in accordance with standards, industry guidelines, and contracts.**

☐ **Prepare for roofing projects by** [☐ performing on-site reviews | ☐ reviewing surveys | ☐ taking dimensions | ☐ developing drawings | ☐ interpreting roofing plans, specifications, and standards | ☐ conducting roofing tests to provide architect with necessary information for contract completion | ☐ identifying and resolving project deficiencies | ☐ estimating materials, hours, and (replacement) costs | ☐ ordering required roofing materials | ☐ other: _____].

Safety & Responsibility for Others

See also "Environment, Safety & Health Management Compliance."

☐ **Ensure that** [☐ employees | ☐ buildings | ☐ facilities | ☐ grounds | ☐ customers and others] **are safe and secure by** [☐ following safe work procedures | ☐ exercising a high degree of awareness | ☐ complying with all safety codes | ☐ other: _____].

☐ **Safeguard lives by** [☐ following safe work procedures | ☐ exercising a high degree of awareness | ☐ complying with all safety guidelines and precautions | ☐ other: _____].

☐ **Follow safety precautions using protective equipment around exposure to** [☐ extreme temperatures | ☐ toxic chemicals | ☐ biohazardous materials | ☐ smoke and fumes | ☐ other: _____].

☐ **Ensure proper safety precautions and regulations are observed during all** _____ *[type of]* [☐ installations | ☐ repairs | ☐ construction] **by** _____ *[doing what?]* **to prevent physical injury to self and others**.

ACHIEVEMENT SAMPLES:

☐ **Achieved safety performance levels to** _____ *[what level?]* **from previous incident rate of** _____ *[what level?]* **by** _____ *[doing what?]*, **ensuring overall business and personnel safety and security.**

☐ **Decreased controllable expenses $**_____ *[amount]* **over previous year by implementing improved** _____ *[type of]* [☐ safety programs | ☐ security programs | ☐ safety awareness training | ☐ other: _____] **that** _____ *[did what?]*, **resulting in** _____ *[what benefits?]*.

☐ **Maintained optimum** [☐ company | ☐ plant | ☐ other: _____] **safety and security by** _____ *[doing what?]* **and implementing safety procedures in accordance with** [☐ OSHA | ☐ other: _____] **regulations**.

☐ **Achieved and maintained high levels of** [☐ employee | ☐ crew | ☐ customer | ☐ others: _____] **safety by** _____ *[doing what?]*.

Safety & Security Compliance

See "Environmental, Safety & Health Management Compliance."

Staff Management & Supervision – General

See also "Staff Management & Supervision – Construction Teams," "Staff Management & Supervision – Carpentry / Labor Teams," "Team Leadership & Direction," and "Work Collaboration," as applicable.

☐ **Provide strategic, comprehensive** [☐ leadership and direction | ☐ supervision and guidance | ☐ assistance and support] **to the** _____ *[which?]* **staff in the areas of** _____, _____ **and** _____ *[which areas?]* **that leads to** _____ *[what?]* **and the successful completion of all jobs.**

☐ **Supervise, coordinate, and oversee the day-to-day activities of the** _____ *[which?]* **Department team of** _____ *[#]* **including** _____, _____, **and** _____ *[titles or functions]* **including** [☐ prioritizing work assignments and project tasks | ☐ analyzing scope and importance of work | ☐ determining deadlines | ☐ strategizing best approach to meet commitments | ☐ delegating assignments | ☐ providing guidance and support | ☐ other: _____] **ensuring quality performance in all areas.**

☐ **Oversee the supervision of the** _____ *[which?]* **staff in the areas of** [☐ work prioritization | ☐ work allocation | ☐ job assignments | ☐ delegating | ☐ scheduling | ☐ employee development | ☐ performance evaluations | ☐ personnel actions | ☐ productivity and performance improvement | ☐ technical support | ☐ problem resolution | ☐ other: _____], **and motivate employees to achieve peak productivity and performance.**

☐ **Manage a(n)** _____ *[type of]* **team of** _____ *[#]* **ensuring** [☐ the highest quality work | ☐ fulfillment of all expected deliverables | ☐ timely development and completion of all projects | ☐ quality standards are adhered to | ☐ compliance with all company guidelines | ☐ measurable member participation and progress | ☐ other: _____].

☐ **Supervise and oversee the daily activities of the** _____ *[which?]* **staff including** [☐ assignment delegating | ☐ purchasing | ☐ payroll processing | ☐ administrative support | ☐ report generation | ☐ contract administration | ☐ other: _____] **ensuring quality performance in all areas.**

☐ **Monitor, fairly evaluate, and document subordinates' progress to ensure that** [☐ all required goals are met for the position | ☐ quality of work or customer service delivered meets firm's high standards of excellence | ☐ other requirements: _____].

☐ **Oversee personnel management functions including** [☐ new hire selections | ☐ training and development | ☐ performance ratings | ☐ commendatory and disciplinary actions | ☐ promotions | ☐ demotions | ☐ transfers | ☐ terminations | ☐ other: _____] **to** [☐ optimize staffing needs | ☐ maintain work force productivity | ☐ ensure quality workmanship ☐ other: _____].

☐ **Influence, energize, and motivate** _____ *[type of]* **staff to apply** _____ *[type of]* **skills to help them** [☐ solve dynamic challenges | ☐ overcome obstacles | ☐ other: _____] **to bring projects to a successful completion.**

☐ [☐ Manage | ☐ Supervise] **and oversee a team of** _____ *[#]* **in the initiation, planning, and development of** _____ *[type of]* **projects ranging from $**_____ **to $**_____ **and resulting in** [☐ delivering bottom-line business value | ☐ business transformation | ☐ new product offerings | ☐ the translation of enterprise strategies into projects | ☐ increased productivity | ☐ other benefits: _____].

☐ **Supervise and direct a staff of** _____ *[#]* _____ *[titles]* **and oversee their daily activities ensuring** [☐ quality performance in all areas | ☐ all work is completed on time and to expectations | ☐ other: _____].

☐ **Guide and oversee a** _____ *[which?]* **staff of** _____ *[#]* **ensuring** [☐ the highest quality work | ☐ fulfillment of all expected deliverables | ☐ all functions are performed in a timely, cost-effective manner | ☐ measurable member participation and progress | ☐ quality deliverables | ☐ other: _____] **which** [☐ meet customer needs | ☐ achieve business objectives].

☐ **Successfully delegate and follow up on** _____ *[what?]* **to ensure staff completes all assigned functions correctly and in accordance with** _____ *[what?]* [☐ policies and procedures | ☐ rules and regulations | ☐ other: _____], **resulting in** _____ *[what benefits?].*

☐ **Manage and oversee** _____ *[#]* _____ *[whom?]* **in a** _____ *[type of]* **environment including** [☐ recruiting staff | ☐ preparing work schedules | ☐ developing training programs | ☐ conducting performance appraisals | ☐ other: _____].

☐ **Supervise and guide** _____ *[#]* **employees in the** _____ *[which?]* [☐ division | ☐ department | ☐ unit | ☐ store | ☐ other: _____], **including** _____ *[#]* **directly and** _____ *[#]* **indirectly for this** _____ *[type of]* **firm.**

☐ **Hire, schedule, and supervise a** [☐ direct | ☐ indirect] **support staff of from** _____ *[#]* **to** _____ *[#].*

ACHIEVEMENT SAMPLES:

☐ **Built a strong, supportive team environment by exhibiting and modeling leadership skills in** [☐ communication | ☐ negotiation | ☐ problem-solving | ☐ obstacle tackling | ☐ other: _____].

☐ **Gained** _____ *[which?]* **team member cooperation, commitment, and buy-in by** [☐ providing clear direction | ☐ soliciting feedback | ☐ serving as primary resource hub | ☐ insisting on mutual support | ☐ sharing information | ☐ modeling professional behavior | ☐ building a collaborative environment | ☐ removing all obstacles to project success | ☐ other: _____].

☐ **Energized, inspired, and motivated the** _____ *[which?]* **Department staff of** _____ *[#]* **to** _____ *[perform what?]* **by** _____ *[doing what well?].*

☐ **Provided strategic, comprehensive** [☐ leadership | ☐ direction | ☐ guidance | ☐ assistance | ☐ support] **to the** _____ *[which?]* **staff in the areas of** _____, _____, **and** _____ *[which areas?]* **that led to** _____ *[what?]* **and the successful completion of all jobs.**

☐ **Developed and maintain a** [☐ strong | ☐ knowledgeable | ☐ cooperative | ☐ supportive | ☐ high-energy | ☐ productive | ☐ creative | ☐ winning | ☐ other: _____] _____ *[which?]* **management team environment in the coordination and completion of all** _____ *[what?]* **activities by exhibiting and modeling influential leadership skills in** [☐ communication | ☐ problem-solving | ☐ obstacle tackling | ☐ negotiation | ☐ other: _____].

☐ **Developed and implemented a** _____ *[type of]* **employee incentive program to** _____ *[accomplish what?]*, **which resulted in** _____ *[what benefits?]*.

☐ **Instilled** _____ *[what?]* **in a project team of** _____ *[#]* **that resulted in attaining** [☐ the highest quality work | ☐ fulfillment of all expected deliverables regardless of obstacles | ☐ all projects staying on schedule and within budget | ☐ timely development and completion of all projects | ☐ meeting project success criteria | ☐ adherence to quality standards | ☐ lower turnover | ☐ compliance with all company guidelines and ordinances | ☐ other: _____].

☐ **Influenced, energized, and motivated team members to develop and maintain positive working relationships with all levels of management and to apply** _____ *[type of]* **skills to help them** [☐ set realistic expectations | ☐ solve dynamic challenges | ☐ overcome obstacles | ☐ understand the impact of change | ☐ tackle political or bureaucratic obstacles | ☐ other: _____] **to bring** _____ *[type of]* **projects to a successful completion**.

☐ **Tackled challenging** _____ *[type of]* **employee situations through the means of** _____ *[what?]* **methods, which has resulted in** [☐ a smooth workflow | ☐ less downtime | ☐ more productivity | ☐ more motivated employees | ☐ other: _____].

☐ **Developed effective relationships with** _____ *[which?]* **staff by** [☐ fostering a cooperative team environment | ☐ promoting a cooperative working atmosphere | ☐ maximizing employee morale | ☐ other: _____].

Staff Management & Supervision – Carpentry / Labor Teams

See also "Staff Management & Supervision – General," "Trades / Crew Supervision – All Trades" and "Trades Coordination & Oversight."

☐ **Lead and direct a crew of** _____ *[#]* [☐ carpenters | ☐ laborers] **involved in all aspects of** [☐ carpentry | ☐ construction] **including** [☐ reviewing project plans | ☐ reading and interpreting blueprints | ☐ estimating time | ☐ developing work schedules | ☐ assigning crews | ☐ delegating jobs | ☐ preparing work orders | ☐ ordering and setting up equipment | ☐ purchasing supplies | ☐ preparing job sites | ☐ performing rough and finish carpentry | ☐ inspecting work area | ☐ other: _____] **ensuring all jobs are completed in compliance with all specifications and building codes.**

☐ **Lead and supervise from** _____ *[#]* **to** _____ *[#]* **laborers in the construction and installation of** [☐ walls | ☐ doors | ☐ door jambs | ☐ roofs | ☐ floors | ☐ wall coverings | ☐ ceilings | ☐ paneling | ☐ plastic laminates | ☐ platforms | ☐ partitions | ☐ fences | ☐ ramps | ☐ insulation | ☐ weather stripping | ☐ other: _____] **for this** _____ *[type of]* **firm.**

☐ **Oversee personnel management and job operations including** [☐ coordinating steel and concrete trades | ☐ scheduling laborers | ☐ managing construction | ☐ overseeing site materials and equipment set-up | ☐ other: _____].

☐ **Supervise and oversee laborers in all phases of construction projects including** [☐ pouring foundations | ☐ framing walls and partitions | ☐ installing sheetrock | ☐ building and installing (☐ stairs / ☐ windows / ☐ doors / ☐ brattices / ☐ roofing) | ☐ taping and spackling | ☐ painting | ☐ trim work | ☐ flooring | ☐ tiling | ☐ ceilings | ☐ cabinets | ☐ other: _____].

☐ **Oversee the work of** _____ *[#]* [☐ carpenters | ☐ laborers | ☐ contractors] **in the measuring, cutting, and fitting of wallboard panels to wood and metal framework, cutting holes in panels for** [☐ windows | ☐ doors | ☐ electrical outlets | ☐ air-conditioning units | ☐ plumbing | ☐ other: _____] **and applying textured surfaces to** [☐ walls | ☐ ceilings | ☐ floors | ☐ other: _____].

☐ **Provide construction support, feedback, and inspiration to a carpentry staff of** _____ *[#]* _____ *[titles]* **in the development and coordination of major and minor** _____ *[type of]* **projects.**

☐ **Oversee laborers in the set-up of prefabricated components including** [☐ frames | ☐ stairs | ☐ wall panels | ☐ other: _____] **to construct and build** _____ *[what?]*.

☐ **Supervise home** [☐ construction | ☐ improvement | ☐ renovation | ☐ additions | ☐ finished attics and basements | ☐ other: _____] **carpenters and other contractors for individual clients** [☐ on a consultant basis].

☐ **Oversee** _____ *[#]* **laborers in fastening of drywall panels to framework of** [☐ residential houses | ☐ commercial buildings | ☐ other: _____]; **and prepare panels for painting by filling, taping, troweling, and finishing joints**.

☐ **Direct and oversee all** [☐ carpentry | ☐ plumbing | ☐ electrical | ☐ HVAC | ☐ welding | ☐ landscaping | ☐ other: _____] [☐ installation | ☐ replacement | ☐ maintenance | ☐ repair | ☐ other: _____] **work required in** _____ *[type of]* **jobs for this $** _____ *[revenues]* _____ *[type of]* **firm.**

☐ **Monitor job progress through on-site field inspection and review to ensure conformance to** [☐ design specifications | ☐ cost estimates | ☐ time schedules | ☐ electrical codes | ☐ other: _____], **immediately resolving any problems.**

ACHIEVEMENT SAMPLES: *See Achievements under "Staff Management & Supervision – General."*

Staff Management & Supervision – Construction Teams

See also "Staff Management & Supervision – General," "Trades / Crew Supervision – All Trades"
and "Trades Coordination & Oversight."

☐ **Direct and supervise the** [☐ engineering | ☐ architect | ☐ drafting | ☐ project management | ☐ technical | ☐ construction | ☐ other: _____] **staff(s) of** _____ *[#]* **in all related aspects of** [☐ engineering applications | ☐ architectural renderings | ☐ construction management | ☐ other: _____] **for the design and support of** [☐ major | ☐ complex | ☐ high-dollar | ☐ other: _____] _____ *[type of]* **projects and sound architectural standards for this** _____ *[type of]* **firm.**

☐ **Lead, direct, and mentor an engineering staff of** _____ *[#]* **in the** [☐ design and] **construction of** [☐ buildings | ☐ structures | ☐ highways | ☐ transportation systems | ☐ public utilities | ☐ transit systems | ☐ water quality systems | ☐ water resource management systems | ☐ agricultural systems | ☐ environmentally-friendly systems | ☐ other: _____] **for this** _____ *[type of firm/agency].*

☐ **Provide strong leadership and direction to the** [☐ engineering | ☐ architectural ☐ project management | ☐ construction | ☐ other: _____] **staff(s) through** [☐ strategic vision and planning | ☐ innovative research | ☐ engineering | ☐ effective communication | ☐ other: _____] **in the** [☐ concept | ☐ schematic design | ☐ site planning | ☐ construction | ☐ cost management | ☐ quantity control | ☐ other: _____] **of** [☐ interior spaces | ☐ exterior spaces | ☐ physical environments | ☐ other: _____] **of** _____ *[type of]* **projects.**

☐ **Direct and oversee various engineering and administrative functions including** [☐ research and analysis | ☐ assessments and evaluations | ☐ architectural renderings | ☐ profile sheet plotting and drafting | ☐ client presentations | ☐ project time and cost estimates | ☐ project prioritization | ☐ planning | ☐ conceptualization | ☐ establishing priorities, scheduling, and deadlines | ☐ quality control | ☐ change orders | ☐ other: _____].

☐ **Coordinate work of** _____ *[#]* [☐ Project Engineers | ☐ Design Engineers | ☐ CAD Technicians | ☐ others: _____] **from initial planning stages through final construction.**

☐ **Provide strong leadership and direction to the** _____ *[which?]* **engineering staff through** [☐ strategic vision and planning | ☐ effective communication | ☐ other: _____] **in the** [☐ concept | ☐ schematic design | ☐ site planning | ☐ construction | ☐ cost management | ☐ quantity control | ☐ other: _____] **of** _____ *[type of]* **projects.**

☐ **Oversee and direct the work of** [☐ Engineers | ☐ structural engineering staff | ☐ drafting professionals | ☐ other: _____] **in the design and construction of** _____ *[what?].*

☐ **Lead and direct** _____ *[which?]* **project teams in the planning and design of** _____ *[what?]* **and other structures for** [☐ highway | ☐ railroad | ☐ other: _____] **facilities with projects ranging from simple to complex including** [☐ multispan bridges | ☐ curved steel bridges | ☐ pre-stressed concrete | ☐ post-tensioned concrete | ☐ variety of retaining walls | (☐ single | ☐ multi-cell) culverts | ☐ other: _____].

☐ **Provide leadership and direction to an engineering staff of** _____ *[#]* **in the design of** _____ *[what?]* **for this** [☐ full-service] [☐ architectural and engineering design | ☐ design-and-build | ☐ other: _____] **firm.**

☐ **Supervise an engineering staff of** _____ *[#]* **who** [☐ calculates operating budgets | ☐ generates _____ *(type of)* reports | ☐ performs _____ *(type of)* investigations | ☐ other: _____] **to evaluate the efficiency of** _____ *[type of]* **engineering** [☐ programs | ☐ operations | ☐ processes | ☐ projects | ☐ other: _____].

☐ **Plan and direct the work of** _____ *[#]* [☐ Stationary | ☐ Utility | ☐ Staff | ☐ Mechanical | ☐ Maintenance | ☐ other: _____] **Engineers in the** [☐ installation | ☐ operation | ☐ maintenance | ☐ repair] **of** [☐ heating | ☐ ventilating | ☐ air conditioning | ☐ refrigeration | ☐ electrical | ☐ plumbing | ☐ pneumatic control | ☐ life safety | ☐ water treatment | ☐ building management | ☐ other: _____] **systems as well as** [☐ natural gas distribution lines | (☐ water / ☐ steam / ☐ sewage) lines | (☐ diesel / ☐ emergency) generators | ☐ sewage lift stations | ☐ boilers | ☐ electric fire pumps | ☐ water wells | ☐ irrigation pumps | ☐ power equipment | ☐ lighting | ☐ preventive maintenance | ☐ switch rooms | ☐ electrical substations | ☐ grounds | ☐ other: _____].

☐ **Provide leadership and direction in the** [☐ concept | ☐ schematic design | ☐ site planning | ☐ construction | ☐ cost management | ☐ quality control | ☐ other: _____] **of** [☐ interior spaces | ☐ exterior spaces | ☐ physical environments | ☐ other: _____] **of** _____ *[type of]* **projects.**

☐ **Manage and oversee** [☐ trades supervision | ☐ construction inspection | ☐ quality control | ☐ building and safety codes enforcement | ☐ design guidelines and specifications standards development | ☐ other: _____].

☐ **Lead a project team of** _____ [#] [☐ Engineers | ☐ Architects | ☐ Project Managers | ☐ other: _____] **in the design and construction of high quality, cost-effective** _____ [type of] **solutions that successfully address** [☐ firm's | ☐ clients'] **requirements**.

☐ **Oversee and direct the daily activities of the project team and contract staff including** [☐ assignment delegating | ☐ purchasing | ☐ payroll processing | ☐ administrative support | ☐ report generation | ☐ contract administration | ☐ other: _____] **ensuring quality performance in the successful completion of all projects.**

☐ **Manage a project team ensuring** [☐ the highest quality work | ☐ fulfillment of all expected deliverables | ☐ all projects stay on schedule and within budget | ☐ timely development and completion of all projects | ☐ project success criteria are met | ☐ quality and project management standards are adhered to | ☐ compliance with all company guidelines and ordinances | ☐ other: _____].

☐ **Provide technical direction, leadership, and training of an engineering staff of** _____ [#] **in the areas of** _____, _____, **and** _____ [which areas?].

ACHIEVEMENT SAMPLES: *See Achievements under "Staff Management & Supervision – General."*

Staff Management & Supervision – Office Support Staff

See also "Staff Management & Supervision – General."

☐ **Manage and oversee the daily activities of an office support staff of** _____ [#] **including** _____, _____, **and** _____ [job titles] **in the areas of** [☐ work scheduling | ☐ assignment delegating | ☐ administrative support | ☐ report generation | ☐ payroll processing | ☐ report generation | ☐ purchasing | ☐ contract administration | ☐ other: _____] **ensuring quality performance in all areas.**

☐ **Lead a team of** _____ [#] _____ [titles] **in the** [☐ development | ☐ implementation | ☐ sale | ☐ performance | ☐ other: _____] **of** [☐ high quality | ☐ cost-effective | ☐ other: _____] [☐ products | ☐ services | ☐ business solutions | ☐ other: _____] **that successfully ensure** [☐ quality standards are adhered to | ☐ compliance with all company guidelines | ☐ other: _____].

☐ **Prioritize work assignments and project tasks by** [☐ determining deadlines | ☐ analyzing scope and importance of work | ☐ strategizing best approach to meet commitments | ☐ other: _____].

☐ **Supervise a staff of** _____ [#] _____ [what titles?] **including accountability for their** [☐ customer service | ☐ client relations | ☐ sales support | ☐ other: _____], **ensuring prompt** [☐ sales | ☐ deliveries | ☐ order fulfillment | ☐ other: _____].

☐ **Supervise diversified office activities, including** [☐ correspondence | ☐ bookkeeping | ☐ billing | ☐ travel arrangements | ☐ insurance | ☐ dispatch | ☐ timekeeping | ☐ job inquiries | ☐ payroll reports | ☐ other: _____].

☐ **Manage an office-support staff of** _____ [#] _____ [position titles] **in the functions of** [☐ accounting | ☐ billing | ☐ filing | ☐ emailing | ☐ word processing | ☐ faxing | ☐ other: _____].

☐ **Oversee** _____ [#] **first-line supervisors from** _____ [which?] **departments, including the** [☐ administrative | ☐ secretarial | ☐ clerical | ☐ other: _____] **staff(s) that involves hiring and dismissing employees.**

ACHIEVEMENT SAMPLES: *See Achievements under "Staff Management & Supervision – General."*

Staff Management & Supervision – Project Management Team

See also "Staff Management & Supervision – General."

☐ **Guide a** _____ [job title] **team of** _____ [#] **to effectively** [☐ analyze project needs | ☐ establish strategy | ☐ determine project logistics | ☐ provide management consulting support | ☐ identify and mitigate risks | ☐ handle issue escalation and resolution | ☐ ensure quality deliverables | ☐ other: _____] **to meet client needs**.

☐ **Plan and coordinate all activities of** [☐ small- | ☐ medium- | ☐ large-] **scale** _____ [type of] **projects for this** _____ [type of] **firm with** _____ [#] [☐ locations | ☐ employees | ☐ partners | ☐ other: _____] **that generates fiscal-year revenues of $**_____ [amount].

☐ **Provide leadership, vision, and direction to a project management team of** _____ [#] **to initiate, plan, and implement** _____ [type of] **projects ranging from $**_____ **to $**_____ **and resulting in** [☐ delivering bottom-line business value | ☐ business transformation | ☐ new product offerings | ☐ the translation of enterprise strategies into projects | ☐ increased productivity | ☐ other benefits: _____].

☐ **Lead the project team of** _____ [#] **that defines, plans, and implements new** _____ [type of] **projects; and oversee the development, execution, tracking, and reporting of those projects in support of the firm's business vision and objectives.**

☐ **Plan, schedule, and coordinate all** _____ *[type of?]* [☐ projects | ☐ functions | ☐ activities | ☐ work] **by effectively prioritizing and delegating assignments and ensuring sufficient project manning to** [☐ meet client needs | ☐ perform required functions | ☐ facilitate job specifications | ☐ other: _____].

☐ **Lead the project team of** _____ *[#]* **that defines, plans, and implements new** _____ *[type of]* **projects; and oversee the development, execution, tracking, and reporting of those projects to support the business vision and objectives of the firm.**

☐ **Manage a(n)** _____ *[which?]* **project team ensuring** [☐ the highest quality creative work | ☐ all projects stay on schedule and within budget | ☐ timely development and completion of all projects | ☐ quality standards | ☐ adherence to all objectives | ☐ other: _____].

☐ **Lead and direct a** _____ *[type of]* **project implementation team of** _____ *[#]* **in the development and execution of effective** [☐ marketing campaigns | ☐ Internet marketing programs | ☐ leads generation | ☐ market segmentation | ☐ website trafficking | ☐ data tracking methods | ☐ other: _____].

☐ **Instilled** _____ *[what?]* **in a project team of** _____ *[#]* **that resulted in attaining** [☐ the highest quality work | ☐ fulfillment of all expected deliverables regardless of obstacles | ☐ all projects staying on schedule and within budget | ☐ timely development and completion of all projects | ☐ meeting project success criteria | ☐ adherence to quality standards | ☐ lower turnover | ☐ compliance with all company guidelines and ordinances | ☐ other: _____].

☐ **Provide strategic, comprehensive leadership to a** _____ *[which?]* **team of** _____ *[#]* **to initiate, and design complex** _____ *[type of]* **projects ranging from $**_____ **to $**_____ *[amounts]* **and resulting in resulting in** [☐ new product offerings | ☐ the translation of enterprise strategies into projects | ☐ delivering bottom-line business value | ☐ other benefits: _____].

☐ **Direct and oversee a project management of** _____ *[#]*—**from design and coordination to implementation and delivery**—[☐ using standardized project management methodology | ☐ for multiple implementation projects | ☐ for projects that vary in scope and size | ☐ in support of firm's strategic visions | ☐ to support client objectives | ☐ in accordance with all project timelines and budget].

ACHIEVEMENT SAMPLES: *See Achievements under **"Staff Management & Supervision – General."***

Team Leadership & Direction – Construction Management Team

*See also **"Team Leadership & Direction – Project Management Team."***

☐ **Lead and direct the construction management staff of** _____ *[#]* **in the** [☐ design and] **construction of** [☐ buildings | ☐ structures | ☐ highways | ☐ transportation systems | ☐ public utilities | ☐ transit systems | ☐ water quality systems | ☐ water resource management systems | ☐ agricultural systems | ☐ environmentally-friendly systems | ☐ other: _____] **by providing** [☐ strategic vision and planning | ☐ innovative research | ☐ effective communication | ☐ other: _____] **in the** [☐ concept | ☐ schematic design | ☐ site planning | ☐ construction | ☐ production | ☐ cost management | ☐ quantity control | ☐ other: _____] **of** _____ *[type of]* **projects.**

☐ **Provide executive leadership and direction to the** [☐ construction project | ☐ project delivery | ☐ field supervision | ☐ other: _____] **management team(s) in** [☐ strategy execution | ☐ financial management | ☐ procurement | ☐ resource acquisition | ☐ approval management | ☐ municipal permit attainment | ☐ quality assurance | ☐ safety | ☐ estimating | ☐ subcontracting | ☐ other: _____] **activities to develop, coordinate, and administer the design and construction of new and refurbished** _____ *[type of]* [☐ buildings | ☐ facilities | ☐ properties | ☐ other: _____].

☐ **Oversee Construction Project Managers in their daily functions including** [☐ job estimates and proposals | ☐ contract negotiations | ☐ trades hiring and scheduling | ☐ permit obtainment | ☐ materials purchasing | ☐ expense monitoring and approval | ☐ other: _____] **ensuring the completion of all projects on time, within budget, and at the clients' satisfaction.**

☐ **Lead, direct, and monitor the** [☐ construction | ☐ project management | ☐ contract management | ☐ estimating | ☐ other: _____] [☐ management | ☐ consulting | ☐ contracting | ☐ other: _____] **team(s) in support of** [☐ major | ☐ complex | ☐ high-dollar | ☐ other: _____] _____ *[type of]* [☐ demolition | ☐ construction | ☐ alteration | ☐ remodel | ☐ other: _____] **projects.**

☐ **Manage and oversee the construction management staff in support of** [☐ major | ☐ complex | ☐ high-dollar | ☐ other: _____] _____ *[type of]* **projects and sound architectural standards for this** _____ *[type of]* **firm.**

☐ **Direct, control, and supervise the Construction** [☐ Division | ☐ Department] **and activities of** _____ *[#]* _____ *[title]* Construction Managers **including formulating** [☐ plans | ☐ specifications | ☐ designs | ☐ cost estimates | ☐ other: _____] **for** _____ *[type of]* **projects.**

☐ **Coordinate and oversee construction management team activities at a strategic level**—**from** [☐ procurement | ☐ demolition | ☐ construction | ☐ other: _____] **through to completion.**

☐ **Lead and direct** _____ *[whom?]* **by providing via** [☐ strategic vision and planning | ☐ innovative research | ☐ engineering | ☐ effective communication | ☐ other: _____] **in the** [☐ site planning | ☐ construction | ☐ cost management | ☐ quantity control | ☐ other: _____] **of** [☐ interior spaces | ☐ exterior spaces | ☐ physical environments] **of** _____ *[type of]* **projects**.

☐ **Supervise a construction management staff of** _____ *[#]* **in the preparation of** [☐ master plans | ☐ cost estimates | ☐ specifications | ☐ construction drawings | ☐ other: _____] **and all related aspects of engineering applications for the construction of** _____ *[what?]*.

☐ **Supervise and mentor an engineering staff of** _____ *[#]* **who** [☐ calculates operating budgets | ☐ generates _____ *(type of)* reports | ☐ performs _____ *(type of)* investigations | ☐ other: _____] **to evaluate the efficiency of** _____ *[type of]* **engineering** [☐ programs | ☐ operations | ☐ processes | ☐ projects | ☐ other: _____].

☐ **Assess the knowledge, skills, and abilities of the construction management staff, and address their training needs in the areas of** _____ *[which areas?]* **to ensure quality accomplishment of goals and professional development.**

☐ **Provide strategic, comprehensive** [☐ leadership | ☐ direction | ☐ guidance | ☐ consultation | ☐ assistance | ☐ support] **to construction management staff in all areas of** _____ *[what?]*.

Team Leadership & Direction – Project Management Team

See also "Team Leadership & Direction – Construction Management Team."

☐ **Oversee** _____ *[#]* **Construction Project Managers in their daily functions Including** [☐ review and/or modification of construction drawings | ☐ job estimates and proposals | ☐ securing competitive bids | ☐ contract negotiations | ☐ trades hiring, coordinating, and scheduling | ☐ permit obtainment | ☐ on-site supervision | ☐ maintaining direct client relationships | ☐ materials purchasing | ☐ expense monitoring and approval | ☐ change orders negotiations and processing | ☐ other: _____] **ensuring the completion of all projects on time, within budget, and at the clients' satisfaction.**

☐ **Provide proactive leadership, vision, and direction to a project management team of** _____ *[#]* _____ *[titles]* **in the initiation, planning, design, and construction of** _____ *[type of]* **projects ranging from $**_____ **to $**_____ *[amounts]* **and resulting in** [☐ delivering bottom-line business value | ☐ business transformation | ☐ new product offerings | ☐ the translation of enterprise strategies into projects | ☐ increased productivity | ☐ other benefits: _____].

☐ **Direct and lead** _____ *[#]* **Construction Project Managers in all project management phases—from concept development through the operational evaluation phases of** _____ *[what?]* **considering** [☐ costs | ☐ resource requirements | ☐ scheduling | ☐ technical requirements | ☐ other: _____].

☐ **Lead a project team of** _____ *[#]* **in the construction of high quality, cost-effective** _____ *[type of]* **solutions that successfully address** [☐ the firm's | ☐ clients'] **requirements by** [☐ establishing clear guidelines | ☐ offering feedback on completed projects | ☐ providing methods to increase productivity | ☐ other: _____].

☐ **Provide leadership and direction to project staff in** [☐ project planning and coordination | ☐ determining costs | ☐ performing feasibility studies and estimates | ☐ developing specifications | ☐ preparing bills of materials | ☐ negotiating contracts | ☐ identifying resources | ☐ identifying materials | ☐ recordkeeping | ☐ other: _____] **to ensure timely and efficient completion of** _____ *[type of]* [☐ construction | ☐ renovation | ☐ remodel | ☐ extensions | ☐ ground improvement | ☐ other: _____] **projects.**

☐ **Supervise and support the work of** _____ *[#]* **Construction Project Managers in the management of** _____ *[type of]* **projects and the preparation of** [☐ master plans | ☐ architectural renderings | ☐ cost estimates | ☐ specifications | ☐ construction drawings | ☐ other: _____].

☐ **Lead by example a project management staff of** _____ *[#]* **in the** [☐ delegation of assignments | ☐ monitoring of work performance | ☐ development of performance evaluations | ☐ performance improvement coaching | ☐ other methods: _____].

☐ **Oversee and direct the daily activities of the project team** [☐ and contract staff] **including** [☐ assignment delegating | ☐ purchasing | ☐ payroll processing | ☐ administrative support | ☐ report generation | ☐ contract administration | ☐ other: _____] **ensuring quality performance in the successful completion of all projects.**

☐ **Provide construction project team leadership and support in the development and coordination of major and minor projects in the areas of** _____ , _____ , **and** _____ *[which areas?]*.

ACHIEVEMENT SAMPLES: *See "Staff Management & Supervision Achievement Samples."*

Testing & Inspections – Trades

See "Inspections & Compliance" and "Equipment, Tools & Testing Devices."

Tools & Testing Devices

See *"Equipment, Tools & Testing Devices"* (various categories).

Trades Coordination & Oversight – General

See also *"Trades/Crew Supervision – All Trades,"* *"Work Collaboration,"* *"Contractor/Subcontractor Influence & Collaboration,"* *"Inspections & Compliance – Trades,"* and *"Job Preparation,"* as applicable.

☐ **Provide decisive leadership and clear direction in all phases of** [☐ large-scale | ☐ complex] _____ *[type of]* **projects for** [☐ commercial | ☐ residential | ☐ industrial | ☐ other: _____] **clients overseeing a top-performing team of** _____ *[#]* _____ *[title(s)]*.

☐ **Coordinate and oversee trades including** [☐ demolition | ☐ framing | ☐ carpentry | ☐ electrical | ☐ plumbing | ☐ HVAC | ☐ roofing | ☐ insulation | ☐ sheetrock | ☐ tape and spackle | ☐ painting | ☐ tiling | ☐ flooring | ☐ ceilings | ☐ interior design | ☐ landscaping | ☐ masonry | ☐ other: _____] **in the** [☐ design and] **construction of** _____ *[what?]*.

☐ **Provide a full array of** [☐ plumbing | ☐ HVAC | ☐ refrigeration | ☐ steamfitting | ☐ welding | ☐ carpentry | ☐ other: _____] **installation, maintenance, and repair services including** [(☐ plumbing / ☐ electrical / ☐ general contracting) work | (☐ bathroom / ☐ kitchen / ☐ tile) installations | ☐ other: _____] **for this** [☐ local] [☐ plumbing | ☐ general contracting | ☐ construction | ☐ other: _____] **firm.**

☐ **Exercise supervision over all trades including** [☐ Carpenters | ☐ Framers | ☐ Insulation Workers | ☐ Sheetrock Installers | ☐ Painters | ☐ Roofers | ☐ Electricians | ☐ Plumbers | ☐ HVAC Specialists | ☐ Carpet and Floor Installers | ☐ Tile Installers | ☐ Ceiling Installers | ☐ Space Planners | ☐ Interior Designers | ☐ Interior Decorators | ☐ Cabinet Makers | ☐ Landscape Technicians | ☐ Masons | ☐ Glaziers | ☐ other: _____].

☐ **Oversee** [☐ apprentice- | ☐ journeyman-] **level** _____ *[type of]* **work related to the installation and/or repair of** [☐ air conditioning systems | ☐ boilers | ☐ refrigeration | ☐ hot and cold air ducts | ☐ heat exchangers | ☐ other: _____] **ensuring compliance with all codes.**

☐ **Coordinate, schedule, and supervise all trades including** [☐ demolition | ☐ concrete | ☐ welding | ☐ masonry | ☐ other: _____] **on** _____ *[type of]* **projects.**

☐ **Supervise and inspect work performed by technicians and** [☐ contractors | ☐ subcontractors | ☐ contract service providers] **ensuring** [☐ safe working conditions | ☐ high quality | ☐ work completed properly and timely | ☐ compliance with all codes, OSHA, EPA, ADA, and MSDS | ☐ other: _____].

☐ **Obtain permits, estimate jobs, and hire and schedule trades acting as liaison with** [☐ building managers | ☐ client reps | ☐ inspectors | ☐ union delegates | ☐ architects | ☐ engineers | ☐ contractors | ☐ others: _____].

☐ **Coordinate, schedule, and supervise** _____ *[type of]* **projects including** [☐ building construction | ☐ asbestos abatement | ☐ roofing repairs | ☐ other: _____] **with sensitivity to client deadlines and project requirements, assigning projects based on staff's unique skills.**

☐ **Ensure all jobs are completed in compliance with building codes, zoning laws, fire regulations, and ordinances by** [☐ proactively monitoring work performance | ☐ ensuring effective quality control | ☐ other methods: _____].

☐ **Manage and oversee the work of** [☐ technical | ☐ construction | ☐ other: _____] [☐ contractors | ☐ subcontractors | ☐ staff] **involved in project activities including** _____, _____, **and** _____ *[which functions?]*.

☐ **Work with** _____ *[which?]* **trades to coordinate the** [☐ design | ☐ construction | ☐ installation | ☐ repair | ☐ other: _____] **of** _____ *[what projects?]* **for** _____ *[whom or what?]*.

☐ [☐ Oversee | ☐ Assist] [☐ HVAC | ☐ plumbing | ☐ electrical | ☐ maintenance | ☐ carpentry | ☐ crafts | ☐ other: _____] **staff(s) in performing the** [☐ construction | ☐ assembly | ☐ installation | ☐ repair | ☐ maintenance | ☐ monitoring | ☐ testing | ☐ upkeep | ☐ other: _____] **of** _____ *[what?]*.

☐ **Coordinate various aspects of projects with** [☐ subcontractors | ☐ general contractors | ☐ architects | ☐ municipal officials | ☐ code officials | ☐ others: _____] **in the** _____ *[what phases of construction?]*.

☐ **Oversee all** [☐ plumbing | ☐ HVAC | ☐ refrigeration | ☐ steamfitting | ☐ welding | ☐ carpentry | ☐ landscaping | ☐ masonry | ☐ painting | ☐ other: _____] **functions for this** [☐ general contracting | ☐ construction | ☐ other: _____] **firm.**

☐ **Supervise all** _____ *[type of]* **trade activities required in the installation, maintenance, and/or repair of** _____ *[what?]* **including** _____, _____, **and** _____ *[which functions?]*.

☐ **Manage and oversee the building of** _____ *[type of]* **structures with precision and uniformity by** _____ *[doing what?]* **depending on job complexity and blueprint specifications.**

☐ **Working closely with related trades to create** _____ *[type of]* **structures to ensure** _____ *[what?]*.

☐ **Oversee the planning, design, and [**☐ construction | ☐ installation | ☐ repair | ☐ other: _____**] of** _____ *[what?]* **including** _____**,** _____**, and** _____ *[which functions?]* **taking into account** _____ *[which]* **conditions**.

☐ **Direct and oversee the completion of** _____ *[type of]* **services for [**☐ residential | ☐ commercial | ☐ industrial | ☐ other: _____**] clients for** _____ *[type of]* **projects**.

☐ **Review client contracts to determine required** _____ *[type of]* **services, equipment, methods, materials, and labor and make project determinations based on** _____ *[what?]*.

ACHIEVEMENT SAMPLES:

☐ **Built a strong, supportive contractor / subcontractor team environment by exhibiting and modeling leadership skills in** [☐ communication | ☐ negotiation | ☐ problem-solving | ☐ obstacle tackling | ☐ other: _____].

☐ **Serving on a team of** _____ *[#]* **laborers, performed all** _____ *[type of]* **project [**☐ construction | ☐ remodels | ☐ repairs | ☐ other: _____**] to a successful completion in support of the [**☐ firm's | ☐ clients' | ☐ firm and clients'**] objectives and requirements**.

☐ **Influenced [**☐ contractors | ☐ subcontractors | ☐ vendors | ☐ others: _____**] to develop and maintain positive working relationships with all levels of [**☐ internal | ☐ external**] management by** _____ *[doing what well?]*.

Trades Coordination & Oversight – Ceiling, Lathing, Insulation & Drywall

See also "Trades Coordination & Oversight – General" and other "Trades Coordination & Oversight" categories.

☐ **Oversee drywall mounting and spackling as well as [**☐ acoustical tiles | ☐ shock-absorbing materials | ☐ other: _____**] to reduce / reflect sound to ceilings and walls for** _____**,** _____**, and** _____ *[type of projects or companies]*.

☐ **Supervise the preparation of ceiling and drywall installation jobs by first inspecting [**☐ electrical wire | ☐ ductwork | ☐ piping | ☐ other: _____**] to ensure correct [**☐ removal of existing plaster, drywall, or paneling | ☐ surface measurement | ☐ materials and installation methods | ☐ dry lines hanging | ☐ furring strips installation | ☐ wall studs, light fixtures, and electrical boxes marking | ☐ use of T-braces for leverage and support | ☐ hanging and affixing of drywall sheets | ☐ taping and spackling | ☐ other: _____].

☐ **Ensure all [**☐ metal | ☐ rockboard | ☐ wood | ☐ other: _____**] laths are correctly fastened to inside framing of [**☐ walls | ☐ ceilings | ☐ partitions | ☐ other: _____**] for** _____ *[type of]* **[**☐ commercial | ☐ residential | ☐ other: _____**] buildings**.

☐ **Coordinating work with drywall finishers and insulation installers, project manage all [**☐ ceiling | ☐ lathing | ☐ drywall**] installation functions including [**☐ lath cutting, bending, and fastening | ☐ metal frame supports welding | ☐ wallboards fitting and fastening | ☐ outlet, plumbing, vent, and window openings | (☐ furrings / ☐ masonry) surface inspecting | ☐ tile installation | ☐ joints sealing | ☐ insulation | ☐ metal casings | ☐ decorative trim | ☐ other: _____].

☐ **Ensure [**☐ buildings | ☐ attics | ☐ exterior walls | ☐ ceilings | ☐ boilers | ☐ steam and hot water pipes | ☐ other: _____**] are properly insulated with [**☐ fiberglass | ☐ foam | ☐ cellulose | ☐ rock wool batt | ☐ other: _____**] insulation [**☐ using wire meshes to spray foam insulation | ☐ wrapping it with (☐ aluminum / ☐ plastic / ☐ canvas / ☐ other: _____) | ☐ screwing sheet metal around insulated pipes | ☐ applying drywall and plaster | ☐ other: _____].

☐ **Supervise drywall panel fastening to framework of** _____ *[type of]* **buildings and preparation of panels including filling, taping, troweling, and joint finishing**.

☐ **Oversee the insulation of** _____ *[type of]* **projects ensuring safe and correct use of [**☐ stapling guns | ☐ power saws | ☐ compressors | ☐ welding machines | ☐ trowels | ☐ brushes | ☐ knives | ☐ saws | ☐ pliers | ☐ stapling guns | ☐ tape | ☐ other: _____**], following all safety guidelines**.

ACHIEVEMENT SAMPLES: *See also "Construction Projects."*

☐ **Increased productivity** _____**%** *[percentage]*, **slashed** _____ *[type of]* **project times, and decreased man hours from** _____ *[#]* **[**☐ hours | ☐ days**] to** _____ **[**☐ hours | ☐ days**] by using [**☐ ratcheting cargo jacks and telescopic paint roller handles to attach to beams and ladder treads to support sheetrock | ☐ other methods: _____**] allowing for one-person drywall ceiling installations**.

☐ **Reduced energy consumption** _____**%** *[percentage]* **on** _____ *[type of]* **project by properly insulating [**☐ buildings | ☐ attics | ☐ exterior walls | ☐ ceilings | ☐ plaster walls | ☐ paneling | ☐ boilers | ☐ steam and hot water pipes | ☐ storage rooms | ☐ vats | ☐ tanks | ☐ other: _____**] with [**☐ fiberglass | ☐ foam | ☐ cellulose | ☐ rock wool | ☐ other: _____**] insulation protecting from weather conditions and damage**.

Trades Coordination & Oversight – Concrete Pouring, Setting & Finishing Projects

See also "Trades Coordination & Oversight – General" and other "Trades Coordination & Oversight" categories.

☐ **Oversee trades in the concrete and steel reinforcement of** [☐ residential | ☐ commercial | ☐ highway | ☐ other: _____] **construction projects and the finishing of** _____ *[type of]* **walls with** [☐ wood | ☐ structural metal | ☐ lath | ☐ plaster | ☐ other: _____] **materials meeting all project budgets and deadlines on or ahead of schedule.**

☐ **Manage and oversee project team crew activities in the areas of** [☐ scheduling | ☐ concrete preparation and pouring | ☐ building to specifications | ☐ concrete measurements | ☐ formwork | ☐ mixing | ☐ installation | ☐ application of chemical additives | ☐ surface finishing | ☐ problem troubleshooting | ☐ other: _____] **ensuring accurate measurements, quality of finished concrete projects, and compliance with all safety policies, practices, and procedures.**

☐ **Supervise and direct** _____ *[#]* **Concrete** [☐ Masons | ☐ Installers | ☐ Form Setters | ☐ Layers | ☐ Finishers | ☐ Smoothers | ☐ Laborers | ☐ Carpenters | ☐ Patchers | ☐ Grinder Operators | ☐ Curb Builders | ☐ Joint Setters | ☐ Joint Finishers | ☐ Stone Finishers | ☐ Material Testers | ☐ Floaters | ☐ Terrazzo Finishers | ☐ other: _____] [☐ as well as field supervisors and other contractors] **to ensure** [☐ efficient use of equipment and materials | ☐ correct elevation | ☐ all project objectives are met with quality | ☐ project is constructed in accordance with design, budget, and schedule | ☐ contractual performance of projects are met | ☐ other: _____].

☐ **Provide project management oversight in concrete operations including** [☐ quality control | ☐ monitoring labor budget | ☐ interpreting plans and specifications | ☐ ordering and maintaining sufficient supplies | ☐ inventory management and control | ☐ interviewing, hiring, and training (☐ employees / ☐ laborers) | ☐ equipment scheduling | ☐ identifying potential design or construction problems | ☐ clarifying discrepancies | ☐ administering Safety Program | ☐ scheduling equipment | ☐ monitoring how the weather affects the curing process | ☐ completing _____ *(type of)* paperwork | ☐ other: _____].

☐ **Collaborate with other on-site labor teams including** _____ *[which?]* [☐ contractors | ☐ subcontractors | ☐ others: _____], **to resolve problems and ensure quality, safety, and support of** _____ *[type of]* **project objectives.**

Trades Coordination & Oversight – Glazier Projects

See also "Trades Coordination & Oversight – General" and other "Trades Coordination & Oversight" categories.

☐ **Oversee** [☐ small to large | ☐ multiple | ☐ complex | ☐ other: _____] _____ *[type of]* [☐ residential | ☐ commercial | ☐ other: _____] **glazing projects, handling the full project scope—from contract award through closeout for this** [☐ commercial glazing company | ☐ contractor | ☐ other: _____] **including** _____ *[type of]* [☐ windows | ☐ glass doors | ☐ tempered glass | ☐ glass panels | ☐ blast resistant windows | ☐ skylights | ☐ doors | ☐ entrance enclosures | ☐ sun rooms | ☐ storefronts | ☐ shower enclosures | ☐ aluminum curtain walls | ☐ backsplashes | ☐ display cases | ☐ table tops | ☐ decorative room dividers | ☐ security windows | ☐ metal framework extrusions | ☐ windshields | ☐ aluminum storefronts | ☐ glass railing systems | ☐ mirrors | ☐ other: _____] **using** [☐ glass cutters | ☐ glazing knives | ☐ power saws | ☐ suction cups | ☐ drills | ☐ grinders | ☐ other: _____] **for various** _____ *[type of]* **projects ranging $**_____ **to $**_____ *[amounts].*

☐ **Supervise and oversee the work of** _____ *[#]* **commercial glaziers upholding a high quality of work standards and ensuring the completion of successful projects on time and within budget.**

☐ **Coordinate and collaborate with** _____ *[which?]* **trades in the installation of** _____ *[type of]* **glass projects for** [☐ commercial | ☐ residential | ☐ automotive | ☐ other: _____] **clients** [☐ using precision-cutting methods | ☐ cutting glass panes manually | ☐ spreading glazing compound around molding edges | ☐ trimming excess material | ☐ other: _____] **for a perfect fit and polished, professional look.**

☐ **Work closely with** [☐ plastics | ☐ granite | ☐ marble | ☐ steel | ☐ aluminum | ☐ other: _____] **laborers to** [☐ install | ☐ replace] **glass and** [☐ mount sashes | ☐ install frames | ☐ attach locks, hinges, rubber gaskets, and moldings | ☐ other: _____] **resulting in a** [☐ professional look | ☐ unique design | ☐ decorative finish | ☐ other: _____].

☐ **Communicate with** [☐ customers | ☐ Project Manager | ☐ Superintendent | ☐ Shop Foreman | ☐ Estimator | ☐ Glaziers | ☐ draftsmen | ☐ vendors | ☐ Architects | ☐ General Contractor | ☐ co-workers | ☐ others: _____] **regarding** [☐ project scope and requirements | ☐ setting and managing expectations | ☐ project specifications | ☐ project scheduling | ☐ daily work schedules | ☐ materials lead time | ☐ equipment requirements | ☐ material deliveries | ☐ project progress | ☐ labor coordination with other contractors | ☐ scope changes | ☐ risks and liabilities | ☐ quality | ☐ production | ☐ other: _____] **throughout project stages—taking project from inception through completion.**

☐ **Inspect and monitor work to ensure quality installation, compliance, and customer satisfaction according to** [☐ contractual obligations | ☐ manufacturer's installation instructions | ☐ industry standards | ☐ estimated manhours and benchmarks | ☐ safety program | ☐ other: _____].

☐ **Handle various project-related administrative functions including** [☐ reviewing and verifying project drawings | ☐ interpreting specifications | ☐ securing material quotes | ☐ negotiating vendor pricing | ☐ estimating project costs | ☐ preparing bid proposals | ☐ issuing purchase orders | ☐ determining equipment costs | ☐ reviewing and approving project contracts | ☐ ordering and scheduling materials | ☐ documenting project progress and conditions | ☐ maintaining accurate progress records | ☐ photographing progress and results | ☐ approving invoices for payment | ☐ managing shop drawing process | ☐ closeout processing | ☐ processing change orders | ☐ closeout processing | ☐ records management | ☐ other: _____].

☐ **Apply** [☐ working | ☐ proficient] **knowledge and experience in** [☐ the glass industry | ☐ reading and interpreting blueprints and instructions | ☐ calculating figures including area, circumference, and volume | ☐ measuring and cutting glass to size or pattern | ☐ installing frames | ☐ insulating glass | ☐ using (☐ sanding / ☐ beveling / ☐ polishing) machines | ☐ other: _____].

Trades Coordination & Oversight – Highway & Bridge Maintenance Projects

See also "Trades Coordination & Oversight – General" and other "Trades Coordination & Oversight" categories.

☐ [☐ Manage and oversee | ☐ Perform] **various highway maintenance activities including** [☐ traffic control | ☐ highway inspection and repair | ☐ preventative maintenance | ☐ herbicide and pesticide application | ☐ roadway right of way maintenance during emergencies | ☐ excessive foliage removal in right-of-way areas | ☐ following up on road complaints | ☐ other: _____] **for the** _____ *[state]* **Department of Transportation (DOT).**

☐ [☐ Perform | ☐ Supervise] **maintenance crew work including** [☐ flagging motorists | ☐ diverting traffic around work areas | ☐ removing debris and litter from roadways | ☐ controlling snow and ice | ☐ spreading (☐ sand / ☐ salt / ☐ gravel) | ☐ erecting guardrails | ☐ installing sign and warning signals | repairing highway lighting | ☐ mowing grass | ☐ operating heavy machinery | ☐ driving trucks to transport crews and equipment to work sites | ☐ preventive maintenance of heavy equipment | ☐ other: _____] **and other physical maintenance work.**

☐ [☐ Perform | ☐ Supervise a crew of _____ (#) in] **bridge maintenance work including the** [☐ repair | ☐ construction] **of** _____ *[type of]* **bridge-building structures and** [☐ bridge opening machinery | ☐ engine generator sets | ☐ routine maintenance | ☐ other: _____] **to ensure efficient and dependable bridge operations including all electrical and mechanical systems.**

☐ **Work on a wide range of highway projects including** [☐ picking up roadside litter | ☐ repairing ditches and other drainage structures | ☐ repairing highway signs | ☐ cleaning roadway signs and markers | ☐ acting as flag person | ☐ closing lanes | ☐ sealing road patches and cracks | ☐ removing undergrowth from highway rights of ways | ☐ working on traffic control using traffic cones and flares | ☐ sweeping, shoveling, and raking asphalt | ☐ plowing snow | ☐ hauling garbage | ☐ other: _____].

☐ [☐ Oversee | ☐ Perform] [☐ bridge and work zone inspections | ☐ repair functions | ☐ bridge cleaning | ☐ traffic control functions | ☐ preventive maintenance and repairs | ☐ concrete repairs | ☐ vegetative activities | ☐ debris cleaning around structures | ☐ snow removal | ☐ other: _____] **to ensure bridge safety, proper traffic control, and compliance with all safety and environmental regulations as well as** [☐ proper methods | ☐ quality control | ☐ timely project completion | ☐ other: _____].

☐ [☐ Perform | ☐ Supervise] **Inspections and repairs on damaged bridge** [☐ components | ☐ guardrails | ☐ pavement | ☐ barrier walls | ☐ overpass structures | ☐ drainage structures | ☐ signs | ☐ delineators | ☐ lighting | ☐ fencing | ☐ other: _____].

☐ **Plan, direct, and supervise** [☐ a crew of _____ (#) | ☐ multiple crews] **engaged in** [☐ new | ☐ reconstruction] **highway work including** [☐ clearing | ☐ filling | ☐ grading | ☐ laying | ☐ other: _____] **of new surfaces.**

☐ **Supervise a** [☐ district-wide | ☐ maintenance patrol | ☐ other: _____] [☐ highway | ☐ bridge | ☐ other: _____] **maintenance crew of** _____ *[#]* **in their performance of** _____, _____, **and** _____ *[what functions?].*

☐ **Supervise and oversee** [☐ pavement care | ☐ roadside shoulder restoration and repairs | ☐ equipment deliveries | ☐ snow removal operations | ☐ other: _____] **ensuring environmental compliance in all areas.**

☐ **Maintain** [☐ local | ☐ interstate | ☐ country | ☐ township] **highways and adjacent right-of-way properties including** [☐ roadways | ☐ municipal roads | ☐ rural roads | ☐ airport runways | ☐ other: _____] **through** [☐ road repair | ☐ brush removal | ☐ tree trimming and pruning | ☐ litter removal | ☐ snow and ice containment | ☐ fence and guard rail repair | ☐ other: _____].

☐ **Ensure all incident responses to highway emergencies are handled timely and professionally.**

☐ **Work closely with the** [☐ Department of Transportation (DOT) | ☐ State Police | ☐ Traffic Management Center | ☐ government officials | ☐ private entities | ☐ the public | ☐ others: _____] **in the areas of** _____, _____, **and** _____ *[which areas?]* **to minimize traffic flow interruptions and ensure public safety is maintained.**

☐ **Oversee the** _____ *[which?]* **maintenance section to provide for safe driving thoroughfare within** _____ *[what?]* **area(s) covering** _____ *[#]* **miles of highways and roadways by ensuring the maintenance of all roads, structures, and rights-of-way.**

☐ **Supervise and coordinate maintenance crew activities in the installation and repair of** [☐ traffic signals | ☐ signs | ☐ traffic islands | ☐ barriers | ☐ other: _____].

☐ **Inspect** [☐ construction | ☐ maintenance | ☐ repair] **of** _____ *[type of]* [☐ highway | ☐ bridge | ☐ other: _____] **projects to determine and order the materials and equipment needed for** _____ *[what?]* **in order to maximize production and ensure highest standards of performance.**

ACHIEVEMENT SAMPLES: *See also "Construction Projects."*

☐ **Facilitated restoration and repair of** _____ *[which?]* **roadway surfaces which helped maintain the integrity of state** [☐ highways | ☐ bridges | ☐ other: _____]. **Performed roadway, roadside, and structural maintenance activities keeping** [☐ pavement surfaces | ☐ shoulders | ☐ clear zones | ☐ roadways | ☐ other: _____] **in good repair.**

☐ **By promoting and practicing a culture of safety,** [(☐ reduced / ☐ eliminated) accidents and injuries | ☐ other achievements: _____].

☐ **As part of the** _____ *[which?]* **Committee, evaluated the** *Safety and Accident Prevention Program* **and recommended** _____ *[what?]*, **which helped improve the state's DOTs safety rating from** _____ *[previous rating]* **to** _____ *[current rating]* **by** _____ *[doing what?]* **and reduced risk in the area(s) of** _____ *[which area(s)?]*.

☐ **Recipient of** [☐ "Highway Safety" | ☐ "Snow Fighter" | ☐ other: "_____"] **Award** _____ *[#]* **consecutive years for** [☐ having no accidents | ☐ reducing company liability | ☐ work at Ground Zero | ☐ other: _____].

☐ **Often requested by** _____ *[whom?]* **to** _____ *[perform what?]* **due to** [☐ my safety precautions | ☐ diligent highway work oversight | ☐ other: _____].

☐ **Received** [☐ excellent | ☐ above average] **performance evaluations for** [☐ safety measures | ☐ damage control methods | ☐ machinery knowledge | ☐ diligence in completing _____ *(what?)* | ☐ other achievements: _____].

Trades Coordination & Oversight – HVAC / HVAC-R Projects

See also "Trades/Crew Supervision," "Inspections & Compliance," and "Contractor / Subcontractor Influence & Collaboration."

☐ **Manage and lead the installation and servicing of** [☐ heating and air conditioning systems | ☐ refrigeration systems | ☐ industrial and commercial refrigerant systems | ☐ fuel supply lines | ☐ water supply and drain lines | ☐ steam lines | ☐ water heaters | (☐ gas / ☐ electric / ☐ open flame) boilers | ☐ pipes, faucets, and valves | ☐ specialty items | ☐ other: _____] **and test units to ensure proper control of temperature, humidity, and air quality in** [☐ residential | ☐ commercial | ☐ industrial | ☐ other: _____] **buildings**.

☐ **Provide a full array of** [☐ plumbing | ☐ HVAC | ☐ refrigeration | ☐ steamfitting | ☐ welding | ☐ carpentry | ☐ other: _____] **services including** [(☐ plumbing / ☐ electrical / ☐ general contracting) work | (☐ bathroom / ☐ kitchen / ☐ tile) installations | ☐ other: _____] **for this** [☐ HVAC | ☐ general contracting | ☐ construction | ☐ other: _____] **firm**.

☐ **Oversee and supervise air conditioning installations and repair for** [☐ commercial | ☐ industrial | ☐ residential] **customers including** _____ *[what functions?]* **for this $**_____ *[revenues]* _____ *[type of]* **firm.**

☐ **Direct day-to-day operations of this** [☐ HVAC | ☐ plumbing | ☐ general contracting | ☐ construction | ☐ other: _____] **firm providing a full array of** [☐ HVAC | ☐ plumbing | ☐ steamfitting | ☐ carpentry | ☐ other: _____] **services including** [☐ bathroom and kitchen installation | ☐ plumbing, electrical, and general contracting work | ☐ other: _____].

☐ **Supervise and perform the installation, maintenance, repair, and/or replacement of all required HVAC** [☐ equipment | ☐ systems | ☐ pipes | ☐ fixtures | ☐ valves | ☐ pumps | ☐ other: _____] **to** [☐ set up | ☐ operate | ☐ maintain] **the** [☐ water distribution | ☐ heating and cooling | ☐ other: _____] **system(s) and related equipment of** _____ *[what?]*.

☐ **Lead and direct approximately** _____ *[#]* **HVAC jobs** [☐ weekly | ☐ monthly | ☐ annually] [☐ averaging $_____ to $_____ *(amounts)* | ☐ totaling $_____ *(amount)*] **including** [☐ estimating job times and costs | ☐ selecting materials | ☐ preparing materials estimates | ☐ reviewing bids | ☐ ordering required job-related materials | ☐ scheduling jobs | ☐ performing HVAC functions | ☐ inspecting completed jobs | ☐ other: _____].

☐ **Supervise** [☐ journey- | ☐ apprentice- | ☐ masters-] **level** [☐ installation | ☐ maintenance | ☐ servicing | ☐ repair] **of HVAC systems for this $**_____ *[revenues]* _____ *[type of]* **firm that services** _____ *[type of]* **clientele.**

☐ **Supervise all** [☐ HVAC | ☐ HVAC-R | ☐ mechanical systems | ☐ other: _____] **related activities including** [☐ preventive maintenance | ☐ heating and cooling equipment inspections | ☐ duct airflow readings | ☐ HVAC systems balancing | ☐ fuel system components maintenance | ☐ building and automation systems monitoring | ☐ production and injection systems repair | ☐ water treatment tests | ☐ firing and fuel ratio controls upkeep | ☐ other: _____].

☐ **Provide leadership and direction to** _____ *[#]* **HVAC Technicians in the installation and maintenance of** [☐ central air conditioning systems | ☐ fuel and water supply lines | ☐ gas | ☐ oil | ☐ electric | (☐ solid-fuel / ☐ multiple-fuel) heating | ☐ other: _____]; **and test units for proper installation and operation ensuring compliance with** [☐ blueprints | ☐ specifications].

☐ **Supervise and oversee** _____ *[#]* **HVAC Technicians in the service and repair of climate-control equipment in** [☐ residential homes | ☐ office buildings | ☐ stores | ☐ schools | ☐ hospitals | ☐ restaurants | ☐ factories | ☐ hotels ☐ other: _____].

☐ **Direct the HVAC** [☐ installation | ☐ replacement | ☐ maintenance | ☐ repair | ☐ administrative | ☐ other: _____] **operations including all aspects of plumbing required in** [☐ new construction | ☐ remodel | ☐ maintenance | ☐ repair | ☐ other: _____] **jobs for this $**_____ *[revenues]* _____ *[type of]* **firm.**

☐ [☐ Lead and direct] [☐ Supervise and perform] **the installation, maintenance, repair, and/or replacement of all required HVAC** [☐ equipment | ☐ systems | ☐ pipes | ☐ fixtures | ☐ valves | ☐ pumps | ☐ other: _____] **to** [☐ set up | ☐ operate | ☐ maintain] **the** [☐ water distribution | ☐ heating and cooling | ☐ other: _____] **system(s) and related equipment of** _____ *[what?].*

☐ **Supervise HVAC** [☐ installation | ☐ replacement | ☐ repair | ☐ other: _____] **functions including all aspects of plumbing required in** [☐ new construction | ☐ remodel | ☐ maintenance | ☐ other: _____] **jobs on** _____ *[type of]* **projects.**

☐ **Oversee the installation, maintenance, and servicing of** [☐ heating and air conditioning systems | ☐ industrial and commercial refrigerant systems | ☐ other: _____] **to ensure control of temperature, humidity, and air quality in** [☐ residential | ☐ commercial | ☐ industrial | ☐ manufacturing | ☐ other: _____] **buildings for this** _____ *[type of]* **firm.**

☐ **Review and evaluate HVAC** [☐ plans | ☐ specifications | ☐ drawings] **and other** [☐ blueprints | ☐ diagrams | ☐ schematics | ☐ specifications] **to** [☐ determine compatibility and adaptability with existing systems | ☐ ensure compliance with all codes | ☐ advise (☐ Project Engineer / ☐ HVAC Foreman / ☐ Lead Plumber / ☐ other: _____) on code requirements | ☐ other: _____]; **and modify blueprints to meet as-built specifications and dimensions.**

☐ **Managed the upgrade of plant-wide** [☐ heating systems | ☐ cooling systems | ☐ computer rooms | ☐ other: _____] **that involved** _____ *[what?]* **resulting in** _____ *[what benefits?].*

Trades Coordination & Oversight – Landscape Projects

See also "Trades Coordination & Oversight – General" and other "Trades Coordination & Oversight" categories as well as "Landscape Design," and "Trades Coordination & Oversight – Masonry Projects," as applicable.

☐ **Oversee landscaping and masonry trades in their landscape work for** [☐ commercial | ☐ residential | ☐ public] _____ *[type of]* **properties including** [☐ condominiums | ☐ apartment complexes | ☐ residential properties | ☐ commercial grounds | ☐ public facilities | ☐ parks | ☐ shopping centers | ☐ golf courses | ☐ botanical gardens | ☐ nurseries | ☐ garden centers | ☐ banks | ☐ factories | ☐ school grounds | ☐ parking lots | ☐ train stations | ☐ club houses | ☐ hotels | ☐ athletic fields | ☐ cemeteries | ☐ college campuses | ☐ large estates | ☐ highways and roadways | ☐ communities | ☐ other: _____].

☐ **Manage and oversee all aspects of this** _____ *[type of]* **landscaping business including** [☐ sales | ☐ customer service | ☐ installations | ☐ maintenance | ☐ account servicing | ☐ administration | ☐ cash management | ☐ client and financial database | ☐ hiring, training, and scheduling employees | ☐ equipment maintenance | ☐ budgeting | ☐ other: _____].

☐ **Schedule and supervise the daily operations and landscaping activities of a crew of** _____ *[#]*; **and oversee the complete upkeep of the** _____ *[which?]* **grounds for this** _____ *[type of]* [☐ landscaping | ☐ groundskeeping | ☐ lawn maintenance | ☐ general contracting | ☐ public services | ☐ other: _____] **company.**

☐ **Supervise all** [☐ landscaping | ☐ grounds maintenance | ☐ other: _____] **activities including the installation of** [☐ structural wall panels | ☐ retainer walls | ☐ pathways | ☐ patios | ☐ decks | ☐ firebrick linings | ☐ refractory tile | ☐ soaking pits | ☐ other: _____] **and the application of** [☐ marble | ☐ granite | ☐ limestone | ☐ concrete block | ☐ marble chips | ☐ brick veneer | ☐ tile | ☐ other: _____] **and other masonry projects.**

☐ **Manage and oversee all aspects of grounds maintenance services including** [☐ lawn mowing | ☐ leaf removal | ☐ tree trimming | ☐ weed control | ☐ fertilizing | ☐ insect control | ☐ pest elimination | ☐ flower gardening | ☐ shrub pruning | ☐ horticulture | ☐ grading | ☐ seeding | ☐ detaching | ☐ aerating | ☐ planting | ☐ plant damage care | ☐ snow removal | ☐ other: _____].

☐ **Direct the installation of** _____ *[#]* **acres of** _____ *[type of]* **landscapes for** _____ *[whom or what?]* **covering all aspects of** _____ *[what?]* **including** [☐ installing landscaped areas | ☐ building walkways, terraces, patios, decks | ☐ grading property | ☐ installing lighting | ☐ planting new gardens | ☐ maintaining swimming pools | ☐ controlling weeds, disease, and insect infestation | ☐ other: _____].

☐ **Coordinate and oversee all aspects of landscaping** [☐ design | ☐ installations | ☐ activities] **with other trades including the installation of** [☐ retainer walls | ☐ pathways | ☐ patios | ☐ sidewalks | ☐ walkways | ☐ retainer walls | ☐ decks | ☐ porches | ☐ patios | ☐ terraces | ☐ arbors | ☐ gazebos | ☐ pools | ☐ cabanas | ☐ fountains | ☐ fences | ☐ planters | ☐ parking lots | ☐ sprinkler systems | ☐ lighting | ☐ flower beds | ☐ borders | ☐ other: _____].

☐ **Supervise the installation of** [☐ retainer walls | ☐ flower beds | ☐ landscape borders | ☐ walkways | ☐ sprinkler systems | ☐ concrete masonry wall units | ☐ other: _____] **including** [☐ grading | ☐ planting | ☐ sod laying | ☐ transplanting | ☐ trimming | ☐ masonry | ☐ other: _____] **of** [☐ lawns | ☐ flowers | ☐ plants | ☐ shrubbery | ☐ shade and ornamental trees | ☐ annuals

| □ perennials | □ other: _____] **taking into account** [□ sun exposure | □ shading | □ existing soil | □ other: _____] **conditions.**

☐ **Oversee a landscaping team of** _____ *[#]* **including hiring, training, scheduling, and evaluating crew; and supervise and coordinate daily crew operations for this** _____ *[type of]* **firm.**

☐ **Plan, organize, coordinate, and direct** [□ landscaping | □ groundskeeping | □ lawn service] **activities including** □ planting trees, shrubs, flowers | □ maintaining lawns | □ applying fertilizers and pesticides | □ other: _____] **to meet contract specifications.**

☐ **Manage and oversee all** [□ landscaping | □ landscaping installations | □ grounds maintenance] including [□ lawn | □ shrub | □ flower] acreage care for _____ *[what?]* **including** [□ building retainer walls | □ constructing pathways | □ installing patios | □ other: _____].

☐ **Provide decisive leadership and clear direction in all phases of** [□ large-scale | □ complex] _____ *[type of]* **projects for** [□ residential | □ commercial | □ industrial | □ other: _____] **clients overseeing a top-performing team of** _____ *[#]* **landscapers.**

☐ **Direct and schedule landscape crew's functions and oversee the complete upkeep of the** _____ *[which?]* **grounds for this** _____ *[type of]* **firm with** _____ *[#]* **clients to maximize property potential and aesthetics.**

☐ **Supervise and coordinate the activities of a crew of** _____ *[#]* [□ skilled | □ semi-skilled | □ unskilled] [□ Landscape Laborers | □ Greenhouse Workers | □ Park Caretakers | □ Nursery Workers | □ other: _____] **in the grounds upkeep of** _____ *[what?].*

☐ **Oversee and supervise the** _____ *[type of]* **activities of a team of** _____ *[#]* **skilled** [□ Landscape Architects | □ Ornamental Horticulturists | □ Park Naturalists | □ other: _____] **in the design and installation of** _____ *[what?].*

☐ **Manage daily activities of a landscaping team of** _____ *[#]* **coordinating all** [□ landscaping | □ grounds maintenance | □ horticulture | □ other: _____] **work functions for** _____ *[#]* [□ commercial | □ residential | □ public] **accounts including** _____ *[type of accounts]* **ensuring all work is completed according to landscaping plans and schedules.**

☐ **Coordinate landscaping and masonry functions with other trades in the design and installation of** _____ *[what?].*

☐ **Direct concrete casting and supervise** _____ *[#]* **laborers who spread, level, float, and smooth concrete, create joints, and trowel surfaces to ensure wedges, plumblines, levels, and brackets create a precision fit and attractive finish.**

☐ **Oversee the performance of various landscaping functions including installing** [□ landscaped areas | □ sod | □ retainer walls | □ terraces | □ patios | □ decks and porches | □ flower beds | □ botanical crops | □ landscape borders | □ walkways | □ sprinkler systems | □ concrete masonry wall units | □ lighting | □ irrigation systems | □ shade and ornamental trees | □ annuals | □ perennials | □ other: _____] **and** [□ grading | □ planting | □ transplanting | □ trimming | □ thatching | □ seeding | □ raking | □ masonry | □ other: _____] **lawns.**

☐ **Review client contracts to determine required services, equipment, methods, materials, and labor and make project determinations based on** _____ *[what?].*

☐ **Plan, organize, and coordinate landscaping and masonry activities including** [□ planting trees, shrubs, and flowers | □ installing lawns | □ applying fertilizers and pesticides | □ other: _____] **to meet** [□ client needs | □ contract specifications].

☐ **Schedule and supervise the daily operations and all landscaping activities of a crew of** _____ *[#];* **and oversee the complete upkeep of the** _____ *[which?]* **grounds.**

☐ **Inspect** [□ lawns | □ trees | □ shrubs | □ plants | □ crops | □ other: _____] **for** [□ disease | □ insect | □ pest | □ other: _____] **problems and apply** [□ fertilizers | □ insecticides | □ pesticides | □ herbicides | □ fungicides | □ _____ *(type of)* chemicals] **to** [□ eradicate weeds | □ stimulate growth | □ eliminate insect infestation | □ rid of pests | □ other: _____] **resulting in** _____ *[what outcome?].*

Trades Coordination & Oversight – Masonry Projects

See also **"Trades Coordination & Oversight – General"** *and other* **"Trades Coordination & Oversight"** *categories.*

☐ **Project manage the design and build of attractive landscape designs including** [□ walkways | □ sidewalks | □ patios | □ roadways | □ flooring | □ concrete surfaces | □ exposed aggregate walls | □ concrete beams | □ columns | □ panels | □ other: _____] **for this** [□ masonry | □ landscaping | □ general contracting | □ other: _____] **firm that services** [□ residential | □ commercial | □ other: _____] **clients.**

☐ **Oversee the use of a variety of masonry techniques to build creative and functional projects, such as** [□ colorizing concrete for a decorative finish | □ polishing and sealing masonry surfaces to prevent breakage, separation, and chipping | □ installing decorative interlocking pavers and edging materials | □ staggering blocks to create unique designs | □ creating ornate stone walls |

☐ designing and installing decorative patios and steps | ☐ embedding gravel chips for a pebble finish | ☐ brushing surfaces for a coarse, nonskid finish | ☐ creating unique finishes by applying _____ *(what?)* | ☐ using various masonry materials that create contrast and visual interest | ☐ other: _____].

☐ **Supervise the installation of** [☐ structural wall panels | ☐ firebrick linings in industrial furnaces | ☐ refractory tile in boilers and furnaces | ☐ soaking pits in industrial establishments | ☐ other: _____ **] applying the use of** [☐ marble | ☐ granite | ☐ limestone | ☐ concrete block | ☐ marble chips | ☐ brick veneer | ☐ tile | ☐ glass | ☐ other: _____ **] and other masonry materials.**

☐ **Oversee the installation of a variety of interlocking pavers and edging materials for decorative** [☐ landscape designs | ☐ walkways | ☐ paths | ☐ driveways | ☐ patios | ☐ panels | ☐ playgrounds | ☐ steps | ☐ other: _____].

☐ **Ensure** _____ *[type of]* **structures are built with precision and uniformity and** [☐masonry materials are aligned with wedges, plumb lines, levels, and brackets for a precision fit | ☐ corner lead and corner pole methods are used correctly | ☐ other technique: _____ **] depending on job complexity and blueprint specifications.**

☐ **Oversee the installation of** _____ *[type of]* [(☐ structural / ☐ insulated / ☐ other: _____) wall panels | ☐ exposed aggregate and retainer walls | ☐ roadways | ☐ driveways | ☐ walkways | ☐ paths | ☐ playgrounds | ☐ stone walls | ☐ ornate exteriors | ☐ concrete beams and columns | ☐ other: _____].

☐ **Design and install decorative, durable** _____ *[type of]* **masonry** [☐ surfaces | ☐ structures | ☐ other: _____ **] with varying complexity for** _____ *[type of]* **clients including** [☐ stone walls | ☐ masonry walkways | ☐ structural wall panels | ☐ concrete foundations | ☐ ornate exteriors | ☐ roadways | ☐ driveways | ☐ other: _____ **] on** [☐ high-rise buildings | ☐ office buildings | ☐ residential homes | ☐ lobbies | ☐ other: _____ **] by** _____ *[doing what?].*

☐ **Manage and oversee the concrete demolition, installation, and/or repair functions including** [☐ removing existing pavement | ☐ grading soil | ☐ installing and compacting base material | ☐ accurately setting and aligning concrete forms | ☐ casting concrete | ☐ spreading, leveling, floating, and smoothing concrete | ☐ building solid, level concrete foundations | ☐ using corner lead and corner pole methods | ☐ troweling surface and creating joints | ☐ monitoring how the wind, heat, and cold affect concrete curing to prevent defects | ☐ laying pavers | ☐ grinding terrazzo | ☐ filling spaces with sand | ☐ installing edging materials | ☐ cleaning, polishing, and sealing surfaces | ☐ repairing cracks | ☐ other: _____ **] on** _____ *[type of]* **projects.**

☐ **Working closely with related trades to create** _____ *[type of]* **structures, ensure the precise alignment of all** [☐ stones | ☐ bricks | ☐ pavers | ☐ edgers | ☐ other: _____ **] with wedges, plumblines, levels, and brackets for a precision fit and attractive finish.**

☐ **Ensure that all concrete** [☐ foundations | ☐ panels | ☐ forms | ☐ other: _____ **] are accurately set and aligned, joints are created properly, and all necessary preventive measures are taken to prevent defects from occurring.**

☐ **Supervise** _____ *[#]* **laborers who spread, level, float, and smooth concrete, create joints, and trowel surfaces.**

Trades Coordination & Oversight – Painting Projects

See also "Trades Coordination & Oversight – General" and other "Trades Coordination & Oversight" categories.

☐ **Oversee the planning, organization, and supervision of surface preparation and application of** [☐ paint | ☐ stain | ☐ varnish | ☐ other: _____ **] products on** [☐ interiors | ☐ exteriors] **of** [☐ residential homes | ☐ commercial buildings | ☐ other: _____ **] on** _____ *[type of]* **projects.**

☐ **Project manage and oversee approximately** _____ *[#]* **painting jobs per** [☐ week | ☐ month] **ranging from $_____ to $_____** *[amounts]* **for** _____ *[type of]* **clients.**

☐ **Provide decisive leadership and clear project management direction in all phases of** [☐ large-scale | ☐ complex] _____ *[type of]* **painting and staining projects for** [☐ residential | ☐ commercial | ☐ industrial | ☐ other: _____ **] clients.**

☐ **Ensure all surfaces of** _____ *[type of]* **painting jobs are cleared of dirt, mold, and peeling paint; that cracks and holes are patched; and areas protected to prevent damage to location and ensure a professional outcome.**

☐ **Ensure paints and stains are mixed, matched, and color-coordinated through the use of correct** [☐ tinting bases | ☐ liquid colors | ☐ primers | ☐ other: _____ **] for application on** _____ *[type of]* **projects.**

☐ **Oversee painters and monitor painting projects to ensure effective and productive work, troubleshooting and resolving any project or customer concerns by** [☐ listening carefully to their needs | ☐ immediately rectifying problems | ☐ offering alternative solutions | ☐ other methods: _____].

☐ **Supervise a variety of painting and other projects including** [☐ hanging wallpaper | ☐ staining furniture | ☐ painting stripes in _____ *(which?)* (☐ parking lots / ☐ football fields / ☐ gym floors / ☐ other: _____) | ☐ other: _____ **] ensuring all projects are completed on time.**

☐ **Coordinate painting work with** _____ *[which?]* **contractors to ensure it is completed according to agreement and complies with standards.**

Trades Coordination & Oversight – Plumbing Projects

See also **"Trades Coordination & Oversight – General"** *and other* **"Trades Coordination & Oversight"** *categories.*

☐ **Oversee the installation of all required plumbing** [☐ equipment | ☐ systems | ☐ pipes | ☐ fixtures | ☐ valves | ☐ pumps | ☐ other: _____] **to** [☐ set up | ☐ operate | ☐ maintain] **the** [☐ water distribution | ☐ drainage | ☐ heating and cooling | ☐ sewage collection | ☐ sprinkler | ☐ other: _____] **system(s) and related equipment of** _____ *[what?].*

☐ **Project manage and oversee the installation of** [☐ plumbing | ☐ heating | ☐ cooling | ☐ ventilating | ☐ refrigeration | ☐ water supply | ☐ sewer | ☐ fire | ☐ sprinkler | ☐ steamfitting | ☐ other: _____] **systems including** [☐ drain lines | ☐ steam lines | ☐ roof drains | ☐ water heaters | (☐ gas / ☐ electric / ☐ open flame) ☐ boilers | ☐ storm drains | ☐ cesspools | ☐ septic tanks | ☐ pipes, faucets, valves, fixtures, and fittings | ☐ specialty plumbing items | ☐ other: _____].

☐ **Direct and oversee the plumbing** [☐ installation | ☐ replacement | ☐ maintenance | ☐ repair] **work required in** [☐ new construction | ☐ remodel | ☐ other: _____] **jobs for this** [☐ plumbing | ☐ general contracting | ☐ construction management | ☐ other: _____] **firm.**

☐ **Manage and oversee plumbing jobs ranging from $**_____ **to $**_____ *[average job amount]* **and handle** [☐ estimating of job times, materials, and costs | ☐ reviewing materials bids | ☐ ordering materials and hardware | ☐ scheduling jobs | ☐ performing plumbing functions | ☐ inspecting completed jobs for code compliance | ☐ other: _____].

☐ **Oversee the installation of all** [☐ heating | ☐ ventilating | ☐ cooling | ☐ systems] of _____ *[what?]* by [☐ monitoring equipment | ☐ inspecting energy management systems | ☐ using _____ *(type of)* control software | ☐ making frequent on-site visits to check computer programming | ☐ verifying temperature controls | ☐ adjusting temperatures | ☐ maximizing the efficiency of control systems | ☐ adjusting (☐ mixed / ☐ return / ☐ discharge) air | ☐ performing combustion analyses | ☐ other methods: _____].

☐ **Supervise all plumbing activities required in the installation, maintenance, and/or repair of** _____ *[what?]* **including** _____, _____, **and** _____ *[which functions?].*

☐ **Lead and direct a variety of plumbing activities including** [☐ cutting and threading _____ *(type of)* pipes | ☐ winterizing piping (☐ and sprinkler) systems | ☐ soldering copper | ☐ installing PVC piping | ☐ installing (☐ waste / ☐ gas) pipes and pipe fittings | ☐ repairing drain systems | ☐ dismantling and repairing plumbing devices | ☐ plumbing kitchen facilities | ☐ inspecting piping systems | ☐ responding to client emergency situations | ☐ other: _____] **for** _____ *[what or whom?].*

☐ **Facilitate plumbing management functions including** [☐ reviewing and evaluating plumbing specifications | ☐ coordinating bid selections | ☐ estimating project time, materials, and costs | ☐ preparing estimates | ☐ negotiating contracts | ☐ writing purchase requests | ☐ evaluating subcontractor bids | ☐ prioritizing work assignments | ☐ scheduling jobs | ☐ supervising various trades | ☐ setting up projects with materials | ☐ determining safety requirements | ☐ coordinating materials shipping | ☐ purchasing or leasing equipment | ☐ preparing cost estimates | ☐ ensuring plumbing safety practices | ☐ maintaining plumbing tools and equipment | ☐ ordering and maintaining plumbing parts | ☐ obtaining required permits | ☐ making on-site visits | ☐ inspecting work for compliance with codes | ☐ maintaining plumbing tools and equipment | ☐ training staff in plumbing techniques | ☐ handling inventory management and control | ☐ coordinating projects with (☐ engineers / ☐ architects) | ☐ monitoring equipment | ☐ other: _____].

☐ **Oversee the repair and maintenance of all** [☐ plumbing | ☐ electrical | ☐ HVAC | ☐ motors | ☐ appliances | ☐ fixtures | ☐ lights | ☐ ballasts | ☐ receptacles | ☐ switches | ☐ other: _____] **to** [☐ help improve the work environment | ☐ maintain proper operation of all equipment | ☐ maintain compliance with all OSHA and environmental regulations | ☐ other: _____].

☐ **Lead and direct the installation, maintenance, repair, and/or replacement of all required plumbing** [☐ equipment | ☐ systems | ☐ pipes | ☐ fixtures | ☐ valves | ☐ pumps | ☐ other: _____] **to** [☐ set up | ☐ operate | ☐ maintain] **the** [☐ water distribution | ☐ drainage | ☐ heating and cooling | ☐ sewage collection | ☐ sprinkler | ☐ other: _____] **system(s) and related equipment.**

☐ **Coordinate with other trades and oversee plumbing installations in** [☐ new construction | ☐ remodel | ☐ restoration | ☐ other: _____] **of** _____ *[type of]* **projects.**

☐ **Coordinate and oversee the installation of** [☐ plumbing | ☐ heating | ☐ cooling | ☐ ventilating | ☐ refrigeration | ☐ water supply | ☐ sewer | ☐ fire | ☐ sprinkler | ☐ other: _____] **systems including** [☐ drain lines | ☐ steam lines | ☐ roof drains | ☐ water heaters | (☐ gas / ☐ electric / ☐ open flame) boilers | ☐ storm drains | ☐ cesspools | ☐ septic tanks | ☐ pipes, faucets, valves, fixtures, and fittings | ☐ specialty plumbing items | ☐ other: _____].

☐ **Perform** [☐ machining | ☐ rigging | ☐ industrial pipefitting | ☐ other: _____] **for** _____ *[what?].*

☐ **Handle approximately** _____ *[#]* **plumbing jobs** [☐ daily | ☐ weekly | ☐ monthly | ☐ annually] [☐ averaging $_____ to $_____ *(amounts)* | ☐ totaling $_____] **including** [☐ estimating job times, materials, and costs | ☐ selecting materials and hardware | ☐ preparing materials estimates | ☐ reviewing materials bids | ☐ ordering required job-related materials | ☐ scheduling jobs | ☐ performing plumbing functions | ☐ inspecting completed plumbing jobs for code compliance | ☐ other: _____].

Trades Coordination & Oversight – Roofing Projects

See also "Trades Coordination & Oversight – General" and other "Trades Coordination & Oversight" categories.

☐ [☐ Manage | ☐ Perform] _____ *[type of]* **roofing construction projects for** [☐ general commercial construction | ☐ residential homes | ☐ decks and porches | ☐ sunrooms | ☐ cabanas | ☐ other: _____] **according to company's established policies, procedures, and guidelines and in compliance with all codes.**

☐ **Plan and direct roofing surveys of** _____ *[what?]* **to determine** _____ *[type of]* **maintenance and new roof requirements.**

☐ **Apply** [☐ proficiency in | ☐ considerable knowledge of | ☐ other: _____] **various** [☐ commercial | ☐ residential | ☐ other: _____] **roofing systems, materials, and installation methods;** [☐ state and local building codes | ☐ Uniform Building Code | ☐ electrical codes | ☐ plumbing codes | ☐ other: _____]; **and** [☐ construction site development | ☐ commercial construction | ☐ demolition | ☐ other: _____] **procedures in the installation of** _____ *[type of]* **roofs.**

☐ [☐ Direct | ☐ Facilitate] [☐ large-scale | ☐ mid-size | ☐ other: _____] _____ *[type of]* **commercial roofing projects ensuring all quality standards are followed and all work is completed in accordance with standards, industry guidelines, and contracts.**

☐ **Prepare for roofing projects by** [☐ performing on-site reviews | ☐ reviewing surveys | ☐ taking dimensions | ☐ developing drawings | ☐ interpreting roofing plans, specifications, and standards | ☐ conducting roofing tests to provide architect with necessary information for contract completion | ☐ identifying and resolving project deficiencies | ☐ estimating materials, hours, and (replacement) costs | ☐ ordering required roofing materials | ☐ other: _____].

Trades Coordination & Oversight – Welding / Steamfitting Projects

See also "Trades Coordination & Oversight – General," "Trades / Crew Supervision – All Trades,"
"Inspections & Compliance – Welding / Steamfitting," and "Contractor / Subcontractor Influence & Collaboration."

☐ **Coordinate and oversee steamfitting trade functions for** [☐ large office buildings | ☐ industrial (☐ welding / ☐ pipefitting / ☐ plumbing) | ☐ domestic water systems | ☐ sprinkler systems | ☐ HVAC piping | ☐ compressed air systems | ☐ fire sprinklers | ☐ other: _____] **on** _____ *[type of]* **projects to ensure quality control, regulation compliance, and machinery and equipment safety.**

☐ **Provide decisive leadership and clear direction in all phases of** [☐ large-scale | ☐ complex] _____ *[type of]* **projects for** [☐ commercial | ☐ residential | ☐ industrial | ☐ other: _____] **clients overseeing a team of** _____ *[#]* [☐ welders | ☐ steamfitters | ☐ other: _____].

☐ **Oversee various types of** [☐ welding | ☐ joint welding | ☐ steamfitting | ☐ soldering | ☐ arc welding | ☐ torch cutting | ☐ other: _____] **projects for this** _____ *[type of]* **firm including** [☐ industrial |☐ welding | ☐ pipefitting | ☐ plumbing] **and** [☐ domestic water systems | ☐ sprinkler systems | ☐ HVAC piping | ☐ compressed air systems | ☐ fire sprinklers | ☐ other: _____].

☐ **Manage and oversee welding jobs averaging $**_____ **to $**_____ *[amounts]* **including** [☐ estimating job times, materials, and costs | ☐ selecting materials and hardware | ☐ preparing materials estimates | ☐ reviewing bids | ☐ ordering required job-related materials | scheduling jobs | ☐ inspecting completed jobs for quality and code compliance | ☐ other: _____].

☐ **Supervise the installation, servicing, and maintenance of new and existing domestic** [☐ water systems | ☐ sanitary piping | ☐ HVAC piping and equipment | ☐ other: _____].

☐ **Oversee** [☐ welding | ☐ arc welding | ☐ joint welding | ☐ soldering | ☐ steamfitting | ☐ torch cutting | ☐ industrial welding | ☐ other: _____] **trades in their installation of new and repair of existing domestic** [☐ water | ☐ steam | ☐ sanitary | ☐ HVAC | ☐ electrical | ☐ hydraulic | ☐ gas | ☐ vacuum | ☐ sprinkler | ☐ other: _____] **systems.**

☐ **Supervise the installation and repair of** _____ *[type of]* [(☐ electrical / ☐ hydraulic) systems | (☐ low / ☐ high) pressure steam piping | ☐ gas piping | ☐ air compressor piping | ☐ HVAC piping and equipment | (☐ gas / ☐ vacuum) piping | ☐ low- and high-pressure steam piping and equipment | ☐ truck beds | ☐ other: _____] **for** _____ *[what?]*.

☐ **Oversee all types of welding projects including** [☐ connecting water, steam, gas, oxygen, and air lines | ☐ performing fabrication of metals and alloys | ☐ heating, tempering, straightening, and shaping metals | ☐ working with (☐ water / ☐ steam / ☐ gas / ☐ oxygen / ☐ argon / ☐ helium / ☐ acetylene) | ☐ constructing specialized devices and structures | ☐ performing (☐ machining / ☐ rigging) | ☐ repairing (☐ electrical / ☐ hydraulic) systems | ☐ performing industrial pipefitting | ☐ welding exotic metals | ☐ installing (☐ low- and high-pressure steam / ☐ HVAC / ☐ gas / ☐ vacuum / ☐ air compressor) piping | ☐ maintaining and servicing steam boilers | ☐ constructing specialized devices and structures | ☐ designing, laying out, and cutting special parts | ☐ developing items from (☐ ferrous / ☐ nonferrous) metals | ☐ repairing (☐ electrical / ☐ hydraulic) systems | ☐ other: _____].

☐ **Ensure the safety in use of all gases including** [☐ argon | ☐ helium | ☐ oxygen | ☐ acetylene | ☐ other: _____].

☐ **Manage and oversee various** _____ *[type of]* **welding projects including** [☐ connecting and working with (☐ water / ☐ steam / ☐ gas / ☐ oxygen / ☐ air lines / ☐ argon / ☐ helium / ☐ acetylene / ☐ other: _____) | ☐ fabrication of metals and alloys | ☐ heating, tempering, straightening, and shaping metals | ☐ constructing specialized devices and structures | ☐ conducting (☐ machining / ☐ rigging) | ☐ repairing (☐ electrical / ☐ hydraulic) systems | ☐ performing industrial pipefitting | ☐ welding exotic metals | ☐ installing (☐ low and high pressure steam / ☐ air compressor / ☐ HVAC / ☐ gas / ☐ vacuum / ☐ other: _____) piping | ☐ maintaining and servicing steam boilers | ☐ constructing specialized devices and structures | ☐ designing, laying out, and cutting special parts | ☐ repairing (☐ electrical / ☐ hydraulic) systems | ☐ other: _____].

☐ **Oversee** [☐ welding | ☐ arc welding | ☐ joint welding | ☐ torch cutting | ☐ soldering | ☐ steamfitting | ☐ other: _____] **of** _____ *[what?]* **including** [☐ reading and interpreting blueprints | ☐ preparing job sites | ☐ using precision-measuring instruments | ☐ ensuring safety in use of all gases | ☐ modifying, repairing, and servicing existing systems | ☐ ensuring structural support | ☐ determining best welding methods and techniques for the job at hand | ☐ maintaining supplies and inventory | ☐ designing, laying out and cutting special parts | ☐ fabricating and fitting equipment and parts | ☐ determining dimensions and tolerances | ☐ training staff on welding and machining equipment | ☐ determining project time and costs | ☐ cleaning, lubricating, and maintaining shop equipment | ☐ operating metal forming equipment | ☐ repairing heavy equipment | ☐ operating (☐ drill presses / ☐ milling / ☐ gear-cutting / ☐ CNC / ☐ Atlas / ☐ metal-removing machines / ☐ other: _____) | ☐ operating centrifugal chiller and steam absorption machines | ☐ other: _____].

☐ **Oversee the construction of** _____ *[type of]* [☐ specialized devices and structures | ☐ items from (☐ ferrous / ☐ nonferrous) metals | ☐ other: _____] **through the** [☐ heating, tempering, straightening, and shaping metals | ☐ designing, laying out, and cutting special parts | ☐ other: _____] **and** _____ *[doing what?]* **for** _____ *[purpose]*.

ACHIEVEMENT SAMPLES: *See also "Construction Projects."*

☐ **Managed and oversaw the installation of low- and high-pressure steam piping, including** [☐ heating | ☐ ventilating | ☐ air condition | ☐ sterilization equipment | ☐ other: _____] **for a** _____ *[#]*-**floor,** _____ *[#]*-**room** [☐ plant | ☐ commercial building | ☐ facility | ☐ other: _____].

☐ **Oversaw the construction of** _____ *[type of]* **specialized** [☐ structures | ☐ devices | ☐ programs | ☐ other: _____] **that** _____ *[did what?]* **while benefiting the** [☐ client | ☐ firm | ☐ other: _____] **by** _____ *[what means?]*.

☐ **Managed** [☐ welding | ☐ steamfitting | ☐ other: _____] **projects for** [☐ large office buildings | ☐ truck bed body work | ☐ industrial welding | ☐ industrial pipefitting | ☐ industrial plumbing | ☐ domestic water systems | ☐ sprinkler systems | ☐ HVAC piping | ☐ compressed air systems | ☐ other: _____] **for** _____ *[type of clients]*.

☐ **Supervised medical gas piping, including** [☐ oxygen | ☐ nitrogen | ☐ medical air | ☐ vacuum | ☐ other: _____] **piping which required tying into existing systems while** [☐ clients | ☐ patrons | ☐ patients | ☐ other: _____] **were living off systems, ensuring proper safety and precautions at all times.**

☐ **Oversaw on-site** [☐ welding | ☐ steamfitting | ☐ other: _____] **while** [☐ company remained open for business | ☐ homeowners remained on premises | ☐ other: _____] **by** _____ *[doing what?]*, **which minimized the work impact so** [☐ business | ☐ home] **operations remained functional.**

Trades / Crew Supervision – All Trades

See also "Inspections & Compliance – Trades Work" "Contractor / Subcontractor Influence & Collaboration," "Staff Management & Supervision," "Team Leadership & Direction," "Trades Coordination & Oversight," and "Work Collaboration," as applicable.

☐ **Supervise the day-to-day activities of** _____ *[#]* **laborers on** _____ *[type of]* **jobs ensuring quality control in all activities and that all work is performed according to job specs and code.**

☐ **Oversee an average of** _____ *[#]* **laborers on** _____ *[type of]* **jobs to ensure all work is performed according to job specs and code, on time and within budgets.**

☐ **Lead and oversee a team of** _____ *[#]* **laborers in the** [☐ installation | ☐ construction | ☐ maintenance | ☐ other: _____] **of** _____ *[what?]* **projects ranging from $** _____ **to $** _____ *[amounts]* **and resulting in** _____ *[what outcome?]*.

☐ **Coordinate, lead, and train** _____ *[type of]* **crew(s) to complete** _____ *[type of]* [☐ commercial | ☐ industrial | ☐ residential | ☐ other: _____] **projects within established guidelines, timeframes, and budget with an emphasis on** [☐ quality | ☐ safety | ☐ attention to detail | ☐ regulatory compliance | ☐ other: _____].

☐ **Supervise and coordinate the activities of a crew of** _____ *[#]* **skilled** [☐ Plumbers | ☐ Electricians | ☐ HVAC Technicians | ☐ Carpenters | ☐ others: _____] [☐ in the design and installation of _____ *(what?)* | ☐ and oversee the complete upkeep of _____ *(what?)*] **for this** _____ *[type of]* **firm with** _____ *[#]* **clients** [☐ to maximize property potential].

☐ **Lead and direct a crew of** _____ *[#]* _____ *[titles]* **involved in all aspects of** _____ *[which trade?]* **including** [☐ reviewing project plans | ☐ reading and interpreting blueprints | ☐ estimating time | ☐ developing work schedules | ☐ assigning crews | ☐ delegating jobs | ☐ preparing work orders | ☐ ordering and setting up equipment | ☐ purchasing supplies | ☐ preparing job sites | ☐ inspecting work area | ☐ other: _____] **ensuring all jobs are completed in compliance with specifications and codes.**

☐ **Provide decisive leadership and clear direction in all phases of** [☐ large-scale | ☐ complex] _____ *[type of]* **projects for** [☐ commercial | ☐ residential | ☐ industrial | ☐ other: _____] **clients overseeing a top-performing team of** _____ *[#]* _____ *[titles].*

☐ **Manage the daily activities of a team of** _____ *[#]* _____ *[titles]* **coordinating all job functions for** [☐ commercial | ☐ residential | ☐ public | ☐ other: _____] **accounts including** _____ *[type of projects]* **ensuring all work is completed according to plans, specifications, and schedules.**

☐ **Schedule, coordinate, and supervise the daily operations and all** _____ *[which trade?]* **activities of a crew of** _____ *[#]* **including** _____, _____, **and** _____ *[what functions?]* **to ensure quality workmanship and compliance with all codes.**

☐ **Successfully lead a** _____ *[which?]* [☐ crew | ☐ project team] **of** _____ *[#]* **in the completion of** _____ *[type of]* **projects enforcing compliance with all safety, fire, and other regulations and ensuring** [☐ the highest quality work | ☐ fulfillment of all expected deliverables | ☐ timely completion of all work | ☐ quality standards are adhered to | ☐ measurable member participation and progress | ☐ all jobs are performed to code | ☐ other: _____].

☐ **Manage and oversee the day-to-day activities of a team of** _____ *[#]* **skilled** _____ *[titles]* **in the design and installation of** _____ *[what?]* **including** [☐ hiring, training, scheduling, and evaluating crew | ☐ supervising and coordinating daily crew operations and work functions | ☐ other: _____], **ensuring quality control in all activities.**

☐ **Direct and oversee all** [☐ carpentry | ☐ plumbing | ☐ electrical | ☐ HVAC-R | ☐ welding | ☐ landscaping | ☐ other: _____] [☐ installation | ☐ replacement | ☐ maintenance | ☐ repair | ☐ other: _____] **work required in** _____ *[type of]* **jobs.**

☐ **Coordinate, schedule, and supervise trades for** _____ *[type of]* **projects including** [☐ building construction | ☐ asbestos abatement | ☐ roofing repairs | ☐ other: _____] **with sensitivity to client deadlines and project requirements, assigning projects based on staff's unique skills.**

☐ **Manage a** _____ *[which trade?]* **team of** _____ *[#]* **including hiring, training, scheduling, and evaluating crew; and supervising and coordinating daily crew operations and work functions for this** _____ *[type of]* **firm.**

☐ **Schedule and supervise the daily activities of a team of** _____ *[#]* _____ *[titles]* **coordinating all functions for** [☐ commercial | ☐ residential | ☐ public | ☐ other: _____] **accounts including** _____, _____, **and** _____ *[what functions?]* **ensuring all work is completed according to plans, specifications, codes, and schedules.**

☐ **Oversee and supervise a staff of** _____ *[#]* _____ *[type of]* **technicians in their various functions including accountability for their** [☐ client relations | ☐ workmanship | ☐ other: _____] **and enforcing all codes.**

☐ **Provide** [☐ architectural | ☐ engineering | ☐ construction | ☐ other: _____] **support and inspiration to a staff of** _____ *[#]* _____ *[titles]* **in the development and coordination of major and minor projects in the areas of** _____, _____, **and** _____ *[which areas?].*

☐ **Provide support and feedback to** _____ *[whom?]* **regarding** [☐ maintenance | ☐ structural | ☐ renovation | ☐ mechanical | ☐ environmental | ☐ other: _____] **issues at the site.**

Trades / Crew Supervision – Carpentry & Construction

☐ **Coordinate, schedule, and supervise** _____ *[type of]* **projects including** [☐ building construction | ☐ asbestos abatement | ☐ roofing repairs | ☐ other: _____] **with sensitivity to client deadlines and project requirements, assigning projects based on staff's unique skills.**

☐ **Lead and direct a crew of** _____ *[#]* [☐ carpenters | ☐ laborers] **involved in all aspects of** [☐ carpentry | ☐ construction] **including** [☐ reviewing project plans | ☐ reading and interpreting blueprints | ☐ estimating time | ☐ developing work schedules | ☐ assigning crews | ☐ delegating jobs | ☐ preparing work orders | ☐ ordering and setting up equipment | ☐ purchasing supplies | ☐ preparing job sites | ☐ performing rough and finish carpentry | ☐ inspecting work area | ☐ other: _____] **ensuring all jobs are completed in compliance with all specifications and building codes.**

☐ **Oversee personnel management and job operations including** [☐ coordinating steel and concrete trades | ☐ scheduling laborers | ☐ managing construction | ☐ overseeing site materials and equipment set-up | ☐ other: _____].

☐ **Lead and supervise from** _____ *[#]* **to** _____ *[#]* **laborers in the construction and installation of** [☐ walls | ☐ doors | ☐ door jambs | ☐ roofs | ☐ floors | ☐ wall coverings | ☐ ceilings | ☐ paneling | ☐ plastic laminates | ☐ platforms | ☐ partitions | ☐ fences | ☐ ramps | ☐ insulation | ☐ weather stripping | ☐ other: _____] **for this** _____ *[type of]* **firm.**

☐ **Provide construction support, feedback, and inspiration to a carpentry staff of** _____ *[#]* _____ *[titles]* **in the development and coordination of major and minor** _____ *[type of]* **projects.**

☐ **Supervise and oversee laborers in all phases of construction projects including** [☐ pouring foundations | ☐ framing walls and partitions | ☐ installing sheetrock | ☐ building and installing (☐ stairs / ☐ windows / ☐ doors / ☐ brattices / ☐ roofing) | ☐ taping and spackling | ☐ painting | ☐ trim work | ☐ flooring | ☐ tiling | ☐ ceilings | ☐ cabinets | ☐ other: _____].

☐ **Oversee laborers in the set-up of prefabricated components including** [☐ frames | ☐ stairs | ☐ wall panels | ☐ other: _____] **to construct and build** _____ *[what?]*.

☐ **Oversee the work of** _____ *[#]* [☐ carpenters | ☐ laborers | ☐ contractors] **in the measuring, cutting, and fitting of wallboard panels to wood and metal framework, cutting holes in panels for** [☐ windows | ☐ doors | ☐ electrical outlets | ☐ air-conditioning units | ☐ plumbing | ☐ other: _____] **and applying textured surfaces to** [☐ walls | ☐ ceilings | ☐ floors | ☐ other: _____].

☐ **Supervise home** [☐ construction | ☐ improvement | ☐ renovation | ☐ additions | ☐ finished attics and basements | ☐ other: _____] **carpenters and other contractors for individual clients** [☐ on a consultant basis].

☐ **Oversee** _____ *[#]* **laborers in fastening of drywall panels to framework of** [☐ residential houses | ☐ commercial buildings | ☐ other: _____]; **and prepare panels for painting by filling, taping, troweling, and finishing joints.**

☐ **Direct and oversee all** [☐ carpentry | ☐ plumbing | ☐ electrical | ☐ HVAC | ☐ welding | ☐ landscaping | ☐ other: _____] [☐ installation | ☐ replacement | ☐ maintenance | ☐ repair | ☐ other: _____] **work required in** _____ *[type of]* **jobs for this $**_____ *[revenues]* _____ *[type of]* **firm.**

☐ **Monitor job progress through on-site field inspection and review to ensure conformance to** [☐ design specifications | ☐ cost estimates | ☐ time schedules | ☐ electrical codes | ☐ other: _____], **immediately resolving any problems.**

Turnaround Times

ACHIEVEMENT SAMPLES:

☐ **Decreased a** _____ *[#]*-**week delivery delay to a** _____ *[#]*-**day waiting period by** [☐ negotiating with suppliers allowing for job to finish on time and under budget | ☐ other method(s): _____].

☐ **Completed** _____ *[name of]* **project in record time and ahead of schedule; achieved by** [☐ getting the most productivity out of laborers | ☐ organizing and planning daily workloads | ☐ other: _____] **resulting in** [☐ company being awarded state bonuses | ☐ other achievement: _____].

☐ **Complete all projects on time and within budget and at the client reps' and company's satisfaction by** _____ *[doing what well?]*.

☐ **Assigned to take over** _____ *[type of project]* **to smooth out conflicts; handled through firm negotiations and teamwork with client rep and all trades to put project back on track, successfully completing it on schedule and within budget.**

Union Functions

*See also "**Grievance Investigations**," "**Union Leadership**," and "**Compliance**" categories.*

☐ **Thoroughly investigate all employee complaints and disputes to determine if a violation of employee rights occurred by reviewing the circumstances and facts and researching** [☐ the Collective Agreement | ☐ Federal law | ☐ Workers Compensation Board regulations | ☐ Company safety policies and rules and regulations | ☐ established past practices | ☐ other: _____].

☐ **Make work site visits to monitor and enforce** _____ *[which?]* **collective bargaining agreement provisions ensuring the firm and union workers are in compliance with all contractual terms such as** _____, _____, **and** _____ *[what?]*.

☐ **As the** _____ *[which?]* **Union's primary advisor on** [☐ employee engagement | ☐ pro-employer campaigns | (☐ national | ☐ local) labor relations | ☐ other: _____], [☐ formulate and recommend program goals | ☐ participate in contract negotiations | ☐ administer labor agreements | ☐ implement grievance procedures | ☐ other: _____].

☐ **Support administration of all** [☐ contract settlements | ☐ release agreements | ☐ Memorandum Agreements (MOA) | ☐ Side Letter Agreements (SLA) | ☐ other: _____] **between the company and Union including** [☐ negotiations with stakeholders | ☐ cost determinations | ☐ case-specific language | ☐ other: _____].

☐ **Apply expertise in** [☐ organizing | ☐ bargaining | ☐ representation | ☐ arbitration | ☐ coalition building | ☐ contract enforcement | ☐ grievance handling | ☐ political activity | ☐ analyzing and interpreting complex contract language | ☐ creating innovative problem-solving ideas | ☐ developing strategically sound contract campaigns | ☐ servicing large bargaining units | ☐ building effective union power and worker leadership | ☐ upholding union standards | ☐ other: _____] **in the development, negotiation, and/or ratification of contracts.**

☐ **Effectively negotiate with management on employee** [☐ hours | ☐ wages | ☐ benefits | ☐ grievances | ☐ other: _____] **and other work-related matters by** _____ [doing what?].

☐ **Studied and ensured familiarization with all** [☐ union policies and activities | ☐ jobs | ☐ rates of pay | ☐ member seniority | ☐ company rules | ☐ health and safety policy | ☐ departmental operations | ☐ other: _____] **in order to better represent members.**

☐ **Working in the spirit of cooperation and teamwork, ensure Collective Agreements include the rights and responsibilities of both employees and management including** [☐ work hours | ☐ overtime | ☐ wages | ☐ benefits | ☐ vacations | ☐ holidays | ☐ working conditions | ☐ seniority provisions | ☐ job security provisions | ☐ other: _____] **by presenting the facts and using effective listening and bargaining skills.**

☐ **Educate new Union Members on the Union and its role as well as** [☐ the collective agreement | ☐ _____ (type of) programs | ☐ the importance of the labor movement | ☐ attending rallies and sponsored events | ☐ assistance resources | ☐ counseling organizations | ☐ other: _____] **so they have an understanding about their rights and responsibilities, health and safety issues, and other workplace matters.**

☐ **As Union Representative,** [☐ enforce the union contract | ☐ ensure changes do not violate contract terms and conditions | ☐ orient new employees | ☐ identify and train new union activists | ☐ discuss members concerns | ☐ accompany employees to (☐ disciplinary | ☐ grievance | ☐ arbitration | ☐ administrative | ☐ formal dispute resolution) meetings and hearings | ☐ represent members in collective bargaining negotiations | ☐ meet with employer to find best possible solutions to workplace issues | ☐ develop health and safety procedures | ☐ develop campaign materials | ☐ hold training sessions | ☐ organize membership rallies | ☐ participate in organizing demonstrations | ☐ other: _____].

☐ **Interact with company management on behalf of union members and engage in collective bargaining regarding employee** [☐ hours | ☐ wages | ☐ grievances | ☐ other: _____] **and other work-related matters resulting in** _____ [benefits].

☐ **As Organizer, handle various functions including** [☐ signing up members to ensure their job security, fair pay, and equal treatment | ☐ initiating contact with any employees dissatisfied with working conditions | ☐ scheduling union membership benefits meetings | ☐ providing employee opportunities to be active union leaders | ☐ other: _____].

☐ **As Contract Negotiator,** [☐ engage in collective bargaining on behalf of union members, working to achieve good wages and benefits that the entire employee base can live with | ☐ meet at the bargaining table with management and present what they believe are the best options for working conditions | ☐ to act in the best interest of the collective body | ☐ address ongoing work issues during collective bargaining season | ☐ other: _____].

☐ **Represent all workers fairly, completely, and free from bias and ensure compliance with the National Labor Relations Act by** _____ [doing what?].

ACHIEVEMENT SAMPLES: *See Achievements under "Union Leadership."*

Union Leadership

See also "Grievance Investigations," "Union Functions," and "Compliance" categories.

☐ **Manage and oversee all labor relations matters including** [☐ strategy | ☐ negotiations | ☐ interpretation | ☐ grievances | ☐ direction and advice | ☐ union relationship(s) | ☐ other: _____] **for this** _____ [which?] **Union representing** _____ [#] **employees in** _____ [#] **units throughout the state of** _____ [state].

☐ **Direct and coordinate the** _____ [which?] **labor organization functions including** [☐ promoting local membership | ☐ placing union members on jobs | ☐ maintaining labor organization and employer relations | ☐ developing safety and health measures | ☐ arranging local meetings | ☐ visiting work sites to ensure adherence to contractual specifications and labor codes | ☐ engaging in collective bargaining | ☐ acting as employee advocate | ☐ planning and implementing organizing campaigns | ☐ maintaining relations between union and employer's press representatives | ☐ other: _____].

☐ **Manage the business affairs of the** _____ [which?] **labor union including the coordination and direction of** [☐ local membership | ☐ job placement | ☐ work site visits | ☐ other: _____] **as well as strategic negotiations and the implementation of employee relations, employee engagement programs, and labor relations.**

☐ **Conduct** [☐ benefits orientations | ☐ job safety workshops | ☐ _____ (type of) meetings | ☐ other: _____] **that cover** [☐ rights and responsibilities | ☐ health and safety issues | ☐ workplace issues | ☐ other: _____] **and ensure compliance with OSHA standards.**

☐ **Act as** [☐ liaison between | ☐ subject matter expert to] **department managers, Union Representatives, and employees by** [☐ providing personnel policies and employment laws advice | ☐ responding to inquiries relating to _____ *(what?)* | ☐ interpreting labor agreements | ☐ participating in contract negotiations | ☐ providing labor relations support during negotiations | ☐ other: _____].

☐ **Play a leading role in union meetings and act as a conduit of information between workers and** [☐ the firm | ☐ management | ☐ union leadership] **by** _____ *[doing what?].*

☐ **Work with the firm's Human Resource Department to ensure all employee job descriptions are legally compliant in the areas of** [☐ job titles | ☐ job functions and responsibilities | ☐ education and experience required to perform jobs | ☐ reasoning abilities | ☐ physical demands | ☐ work environment | ☐ other: _____] **and other requirements for each job description.**

☐ **Interact with company representatives, assist local Union Stewards, and liaise with the National Labor Relations Board on matters concerning** _____ *[what?].*

☐ **Perform various union leadership functions including** [(☐ formulating | ☐ recommending) program goals and objectives | ☐ conducting risk assessments | ☐ creating risk mitigation solutions | ☐ monitoring program costs | ☐ conducting investigations and evaluating information | ☐ making policy change recommendations to the Human Resources Vice President | ☐ executing grievance procedures | ☐ researching and evaluating grievances and identifying effective solutions | ☐ reviewing liability reports | ☐ increasing employee engagement | ☐ act as Chief Spokesperson | ☐ developing budget and expense proposals | ☐ serving as Union Representative during arbitration hearings | ☐ other: _____].

ACHIEVEMENT SAMPLES:

☐ **Negotiated fair and equitable** _____ *[type of]* **contracts through** [☐ effective listening and understanding to both sides | ☐ thorough research and preparation | ☐ exhibiting honesty | ☐ providing information | ☐ other: _____], **resulting in** [☐ increased productivity for management | ☐ fair wages and benefits for employees | ☐ other: _____].

☐ **Significantly decreased arbitrations by** _____% *[percentage]* **by** [☐ setting up union/management meetings | ☐ resolving _____ *(type of)* problems | ☐ other: _____] **resulting in a cost savings of $**_____ *[amount]..*

☐ **Build a united and involved membership in the workplace by** [☐ organizing the workplace | ☐ compiling research | ☐ handling grievances | ☐ solving problems | ☐ working out agreeable contracts | ☐ mitigating circumstances | ☐ negotiating with and providing solutions to management | ☐ educating workers on health and safety regulations and labor laws | ☐ other: _____] **for this** _____ *[type of company].*

☐ **Ratified** _____% *[percentage]* **of all** _____ *[type of]* **contracts without having a strike by** _____ *[doing what?].*

☐ **Established effective shop steward meetings that** [☐ better informed membership of _____ *(what?)* | ☐ resolved _____ *(type of)* potential problems before they became serious | ☐ helped ensure compliance with OSHA standards | ☐ other: _____], **which benefited by way of** _____ *[what results?].*

☐ **Selected out of** _____ *[#]* **union members to oversee regulatory compliance on all** _____ *[type of]* **projects in** _____ *[#]* [☐ counties | ☐ boroughs | ☐ regions | ☐ states | ☐ countries | ☐ other: _____].

☐ **Contributed to the strength of the Union by recruiting** _____ *[#]* **new Union members and growing its size from** _____ *[#]* **to** _____ *[#]* **by successfully** _____ *[doing what?].*

☐ **Reviewed and evaluated** _____ *[type of]* **documents in order to enhance union member job performance and workplace environment by** _____ *[doing what?]* **and ensured overall consistency, accuracy, and fairness by way of** _____ *[what measures?].*

☐ **Serviced over** _____ *[#]* **members, including** _____ *[which?]* **staffs, to investigate and resolve grievances in** _____ *[which]* [☐ public | ☐ private] **sector(s).**

☐ **Supported the** [☐ Human Resources Vice President | ☐ Union Officer | ☐ Labor Relations Director | ☐ other: _____] **in a major** _____ *[type of]* [☐ project | ☐ initiative] **that** _____ *[did what?],* **which ultimately benefited the firm and its employees by** _____ *[how?].*

☐ **While inspecting the worksite for health or safety issues, found and documented** _____ *[type of]* [☐ health | ☐ safety | ☐ other: _____] **OSHA (Occupational Safety and Health Administration) violations, resulting in** _____ *[what?].*

☐ **Established excellent communication networks throughout all organizational levels by** _____ *[doing what well?].*

☐ [☐ Developed and mentored | ☐ Motivated and empowered] _____ *[title of]* **leaders to act collectively and strategically in the** [☐ protection of their rights | ☐ improvement of the quality of union members' work lives | ☐ fight of unfairness | ☐ other: _____] **by** _____ *[doing what well?].*

☐ **Contributed to the** _____ *[which?]* **internal and external communications strategy and material by** _____ *[doing what?].*

☐ [☐ Developed and implemented | ☐ Assisted in developing] [☐ plant production | ☐ safety health | ☐ other: _____] **measures that** _____ *[did what?]* **and resulted in** _____ *[what benefits?].*

☐ **Formulated and delivered** _____ *[type of]* [☐ short-term | ☐ long-term] [☐ organizing plans | ☐ member development goals | ☐ capacity-building objectives | ☐ other: _____] **that** _____ *[did what?].*

☐ **Elected by union members as the** _____ *[which?]* **Union's Trade Union Representative and applied the National Occupational Standards for Trade Union Reps in the performance of** _____ *[what?].*

Vendor Bids & Proposals

See "Bids & Proposals."

Welding / Steamfitting Scope

See also "Welding / Steamfitting – Functions & Projects" "Trades / Crew Supervision – All Trades," "Inspections & Compliance – Welding / Steamfitting," and "Contractor / Subcontractor Influence & Collaboration."

☐ **Provide decisive leadership and clear direction in all phases of** [☐ large-scale | ☐ complex] _____ *[type of]* **projects for** [☐ commercial | ☐ residential | ☐ industrial | ☐ other: _____] **clients overseeing a top-performing team of** _____ *[#]* [☐ welders | ☐ steamfitters | ☐ other: _____].

☐ **Handle various types of** [☐ welding | ☐ joint welding | ☐ steamfitting | ☐ soldering | ☐ arc welding | ☐ torch cutting | ☐ other: _____] **projects for this** _____ *[type of]* **firm including** [☐ industrial welding | ☐ industrial pipefitting | ☐ industrial plumbing | ☐ domestic water systems | ☐ sprinkler systems | ☐ HVAC piping | ☐ compressed air systems | ☐ fire sprinklers | ☐ truck bed body work | ☐ other: _____].

☐ **Perform** _____ *[#]* **welding projects** [☐ daily | ☐ weekly | ☐ monthly] **for this** [☐ industrial | ☐ mechanical | ☐ manufacturing | ☐ residential | ☐ commercial | ☐ public | ☐ other: _____] _____ *[type of]* **company**.

☐ **Handle approximately** _____ *[#]* **welding jobs** [☐ daily | ☐ weekly | ☐ monthly | ☐ annually] [☐ averaging $_____ to $_____ *(amounts)* | ☐ totaling $_____ *(amount)*] **including** [☐ estimating job times, materials, and costs | ☐ selecting materials and hardware | ☐ preparing materials estimates | ☐ reviewing bids | ☐ ordering required job-related materials | scheduling jobs | ☐ inspecting completed jobs for quality and code compliance | ☐ other: _____].

☐ **Supervise the installation, servicing, and maintenance of new and existing domestic** [☐ water systems | ☐ sanitary piping | ☐ HVAC piping and equipment | ☐ other: _____].

☐ **Oversee** [☐ welding | ☐ arc welding | ☐ joint welding | ☐ soldering | ☐ steamfitting | ☐ torch cutting | ☐ industrial welding | ☐ other: _____] **trades in their installation of new and repair of existing** [☐ domestic | ☐ commercial] [☐ water | ☐ steam | ☐ sanitary | ☐ HVAC | ☐ electrical | ☐ hydraulic | ☐ gas | ☐ vacuum | ☐ sprinkler | ☐ other: _____] **systems**.

☐ **Install and repair** _____ *[type of]* [(☐ electrical / ☐ hydraulic) systems | (☐ low / ☐ high) pressure steam piping | ☐ gas piping | ☐ air compressor piping | ☐ HVAC piping and equipment | (☐ gas / ☐ vacuum) piping | ☐ low- and high-pressure steam piping and equipment | ☐ truck beds | ☐ other: _____] **for** _____ *[what?].*

☐ **Maintain and service new and existing** [☐ domestic water systems | ☐ sanitary piping | ☐ HVAC piping and equipment | ☐ other: _____] **by** _____ *[doing what?].*

☐ [☐ Perform | ☐ Oversee] **all types of welding projects including** [☐ connecting water, steam, gas, oxygen, and air lines | ☐ performing fabrication of metals and alloys | ☐ heating, tempering, straightening, and shaping metals | ☐ working with (☐ water / ☐ steam / ☐ gas / ☐ oxygen / ☐ argon / ☐ helium / ☐ acetylene) | ☐ constructing specialized devices and structures | ☐ performing (☐ machining / ☐ rigging) | ☐ repairing (☐ electrical / ☐ hydraulic) systems | ☐ performing industrial pipefitting | ☐ welding exotic metals | ☐ installing (☐ low- and high-pressure steam / ☐ HVAC / ☐ gas / ☐ vacuum / ☐ air compressor) piping | ☐ maintaining and servicing steam boilers | ☐ constructing specialized devices and structures | ☐ designing, laying out, and cutting special parts | ☐ developing items from (☐ ferrous / ☐ nonferrous) metals | ☐ repairing (☐ electrical / ☐ hydraulic) systems | ☐ other: _____].

☐ **Install, service, and maintain fire suppression sprinkler systems, including** [☐ wet systems | ☐ dry systems | ☐ deluge systems | ☐ other: _____] **for** _____ *[what?].*

☐ **Weld** [☐ exotic metals | ☐ alloys | (☐ ferrous / ☐ nonferrous) metals | ☐ other: _____] **including** [☐ carbon | ☐ stainless steel | ☐ aluminum | ☐ tungsten | ☐ cast iron | ☐ other: _____] **in the steamfitting of** _____ *[what?]* **and ensure safety in use of all gases including** [☐ argon | ☐ helium | ☐ oxygen | ☐ acetylene | ☐ other: _____].

ACHIEVEMENT SAMPLES: *See "Welding/Steamfitting Functions & Projects" and "Construction Projects."*

Welding / Steamfitting Functions & Projects

See also "Welding / Steamfitting – General," "Equipment, Tools & Testing Devices – Welding / Steamfitting," and "Inspections & Compliance – Trades," as applicable.

☐ **Conduct various** [☐ welding | ☐ arc welding | ☐ joint welding | ☐ torch cutting | ☐ soldering | ☐ steamfitting | ☐ other: _____] **functions including** [☐ interpreting blueprints | ☐ preparing job sites | ☐ determining dimensions and tolerances | ☐ modifying, servicing, and repairing existing _____ *(type of)* systems | ☐ ensuring safety in use of all gases | ☐ maintaining supplies | ☐ designing, laying out, and cutting special parts | ☐ fabricating and fitting equipment and parts | ☐ ensuring structural support | ☐ determining best welding methods and techniques | ☐ training staff on welding and machining equipment | ☐ determining project time and costs | ☐ cleaning, lubricating, and maintaining shop equipment | ☐ repairing heavy equipment | ☐ other: _____].

☐ **Perform all aspects of joint welding including** [☐ groove | ☐ bead | ☐ edge | ☐ plug | ☐ slot | ☐ fillet | ☐ arc-seam | ☐ other: _____] **in the welding of** _____ *[what?]* **for** _____ *[purpose]*.

☐ **Prepare for** _____ *[type of]* **welding work by** [☐ reading and interpreting blueprints | ☐ determining dimensions and tolerances | ☐ estimating project time and costs | ☐ specifying best welding methods and techniques for the job | ☐ prioritizing work assignments | ☐ determining equipment needed | ☐ ordering required inventory | ☐ preparing job site for welding | ☐ setting up project with materials | ☐ coordinating vendors | ☐ determining safety requirements | ☐ identifying replacements and/or repairs | ☐ ensuring structural support where needed | ☐ maintaining inventory and supplies | ☐ other: _____].

☐ **Handle** [☐ welding | ☐ arc welding | ☐ joint welding | ☐ torch cutting | ☐ soldering | ☐ steamfitting | ☐ other: _____] **of** _____ *[what?]* **including** [☐ reading and interpreting blueprints | ☐ preparing job sites | ☐ using precision-measuring instruments | ☐ ensuring safety in use of all gases | ☐ modifying, repairing, and servicing existing systems | ☐ ensuring structural support | ☐ determining best welding methods and techniques for the job at hand | ☐ maintaining supplies and inventory | ☐ designing, laying out and cutting special parts | ☐ fabricating and fitting equipment and parts | ☐ determining dimensions and tolerances | ☐ training staff on welding and machining equipment | ☐ determining project time and costs | ☐ cleaning, lubricating, and maintaining shop equipment | ☐ operating metal forming equipment | ☐ repairing heavy equipment | ☐ operating (☐ drill presses / ☐ milling / ☐ gear-cutting / ☐ CNC / ☐ Atlas / ☐ metal-removing machines / ☐ other: _____) | ☐ operating centrifugal chiller and steam absorption machines | ☐ other: _____].

☐ **Construct** _____ *[type of]* [☐ specialized devices and structures | ☐ items from (☐ ferrous / ☐ nonferrous) metals | ☐ other: _____] **by** [☐ heating, tempering, straightening, and shaping metals | ☐ designing, laying out, and cutting special parts | ☐ other: _____] **and** _____ *[doing what?]* **for** _____ *[purpose]*.

☐ [☐ **Perform** | ☐ **Manage and oversee**] **various** _____ *[type of]* **welding projects including** [☐ connecting and working with (☐ water / ☐ steam / ☐ gas / ☐ oxygen / ☐ air lines / ☐ argon / ☐ helium / ☐ acetylene / ☐ other: _____) | ☐ fabrication of metals and alloys | ☐ heating, tempering, straightening, and shaping metals | ☐ constructing specialized devices and structures | ☐ conducting (☐ machining / ☐ rigging) | ☐ repairing (☐ electrical / ☐ hydraulic) systems | ☐ performing industrial pipefitting | ☐ welding exotic metals | ☐ installing (☐ low and high pressure steam / ☐ air compressor / ☐ HVAC / ☐ gas / ☐ vacuum / ☐ other: _____) piping | ☐ maintaining and servicing steam boilers | ☐ constructing specialized devices and structures | ☐ designing, laying out, and cutting special parts | ☐ repairing (☐ electrical / ☐ hydraulic) systems | ☐ other: _____].

☐ **Work with** [☐ water | ☐ steam | ☐ gas | ☐ oxygen | ☐ argon | ☐ air lines | ☐ helium | ☐ acetylene | ☐ other: _____] **in the fabrication of** _____ *[what?]* **for** _____ *[purpose]*.

☐ **Facilitate** [☐ machining | ☐ rigging | ☐ industrial pipefitting | ☐ fabrication of metals and alloys | ☐ other: _____] **for** _____ *[what?]*.

ACHIEVEMENT SAMPLES: *See also "Construction Projects."*

☐ **Installed and repaired low- and high-pressure steam piping, including** [☐ heating | ☐ ventilating | ☐ air condition | ☐ sterilization equipment | ☐ other: _____] **for a** _____ *[#]*-**floor,** _____ *[#]*-**room** [☐ plant | ☐ commercial building | ☐ facility | ☐ other: _____].

☐ **Constructed** _____ *[type of]* **specialized** [☐ structures | ☐ devices | ☐ programs | ☐ other: _____] **that** _____ *[did what?]* **while benefiting the** [☐ client | ☐ firm | ☐ other: _____] **by** _____ *[what means?]*.

☐ **Handled** [☐ welding | ☐ steamfitting | ☐ other: _____] **projects for** [☐ large office buildings | ☐ truck bed body work | ☐ industrial welding | ☐ industrial pipefitting | ☐ industrial plumbing | ☐ domestic water systems | ☐ sprinkler systems | ☐ HVAC piping | ☐ compressed air systems | ☐ other: _____] **for** _____ *[type of clients]*.

☐ **Installed medical gas piping, including** [☐ oxygen | ☐ nitrogen | ☐ medical air | ☐ vacuum | ☐ other: _____] **piping which required tying into existing systems while** [☐ clients | ☐ patrons | ☐ patients | ☐ other: _____] **were living off systems, ensuring proper safety and precautions at all times.**

☐ **Handled on-site** [☐ welding | ☐ steamfitting | ☐ other: _____] **while** [☐ company remained open for business | ☐ homeowners remained on premises | ☐ other: _____] **by** _____ *[doing what?]*, **which minimized the work impact so** [☐ business | ☐ home] **operations remained functional.**

Welding / Steamfitting Equipment Use

See "Equipment, Tools & Testing Devices – Welding / Steamfitting."

Welding / Steamfitting Projects Oversight

See also "Welding/Steamfitting Functions & Projects" "Trades/Crew Supervision – All Trades,"
"Inspections & Compliance – Welding/Steamfitting," and "Contractor/Subcontractor Influence & Collaboration."

☐ **Provide decisive leadership and clear direction in all phases of** [☐ large-scale | ☐ complex] _____ *[type of]* **projects for** [☐ commercial | ☐ residential | ☐ industrial | ☐ other: _____] **clients overseeing a top-performing team of** _____ *[#]* [☐ welders | ☐ steamfitters | ☐ other: _____].

☐ **Coordinate and oversee steamfitting trade functions for** [☐ large office buildings | ☐ industrial welding | ☐ industrial pipefitting | ☐ industrial plumbing | ☐ domestic water systems | ☐ sprinkler systems | ☐ HVAC piping | ☐ compressed air systems | ☐ fire sprinklers | ☐ other: _____] **on** _____ *[type of]* **projects to ensure quality control, regulation compliance, and machinery and equipment safety.**

☐ **Oversee various types of** [☐ welding | ☐ joint welding | ☐ steamfitting | ☐ soldering | ☐ arc welding | ☐ torch cutting | ☐ other: _____] **projects for this** _____ *[type of]* **firm including** [☐ industrial welding | ☐ industrial pipefitting | ☐ industrial plumbing | ☐ domestic water systems | ☐ sprinkler systems | ☐ HVAC piping | ☐ compressed air systems | ☐ fire sprinklers | ☐ truck bed body work | ☐ other: _____].

☐ **Manage and oversee welding jobs averaging $**_____ **to $**_____ *[amounts]* **including** [☐ estimating job times, materials, and costs | ☐ selecting materials and hardware | ☐ preparing materials estimates | ☐ reviewing bids | ☐ ordering required job-related materials | scheduling jobs | ☐ inspecting completed jobs for quality and code compliance | ☐ other: _____].

☐ **Oversee** [☐ welding | ☐ arc welding | ☐ joint welding | ☐ torch cutting | ☐ soldering | ☐ steamfitting | ☐ other: _____] **of** _____ *[what?]* **including** [☐ reading and interpreting blueprints | ☐ preparing job sites | ☐ using precision-measuring instruments | ☐ ensuring safety in use of all gases | ☐ modifying, repairing, and servicing existing systems | ☐ ensuring structural support | ☐ determining best welding methods and techniques for the job at hand | ☐ maintaining supplies and inventory | ☐ designing, laying out and cutting special parts | ☐ fabricating and fitting equipment and parts | ☐ determining dimensions and tolerances | ☐ training staff on welding and machining equipment | ☐ determining project time and costs | ☐ cleaning, lubricating, and maintaining shop equipment | ☐ operating metal forming equipment | ☐ repairing heavy equipment | ☐ operating (☐ drill presses / ☐ milling / ☐ gear-cutting / ☐ CNC / ☐ Atlas / ☐ metal-removing machines / ☐ other: _____) | ☐ operating centrifugal chiller and steam absorption machines | ☐ other: _____].

☐ **Supervise the installation and repair of** _____ *[type of]* [(☐ electrical / ☐ hydraulic) systems | (☐ low / ☐ high) pressure steam piping | ☐ gas piping | ☐ air compressor piping | ☐ HVAC piping and equipment | (☐ gas / ☐ vacuum) piping | ☐ low- and high-pressure steam piping and equipment | ☐ truck beds | ☐ other: _____] **for** _____ *[what?]*.

☐ **Oversee** [☐ welding | ☐ arc welding | ☐ joint welding | ☐ soldering | ☐ steamfitting | ☐ torch cutting | ☐ industrial welding | ☐ other: _____] **trades in their installation of new and repair of existing domestic** [☐ water | ☐ steam | ☐ sanitary | ☐ HVAC | ☐ electrical | ☐ hydraulic | ☐ gas | ☐ vacuum | ☐ sprinkler | ☐ other: _____] **systems**.

☐ **Ensure the safety in use of all gases including** [☐ argon | ☐ helium | ☐ oxygen | ☐ acetylene | ☐ other: _____].

☐ **Oversee all types of welding projects including** [☐ connecting water, steam, gas, oxygen, and air lines | ☐ performing fabrication of metals and alloys | ☐ heating, tempering, straightening, and shaping metals | ☐ working with (☐ water / ☐ steam / ☐ gas / ☐ oxygen / ☐ argon / ☐ helium / ☐ acetylene) | ☐ constructing specialized devices and structures | ☐ performing (☐ machining / ☐ rigging) | ☐ repairing (☐ electrical / ☐ hydraulic) systems | ☐ performing industrial pipefitting | ☐ welding exotic metals | ☐ installing (☐ low- and high-pressure steam / ☐ HVAC / ☐ gas / ☐ vacuum / ☐ air compressor) piping | ☐ maintaining and servicing steam boilers | ☐ constructing specialized devices and structures | ☐ designing, laying out, and cutting special parts | ☐ developing items from (☐ ferrous / ☐ nonferrous) metals | ☐ repairing (☐ electrical / ☐ hydraulic) systems | ☐ other: _____].

☐ **Supervise the installation, servicing, and maintenance of new and existing domestic** [☐ water systems | ☐ sanitary piping | ☐ HVAC piping and equipment | ☐ other: _____].

☐ **Oversee the construction of** _____ *[type of]* [☐ specialized devices and structures | ☐ items from (☐ ferrous / ☐ nonferrous) metals | ☐ other: _____] **through the** [☐ heating, tempering, straightening, and shaping metals | ☐ designing, laying out, and cutting special parts | ☐ other: _____] **and** _____ *[doing what?]* **for** _____ *[purpose]*.

☐ **Manage and oversee various** _____ *[type of]* **welding projects including** [☐ connecting and working with (☐ water / ☐ steam / ☐ gas / ☐ oxygen / ☐ air lines / ☐ argon / ☐ helium / ☐ acetylene / ☐ other: _____) | ☐ fabrication of metals and alloys | ☐ heating, tempering, straightening, and shaping metals | ☐ constructing specialized devices and structures | ☐ conducting

(☐ machining / ☐ rigging) | ☐ repairing (☐ electrical / ☐ hydraulic) systems | ☐ performing industrial pipefitting | ☐ welding exotic metals | ☐ installing (☐ low and high pressure steam / ☐ air compressor / ☐ HVAC / ☐ gas / ☐ vacuum / ☐ other: _____) piping | ☐ maintaining and servicing steam boilers | ☐ constructing specialized devices and structures | ☐ designing, laying out, and cutting special parts | ☐ repairing (☐ electrical / ☐ hydraulic) systems | ☐ other: _____].

ACHIEVEMENT SAMPLES: *See also "Construction Projects."*

☐ **Managed and oversaw the installation of low- and high-pressure steam piping, including** [☐ heating | ☐ ventilating | ☐ air condition | ☐ sterilization equipment | ☐ other: _____] **for a** _____ *[#]*-**floor,** _____ *[#]*-**room** [☐ plant | ☐ commercial building | ☐ facility | ☐ other: _____].

☐ **Oversaw the construction of** _____ *[type of]* **specialized** [☐ structures | ☐ devices | ☐ programs | ☐ other: _____] **that** _____ *[did what?]* **while benefiting the** [☐ client | ☐ firm | ☐ other: _____] **by** _____ *[what means?]*.

☐ **Managed** [☐ welding | ☐ steamfitting | ☐ other: _____] **projects for** [☐ large office buildings | ☐ truck bed body work | ☐ industrial welding | ☐ industrial pipefitting | ☐ industrial plumbing | ☐ domestic water systems | ☐ sprinkler systems | ☐ HVAC piping | ☐ compressed air systems | ☐ other: _____] **for** _____ *[type of clients]*.

☐ **Supervised medical gas piping, including** [☐ oxygen | ☐ nitrogen | ☐ medical air | ☐ vacuum | ☐ other: _____] **piping which required tying into existing systems while** [☐ clients | ☐ patrons | ☐ patients | ☐ other: _____] **were living off systems, ensuring proper safety and precautions at all times.**

☐ **Oversaw on-site** [☐ welding | ☐ steamfitting | ☐ other: _____] **while** [☐ company remained open for business | ☐ homeowners remained on premises | ☐ other: _____] **by** _____ *[doing what?]*, **which minimized the work impact so** [☐ business | ☐ home] **operations remained functional**.

Work Collaboration – Construction

See also "Work Collaboration – General."

☐ **Conduct preconstruction meetings and confer with** [☐ architects | ☐ engineers | ☐ contractors | ☐ builders | ☐ project managers | ☐ superintendents | ☐ the general public | ☐ others: _____] **to review building requirements and restrictions**.

☐ **Coordinate all aspects of** [☐ drafting | ☐ construction | ☐ production | ☐ other: _____] **projects with** [☐ clients | ☐ engineers | ☐ architects | ☐ municipal officials | ☐ county officials | ☐ code officers | ☐ others: _____] **ensuring compliance with all codes and quality standards throughout project phases.**

☐ **Collaborate with various trades in the coordination of job functions including** [☐ plumbing | ☐ electrical | ☐ building maintenance | ☐ carpentry | ☐ HVAC | ☐ masonry | ☐ framing | ☐ landscaping | ☐ other: _____].

☐ **Interact with** [☐ clients | ☐ architects | ☐ engineers | ☐ general contractors | ☐ subcontractors | ☐ project managers | ☐ urban planners | ☐ interior designers | ☐ landscape architects | ☐ expeditors | ☐ zoning officials | ☐ inspectors | ☐ homeowners | ☐ (custom home) builders | ☐ electricians | ☐ plumbers | ☐ roofers | ☐ others: _____] **during the** [☐ design | ☐ design-and-build | ☐ construction | ☐ engineering | ☐ development] **process to** [☐ define project parameters | ☐ develop detailed project plans | ☐ schedule projects | ☐ identify and problem solve issues | ☐ manage construction | ☐ procure permits | ☐ other: _____].

☐ **Meet and coordinate jobs with** [☐ building managers | ☐ homeowners | ☐ subcontractors | ☐ zoning officials | ☐ architects | ☐ engineers | ☐ inspectors | ☐ union delegates | ☐ zoning officials | ☐ lumber yards | ☐ vendors | ☐ others: _____] **during the** _____ *[which trade(s)?]* **process**.

☐ **Work with** _____ *[which?]* **trades to coordinate the** [☐ design and] **installation of** _____ *[what projects?]* **for** _____ *[whom or what?]*.

☐ **Work collaboratively in a team environment with** [☐ management | ☐ laborers | ☐ maintenance crew | ☐ subcontractors | ☐ others: _____] **while** [☐ leading | ☐ handling] **multiple projects and adapting to frequently changing priorities.**

☐ **Interface and work closely with** [☐ architects | ☐ designers | ☐ builders | ☐ general contractors | ☐ homeowners | ☐ project engineers | ☐ builders | ☐ electricians | ☐ plumbers | ☐ roofers | ☐ lumber yards | ☐ others: _____] [☐ on all relevant issues and project phases | ☐ to identify problems and recommend solutions | ☐ to modify plans as needed | ☐ other: _____].

☐ **Coordinate the implementation and monitoring of** _____ *[what?]* **with other departments, successfully producing results through others by** _____ *[doing what well?]*.

☐ **Collaborate with** _____ *[which?]* **staff to** [☐ ensure positive (☐ customer / ☐ internal / ☐ external) relationships | ☐ maintain service quality | ☐ address and resolve issues | ☐ communicate project milestones | ☐ properly identify and process scope changes | ☐ other: _____].

☐ **Establish and maintain effective working relations with** _____ *[whom?]* **for** _____ *[purpose, process, or project]*.

☐ **Participate in work collaboration meetings with** _____ *[whom?]* **regarding** _____ *[what?]*.

☐ **Collaborate with** [☐ state officials | ☐ state agencies | ☐ politicians | ☐ others: _____] **to improve conditions for** _____ *[what trade(s)?]* **regarding** [☐ licensing | ☐ safety | ☐ general welfare | ☐ other: _____].

☐ **Work as a team with** _____ *[#]* **laborers in the construction and installation of** [☐ walls | ☐ doors | ☐ door jambs | ☐ roofs | ☐ floors | ☐ wall coverings | ☐ ceilings | ☐ paneling | ☐ plastic laminates | ☐ platforms | ☐ hardware | ☐ podiums | ☐ partitions | ☐ fences | ☐ ramps | ☐ insulation | ☐ weather stripping | ☐ other: _____] **for this** _____ *[type of]* **firm.**

☐ **Work with** [☐ architects | ☐ engineers | ☐ urban planners | ☐ interior designers | ☐ other: _____] **and other professionals during the** [☐ design and] **construction process.**

☐ **Collaborate with** _____ *[whom?]* **on** _____ *[type of]* **projects using** [☐ tact | ☐ diplomacy | ☐ project management skills | ☐ other: _____] **and a thorough understanding of the project planning process.**

☐ **Liaise and interface regularly with** _____, _____, **and** _____ *[whom?]* **to** [☐ determine project scope | ☐ develop project plans | ☐ review feedback on project goals and timelines | ☐ develop project plans | ☐ schedule projects | ☐ identify and problem solve issues | ☐ manage construction | ☐ track projects | ☐ other: _____] **in the various phases of the project.**

☐ **Work with owners to maintain customer satisfaction by** [☐ listening to and interpreting their needs | ☐ giving careful attention to detail | ☐ other: _____].

☐ **Interface and work closely with client representatives to** [☐ develop project strategies | ☐ determine project scope | ☐ execute project plans | ☐ determine required materials and resources | ☐ coordinate trades | ☐ apprise management of status | ☐ other: _____].

☐ **Coordinate various aspects of projects with** [☐ subcontractors | ☐ general contractors | ☐ architects | ☐ municipal officials | ☐ code officials | ☐ others: _____] **in the** _____ *[what phases of construction?]*.

☐ **Act as liaison with** [☐ architects | ☐ designers | ☐ builders | ☐ general contractors | ☐ homeowners | ☐ project engineers | ☐ supervisors | ☐ custom home builders | ☐ electricians | ☐ plumbers | ☐ roofers | ☐ lumber yards | ☐ others: _____] [☐ on all relevant issues and project phases | ☐ to modify plans as needed | ☐ to identify problems and recommend solutions | ☐ other: _____].

☐ **Interface and work closely with client representatives to** [☐ develop project strategies | ☐ determine project scope | ☐ execute project plans | ☐ determine required materials and resources | ☐ coordinate trades | ☐ apprise management of status | ☐ other: _____].

ACHIEVEMENT SAMPLES:

☐ **Coordinated** _____ *[type of]* **projects with** [☐ subcontractors | ☐ general contractors | ☐ engineers | ☐ architects | ☐ municipal officials | ☐ code officials | ☐ county officials | ☐ clients | ☐ others: _____] **in all phases of construction, which enhanced compliance with codes and quality standards toward the successful completion of all jobs.**

☐ **Established and maintain** [☐ collaborative relationships | ☐ useful interfaces | ☐ effective working relations | ☐ other: _____] **with** [☐ clients | ☐ internal staff | ☐ end users | ☐ management | ☐ other: _____] **as well as** _____ *[whom?]* **regarding all contractual issues and matters.**

☐ **In collaboration with the** _____ *[whom?]* [☐ created accurate project estimates | ☐ prepared schedules | ☐ allocated resources | ☐ other: _____] **that support company-wide projects and maintain project management practices.**

☐ **Developed a cooperative team effort with** _____ *[whom?]* **enhancing the coordination and successful completion of all** _____ *[type of]* **projects by** _____ *[doing what successfully?]*.

Work Collaboration & Coordination – Plumbing Projects

See also "Work Collaboration – General."

☐ **Confer with** _____ *[whom?]* **concerning** _____ *[type of]* **plumbing** [☐ projects | ☐ programs | ☐ matters] **to** [☐ define needs | ☐ determine schedules | ☐ make changes | ☐ keep projects running smoothly | ☐ other: _____].

☐ **Establish and maintain effective working relations with** _____ *[whom?]* **for** _____ *[what purpose, process, or project?]*.

☐ **Collaborate and coordinate** _____, _____, **and** _____ *[what activities?]* **with** _____ *[whom?]* **on** _____ *[type of]* **plumbing projects using** [☐ tact | ☐ diplomacy | ☐ project management skills | ☐ other: _____] **and a thorough understanding of the project planning process.**

☐ **Liaise and interface with** _____ *[whom?]* **to** [☐ determine project scope | ☐ develop strategies | ☐ gather data | ☐ define project parameters | ☐ create project plans | ☐ identify required materials and resources | ☐ execute plans | ☐ schedule projects | ☐ identify and problem solve issues | ☐ overcome obstacles | ☐ modify plans as needed | ☐ other: _____].

☐ **Coordinate all aspects of plumbing projects with** [☐ clients | ☐ engineers | ☐ architects | ☐ municipal officials | ☐ county officials | ☐ code officers | ☐ others: _____] **ensuring compliance with all** [plumbing codes | quality standards | work schedules | other: _____].

☐ **Develop and maintain a cooperative team effort with** [☐ architects | ☐ engineers | ☐ superintendents | ☐ foremen | ☐ project managers | ☐ electricians | ☐ other departments | ☐ others: _____] **in the coordination and completion of all plumbing jobs** [☐ throughout the construction process].

☐ **Act as liaison with** _____ *[which?]* **staff to** [☐ ensure positive (☐ customer / ☐ internal / ☐ external) relationships | ☐ maintain service quality | ☐ address and resolve issues | ☐ communicate project milestones | ☐ properly identify and process scope changes | ☐ other: _____].

☐ **Collaborate at all levels of the firm on** _____ *[type of]* **projects using tact and diplomacy to** [☐ define needs | ☐ clarify scope | ☐ identify issues | ☐ determine schedules | ☐ make changes | ☐ solve problems | ☐ overcome obstacles | ☐ recommend solutions | ☐ obtain solutions acceptance | ☐ keep projects running smoothly | ☐ reach _____ *(type of)* decisions | ☐ other: _____] **during the development and implementation of** _____ *[type of]* **projects.**

☐ **Participate in work collaboration meetings with** _____ *[whom?]* **regarding** _____ *[what?].*

ACHIEVEMENT SAMPLES:

☐ **Established and maintain** [☐ collaborative relationships | ☐ useful interfaces | ☐ effective working relations | ☐ other: _____] **with** [☐ clients | ☐ internal staff | ☐ end users | ☐ management | ☐ other: _____] **as well as** _____ *[whom?]* **regarding all contractual issues and matters.**

☐ **Developed a cooperative team effort with** _____ *[whom?]* **enhancing the coordination and successful completion of all** _____ *[type of]* **projects by** _____ *[doing what successfully?].*

☐ **Developed positive working relationships with** _____ *[type of]* [☐ clients | ☐ staff | ☐ vendors | ☐ others: _____] **by** [☐ using effective listening skills | ☐ providing responses to special issues | ☐ other methods: _____], **which resulted in** _____ *[what benefits?].*

Work Collaboration & Coordination – Project Management

See also "Work Collaboration – General."

☐ **Collaborate at all levels of the firm on** _____ *[type of]* **projects using** [☐ tact | ☐ diplomacy | ☐ project management skills | ☐ other: _____] **to** [☐ define needs | ☐ clarify scope | ☐ identify issues | ☐ determine schedules | ☐ make changes | ☐ solve problems | ☐ overcome obstacles | ☐ recommend solutions | ☐ obtain solutions acceptance | ☐ keep projects running smoothly | ☐ reach _____ *(type of)* decisions | ☐ other: _____] **during the construction of** _____ *[type of]* **projects.**

☐ **Liaise and interface regularly with** _____ *[whom?]* **to** [☐ determine project scope | ☐ develop strategies | ☐ gather data | ☐ define project parameters | ☐ create project plans | ☐ identify required materials and resources | ☐ execute plans | ☐ schedule projects | ☐ identify and problem solve issues | ☐ overcome obstacles | ☐ modify plans as needed | ☐ other: _____].

☐ **Interact and liaise with** _____ *[whom?]* **to ensure that construction work is within parameters identified by the firm and in compliance with** _____ *[what?].*

☐ **Work collaboratively in a team environment with** _____ *[whom?]* [☐ while leading multiple projects | ☐ adapting to frequently changing priorities | ☐ demonstrating a strong commitment to improvement | ☐ other: _____].

☐ **Participate as a member of a project team of** _____ *[#]* **to** [☐ prepare and distribute project schedules | ☐ provide support | ☐ communicate project status | ☐ resolve issues | ☐ other: _____] **that meet schedule requirements.**

☐ **Serve on a project team of** _____ *[#]* **including** _____ *[whom?]* **that defines, plans, and implements new** _____ *[type of]* **projects; and perform the** [☐ design | ☐ development | ☐ deployment | ☐ other: _____] **of those projects in support of the** [☐ firm's | ☐ clients'] **objectives.**

☐ **In collaboration with the** _____ *[what team?]* [☐ create accurate project estimates | ☐ prepare schedules | ☐ allocate resources | ☐ other: _____] **that support company-wide projects and maintain project management practices.**

☐ **Oversee staff interactions with** _____ *[whom?]* **to** [☐ maintain productive working relationships with _____ *(whom?)* | ☐ schedule projects | ☐ facilitate inspections | ☐ ensure proper handling and receipt of payments | ☐ other: _____].

☐ **Foster strong internal and external client relationships by** [☐ ensuring all client challenges are effectively solved | ☐ other: _____].

☐ **Interface and work closely with clients to** [☐ develop project strategies | ☐ determine project scope | ☐ execute project plans | ☐ determine required materials and resources | ☐ apprise project management team of status | ☐ other: _____].

☐ **Liaise with** _____ *[whom?]* **to maintain customer satisfaction by** [☐ listening to and interpreting their needs | ☐ giving careful attention to detail | ☐ other: _____].

ACHIEVEMENT SAMPLES: *See also Achievements under "Work Collaboration & Coordination – General."*

☐ **In collaboration with the** _____ *[whom?]* [☐ created accurate project estimates | ☐ prepared schedules | ☐ allocated resources | ☐ other: _____] **that support company-wide projects and maintain project management practices.**

☐ **Developed a cooperative team effort with** _____ *[whom?]* **enhancing the coordination and successful completion of all** _____ *[type of]* **projects by** _____ *[doing what successfully?].*

Now you have everything you need to pull your resume together!

STEP 6
PULL YOUR RESUME TOGETHER

CONTENTS OF STEP 6

☐ **Step-by-Step Instructions**

1. Decide on Your Resume Design and Start Your Resume.
2. Input the Information You Compiled in Your Resume Worksheet.
3. Transfer Over Your "Professional Summary" and Slogan.
4. List Your Core Competencies.
5. Consider Using a "Key Accomplishments" Section.
6. Add Your "Professional Experience" Bullets.
7. Verify that all of Your Critical Keywords are Included in Your Resume.
8. Ensure Your Resume Bullets Start with Action Verbs.
9. Infuse Descriptive Adjectives and Adverbs.
10. Add Company and Position Descriptors Under Your Employers.
11. Edit Your Resume.
12. Include Your Testimonials.
13. Consider Adding "Wow" Elements to Your Resume.
14. Determine Your Resume Length.
15. Make Sure Your Resume is Targeted and Compelling.
16. Ensure You Have Left No Stone Unturned.
17. Create an ASCII (Text-Only) Version of Your Resume.
18. Compose Your Cover Letter.
19. Print Out Your Resume and Cover Letter.

☐ **Action Verbs: Resume Bullet Starters**

☐ **Descriptive Adjectives and Adverbs**

☐ **Add Company and Position Descriptors**

☐ **"100 Components of an Exemplary Resume: How Does Your Resume Fare?"**

☐ **Resume Design Layout Samples**

STEP-BY-STEP INSTRUCTIONS

INTRODUCTION

Everything you need to compile your resume you have completed within this Book. This chapter provides the instructions to pull the various components together to finalize your resume.

Take your time in completing these steps to ensure your resume is the best it can be and ready for distribution.

1. DECIDE ON YOUR RESUME DESIGN AND START YOUR RESUME.

Just as your resume content is important, so too is its layout and design to first get your resume noticed. In a pile of bland resumes, the ones that will get noticed first are those that attract the attention of hiring managers. And if after getting their attention, the content compels them to call, you have met your goal of getting yourself noticed above your competition.

Ensure your resume presentation is visually-appealing and professional by keeping the design clean and organized. Including bold headers, rules, and white space will make it easier to read and invite hiring managers in to want to read your resume. I generally set my resume margins at .5 at the top and bottom and .75 on the left and right sides. If you are savvy in MS Word, a two-column resume works well when you have a lot of information to include. Save your resume and entitle it, *"(Your Name) Resume.docx"* or *.doc.*

Use basic fonts such as Arial, Arial Narrow, Helvetica, Times, Times New Roman, Garamond, Trebuchet MS, or Verdana to ensure hiring managers have the fonts on their computer and your resume looks the same when they view it. Alternating serif and sans serif fonts for your headers and body copy organizes your content and creates visual interest. (More on font sizes in *"Determine Your Resume Length"* below.)

Consider adding a splash of color to your personal header and/or resume category headings. Deep blues, burgundies, and greens are professional and work well. If you selected brand colors in **Step 4: Develop Your Personal Brand and Professional Summary,"** you might consider infusing those colors instead.

At the end of this chapter you will find five resume design layouts you can use as a guide to lay out your resume. For actual layouts you can load onto your computer, my **Step-by-Step Resumes: Build an Outstanding Resume in 10 Easy Steps!** book *(published by JIST Publishing, $19.95)* includes a CD that contains 24 design templates in MS Word, which may make it easier for you to compile and customize your resume.

2. INPUT THE INFORMATION YOU COMPILED IN YOUR RESUME WORKSHEET.

From **Step 1: Start Your Resume,** start by including all of the information you completed in your *Resume Worksheet:*

- **ENTER YOUR PERSONAL INFORMATION.** Add your name, address, phone number(s), email address, and the URLs for your LinkedIn account and/or Web Portfolio at the top of your resume. You can also include your Twitter and/or Facebook URLs if your posts are professional. (More on that in **Step 7: Market Yourself!**)

- **SET UP YOUR HEADINGS.** Key in all of the resume headings you identified in **Step 1: Start Your Resume:** *"Licenses & Certifications," "Professional Summary" / "Executive Profile," "Core Competencies" / "Areas of Expertise," "Key Accomplishments" / "Highlighted Achievements"* (addressed in #5 below), *"Professional Experience," "Education & Training," "Publications,"* and so on in that order. Make your headings in bold caps and add a rule under each. Leave space between each category so you can input your information from the remaining steps.

- **START YOUR "PROFESSIONAL EXPERIENCE" SECTION.** Chronologically set up your employment information by first keying in your current or most recent Job Title (in bold caps), your employers' Company Name (with Town and State) (in bold), and years of employment (months can be excluded) according to your chosen design layout. Include the responsibilities and achievements you listed in your **Resume Worksheet** under your applicable employers. You will go back and check, edit, and/or delete some content after you add your Resume ClipBullets *(in No. 6 below)*.

  <u>NOTE:</u> *Since hiring managers prefer the Reverse-Chronological Resume format, this Book addresses that format. If, however, your employment record shows a number of unexplained gaps, you are changing careers and cannot substantiate any experience in your targeted profession, you are re-entering the job market after a number of years, or otherwise require a nontraditional resume format, the four formats (Reverse Chronological, Combination, Functional, and Curriculum Vitae) are addressed in and contain templates for these on CD in my more generalized* **Step-by-Step Resumes: Build an Outstanding Resume in 10 Easy Steps!** *book (JIST Publishing).*

- **ADD YOUR EDUCATION AND TRAINING.** If you are a recent grad, your *"Education & Training"* section belongs at the beginning of your resume. Include the year(s) you attended or obtained your degree. If you already have experience in your field, add your Education at the end of your resume. If you attended college more than ten years ago, you can omit the years. Leave off an Associate's degree if you obtained a Bachelor's degree. Be sure to include any related training in your field and where you obtained it. Again, if it is recent, include the years; if not, omit them.

3. TRANSFER OVER YOUR "PROFESSIONAL SUMMARY" AND SLOGAN.

Key in the personally branded *"Professional Summary"* / *"Executive Profile"* you developed in **Step 4: Develop Your Personal Brand and Professional Summary** onto the top portion of your resume under your main header (or under your *"Education"* section if you are a new grad). Make sure it contains all of your *"Primary Resume Keywords"* identified in **Step 2: Check Off Your Resume Keywords.** Check also that you have included your *"Primary Personal Attributes"* you listed in **Step 3: Check Off Your Personal Attributes**. If not, infuse some of them within your Summary. If you created a slogan in **Step 4,** include it as well directly under your header.

4. LIST YOUR "CORE COMPETENCIES."

Input your "Secondary Resume Keywords" (from **Step 2: Check Off Your Resume Keywords**) into a "Core Competencies" or "Areas of Expertise" section positioned under your "Professional Summary." If you are laying out your resume in a two-column format, your core competencies work well in a left-hand column that consumes about one-fourth of the page.

Should you have expertise in several areas and/or have a long list of keywords, section them off under applicable headings, such as "Human Resource Management," "Employee Engagement," "Talent Acquisition," and so on. Those headings should generally be the same as your "Primary Keywords" you included above in #3. Alternatively, you can use the keyword categories listed in **Step 2.** Since this Book covers various levels of experience, you may have knowledge of lower-level functions / keywords that may not be as relevant to the position you are seeking. Those can be omitted unless hands-on knowledge is required in your targeted position.

5. CONSIDER INCLUDING A "KEY ACCOMPLISHMENTS" SECTION.

If you are an executive or manager or otherwise have quite a number of significant accomplishments that exhibit your value proposition, or if when developing your resume at least some of your primary accomplishments do not appear on its first page, consider adding a *"Key Accomplishments"* or *"Achievement Highlights"* section under your *"Professional Summary"* and *"Core Competencies"* sections to include them. Put your "heavy hitter" accomplishments at the top, such as where you made or saved the most amount of money for your employer, significantly increased percentages in productivity or customer service satisfaction levels, won a notable award for your employer, and so on. Hiring managers typically view the first page of prospective candidates' resumes during their first screening to decide which candidates to call. You will want to make sure they see your value with some of your matching achievements during their first screening.

6. ADD YOUR "PROFESSIONAL EXPERIENCE" BULLETS.

- **ENTER THE RESUME CLIPBULLETS** you checked off and completed throughout **Step 5: Select Your Resume ClipBullets** under your employers where they are applicable, adding them after the *"Responsibilities"* and *"Achievements"* you brought over from your *"Resume Foundation."* Omit the word "Responsibilities." At this time, do not worry about how long your resume draft will become. *(You will be editing these down in #11 below.)*

- **REVIEW AND PRIORITIZE YOUR BULLETS**. Verify that all of the functions your targeted position requires and you have performed have been included (from the *"Job Descriptions"* you Googled in **Step 4: Develop Your Personal Brand & Professional Summary**). Include those at the top of your bullets under each employer. Then prioritize the bullets under each of your jobs in order of their importance to your targeted position.

- **CHECK THAT YOUR BULLETS ARE "CAR" STATEMENTS.** Always try to show how well you accomplished your responsibilities by including the **C**hallenge you were faced with, the **A**ctions you took to make it happen, and the **R**esults / Benefits your company or its clients derived from your efforts. Add if not already noted.

  Ensure quantifying information is included in your bullets by adding numbers *(dollars, percentages, measurements, and other statistics)* wherever you can to show *how well* you accomplished your functions. Ask yourself, *how large, how big, how much, how fast, how often?* Compare those numbers against the company or industry "norm." If better, include them.

- **IF YOU HAVE MANY BULLETS, CATEGORIZE THEM.** If you find you have a dozen or more bullets under your individual employers, separate out your accomplishments under an *"Achievements"* heading under those employers.

7. VERIFY THAT ALL OF YOUR CRITICAL KEYWORDS ARE INCLUDED IN YOUR RESUME.

Double-check that the resume keywords you identified in **Step 2: Check Off Your Resume Keywords** have all been included. That is, your **Primary Keywords** are contained within your *"Professional Summary"* and/or a slogan at the top of your resume under your header, your **Secondary Keywords** are listed under *"Core Competencies,"* and any **remaining keywords** have been included within the bullets in your *"Professional Experience"* section.

8. ENSURE YOUR RESUME BULLETS START WITH ACTION VERBS.

In essence, Action Verbs *(such as advocate, build, champion, approve, collaborate, and so on)* are the most basic form of a job function. All of your resume bullets in your *"Professional Experience"* section should start with an Action Verb. The exception to the rule is when you precede the Action Verb with an Adverb *(addressed next)*. Never start your bullets with *"Responsible for..."* Instead, omit those words and jump right into the actions you perform(ed).

All of the *Resume ClipBullets* contained in this Book already contain Action Verbs, but a complete list is included in this chapter for you to ensure any bullets you created on your own include them and/or to check if there are any important "functions" you may have omitted and still require in your resume.

EXAMPLES BY POSITION TITLE

- **Executive** – spearhead, strategize, manage, oversee, direct, establish, forecast, increase, orchestrate
- **Social Worker** – assess, advocate, link, coordinate, counsel, evaluate, investigate, place
- **Attorney** – advise, consult, depose, examine, litigate, research, settle, summon
- **Graphic Designer** – conceptualize, create, design, render, strategize, synthesize
- **Programmer** – develop, configure, test, code, program, analyze, monitor, diagnose

9. INFUSE DESCRIPTIVE ADJECTIVES AND ADVERBS.

You can further show *how well* you performed a certain task, responsibility, or achievement by preceding the *Action Verb* with a *Descriptive Adverb* or by adding a *Descriptive Adjective* in front of a *Noun* within your bullets. (See examples.) Include some in your resume to help describe how well you accomplished your job functions or achievements.

Descriptive Adverb Examples: *Accurately* invoice, *Diplomatically* negotiate, *Efficiently* conduct, *Continuously* improve, *Virtually* eliminated, *Quickly* intervene, *Successfully* spearhead, *Regularly* monitor, *Dramatically* reduced, and so on.

Descriptive Adjective Examples: Allocate *appropriate* resources, Conceptualize *creative* designs, Offer *encouraging* support, Facilitate *timely* negotiations, Develop *effective* solutions, Prepare *accurate* records, and so on.

10. ADD COMPANY AND POSITION DESCRIPTORS UNDER YOUR EMPLOYERS.

At the end of this chapter, you will find foundations for **Company and Position Descriptors** to include under your employers in your *"Professional Experience"* Section. Although not mandatory, adding a short italicized paragraph under each of your jobs detailing the purpose for which you were hired, your primary responsibilities, and information about your firm is especially beneficial if you have a number of bullets where you can cull out some of this information to include in a Position Descriptor.

11. EDIT YOUR RESUME.

- **REVIEW AND EDIT ALL OF YOUR EMPLOYMENT BULLETS.** Because this Book contains so much relevant information for each position, when your first draft is complete, chances are good that you will have more bullets than you need to finalize your resume. Now is the time to edit down your information as much as possible *without* losing any important content. Review all of your bullets to check for redundancy. Join like bullets into one. Delete any less important bullets that are not as significant to or required in the position(s) you seek.

- **MAKE YOUR BULLETS CONCISE.** Condense everything down to the most concise sentences possible—what I call *"the lowest common denominator."* Always try to say the same thing in less words until you cannot edit down any further without losing substance. Omit words such as pronouns (I, me, my), "the," "that," and other nonessential words.

- **VARY YOUR BULLET LINE LENGTH.** To maintain the interest of your reader, vary your bullet line length alternating between one-, two-, three-, and four-line bulleted sentences (bearing in mind what you have already prioritized). Keep long bullets to a minimum. If you have a number of four- or five-line bullets, try condensing or splitting them.

- **MAKE SENSIBLE PAGE BREAKS.** If you can, end your resume pages with the completion of a particular position, starting the next position at the top of the following page. If you are off a bit, try to edit down further until it fits properly and/or adjust your spacing.

- **CHECK FOR CONSISTENCY.** To ensure your completed resume has a polished look, check for consistency in your fonts, verbiage, spacing, line breaks, rules, and other areas and that your margins are pretty much even all around.

- **SPELL-CHECK AND PROOFREAD YOUR RESUME.** Several times. It can take only one spelling error to disqualify you as an eligible candidate (in many positions). Be sure everything is accurate, there are no spelling errors, and all information is "true" before you consider it "done." If this is not your forte, have someone with good spelling, grammar, and punctuation skills do this for you.
- **EDIT EVERYTHING AGAIN AND AGAIN.** This is what professional resume writers do. Sleep on it and look it over again the next day and the following before considering it finished. There is usually always room for improvement—that is, more content you can edit down and perfect.

12. INCLUDE YOUR TESTIMONIALS.

Another way to add interest to your resume presentation is to include (three) *"Testimonials."* Testimonials from others in your industry add credence to your resume content by exhibiting what others say about you. Prospective employers generally ask for your references during an interview, but including testimonials in your resume can spark their interest in the first place and increase your interview odds. Testimonials can be added as call-outs in the scholar's margin of your resume, as a category at the end of your resume, or on a separate addendum page.

Include your *"Testimonials"* from **Step 4: Develop Your Personal Brand and Professional Summary.** Select testimonials and endorsements from LinkedIn, performance evaluations, letters of recommendation, client thank you letters, internship summaries, vendor satisfaction letters, and the like. If you don't have any reference letters, now is a good time to ask for them. Select comments that speak to your value and various abilities from a variety of sources, such as superiors, peers, subordinates, professors, clients, vendors, and others. If the testimonial is long, paraphrase it using an ellipse (…) to connect thoughts and indicate something was omitted.

13. CONSIDER ADDING "WOW" FACTORS TO YOUR RESUME.

Following are additional ways you can add interest to your resume presentation while showcasing your skills and abilities. Consider including a Mission Statement, Success Stories, Case Studies, Work Samples, Charts, and/or Graphs.

• A MISSION STATEMENT

A way to immediately capture a hiring manager's attention and show you are passionate about your profession is by creating a short mission statement (a promise or belief) that exhibits what you have to offer a prospective employer. You can include your mission statement in the margin of your resume and/or cover letter or at the bottom of your resume in a footer so it appears on each page.

EXAMPLES BY POSITION TITLE:

Executive Chef: *"An Executive Chef's talent lies in his ability to create innovative cuisine, instruct it masterfully, and wow his patrons."*
Service Manager: *"I believe the true quality of a good Service Manager is the ability to run an operation with an eye towards profitability while servicing the customer in a fair and honest way."*
Case Manager: *"An effective Case Manager takes time to listen, treats others the way she wants to be treated, inspires positive changes in people's lives, and is accountable for her actions and reactions."*
Teacher: *"Each step a child takes in his life has an effect on his future. I would like to help students take positive steps by creating an educational experience conducive to learning."*
Sales Associate: *"If the customer is happy and you are making a sale, it's a win/win."*

• CHARTS AND GRAPHS

Executives, managers, and others who have, for example, increased revenues, sales, productivity, or customer service satisfaction levels and/or decreased costs, labor, or employee turnover might consider putting this information in a chart or graph that depicts these numbers and include it in your resume. Doing so is a great way to showcase your achievements in a visual that readers will see first.

• SUCCESS STORIES OR CASE STUDIES

By including a "Success Stories" or "Case Studies" Addendum Page at the end of your resume, prospective employers can see first-hand how you have successfully performed your job and achieved your position goals. Always include the challenge you were faced with, the actions you took to solve it, and the end result to show the benefits of your work. Chances are your readers will flip through your resume and read this first.

EXAMPLES FOR A SOCIAL WORKER:

Success Story No. 1: An adoptive adolescent with a tough exterior and intimidating mannerisms was in the Mercy Residential Treatment Center because of her negative behaviors. Though Jane was intelligent, she was told she had to attend until her behaviors improved. She wanted to leave at the end of the year to be mainstreamed into her district public school; however, during the year her behavior fluctuated. Although several counselors had chosen not to work with her, I found that by working on her conflicts and offering my client a working relationship built on trust, it helped empower her to focus on her behavioral and academic goals. At the end of the school year, Jane was mainstreamed back into her district high school.

<u>Success Story No. 2:</u> A bi-polar patient felt very upset when her mom yelled at her. After inviting Mary's mom in for a meeting and discussing with her the impact it had on her daughter, while teaching Mary how to communicate with her mom, she learned to express her feelings when she was upset, and her mom became more understanding of the impact she had on her daughter. The relationship became more of a working one, and Mary responded better to treatment because she and her mom were talking things out.

<u>Success Story No. 3:</u> Derek, a 15-year-old client with impaired intelligence, was to receive a prison sentence of 15 years to life for sexual offenses. I built a relationship with his mother who found it very difficult to deal with the situation, was preoccupied with her own life, and resisted putting in time. Together, we worked on getting her son treatment instead of going to jail and I found a parent support group for her to attend. I followed through with appropriate agencies so he could receive psychiatric treatment and sent a detailed report to the District Attorney to present to the judge before trial. Now Derek is undergoing psychiatric care at the Children's Services Treatment Center with intense supervision.

<u>Success Story No. 4:</u> Jane, an alcoholic 17-year-old client who lived in a group home, had experienced difficulty living at home. Her mother was concerned with her living at home because she engaged herself in self-hazardous situations. My client didn't believe her mother listened to her side. By creating a neutral environment during sessions, building trust, and following up on issues, my client eventually disclosed her distrust for authoritative figures due to past experiences where she had been misled. The counseling helped Jane come to terms with her alcoholism that originated from her father and grandfather before her, and helped build a communicative relationship between mother and daughter.

- **WORK SAMPLES**

Especially helpful for Graphic Designers, Marketing professionals, Teachers, Architects, Construction Managers, Interior Decorators, Chefs, Artists, and Photographers, for example, **Work Samples** can show first-hand what you are capable of by including photos or illustrations of work you performed. You can include *Work Samples* under your specific employers where you performed this work, in the margin of your resume, or on an Addendum Page at the end of your resume.

Additional information regarding these and many other visual and verbal branding elements are contained in my more generalized book, **Step-by-Step Resumes: Build an Outstanding Resume in 10 Easy Steps!** *(JIST Publishing).*

14. DETERMINE YOUR RESUME LENGTH.

There is no "magical number" of pages a resume should be, though some may tell you otherwise. You want to enthral hiring managers to *want to* read your resume and *compel* them to call you. So if you hand them a four-page resume with just copy that is all in the same font and not organized or sectioned off in any way to invite your reader in, then it is too long and will likely not be read. View the resume design layouts at the end of this chapter as a guide, and ensure all of your information is organized and easy to read. Here are some guidelines:

- Your resume should be as long as it needs to be to include all of your critical content in its *most concise* form. Edit, edit, edit is the key.

- Executives and others with a lot of achievements will have longer resumes, such as three to five pages. If you are responsible for profit and loss, for example, your achievements will take up more space. A Project Engineer may also have many projects important to include. You can list the projects with their critical information under your employers and note *"See 'Completed Projects' for details on the addendum page,"* where you can provide more information, perhaps along with "before and after" photos.

- Your more recent position and/or those positions related to your targeted job should include more bullets, with successively less bullets for older positions as you go back chronologically. If you find your position content is longer than say two-thirds of a page, consider breaking out your achievements into a *"Key Accomplishments"* section *(see #5 above).* Try to keep your responsibility / function-related bullets to 8 to 12 in your more recent positions, depending upon how long your bullets are (again, not a "magical number").

- Font style and size makes a difference insofar as how long your resume is. Depending upon the font, it can actually be smaller or larger at the same size. Font examples in their indicated and recommended font sizes: <u>Times New Roman at 11 point</u>, <u>Arial at 10 point,</u> <u>Verdana at 9.5 point</u>. If your resume is long, I recommend using <u>Arial Narrow at 10.5 point</u>. If space allows, make your cover letter one-half to one point size larger.

- Your resume length could also depend upon the country you work in. In the United States for example, two to three pages is quite the norm. In Australia, if you submit a two-page resume, hiring managers will wonder where the "rest of the resume" is, and five to six pages is not unusual.

15. MAKE SURE YOUR RESUME IS TARGETED AND COMPELLING.

- **VERIFY THAT YOUR RESUME IS TARGETED.** Go back to when you Googled job descriptions in **Step 4: Develop Your Personal Brand and Professional Summary.** Check that everything required in the position(s) you seek in which you have accomplished during your career has been included. If not, add it. Also, double-check that all relative skills, keywords, and other requirements listed in the job descriptions are included as they are applicable to you.

- **IS YOUR FINAL RESUME COMPELLING?** When you feel your resume is done, take a look at it and ask yourself if it compels you to want to delve into and read it. When you read your resume, are you impressed with yourself? Does your resume contain your unique personal brand? Have you provided enough value that a hiring manager would feel compelled to want to call you in for an interview and hire you? If there is any question, go back to **Step 4** to make sure you have included all of your brand components.

16. ENSURE YOU HAVE LEFT NO STONE UNTURNED.

To ensure you have done absolutely everything you could possibly do to make your resume the best it can be, test yourself by reviewing my **100 Components of an Exemplary Resume: How Does Your Resume Fare?** article in this chapter by checking off what you feel you have included in your resume and revisiting any areas not taken care of.

17. CREATE AN ASCII (TEXT-ONLY) VERSION OF YOUR RESUME.

Some prospective employers and recruiters request a plain text version of your resume. Also, when you post your resume to job boards and attaching your resume does not automatically flow your information into their specific categories, you will need to copy and paste the sections in yourself. It is easier to use this plain resume version to do that.

Once you are 100% sure that your resume is complete, edited, and proofread, save an additional copy as "Text Only" within MS Word. Then close the document and reopen the ".txt" file. You will see that all font attributes and rules have been removed. Review the content for correct line breaks, any excess spacing between sections, and that everything is consistent. If you added headers for page breaks, delete them.

18. COMPOSE YOUR COVER LETTER.

Think of your Cover Letter as a sales tool to sell yourself. A marketing-savvy cover letter entices the reader to want to read your resume and can actually intrigue hiring managers to call you even before they review your resume. Catch their attention with a cover letter that clearly shows your value proposition (that you developed in **Step 4: Develop Your Personal Brand and Professional Summary**), explains how your qualifications match the position requirements, includes a summary of your key accomplishments, and states why you feel you can be an asset to the firm.

Here are some guidelines:

- Start your cover letter by including your value proposition and/or other components of your personal brand. Consider using your *Elevator Pitch* you developed in **Step 4**. Include the position title you are seeking and where you heard about the job opening.

- The second paragraph should sell yourself as a qualified candidate based on your experience, education, and skills. Explain what you have to offer through your matching qualifications, and include the primary requirements in the job posting insofar as how they pertain to your expertise and skills in those areas.

- In the third paragraph, summarize some related achievements (in bulleted or paragraph form) to exemplify how you can be an asset to their firm and help them achieve their goals. When stating your achievements, leave out the details and indicate *"See resume for details."*

- A fourth paragraph could include additional information about your primary attributes and skills, a related story of why you are passionate about or interested in the profession, and/or other compelling information that might be of specific interest to a prospective employer in your industry.

- In the last paragraph, close with a statement of interest, include your call-to-action, and thank the reader for their consideration.

- Keep your cover letter to one page (4 to 5 paragraphs work well). Be sure it includes all of your primary keywords.

For more information on how to compose a superb cover letter, my book, **Step-by-Step Cover Letters: Build a Cover Letter in 10 Easy Steps Using Personal Branding** (JIST Publishing), takes you step by step through the process and includes a CD containing a number of cover letter foundations you can load into your computer and use to fill in your related information.

19. PRINT OUT YOUR RESUME AND COVER LETTER.

Use a high-quality (28 to 32 lb.) resume paper found in office supply stores for printing and mailing your resume and cover letter to prospective employers. If the targeted position includes both a physical and email address, use both methods to send out your resume. And always bring extra copies with you when you go on interviews.

ACTION VERBS:
Resume Bullet Starters

☐ Abate	☐ Abbreviate	☐ Abide	☐ Abolish	☐ Absolve	☐ Absorb
☐ Abstract	☐ Accelerate	☐ Access	☐ Acclaim	☐ Acclimate	☐ Accommodate
☐ Accompany	☐ Accomplish	☐ Account for	☐ Accredit	☐ Accrue	☐ Accumulate
☐ Achieve	☐ Acknowledge	☐ Acquire	☐ Act as	☐ Activate	☐ Adapt
☐ Add	☐ Address	☐ Adhere to	☐ Adjudicate	☐ Adjust	☐ Administer
☐ Admit	☐ Adopt	☐ Advance	☐ Advise	☐ Advocate	☐ Affiliate with
☐ Affirm	☐ Affix	☐ Affray	☐ Aid	☐ Align	☐ Allocate
☐ Ambulate	☐ Amend	☐ Amplify	☐ Analyze	☐ Anchor	☐ Anesthetize
☐ Animate	☐ Answer	☐ Appease	☐ Apply	☐ Appoint	☐ Appraise
☐ Apprehend	☐ Apprise	☐ Approach	☐ Appropriate	☐ Approve	☐ Arbitrate
☐ Archive	☐ Arraign	☐ Arrange	☐ Arrest	☐ Articulate	☐ Ascertain
☐ Ascribe	☐ Assemble	☐ Assert	☐ Assess	☐ Assign	☐ Assimilate
☐ Assist	☐ Assure	☐ Attach	☐ Attain	☐ Attend	☐ Attest to
☐ Auction	☐ Audit	☐ Augment	☐ Authenticate	☐ Author	☐ Authorize
☐ Automate	☐ Award	☐ Backtrack	☐ Bag	☐ Balance	☐ Base
☐ Batch	☐ Begin	☐ Bestow	☐ Bid	☐ Bill	☐ Bind
☐ Bisect	☐ Blend	☐ Block	☐ Board	☐ Book	☐ Brace
☐ Brainstorm	☐ Brand	☐ Break down	☐ Break up	☐ Breed	☐ Bridge
☐ Brief	☐ Bring about	☐ Broach	☐ Broadcast	☐ Broaden	☐ Browse
☐ Budget	☐ Build	☐ Bulk	☐ Bundle	☐ Buy	☐ Calculate
☐ Calibrate	☐ Call	☐ Cancel	☐ Canvas	☐ Capitalize on	☐ Captivate
☐ Capture	☐ Care for	☐ Carry out	☐ Carry over	☐ Carve	☐ Cash
☐ Cash out	☐ Cast	☐ Catalog	☐ Catalyze	☐ Catapult	☐ Catch
☐ Categorize	☐ Cater to	☐ Centralize	☐ Certify	☐ Chair	☐ Challenge
☐ Champion	☐ Change	☐ Channel	☐ Characterize	☐ Charge	☐ Charge off
☐ Check	☐ Check in	☐ Check out	☐ Check up	☐ Choose	☐ Circulate
☐ Cite	☐ Claim	☐ Classify	☐ Cleanse	☐ Clear out	☐ Clear up
☐ Climb	☐ Clip	☐ Clock	☐ Close	☐ Close out	☐ Close up
☐ Co-administer	☐ Co-arrange	☐ Coat	☐ Co-author	☐ Co-chair	☐ Co-compose
☐ Co-contribute	☐ Co-coordinate	☐ Co-create	☐ Code	☐ Co-defend	☐ Co-design
☐ Co-develop	☐ Co-direct	☐ Co-edit	☐ Co-handle	☐ Co-head	☐ Co-here
☐ Co-invent	☐ Co-lead	☐ Collaborate	☐ Collate	☐ Collect	☐ Co-manage
☐ Combine	☐ Commence	☐ Comment on	☐ Commit to	☐ Communicate	☐ Compare
☐ Compensate	☐ Compete with	☐ Compile	☐ Complete	☐ Comply with	☐ Compose
☐ Composite	☐ Compound	☐ Compress	☐ Compute	☐ Concentrate on	☐ Conceptualize
☐ Conclude	☐ Condense	☐ Condition	☐ Conduct	☐ Confect	☐ Confer with
☐ Configure	☐ Confirm	☐ Confiscate	☐ Conform to	☐ Congregate	☐ Connect
☐ Conserve	☐ Consider	☐ Consign	☐ Console	☐ Consolidate	☐ Consort
☐ Constrain	☐ Constrict	☐ Construct	☐ Consult with	☐ Contact	☐ Contain
☐ Contemplate	☐ Contest	☐ Contract	☐ Contribute to	☐ Contrive	☐ Control
☐ Converge	☐ Convert	☐ Convey	☐ Cooperate with	☐ Coordinate	☐ Co-partner
☐ Co-present	☐ Co-produce	☐ Co-promote	☐ Copy	☐ Copy Write	☐ Copyright
☐ Correct	☐ Correlate	☐ Correspond	☐ Corroborate	☐ Co-sponsor	☐ Counsel
☐ Count	☐ Counteract	☐ Counterbalance	☐ Counterbid	☐ Counterdemand	☐ Countermand
☐ Counterplea	☐ Countersign	☐ Couple	☐ Cover	☐ Co-write	☐ Crack down on
☐ Craft	☐ Create	☐ Credit	☐ Critique	☐ Crop	☐ Cross-check
☐ Cross-file	☐ Cross-index	☐ Cross-link	☐ Cross-reference	☐ Cross-section	☐ Cross-sell
☐ Cultivate	☐ Cumulate	☐ Curtail	☐ Cut	☐ Cut back	☐ Cut down
☐ Cycle	☐ Deactivate	☐ Deal	☐ Debate	☐ Debit	☐ Debrief
☐ Debug	☐ Decide	☐ Decipher	☐ Declare	☐ Declassify	☐ Decline
☐ Decode	☐ Decompress	☐ Decorate	☐ Decrease	☐ Dedicate	☐ Deduce
☐ Deduct	☐ Defeat	☐ Defend	☐ Defer	☐ Deflate	☐ Deflect
☐ Defray	☐ Dehydrate	☐ Delay	☐ Delegate	☐ Delete	☐ Deliberate
☐ Delineate	☐ Deliver	☐ Demagnetize	☐ Demise	☐ Demolish	☐ Demonstrate
☐ Demount	☐ Demystify	☐ Denote	☐ Densify	☐ Deny	☐ Deploy
☐ Deport	☐ Depose	☐ Deposit	☐ Depreciate	☐ Depute	☐ Deputize
☐ Describe	☐ Deselect	☐ Design	☐ Designate	☐ Detach	☐ Detain

288

- [ ] Detect
- [ ] Determine
- [ ] Develop
- [ ] Deviate
- [ ] Devise
- [ ] Diagnose
- [ ] Diffract
- [ ] Diffuse
- [ ] Dig
- [ ] Digitize
- [ ] Direct
- [ ] Disable
- [ ] Disallow
- [ ] Disarm
- [ ] Disassemble
- [ ] Disband
- [ ] Disburse
- [ ] Discard
- [ ] Disclaim
- [ ] Disclose
- [ ] Disconnect
- [ ] Discontinue
- [ ] Discount
- [ ] Discover
- [ ] Discuss
- [ ] Dismantle
- [ ] Dismiss
- [ ] Dispatch
- [ ] Dispense
- [ ] Disperse
- [ ] Display
- [ ] Dispose of
- [ ] Disprove
- [ ] Dispute
- [ ] Dissect
- [ ] Dissipate
- [ ] Dissolve
- [ ] Dissuade
- [ ] Distribute
- [ ] Disunite
- [ ] Diversify
- [ ] Divert
- [ ] Divest
- [ ] Divide
- [ ] Dock
- [ ] Document
- [ ] Dodge
- [ ] Dogmatize
- [ ] Double
- [ ] Draft
- [ ] Draw
- [ ] Drive
- [ ] Duplicate
- [ ] Edit
- [ ] Educate
- [ ] Elect
- [ ] Elevate
- [ ] Eliminate
- [ ] Embrace
- [ ] Employ
- [ ] Encourage
- [ ] Endure
- [ ] Energize
- [ ] Enforce
- [ ] Engage in
- [ ] Engineer
- [ ] Enhance
- [ ] Ensure
- [ ] Enter
- [ ] Entertain
- [ ] Entrench
- [ ] Entrust
- [ ] Enumerate
- [ ] Equalize
- [ ] Equate
- [ ] Escort
- [ ] Establish
- [ ] Estimate
- [ ] Evaluate
- [ ] Examine
- [ ] Exceed
- [ ] Execute
- [ ] Exemplify
- [ ] Exercise
- [ ] Exhibit
- [ ] Expand
- [ ] Expedite
- [ ] Explain
- [ ] Explore
- [ ] Fabricate
- [ ] Facilitate
- [ ] Fasten
- [ ] File
- [ ] Fill
- [ ] Finance
- [ ] Fine-tune
- [ ] Fix
- [ ] Follow up on
- [ ] Forecast
- [ ] Formulate
- [ ] Foster
- [ ] Founded
- [ ] Frequent
- [ ] Fulfill
- [ ] Furnish
- [ ] Fuse
- [ ] Garnish
- [ ] Gather
- [ ] Generate
- [ ] Give
- [ ] Govern
- [ ] Greet
- [ ] Grow
- [ ] Handle
- [ ] Harmonize
- [ ] Heighten
- [ ] Help
- [ ] Hire
- [ ] Identify
- [ ] Illustrate
- [ ] Impact
- [ ] Implement
- [ ] Improve
- [ ] Incorporate
- [ ] Increase
- [ ] Induce
- [ ] Inform
- [ ] Initiate
- [ ] Inspect
- [ ] Inspire
- [ ] Install
- [ ] Instill
- [ ] Instruct
- [ ] Instrumental in
- [ ] Integrate
- [ ] Intensify
- [ ] Interact with
- [ ] Interface with
- [ ] Interpret
- [ ] Intervene
- [ ] Interview
- [ ] Introduce
- [ ] Invent
- [ ] Investigate
- [ ] Invite
- [ ] Involved in
- [ ] Irrigate
- [ ] Join
- [ ] Juggle
- [ ] Launch
- [ ] Layout
- [ ] Lead
- [ ] Learned
- [ ] Lend
- [ ] Lessen
- [ ] Link
- [ ] List
- [ ] Litigate
- [ ] Locate
- [ ] Lower
- [ ] Maintain
- [ ] Manufacture
- [ ] Mark
- [ ] Market
- [ ] Maximize
- [ ] Measure
- [ ] Mediate
- [ ] Meet
- [ ] Mentor
- [ ] Merchandise
- [ ] Minimize
- [ ] Model
- [ ] Moderate
- [ ] Modify
- [ ] Mold
- [ ] Monitor
- [ ] Motivate
- [ ] Mount
- [ ] Negotiate
- [ ] Network with
- [ ] Nullify
- [ ] Observe
- [ ] Obtain
- [ ] Offer
- [ ] Open
- [ ] Operate
- [ ] Optimize
- [ ] Orchestrate
- [ ] Order
- [ ] Organize
- [ ] Orient
- [ ] Originate
- [ ] Outline
- [ ] Overcome
- [ ] Oversee
- [ ] Package
- [ ] Paint
- [ ] Participate in
- [ ] Partition
- [ ] Penetrate
- [ ] Perform
- [ ] Perpetuate
- [ ] Persist
- [ ] Persuade
- [ ] Place
- [ ] Plan
- [ ] Plant
- [ ] Post
- [ ] Practice
- [ ] Preapprove
- [ ] Prearrange
- [ ] Pre-establish
- [ ] Prep
- [ ] Prepare
- [ ] Present
- [ ] Preserve
- [ ] Prevent
- [ ] Price
- [ ] Print
- [ ] Prioritize
- [ ] Problem-solve
- [ ] Process
- [ ] Produce
- [ ] Project
- [ ] Promote
- [ ] Proofread
- [ ] Protect
- [ ] Prove
- [ ] Provide
- [ ] Publish
- [ ] Purchase
- [ ] Pursue
- [ ] Quadruple
- [ ] Quantify
- [ ] Question
- [ ] Raise
- [ ] Rank
- [ ] Reach out to
- [ ] Realign
- [ ] Rearrange
- [ ] Reassemble
- [ ] Reassess
- [ ] Reassure
- [ ] Rebuild
- [ ] Recalculate
- [ ] Receive
- [ ] Recheck
- [ ] Recommend
- [ ] Reconcile
- [ ] Recondition
- [ ] Reconstruct
- [ ] Reconvert
- [ ] Record
- [ ] Recreate
- [ ] Recruit
- [ ] Rectify
- [ ] Recultivate
- [ ] Redesign
- [ ] Redevelop
- [ ] Redirect
- [ ] Redistribute
- [ ] Reduce
- [ ] Reengineer
- [ ] Reestablish
- [ ] Reevaluate
- [ ] Re-examine
- [ ] Re-explore
- [ ] Refer
- [ ] Refill
- [ ] Refinance
- [ ] Refute
- [ ] Regenerate
- [ ] Rehabilitate
- [ ] Reinforce
- [ ] Reinstall
- [ ] Reintroduce
- [ ] Reinvent
- [ ] Relate
- [ ] Relay
- [ ] Relocate
- [ ] Remanufacture
- [ ] Remarket
- [ ] Remerchandise
- [ ] Remind
- [ ] Render
- [ ] Reorchestrate
- [ ] Reorder
- [ ] Reorganize
- [ ] Repackage
- [ ] Repair
- [ ] Replace
- [ ] Replant
- [ ] Report
- [ ] Repossess
- [ ] Represent
- [ ] Reprint
- [ ] Reprioritize
- [ ] Reprocess
- [ ] Reproduce
- [ ] Rerun
- [ ] Reschedule
- [ ] Research
- [ ] Reselect
- [ ] Resell
- [ ] Resend
- [ ] Resolve
- [ ] Respond to
- [ ] Restructure
- [ ] Resurvey
- [ ] Retest
- [ ] Retouch
- [ ] Retrain
- [ ] Reuse
- [ ] Review
- [ ] Revisit
- [ ] Rewrite
- [ ] Ride
- [ ] Run
- [ ] Safeguard
- [ ] Sample
- [ ] Satisfy
- [ ] Saturate
- [ ] Save
- [ ] Scale
- [ ] Scan
- [ ] Schedule
- [ ] Screen
- [ ] Script
- [ ] Search
- [ ] Secure
- [ ] Seize
- [ ] Select
- [ ] Selected to
- [ ] Sell
- [ ] Send
- [ ] Separate
- [ ] Serve
- [ ] Serve as
- [ ] Service
- [ ] Set up
- [ ] Settle
- [ ] Ship
- [ ] Sign
- [ ] Simplify
- [ ] Solicit
- [ ] Solve
- [ ] Sort
- [ ] Spearhead
- [ ] Specialize in
- [ ] Specify
- [ ] Split
- [ ] Standardize
- [ ] Strategize
- [ ] Streamline
- [ ] Strengthen
- [ ] Structure
- [ ] Study
- [ ] Sub out
- [ ] Substantiate
- [ ] Succeed
- [ ] Successful in
- [ ] Summarize
- [ ] Summon
- [ ] Supervise
- [ ] Support
- [ ] Surpass
- [ ] Survey
- [ ] Synchronize
- [ ] Synthesize
- [ ] Tackle
- [ ] Tailor
- [ ] Take

- [ ] Teach
- [ ] Transition
- [ ] Troubleshoot
- [ ] Unite
- [ ] View
- [ ] Work with
- [ ] Test
- [ ] Translate
- [ ] Turn around
- [ ] Upsell
- [ ] Visit
- [ ] Write
- [ ] Testify
- [ ] Transmit
- [ ] Tutor
- [ ] Use
- [ ] Vote
- [ ] Thwart
- [ ] Transport
- [ ] Uncover
- [ ] Utilize
- [ ] Warn
- [ ] Track
- [ ] Treat
- [ ] Underwrite
- [ ] Validate
- [ ] Work as
- [ ] Train
- [ ] Triple
- [ ] Unify
- [ ] Verify
- [ ] Work out

DESCRIPTIVE ADJECTIVES & ADVERBS

DESCRIPTIVE ADVERB SAMPLES

- [ ] Accurately invoice...
- [ ] Analytically review...
- [ ] Carefully inspect...
- [ ] Concisely edit...
- [ ] Creatively develop...
- [ ] Dramatically reduced...
- [ ] Encouragingly assist...
- [ ] Finitely define...
- [ ] Independently test...
- [ ] Patiently cater to...
- [ ] Proactively provide...
- [ ] Regularly monitor...
- [ ] Strategically plan...
- [ ] Succinctly write...
- [ ] Thoroughly investigate...
- [ ] Voluntarily serve...

- [ ] Actively explore...
- [ ] Appropriately allocate...
- [ ] Clearly communicate...
- [ ] Consistently attain...
- [ ] Diligently perform...
- [ ] Effectively enhance...
- [ ] Expediently route...
- [ ] Fruitfully completed...
- [ ] Intriguingly captivate...
- [ ] Persistently follow up on...
- [ ] Professionally greet...
- [ ] Significantly improved...
- [ ] Successfully coordinated...
- [ ] Tactically manage...
- [ ] Virtually eliminated...
- [ ] Warmly greet...

- [ ] Actively network with...
- [ ] Architecturally design...
- [ ] Collaboratively tackle...
- [ ] Continuously improve...
- [ ] Diplomatically negotiate...
- [ ] Efficiently conduct...
- [ ] Financially manage...
- [ ] Impartially determine...
- [ ] Intuitively foresee...
- [ ] Persuasively present...
- [ ] Quickly intervene...
- [ ] Simultaneously tackle...
- [ ] Successfully spearheaded...
- [ ] Tastefully decorate...
- [ ] Vividly demonstrate...

DESCRIPTIVE ADJECTIVE SAMPLES

- [ ] Allocate appropriate resources...
- [ ] Create vogue fashions...
- [ ] Devise captivating presentations...
- [ ] Implement seasonal planograms...
- [ ] Negotiate diplomatic negotiations...
- [ ] Prepare accurate records...
- [ ] Recommend analytic solutions...

- [ ] Conceptualize creative designs...
- [ ] Develop contemporary programs...
- [ ] Execute successful new policies...
- [ ] Make a visible difference...
- [ ] Offer encouraging support...
- [ ] Prepare essential reports...
- [ ] Showcase attractive displays...

- [ ] Conduct regular reviews...
- [ ] Develop effective solutions...
- [ ] Facilitate timely negotiations...
- [ ] Make thorough recommendations...
- [ ] Perform preventive maintenance...
- [ ] Present stimulating ideas...
- [ ] Write succinct outlines...

ADD COMPANY & POSITION DESCRIPTORS
For Your "Professional Experience" Section

INTRODUCTION

Adding a "Position Descriptor" under each of your jobs encapsulates your company and job responsibility information into a few lines to make it easier for hiring managers to get a full perspective of what you are/were engaged in before reading all of your function- and achievement-related bullets. It is especially beneficial if you have quite a number of bullets listed under your positions where you can cull out some of this information to include in your Position Descriptor and condense some of your bullet content.

This short italicized (two- to five-line) sentence or paragraph will describe the purpose for which you were hired, your primary responsibilities and accountabilities, and specific information about your firm, such as its size, revenues, number of locations and/or employees, products and services it offers, and so on. You can obtain company information from your employers' websites, annual report, and/or marketing materials.

Below are some foundations to use as a guide in developing your own company and position descriptors for each of your positions, followed by samples for various different positions. Add or adjust information as appropriate for your position and company.

COMPANY & POSITION DESCRIPTOR FOUNDATION #1

Recruited as _____ *[what function or title?]* **to** _____ *[do what?]* [□ **for** _____ *(whom or what?)* | □ **with focus on** _____ *(what?)*] **and to** [□ lead and direct | □ manage and oversee | □ conduct | □ perform | □ other: _____] **all aspects of** _____ , _____ , **and** _____ *[your primary keywords]* **as well as** _____ *[what areas?]* **for this** [□ multibillion-dollar | □ multimillion-dollar | □ $_____ *(revenues)*] _____ *[type of]* **firm with** _____ [□ locations | □ employees | □ other: _____] **that provides** _____ *[type of]* [□ products | □ services | □ other: _____] **to (the)** _____ *[type of clients or industry].* [□ _____ *(additional information).*] (_____ *[#]* **direct reports** | _____ *[#]* **indirect reports**)

SAMPLE FOR A FINANCIAL VICE PRESIDENT

Recruited as Vice President of Finance **to** revamp financial support and control **for** the Portfolio Solutions Group **and to manage** all aspects of investment, overhead, research and development, and a $9 million sales support budget **as well as** all financial aspects of the Service Delivery Center **for this** $3 billion investment **firm that provides** investment portfolios **services to** middle- to upper-income clients. (5 **direct reports** | 25 **indirect reports**)

SAMPLE FOR A UNION LEADER

Recruited to lead the expansion of the Nationwide Operations' Business Unit **with focus on** new business development in the Northeast markets **and to manage and oversee** operations and spearhead new projects **for this** multimillion-dollar construction management **firm. Provide** representation **services to** union members **including** contract negotiations and enforcement, grievance handling, collective bargaining, union organizing activities, **and** development and enforcement of health and safety procedures. (7 **direct reports** | 15 **indirect reports**)

SAMPLE FOR A TURNAROUND SPECIALIST

Recruited as part of the Turnaround Team **to** direct and manage strategic planning and operations for front- and back-of-the-house operations including restaurant supervision, kitchen management, inventory control, food cost control, and staff training and development **for this** full-service fine dining restaurant **with** 3 **locations,** 75 **employees,** a seating capacity of 250, **and** annual sales of $25 million. (14 **direct reports and** 20 **indirect reports**)

COMPANY & POSITION DESCRIPTOR FOUNDATION #2

[□ **Appointed by the** _____ *(title)* | (□ **Selected** / □ **Recruited**) **as** _____ *(what function?)*] **to** _____ *[do what?]* **in support of** _____ *[what?]* **for this** _____ *[type of]* [□ **company** | □ **agency** | □ **organization** | □ **other:** _____] **with** [□ **revenues** | □ **locations** □ **employees** □ **other:** _____] **of** _____ *[number / amount].* [□ _____ *(additional information).*] (_____ *[#]* **direct reports** | _____ *[#]* **indirect reports**)

SAMPLE FOR AN ASSISTANT VICE PRESIDENT

Appointed by the President **as** a special representative **to** lead Far East operations and to serve as interim Chief of Staff **in support of** organizational restructuring vis-á-vis a holistic approach **for this** governmental agency **with revenues of** $2.9 Million ensuring all program activities operate consistently and ethically within the mission and values of the firm.

SAMPLE FOR A HIGHER-EDUCATION MENTOR / LEADER

Selected by the Administrator **to** help facilitate this brick-and-mortar, traditional college's learning communities with a student body of 3500 **in support of** providing academic advisement, mentoring, and coaching to an adult student body of nontraditional, first generation college students with different learning styles **for this** higher-education facility. Spearheading various strategic initiatives drove the student body population to 18,000.

SAMPLE FOR A OPERATIONS DIRECTOR / GENERAL MANAGER

Recruited as turnaround specialist **for** the corporation's multiple holdings of 3 **locations** including ABC, Inc.; DEF Corporation; and GHI Company establishments. 7 **direct reports and** 150 **indirect reports.**

COMPANY & POSITION DESCRIPTOR FOUNDATION #3

Provide _____ *[what?]* **to/for** _____ *[whom or what?]* **including** _____, _____, _____, **and** _____ *[what activities?]* **for this $**_____ *[revenues]* _____ *[type of]* **firm [☐ with** _____ *[#]* **locations and** _____ *[#]* **employees | ☐ serving the** _____ *(what?)* **industry]. [☐ Manage and oversee a $**_____ *(amount)* _____ *(type of)* **budget.] [☐**_____ *(additional information).]*

SAMPLE FOR A CLIENT FINANCIAL MANAGEMENT ANALYST

Provide key support **to** the P&L budgeting and forecasting process **including** detailed analytics focused on expenses, taxes, **and** net income **for this** multibillion-dollar global management consulting, technology services, and outsourcing **firm with** 12 **locations and** 25,000+ **employees.** Assist with the preparation of engagement, project, program reporting, and finance control processes. **Manage and oversee a** $12 million department **budget.**

SAMPLE FOR A STRUCTURAL ENGINEER

Provide structural engineering and drafting services **to** architects, contractors, developers, and owners of commercial and industrial facilities with client goals driving every design solution **for this** engineering **firm serving the** energy, manufacturing, and process industries. Blending architectural creativity with practical engineering solutions, manage all phases of development—from renderings to completion.

SAMPLE FOR A POWER GENERATION MANAGER

Provide power plant maintenance and operations management **including** safety and environmental oversight, manpower planning, process improvements, energy reductions, and outage coordination **for this** $26 billion paper, packaging, and forest products **firm.** Maximize production growth and opportunities through strategic planning, prioritizing, and scheduling.

COMPANY & POSITION DESCRIPTOR FOUNDATION #4

[☐ Manage and drive | ☐ Lead and direct | ☐ Strategize | ☐ Perform | ☐ other: _____] _____ *[what?]* **of** _____, _____, **and** _____ *[what?]* **for this** _____ *[type of]* **firm with [☐ $**_____ *(amount)* **in revenues | ☐** _____ *(#)* **locations |** _____ *[#]* **employees | ☐ other:** _____] **that [☐ serves | ☐ provides | ☐ includes]** _____, _____, **and** _____ *[what?]*. [☐_____ *(additional information)]*. **Direct reports:** _____ *[#]*. **Indirect reports:** _____ *[#]*.

SAMPLE FOR AN AUTOMOTIVE SALES & TECHNICAL MANAGER

Manage and drive regional sales of all automotive refinish products and computer systems, generate and support new business, conduct field sales, and provide technical support **for this** national platinum distributorship **with** $275 million **in revenues,** 25 **locations, and** 325 **employees. Direct reports:** 5. **Indirect reports**: 13.

SAMPLE FOR A CHIEF OF DENTISTRY / CLINICAL DIRECTOR

Lead and direct the continuous strategic planning **of** innovative business model development and issue management; **and oversee** Fiscal Management, Human Resources, Administration, Facility Management, **and** Information Technology **for this** $25 million multispecialty diagnostic and treatment center **that provides** a wide range of specialty health care services including medical, dental, mental health, rehabilitative, and support services **to** 3,000 patients annually. **Direct reports:** 15. **Indirect reports:** 23.

SAMPLE FOR AN INFORMATION TECHNOLOGY REGIONAL MANAGER

Strategize and lead execution **of all** field sales and sales support **for** Optical Transport, IP RAN, and Metro Ethernet product lines **for** the new ABC brand including calling on science and technology organization, product management, **and** network operations across 9 states. **Direct reports:** 10. **Indirect reports:** 28.

COMPANY & POSITION DESCRIPTOR FOUNDATION #5

[☐ Founded | ☐ Co-founded | ☐ Built | ☐ Started] **this** _____ *[type of]* **firm from the ground up** [☐ to a leading _____ *(type of)* firm specializing in _____ *(what?)* | ☐ and championed the growth of the firm to _____ *(#)* offices, $_____ *(amount)* in annual sales, and _____ *(#)* employees]. [☐ Lead and direct | ☐ Oversee | ☐ Perform | ☐ Conduct | ☐ other: _____] **all aspects** of _____, _____, **and** _____ *[what?]* [☐ that provides _____ *(what?)*]. [☐_____ *(additional information)*].

SAMPLE FOR A MORTGAGE BROKER / BANKER

Started this mortgage bank / brokerage **firm from the ground up and championed the growth of the firm to** three offices, $156 million **in annual sales, and** 90 **employees. Oversee all aspects of** mortgage sales, marketing, **and** brokering—from new business development and loan originations through to sale closing, loan underwriting, and processing—tackling changing market conditions.

SAMPLE FOR A SENIOR MEDICAL ADVISOR / CHIEF EXECUTIVE OFFICER

Co-founded this firm from the ground up to a leading full-service medical claims evaluation firm specializing in independent medical evaluations and medical claims solutions, management, and staffing. **Lead and direct all aspects of** new business, joint venture, **and** physician panel development **that provides** second opinion diagnostic reviews and medical evaluations in all medical specialties.

SAMPLE FOR A PROJECT MANAGER

Founded this construction management **firm from the ground up to a leading full-service construction firm specializing in apartment rehabilitations,** managing the $2.5 million, 75-unit ABC apartments rehabilitation project on time and within budget. **Manage and monitor** key outside personnel, wages, bidding, purchasing, budgeting, scheduling, permitting, change orders, lien releases, and contracts for the construction of all units.

100 COMPONENTS OF AN EXEMPLARY RESUME:
How Does Your Resume Fare?

Did you know that a full 98 percent of the general public prepares their resume incorrectly? That's because resume writing is an art and a science that takes even professional resume writers years to perfect.

Job seekers generally do not target their resumes precisely to the positions they seek, match their qualifications with the position requirements, incorporate all of the relative resume keywords, showcase their value proposition and matching achievements to prospective employers, and they do not know how to brand themselves. These and other areas are critical to demonstrate to prospective employers how suitable of a candidate you are for them.

If your resume and cover letter are well crafted, it will help you increase your interview odds manyfold, heighten your confidence level, gain renewed enthusiasm for the job search, feel empowered in the interview stage, land the position you seek sooner, and obtain your highest salary potential possible.

The following list of requirements for successful resumes focuses on all of the critical resume and cover letter areas to help you make your presentation the best it can be in order to maximize your interview odds and salary potential. As a Certified Resume Writer and Career Coach, these are the areas I personally include in all of my clients' resumes.

A. Overall Targeted Resume and Cover Letter Strategy

A building is only as strong as the foundation on which it sits. Similarly, resume strategy is key in developing your resume to ensure it is a success. The correct resume format should be used, your overall resume should precisely target the position for which you seek, any "red flags" must be skillfully handled, and it should portray how you can help prospective employers reach their goals.

CRITERIA CHECKLIST:

1. Resume and cover letter target prospective employers' needs with matching qualifications and demonstrate a fit between your qualifications and their needs.
2. Correct resume format (Chronological, Functional, Combination, or Curriculum Vitaé) is used for your situation.
3. Most important targeted information is contained in the top one-third of your resume.
4. All of your key transferable skills (skills used in one profession or position that can be transferred over to another) are included in your cover letter and resume.
5. Work history goes back 10 or, max, 15 years (if relative experience cannot be shown in the past 10 years).
6. Employment related to your targeted profession is documented under "Professional Experience." Any earlier, unrelated experience is listed under "Earlier Career Development," "Additional Experience," or "Other Employment" at the end of your resume.
7. No employment gaps are evident or are skillfully handled.
8. "Red flags" are omitted or tactfully handled by turning them into assets wherever possible.
9. Resume plays up strengths and minimizes weaknesses.
10. Unrelated jobs include targeted job functions wherever possible. *(Example: Someone applying for a railroad conductor might include customer service and money handling functions in an unrelated position.)*
11. Activities, hobbies, professional affiliations, and/or special interests are included when relative and omitted when not.
12. Promotions are included and demonstrate progressive experience in your field.
13. Resume incorporates all relevant information and omits or de-emphasizes irrelevant information.
14. All resume and cover letter components meet strict Resume-Writing Standards.
15. Ensure that all pertinent qualifications (those targeted to your goal) are included.

B. Your Cover Letter

Your Cover Letter, if written well in marketing-savvy language, attracts your audience to want to read your resume and can even compel hiring managers to call you in for an interview based on your cover letter's content alone.

CRITERIA CHECKLIST:

16. The first paragraph attracts your audience via your personal brand message (your assets, benefits, competitive edge, value proposition, and return on investment) or other "wow" factor.
17. First paragraph also includes position sought and where heard of.
18. The second paragraph explains what you have to offer through your matching qualifications and value proposition.
19. The third paragraph validates your value proposition by summarizing your related achievements.
20. The fourth (optional) paragraph sparks additional interest via a related story or eye-opening comment that shows hiring managers why

you are interested in and/or passionate about the position.

21. The last paragraph closes with a statement of interest, includes your call-to-action, and thanks the reader.

22. Overall cover letter uses benefit-driven sentences to entice the reader to want to read your resume, and if it's a really good cover letter, to call you in for an interview before even reading the resume.

23. Shows how you are a match for a position opening by including the primary requirements in the original job posting and noting your expertise and qualifications in these areas.

24. Portrays how you can help prospective employers reach their goals with an explanation of how your assets and benefits can serve the firm.

25. Provides a human touch for the person behind the piece of paper so hiring managers can envision you in their firm and its culture performing the position they need filled.

26. Cover letter should be kept to within one page (4 to 5 paragraphs work well).

27. Summarizes your major achievements in brief statements, substantiates how you can be an asset to their firm, and sells you as a qualified candidate based on your experience, education, skills, and qualifications.

28. Contains persuasive benefit-driven statements that make hiring managers want to meet with you.

29. States what your return on investment is to prospective employers if they were to hire you.

30. Includes all of your primary industry-specific keywords. (Check Job Descriptions found on the Internet for your position title, and include all keywords in which you have experience.)

31. Includes specific ways you might be able to help the prospective employer. (View their website to get a feel for what the firm's mission and goals are and any other information where you might be able to fill a need.)

32. Contains any additional compelling information as to why this particular field or position is important to you.

C. Professional Summary Section

The "Professional Summary" section is an encapsulated first paragraph of your resume that states what you have to offer in a concise format. The purpose of this section is to match your qualifications with your prospective employers' requirements, to demonstrate you are a good fit for the position you seek, and to invite the reader in to want to read the rest of your resume.

CRITERIA CHECKLIST:

33. "Professional Summary" is well constructed and summarizes your experience in a nutshell (one to two paragraphs work well).

34. Includes your Personal Brand Message (your assets, benefits, competitive edge, value proposition, and return on investment).

35. Invites the reader to want to read the rest of your resume.

36. States your targeted position in the first sentence (so it is not necessary to include an "Objective" section in your resume).

37. All primary targeted skills and qualifications are included.

38. Primary personal attributes are contained within your "Professional Summary" section.

39. Matches your qualifications with the prospective employers' requirements to demonstrate you are a good fit for the position.

40. Includes all of the primary keywords for the targeted position.

41. Contains heavy-hitting, marketing-savvy, and impactful statements.

42. Includes good use of varied sentence types.

D. Core Competencies or Areas of Experience Section: Resume Keywords

Many firms scan in resumes to search for all relative keywords that match the position opening to determine if you are a qualified candidate. The purpose of including resume keywords is to pass the first electronic screening of your resume so that it is put in the hands of a hiring manager. If your resume does not include all relative keywords, it may not be read or even seen by a human.

CRITERIA CHECKLIST:

43. All related keywords are including in list form under a *"Core Competencies"* or *"Areas of Experience"* section of your resume right under your *"Professional Summary"* section.

44. Infuses the important industry-specific keywords for your profession within your resume and cover letter.

45. Profession-specific keywords are included within responsibility bullets wherever applicable.

46. Transferable skills you may have used in other positions are also included.

47. All technical skills pertinent to the position are identified and included.

E. Professional Experience Section: Job Responsibility and Achievement Bullets

Most jobseekers who prepare their own resumes just list their job functions under each employer. That's what job descriptions are for. Your resume, on the other hand, must showcase how well you accomplished these job functions in order to demonstrate that you are a qualified candidate for the position, or it will not generate many interviews. Achievements are the most important part of your resume. They should target the position you seek and showcase measurable employer benefits.

CRITERIA CHECKLIST:

48. Job years are placed to best advantage: before job title if there are no employment gaps, tucked at end of employment line if gaps are evident.
49. Primary profession-specific bullets start with responsibilities that target the position you seek.
50. Action verbs are used (in their natural sequence) to start each resume bullet, such as manage, develop, and implement…
51. Resume bullets for each position are in good sequential order relative to the targeted position you seek: most relevant bullets appear first, companion bullets thereafter, less important bullets last.
52. Wherever possible resume does not show job hopping. Jobs held for less than a year can be omitted if unrelated to position sought and employment gaps are explained as an asset, wherever possible.
53. The number of jobs included in your resume does not exceed five, or when there are more, they are categorized differently to provide the "look" of five or less. For example: older jobs with the same position title can be categorized as one by listing the three employers followed by bullets related to all three.
54. Job promotions are included and skillfully handled and/or progressive experience in your field is evident, if applicable. Job promotions are included in a way that shows progression under one employer, not as separate positions.
55. Management or supervisory bullets, if applicable, are included to demonstrate how well you can lead, manage, mentor, and train staff.
56. Bland job function bullets are converted into action-packed **CAR (Challenge-Action-Result)** achievement statements. They state the challenge you were faced with, the action you took to meet that challenge, and the benefits your employer or clients derived from your efforts.
57. Job functions are quantified with measurable employer benefits (how much, how many, how big, how fast, how well, how often, and so on) in percentages and dollar amounts.
58. Current and most relevant positions contain the most bullets; older and less relevant positions contain fewer bullets.
59. Bullets are worked up comprehensively so anyone who reads your resume has a full understanding of what you accomplished.
60. Each achievement bullet is concisely edited down to its "lowest common denominator" so it is impactful and does not leave out any important content.
61. Bullet line length is varied throughout resume from one to four lines.
62. Resume includes a "Key Accomplishments" section when achievements are many (such as for Executives, managers, and/or technical positions).

F. Resume Format and Design

For your resume to stand out and be read, it must first attract interest. Using graphic elements and rules and a resume format and design that invites the reader in will help it to stand out from your competition and get read.

CRITERIA CHECKLIST:

63. Resume immediately attracts attention through exceptional formatting and design that helps it stand out from your competition and entices the reader to want to read your resume.
64. Incorporates effective marketing, design, and presentation strategies.
65. Resume design is suitable for your profession and targeted market.
66. Placement of most important information (that which targets your audience and the position you seek) is in the top one-third of your resume.
67. Job titles are clearly indicated in bold, caps, and a larger font size.
68. Proper use of fonts and font sizes has been applied for headings and body copy.
69. There is good organization and division of material and content flows well.
70. Important information is bold-faced (section titles, job titles, employers).
71. There is sufficient white space around content so resume does not look crowded.
72. Individual pages end with full paragraphs, or better, full positions.
73. Spacing is consistent throughout and formatting looks professional.
74. Resume sections are organized and titled well (*"Professional Summary," "Areas of Expertise," "Key Accomplishments," "Professional Experience," "Education and Training," etc.*).
75. Contact information is clear and readable (be sure to verify accuracy).

G. Education and Training

All relative education and additional training are important to include in your resume. The way your education is presented plays an important part in your resume.

CRITERIA CHECKLIST:

76. Education includes college or university name, town and state, and degree received (or related coursework, if none).

77. Include Grade Point Averages of 3.0 or above or GPA in major when overall GPA is less than 3.0 and it is higher. Otherwise omit GPA altogether.
78. Year of completion is included if within the past 10 years; omitted if earlier in life.
79. All Degrees are included except when both a Bachelor's and Associate's Degree have been attained, in which case the Associate's Degree can be omitted.
80. When a new grad, education belongs up front. When experience is more relative than education, education belongs towards the end of the resume.
81. Any additional training you received related to your targeted position is included in your resume. Include training course titles and where received. Add years attained if recent.

H. Resume Grammar, Punctuation, Spelling, and Editing

There are few, if any, excusable mistakes allowable in a resume. Grammar, punctuation, and spelling are not any of them. Many firms toss resumes with misspellings and misuse of grammar and punctuation. Be sure your resume has no typos and each sentence flows well.

CRITERIA CHECKLIST:

82. Information is comprehensive but concise; one gets a complete understanding of what you are capable of and have achieved in your career.
83. Your resume does not include personal pronouns. "I," "me," and "my" are understood and do not belong in resumes.
84. Bullets are prioritized within each position in order of their importance to the targeted profession.
85. Action verbs start off each resume bullet and are used correctly (unless they are preceded by an adverb to show how well you handled that function). Such as "Finitely edited..."
86. Descriptive adjectives or adverbs are included, but not overused.
87. Resume is edited down without losing content.
88. Redundant or superfluous words are eliminated.
89. Irrelevant information is omitted.
90. Quantifying information (in numbers) is included wherever possible.
91. Your resume and cover letter contains powerful, persuasive marketing phrases.
92. Personal information (marriage status, children, etc.) is left out.
93. Your resume engages reader and maintains interest through well-written content, compelling copy, and concise editing.

I. Personal Branding

Personal Branding is critical in today's world of work. It sets you apart from your competition and actually helps position you in the top 2% of candidates who are called for interviews and receive job offers.

CRITERIA CHECKLIST:

94. Your cover letter should include all elements of your personal brand: assets, benefits, competitive edge, value proposition, and return on investment.
95. Your personal brand message is finitely written and edited and makes a "wow" statement.
96. Your resume must back up your personal brand with matching achievements.
97. Some use of Visual Branding (Occupational Icon™, graphic elements, charts, graphs, work samples, etc.) is contained within your resume and cover letter, if applicable.
98. Good use of Verbal Branding (slogan, testimonials, mission statement, success stories, case studies, etc.) is included in your cover letter and/or resume.
99. When you read your finalized resume and cover letter, you say *"Wow! I'd hire me!"*
100. To ensure you have left no stone unturned in making you shine, modify any areas that can use enhancement.

RESUME DESIGN LAYOUT SAMPLES

RESUME DESIGN LAYOUT #1

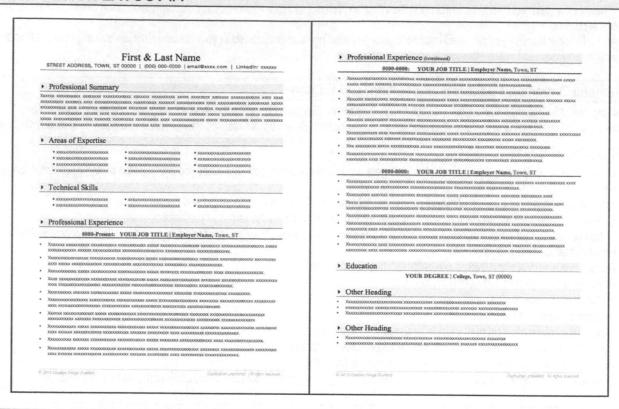

RESUME DESIGN LAYOUT #2

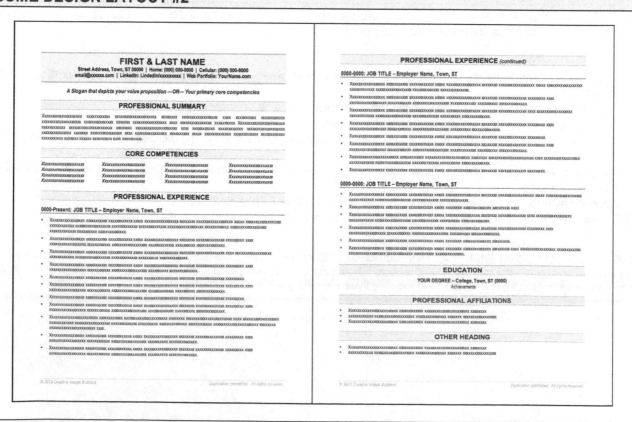

RESUME DESIGN LAYOUT #3

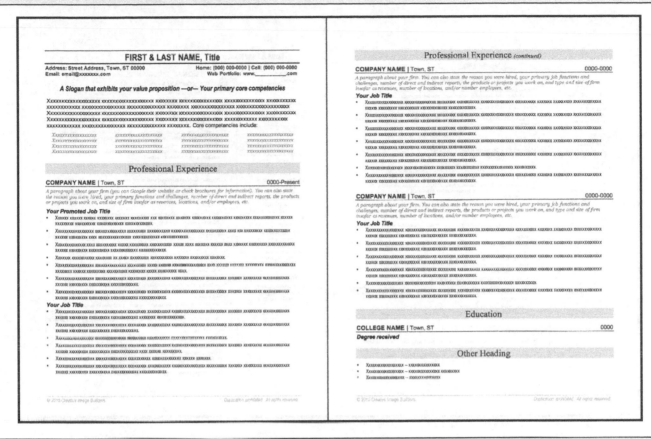

RESUME DESIGN LAYOUT #4

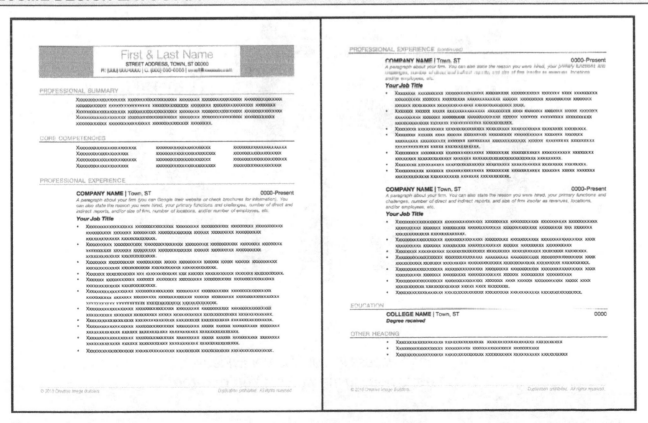

RESUME DESIGN LAYOUT #5

Much Success in Your Career Endeavors!
Here's to hearing the words, "You're Hired!"

INDEX
OF ALL POSITION TITLES

Concrete Floor Installer	Concrete Foreman	Concrete Form Laborer
Concrete Form Setter	Concrete Grinder Operator	Concrete Installer
Concrete Laborer	Concrete Layer	Concrete Materials Tester
Concrete Placement Equipment Operator	Concrete Pointer	Concrete Polisher
Concrete Safety Manager	Concrete Smoother	Concrete Stone Finisher
Concrete Swimming Pool Installer	Concreting Supervisor	Construction & Building Inspector
Construction & Estimator Assistant	Construction & Service Coordinator	Construction Administrative Coordinator
Construction Administrator	Construction Area Manager	Construction Assistant Superintendent
Construction Carpenter	Construction Coordinator	Construction Cost Estimator
Construction Customer Service Manager	Construction Electrician Journeyman	Construction Equipment Operator
Construction Estimator	Construction Expeditor	Construction Field Engineer
Construction Field Estimator	Construction Field Supervisor	Construction Foreman
Construction Form Setter	Construction Inspector	Construction Journeyman
Construction Journeyman Electrician	Construction Labor / Equipment Operator	Construction Laborer
Construction Manager	Construction Manager	Construction Mason
Construction Materials Technician	Construction Office Manager	Construction Operations Manager
Construction Operations Supervisor	Construction Project Administrator	Construction Project Coordinator
Construction Project Engineer	Construction Project Manager	Construction Project Manager / Designer
Construction Project Manager / Site Superintendent	Construction Project Specialist	Construction Project Supervisor
Construction QA / QC Engineer	Construction Quality Assurance Inspector	Construction Quality Control Manager
Construction Quality Specialist	Construction Representative	Construction Services Assistant
Construction Services Manager	Construction Site Manager	Construction Site Superintendent
Construction Superintendent	Construction Supervisor	Construction Supervisor
Construction Tradesman	Construction Trainee	Construction Worker
Contract (Site) Manager	Contract Administrator	Contractor
Cost Analyst	Cost Estimator	Craftsman
Crane Manager	Crane Operator	Crane Rigger
Crew Chief	Crew Leader	Crew Leader – Maintenance
Curb Builder	Custodial Manager	Custodial Supervisor
Custodial Worker	Custodian	Custodian Engineer
Customer Service Representative – Construction	Customer Service Superintendent	Deck Builder
Deck Installer	Deck Worker	Demolition Contractor
Demolition Foreman	Demolition Superintendent	Demolition Worker
Directional Bore Operator	Directional Drill Operator	Director, Labor Relations
Dirt Foreman / Superintendent	Door & Window Installer	Dragline Operator
Dredge Operator	Dredger	Dredging Inspector
Driller	Drilling Foreman	Drywall & Ceiling Tile Installer
Drywall & Make-ready Technician	Drywall Applicator	Drywall Boardhanger
Drywall Carpenter	Drywall Finisher	Drywall Hanger
Drywall Installer	Drywall Mechanic	Drywall Metal Stud Worker
Drywall Sander	Drywall Stripper	Drywall Taper
Drywall Worker	Drywaller	Dump Truck Backhoe Operator
Dump Truck Driver	Electric Service Worker	Electrical Apprentice
Electrical Construction Foreman	Electrical Contractor	Electrical Design Engineer
Electrical Engineering Technician	Electrical Foreman	Electrical Inspector
Electrical Project Manager	Electrical Systems Design Engineer	Electrical Systems Supervisor
Electrician	Electrician Apprentice	Electrician Contractor
Electrician Foreman	Electrician Helper	Electrician Supervisor
Elevator Installer	Engineer – Electrical Systems Design	Engineering Equipment Operator
Equipment Operator	Estimating / Bidding Assistant	Estimating / Change Manager
Estimating Assistant	Estimating Supervisor	Estimator
Estimator – High-end General Construction	Estimator – Specialty Construction	Estimator – Structural & Miscellaneous Steel Fabrication
Estimator / Assistant Project Manager	Estimator / Purchaser	Estimator Project Manager
Excavating Contractor	Excavating Machine Operator	Excavator Foreman
Excavator Operator	Facilities Construction Coordinator	Facilities Construction Project Specialist
Facilities Construction Trades Worker	Facilities Foreperson	Facilities Generalist
Facilities Maintenance Mechanic	Facilities Superintendent	Facility Maintenance Specialist
Facility Operations Project Manager	Fence Builder	Field Construction Coordinator
Field Foreman	Field Helper	Field Inspector

Field Install Site Supervisor
Field Manager – Residential Construction
Field Superintendent
Field-based Construction Manager
Finish Superintendent
Fire Sprinkler Fitter
Flat Glass Glazier Technician
Floor Laying Contractor
Foreman / Foreperson
Framing Carpenter
Garden Center Worker
Gas Welder
General Construction Laborer
General Engineering Contractor
General Highway Worker
General Maintenance Technician
General Superintendent
Glass Fitter
Glass Technician
Glazier Supervisor
Golf Course Laborer
Grader Operator
Greenhouse Foreman
Greens Foreman
Greenskeeper
Ground Worker
Groundskeeper
Hand Arc Welder
Hazardous Materials Removal Worker
Heating Mechanic
Heavy Civil Project Engineer
Hedge Trimmer
Highway Foreman
Highway Maintenance Laborer
Highway Maintenance Worker
Home Building Superintendent
Home Remodeling Contractor
Housing Inspector
HVAC Foreman
HVAC Mechanic
HVAC Specialist
HVAC/R Mechanic
HVAC/R Technician
Indoor Gardener
Inspecting Engineer
Installation Supervisor
Insulation Installer
Inventory Control Assistant – Construction
Irrigation Project Superintendent
Janitor
Joint Finisher
Journeyman Carpenter
Journeyman Fire Sprinkler Fitter
Junior Site Surveyor
Labor Foreman
Labor Relations Director
Laborer
Land Development Manager
Landscape Foreman
Landscape Laborer

Field Manager
Field Operations Supervisor
Field Supervisor
Field-based Facilities Manager
Finish-Pour Assistant
Fire Sprinkler Helper
Floor Installer
Floor Systems Carpenter
Forklift Operator
Front-End Loader Operator
Gardener
General Building Contractor
General Contractor
General Foreman
General Laborer
General Maintenance Worker
Glass & Glazing Contractor
Glass Installer
Glazier
Glazing Project Manager
Gradall Operator
Grass Cutter
Greenhouse Worker
Greens Laborer
Greenskeeper Foreman
Grounds Caretaker
Groundskeeper Foreman
Handyman
Heating Foreman
Heating Specialist
Heavy Equipment Operator
Helliarc Welder
Highway Inspector
Highway Maintenance Lead Worker
Highway Safety Specialist
Home Improvement Contractor
Horizontal Directional Drill Operator
HVAC / Skilled Tradesman
HVAC Helper
HVAC Project Manager
HVAC Systems Foreman
HVAC/R Service Technician
HVAC-R Inspector
Industrial Brick Mason Foreman
Inspector
Installer
Insulation Worker
Inventory Control Manager – Construction
Janitorial Manager
Janitor Cleaner Custodian
Joint Setter
Journeyman Construction Carpenter
Junior Construction Estimator
Junior Superintendent
Labor Organization Representative
Labor Supervisor
Land Assistant Project Manager
Landfill Heavy Equipment Operator
Landscape Gardener
Landscape Maintenance Worker

Field Manager – Homebuilding
Field Representative
Field Survey Specialist
Finish Carpenter
Fire Sprinkler Designer
Fire Sprinkler Installer
Floor Layer
Foreman
Framer
Furniture Maker
Gas Inspector
General Construction Equipment Operator
General Contractor
General Foreman – Civil
General Maintenance Mechanic
General Manager – Construction
Glass Combo Technician
Glass Setter
Glazier Contractor
Golf Course Keeper
Grade Checker
Grass Mower
Greens Cutter
Greens Superintendent
Ground Crewman
Grounds Cleaner
Groundskeeping Maintenance Worker
Handyman / Service Technician
Heating Installer
Heating Technician
Heavy Equipment Operator Apprentice
Highway Construction Inspector
Highway Maintenance Foreman
Highway Maintenance Technician
Highway Technician
Home Inspector
Horticulturist
HVAC Contractor
HVAC Installer & Service Technician
HVAC Service Technician
HVAC Technician
HVAC/R Specialist
Independent Contractor
Industrial Electrician
Installation / Service Technician
Installer Technician
Interior Finish Carpenter
Iron Worker
Janitorial Supervisor
Job Superintendent
Journey Lineworker
Journeyman Electrician
Junior Estimator
Labor Business Representative
Labor Organizer
Labor Union Business Representative
Land Construction Manager
Landscape Design & Build Project Manager
Landscape Irrigation Project Superintendent
Landscape Management Technician

Landscape Technician	Landscaper	Landscaper Helper
Lath & Plaster	Lath Hand	Lather
Lather Apprentice	Lawn Caretaker	Lawn Maintenance Laborer
Lawn Mower Operator	Lawn Service Worker	Lawn Sprinkler Installer
Lawn Sprinkler Servicer	Lead Carpenter	Lead Electrician
Lead Glazer	Lead Plumber	Lead Project Coordinator
Lead Superintendent	Lead Welder	Leadman / Lead Person
Leadman Construction Laborer	Licensed Journeyman Electrician	Licensed Plumber
Loader Operator	Loading Machine Operator	Low Boy Driver
Maintenance & Operations Supervisor	Maintenance Aide	Maintenance Carpenter
Maintenance Contractor	Maintenance Electrician	Maintenance Engineer
Maintenance Groundsman	Maintenance Helper	Maintenance Journeyman
Maintenance Mechanic	Maintenance of Traffic	Maintenance Project Superintendent
Maintenance Project Supervisor	Maintenance Repair Worker	Maintenance Repair Worker Assistant
Maintenance Specialist	Maintenance Worker	Manager Construction Projects, Facility Engineering
Marble Setter	Mason	Mason Carpenter
Mason Laborer	Mason Tender	Mason-Plasterer
Masonry & Stone Setting Contractor	Masonry Contractor	Masonry Foreman
Masonry Outfitter	Masonry Specialist	Masonry Superintendent
Masonry Tuck-pointer Laborer	Masonry Worker	Master Carpenter
Master Electrician	Master Plumber	Material Coordinator
Metal Framer	Metal Furrer	Metal Lather
Metal Roofing Technician	Metal Stud Framer	Metal Welder
Midlevel Estimator	Motor Grader Operator	Multi-Family Construction Project Supervisor
Multifamily Superintendent	Multiskilled Craftsman / Remodeler	Multiterrain Loader
New Homes Superintendent	Nursery Helper	Nursery Manager
Office Administrator – Construction	Office Manager – Construction	Operations Manager – Construction
Operations Manager – Construction	Operations Supervisor	Owner / Operator (Contractor)
Painter	Painter – Commercial	Painter – Industrial
Painter – Residential	Painter / Crew Leader	Painter Helper / Prepper
Painter Leader	Painting Contractor	Painting Contractor
Painting Foreman	Park Caretaker	Park Caretaker Keeper
Park Caretaker Worker	Park Crew Chief	Park Foreman
Park Keeper	Park Worker	Paving Equipment Operator
Paving Inspector	Pay Loader Operator	Pesticide Handler
Pesticide Sprayer	Pile-Driver Operator	Pipe Welder
Pipefitter	Pipefitter Helper	Pipefitter Trade Foreman
Planning & Coordination Specialist	Plant Maintenance Mechanic	Plant-Care Worker
Planting Foreman	Plaster Lather	Plasterer
Plastering, Drywall, Acoustical & Insulation Contractor	Plumber	Plumber Apprentice / Helper
Plumbing / Mechanical Inspector	Plumbing Contractor	Plumbing Contractor
Plumbing Designer	Plumbing Foreman	Plumbing Foreman (Multifamily)
Plumbing Inspector	Plumbing Inspector / Plans Reviewer	Plumbing Installer
Plumbing, Heating & Air Conditioning Contractor	Preconstruction Manager	Preconstruction Manager – Renovation
Prefabricated Structures Carpenter	Principal Landscape Architect	Project Assistant – Jobsite
Project Associate – Construction	Project Control Coordinator	Project Coordination Specialist
Project Coordinator	Project Engineer – Electrical	Project Engineer / Finish Carpenter
Project Environmental Engineer	Project Foreman	Project Lead
Project Leader	Project Management Administrator	Project Manager
Project Manager – Electrical	Project Manager – HVAC	Project Manager – Metal Construction
Project Manager – Plumbing	Project Manager – Residential Remodeling	Project Manager – Sheet Metal
Project Manager / General Contractor	Project Manager / Installation Manager	Project Manager / Site Superintendent
Project Manager Assistant	Project Material Coordinator	Project Principal Work Planner
Project Scheduler	Project Specialist	Project Superintendent
Project Superintendent	Project Superintendent / Engineer	Project Supervisor
Property Compliance Inspector	Property Maintenance Worker	Property Manager – Construction
Property Manager – Groundskeeping	Property Manager – Landscaping	Pruner
Public Works Inspector	Public Works Manager	Purchasing / Estimating Assistant
Purchasing Administrator	Purchasing Agent – Construction	Purchasing Manager – Construction
Purchasing Trade Agent	Refrigeration Apprentice	Refrigeration Foreman

Refrigeration Installer
Refrigeration Technician
Regional Purchasing Manager
Resident Project Representative
Residential Electrical Foreman
Retail Construction Manager
Rockboard Lather
Roofing Apprentice
Roofing Foreman
Scaffold Erector
Senior Building Maintenance Mechanic
Senior Building Technician
Senior Facilities Maintenance Mechanic
Senior Plant Maintenance Mechanic
Services Manager
Sheet Metal Worker
Sheetrock Finisher
Sheetrock Layer
Sheetrock Worker
Shrub Planter
Siding Foreman
Site Supervisor
Skid Steer Loader Operator
Skilled Trades Specialist
Solar Installation / Production Manager
Special Trade Contractor
Sprinkler Fitter
Stonemason
Structural Contractor
Structural Tradesworker
Superintendent – Installation
Superintendent – White Paving
Support Specialist
Swimming Pool Installer
Terrazzo Contractor
Terrazzo Setter
Tile Installer
Track Hoe Operator
Trades Specialist – HVAC
Tree Maintenance Worker
Tree Surgeon
Truck Driver / Equipment Operator
Union Negotiator
Union Staff Representative
Utility Maintenance Worker
Waterproofer
Weed Sprayer
Welding Contractor
Wiring Technician
Working Superintendent
Yard Worker

Refrigeration Mechanic
Regional Property Manager
Remodel Contractor
Residential Construction Estimator
Residential General Contractor
Roadway Construction Laborer
Roofer
Roofing Carpenter
Scaffold Builder
Scenic Carpenter
Senior Building Maintenance Technician
Senior Estimator
Senior Field Manager
Senior Project Manager / Estimator
Sheet Metal Contractor
Sheetrock Applicator
Sheetrock Hanger
Sheetrock Nailer
Sheetrocker
Shrub Trimmer
Site Manager
Site Surveyor
Skilled Carpenter
Skilled Trades Worker
Solar Photovoltaic Installer
Specialty Contractor
Steamfitter
Stonesetter
Structural Superintendent
Subcontractor
Superintendent – Specialty Construction
Superintendent of Facilities Maintenance
Surfacing Equipment Operator
Tack Welder
Terrazzo Finisher
Terrazzo Worker
Tile Setter
Trade Professional Manager
Tradesworker – Bridges
Tree Pruner
Tree Trimmer
Union Business Representative
Union Organizer
Union Steward
Utility Worker – Heavy Equipment
Weed Controller
Weeder
Window Washer
Wood Lather
Working Superintendent – Retail / Commercial
Zone Chief (HVAC)

Refrigeration Specialist
Regional Purchasing Administrator
Remodeling Tradesman
Residential Construction Project Manager
Restoration Carpenter
Rock Lather
Roofing & Siding Contractor
Roofing Contractor
Scaffold Construction Manager
Senior Building Facilities Technician
Senior Building Maintenance Worker
Senior Estimator, Home Building Construction
Senior Maintenance Mechanic
Service Plumber
Sheet Metal Helper
Sheetrock Applier
Sheetrock Installer
Sheetrock Sander
Shop Steward
Side Boom Tractor Operator
Site Superintendent
Sitework Manager
Skilled Trades Apprentice
Solar Heating Cooling System Installer
Solar Project Manager
Spot Welder
Steward
Structural Concrete Superintendent
Structural Trades Superintendent
Superintendent – Concrete
Superintendent – Steel
Supervisor of Building Trades
Swimming Pool Installer
Tamping Equipment Operator
Terrazzo Grinder
Territory Facilities Manager
Torch Welder
Trade Union Representative
Tradesworker – Welding
Tree Specialist
Trencher Operator
Union Carpenter
Union Representative
Utility Line Locator
Vocational Assistant / General Laborer
Weed Inspector
Welder
Wire Lather
Working Foreman
Yard Work Laborer
Other related positions

CAREER MANAGEMENT RESOURCES

ResumeProducts.com
FOR RESUME & CAREER PRODUCTS

StepByStepResumes.com
FOR RESUME BOOKS IN ALL PROFESSIONS

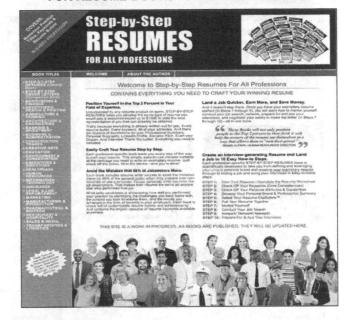

Get the Companion Books:

STEP-BY-STEP COVER LETTERS:
Create Your Cover Letter in 10 Easy Steps Using Personal Branding
(Evelyn Salvador, JIST Publishing)
Explains exactly how to write your cover letter to gain interviews in easy-to-follow steps. It is loaded with foundation templates and examples. $29.95

RESUME KEYWORDS FOR ALL PROFESSIONS
(Evelyn Salvador)
Contains 35,000+ Keywords, 4150+ Attributes and 2000+ Technical Skills. As the largest Keywords resource on the planet, you can be sure all of your critical keywords are included in your resume. $29.95

LAND THAT JOB!
A Step-by-Step Guide to Winning the Job You Desire
(Evelyn Salvador)
Strategic advice on marketing yourself, conducting your job search, networking, acing your interviews, and winning the job at your highest salary potential. $29.95

PERSONAL BRANDING HOW TO
(Evelyn Salvador)
Takes you step by step to build your brand and contains many customizable paragraphs for your Branded Biography, LinkedIn Profile, and Professional Summary—even your Elevator Pitch and Tagline. Plus unique visual tactics to get you noticed first. $29.95

Step-by-Step Resumes For All Professions

   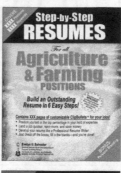 

Step-by-Step Resumes Books
are in various stages of completion.
Visit **ResumeProducts.com**
or **StepByStepResumes.com**
for more information.